12TH EDITION

ARMSTRONG'S HANDBOOK

OF HUMAN RESOURCE MANAGEMENT PRACTICE

Michael Armstrong

First edition published in 1977 as *A Handbook of Personnel Management Practice* by Kogan Page Limited
Seventh edition published in 1999 as *A Handbook of Human Resource Management Practice*
Eleventh edition published in 2009 as *Armstrong's Handbook of Human Resource Management Practice*
Twelfth edition 2012

120 Pentonville Road
London N1 9JN
United Kingdom
www.koganpage.com

1518 Walnut Street, Suite 1100
Philadelphia PA 19102
USA

4737/23 Ansari Road
Daryaganj
New Delhi 110002
India

© Michael Armstrong, 1977, 1984, 1988, 1991, 1995, 1996, 1999, 2001, 2003, 2006, 2009, 2012

ISBN   978 0 7494 6550 6
E-ISBN   978 0 7494 6551 3

British Library Cataloguing-in-Publication Data

A CIP record for this book is available from the British Library.

Library of Congress Cataloging-in-Publication Data

Armstrong, Michael, 1928–
    Armstrong's handbook of human resource management practice / Michael Armstrong. – 12th ed.
       p. cm.
    ISBN 978-0-7494-6550-6 – ISBN 978-0-7494-6551-3   1. Personnel management–Handbooks,
manuals, etc.   I. Title.   II. Title: Handbook of human resource management practice.
    HF5549.17.A76 2012
    658.3–dc23
                                                                                    2011043139

Typeset by Graphicraft Ltd, Hong Kong
Print production managed by Jellyfish
Printed and bound in the UK by Ashford Colour Press

ARMSTRONG'S HANDBOOK

OF HUMAN RESOURCE
MANAGEMENT PRACTICE

CONTENTS IN BRIEF

PART III People resourcing 201

PART IV Learning and development 271

PART V Performance and reward 319

PART VI Employee relations 391

PART VII Employee wellbeing 429

PART VIII HR policies, procedures and systems 449

PART IX HR skills 473

PART X HRM toolkits 601

CONTENTS

PART VI Employee relations 391

30 Strategic employee relations 393

31 The employment relationship 401

32 The psychological contract 407

SUPPORTING RESOURCES FOR INSTRUCTORS AND STUDENTS

As a reader of *Armstrong's Handbook of Human Resource Management Practice* you have automatic access to a range of additional resources designed to enhance your experience and use of the book. Full details are provided below.

For practitioners

- 78 questionnaires and checklists included in the 14 toolkits for use as diagnostics.
- 58 action points and checklists for HR activities.

For lecturers and instructors

- 615 PowerPoint slides virtually all containing additional notes covering 56 of the 70 chapters (the remaining 14 chapters contain toolkits).
- Session outlines for each chapter other than the toolkits.
- A glossary of 950 HRM terms.

A bibliography of 706 books and articles.

A selection of multiple-choice questions.

51 case studies.

A literature review covering 382 publications.

For students

- Flash cards for revision purposes containing answers to the 454 questions posed in the text.
- Student learning notes – with key learning points for each chapter.
- A glossary of 950 HRM terms.
- A bibliography of 706 books and articles.
- A literature review covering 382 publications.

These online resources can be found on the Kogan Page website. To access, go to **www.koganpage.com/editions/armstrongs-handbook-of-human-resource-management-practice/9780749465506**

LIST OF FIGURES

LIST OF TABLES

LIST OF EXHIBITS

PREFACE

A number of radical changes have been made to this 12th edition of the *Handbook*. Two whole new parts have been added. One covers 16 key skills required by human resource management (HRM) professionals, the other contains 14 toolkits that provide practical guidance on developing and implementing fundamental HRM practices. These additional parts recognize that, however important the conceptual framework of HRM is as dealt with in the first two parts of the book and however important it is to know about the different areas of HRM as covered in the next six parts, ultimately HRM is all about putting things into practice. This needs a wide range of skills and a systematic approach to managing development and implementation programmes.

Other innovations include many more illustrations of HRM in action by means of case studies and examples, and a number of critical evaluations of significant HRM concepts or approaches.

Apart from these substantial changes, the *Handbook* has been brought up to date by reference to the findings of a number of recent significant research projects and other investigations into how HRM operates in practice. The plan of the book is illustrated in the 'route map' shown in Figure 0.1.

The companion website provides further resources for students and lecturers, as described on page xxv.

FIGURE 0.1   *Handbook of Human Resource Management Practice* route map

Part I The Practice of Human Resource Management
1. The concept of human resource management
2. Strategic HRM
3. Delivering HRM
4. HRM and performance
5. International HRM
6. Human capital management
7. Knowledge management
8. Competency-based HRM
9. The ethical dimension of HRM
10. Corporate social responsibility

Part II People and Organizations
11. Organizational behaviour
12. Work, organization and job design
13. Organization development
14. Employee engagement
15. Motivation
16. Commitment

Part III People Resourcing
17. Strategic resourcing
18. Workforce planning
19. Recruitment and selection
20. Resourcing practice
21. Talent management

Part IV Learning and Development
22. Strategic learning and development
23. The process of learning and development
24. The practice of learning and development
25. Leadership and management development

Part V Performance and Reward
26. Performance and reward basics
27. The practice of performance management
28. Strategic reward
29. The practice of reward management

Part VI Employee Relations
30. Strategic employee relations
31. The employment relationship
32. The psychological contract
33. The practice of industrial relations
34. Employee voice
35. Employee communications

Part VII Employee Wellbeing
36. The practice of employee wellbeing
37. Health and safety

Part VIII HR Policies, Procedures and Systems
38. HR policies
39. HR procedures
40. HR information systems

Part IX HR Skills
41. Strategic HRM skills
42. Business skills
43. Problem-solving skills
44. Analytical and critical skills
45. Research skills
46. Statistical skills
47. Selection interviewing skills
48. Job, role, competency and skills analysis
49. Learning and development skills
50. Negotiating skills
51. Leading and facilitating change
52. Leadership skills
53. Influencing skills
54. Handling people problems
55. Managing conflict
56. Political skills

Part X HRM Toolkits
57. Strategic HRM
58. Human capital management
59. Organization design
60. Organization development
61. Engagement
62. Workforce planning
63. Talent management
64. Planning and delivering learning events
65. Performance management
66. Strategic reward
67. Total rewards
68. Job evaluation
69. Grade and pay structure design
70. Attitude surveys

PART I

The practice of human resource management

PART I CONTENTS

Introduction

Human resource management (HRM) is a comprehensive and coherent approach to the employment and development of people. HRM can be regarded as a philosophy about how people should be managed that is underpinned by a number of theories relating to the behaviour of people and organizations. It is concerned with the contribution it can make to improving organizational effectiveness through people but it is, or should be, equally concerned with the ethical dimension – how people should be treated in accordance with a set of moral values. HRM involves the application of policies and practices in the fields of organization design and development, employee resourcing, learning and development, performance and reward, and the provision of services that enhance the wellbeing of employees. These are based on human resource (HR) strategies that are integrated with one another and aligned to the business strategy.

Some people criticize the notion of referring to people as 'resources' as if they were any other factor of production. Osterby and Coster (1992: 31) argued that: 'The term "human resources" reduces people to the same category of value as materials, money and technology – all resources, and resources are only valuable to the extent they can be exploited or leveraged into economic value.' 'People management' is sometimes preferred as an alternative, but in spite of its connotations, 'HRM' is the term most commonly used.

Whatever term is adopted the approach should be based on the principle laid down by Schneider (1987: 450) that: 'Organizations are the people in them; that people make the place ... Positive job attitudes for workers in an organization can be expected when the natural inclinations of the persons there are allowed to be reflected in their behaviours by the kinds of processes and structures that have evolved there.'

But as Keegan and Francis (2010: 873) observed, HR work is now 'largely framed as a business issue'. The emphasis is on business alignment and strategic fit. These are important requirements, but focusing on them can lead HR professionals to place correspondingly less emphasis on employee needs and motivations when developing their new and altered arrangements. A simplistic view of the business imperative permits little room for considering how HR strategy should impact on individual employees. HRM indeed aims to support the achievement of business goals but, equally, it should aim to build a relationship based on trust, openness and personal fulfilment.

This first part of the handbook deals with the broad areas and concerns of the practice of HRM, covering its conceptual basis, the strategic framework within which HRM activities take place and the various factors that affect it, including the impact of HRM on performance, the international context, the specific functions of human capital management, knowledge management and competency-based HRM and, importantly, the ethical and social responsibility considerations that need to be taken into account when practising HRM.

REFERENCES

Keegan, A and Francis, H (2010) Practitioner talk: the changing textscape of HRM and emergence of HR business partnership, *The International Journal of Human Resource Management*, **21** (6), pp 873–98

Osterby, B and Coster, C (1992) Human resource development – a sticky label, *Training and Development*, April, pp 31–2

Schneider, B (1987) The people make the place, *Personnel Psychology*, **40** (3), pp 437–53

01
The concept of human resource management

LEARNING OUTCOMES

On completing this chapter you should be able to define these key concepts. You should also know about:

- The meaning of HRM
- The hard and soft versions of HRM
- The reservations about HRM

- How HRM developed
- The conceptual framework of HRM
- The position of HRM today

Introduction

Human resource management (HRM) is concerned with all aspects of how people are employed and managed in organizations. It covers activities such as strategic HRM, human capital management, knowledge management, corporate social responsibility, organization development, resourcing (workforce planning, recruitment and selection and talent management), learning and development, performance and reward management, employee relations, employee wellbeing and the provision of employee services.

HRM as conceived in the 1980s had a conceptual framework consisting of a philosophy underpinned by a number of theories drawn from the behavioural sciences and from the fields of strategic management, human capital and industrial relations. The HRM philosophy was heavily criticized in the 1990s by academics, but this criticism has subsided, perhaps because it became increasingly evident that the term 'HRM' was being used as a synonym for what used to be called 'personnel management'. HRM practice is no longer governed by the original philosophy, if it ever was. HRM today is simply what HR people and line managers do. Few references are now made to the HRM conceptual framework. This is a pity – an appreciation of the philosophy and underpinning theories of HRM provides a sound basis for understanding and developing HR practice.

The aim of this chapter is to remedy this situation. It starts with an overview of HRM and continues with analyses of the concept of HRM and its underpinning theories. Reference is made to the reservations about HRM and this leads to an assessment of where HRM has got to now. Following this analysis the next two chapters explain how in general terms HRM is planned through the processes of strategic HRM and delivered through the HR architecture and system, by the HR function and its members, and by line managers.

HRM overview

The following overview of HRM explains what it is, sets out its main concerns and summarizes the contribution of those who originated and developed the concept. This provides the backcloth to the analysis of the conceptual framework in the next section.

HRM defined

Human resource management can be defined in line with the original concept as a strategic, integrated and coherent approach to the employment, development and wellbeing of the people working in organizations. It was described more pragmatically by Boxall and Purcell (2003: 1) as 'all those activities associated with the management of employment relationships in the firm'. A later more comprehensive definition was offered by Watson (2010: 919):

> HRM is the managerial utilisation of the efforts, knowledge, capabilities and committed behaviours which people contribute to an authoritatively co-ordinated human enterprise as part of an employment exchange (or more temporary contractual arrangement) to carry out work tasks in a way which enables the enterprise to continue into the future.

The development of the HRM concept

What might be called the founding fathers of HRM were the US academics Michael Beer and Charles Fombrun and their colleagues. In the UK they were followed by a number of commentators who developed, explained and frequently criticized the concept.

Beer *et al* (1984) produced what has become known as the 'Harvard framework'. They started with the proposition that: 'Human resource management (HRM) involves all management decisions and actions that affect the nature of the relationship between the organization and employees – its human resources' (*ibid*: 1). They believed that: 'Today ... many pressures are demanding a broader, more comprehensive and more strategic perspective with regard to the organization's human resources' (*ibid*: 4). They also stressed that it was necessary to adopt 'a longer-term perspective in managing people and consideration of people as a potential asset rather than merely a variable cost' (*ibid*: 6). Beer and his colleagues were the first to underline the HRM tenet that it belongs to line managers. They suggested that HRM had two characteristic features: 1) line managers accept more responsibility for ensuring the alignment of competitive strategy and HR policies; and 2) HR has the mission of setting policies that govern how HR activities are developed and implemented in ways that make them more mutually reinforcing.

The other major early contributors to the development of the philosophy of HRM – Fombrun *et al* (1984) – produced what has been termed the 'matching model', which indicated that HR systems and the organization structure should be managed in a way that is congruent with organizational strategy. This point was made in their classic statement that: 'The critical management task is to align the formal structure and human resource systems so that they drive the strategic objectives of the organization' (*ibid*: 37). Thus they took the first steps towards the concept of strategic HRM.

Following these US pioneers, as Legge (2005: 101) commented, 'the term [HRM] was taken up by both UK managers (for example, Armstrong, 1987; Fowler, 1987) and UK academics'. Hendry and Pettigrew (1990: 18) observed that: HRM was 'heavily normative from the start: it provided a diagnosis and proposed solutions'. They also commented that: 'What HRM did at this point was to provide a label to wrap around some of the observable changes, while providing a focus for challenging deficiencies – in attitudes, scope, coherence, and direction – of existing personnel management' (*ibid*: 20).

The goals of HRM

The goals of HRM are to:

- support the organization in achieving its objectives by developing and implementing HR strategies that are integrated with the business strategy (strategic HRM);
- contribute to the development of a high-performance culture;
- ensure that the organization has the talented, skilled and engaged people it needs;
- create a positive employment relationship between management and employees and a climate of mutual trust;
- encourage the application of an ethical approach to people management.

HRM is delivered in most organizations by HR specialists working in partnership with line managers.

The diversity of HRM

The practice of HRM can be diverse. Dyer and Holder (1988) pointed out that HRM goals vary according to competitive choices, technologies, characteristics of employees (eg could be different for managers) and the state of the labour market. Boxall (2007: 48) observed that: 'Human resource management covers a vast array of activities and shows a huge range of variations across occupations, organizational levels, business units, firms, industries and societies.'

Hard and soft HRM

One aspect of diversity is the distinction made by Storey (1989: 8) between the 'hard' and 'soft' versions of HRM. He wrote that:

> The hard one emphasizes the quantitative, calculative and business-strategic aspects of managing human resources in as 'rational' a way as for any other economic factor. By contrast, the soft version traces its roots to the human-relations school; it emphasizes communication, motivation and leadership.

However, it was pointed out by Keenoy (1997: 838) that 'hard and soft HRM are complementary rather than mutually exclusive practices' and research in eight UK organizations by Truss *et al* (1997) indicated that the distinction between hard and soft HRM was not as precise as some commentators have implied. Their conclusions are set out below.

Source review

Conclusions on hard and soft models of HRM – Truss *et al* (1997: 70)

Even if the rhetoric of HRM is 'soft', the reality is almost always 'hard', with the interests of the organization prevailing over those of the individual. In all the organizations, we found a mixture of both hard and soft approaches. The precise ingredients of this mixture were unique to each organization, which implies that factors such as the external and internal environment of the organization, its strategy, culture and structure all have a vital role to play in the way in which HRM operates.

The philosophy of human resource management

The following explanation of HRM philosophy was made by Legge (1989: 25) whose analysis of a number of HRM models identified the following common themes:

> That human resource policies should be integrated with strategic business planning and used to reinforce an appropriate (or change an inappropriate) organizational culture, that human resources are valuable and a source of competitive advantage, that they may be tapped most effectively by mutually consistent policies that promote commitment and which, as a consequence, foster a willingness in employees to act flexibly in the interests of the 'adaptive organization's' pursuit of excellence.

Storey (2001: 7) noted that:

> the beliefs of HRM included the assumptions that it is the human resource which gives competitive edge, that the aim should be to enhance employee commitment, that HR decisions are of strategic importance and that therefore HR policies should be integrated into the business strategy.

Underpinning theories of HRM

The original notion of HRM had a strong theoretical base. Guest (1987: 505) commented that: 'Human resource management appears to lean heavily on theories of commitment and motivation and other ideas derived from the field of organizational behaviour.' These theories are summarized below.

Commitment

The significance in HRM theory of organizational commitment (the strength of an individual's identification with, and involvement in, a particular organization) was highlighted in a seminal *Harvard Business Review* article by Richard Walton.

Source review

From control to commitment – Walton (1985: 77)

Workers respond best – and most creatively – not when they are tightly controlled by management, placed in narrowly defined jobs and treated as an unwelcome necessity, but, instead, when they are given broader responsibilities, encouraged to contribute and helped to take satisfaction in their work. It should come as no surprise that eliciting commitment – and providing the environment in which it can flourish – pays tangible dividends for the individual and for the company.

The traditional concept of organizational commitment resembles the more recent notion of organizational engagement (see Chapter 14).

Organizational behaviour theory

Organizational behaviour theory describes how people within their organizations act individually or in groups and how organizations function in terms of their structure, processes and culture. It therefore influences HRM approaches to organization design and development and enhancing organizational capability (the capacity of an organization to function effectively in order to achieve desired results).

Motivation theory

Motivation theory explains the factors that affect goal-directed behaviour and therefore influences the approaches used in HRM to enhance engagement (the situation in which people are committed to their work and the organization and are motivated to achieve high levels of performance).

AMO theory

The 'AMO' formula as set out by Boxall and Purcell (2003) states that performance is a function of

Ability + Motivation + Opportunity to Participate. HRM practices therefore impact on individual performance if they encourage discretionary effort, develop skills and provide people with the opportunity to perform. The formula provides the basis for developing HR systems that attend to employees' interests, namely their skill requirements, motivations and the quality of their job.

Human capital theory

Human capital theory is concerned with how people in an organization contribute their knowledge, skills and abilities to enhancing organizational capability and the significance of that contribution.

Resource dependence theory

Resource dependence theory states that groups and organizations gain power over each other by controlling valued resources. HRM activities are assumed to reflect the distribution of power in the system.

Resource-based theory

Resource-based theory states that competitive advantage is achieved if a firm's resources are valuable, rare and costly to imitate. HRM can play a major part in ensuring that the firm's human resources meet those criteria.

Institutional theory

Organizations conform to internal and external environmental pressures in order to gain legitimacy and acceptance.

Transaction costs theory

Transaction costs economics assumes that businesses develop organizational structures and systems that economize the costs of the transactions (interrelated exchange activities) that take place during the course of their operations.

Agency theory

Agency theory states that the role of the managers of a business is to act on behalf of the owners of the business as their agents. But there is a separation between the owners (the principals) and the agents (the managers) and the principals may not have complete control over their agents. The latter may therefore act in ways that are against the interests of those principals. Agency theory indicates that it is desirable to operate a system of incentives for agents, ie directors or managers, to motivate and reward acceptable behaviour.

Contingency theory

Contingency theory states that HRM practices are dependent on the organization's environment and circumstances. This means that, as Paauwe (2004: 36) explained:

> The relationship between the relevant independent variables (eg HRM policies and practices) and the dependent variable (performance) will vary according to the influences such as company size, age and technology, capital intensity, degree of unionization, industry/sector ownership and location.

Contingency theory is associated with the notion of *fit* – the need to achieve congruence between an organization's HR strategies, policies and practices and its business strategies within the context of its external and internal environment. This is a key concept in strategic HRM.

Reservations about the original concept of HRM

On the face of it, the original concept of HRM had much to offer, at least to management. But for some time HRM has been a controversial topic in academic circles. The main reservations have been that HRM promises more than it delivers and that its morality is suspect:

- Guest (1991: 149) referred to the 'optimistic but ambiguous label of human resource management'.

- 'The HRM rhetoric presents it as an all or nothing process which is ideal for any organization, despite the evidence that different business environments require different approaches' (Armstrong, 2000: 577).

- HRM is simplistic – as Fowler (1987: 3) wrote: 'The HRM message to top management tends to be beguilingly simple. Don't bother too much about the content or techniques of personnel management, it says. Just manage the context. Get out from behind your desk, bypass the hierarchy, and go and talk to people. That way you will unlock an enormous potential for improved performance.'

- The unitarist approach to employee relations implicit in HRM (the belief that management and employees share the same concerns and it is therefore in both their interests to work together) prompted Fowler (1987: 3) to write: 'At the heart of the concept is the complete identification of employees with the aims and values of the business – employee involvement but on the company's terms. Power in the HRM system remains very firmly in the hands of the employer. Is it really possible to claim full mutuality when at the end of the day the employer can decide unilaterally to close the company or sell it to someone else?'

- HRM is 'macho-management dressed up as benevolent paternalism' (Legge, 1998: 42).

- HRM is manipulative: Wilmott (1993: 534) asserted that, 'any (corporate) practice/value is as good as any other so long as it secures the compliance of employees'.

- HRM is managerialist: 'The analysis of employment management has become increasingly myopic and progressively more irrelevant to the daily experience of being employed. While the reasons for this development are immensely complex ... it is primarily a consequence of the adoption of the managerialist conception of the discourse of HRM' (Delbridge and Keenoy, 2010: 813).

HRM today

These are valid concerns but the more important messages of HRM, such as the need for strategic

integration, the desirability of gaining commitment, the virtues of partnership and participation and the key role of line managers are now generally accepted. However, the increasing emphasis on the business partnership role of HR at the expense of its function as an employee champion has been rightly criticized (Keegan and Francis, 2010). But the underpinning theories are as relevant today as they ever were.

As a description of people management activities in organizations, the term 'HRM' is here to stay even if it is applied diversely or only used as a label to describe traditional personnel management practices. Emphasis is now placed on the need for HR to be strategic and business-like and to add value, ie to generate extra value (benefit to the business) by the expenditure of effort, time or money on HRM activities. There have been plenty of new interests and developments including human capital management, engagement, talent management, competency-based HRM, e-HRM, high-performance work systems, and performance and reward management. But these have not been introduced under the banner of the HRM concept as originally defined.

Source review

The meaning of HRM – Boxall et al (2007: 1)

Human resource management (HRM), the management of work and people towards desired ends, is a fundamental activity in any organization in which human beings are employed. It is not something whose existence needs to be radically justified: HRM is an inevitable consequence of starting and growing an organization. While there are a myriad of variations in the ideologies, styles, and managerial resources engaged, HRM happens in some form or other. It is one thing to question the *relative* performance of particular models of HRM in particular contexts ... It is quite another thing to question the necessity of the HRM process itself, as if organizations cannot survive or grow without making a reasonable attempt at organizing work and managing people.

HRM has become something that organizations *do* rather than an aspiration or a philosophy and the term is generally in use as a way of describing the process of managing people. In the words of Storey (2001: 5), HRM has become 'a generic term simply denoting any approach to employment management'.

The convincing summary set out on page 8 of what HRM means today, which focuses on what HRM *is* rather than on its philosophy, was provided by Peter Boxall, John Purcell and Patrick Wright (2007), representing the new generation of commentators.

Key learning points: The concept of HRM

HRM defined

Human resource management is concerned with all aspects of how people are employed and managed in organizations.

Goals of HRM

The goals of HRM are to:

- support the organization in achieving its objectives by developing and implementing HR strategies that are integrated with the business strategy (strategic HRM);

- contribute to the development of a high-performance culture;

- ensure that the organization has the talented, skilled and engaged people it needs;

- create a positive employment relationship between management and employees and a climate of mutual trust;

- encourage the application of an ethical approach to people management.

Philosophy of HRM

The beliefs of HRM included the assumptions that it is the human resource which gives competitive edge, that the aim should be to enhance employee commitment, that HR decisions are of strategic importance and that therefore HR policies should be integrated into the business strategy. (Storey, 2001: 7)

Underpinning theories

'Human resource management appears to lean heavily on theories of commitment and motivation and other ideas derived from the field of organizational behaviour' (Guest, 1987: 505).

The diversity of HRM

Many HRM models exist, and practices within different organizations are diverse, often only corresponding to the conceptual version of HRM in a few respects.

Reservations about HRM

On the face of it, the concept of HRM has much to offer, at least to management. But reservations have been expressed about it. There may be something in these criticisms but the fact remains that as a description of people management activities in organizations, HRM is here to stay even if it is applied diversely or only used as a label to describe traditional personnel management practices.

Questions

1 What is HRM?

2 What was the main message of the Harvard framework?

3 What was the main message of the matching model?

4 What are the goals of HRM?

5 What is the difference between hard and soft HRM?

6 What is the essence of the philosophy of HRM?

7 What is resource-based theory?

8 What is the significance of contingency theory?

9 What are the key reservations expressed by commentators about the early version of HRM?

10 What is the position of HRM today?

References

Armstrong, M (1987) Human resource management: a case of the emperor's new clothes, *Personnel Management*, August, pp 30–35

Armstrong, M (2000) The name has changed but has the game remained the same?, *Employee Relations*, 22 (6), pp 576–89

Beer, M, Spector, B, Lawrence, P, Quinn Mills, D and Walton, R (1984) *Managing Human Assets*, New York, The Free Press

Boxall, P F (2007) The goals of HRM, in (eds) P Boxall, J Purcell and P Wright, *Oxford Handbook of Human Resource Management*, Oxford, Oxford University Press, pp 48–67

Boxall, P F and Purcell, J (2003) *Strategy and Human Resource Management*, Basingstoke, Palgrave Macmillan

Boxall, P F, Purcell, J and Wright, P (2007) Human resource management: scope, analysis and significance, in (eds) P Boxall, J Purcell and P Wright, *The Oxford Handbook of Human Resource Management*, Oxford, Oxford University Press, pp 1–16

Delbridge, R and Keenoy, T (2010) Beyond managerialism?, *The International Journal of Human Resource Management*, 21(6), pp 799–817

Dyer, L and Holder, G W (1988) Strategic human resource management and planning, in (ed) L Dyer, *Human Resource Management: Evolving roles and responsibilities*, Washington, DC, Bureau of National Affairs, pp 1–46

Fombrun, C J, Tichy, N M and Devanna, M A (1984) *Strategic Human Resource Management*, New York, Wiley

Fowler, A (1987) When chief executives discover HRM, *Personnel Management*, January, p 3

Guest, D E (1987) Human resource management and industrial relations, *Journal of Management Studies*, 24 (5), pp 503–21

Guest, D E (1991) Personnel management: the end of orthodoxy, *British Journal of Industrial Relations*, 29 (2), pp 149–76

Hendry, C and Pettigrew, A (1990) Human resource management: an agenda for the 1990s, *International Journal of Human Resource Management*, 1 (1), pp 17–44

Keegan, A and Francis, H (2010) Practitioner talk: the changing textscape of HRM and emergence of HR business partnership, *The International Journal of Human Resource Management*, 21 (6), pp 873–98

Keenoy, T (1997) HRMism and the images of re-presentation, *Journal of Management Studies*, 34 (5), pp 825–41

Legge, K (1989) Human resource management: a critical analysis, in (ed) J Storey, *New Perspectives in Human Resource Management*, London, Routledge, pp 19–40

Legge, K (1998) The morality of HRM, in (eds) C Mabey, D Skinner and T Clark, *Experiencing Human Resource Management*, London, Sage, pp 14–32

Legge, K (2005) *Human Resource Management – Rhetorics and realities*, Basingstoke, Macmillan

Paauwe, J (2004) *HRM and Performance: Achieving long-term viability*, Oxford, Oxford University Press

Storey, J (1989) From personnel management to human resource management, in (ed) J Storey, *New Perspectives on Human Resource Management*, London, Routledge, pp 1–18

Storey, J (2001) Human resource management today: an assessment, in (ed) J Storey, *Human Resource Management: A critical text*, London, Thompson Learning, pp 3–20

Truss, C, Gratton, L, Hope-Hailey, V, McGovern, P and Stiles, P (1997) Soft and hard models of human resource management: a re-appraisal, *Journal of Management Studies*, 34 (1), pp 53–73

Walton, R E (1985) From control to commitment in the workplace, *Harvard Business Review*, March–April, pp 77–84

Watson, T J (2010) Critical social science, pragmatism and the realities of HRM, *The International Journal of Human Resource Management*, 21 (6), pp 915–31

Wilmott, H (1993) Strength is ignorance, slavery is freedom: Managing culture in modern organizations, *Journal of Management Studies*, 30 (4), pp 515–52

02
Strategic HRM

KEY CONCEPTS AND TERMS

Best fit	Best practice
Bundling	Business model
Business model innovation	Competency framework
Competitive advantage	Configuration
Contingent determinism	High-commitment management
High-involvement management	High-performance management
High-performance work system	Human resource advantage
Lifecycle model	Resource-based view
Resource dependence theory	Strategic configuration
Strategic fit	Strategic HRM
Strategic management	Strategy

LEARNING OUTCOMES

On completing this chapter you should be able to define these key concepts. You should also understand:

- The conceptual basis of strategic HRM
- The fundamental characteristics of strategy
- How strategy is formulated
- The aims of strategic HRM
- The resource-based view and its implications
- The meaning of strategic fit
- The three HRM 'perspectives' of Delery and Doty
- The significance of bundling
- The significance of the concepts of 'best practice' and 'best fit'
- The significant features of strategic HRM
- The content and formulation of HR strategies

Introduction

Strategic human resource management (strategic HRM or SHRM) is an approach to the development and implementation of HR strategies that are integrated with business strategies and support their achievement. SHRM has been described by Boxall (1996) as the interface between HRM and strategic management. Schuler and Jackson (2007: 5) stated that SHRM is fundamentally about 'systematically linking people with the firm'.

Baird and Meshoulam (1988: 116) pointed out that: 'Business objectives are accomplished when human resource practices, procedures and systems are developed and implemented based on organizational needs, that is, when a strategic perspective to human resource management is adopted.' Wright and McMahan (1992: 295) explained that the field of HRM has 'sought to become integrated with the strategic management process through the development of a new discipline referred to as strategic human resource management'.

In essence, strategic HRM is conceptual; it is a general notion of how integration or 'fit' between HR and business strategies is achieved, the benefits of taking a longer-term view of where HR should be going and how to get there, and how coherent and mutually supporting HR strategies should be developed and implemented. Importantly, it is also about how members of the HR function should adopt a strategic approach on a day-to-day basis. This means that they operate as part of the management team, ensure that HR activities support the achievement of business strategies on a continuous basis, and add value.

The aim of this chapter is to explore what this involves. It starts with an analysis of the meaning of SHRM. It then covers: an examination of its nature and its aims; an analysis of its underpinning concepts – the resource-based view and strategic fit; and a description of how strategic HRM works, namely the universalistic, contingency and configurational perspectives defined by Delery and Doty (1996) and the three approaches associated with those perspectives – best practice, best fit and bundling. The chapter continues with a summary of the distinctive features of strategic HRM and ends with an examination of how HR strategies are developed and implemented when an SHRM approach is adopted.

The conceptual basis of strategic HRM

Strategic HRM takes the notion of HRM as a strategic, integrated and coherent process and associates it with an approach to management that involves adopting a broad and long-term view of where the business is going and managing it in ways that ensure that this strategic thrust is maintained. It is influenced by the concepts of strategic management and strategy.

Strategic management

According to Boxall and Purcell (2003: 44): 'Strategic management is best defined as a process. It is a process of strategy making, of forming and, if the firm survives, reforming its strategy over time.' Strategic management was described by Johnson *et al* (2005: 6) as 'understanding the strategic position of an organization, making strategic choices for the future, and turning strategy into action'. The purpose of strategic management has been expressed by Kanter (1984: 288) as being to: 'elicit the present actions for the future' and become 'action vehicles – integrating and institutionalizing mechanisms for change' (*ibid*: 301).

The key strategic management activity identified by Thompson and Strickland (1996: 3) is: 'deciding what business the company will be in and forming a strategic vision of where the organization needs to be headed – in effect, infusing the organization with a sense of purpose, providing long-term direction, and establishing a clear mission to be accomplished.'

The focus is on identifying the organization's mission and strategies, but attention is also given to the resource base required to make it succeed. Managers who think strategically will have a broad and long-term view of where they are going. But they will also be aware that they are responsible, first, for planning how to allocate resources to opportunities that contribute to the implementation of strategy, and secondly, for managing these opportunities in ways that will add value to the results achieved by the firm.

The concept of strategy

Strategy is the approach selected to achieve specified goals in the future. As defined by Chandler (1962: 13) it is: 'The determination of the long-term goals and objectives of an enterprise, and the adoption of courses of action and the allocation of resources necessary for carrying out those goals.' The formulation and implementation of corporate strategy is a process for developing a sense of direction, making the best use of resources and ensuring strategic fit.

Strategy has three fundamental characteristics. First, it is forward looking. It is about deciding where you want to go and how you mean to get there. It is concerned with both ends and means. In this sense a strategy is a declaration of intent: 'This is what we want to do and this is how we intend to do it.' Strategies define longer-term goals but they also cover how those goals will be attained. They guide purposeful action to deliver the required result. A good strategy is one that works, one that in Abell's (1993: 1) phrase enables organizations to adapt by 'mastering the present and pre-empting the future'. As Boxall (1996: 70) explained: 'Strategy should be understood as a framework of critical ends and means.'

The second characteristic of strategy is the recognition that the organizational capability of a firm (its capacity to function effectively) depends on its resource capability (the quality and quantity of its resources and their potential to deliver results). This is the resource-based view as described later in this chapter.

The third characteristic of strategy is that it aims to achieve strategic fit – the need when developing functional strategies such as HR to achieve congruence between them and the organization's business strategies within the context of its external and internal environment.

Implementation of strategy

'Implementation entails converting the strategic plan into action and then into results' (Thompson and Strickland, 1996: 20). Dreaming up a strategy is fairly easy; getting it to work is hard. Kanter (1984: 305) noted that: 'Many companies, even very sophisticated ones, are much better at generating impressive plans on paper than they are at getting "ownership" of the plans so that they actually guide operational decisions.'

Critical evaluation of the concept of strategy

The development of corporate strategy is often assumed to be a logical, step-by-step affair, the outcome of which is a formal written statement that provides a definitive guide to the organization's intentions. Many people still believe and act as if this were the case, but it is a misrepresentation of reality. In practice the formulation of strategy may not be as rational and linear a process as some writers describe it or as some managers attempt to make it. There are limitations to the totally logical model of management that underpins the concept of strategic human resource management. In the words of Mabey et al (1998: 74): 'The reality is … that strategies may not always be easy to discern, that the processes of decision making may be implicit, incremental, negotiated and compromised.'

Sparrow et al (2010: 4) asserted succinctly that: 'Strategy is not rational and never has been.' Strategy formulation can best be described as 'problem solving in unstructured situations' (Digman, 1990: 53) and strategies will always be formed under conditions of partial ignorance. Quinn (1980: 9) stated that a strategy may simply be 'a widely held understanding resulting from a stream of decisions'. He believed that strategy formulation takes place by means of 'logical incrementalism', ie it evolves in several steps rather than being conceived as a whole. Pettigrew and Whipp (1991: 26) observed that: 'strategy does not move forward in a direct linear way, nor through easily discernable sequential phases. Quite the reverse; the pattern is much more appropriately seen as continuous, iterative and uncertain.'

Another difficulty is that strategies are often based on the questionable assumption that the future will resemble the past. Some years ago, Heller (1972: 150) had a go at the cult of long-range planning: 'What goes wrong' he wrote, 'is that sensible anticipation gets converted into foolish numbers: and their validity always hinges on large loose assumptions.' Faulkner and Johnson (1992: 17–18) said of long-term planning that it:

> was inclined to take a definitive view of the future, and to extrapolate trend lines for the key business variables in order to arrive at this view. Economic turbulence was insufficiently considered, and the reality that much strategy is formulated and

implemented in the act of managing the enterprise was ignored. Precise forecasts ending with derived financials were constructed, the only weakness of which was that the future almost invariably turned out differently.

Strategy formulation is not necessarily a deterministic, rational and continuous process, as was emphasized by Mintzberg (1987). He noted that, rather than being consciously and systematically developed, strategy reorientation happens in what he calls brief 'quantum loops'. A strategy, according to Mintzberg, can be deliberate – it can realize the intentions of senior management, for example to attack and conquer a new market. But this is not always the case. In theory, he says, strategy is a systematic process: first we think, then we act; we formulate then we implement. But we also 'act in order to think'. In practice, 'a realized strategy can emerge in response to an evolving situation' (*ibid*: 68) and the strategic planner is often 'a pattern organizer, a learner if you like, who manages a process in which strategies and visions can emerge as well as be deliberately conceived' (*ibid*: 73). This concept of 'emergent strategy' conveys the essence of how in practice organizations develop their business and HR strategies.

Boxall and Purcell (2003: 34) suggested that, 'it is better if we understand the strategies of firms as *sets of strategic choices* some of which may stem from planning exercises and set-piece debates in senior management, and some of which may emerge in a stream of action'. Research conducted by Tyson (1997: 280) confirmed that, realistically, strategy:

- has always been emergent and flexible – it is always 'about to be', it never exists at the present time;
- is not only realized by formal statements but also comes about by actions and reactions;
- is a description of a future-oriented action that is always directed towards change;
- is conditioned by the management process itself.

The nature of strategic HRM

Strategic HRM is an approach that defines how the organization's goals will be achieved through people by means of HR strategies and integrated HR policies and practices. It was defined by Mabey

et al (1998: 25) as the process of, 'developing corporate capability to deliver new organizational strategies'. It is based on two key ideas, namely, the resource-based view and the need for strategic fit, as discussed later in this chapter.

SHRM can be regarded as a mindset underpinned by certain concepts rather than a set of techniques. It provides the foundation for strategic reviews in which analyses of the organizational context and existing HR practices lead to decisions on strategic plans for the development of overall or specific HR strategies. SHRM involves the exercise of strategic choice (which is always there) and the establishment of strategic priorities. It is essentially about the integration of business and HR strategies so that the latter contribute to the achievement of the former.

Strategic HRM is not just about strategic planning, nor does it only deal with the formulation of individual HR strategies. Its main concern is with integrating what HR does and plans to do with what the business does and plans to do. As modelled in Figure 2.1, SHRM is about both HR strategies and the strategic management activities of HR professionals.

Aims of SHRM

The fundamental aim of strategic HRM is to generate organizational capability by ensuring that the organization has the skilled, engaged, committed and well-motivated employees it needs to achieve sustained competitive advantage. Alvesson (2009: 52) wrote that strategic HRM is about, 'how the employment relationships for all employees can be managed in such a way as to contribute optimally to the organization's goal achievement'.

SHRM has three main objectives: first to achieve integration – the vertical alignment of HR strategies with business strategies and the horizontal integration of HR strategies. The second objective is to provide a sense of direction in an often turbulent environment so that the business needs of the organization and the individual and collective needs of its employees can be met by the development and implementation of coherent and practical HR policies and programmes. The third objective is to contribute to the formulation of business strategy by drawing attention to ways in which the business can capitalize on the advantages provided by the strengths of its human resources.

FIGURE 2.1   Strategic HRM model

Critical evaluation of the concept of SHRM

The whole concept of SHRM is predicated on the belief that HR strategies should be integrated with corporate or business strategies. Vertical integration (strategic fit between business and HR strategies) may be desirable but it is not easy to achieve for the following reasons.

Diversity of strategic processes, levels and styles

The different levels at which strategy is formulated and the different styles adopted by organizations may make it difficult to develop a coherent view of what sort of HR strategies will fit the overall strategies and what type of HR contributions are required during the process of formulation.

The complexity of the strategy formulation process

Business strategy formulation and implementation is a complex, interactive process heavily influenced by a variety of contextual and historical factors. In these circumstances, as Guest (1991) has asked, how

can there be a straightforward flow from the business strategy to the HR strategy? It has been pointed out by Truss (1999) that the assumption of some matching models of strategic HRM is that there is a simple linear relationship between business strategy and human resource strategy, but this assumption 'fails to acknowledge the complexities both between and within notions of strategy and human resource management ... (It) is based on a rational model of organizations and individuals which takes no account of the significance of power, politics and culture'.

The evolutionary nature of business strategy

The evolutionary and incremental nature of strategy making may make it difficult to pin down the HR issues that are likely to be relevant. Hendry and Pettigrew (1990) suggest that there are limits to the extent to which rational HR strategies can be drawn up if the process of business strategic planning is itself irrational.

The absence of articulated business strategies

If, because of its evolutionary nature, the business strategy has not been clearly articulated, this would add to the problems of clarifying the business strategic issues that human resource strategies should address.

The qualitative nature of HR issues

Business strategies tend, or at least aim, to be expressed in the common currency of figures and hard data on portfolio management, growth, competitive position, market share, profitability, etc. HR strategies may deal with quantifiable issues such as resourcing and skill acquisition but are equally likely to refer to qualitative factors such as engagement, commitment, motivation, good employee relations and high employment standards. The relationship between the pursuit of policies in these areas and individual and organizational performance may be difficult to establish.

Integration with what?

The concept of SHRM implies that HR strategies must be totally integrated with corporate/business strategies in the sense that they both flow from and contribute to such strategies. But as Brewster (2004) argued, HR strategy will be subjected to considerable external pressure; for example, in Europe, legislation about involvement. These may mean that HR strategies cannot be entirely governed by the corporate/business strategy.

The question: 'To what extent should HR strategy take into account the interests of all the stakeholders in the organization, employees in general as well as owners and management?' also needs to be answered.

Conclusions

The difficulties mentioned above are real, but they are frequently glossed over in rhetorical statements about the need for integration. Too often the outcome is a platitudinous statement such as, 'Our HR strategy is to develop a performance culture' or, 'Our HR strategy is to ensure that the organization has the talented people it needs.' These are perfectly laudable broad objectives but they need to be more specific about how the aims will be achieved and how they will support the achievement of business goals.

Matching HR and business strategies is a problematic process but this doesn't mean that the attempt to do should be abandoned. HR strategists must make every effort to understand the business model of their organization (ie a picture of an organization that explains how it achieves competitive advantage and makes money) and the plans for business model innovation (the process followed by an organization to develop a new business model or change an existing one). They have to take into account the difficulties mentioned above but they need to overcome these by persistent efforts designed to obtain insight into the real issues facing the organization, leading to plans for practical interventions that address those issues.

The resource-based view of SHRM

To a very large extent, the philosophy of SHRM is underpinned by the resource-based view. This states that it is the range of resources in an organization, including its human resources, that produces its unique character and creates competitive advantage. The resource-based view is founded on the ideas of Penrose (1959: 24–5), who wrote that the firm is, 'an administrative organization and a collection of productive resources' and saw resources as 'a bundle of potential services'. It was expanded by Wernerfelt (1984: 172), who explained that strategy, 'is a balance between the exploitation of existing resources and the development of new ones'. Resources were defined by Hunt (1991: 322), as, 'anything that has an enabling capacity'.

The concept was developed by Barney (1991: 102), who stated that, 'a firm is said to have a competitive advantage when it is implementing a value-creating strategy not simultaneously being implemented by any current or potential competitors *and* when these other firms are unable to duplicate the benefits of this strategy'. This will happen if their resources are valuable, rare, inimitable and non-substitutable. He noted later (Barney 1995: 49) that an environmental (SWOT) analysis of strengths, weaknesses, opportunities and threats was only half the story: 'A complete understanding of sources of a firm's competitive advantage requires the analysis of a firm's internal strengths and weaknesses as well.' He emphasized that:

> Creating sustained competitive advantage depends on the unique resources and capabilities that a firm brings to competition in its environment. To discover these resources and capabilities, managers must look inside their firm for valuable, rare and costly-to-imitate resources, and then exploit these resources through their organization. (*ibid*: 60)

The following rationale for resource-based strategy was produced by Grant.

Source review

Rationale for resource-based strategy – Grant (1991: 13)

The resources and capabilities of a firm are the central considerations in formulating its strategy: they are the primary constants upon which a firm can establish its identity and frame its strategy, and they are the primary sources of the firm's profitability. The key to a resource-based approach to strategy formulation is understanding the relationships between resources, capabilities, competitive advantage and profitability – in particular, an understanding of the mechanisms through which competitive advantage can be sustained over time. This requires the design of strategies which exploit to maximum effect each firm's unique characteristics.

Resource-based SHRM can produce what Boxall and Purcell (2003) referred to as 'human resource advantage'. The aim is to develop strategic capability. This means strategic fit between resources and opportunities, obtaining added value from the effective deployment of resources, and developing managers who can think and plan strategically in the sense that they understand the key strategic issues and ensure that what they do enables the strategic goals of the business to be achieved. In line with human capital theory, the resource-based view emphasizes that investment in people increases their value to the firm. It proposes that sustainable competitive advantage is attained when the firm has a human resource pool that cannot be imitated or substituted by its rivals.

Boxall (1996: 66) suggested that, 'the resource-based view of the firm provides a conceptual basis, if we needed one, for asserting that key human resources are sources of competitive advantage'. He noted that human resource advantage is achieved by a combination of 'human capital advantage', which results from employing people with competitively valuable knowledge and skills, and 'human process advantage', which follows from the establishment of, 'difficult to imitate, highly evolved processes within the firm, such as cross-departmental cooperation and executive development'. Accordingly, 'human resource advantage', the superiority of one firm's labour management over another's, can be thought of as the product of its human capital and human process advantages. He also observed (*ibid*: 66) that the strategic goal emerging from the resource-based view was to, 'create firms which are more intelligent and flexible than their competitors' by hiring and developing more talented staff and by extending their skills base. Resource-based strategy is therefore concerned with the enhancement of the human or intellectual capital of the firm. As Ulrich (1998: 126) commented: 'Knowledge has become a direct competitive advantage for companies selling ideas and relationships. The challenge to organizations is to ensure that they have the capability to find, assimilate, compensate and retain the talented individuals they need.'

The strategic goal emerging from the resource-based view is to create firms that are more intelligent and flexible than their competitors (Boxall, 1996) by hiring and developing more talented staff and by extending their skills base. Resource-based strategy is therefore concerned with the enhancement of the human or intellectual capital of the firm. Resource dependence theory (Pfeffer and Davis-Blake, 1992) suggests that HR strategies such as those concerned with reward are strongly influenced by the need to attract, retain and energize high-quality people.

Critical evaluation of the resource-based view

The resource-based view has had considerable influence on thinking about human resource management. It provides a justification for attaching importance to resourcing activities, especially those concerned with talent management. It can also be used to enhance the value of the HR contribution in achieving competitive advantage. But it has the following limitations:

- it may be difficult to find resources that satisfy all the criteria;
- external factors such as product market pressures are ignored;
- it provides only generalized guidance on what resources are suitable;
- different resource configurations can provide the same value for firms;
- as Priem and Butler (2001) pointed out, the theory is tautological because valuable resources and competitive advantage are defined in the same terms.

Strategic fit

The concept of strategic fit stresses that when developing HR strategies it is necessary to achieve congruence between them and the organization's business strategies within the context of its external and internal environment. This notion is fundamental to SHRM, as was stressed by Wright and Snell (1998: 758) who wrote that: 'The primary role of strategic HRM should be to promote a fit with the demands of the competitive environment.' In more detail, Schuler (1992: 18) stated that:

> Strategic human resource management is largely about integration and adaptation. Its concern is to ensure that: (1) human resources (HR) management is fully integrated with the strategy and strategic needs of the firm (vertical fit); (2) HR policies cohere both across policy areas and across hierarchies (horizontal fit); and (3) HR practices are adjusted, accepted and used by line managers and employees as part of their everyday work.

Perspectives on SHRM

Taking into account the concepts of the resource-based view and strategic fit, Delery and Doty (1996: 802) contended that, 'organizations adopting a particular strategy require HR practices that are different from those required by organizations adopting different strategies' and that organizations with 'greater congruence between their HR strategies and their (business) strategies should enjoy superior performance' (*ibid*: 803). They identified these three HRM perspectives:

1 *The universalistic perspective* – some HR practices are better than others and all organizations should adopt these best practices. There is a universal relationship between individual 'best' practices and firm performance.

2 *The contingency perspective* – to be effective an organization's HR policies must be consistent with other aspects of the organization. The primary contingency factor is the organization's strategy. This can be described as 'vertical fit'.

3 *The configurational perspective* – this is a holistic approach that emphasizes the importance of the *pattern* of HR practices and is concerned with how this pattern of independent variables is related to the dependent variable of organizational performance.

This typology provided the basis for what has become the most commonly used classification of approaches as used by Richardson and Thompson (1999), which is to adopt the terms 'best practice' and 'best fit' for the universalistic and contingency perspectives, and 'bundling' as the third approach. This followed the classification made by Guest (1997) of fit as an ideal set of practices, fit as contingency and fit as bundles.

The best practice model

This model is based on the assumption that there is a set of best HRM practices that are universal in the sense that they are best in any situation, and that adopting them will lead to superior organizational performance.

A number of lists of 'best practices' have been produced, the best known being by Pfeffer (1998):

1   employment security;

2   selective hiring;

3   self-managed teams;

4   high compensation contingent on performance;

5   training to provide a skilled and motivated workforce;

6   reduction of status differentials;

7   sharing information.

The best fit model

The best fit model is in line with contingency theory. It emphasizes that HR strategies should be congruent with the context and circumstances of the organization. 'Best fit' can be perceived in terms of vertical integration or alignment between the organization's business and HR strategies. There are three models: lifecycle, competitive strategy, and strategic configuration.

The lifecycle model

The lifecycle model is based on the theory that the development of a firm takes place in four stages: start-up, growth, maturity and decline. This is in line with product lifecycle theory. The basic premise of this model was expressed by Baird and Meshoulam (1988: 117) as follows:

> Human resource management's effectiveness depends on its fit with the organization's stage of development. As the organization grows and develops, human resource management programmes, practices and procedures must change to meet its needs. Consistent with growth and development models it can be suggested that human resource management develops through a series of stages as the organization becomes more complex.

Best fit and competitive strategies

Three strategies aimed at achieving competitive advantage were identified by Porter (1985):

1   *Innovation* – being the unique producer.

2   *Quality* – delivering high-quality goods and services to customers.

3   *Cost leadership* – the planned result of policies aimed at 'managing away' expense.

It was argued by Schuler and Jackson (1987) that to achieve the maximum effect it is necessary to match the role characteristics of people in an organization with the preferred strategy.

Strategic configuration

Another approach to best fit is the proposition that organizations will be more effective if they adopt a policy of strategic configuration (Delery and Doty, 1996) by matching their strategy to one of the ideal types defined by theories such as those produced by Miles and Snow (1978). This increased effectiveness is attributed to the internal consistency or fit between the patterns of relevant contextual, structural and strategic factors. They identified the following four types of organizations, classifying the first three types as 'ideal' organizations:

1   *Prospectors*, which operate in an environment characterized by rapid and unpredictable changes. Prospectors have low levels of formalization and specialization and high levels of decentralization. They have relatively few hierarchical levels.

2   *Defenders*, which operate in a more stable and predictable environment than prospectors and engage in more long-term planning. They have more mechanistic or bureaucratic structures than prospectors and obtain coordination through formalization, centralization, specialization and vertical differentiation.

3   *Analysers*, which are a combination of the prospector and defender types. They operate in stable environments like defenders and also in markets where new products are constantly required, like prospectors. They are usually not the initiators of change like prospectors but they follow the changes more rapidly than defenders.

4   *Reactors*, which are unstable organizations existing in what they believe to be an unpredictable environment. They lack consistent well-articulated strategies and do not undertake long-range planning.

Critical evaluation of the best practice and best fit models

The best practice model

The notion of best practice incorrectly assumes that there are universally effective HR practices that can readily be transferred. The 'best practice' rubric has been attacked by a number of commentators. Cappelli and Crocker-Hefter (1996: 7) commented that the notion of a single set of best practices has been over-stated: 'There are examples in virtually every industry of firms that have very distinctive management practices. ... Distinctive human resource practices shape the core competencies that determine how firms compete.'

Purcell (1999: 26) noted that 'the search for best practice tends to take on the flavour of a moral crusade'. He has also criticized the best practice or universalist view by pointing out the inconsistency between a belief in best practice and the resource-based view, which focuses on the intangible assets, including HR, that allow the firm to do better than its competitors. He asked how can 'the universalism of best practice be squared with the view that only some resources and routines are important and valuable by being rare and imperfectly imitable?' He stated that: 'The claim that the bundle of best practice HRM is universally applicable leads us into a utopian cul-de-sac' (*ibid*: 36). Boxall (2007: 5) concluded that he was, 'deeply sceptical about claims for universal applicability for particular HRM practices or clusters of practices [but] this does not rule out the search for general principles in the management of work and people'.

However, a knowledge of what is assumed to be best practice can be used to inform decisions on what practices are most likely to fit the needs of the organization, as long as it is understood *why* a particular practice should be regarded as a best practice and what needs to be done to ensure that it will work in the context of the organization. Becker and Gerhart (1996) argued that the idea of best practice might be more appropriate for identifying the principles underlying the choice of practices, as opposed to the practices themselves.

The best fit model

The best fit model seems to be more realistic than the best practice model. As Dyer and Holder (1988:

31) observed: 'The inescapable conclusion is that what is best depends.' But there are limitations to the concept. Paauwe (2004: 37) emphasized that: 'It is necessary to avoid falling into the trap of "contingent determinism" (ie claiming that the context absolutely determines the strategy). There is, or should be, room for making strategic choices.'

There is a danger of mechanistically matching HR policies and practices with strategy. It is not credible to claim that there are single contextual factors that determine HR strategy, and internal fit cannot therefore be complete. Purcell (1999: 35) pointed out that: 'each firm has to make choices not just on business and operational strategies but on what type of HR system is best for its purposes'. As Boxall (2007: 61) asserted: 'It is clearly impossible to make *all* HR policies reflective of a chosen competitive or economic mission.' They may have to fit with social legitimacy goals. And Purcell (1999: 37) commented that: 'The search for a contingency or matching model of HRM is also limited by the impossibility of modelling all the contingent variables, the difficulty of showing their interconnection, and the way in which changes in one variable have an impact on others.'

Best fit models tend to be static and don't take account of the processes of change. They neglect the fact that institutional forces shape HRM – it cannot be assumed that employers are free agents able to make independent decisions.

Conclusions

It is often said that best fit is better than best practice but this statement can only be accepted with reservations. As Stavrou *et al* (2010: 952–3) argued:

There may be merit in both approaches where the debate is between general principles/bundles (training and development, staffing, compensation and benefits, communication and participation, and planning) and the manner in which they are carried out ... It seems that the 'best fit' and 'best practice' approaches of the HR-performance relationship are not necessarily mutually exclusive. On the contrary, they may be combined to provide a more holistic picture.

This is particularly the case if the term 'best practice' is replaced by 'good practice', thus avoiding the notion of universality implied by the former term. For example, the meta-analysis carried out by

Schmidt and Hunter (1998) established conclusively that when selecting people, the best levels of predictive validity are achieved by a combination of structured interviews and intelligence tests. But a decision on what sort of structured interview should be adopted and whether or not to use intelligence tests would depend on the situation in which the decision was made.

Bundling

'Bundling' is the development and implementation of several HR practices together so that they are interrelated and therefore complement and reinforce each other. This is the process of horizontal integration, which is also referred to as the use of 'complementarities'. Richardson and Thompson (1999) suggested that a strategy's success turns on combining vertical or external fit and horizontal or internal fit. They concluded that a firm with bundles of associated HR practices should have a higher level of performance, provided it also achieves high levels of fit with its competitive strategy.

Dyer and Reeves (1995: 656–7) noted that: 'The logic in favour of bundling is straightforward … Since employee performance is a function of both ability and motivation, it makes sense to have practices aimed at enhancing both.' Thus there are several ways in which employees can acquire needed skills (such as careful selection and training) and multiple incentives to enhance motivation (different forms of financial and non-financial rewards). Their study of various models listing HR practices that create a link between HRM and business performance found that the activities appearing in most of the models were involvement, careful selection, extensive training and contingent compensation.

The process of bundling HR strategies is an important aspect of the concept of strategic HRM. In a sense, SHRM is holistic: it is concerned with the organization as a total system or entity and addresses what needs to be done across the organization as a whole. It is not interested in isolated programmes and techniques, or in the ad hoc development of HR strategies and practices.

Bundling can take place in a number of ways. For example, competency frameworks (a set of definitions of the competencies that describe the types of behaviour required for the successful performance of a role) can be devised that are used in a number of ways, for example to specify recruitment standards, provide a framework for competency-based interviews, identify learning and development needs and indicate the standards of behaviour or performance required. Job evaluation can also be used to clarify and define levels in an organization. Grade structures can define career ladders in terms of competency requirements (career family structures) and thus provide the basis for learning and development programmes. Total reward approaches 'bundle' financial and non-financial rewards together. High-performance systems are in effect based on the principle of bundling because they group a number of HR practices together to produce synergy and thus increase their impact.

Critical evaluation of bundling

Bundling sounds like a good idea. The research by MacDuffie (1995) and others has shown that bundling can improve performance. But there are a number of inhibiting factors, namely:

- deciding which bundles are likely to be best – there is no evidence that one bundle is generally better than another;
- actually linking practices together – it is always easier to deal with one practice at a time;
- managing the interdependencies between different parts of a bundle;
- convincing top management and line managers that bundling will benefit the organization and them.

These can be overcome by dedicated HR professionals, but it is hard work. What can be done, with difficulty, is to find ways in which different HR practices can support one another, as in the examples given above.

HR strategies

HR strategies indicate what the organization wants to do about its human resource management policies and practices and how they should be integrated with the business strategy and each other. They set out aspirations that are expressed as intentions, which are then converted into actions. As suggested by Chesters (2011: 32), they should be regarded as a statement of the organization's collective endeavour.

They are not just a laundry list of everything the organization would like to do.

HR strategies were described by Dyer and Reeves (1995: 656) as, 'internally consistent bundles of human resource practices'. Richardson and Thompson (1999: 3) observed that:

> A strategy, whether it is an HR strategy or any other kind of management strategy must have two key elements: there must be strategic objectives (ie things the strategy is supposed to achieve), and there must be a plan of action (ie the means by which it is proposed that the objectives will be met).

Purcell (2001: 72) made the point that: 'Strategy in HR, like in other areas, is about continuity and change, about appropriateness in the circumstances, but anticipating when the circumstances change. It is about taking strategic decisions.'

The purpose of HR strategies is to articulate what an organization intends to do about its HRM policies and practices now and in the longer term to ensure that they contribute to the achievement of business objectives. However, it is necessary to bear in mind the dictum of Fombrun *et al* (1984) that business and managers should perform well in the present to succeed in the future.

HR strategies may be defined formally as part of a strategic HRM process that leads to the development of overall or specific strategies for implementation by HR *and*, vitally, line managers. But an organization that has developed an HR strategy will not be practising SHRM unless that HR strategy has strategic relevance to the organization's success. As Wright and McMahan (1999: 52) indicated, HRM can only be considered to be strategic if 'it enables an organization to achieve its goals'.

Pettigrew and Whipp (1991: 30) emphasized that strategy, 'far from being a straightforward, rational phenomenon, is in fact interpreted by managers according to their own frame of reference, their particular motivations and information'. They were writing about business strategy, but the same applies to HR strategy, which can appear through an emergent, evolutionary and possibly unarticulated process influenced by the business strategy as it develops and changes in the internal and external environment. But there are still strong arguments for a systematic approach to identifying strategic directions that can provide a framework for decision making and action. The main argument for articulating HR strategies is that unless you know where you are going, you will not know how to get there or when you have arrived.

Because all organizations are different, all HR strategies are different. There is no such thing as a standard strategy. Research into HR strategy conducted by Armstrong and Long (1994) and Armstrong and Baron (2002) revealed many variations. Some strategies are simply very general declarations of intent. Others go into much more detail. The two types of HR strategies are: 1) general strategies such as high-performance working, and 2) specific strategies relating to the different aspects of HRM such as learning and development and reward.

General HR strategies

General strategies describe the overall system or bundle of complementary HR practices that the organization proposes to adopt or puts into effect in order to improve organizational performance. The three main approaches are summarized below.

High-performance management

High-performance management aims, through high-performance work systems (bundles of practices that enhance employee performance and facilitate their engagement, motivation and skill enhancement), to make an impact on the performance of the organization in such areas as productivity, quality, levels of customer service, growth and profits. High-performance working practices include rigorous recruitment and selection procedures, extensive and relevant training and management development activities, incentive pay systems and performance management processes.

High-commitment management

One of the defining characteristics of HRM is its emphasis on the importance of enhancing mutual commitment (Walton, 1985). High-commitment management has been described by Wood (1996) as: 'A form of management which is aimed at eliciting a commitment so that behaviour is primarily self-regulated rather than controlled by sanctions and pressures external to the individual, and relations within the organization are based on high levels of trust.'

High-involvement management

As defined by Benson *et al* (2006: 519): 'High-involvement work practices are a specific set of human resource practices that focus on employee decision-making, power, access to information, training and incentives.' Camps and Luna-Arocas (2009: 1057) observed that: 'High-involvement work practices aim to provide employees with the opportunity, skills and motivation to contribute to organizational success in environments demanding greater levels of commitment and involvement.' The term 'high-involvement' was used by Lawler (1986) to describe management systems based on commitment and involvement, as opposed to the old bureaucratic model based on control.

Examples of general HR strategies

- A local authority. As expressed by the chief executive of this borough council, its HR strategy is about 'having a very strong focus on the overall effectiveness of the organization, its direction and how it's performing; there is commitment to, and belief in, and respect for individuals, and I think that these are very important factors'.

- A public utility. 'The only HR strategy you really need is the tangible expression of values and the implementation of values ... unless you get the human resource values right you can forget all the rest'. *(Managing Director)*

- A manufacturing company. 'The HR strategy is to stimulate changes on a broad front aimed ultimately at achieving competitive advantage through the efforts of our people. In an industry of fast followers, those who learn quickest will be the winners.' *(HR Director)*

- A retail stores group. 'The biggest challenge will be to maintain (our) competitive advantage and to do that we need to maintain and continue to attract very high calibre people. The key differentiator on anything any company does is fundamentally the people, and I think that people tend to forget that they are the most important asset. Money is easy to get hold

of, good people are not. All we do in terms of training and manpower planning is directly linked to business improvement'. *(Managing Director)*

Specific HR strategies

Specific HR strategies set out what the organization intends to do in areas such as:

- *Human capital management* – obtaining, analysing and reporting on data that informs the direction of value-adding people management strategic, investment and operational decisions.

- *Knowledge management* – creating, acquiring, capturing, sharing and using knowledge to enhance learning and performance.

- *Corporate social responsibility* – a commitment to managing the business ethically in order to make a positive impact on society and the environment.

- *Engagement* – the development and implementation of policies designed to increase the level of employees' engagement with their work and the organization.

- *Organization development* – the planning and implementation of programmes designed to enhance the effectiveness with which an organization functions and responds to change.

- *Resourcing* – attracting and retaining high-quality people.

- *Talent management* – how the organization ensures that it has the talented people it needs to achieve success.

- *Learning and development* – providing an environment in which employees are encouraged to learn and develop.

- *Reward* – defining what the organization wants to do in the longer term to develop and implement reward policies, practices and processes that will further the achievement of its business goals and meet the needs of its stakeholders.

- *Employee relations* – defining the intentions of the organization about what needs to be done and what needs to be changed in the ways in which the organization manages its relationships with employees and their trade unions.

- *Employee wellbeing* – meeting the needs of employees for a healthy, safe and supportive work environment.

The following are some examples of specific HR strategies.

The Children's Society

- Implement the rewards strategy of the Society to support the corporate plan and secure the recruitment, retention and motivation of staff to deliver its business objectives.
- Manage the development of the human resources information system to secure productivity improvements in administrative processes.
- Introduce improved performance management processes for managers and staff of the Society.
- Implement training and development that supports the business objectives of the Society and improves the quality of work with children and young people.

Diageo

There are three broad strands to the *Organization and People Strategy*:

1 *Reward and recognition*: use recognition and reward programmes to stimulate outstanding team and individual performance contributions.

2 *Talent management*: drive the attraction, retention and professional growth of a deep pool of diverse, talented employees.

3 *Organizational effectiveness*: ensure that the business adapts its organization to maximize employee contribution and deliver performance goals.

It provides direction to the company's talent, operational effectiveness and performance and reward agendas. The company's underlying thinking is that the people strategy is not for the human resource function to own but is the responsibility of the whole organization, hence the title 'Organization and People Strategy'.

A government agency

The key components of the HR strategy are:

- Investing in people – improving the level of intellectual capital.
- Performance management – integrating the values contained in the HR strategy into performance management processes and ensuring that reviews concentrate on how well people are performing those values.
- Job design – a key component concerned with how jobs are designed and how they relate to the whole business.
- The reward system – in developing reward strategies, taking into account that this is a very hard driven business.

A local authority

The focus is on the organization of excellence. The strategy is broken down into eight sections: employee relations, recruitment and retention, training, performance management, pay and benefits, health and safety, absence management and equal opportunities.

Criteria for an effective HR strategy

An effective HR strategy is one that works in the sense that it achieves what it sets out to achieve. Its criteria are that it:

- will satisfy business needs;
- is founded on detailed analysis and study, not just wishful thinking;
- can be turned into actionable programmes that anticipate implementation requirements and problems;
- is coherent and integrated, being composed of components that fit with and support each other;
- takes account of the needs of line managers and employees generally as well as those of the organization and its other stakeholders.

Formulating HR strategy

Research conducted by Wright *et al* (2004) identified two approaches that can be adopted by HR to strategy formulation. 1. *The inside-out approach* begins with the status quo HR function (in terms of skills, processes, technologies, etc) and then attempts (with varying degrees of success) to identify linkages to the business (usually through focusing on 'people issues'), making minor adjustments to HR activities along the way. 2. *The outside-in approach* in which the starting point is the business and the customer, competitor and business issues it faces. The HR strategy then derives directly from these challenges to add real value.

They commented that HR strategies are more likely to flow from business strategies dominated by product/market and financial considerations. But there is still room for HR to make an essential contribution at the stage when business strategies are conceived, for example by focusing on resource issues. This contribution may be more significant when strategy formulation is an emergent or evolutionary process – HR strategic issues will then be dealt with as they arise during the course of formulating and implementing the corporate strategy.

Implementing HR strategy

As Gratton (2000: 30) commented: 'There is no great strategy, only great execution.' Strategies cannot be left as generalized aspirations or abstractions. But getting strategies into action is not easy: intent does not always lead to action. Too often, strategists act like Mr Pecksmith, who was compared by Dickens (*Martin Chuzzlewit*, Penguin Classics, 2004: 23) to 'a direction-post which is always telling the way to a place and never goes there'. It is necessary to avoid saying, in effect: 'We need to get from here to there but we don't care how.'

If, in Kanter's (1984) phrase, HR strategies are to be action vehicles, they must be translated into HR policies that provide guidelines on decision making and HR practices that enable the strategy to work. These can be the basis for implementation programmes with clearly stated objectives and deliverables.

To a large extent, HR strategies are implemented by line managers. As Purcell *et al* (2003: x) stressed, it is front-line managers who 'bring policies to life'. They pointed out that:

> Implementing and enacting policies is the task of line managers. It is necessary first to involve line managers in the development of HR strategy – bearing in mind that things done *with* line managers are much more likely to work than things done *to* line managers. Second, ensure that the HR policies they are expected to put into practice are *manageable* with the resources available. Third, provide managers with the training, supporting processes and on the spot guidance they need.

Key learning points: Strategic HRM

The conceptual basis of strategic HRM

Strategic HRM is the 'interface between HRM and strategic management'. It takes the notion of HRM as a strategic, integrated and coherent approach and develops that in line with the concept of strategic management (Boxall, 1996).

The fundamental characteristics of strategy

- Forward looking.
- The organizational capability of a firm depends on its resource capability.
- Strategic fit – the need when developing HR strategies to achieve congruence between them and the organization's business strategies within the context of its external and internal environment.

How strategy is formulated

An emergent and flexible process of developing a sense of direction, making the best use of resources and ensuring strategic fit.

The aim of SHRM

To generate organizational capability by ensuring that the organization has the skilled, engaged, committed and well-motivated employees it needs to achieve sustained competitive advantage.

Implications of the resource-based view (RBV)

The RBV emphasizes the importance of creating firms that are 'more intelligent and flexible than their competitors' (Boxall, 1996) by hiring and developing more talented staff and by extending the skills base.

Implications of the concept of strategic fit

The concept of strategic fit means developing HR strategies that are integrated with the business strategy and support its achievement (vertical integration or fit), and the use of an integrated approach to the development of HR practices.

Best practice

There is a set of best HRM practices that are universal in the sense that they are best in any situation and adopting them will lead to superior organizational performance. The notion of best practice incorrectly assumes that there are universally effective HR practices that can readily be transferred.

Best fit

HR strategies should be congruent with the context and circumstances of the organization. More realistic than best practice, but there is a danger of mechanistically matching HR policies and practices with strategy.

The significance of bundling

The process of bundling HR strategies is an important aspect of the concept of SHRM, which is concerned with the organization as a total system or entity and addresses what needs to be done across the organization as a whole.

HR strategies

HR strategies set out what the organization intends to do about its HRM policies and practices and how they should be integrated with the business strategy and each other. The two types of HR strategies are: 1) general strategies such as high-performance working, and 2) specific strategies relating to the different aspects of HRM such as learning and development and reward.

Questions

1 What is strategic HRM?
2 What is strategic management?
3 What is strategy?
4 What is the resource-based view?
5 What is the meaning and significance of strategic fit?
6 What is the best practice model and to what extent is it valid?
7 What is the best fit model and to what extent is it valid?
8 What is bundling?
9 What are HR strategies?
10 What are the criteria for an effective HR strategy?

References

Abell, D F (1993) *Managing with Dual Strategies: Mastering the present, pre-empting the future*, New York, Free Press

Alvesson, M (2009) Critical perspectives on strategic HRM, in (eds) J Storey, P M Wright and D Ulrich, *The Routledge Companion to Strategic Human Resource Management*, Abingdon, Routledge, pp 52–67

Armstrong, M and Baron, A (2002) *Strategic HRM: The route to improved business performance*, London, CIPD

Armstrong, M and Long, P (1994) *The Reality of Strategic HRM*, London, IPM

Baird, L and Meshoulam, I (1988) Managing two fits of strategic human resource management, *Academy of Management Review*, **13** (1), pp 116–28

Barney, J B (1991) Firm resources and sustained competitive advantage, *Journal of Management Studies*, **17** (1), pp 99–120

Barney, J B (1995) Looking inside for competitive advantage, *Academy of Management Executive*, **9** (4), pp 49–61

Becker, B E and Gerhart, S (1996) The impact of human resource management on organizational performance: progress and prospects, *Academy of Management Journal*, **39** (4), pp 779–801

Benson, G S, Young, S M and Lawler, E E (2006) High involvement work practices and analysts' forecasts of corporate performance, *Human Resource Management*, **45** (4), pp 519–27

Boxall, P F (1996) The strategic HRM debate and the resource-based view of the firm, *Human Resource Management Journal*, **6** (3), pp 59–75

Boxall, P F (2007) The goals of HRM, in (eds) P Boxall, J Purcell and P Wright, *The Oxford Handbook of Human Resource Management*, Oxford, Oxford University Press, pp 48–67

Boxall, P F and Purcell, J (2003) *Strategy and Human Resource Management*, Basingstoke, Palgrave Macmillan

Brewster, C (2004) European perspectives of human resource management, *Human Resource Management Review*, **14** (4), pp 365–82

Camps, J and Luna-Arocas, R (2009) High-involvement work practices and firm performance, *International Journal of Human Resource Management*, **20** (5), pp 1056–77

Cappelli, P and Crocker-Hefter, A (1996) Distinctive human resources are firms' core competencies, *Organizational Dynamics*, Winter, pp 7–22

Chandler, A D (1962) *Strategy and Structure*, Boston, MA, MIT Press

Chesters, J (2011) Creating strategic impact: it's how not what, *People Management*, August, pp 32–5

Delery, J E and Doty, H D (1996) Modes of theorizing in strategic human resource management: tests of universality, contingency and configurational performance predictions, *Academy of Management Journal*, **39** (4), pp 802–35

Dickens, C (1843) *Martin Chuzzlewit*, London, Chapman & Hall (Penguin Classics, 2004)

Digman, L A (1990) *Strategic Management – Concepts, decisions, cases*, Georgetown, Ontario, Irwin

Dyer, L and Holder, G W (1988) Strategic human resource management and planning, in (ed) L Dyer, *Human Resource Management: Evolving roles and responsibilities*, Washington, DC, Bureau of National Affairs

Dyer, L and Reeves, T (1995) Human resource strategies and firm performance: what do we know and where do we need to go?, *The International Journal of Human Resource Management*, **6** (3), pp 656–70

Faulkner, D and Johnson, G (1992) *The Challenge of Strategic Management*, London, Kogan Page

Fombrun, C J, Tichy, N M and Devanna, M A (1984) *Strategic Human Resource Management*, New York, Wiley

Grant, R M (1991) The resource-based theory of competitive advantage: implications for strategy formulation, *California Management Review*, **33** (3), pp 114–35

Gratton, L A (2000) Real step change, *People Management*, 16 March, pp 27–30

Guest, D E (1991) Personnel management: the end of orthodoxy, *British Journal of Industrial Relations*, **29** (2), pp 149–76

Guest, D E (1997) Human resource management and performance; a review of the research agenda, *The International Journal of Human Resource Management*, **8** (3), pp 263–76

Heller, R (1972) *The Naked Manager*, London, Barrie & Jenkins

Hendry, C and Pettigrew, A (1990) Human resource management: an agenda for the 1990s, *International Journal of Human Resource Management*, **1** (1), pp 17–44

Hunt, S (1991) The resource-advantage theory of competition, *Journal of Management Inquiry*, **4** (4), pp 317–22

Johnson, G, Scholes, K and Whittington, R (2005) *Explaining Corporate Strategy*, 7th edn, Harlow, FT Prentice Hall

Kanter, R M (1984) The *Change Masters*, London, Allen & Unwin

Lawler, E E (1986) *High Involvement Management*, San Francisco, CA, Jossey-Bass

Mabey, C, Salaman, G and Storey, J (1998) *Human Resource Management: A strategic introduction*, 2nd edn, Oxford, Blackwell

MacDuffie, J P (1995) Human resource bundles and manufacturing performance, *Industrial Relations Review*, **48** (2), pp 199–221

Miles, R E and Snow, C C (1978) *Organizational Strategy: Structure and process*, New York, McGraw-Hill

Mintzberg, H (1987) Crafting strategy, *Harvard Business Review*, July–August, pp 66–74

Paauwe, J (2004) *HRM and Performance: Achieving long-term viability*, Oxford, Oxford University Press

Penrose, E (1959) *The Theory of the Growth of the Firm*, Oxford, Blackwell

Pettigrew, A and Whipp, R (1991) *Managing Change for Strategic Success*, Oxford, Blackwell

Pfeffer, J (1998) *The Human Equation*, Boston, MA, Harvard Business School Press

Pfeffer, J and Davis-Blake, A (1992) Understanding organizational wage structures: a resource dependence approach, *Academy of Management Journal*, 30, pp 437–55

Porter, M E (1985) *Competitive Advantage: Creating and sustaining superior performance*, New York, The Free Press

Priem, R L and Butler, J E (2001) Is the resource-based theory a useful perspective for strategic management research?, *Academy of Management Review*, 26 (1), pp 22–40

Purcell, J (1999) Best practice or best fit: chimera or cul-de-sac, *Human Resource Management Journal*, 9 (3), pp 26–41

Purcell, J (2001) The meaning of strategy in human resource management, in (ed) J Storey, *Human Resource Management: A critical text*, 2nd edn, London, Thompson Learning, pp 59–77

Purcell, J, Kinnie, K, Hutchinson, R, Rayton, B and Swart, J (2003) *People and Performance: How people management impacts on organizational performance*, London, CIPD

Quinn, J B (1980) *Strategies for Change: Logical incrementalism*, Georgetown, Ontario, Irwin

Richardson, R and Thompson, M (1999) *The Impact of People Management Practices on Business Performance: A literature review*, London, IPD

Schmidt, F L and Hunter, J E (1998) The validity and utility of selection methods in personnel psychology: practical and theoretical implications of 85 years of research findings, *Psychological Bulletin*, 124 (2), pp 262–74

Schuler, R S (1992) Strategic human resource management: linking people with the strategic needs of the business, *Organizational Dynamics*, 21 (1), pp 18–32

Schuler, R S and Jackson, S E (1987) Linking competitive strategies with human resource management practices, *Academy of Management Executive*, 9 (3), pp 207–19

Schuler, R S and Jackson, S E (2007) *Strategic Human Resource Management*, 2nd edn, Oxford, Blackwell

Sparrow, P, Hesketh, A, Hird, M and Cooper, C (2010) Introduction: Performance-led HR, in (eds) P Sparrow, A Hesketh, M Hird and C Cooper, *Leading HR*, Basingstoke, Palgrave Macmillan, pp 1–22

Stavrou, E T, Brewster, C and Charalambousa, C (2010) Human resource management and firm performance in Europe through the lens of business systems: best fit, best practice or both?, *The International Journal of Human Resource Management*, 21 (7), pp 933–62

Thompson, A A and Strickland, A J (1996) *Strategic Management, Concepts and Cases*, 9th edn, Chicago, IL, Irwin

Truss, C (1999) Soft and hard models of HRM, in (eds) L Gratton, V H Hailey, P Stiles and C Truss, *Strategic Human Resource Management*, Oxford, Oxford University Press

Tyson, S (1997) Human resource strategy: a process for managing the contribution of HRM to organizational performance, *International Journal of Human Resource Management*, 8 (3), pp 277–90

Ulrich, D (1998) A new mandate for human resources, *Harvard Business Review*, January–February, pp 124–34

Walton, R E (1985) From control to commitment in the workplace, *Harvard Business Review*, March–April, pp 77–84

Wernerfelt, B (1984) A resource-based view of the firm, *Strategic Management Journal*, 5 (2), pp 171–80

Wood, S (1996) High commitment management and organization in the UK, *The International Journal of Human Resource Management*, 7 (1), pp 41–58

Wright, P M and McMahan, G C (1992) Theoretical perspectives for SHRM, *Journal of Management*, 18 (2), pp 295–320

Wright, P M and McMahan, G C (1999) Theoretical perspectives for human resource management, in (eds) R S Schulker and S E Jackson, *Strategic Human Resource Management*, Blackwell, Oxford, pp 49–72

Wright, P M and Snell, S A (1998) Towards a unifying framework for exploring fit and flexibility in strategic human resource management, *Academy of Management Review*, 23 (4), pp 756–72

Wright, P M, Snell, S A and Jacobsen, H H (2004) Current approaches to HR strategies: inside-out versus outside-in, *Human Resource Planning*, 27 (4), pp 36–46

03
Delivering HRM

LEARNING OUTCOMES

On completing this chapter you should be able to define these key concepts. You should also understand:

- The framework for delivering HRM
- What the concept of HR architecture means
- What an HR system looks like
- The HR role of line managers
- The role and organization of the HR function
- The nature of an HR delivery model
- The role of HR professionals

Introduction

The framework for delivering HRM is provided by the HR architecture of an organization, which consists of the HR system, HR practices and the HR delivery model adopted by the HR function. Within that framework HRM is the responsibility of the HR function and the HR professionals who are members of the function and, importantly, line managers.

HR techniques such as organization development, selection testing, talent management, performance management and total reward play an important part in the delivery of HRM. But there is the danger that new and seemingly different techniques become 'flavours of the month' only to be quickly forgotten when they fail to deliver. Some time ago McLean (1981: 4) observed that:

> The history of the management of human
> resources is littered with examples of
> widely acclaimed techniques enthusiastically
> introduced by managers who are keen to
> find solutions to their 'people' problems, only
> to be discarded and discredited by the same
> disillusioned and increasingly cynical managers
> some time later.

Times have not changed. The effective delivery of HRM depends on using techniques that are tried, tested and appropriate, not ones that are have been promoted vigorously as 'best practice' without supporting evidence.

HR architecture

HR architecture consists of the HR systems, processes and structure, and employee behaviours. It is a comprehensive representation of all that is involved in HRM, not simply the structure of the HR function. As explained by Becker *et al* (2001: 12): 'We use the term HR architecture to broadly describe the continuum from the HR professionals within the HR function, to the system of HR related policies and practices, through the competencies, motivation and associated behaviours of the firm's employees.' It was noted by Hird *et al* (2010: 25)

that: 'this architecture is seen as a unique combination of the HR function's structure and delivery model, the HR practices and system, and the strategic employee behaviours that these create'.

Purcell (1999: 38) suggested that the focus should be on 'appropriate HR architecture and the processes that contribute to organizational performance'. Becker and Huselid (2006: 899) stated that: 'It is the fit between the HR architecture and the strategic capabilities and business processes that implement strategy that is the basis of HR's contribution to competitive advantage.'

The HR system

The HR system contains the interrelated and jointly supportive HR activities and practices which together enable HRM goals to be achieved. Becker and Huselid (1998: 95) observed that: 'The HRM system is first and foremost a vehicle to implement the firm's strategy.' Later (2006) they argued that it is the HR system which is the key HR asset. Boselie *et al* (2005: 73) pointed out that in its traditional form HRM can be viewed as 'a collection of multiple discrete practices with no explicit or discernible link between them. The more strategically minded system approach views HRM as an integrated and coherent bundle of mutually reinforcing practices'.

As illustrated in Figure 3.1, an HRM system brings together *HR philosophies* that describe the overarching values and guiding principles adopted in managing people. Taking account of the internal and external environments in which the organization operates, the system incorporates:

- *HR strategies*, which define the direction in which HRM intends to go in each of its main areas of activity.
- *HR policies*, which set out what HRM is there to do and provide guidelines defining how specific aspects of HR should be applied and implemented.
- *HR practices*, which consist of the HRM activities involved in managing and developing people and in managing the employment relationship.

FIGURE 3.1   The HR system

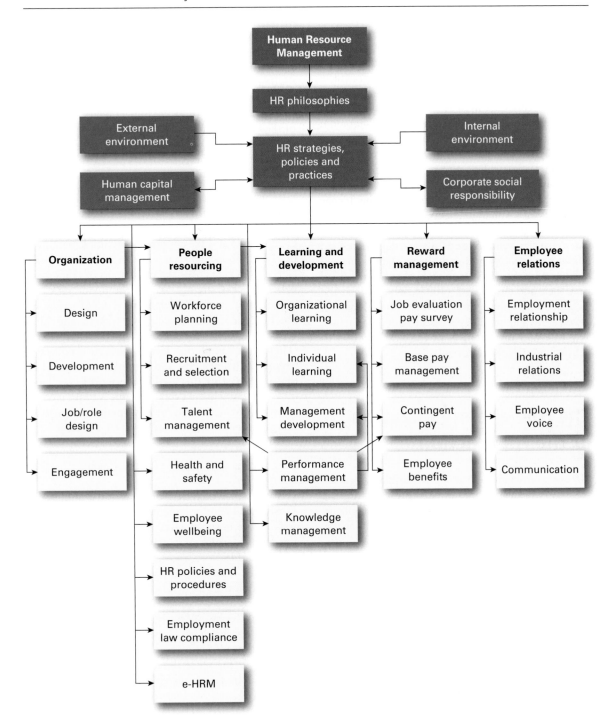

The HR delivery model

In a sense HR is in the delivery business – providing the advice and services that enable organizations to get things done through people. The HR delivery model describes how those services are provided. These methods of delivery take place irrespective of the degree to which what is done corresponds with the conceptual HRM model described in Chapter 1.

The most celebrated delivery model was produced by Dave Ulrich. In his highly influential *Harvard Business Review* article (1998: 124) he wrote that: 'HR should not be defined by what it does but by what it delivers – results that enrich the organization's value to customers, investors, and employees.' More specifically he suggested that HR can deliver in four ways: as a strategic partner, an administrative expert, an employee champion, and a change agent. This first model was later modified by Ulrich and Brockbank (2005), who defined the four roles as employee advocate, human capital developer, functional expert, and strategic partner. The role and organization of the HR function in delivering HRM is explored below.

The role and organization of the HR function

Members of the HR function provide insight, leadership, advice and services on matters affecting the management, employment, learning and development, reward and wellbeing of people and the relationships between management and employees. Importantly, they contribute to the achievement of organizational effectiveness and success (the impact of HRM on performance is considered in Chapter 4).

The basic role of HR is to deliver HRM services. But it does much more than that. It plays a key part in the creation of an environment that enables people to make the best use of their capacities, to realize their potential to the benefit of both the organization and themselves, and to achieve satisfaction through their work.

Increasingly, the role of HR is seen to be business-oriented – contributing to the achievement of sustained competitive advantage. Becker and Huselid (1998: 97) argued that HR should be 'a resource that solves real business problems'. But one of the issues explored by Francis and Keegan (2006) through their research is the tendency for a focus on business performance outcomes to obscure the importance of employee wellbeing in its own right. They quoted the view of Ulrich and Brockbank (2005: 201) that 'caring, listening to, and responding to employees remains a centrepiece of HR work'. The HR function and its members have to be aware of the ethical dimensions of their work.

HR activities

HR activities can be divided into two broad categories: 1) transformational (strategic) activities that are concerned with developing organizational effectiveness and the alignment and implementation of HR and business strategies; and 2) transactional activities, which cover the main areas of HR service delivery – resourcing, learning and development, reward and employee relations. A CEO's view on the HR agenda as quoted by Hesketh and Hird (2010: 105) was that it operates on three levels: 'There's the foundation level, which we used to call personnel, it's just pay and rations, recruitment, all that sort of stuff that makes the world go round, transactional work. Level two to me is tools, it could be engagement, reward, development, those sort of things. Level three is the strategic engagement.'

The organization of the HR function

The ways in which HR operates vary immensely. As Sisson (1990) commented, HR management is not a single homogeneous occupation – it involves a variety of roles and activities that differ from one organization to another and from one level to another in the same organization. Tyson (1987) claimed that the HR function is often 'balkanized' – not only is there a variety of roles and activities but these tend to be relatively self-centred, with little passage between them. Hope-Hailey *et al* (1997: 17) believed that HR could be regarded as a 'chameleon function' in the sense that the diversity of practice established by their research suggests that 'contextual variables dictate different roles for the function and different practices of people management'.

The organization and staffing of the HR function clearly depend on the size of the business, the extent to which operations are decentralized, the type of work carried out, the kind of people employed and the role assigned to the HR function. A survey by Incomes Data Services (IDS, 2010) found that the overall median number of HR staff in the responding organizations was 14. In small and medium-sized companies (with 1–499 staff) the median number was 3.5, and in companies with 500 or more employees it was 20. While, as would be expected, large organizations employed more staff than small and medium-sized enterprises (SMEs), they had on average fewer HR staff per employee. For SMEs the median ratio of employees to HR staff was 62:1; in large employers it was 95:1. The overall ratio was 80:1. The IRS 2011 survey of HR roles and responsibilities found that the median ratio of employees to HR practitioners was 83:1.

A traditional organization might consist of an HR director responsible directly to the chief executive, with functional heads dealing, respectively, with recruitment and employment matters, learning and development, and reward management. Crail (2006: 15) used the responses from 179 organizations to an IRS survey of the HR function to produce a model of an HR department. He suggested that this 'might consist of a team of 12 people serving a workforce of around 1,200. The team would have a director, three managers, one supervisor, three HR officers and four assistants. It would include a number of professionally qualified practitioners, particularly at senior level'. However, there is no such thing as a typical HR function, although the 'three-legged stool' model as described below has attracted a lot of attention.

The three-legged stool model

The notion of delivering HRM through three major areas – centres of expertise, business partners and HR shared service centres – emerged from the HR delivery model produced by Ulrich (1997, 1998), although, as reported by Hird *et al* (2010: 26): 'Ulrich himself has gone on record recently to state that the structures being implemented by HR based on his work are not actually his idea at all but an interpretation of his writing.' They noted that the first reference to the three-legged stool was in an article by Johnson (1999), two years after Ulrich published his delivery model. In this article Johnson quoted David Hilborn, an associate of William Mercer, management consultants, as follows.

Source review

The three-legged stool model – David Hilborn as quoted by Johnson (1999: 44)

The traditional design [of an HR department] typically includes a vice president of HR, then a manager of compensation and benefits, a manager of HRIS and payroll, a manager of employment and so on. However, the emerging model is more like a three-legged stool. One leg of the stool includes an administrative service centre which processes payroll, benefits and the like and focuses on efficiency in transaction functions. The second leg is a centre of excellence (or expertise) in which managers and specialists work. These employees concentrate on design rather than transactions and will have line managers as their customers. HR business partners make up the third leg. They are generalists who usually report to line managers and indirectly to HR. These employees don't get involved in transactions, but instead act as consultants and planners, linking the business with appropriate HR programmes.

This exposition provided the blueprint for all subsequent versions of the model, which has evolved as follows:

1 *Centres of expertise* – these specialize in the provision of high-level advice and services on key HR activities. The CIPD survey on the changing HR function (CIPD, 2007) found that they existed in 28 per cent of respondents' organizations. The most common expertise areas were training and development (79 per cent), recruitment (67 per cent), reward (60 per cent) and employee relations (55 per cent).

2 *Strategic business partners* – these work with line managers to help them reach their goals through effective strategy formulation and execution. They are often 'embedded' in business units or departments.

3 *HR shared service centres* – these handle all the routine 'transactional' services across the

business, which include such activities as recruitment, absence monitoring and advice on dealing with employee issues like discipline and absenteeism.

Critical evaluation of the three-legged stool model

Although this model has attracted a great deal of attention, the 2007 CIPD survey found that only 18 per cent of respondents had implemented all three 'legs', although 47 per cent had implemented one or two elements, with business partners being the most common (29 per cent).

Moreover, there are difficulties with the notion. Gratton (2003: 18) pointed out that: 'this fragmentation of the HR function is causing all sorts of unintended problems. Senior managers look at the fragments and are not clear how the function as a whole adds value'. And as Reilly (2007) commented, respondents to the CIPD survey mentioned other problems in introducing the new model. These included difficulties in defining roles and accountabilities, especially those of business partners, who risk being 'hung, drawn and quartered by all sides', according to one HR director. At the same time, the segmented nature of the structure gives rise to 'boundary management' difficulties, for example when it comes to separating out transactional tasks from the work of centres of expertise. The model can also hamper communication between those engaged in different HR activities. Other impediments were technological failure, inadequate resources in HR and skills gaps.

Hird *et al* (2010: 31) drew attention to the following issues:

- An 'off the shelf' introduction of a new HR structure without careful thought as to how the model fits the organization's requirements.
- A lack of care in dealing with the boundary issues between elements of the HR structure which can easily be fragmented.
- A lack of attention to the new skill sets needed by business partners to ensure they can play at the strategic level.
- A lack of understanding on the part of managers as to the value of a new HR structure.
- A lack of skill on the part of line managers to make the required shift to greater responsibility for people issues implied by the new model.

- What is referred to as the 'polo' problem: a lack of provision of the execution of HR services as the business partner shifts to strategic work, and the centre of expertise to an advisory role.

However, some benefits were reported by respondents to the CIPD (2007) survey. Centres of expertise provide higher quality advice. Business partners exercise better business focus, line managers are more engaged, and the profile of HR is raised. Also, the introduction of shared services results in improved customer service and allows other parts of HR to spend more time on value-adding activities.

Evaluating the HR function

It is necessary to evaluate the contribution of the HR function to ensure that it is effective at both the strategic level and in terms of service delivery and support. The prime criteria for evaluating the work of the function are its ability to operate strategically and its capacity to deliver the levels of services required.

Research conducted by the Institute for Employment Studies (Hirsh, 2008) discovered that the factors that correlated most strongly with line managers' and employees' satisfaction with HR were:

- being well supported in times of change;
- HR giving good advice to employees;
- being well supported when dealing with difficult people or situations;
- HR getting the basics right.

But the results showed that HR could do better in each of these areas. The conclusions reached were that HR must find out what its customers need and what their experiences of HR services are. HR has to be responsive – clear about what it is there for and what services it offers, and easy to contact.

The IRS 2011 survey of HR roles and responsibilities established that the top six measures used by respondents to assess HR effectiveness were:

1 absence management data – 80 per cent;
2 staff turnover data – 78 per cent;
3 discipline and grievance data – 73 per cent;
4 results of employee surveys – 67 per cent;
5 exit interview feedback – 65 per cent;
6 anecdotal/informal feedback – 65 per cent.

CASE STUDIES ON THE ORGANIZATION OF THE HR FUNCTION

HR organization at the National Australia Bank Group

HR at the National Australia Bank Group has a number of centres of expertise, business partners, solutions consultants, project managers, a shared services centre, and telephone advisory service for employees (the people advisory helpline).

Centres of expertise

Centres of expertise cover areas such as reward, employment policy, talent management, culture management, diversity and performance. The staff in the centres are specialists in their respective fields, while the other parts of HR can be found in the HR service centre, with the exception of recruitment, which is conducted by line managers.

Business partners

Business partners attend business unit leadership team meetings and set the company's people strategies and deliver the HR requirements emerging from various projects.

They tend to work in the areas of talent, performance, leadership, diversity and culture and their job is to facilitate the implementation of corporate people initiatives with the relevant specialist HR partners. Unlike shared services staff, they only get involved in HR's daily operational matters if projects escalate and extra help is required.

Solutions consultants

Solutions consultants deal with operational queries referred to them from the people advisory helpline – mainly issues of case management and other more complex enquiries. They are a key point of contact for people leaders on matters of policy and procedure, although they do participate in some transaction work as well.

Project staff

Project staff work on projects that emerge from strategic discussions.

The HR shared services model at PricewaterhouseCoopers (PwC)

The HR shared services model at PwC consists of transactional and professional areas. Transactional functions include payroll, benefits administration and the joiners/leavers process department. The transactional functions also provide services for their professional counterparts. In contrast, professional areas organized into centres of expertise include functions such as recruitment, learning and development, reward, diversity and legal and advisory.

The centres of expertise sit within the central human capital services centre but there are definite lines between them. Every centre of expertise is a cost centre, but for the

annual budgeting process all are looked at together as part of the HR shared services function.

The result of introducing the centres of expertise has been that specialist knowledge is now organized into discrete units enabling know-how and experience to be more easily shared. The new structure means there is less duplication and the improved efficiencies allows more time to be dedicated to strategic issues. Additionally, a decrease in costs has been achieved via a combination of reductions in headcount, economies of scale and related efficiencies.

Reorganizing HR in the Greater Manchester Fire Service

Following major changes in operations, it was decided by senior management that the role of the fire service's HR function was to provide high-level, strategic advice from advisers who could work closely with them, backed

up by specialists. In other words, a business partner model. So the brigade began to recruit business partners – placing a special emphasis on those with expertise in employee relations – and specialists to cover areas such as occupational health, equality and diversity, reward, pensions and recruitment. Finding candidates with sufficient gravitas to act as top-level strategic advisers was difficult. There weren't many true business partners about. A lot of people calling themselves business partners were really HR advisers.

When the team was in place the major developments were:

- to introduce a more transparent promotions process;

- work on the organizational climate and leadership – a series of away-days for leaders using organizational

climate tools such as 360-degree feedback and the Belbin Team Inventory;

- the recruitment process was also modernized by putting together a resourcing team, building a microsite and developing an applicant tracking system;

- reorganize training;

- a departmental competency framework was put in place to ensure HR staff would be able to move easily within the organization rather than becoming bogged down in specialist areas.

The roles of HR professionals

The roles of HR professionals vary widely according to the extent to which they are generalist (eg HR director, HR manager, business partner), or specialist (eg head of learning and development, head of talent management, head of reward), the level at which they work (strategic, executive or administrative) the needs of the organization, the view of senior management about their contribution, the context within which they work and their own capabilities. They can act as strategists, business partners, innovators, change agents, internal consultants, change agents, facilitators and coaches. Tyson and Fell (1986: 7) believed that they were 'specialists in managing the employment relationship'. The competencies required by the role are demanding.

The overall role

HR professionals can play a proactive role, contributing to the formulation of corporate strategy, developing integrated HR strategies and volunteering guidance on matters related to upholding core values and ethical principles. They are involved in business issues and working with line managers to deliver performance targets but they are also concerned with people issues. They help to improve organizational capability – the capacity of the organization to perform effectively and thus reach its goals. They can also be regarded as facilitators;

in the words of Tyson and Fell (1986: 65): 'Their work allows other managerial work to happen.'

The 'Next Generation' research conducted by the CIPD in 2010 emphasized the need for HR professionals to be 'insight-led'. Commenting on the outcomes of the research, Sears (2011: 35) reported that: 'We found that demonstrating a sense of purpose that spans the whole pyramid demands a wide-awake HR function, with a deep understanding of business, contextual and organizational factors.'

Research conducted by Hoque and Noon (2001: 19) established that: 'The growing number of specialists using the HR title are well qualified, are more likely to be involved in strategic decision-making processes and are most likely to be found in workplaces within which sophisticated methods and techniques have been adopted.' However, in some situations they play a mainly reactive and transactional role. They spend much of their time doing what they are told or asked to do, responding to requests for services or advice. They provide the administrative systems required by management. This is what Storey (1992) refers to as the non-interventionary role in which HR people merely provide a service to meet the demands of management and front-line managers.

For many HR practitioners their most important function is service delivery, which includes transactional activities such as recruitment, training and advisory services. The importance of this aspect of their work should not be underestimated by focusing too much on the strategic or business partner roles, as described below.

The strategic role

The strategic role of HR professionals varies according to whether they are operating at strategic levels (as HR directors or heads of the HR function, heads of centres of expertise or key HR functions, and strategic business partners), or at a transactional level (as an HR officer, adviser or assistant delivering basic HR services such as recruitment or training, or working in an HR shared service centre). The strategic HRM skills they need to carry out this role are described in Chapter 41.

Strategic level roles

The roles of HR professionals at a strategic level are:

1   To formulate and implement, in conjunction with their management colleagues, forward-looking HR strategies that are aligned to business objectives and integrated with one another. In doing so they adopt an 'outside-in' approach as described by Wright *et al* (2004) in which the starting point is the business, including the customer, competitor and business issues it faces. The HR strategy then derives directly from these challenges to create real solutions and add real value.

2   To contribute to the development of business strategies. They do this by advising on how the business can achieve its strategic goals by making the best use of its human resources and by demonstrating the particular contribution that can be made by the talented people it employs.

3   To work alongside their line management colleagues and provide on an everyday basis continuous support to the implementation of the business or operational strategy of the organization, function or unit.

The strategic contribution of HR advisers or assistants

The role of HR advisers or assistants is primarily that of delivering effective HR services within their function, or as a member of an HR service centre. While they will not be responsible for the formulation of HR strategies they may contribute to them within their own speciality. They will need to understand the business goals of the departments or managers for whom they provide services in order to ensure that these services support the achievement of those goals.

The business partner role

The notion of HR professionals as business partners has seized the imagination of HR people. In essence, the concept is that, as business partners, HR specialists share responsibility with their line management colleagues for the success of the enterprise and get involved with them in implementing business strategy and running the business.

As business partners, HR practitioners work closely with their line management colleagues. They are aware of business strategies and the opportunities and threats facing the organization. They are capable of analysing organizational strengths and weaknesses and diagnosing the issues facing the enterprise and their human resource implications. They understand the business model and know about the critical success factors that will create competitive advantage. They adopt a 'value-added' approach when making a convincing business case for innovations.

The term 'value added' looms large in the concept of the HR business partner. In the language of accounting, where the phrase originated, added value is defined as the value added to the cost of raw materials and bought-out parts by the process of production and distribution. In HR speak, a value-added approach means creating value through HR initiatives that make a significant contribution to organizational success. Strictly speaking, added value is measured by the extent to which the value of that contribution exceeds its cost or generates a return on investment. But the term is often used more generally to signify the business-oriented approach HR professionals are expected to adopt and how it contributes to the creation of value by the firm. Adding value is about improving performance and results – getting more out of an activity than was put into it.

Critical evaluation of the business partner concept

It can be argued that too much has been made of the business partner model. Perhaps it is preferable to emphasize that the role of HR professionals is to be *part* of the business rather than merely being partners. There is the danger of over-emphasizing the seemingly glamorous role of business or strategic partner at the expense of the service delivery aspect of the HR practitioner's role. Syrett (2006) noted that whatever strategic aspirations senior HR practitioners have, they will amount to nothing if the function they represent cannot deliver the essential transactional services their internal line clients require. As an HR specialist commented to Caldwell (2004): 'My credibility depends on running an extremely efficient and cost-effective administrative machine … If I don't get that right, and consistently, then you can forget about any big ideas.' Another person interviewed during Caldwell's research referred to personnel people as 'reactive pragmatists', a realistic situation in many organizations.

The problem of the over-emphasis on the business partner role has been influenced by the erroneous belief that Ulrich was simply focusing on HR executives as business partners. This has had the unfortunate effect of implying that it was their only worthwhile function. But Ulrich cannot be blamed for this. In 1998 he gave equal emphasis to the need for HR people to be administrative experts, employee champions and change agents, and this was confirmed in the revised model (Ulrich and Brockbank, 2005).

Example – business partnering at the AA

The key competencies required by the AA for its business partners are concerned with commercial decision making, commerciality, influencing people and facilitating change. They have to:

- understand the key factors affecting overall costs and profits;
- understand and interpret financial data;
- understand the connectivity between functional areas of the business;
- understand the impact of actions on cash flow and profitability.

The innovation role

A strategic and therefore proactive approach to HRM will mean that HR specialists will need to innovate – to introduce new processes and procedures they believe will increase organizational effectiveness.

The case for innovation should be established by processes of analysis and diagnosis using an evidence-based management approach to identify the business need and the issues to be addressed. 'Benchmarking' can be used to identify 'best practice' in other organizations. But 'best fit' is more important than 'best practice' – in other words, the innovation should meet the particular needs of the business, which are likely to differ from those of other 'best practice' organizations. It has to be demonstrable that the innovation is appropriate, beneficial, practical in the circumstances and can be implemented without too much difficulty in the shape of opposition from those affected by it or the unjustifiable use of resources – financial and the time of those involved.

The danger, according to Marchington (1995), is that HR people may go in for 'impression management' – aiming to make an impact on senior managers and colleagues through publicizing high profile innovations. HR specialists who try to draw attention to themselves simply by promoting the latest flavour of the month, irrespective of its relevance or practicality, are falling into the trap which Drucker (1955: 243), anticipating Marchington by 40 years, described as follows: 'The constant worry of all personnel administrators is their inability to prove that they are making a contribution to the enterprise. Their preoccupation is with the search for a "gimmick" which will impress their management colleagues.'

As Marchington points out, the risk is that people believe 'all can be improved by a wave of the magic wand and the slaying of a few evil characters along the way'. This facile assumption means that people can too readily devise elegant solutions that do not solve the problem because of the hazards encountered during implementation – for example, the indifference or even open hostility of line managers. These have to be anticipated and catered for.

Guidelines for HR innovations are set out overleaf.

The change agent role

The implementation of strategy means that HR specialists have to act as change agents, facilitating change by providing advice and support on its introduction and management. Caldwell categorizes HR change agents in four dimensions.

Guidelines for HR innovations

1   Be clear on what has to be achieved and why.

2   Ensure that what you do fits the strategy, culture and circumstances of the organization.

3   Don't follow fashion – do your own thing as long as it is relevant and fits the organization's needs.

4   Keep it simple – over-complexity is a common reason for failure.

5   Don't rush – it will take longer than you think.

6   Don't try to do too much at once – an incremental approach is generally best.

7   Assess resource requirements and costs.

8   Pay close attention to project planning and management.

9   Remember that the success of the innovation rests as much on the effectiveness of the process of implementation (line manager buy-in and skills are crucial) as it does on the quality of the concept, if not more so.

10 Focus on change management approaches – communicate, involve and train.

Source review

HR specialists as change agents: the four dimensions – Caldwell (2001)

1   *Transformational change* – a major change that has a dramatic effect on HR policy and practice across the whole organization.

2   *Incremental change* – gradual adjustments of HR policy and practices which affect single activities or multiple functions.

3   *HR vision* – a set of values and beliefs that affirm the legitimacy of the HR function as a strategic business partner.

4   *HR expertise* – the knowledge and skills that define the unique contribution the HR professional can make to effective people management.

Ambiguities in the role of HR practitioners

The activities and roles of HR specialists and the demands made upon them as described above appear to be quite clear cut, but Thurley (1981) pointed out that HR practitioners can be specialists in ambiguity. This continues in the age of Ulrich. As Hope-Hailey *et al* (2005: 51) commented: 'Ulrich highlighted that HR professionals must be both strategic and operational, yet the potential role conflict this could engender was not addressed.'

Caldwell (2004: 212) reached the following conclusions on the basis of his research:

There is the issue of 'powerlessness' or the marginality of HR practitioners in management decision-making processes, especially at a strategic level. The HR function has an inward-looking tendency to identify professional expertise mainly with administrative concerns over who controls HR activities, rather than questions of HR practices or who has responsibility for implementing HR policy.

The status of HR

Over the years, the HR profession has suffered from an inferiority complex. This may arise because the role of HR professionals is ill-defined (they are unsure of where they stand), their status is not fully recognized, or top management and line managers have equivocal views about their value to the organization. Tyson and Fell (1986: 68) remarked that 'the ambiguous character of their work contributes to the problems of convincing others of its value'.

Drucker (1955: 243) observed that: 'The constant worry of all personnel administrators is their inability to prove that they are making a contribution to the organization.' Skinner (1981: 106) in his *Harvard Business Review* article, 'Big hat no cattle', stated that 'the corporate role of personnel has always been problematic'; and Tyson and Fell (1986: 136) argued that: 'Classical personnel management has not been granted a position in decision-making circles because it has frequently not earned one. It has not been concerned with the totality of the organization but often with issues which have not only been parochial but esoteric to boot.'

Fernie *et al* (1994) claimed on the basis of their analysis of WIRS3 that the presence of a personnel manager is associated with a poorer climate of industrial relations, although Guest and Hoque (1994) questioned this conclusion. Watson (1996) referred to the perpetual marginality of the HR function and, as quoted above, Caldwell (2004: 212) raised the 'issue of "powerlessness" or the marginality of HR practitioners in management decision-making processes'.

Traditionally, the HR practitioner's reaction to this problem has been, in the words of Drucker (1955: 243). to 'search for a "gimmick" that will impress their management colleagues'. This was later called adopting 'the flavour of the month'. HR professionals have now become more sophisticated. They have enthusiastically supported approaches that appeal to management such as engagement policies and talent management.

Research conducted by Guthrie *et al* (2011: 1681) confirmed that 'HR departments are still often viewed, collectively, as a function that is more bureaucratic than strategic.' They noted previous research which has shown that, 'it is this role – the strategic role – in which line executives believe that HR is particularly deficient' (*ibid*: 1682). Perhaps this explains why there has been so much emphasis recently on being strategic, although what is meant by that is not always made clear. The following perceptive comment was made on this trend by Keegan and Francis (2010: 878):

> Bearing in mind the history of HR practitioners' struggles for acceptance as key organizational players it is hardly surprising that a way of discursively modelling the concept of HR as 'hard' and relating it to others concepts such as 'business driven agendas' and 'strategic management', has become so popular. It offers perhaps a way out of the dualism when they seek to claim a share of strategic decision making while at the same time struggling to attend to the employee centred and administrative aspects of the role.

They also commented that: 'Exhortations for HR practitioners to pursue strategic roles and downplay their historically embedded administrative and employee championing pose a serious threat to the integrity of HR work and claims to professional expertise' (*ibid*: 894).

HR competencies

The demands made on HR professionals in terms of skills and expected behaviours are considerable although, nowadays, as Keegan and Francis (2010: 884) commented, 'Success in HR roles is measured in terms of developing effective business rather than people skills.' Brockbank *et al* (1999) conducted research that led to a definition of the key HR competency 'domains' and their components, as set out in Table 3.1.

HR behaviours

The CIPD's HR profession map issued in June 2009 (CIPD, 2010) listed the following behaviours needed by HR professionals to carry out their activities:

- curious;
- decisive thinker;
- skilled influencer;
- driven to deliver;
- collaborative;
- personally credible;
- courage to challenge;
- role model.

TABLE 3.1   Key HR specialist competency areas (Brockbank *et al*, 1999)

Competency domain	Components
1. Personal credibility	Live the firm's values, maintain relationships founded on trust, act with an 'attitude' (a point of view about how the business can win, backing up opinion with evidence).
2. Ability to manage change	Drive change: ability to diagnose problems, build relationships with clients, articulate a vision, set a leadership agenda, solve problems and implement goals.
3. Ability to manage culture	Act as 'keepers of the culture', identify the culture required to meet the firm's business strategy, frame culture in a way that excites employees, translate desired culture into specific behaviours, encourage executives to behave consistently with the desired culture.
4. Delivery of human resource practices	Expert in the speciality, able to deliver state-of-the-art innovative HR practices in such areas as recruitment, employee development, compensation and communication.
5. Understanding of the business	Strategy, organization, competitors, finance, marketing, sales, operations and IT.

What it means to be an HR professional

Professionalism in HR as in other fields can be defined generally as the conduct exhibited by people who are providing advice and services that require expertise and which meet defined or generally accepted standards of behaviour. Work done by a professional is usually distinguished by its reference to a framework of fundamental concepts that reflect the skilful application of specialized education, training and experience. It is accompanied by a sense of responsibility and an acceptance of recognized standards. Even more loosely, people can be described as acting 'professionally' when they do their work well and act responsibly.

Professionalism in HR means working in accordance with a professional ethos. As suggested by Fletcher (2004) this is characterized by:

- the possession of specialized knowledge and skills;
- power and status based on expertise;
- self-discipline and adherence to some aspirational performance standards;
- the opportunity to display high levels of autonomy;
- the ability to apply some independence of judgement;
- operating, and being guided by, a code of ethics.

HR professionals are required to uphold the standards laid down by their professional body, the CIPD, but they must also adhere to their own ethical values. Additionally, they are bound by organizational codes of conduct expressed formally or accepted and understood as core values (the basic values adopted by an organization that set out what is believed to be important about how people and organizations should behave).

The HR role of line managers

HR can initiate new policies and practices but it is line managers that have the main responsibility for implementing them. In other words, 'HR proposes but the line disposes.' As Guest (1991: 159) observed: 'HRM is too important to be left to personnel managers.'

If line managers are not inclined favourably towards what HR wants them to do they won't do it or, if compelled to, they will be half-hearted about it. On the basis of their research, Guest and King (2004: 421) noted that 'better HR depended not so much on better procedures but better implementation and ownership of implementation by line managers'.

As pointed out by Purcell *et al* (2003), high levels of organizational performance are not achieved simply by having a range of well-conceived HR policies and practices in place. What makes the difference is how these policies and practices are implemented. That is where the role of line managers in people management is crucial: 'managers … play a vital role in making involvement happen, in communicating, in being open to allow employee concerns to be raised and discussed, in allowing people space to influence how they do their job, and in coaching, guiding and recognizing performance and providing help for the future' (*ibid*: 40). Purcell and his colleagues noted that dealing with people is perhaps the aspect of their work in which line managers can exercise the greatest amount of discretion and they can use that discretion by not putting HR's ideas into practice. As they observed, it is line managers who bring HR policies to life.

A further factor affecting the role of line managers is their ability to do the HR tasks assigned to them. People-centred activities such as defining roles, interviewing, reviewing performance, providing feedback, coaching and identifying learning and development needs all require special skills. Some managers have them; many don't. Performance-related pay schemes sometimes fail because of untrained line managers.

Hutchinson and Purcell made the following recommendations on how to improve the quality of the contribution line managers make to people management.

Source review

Improving the quality of line managers as people managers – Hutchinson and Purcell (2003)

- Provide them with time to carry out their people management duties which are often superseded by other management duties.

- Select them carefully with much more attention being paid to the behavioural competencies required.

- Support them with strong organizational values concerning leadership and people management.

- Encourage the development of a good working relationship with their own managers.

- Ensure they receive sufficient skills training to enable them to perform their people management activities such as performance management.

To which can be added that better implementation and better ownership by line managers of HR practices is more likely to be achieved if: 1) the practice demonstrably benefits them; 2) they are involved in the development and, importantly, the testing of the practices; 3) the practice is not too complicated, bureaucratic or time-consuming; 4) their responsibilities are defined and communicated clearly; and 5) they are provided with the guidance, support and training required to implement the practice.

Key learning points: Delivering HRM

HRM delivery

HRM is delivered through the HR architecture of an organization, which includes the HR system, HR practices, and the HR delivery model adopted by the HR function.

HR architecture

HR architecture includes the HR systems and processes and employee behaviours as well as the structure of the HR function.

The HR system

The HR system as part of the HR architecture consists of the interrelated and jointly supportive HR activities and practices which together enable HRM goals to be achieved.

The HR delivery model

The HR delivery model describes how those services are delivered by the HR function. The best known model was produced by Ulrich in 1998; he suggested that HR could be delivered by specialists in four ways: strategic partner, administrative expert, employee champion and change agent.

The 'three-legged stool' model of the HR function

This model identifies three areas of HR activity: centres of expertise, strategic business partners, and shared service centres.

Roles of HR professionals

They can act as business partners, strategists, innovators, change agents, internal consultants, facilitators and coaches.

Ambiguities in the role of HR practitioners

The activities and roles of HR specialists and the demands made upon them appear to be quite clear cut but in practice the role can be ambiguous.

Professionalism in HR

Professionalism is defined generally as the conduct exhibited by people who are providing advice and services that require expertise and which meet defined or generally accepted standards of behaviour. HR professionals are required to uphold the standards laid down by their professional body, the CIPD, but they must also adhere to their own ethical values.

The HR role of line managers

Line managers play a crucial role in implementing HR policies but they are not always committed or qualified to do so.

Questions

1 How is HRM delivered?

2 What is HRM architecture?

3 What is an HR system?

4 What are the key HR practices?

5 What is the HR delivery model?

6 What is the 'three-legged stool' model for organizing the HR function?

7 What are the main roles of HR professionals?

8 What are the key HR competency domains or areas identified by Brockbank and his colleagues?

9 What does professionalism in HR involve?

10 What is the HR role of line managers?

References

Becker, B E and Huselid, M A (1998) High performance work systems and firm performance: a synthesis of research and managerial implications, *Research on Personnel and Human Resource Management*, **16**, pp 53–101

Becker, B E and Huselid, M A (2006) Strategic human resource management: where do we go from here? *Journal of Management*, **32** (6), pp 898–925

Becker, B E, Huselid, M A and Ulrich, D (2001) *The HR Score Card: Linking people, strategy, and performance*, Boston, MA, Harvard Business School Press

Boselie, P, Dietz, G and Boon, C (2005) Commonalities and contradictions in HRM and performance research, *Human Resource Management Journal*, **15** (3), pp 67–94

Brockbank, W, Ulrich, D and Beatty, D (1999) HR professional development: creating the future creators at the University of Michigan Business School, *Human Resource Management*, **38**, Summer, pp 111–17

Caldwell, R (2001) Champions, adapters, consultants and synergists: the new change agents in HRM, *Human Resource Management Journal*, **11** (3), pp 39–52

Caldwell, R (2004) Rhetoric, facts and self-fulfilling prophesies: exploring practitioners' perceptions of progress in implementing HRM, *Industrial Relations Journal*, **35** (3), pp 196–215

Chartered Institute of Personnel and Development (2007) *The Changing HR Function*, London, CIPD

Chartered Institute of Personnel and Development (2010) *CIPD Next Generation*, London, CIPD

Crail, M (2006) HR roles and responsibilities 2006: benchmarking the HR function, *IRS Employment Review 839*, 20 January, pp 9–15

Drucker, P (1955) *The Practice of Management*, London, Heinemann

Fernie, S, Metcalf, D and Woodland, S (1994) *What Has Human Resource Management Achieved in the Workplace?*, London, Employment Policy Institute

Fletcher, C (2004) *Appraisal and Feedback: Making performance review work*, 3rd edn, London, CIPD

Francis, H and Keegan, A (2006) The changing face of HRM: in search of balance, *Human Resource Management Journal*, **16** (3), pp 231–49

Gratton, L (2003) The Humpty Dumpty effect: a view of a fragmented HR function, *People Management*, 5 January, p 18

Guest, D E (1991) Personnel management: the end of orthodoxy, *British Journal of Industrial Relations*, **29** (2), pp 149–76

Guest, D E and Hoque, K (1994) Yes, personnel management does make the difference, *Personnel Management*, November, pp 40–44

Guest, D E and King, Z (2004) Power, innovation and problem-solving: the personnel managers' three steps to heaven?, *Journal of Management Studies*, **41** (3), pp 401–23

Guthrie, J P, Flood, P C, Liu, W, MacCurtain, S and Armstrong, C (2011) Big hat no cattle? The relationship between the use of high performance work systems and managerial perceptions of HR departments, *The International Journal of Human Resource Management*, **22** (8), pp 1672–85

Hesketh, A and Hird, M (2010) Using relationships between leaders to leverage more value from people: building a golden triangle, in (eds) P Sparrow, A Hesketh, M Hird and C Cooper, *Leading HR*, Basingstoke, Palgrave Macmillan, pp 103–21

Hird, M, Sparrow, P and Marsh, C (2010) HR structures: are they working?, in (eds) P Sparrow, A Hesketh, M Hird, and C Cooper, *Leading HR*, Basingstoke, Palgrave Macmillan, pp 23–45

Hirsh, W (2008) What do people want from you?, *People Management*, 18 September, pp 23–6

Hope-Hailey, V, Farndale, E and Truss, C (2005) The HR department's role in organizational performance, *Human Resource Management Journal*, **15** (3), pp 49–66

Hope-Hailey, V, Gratton, L, McGovern, P, Stiles, P and Truss, C (1997) A chameleon function? HRM in the '90s, *Human Resource Management Journal*, **7** (3), pp 5–18

Hoque, K and Noon, M (2001) Counting angels: a comparison of personnel and HR specialists, *Human Resource Management Journal*, **11** (3), pp 5–22

Hutchinson, S and Purcell, J (2003) *Bringing Policies to Life: The vital role of front line managers in people management*, London, CIPD

IDS (2010) *HR Function Survey*, HR Study 928, October, London, IDS

IRS (2011) *HR Roles and Responsibilities Survey*, http://www.xperthr.co.uk/article/106943/hr-role-and-responsibilities-the-2011-survey, accessed 11 August 2011

Johnson, C (1999) Changing shapes: trends in human resource reorganizations, *HR Magazine*, **44** (3), pp 40–48

Keegan, A and Francis, H (2010) Practitioner talk: the changing textscape of HRM and emergence of HR business partnership, *The International Journal of Human Resource Management*, **21** (6), pp 873–98

McLean, A (1981) Organization development: a case of the emperor's new clothes?, *Personnel Review*, **4** (1), pp 3–14

Marchington, M (1995) Fairy tales and magic wands: new employment practices in perspective, *Employee Relations*, Spring, pp 51–66

Purcell, J (1999) Best practice or best fit: chimera or cul-de-sac, *Human Resource Management Journal*, **9** (3), pp 26–41

Purcell, J, Kinnie, K, Hutchinson, R, Rayton, B and Swart, J (2003) *Understanding the People and Performance Link: Unlocking the black box*, London, CIPD

Reilly, P (2007) Facing up to the facts, *People Management*, 20 September, pp 43–5

Sears, L (2011) A new way of seeing: insight-led HR, *People Management*, April, pp 34–7

Sisson, K (1990) Introducing the Human Resource Management Journal, *Human Resource Management Journal*, **1** (1), pp 1–11

Skinner, W (1981) Big hat no cattle: managing human resources, *Harvard Business Review*, September–October, pp 106–14

Storey, J (1992) *Developments in the Management of Human Resources*, Oxford, Blackwell

Syrett, M (2006) *Four Reflections on Developing a Human Capital Measurement Capability: What's the future for human capital?*, London, CIPD

Thurley, K (1981) Personnel management: a case for urgent treatment, *Personnel Management*, August, pp 24–9

Tyson, S (1987) The management of the personnel function, *Journal of Management Studies*, **24** (5), pp 523–32

Tyson, S and Fell, A (1986) *Evaluating the Personnel Function*, London, Hutchinson

Ulrich, D (1997) *Human Resource Champions*, Boston, MA, Harvard Business School Press

Ulrich, D (1998) A new mandate for human resources, *Harvard Business Review*, January–February, pp 124–34

Ulrich, D and Brockbank, W (2005) *The HR Value Proposition*, Cambridge, MA, Harvard Press

Watson, T (1996) *Management, Organisation and Employment Strategy*, London, Routledge

Wright, P M, Snell, S A and Jacobsen, H H (2004) Current approaches to HR strategies: inside-out versus outside-in, *Human Resource Planning*, **27** (4), pp 36–46

04
HRM and performance

LEARNING OUTCOMES

On completing this chapter you should be able to define these key concepts. You should also understand:

- What impact HRM can make on performance
- How HRM makes that impact
- The nature of a high-performance culture
- How a high-performance work system functions
- The role of performance management
- How HR can contribute

Introduction

All organizations are under an obligation to their stakeholders to perform well. To do this they depend on the quality, dedication, enthusiasm, expertise and skill of the people working in them at all levels. The message of the resource-based view is that HRM delivers added value and helps to achieve sustainable competitive advantage through the strategic development of the organization's rare, hard to imitate and hard to substitute human resources. As Guest (1997: 269) argued: 'The distinctive feature of HRM is its assumption that improved performance is achieved through the people in the organization.' If, therefore, appropriate HR policies and practices are introduced, it can also be assumed that HRM will impact on firm performance.

The chapter begins with a review of the evidence that HRM makes an impact on performance and of the problems met by researchers in establishing what the link is and how it works. It continues with a description of the concept of a high-performance culture and how it can be achieved through a high-performance work system and performance management.

The impact of HR

Much research has been carried out showing that good HRM practice and firm performance are correlated; notable examples in the UK are Guest *et al* (2000a), Patterson *et al* (1997), Purcell *et al* (2003), Thompson (2002) and West *et al* (2002), summarized in Table 4.1.

How HRM makes an impact

Storey *et al* (2009: 4) observed that: 'The premise is that, in some shape or form, HR policies have an effect on HR practices and these in turn influence staff attitudes and behaviours which will, in turn again, impact on service offerings and customer perceptions of value.' The assumption is that good HRM practices will enhance performance. Bowen and Ostroff (2004) argued that the link between HRM and performance is likely to be greater where what they describe as a 'strong' HR system is in place. Core characteristics of their 'strong' system are high levels of distinctiveness, consistency and consensus. Where these are present there will be an organizational climate that supports HR implementation. But they also suggested that it is not enough to have good practices if they are not properly implemented. As Guest (2011: 6) commented: 'What this does is switch the focus to line management.' Nishii *et al* (2008) argued that it is not just the presence of practices that is important but 'perceptions about the intentions behind the practices'.

An extensive research project conducted by Guest and Conway (2011) led to the finding that consensus on HR effectiveness did not support Bowen and Ostroff's (2004) proposition that a strong HR system would have a significant association with outcomes. Guest and Conway commented that their study revealed very low levels of agreement about HR effectiveness. They concluded that: 'There are three elements in a logical model of HR effectiveness. HR practices must be present, they must be effective and they must be effectively implemented' (*ibid*: 1700).

Uncertainties about the link between HRM and performance

As noted earlier, much research has demonstrated an association between HRM and performance. But Guest *et al* (2000b) observed that it left uncertainties about cause and effect. Ulrich (1997: 304) pointed out that: 'HR practices seem to matter; logic says it is so; survey findings confirm it. Direct relationships between performance and attention to HR practices are often fuzzy, however, and vary according to the population sampled and the measures used.' Guest (2011: 11) summed up his article on HRM and performance with the comment that: 'After hundreds of research studies we are still in no position to assert with any confidence that good HRM has an impact on organization performance.'

There are two issues that affect the determination of a link between HRM and firm performance: causal ambiguity, and contingency factors. These contribute to what is known as 'the black box' phenomenon.

Causal ambiguity

The term 'causal ambiguity' refers to the numerous, subtle and often hidden interconnections between the factors influencing cause and effect. Boselie *et al* (2005: 75) referred to the causal distance between an HRM input and an output such as financial performance: 'Put simply, so many variables and events, both internal and external, affect organizations that this direct linkage strains credibility.'

A basic reason for ambiguity is multiple causation, which exists when there is more than one possible cause for an effect. HRM may have caused an improvement in performance but there may be many other economic or business factors that did so, and it could be difficult to unravel them. Another factor is the possibility of reversed causality (a situation where A might have caused B but B might well have caused A). As Purcell *et al* (2003: 2) expressed it: 'Although it is nice to believe that more HR

TABLE 4.1   Research on the link between HRM and firm performance

Researcher(s)	Methodology	Outcomes
Patterson et al (1997)	The research examined the link between business performance and organization culture and the use of a number of HR practices.	HR practices explained significant variations in profitability and productivity (19% and 18% respectively). Two HR practices were particularly significant: 1) the acquisition and development of employee skills, and 2) job design including flexibility, responsibility and variety.
Guest et al (2000a)	An analysis of the 1998 WERS survey which sampled some 2,000 workplaces and obtained the views of about 28,000 employees.	A strong association exists between HRM and both employee attitudes and workplace performance.
Thompson (2002)	A study of the impact of high-performance work practices such as teamworking, appraisal, job rotation, broad-banded grade structures and sharing of business information in UK aerospace establishments.	The number of HR practices and the proportion of the workforce covered appeared to be the key differentiating factor between more and less successful firms.
West et al (2002)	Research conducted in 61 UK hospitals obtaining information on HR strategy, policy and procedures from chief executives and HR directors and mortality rates.	An association between certain HR practices and lower mortality rates was identified. As noted by West: 'If you have HR practices that focus on effort and skill; develop people's skills; encourage cooperation, collaboration, innovation and synergy in teams for most, if not all employees, the whole system functions and performs better.'
Purcell et al (2003)	A University of Bath longitudinal study of 12 companies to establish how people management impacts on organizational performance.	The most successful companies had 'the big idea'. They had a clear vision and a set of integrated values. They were concerned with sustaining performance and flexibility. Clear evidence existed between positive attitudes towards HR policies and practices, levels of satisfaction, motivation and commitment, and operational performance. Policy and practice implementation (not the number of HR practices adopted) is the vital ingredient in linking people management to business performance and this is primarily the task of line managers.

FIGURE 4.1   The black box phenomenon

practices leads to higher economic return, it is just as possible that it is successful firms that can afford more extensive (and expensive) HRM practices.'

Contingency factors

Causation will additionally be affected by the organization's context, ie the internal and external environmental factors that influence what happens within the organization.

The black box phenomenon

Causal ambiguity also stems from the black box phenomenon, as illustrated in Figure 4.1. This is the situation in which, while it may be possible to observe HRM inputs in the form of HR practices and measure firm performance outputs, it may be difficult to ascertain, through research, what happened in between – what the HRM outcomes were that converted the input of HR practices into firm performance outputs. Alvesson (2009: 56) suggested that: 'Research does not proceed beyond attempts to find an empirical association between HR practices and organizational performance. The phenomena are in a black box, only input and output are registered and what is happening remains clouded in the dark.'

Explanations of how HRM makes an impact

Guest (1997: 268) stated that: 'The assumption is that "appropriate" HRM practices tap the motivation and commitment of employees.' He explained how expectancy theory might help to explain the HR/performance link as follows:

The expectancy theory of motivation provides one possible basis for developing a more coherent

rationale about the link between HRM practices and performance. Although expectancy theory is concerned primarily with motivation, it is also a theory about the link between motivation and performance. Specifically, it proposes that high performance, at the individual level, depends on high motivation plus possession of the necessary skills and abilities and an appropriate role and understanding of that role. It is a short step to specify the HRM practices that encourage high skills and abilities, for example careful selection and high investment in training; high motivation, for example employee involvement and possibly performance-related pay; and an appropriate role structure and role perception, for example job design and extensive communication and feedback.

Following this contribution from David Guest, any explanation of the impact of HRM on organizational performance is likely to be based on three propositions: 1) that HR practices can make a direct impact on employee characteristics such as engagement, commitment, motivation and skill; 2) if employees have these characteristics it is probable that organizational performance in terms of productivity, quality and the delivery of high levels of customer service will improve; and 3) if such aspects of organizational performance improve, the financial results achieved by the organization will improve. This can be described as the HR value chain.

The propositions highlight the existence of an intermediate factor between HRM and financial performance. This factor consists of the HRM outcomes in the shape of employee characteristics affected by HR practices. Therefore, HRM does not make a direct impact. A model of the impact of HRM taking into account the considerations of reverse causation and contingency effects mentioned earlier is shown in Figure 4.2.

FIGURE 4.2   Impact of HRM on organizational performance (based on Paauwe, 2004)

But high performance is not just about HR practices. The case-based research by Purcell *et al* (2003) showed that the key to activating what they called the 'people-performance' link lies not only in well-crafted 'bundles' of HR practices, but in their conjunction with a powerful and cohering organizational vision (or 'big idea') and corporate leadership, together with front-line leadership's action and use of its discretionary power.

Developing a high-performance culture

Organizations achieve sustained high performance through the systems of work they adopt, but these systems are managed and operated by people. Ultimately, therefore, high-performance working is about improving performance through people. This can be done through the development and implementation of a high-performance culture involving high-performance work systems in which performance management plays an important part.

High-performance cultures are ones in which the achievement of high levels of performance is a way of life. The characteristics of such cultures are set out below.

Characteristics of a high-performance culture

- Management defines what it requires in the shape of performance improvements, sets goals for success and monitors performance to ensure that the goals are achieved.

- Alternative work practices are adopted such as job redesign, autonomous work teams, improvement groups, team briefing and flexible working.

- People know what's expected of them – they understand their goals and accountabilities.

- People feel that their job is worth doing, and there is a strong fit between the job and their capabilities.

- People are empowered to maximize their contribution.

- There is strong leadership from the top that engenders a shared belief in the importance of continuing improvement.

- There is a focus on promoting positive attitudes that result in an engaged, committed and motivated workforce.

- Performance management processes are aligned to business goals to ensure that people are engaged in achieving agreed objectives and standards.

- Capacities of people are developed through learning at all levels to support performance improvement and they are provided with opportunities to make full use of their skills and abilities.

- A pool of talent ensures a continuous supply of high performers in key roles.

- People are valued and rewarded according to their contribution.

- People are involved in developing high-performance practices.

- There is a climate of trust and teamwork, aimed at delivering a distinctive service to the customer.

- A clear line of sight exists between the strategic aims of the organization and those of its departments and its staff at all levels.

High-performance work systems

High-performance work systems (HPWS) are bundles of HR practices that facilitate employee involvement, skill enhancement and motivation. An HPWS was described by Becker and Huselid (1998: 55) as: 'An internally consistent and coherent HRM system that is focused on solving operational problems and implementing the firm's competitive strategy.' The approach used in a HPWS is sometimes referred to as 'high-performance working'.

Performance cultures are created by HPWSs that embody ways of thinking about performance in organizations and how it can be improved. They are concerned with developing and implementing bundles of complementary practices which, as an integrated whole, will make a much more powerful impact on performance than if they were dealt with as separate entities. Appelbaum et al (2000) stated that HPWSs facilitate employee involvement, skill enhancement and motivation.

Features of an HPWS

There is no generally accepted definition of an HPWS and there is no standard list of the features

or components of such a system. In spite of this problem of definition, an attempt to describe the basic components of an HPWS was made by Shih et al (2005) as follows:

- *Job infrastructure* – workplace arrangements that equip workers with the proper abilities to do their jobs, provide them with the means to do their jobs, and give them the motivation to do their jobs. These practices must be combined to produce their proper effects.

- *Training programmes to enhance employee skills* – investment in increasing employee skills, knowledge and ability.

- *Information sharing and worker involvement mechanisms* – to understand the available alternatives and make correct decisions.

- *Reward and promotion opportunities that provide motivation* – to encourage skilled employees to engage in effective discretionary decision making in a variety of environmental contingencies.

Many descriptions of high-performance systems include lists of desirable features and therefore embody the notion of 'best practice'. However, Gephart (1995) noted that research has not clearly identified any single set of high-performance practices. Becker et al (1997) pointed out that HPWSs were highly idiosyncratic and had to fit the organization's individual circumstances. The lists that have been compiled vary considerably, as is shown in the selection set out in Table 4.2.

Examples

The examples in Table 4.3 of firms that adopt high-performance working policies and practices, assembled by Stevens (2005), illustrate the variety and generalized nature of approaches.

Critical evaluation of the high-performance work system approach

Research conducted by Ramsay et al (2000) aimed to explore linkages from HPWS practices to employee outcomes, and via these to organizational performance. They referred to the existence of the 'black box', meaning that while the introduction of an HPWS may be associated with improved performance, no

TABLE 4.2 Components of an HPWS

US Department of Labor (1993)	Appelbaum et al (2000)	Sung and Ashton (2005)	Thompson and Heron (2005)
• Careful and extensive systems for recruitment, selection and training. • Formal systems for sharing information with employees. • Clear job design. • High-level participation processes. • Monitoring of attitudes. • Performance appraisals. • Properly functioning grievance procedures. • Promotion and compensation schemes that provide for the recognition and reward of high-performing employees.	• Work is organized to permit front-line workers to participate in decisions that alter organizational routines. • Workers require more skills to do their jobs successfully, and many of these skills are firm-specific. • Workers experience greater autonomy over their job tasks and methods of work. • Incentive pay motivates workers to extend extra effort on developing skills. • Employment security provides front-line workers with a long-term stake in the company and a reason to invest in its future.	• High-involvement work practices – eg self-directed teams, quality circles, and sharing/access to company information. • Human resource practices – eg sophisticated recruitment processes, performance appraisals, work redesign and mentoring. • Reward and commitment practices – eg various financial rewards, family friendly policies, job rotation and flexi hours.	• Information sharing. • Sophisticated recruitment. • Formal induction programme. • Five or more days of off-the-job training in the last year. • Semi- or totally autonomous work teams; continuous improvement teams; problem-solving groups. • Interpersonal skill development. • Performance feedback. • Involvement – works council, suggestion scheme, opinion survey. • Team-based rewards, employee share ownership scheme, profit-sharing scheme.

TABLE 4.3   Examples of high-performance working ingredients

Organization	High-performance working ingredients
Halo Foods	• A strategy that maintains competitiveness by increasing added value through the efforts and enhanced capability of all staff. • The integration of technical advance with people development. • Continuing reliance on teamworking and effective leadership, with innovation and self- and team management skills.
Land Registry	• Organizational changes to streamline processes, raise skill levels and release talents. • Managers who could see that the problems were as much cultural as organizational. • Recruitment of people whose attitudes and aptitudes match the needs of high performance work practices.
Meritor Heavy Vehicle Braking Systems	• Skill enhancement, particularly of management and self management skills using competence frameworks. • Teamworking skills and experience used on improvement projects. • Linking learning, involvement and performance management.
Orangebox	• A strategy that relies on constant reinvention of operational capability. • Engagement and development of existing talent and initiative in productivity improvement. • Increasing use of cross-departmental projects to tackle wider opportunities.
Perkinelmer	• A vision and values worked through by managers and supervisors. • Engagement of everyone in the organization and establishment of a continuous improvement culture. • Learning as a basis for change.
United Welsh Housing Association	• Linking of better employment relations with better performance. • Using staff experience to improve customer service. • Focusing management development on the cascading of a partnership culture.

researchers have yet established how this happens. They commented that 'the widely held view that positive performance outcomes from HPWS flow via positive employee outcomes has been shown to be highly questionable' (*ibid*: 521).

Godard (2001) concluded, following his research in Canada, that the actual effects of high-performance work systems can vary considerably and many have a limited lifespan. Following further research, he commented in 2004 that:

The full adoption of this (high performance) paradigm may not yield outcomes that are appreciably more positive than those yielded by practices that have long been associated with good management, including professional personnel practices (eg job ladders, employment security, grievance systems, formal training, above-market pay), group work organization, information sharing and accommodative union relations policies ... There may be positive effects in some workplaces. However, these effects may be inherently more limited than assumed and, in a great many workplaces, may not be sufficient to justify full adoption.

But research conducted by Sung and Ashton (2005), Combs *et al* (2006) and Ericksen (2007) indicated that an HPWS can significantly improve performance. Even so, it is still possible to have reservations about causality and there seems to be no agreement on what constitutes an HPWS except for variable lists of 'best practices', a dubious concept. As Godard (2004) commented, these lists are no more than bundles of long-accepted good personnel practices. Perhaps the virtue of the HPWS model is simply that it makes people think about what can be done to improve performance and how the various approaches can be linked together in a cohesive action programme.

Performance management

Performance management can contribute to the development of a high-performance culture by delivering the message in an organization that high performance is important. The management of organizational performance is the continuing responsibility of top management who, with the help and advice of HR, plan, organize, monitor and control activities and provide leadership to achieve strategic objectives and satisfy the needs and requirements of stakeholders. Individual and team performance management systems play an important part, but they function within the context of what is done to manage organizational performance and to develop effective work systems.

The strategic approach adopted by Johnson & Johnson was described by Wortzel-Hoffman and Boltizar (2007) as follows:

> As we embarked on developing an integrated performance and development process into the organization, we knew that driving change and an enhanced process requires a cultural shift within an organization. The best performance management becomes a continuous process and is not a one time event; it takes time and effort and a dedication to developing people. We also knew that from a business standpoint it was critical to build and develop the talent pipeline of the organization to meet the aggressive business goals and dynamically changing marketplace.

Performance management at organizational, team and individual level defines what high performance is and how managers and their teams should achieve it. It explains how performance should be measured and the steps that should be taken to monitor results in comparison with expectations. The means of achieving high performance are provided by defining the performance expectations implicit in the psychological contract, creating high levels of engagement, motivating people and enhancing skills and competencies through feedback, coaching and personal development planning. Performance management systems are described more fully in Chapter 27.

The contribution of HR

HR contributes to enhancing organizational performance by providing insights on the performance issues affecting the organization and its employees. This means identifying the reasons for the issues, exploring their implications for business and people management and conveying these messages to management. The aim is to find new ways of meeting performance challenges.

HR can advise management on the development of a high performance strategy supported by performance and reward initiatives. Additionally, HR can review policies and practices such as those concerned with organizational development, engagement, resourcing, learning and development, and employee relations. Decisions can then be made to enhance existing policies and practices or introduce new ones. Importantly, consideration needs to be given to how integration of these policies and practices can be achieved by linking them together in a 'bundle' so that they are mutually supportive.

HR has then to prepare a business case for any developments or innovations and persuade management to accept it. Line managers and employees should be involved in the development programme and a communications strategy should be created to inform people about what is going on and how it will affect them.

HR will also be involved in producing and project managing an implementation programme. As necessary, learning and development activities and events will be conducted to ensure that line managers and employees have the skills required.

Key learning points: HRM and performance

The impact of HRM

Much research has been carried out showing that good HRM practice and firm performance are correlated; notable examples in the UK are Guest *et al* (2000a), Patterson *et al* (1997), Purcell *et al* (2003), Thompson (2002) and West *et al* (2002).

How HRM makes an impact

Storey *et al* (2009: 4) observed that: 'The premise is that, in some shape or form, HR policies have an effect on HR practices and these in turn influence staff attitudes and behaviours which will, in turn again, impact on service offerings and customer perceptions of value.'

Explanations of how HRM makes an impact

Guest (1997: 268) stated that: 'The assumption is that "appropriate" HRM practices tap the motivation and commitment of employees.'

An explanation of the impact of HRM is based on three propositions: 1) that HR practices can make a direct impact on employee characteristics such as engagement, commitment, motivation and skill; 2) if employees have these characteristics it is probable that organizational performance in terms of productivity, quality and the delivery of high levels of customer service will improve; and 3) if such aspects of organizational performance improve, the financial results achieved by the organization will improve.

Developing a high-performance culture

Organizations achieve sustained high performance through the systems of work they adopt, but these systems are managed and operated by people. Ultimately, high-performance working is about improving performance through people. This can be done through the development and implementation of a high-performance culture involving HPWSs in which performance management plays an important part.

High-performance work systems

HPWSs are bundles of HR practices that facilitate employee involvement, skill enhancement and motivation. HPWSs provide the means for creating a performance culture.

Performance management

Performance management can contribute to the development of a high-performance culture by delivering the message in an organization that high performance is important.

The contribution of HR

HR can contribute to enhancing organizational performance by providing insight on the performance issues affecting the organization and its employees.

Questions

1 How does HRM make an impact on performance?

2 What is a high-performance culture?

3 What is a high-performance work system?

4 What are the typical features of a high-performance work system?

5 How can performance management contribute?

References

Alvesson, M (2009) Critical perspectives on strategic HRM, in (eds) J Storey, P M Wright and D Ulrich, *The Routledge Companion to Strategic Human Resource Management*, Abingdon, Routledge, pp 53–68

Appelbaum, E, Bailey, T, Berg, P and Kalleberg, A L (2000) *Manufacturing Advantage: Why high performance work systems pay off*, Ithaca, NY, ILR Press

Becker, B E and Huselid, M A (1998) High performance work systems and firm performance: a synthesis of research and managerial implications, *Research on Personnel and Human Resource Management*, **16**, pp 53–101

Becker, B E, Huselid, M A, Pickus, P S and Spratt, M F (1997) HR as a source of shareholder value: research and recommendations, *Human Resource Management*, Spring, **36** (1), pp 39–47

Boselie, P, Dietz, G and Boon, C (2005) Commonalities and contradictions in HRM and performance research, *Human Resource Management Journal*, **15** (3), pp 67–94

Bowen, D and Ostroff, C (2004) Understanding HRM – firm performance linkages: the role of the 'strength' of the HRM system, *Academy of Management Review*, **29** (2), pp 203–21

Combs, J, Liu, Y, Hall, A and Ketchen, D (2006) How much do high performance work practices matter? A meta-analysis of their effects on organizational performance, *Personnel Psychology*, **59** (3), pp 501–28

Ericksen, J (2007) High performance work systems: dynamic workforce alignment and firm performance, *Academy of Management Proceedings*, pp 1–6

Gephart, M A (1995) The road to high performance: steps to create a high performance workplace, *Training and Development*, June, p 29

Godard, J (2001) Beyond the high performance paradigm? An analysis of variation in Canadian managerial perceptions of reform programme effectiveness, *British Journal of Industrial Relations*, **39** (1), pp 25–52

Godard, J (2004) A critical assessment of the high performance paradigm, *British Journal of Industrial Relations*, **42** (2), pp 349–78

Guest, D E (1997) Human resource management and performance; a review of the research agenda, *The International Journal of Human Resource Management*, **8** (3), 263–76

Guest, D E (2011) Human resource management and performance: still searching for some answers, *Human Resource Management Journal*, **21** (1), pp 3–13

Guest, D E and Conway, N (2011) The impact of HR practices, HR effectiveness and a 'strong HR system' on organizational outcomes: a stakeholder perspective, *The International Journal of Human Resource Management*, **22** (8), pp 1686–702

Guest, D E, Michie, J, Sheehan, M and Conway, N (2000a) *Employee Relations, HRM and Business Performance: An analysis of the 1998 Workplace Employee Relations Survey*, London, CIPD

Guest, D E, Michie, J, Sheehan, M, Conway, N and Metochi, M (2000b) *Effective People Management: Initial findings of Future of Work survey*, London, CIPD

Nishii, L, Lepak, D and Schneider, B (2008) Employee attributions of the 'why' of HR practices: their affects on employee attitudes and behaviours, and customer satisfaction, *Personnel Psychology*, **61** (3), pp 503–45

Paauwe, J (2004) *HRM and Performance: Achieving long-term viability*, Oxford, Oxford University Press

Patterson, M G, West, M A, Lawthom, R and Nickell, S (1997) *Impact of People Management Practices on Performance*, London, IPD

Purcell, J, Kinnie, K, Hutchinson, R, Rayton, B and Swart, J (2003) *Understanding the People and Performance Link: Unlocking the black box*, London, CIPD

Ramsay, H, Scholarios, D and Harley, B (2000) Employees and high performance work systems: testing inside the black box, *British Journal of Industrial Relations*, **38** (4), pp 501–31

Shih, H-A, Chiang, Y-H and Hsu, C-C (2005) Can high performance work systems really lead to better performance?, *Academy of Management Conference Paper*, pp 1–6

Stevens, J (2005) *High Performance Wales: Real experiences, real success*, Cardiff, Wales Management Council

Storey, J, Wright, P M and Ulrich, D (2009) Introduction, in (eds) J Storey, P M Wright and D Ulrich, *The Routledge Companion to Strategic Human Resource Management*, Abingdon, Routledge, pp 3–13

Sung, J and Ashton, D (2005) *High Performance Work Practices: Linking strategy and skills to performance outcomes*, DTI in association with CIPD, available at http://www.cipd.co.uk/subjects/corpstrtgy/

Thompson, M (2002) *High Performance Work Organization in UK Aerospace*, London, The Society of British Aerospace Companies

Thompson, M and Heron, P (2005) Management capability and high performance work organization, *International Journal of Human Resource Management*, **16** (6), pp 1029–48

Ulrich, D (1997) *Human Resource Champions*, Boston, MA, Harvard Business School Press

US Department of Labor (1993) *High Performance Work Practices and Work Performance*, Washington, DC, US Government Printing Office

West, M A, Borrill, C S, Dawson, C, Scully, J, Carter, M, Anclay, S, Patterson, M and Waring, J (2002) The link between the management of employees and patient mortality in acute hospitals, *International Journal of Human Resource Management*, **13** (8), pp 1299–310

Wortzel-Hoffman, N and Boltizar, S (2007) Performance and development planning: a culture shift perspective, *Organization Development Journal*, **25** (2), pp 195–200

05
International HRM

LEARNING OUTCOMES

On completing this chapter you should be able to define these key concepts. You should also know about:

- The meaning of international HRM
- Issues in international HRM
- The impact of globalization
- International environmental and cultural differences
- Factors affecting the choice between convergence and divergence
- Global HR policies
- Managing expatriates

Introduction

It has been stated by Brewster *et al* (2005: 949) that: 'A critical challenge for organizations from both the public and private sectors in the twenty-first century is the need to operate across national boundaries.' They identified five distinct, but linked, organizational drivers of international HRM: efficiency orientation, global service provision, information exchange, core business processes and localization of decision making. In this chapter consideration is given to how organizations respond to this challenge through the practice of international HRM.

International HRM defined

International human resource management is the process of managing people across international boundaries by multinational companies. It involves the worldwide management of people, not just the management of expatriates.

Companies that function globally comprise international and multinational firms. International firms are those where operations take place in subsidiaries overseas which rely on the business expertise or manufacturing capacity of the parent company; they may be highly centralized with tight controls. Multinational firms are ones in which a number of businesses in different countries are managed as a whole from the centre; the degree of autonomy they have will vary.

As reported by Welfare (2006: 8), Dr Dickman of the Cranfield School of Management believes that the main contrast between national and global HR practice is the need to see the bigger picture: 'The difference is the higher complexity and the need for sensitivity to different cultures and different business environments.' Dickman stated that understanding the local context is key and an international HR person needs to be asking questions such as: What is the business environment here? What is the role of the trade unions? What is the local labour law? Are these people different? Are their motivation patterns different?

Issues in international HRM

The issues that affect the practice of international as distinct from domestic HRM are the impact of globalization, the influence of environmental and cultural differences, the extent to which HRM policy and practice should vary in different countries (convergence or divergence), and the approaches used to employ and manage expatriates.

Globalization

Globalization is the process of international economic integration in worldwide markets. It involves the development of single international markets for goods or services accompanied by an accelerated growth in world trade.

Any company that has economic interests or activities extending across a number of international boundaries is a global company. This involves some issues not present when the activities of the firm are confined to one country. As Ulrich (1998: 126) contended, globalization requires organizations:

> to move people, ideas, products, and information around the world to meet local needs. They must add new and important ingredients to the mix when making strategy: volatile political situations, contentious global trade issues, fluctuating exchange rates, and unfamiliar cultures. They must be more literate in the ways of international customers, commerce and competition than ever before. In short, globalization requires that organizations increase their ability to learn and collaborate and to manage diversity, complexity, and ambiguity.

Bartlett and Ghoshal (1991) argued that the main issue for multinational companies is the need to manage the challenges of global efficiency and multinational flexibility.

Research conducted over a number of years by Brewster and Sparrow (2007) demonstrated the growth of what they called 'globalized HRM'. They noted that:

> whereas international human resource management has tended to operate in the same way as local HRM but on a wider scale, globalized HRM exploits the new technologies available in order to manage all the company's staff around the world in the same way that it has traditionally managed staff in the home country. (*ibid*: 48)

Global and international HRM

The following distinction was made by Brewster *et al* (2005: 966) between global and international HRM:

> Traditionally, international HR has been about managing an international workforce – the higher level organizational people working as expatriates, frequent commuters, cross-cultural team members and specialists involved in international knowledge transfer. Global HRM is not simply about these staff. It concerns managing all HRM activities, wherever they are, through the application of global rule sets.

Environmental differences

Environmental differences between countries have to be taken into account in managing globally.

As described by Gerhart and Fang (2005: 971) these include 'differences in the centrality of markets, institutions, regulation, collective bargaining and labour-force characteristics'. For example, in Western Europe collective bargaining coverage is much higher than in countries like the United States, Canada and Japan. Works councils are mandated by law in Western European countries like Germany, but not in Japan or the United States. In China, Eastern Europe and Mexico, labour costs are significantly lower than in Western Europe, Japan and the United States.

Cultural differences

Cultural differences must also be taken into account. Hiltrop (1995) noted the following HR areas that may be affected by national culture:

- decisions on what makes an effective manager;

- giving face-to-face feedback;

- readiness to accept international assignments;

- pay systems and different concepts of social justice;

- approaches to organizational structuring and strategic dynamics.

The significance of cultural differences was the influential message delivered by Hofstede (1980) based on his research using worldwide data on IBM employees. He suggested that culture consisted of collective values and involved the collective mental programming of people in an environment and broad tendencies 'to prefer certain states of affairs over others' (*ibid*: 19). One of the conclusions Hofstede reached was that the cultural values within a nation are substantially more similar than the values of individuals from different nations. This has been taken up by subsequent commentators such as Adler (2002) who claimed that Hofstede's study explained 50 per cent of the difference between countries in employees' attitudes and behaviours.

This view has been challenged by Gerhart and Fang (2005). They subjected Hofstede's findings to further analysis and established that at the level of the individual as distinct from the country, only 2 to 4 per cent was explained by national differences and that therefore, 'Hofstede's study should not be interpreted as showing that national culture explains 50 per cent of behaviours' (*ibid*: 977). They also established from Hofstede's data that culture varies more between organizations than between countries. In their view, cross-country cultural differences, while real, have been over-estimated and may well pale in significance when compared with other unique country characteristics when it comes to explaining the effectiveness of HR practices. But they accepted that national culture differences can be critical and that insensitivity to national culture differences can and does result in business failure (as well as failure and career consequences for individual managers).

On the basis of research conducted in 30 multi-national companies by the Global HR Research Alliance, Stiles (2007: 37) commented that 'while national cultural differences were not unimportant … organizational culture actually had more influence on HR practice'. The conclusion from the research was that: 'To think there is one best way to manage human resources is simplistic and wrong, but the variation and contextualization of HR, at least for the companies we studied, owes little to national culture' (*ibid*: 41).

Convergence and divergence

According to Brewster *et al* (2002), the effectiveness of global HRM depends on the ability to judge the extent to which an organization should implement similar practices across the world (convergence) or adapt them to suit local conditions (divergence). The dilemma facing all multinational corporations is that of achieving a balance between international consistency and local autonomy. But Perkins and Shortland (2006) noted that strategic choices on employment relationships may be influenced primarily by 'home country' values and practices.

There is a natural tendency for managerial traditions in the parent company to shape the nature of key decisions, but there are strong arguments for giving as much local autonomy as possible to ensure that local requirements are sufficiently taken into account; hence the mantra, 'Think globally but act nationally.' As Brewster *et al* (2005: 951) pointed out:

Where global integration and coordination are important, subsidiaries need to be globally integrated with other parts of the organization and/or strategically coordinated by the parent. In contrast, where local responsiveness is important, subsidiaries will have far greater autonomy and there is less need for integration.

Brewster (2004) believes that convergence may be increasing as a result of the power of the markets, the importance of cost, quality and productivity pressures, the emergence of transaction cost economies, the development of like-minded international cadres and benchmarking 'best practice'. Stiles (2007: 41) noted that common practices across borders may be appropriate: 'Organizations seek what works and for HR in multinational companies, the range of options is limited to a few common practices that are believed to secure high performance.' Brewster and his colleagues think that it is quite possible for some parts of an HR system to converge while other parts may diverge. But there is choice, and they have listed the following factors affecting it.

Source reviews

Factors affecting the choice between convergence and divergence – Brewster *et al* (2005)

- The extent to which there are well-defined local norms.

- The degree to which an operating unit is embedded in the local environment.

- The strength of the flow of resources – finance, information and people – between the parent and the subsidiary.

- The orientation of the parent to control.

- The nature of the industry – the extent to which it is primarily a domestic industry at local level.

- The specific organizational competencies, including HRM, that are critical for achieving competitive advantage in a global environment.

Welfare (2006) reported Dickman's comment that organizations such as IBM and Oxfam operate a model based on universal principles or values across the organization, which is then implemented differently at regional or national level. Dickman suggested that the extent of integration or convergence depends on the business model of the organization. If the company is basically a McDonald's, where there are only limited local variations but the product is essentially the same all over the world, then the approach is likely to be different to a company like Unilever, whose products and processes tend to be much more responsive to the local market.

Global HR policies and practices

The research conducted by Brewster *et al* (2005) identified three processes that constitute global HRM: talent management/employee branding, international assignments management, and managing an international workforce. They found that organizations such as Rolls Royce had set up centres of excellence operating on a global basis. They observed that global HR professionals are acting as the guardians of culture, operating global values and systems.

It was established by the Global HR Research Alliance study (Stiles, 2007) that global HR policies and practices were widespread in the areas of maintaining global performance standards, the use of common evaluation processes, common approaches to rewards, the development of senior managers, the application of competency frameworks and the use of common performance management criteria. Generally the research has indicated that while global HR policies in such areas as talent management, performance management and reward may be developed, communicated and supported by centres of excellence, often through global networking, a fair degree of freedom has frequently been allowed to local management to adopt their own practices in accordance with the local context as long as in principle these are consistent with global policies.

Managing expatriates

Expatriates are people working overseas on long- or short-term contracts who can be nationals of the parent company or 'third-country nationals' (TCNs) – nationals of countries other than the parent company who work abroad in subsidiaries of that company.

The management of expatriates is a major factor determining success or failure in an international business. Expatriates are expensive: they can cost three or four times as much as employing the same individual at home. They can be difficult to manage because of the problems associated with adapting to and working in unfamiliar environments, concerns about their development and careers, difficulties encountered when they re-enter their parent company after an overseas assignment, and how they should be remunerated. Policies to address all these issues are required, as described below.

Resourcing policies

The challenge is that of resourcing international operations with people of the right calibre. As Perkins (1997) observed, it is necessary for businesses to remain competitive with their employment offering in the market place, to attract and retain high quality staff with worldwide capabilities.

Policies are required on the employment of local nationals and the use of expatriates for long periods or shorter assignments. The advantages of employing local nationals are that they:

- are familiar with local markets, the local communities, the cultural setting and the local economy;
- speak the local language and are culturally assimilated;
- can take a long-term view and contribute for a long period (as distinct from expatriates who are likely to take a short-term perspective);
- do not take the patronizing (neo-colonial) attitude expatriates sometimes adopt.

Expatriates may be required to provide the experience and expertise that local nationals lack, at least for the time being. But there is much to be said for a long-term resourcing policy which states that the aim is to fill all or the great majority of posts with local people. Parent companies that staff their overseas subsidiaries with local nationals always have the scope to 'parachute in' specialist staff to deal with particular issues such as the start-up of a new product or service.

Recruitment and selection policies

Policies for recruitment and selection should deal with specifying requirements, providing realistic previews and preparation for overseas assignments.

Role specifications

Role specifications should take note of the behaviours required for those who work internationally. Leblanc (2001) suggested that they should be able to:

- recognize the diversity of overseas countries;
- accept differences between countries as a fact and adjust to these differences effectively;
- tolerate and adjust to local conditions;
- cope in the long term with a large variety of foreign contexts;
- manage local operations and personnel abroad effectively;
- gain acceptance as a representative of one's company abroad;
- obtain and interpret information about foreign national contexts (institutions, legislations, practices, market specifics, etc);
- inform and communicate effectively with a foreign environment about the home company's policies;
- take into account the foreign environment when negotiating contracts and partnerships;
- identify and accept adjustments to basic product specifications in order to meet the needs of the foreign market;
- develop elements of a common framework for company strategies, policies and operations;
- accept that the practices that will operate best in an overseas environment will not necessarily be the same as the company's 'home' practices.

Realistic previews

At interviews for candidates from outside the organization, and when talking to internal staff about the possibility of an overseas assignment, it is advisable to have a policy of providing a realistic preview of the job. The preview should provide information on the overseas operation, any special features of the work, what will need to be done to adjust to local conditions, career progression overseas, re-entry policy on completion of the assignment, pay and special benefits such as home leave and children's education.

Preparation policy

The preparation policy for overseas assignments should include the provision of cultural familiarization for the country(ies) in which the expatriate will work (sometimes called 'acculturization'), the preferred approach to leading and working in international teams, and the business and HR policies that will apply.

Training policy

Tarique and Caligiri (1995) proposed that the following steps should be taken to design a training programme for expatriates:

1 Identify the type of global assignment, eg technical, functional, tactical, developmental or strategic/executive.

2 Conduct a cross-cultural training needs analysis covering organizational analysis and requirements, assignment analysis of key tasks and individual analysis of skills.

3 Establish training goals and measures – cognitive (eg understanding the role of cultural values and norms) and affective (modifying perception about culture and increasing confidence in dealing with individual behaviours to form adaptive behaviours such as interpersonal skills).

4 Develop the programme – the content should cover both general and specific cultural orientation; a variety of methods should be used.

5 Evaluate training given.

Career management policy

Special attention has to be paid to managing the careers of expatriates either as part of their experience overseas or on return permanently or for a period to their home country.

Assimilation and review policies

Assimilation policies will provide for the adaptation of expatriates to overseas posts and their progress in them to be monitored and reviewed. This may take the form of conventional performance management processes but additional information may be provided on potential and the ability of individuals to cope with overseas conditions. Where a number of expatriates are employed it is customary for someone at headquarters to have the responsibility of looking after them.

Re-entry policies

Re-entry policies should be designed to minimize the problems that can arise when expatriates return to their parent company after an overseas posting. They want to be assured that they will be given positions appropriate to their qualifications, and they will be concerned about their careers, suspecting that their overseas experience will not be taken into account. Policies should allow time for expatriates to adjust. The provision of mentors or counsellors is desirable.

Pay and allowances policies

The factors that are likely to impact on the design of reward systems, as suggested by Bradley *et al* (1999), are the corporate culture of the multinational enterprise, expatriate and local labour markets, local cultural sensitivities and legal and institutional factors. They refer to the choice that has to be made between seeking internal consistency by developing common reward policies to facilitate the movement of employees across borders and preserve internal equity, and responding to pressures to conform to local practices. But they point out that studies of cultural differences suggest that reward system design and management need to be tailored to local values to enhance the performance of overseas operations. As Sparrow (1999) indicated, differences in international reward are not just a consequence of cultural differences but also of differences in international influences, national business systems and the role and competence of managers in the sphere of HRM. The policy of most organizations is to ensure that expatriates are no worse off because they have been posted abroad. In practice, various additional allowances or payments, such as hardship allowances, mean that they are usually better off financially than if they had stayed at home. The basic choice for remunerating expatriates is whether to adopt a home-based or host-based policy.

Home-based pay

The home-based pay approach aims to ensure that the value of the remuneration (pay, benefits and allowances) of expatriates is the same as in their home country. The home-base salary may be a notional one for long-term assignments (ie the salary it is assumed would be paid to expatriates were they employed in a job of equivalent level at the parent company). For shorter-term assignments it may be the actual salary of the individual. The notional or actual home-base salary is used as the foundation upon which the total remuneration package is built. This is sometimes called the 'build-up' or 'balance sheet' approach.

The salary 'build-up' starts with the actual or notional home-base salary. To it is added a cost of living adjustment applied to 'spendable income' – the portion of salary that would be used at home for everyday living. It usually excludes income tax, social security, pensions and insurance and can exclude discretionary expenditure on major purchases or holidays on the grounds that these do not constitute day-to-day living expenses.

The expatriate's salary would then consist of the actual or notional home-base salary plus the cost of living adjustment. In addition, it may be necessary to adjust salaries to take account of the host country's tax regime in order to achieve tax equalization. Moves of less than a year that might give rise to double taxation require particular attention.

Some or all of the following allowances may be added to this salary:

- 'incentive to work abroad' premium;
- hardship and location;
- housing and utilities;
- school fees;
- 'rest and recuperation' leave.

Host-based pay

The host-based pay approach provides expatriates with salaries and benefits such as company cars and holidays that are in line with those given to nationals of the host country in similar jobs. This method ensures equity between expatriates and host country nationals. It is adopted by companies using the so-called 'market rate' system, which ensures that the salaries of expatriates match the market levels of pay in the host country.

Companies using the host-based approach commonly pay additional allowances such as school fees, accommodation and medical insurance. They may also fund long-term benefits like social security, life assurance and pensions from home.

The host-based method is certainly equitable from the viewpoint of local nationals, and it can be less expensive than home-based pay. But it may be much less attractive as an inducement for employees to work abroad, especially in unpleasant locations, and it can be difficult to collect market rate data locally to provide a basis for setting pay levels.

CASE STUDIES

Oxfam

Oxfam is a highly devolved international organization with a strategy of building up local management. Reporting lines for HR staff reflect this devolved approach. Country-based HR staff report to regional HR managers The latter report direct to their regional director but have a 'dotted line' (functional) relationship with Oxfam's head of international HR. This means that they must take account of the principles of Oxfam's international people strategy and its associated policies covering pay, benefits, performance management and other practices that apply to every region. Thus regions will follow Oxfam's international people strategy, pay and benefits framework and other HR procedures unless local legislation has to take precedence; they ultimately decide how to implement policies and pay staff within regional budgets. Oxfam recruits locally when it can but it may be necessary to look elsewhere for people with some specialist skills, although this labour pool is from a global labour market rather than a Western one.

IBM

IBM has over 300,000 employees in more than 160 countries. It has evolved in recent years from a predominately IT manufacturing and sales company to become a business services company. Strategy is global but the human front-end of HR is local, staffed with local nationals. A generally integrated approach to HR is adopted although the extent to which HR policies are tailored to local circumstances varies. This is affected by the need to conform to different legal requirements in each company, which particularly affects employee relations policies.

However, total reward and performance management policies and practices are common across the world. The company claims that it acts on its values, for example equal opportunities, even when they may prove controversial locally. Levels of international mobility are high, especially HR, finance and IT staff.

Key learning points: International HRM

The meaning of international HRM

International human resource management is the process of managing people across international boundaries by multinational companies. It involves the worldwide management of people, not just the management of expatriates.

Issues in international HRM

International HRM issues comprise the impact of globalization, the influence of environmental and cultural differences, the extent to which HRM policy and practice should vary in different countries (convergence or divergence), and the approaches used to employ and manage expatriates.

The impact of globalization

'Globalization requires organizations to move people, ideas, products and information around the world to meet local needs' (Ulrich, 1998).

International environmental differences

Environmental differences between countries have to be taken into account in managing globally. These include markets, institutions, regulation, collective bargaining and labour-force characteristics.

International cultural differences

National culture differences can be critical and insensitivity to them can result in business failure (as well as failure and career consequences for individual managers).

Factors affecting the choice between convergence and divergence (Harris and Brewster, 1999) are:

- The extent to which there are well-defined local norms.
- The degree to which an operating unit is embedded in the local environment.
- The strength of the flow of resources between the parent and the subsidiary.
- The orientation of the parent to control.
- The nature of the industry.
- The specific organizational competencies, including HRM, that are critical for achieving competitive advantage in a global environment.

Global HR policies

Three processes constitute global HRM: talent management/employee branding, international assignments management, and managing an international workforce (Brewster et al, 2005).

Managing expatriates

Expatriates can be difficult to manage because of the problems associated with adapting to and working in unfamiliar environments, concerns about their development and careers, difficulties encountered when they re-enter their parent company after an overseas assignment, and how they should be remunerated. Special policies for them are required covering:

- recruitment and selection;
- assimilation and review;
- training;
- career management;
- re-entry;
- pay and allowances (home-based or host-based pay).

Questions

1 What is international human resource management?

2 What are the main issues in international human resource management?

3 What is the significance of cultural differences?

4 What is the significance of the concepts of convergence and divergence?

5 What are the problems of employing expatriates?

6 What are the advantages of employing local nationals?

7 What polices should be adopted for the re-entry of expatriates to their home country?

8 What are host- and home-based pay policies?

References

Adler, N J (2002) *International Dimensions of Organizational Behaviour*, Cincinnati, OH, South-Western

Bartlett, C A and Ghoshal, S (1991) *Managing Across Borders: The transnational solution*, London, London Business School

Bradley, P, Hendry, C and Perkins, P (1999) Global or multi-local? The significance of international values in reward strategy, in (eds) C Brewster and H Harris, *International HRM: Contemporary issues in Europe*, London, Routledge

Brewster, C (2004) European perspectives of human resource management, *Human Resource Management Review*, **14** (4), pp 365–82

Brewster, C and Sparrow, P (2007) Advances in technology inspire a fresh approach to international HRM, *People Management*, 8 February, p 48

Brewster, C, Harris, H and Sparrow, P (2002) *Globalizing HR*, London, CIPD

Brewster, C, Sparrow, P and Harris, H (2005) Towards a new model of globalizing HRM, *The International Journal of Human Resource Management*, **16** (6), pp 949–70

Gerhart, B and Fang, M (2005) National culture and human resource management: assumptions and evidence, *The International Journal of Human Resource Management*, **16** (6), pp 971–86

Harris, H and Brewster, C (1999) International human resource management: the European contribution, in (eds) C Brewster and H Harris, *International HRM: Contemporary issues in Europe*, London, Routledge

Hiltrop, J M (1995) The changing psychological contract: the human resource challenge of the 1990s, *European Management Journal*, **13** (3), pp 286–94

Hofstede, G (1980) *Cultural Consequences: International differences in work-related values*, Beverley Hills, CA, Sage

Leblanc, B (2001) European competitiveness – some guidelines for companies, in (ed) M H Albrecht, *International HRM*, Oxford, Blackwell

Perkins, S J (1997) *Internationalization: The people dimension*, London, Kogan Page

Perkins, S J and Shortland, S M (2006) *Strategic International Human Resource Management*, London, Kogan Page

Sparrow, P R (1999) *The IPD Guide on International Recruitment, Selection and Assessment*, London, IPD

Stiles, P (2007) A world of difference?, *People Management*, 15 November, pp 36–41

Tarique, I and Caligiri, P (1995) Training and development of international staff, in (eds) A-W Herzorg and J V Ruyssevelde, *International Human Resource Management*, London, Sage

Ulrich, D (1998) A new mandate for human resources, *Harvard Business Review*, January–February, pp 124–34

Welfare, S (2006) A whole world out there: managing global HR, *IRS Employment Review*, **862**, 29 December, pp 8–12

06
Human capital management

LEARNING OUTCOMES

On completing this chapter you should be able to define these key concepts. You should
also understand:

- The nature of human capital management
- The concept of human capital
- Characteristics of human capital
- Constituents of human capital
- Significance of human capital theory
- Importance of human capital measurement
- Reasons for interest in human capital measurement
- Approaches to measurement
- Measurement elements
- Factors affecting choice of measurement
- Criteria for HCM data for managers

Introduction

As defined by Baron and Armstrong (2007: 20), human capital management (HCM) is concerned with obtaining, analysing and reporting on data that inform the direction of value-adding people management, strategic, investment and operational decisions at corporate level and at the level of front line management. It is, as emphasized by Kearns (2005), ultimately about value.

The nature of human capital management

The Accounting for People Task Force report (2003) stated that HCM involves the systematic analysis, measurement and evaluation of how people policies and practices create value. The report emphasized that HCM should be regarded as an approach to people management that deals with it as a high-level strategic issue rather than a matter to be left to HR. However, Wright and McMahan (2011: 102) warned that human capital should not be treated as a form of capital owned and controlled by the firm: 'To do so would miss the complexity of the construct and continue to ignore the "human" in strategic HRM.'

The defining characteristic of HCM is the use of metrics to guide an approach to managing people that regards them as assets and emphasizes that competitive advantage is achieved by strategic investments in those assets through employee engagement and retention, talent management and learning and development programmes. HCM provides a bridge between HR and business strategy. The concept of HCM is underpinned by the concept of human capital, as explained below.

The concept of human capital

Adam Smith, cited by Schultz (1981: 140), originated the idea of human capital (like so many other economic concepts) when he wrote that: 'The acquired wealth of nations derives from the acquired abilities of people – their education, experience, skills and health.' Individuals generate, retain and use knowledge and skill (human capital) and create intellectual capital. Their knowledge is enhanced by the interactions between them (social capital) and generates the institutionalized knowledge possessed by an organization (organizational capital). This concept of human capital is explained below.

Human capital defined

Human capital consists of the knowledge, skills and abilities of the people employed in an organization. As Wright and McMahan (2011: 101) explained:

> Each individual in the organization has characteristics that comprise human capital. He/she also engages in the processing of information, interpretation and reaction to that information in making choices about how to feel and behave. The aggregation of human capital, we propose, constitutes the organization or unit's 'human capital'.

Human capital constitutes a key element of the market worth of a company. A research study conducted in 2003 by CFO Research Services estimated that the value of human capital represented over 36 per cent of total revenue in a typical organization.

The significance of the term was emphasized by Schultz, who defined it as follows.

Source review

Human capital defined – Schultz (1961: 1)

Although it is obvious that people acquire useful skills and knowledge, it is not obvious that these skills and knowledge are a form of capital, that this capital is in substantial part a product of deliberate investment, that it has grown in Western countries at a much faster rate than conventional (non-human) capital, and that its growth may well be the most distinctive feature of the economic system.

He also noted that: 'Attributes ... which are valuable and can be augmented by appropriate investment will be treated as human capital ... Consider all human abilities to be either innate or acquired' (*ibid*: 21).

A later detailed definition was put forward by Bontis *et al*.

Source review

Human capital defined – Bontis *et al* (1999: 393)

Human capital represents the human factor in the organization; the combined intelligence, skills and expertise that gives the organization its distinctive character. The human elements of the organization are those that are capable of learning, changing, innovating and providing the creative thrust which if properly motivated can ensure the long-term survival of the organization.

Scarborough and Elias (2002: *ix*) commented that: 'The concept of human capital is most usefully viewed as a bridging concept – that is, it defines the link between HR practices and business performance in terms of assets rather than business processes.' They pointed out that human capital is to a large extent 'non-standardized, tacit, dynamic, context dependent and embodied in people'. These characteristics make it difficult to evaluate human capital, bearing in mind that the 'features of human capital that are so crucial to firm performance are the flexibility and creativity of individuals, their ability to develop skills over time and to respond in a motivated way to different contexts' (*ibid*: ix).

It is indeed the knowledge, skills and abilities of individuals that create value, which is why the focus has to be on means of attracting, retaining, developing and maintaining the human capital they represent. Davenport (1999: 7) observed that: 'People possess innate abilities, behaviours and personal time. These elements make up human capital, the currency people bring to invest in their jobs. Workers, not organizations, own this human capital.'

The choices they make include how much discretionary behaviour they are prepared to exercise in carrying out their role (discretionary behaviour refers to the discretion people at work can exercise about the way they do their job and the amount of effort, care, innovation and productive behaviour they display). They can also choose whether or not to remain with the organization.

The constituents of human capital

Human capital consists of intellectual, social and organizational capital.

Intellectual capital

The concept of human capital is associated with the overarching concept of intellectual capital, which is defined as the stocks and flows of knowledge available to an organization. These can be regarded as the intangible resources associated with people which, together with tangible resources (money and physical assets), comprise the market or total value of a business.

Social capital

Social capital is another element of intellectual capital. It consists of the knowledge derived from networks of relationships within and outside the organization. The concept of social capital has been defined by Putnam (1996: 66) as 'the features of social life – networks, norms and trust – that enable participants to act together more effectively to pursue shared objectives'. It is important to take into account social capital considerations, that is, the ways in which knowledge is developed through interaction between people. Bontis *et al* (1999) commented that it is flows as well as stocks that matter. Intellectual capital develops and changes over time and a significant part is played in these processes by people acting together.

Organizational capital

Organizational capital is the institutionalized knowledge possessed by an organization that is stored in databases, manuals, etc (Youndt, 2000). It is often called 'structural capital' (Edvinson and Malone, 1997), but the term 'organizational capital' is preferred by Youndt because, he argues, it conveys more clearly that this is the knowledge that the organization actually owns.

Approaches to people management raised by human capital theory

An approach to people management based on human capital theory involves obtaining answers to these questions:

- What are the key performance drivers that create value?
- What skills do we have?
- What skills do we need now and in the future to meet our strategic aims?
- How are we going to attract, develop and retain these skills?
- How can we develop a culture and environment in which organizational and individual learning takes place that meets both our needs and the needs of our employees?
- How can we provide for both the explicit and tacit knowledge created in our organization to be captured, recorded and used effectively?

Human capital theory helps to determine the impact of people on the business and their contribution to shareholder value. It demonstrates that HR practices produce value for money in terms, for example, of return on investment. It also provides guidance on future HR and business strategies and data that will inform strategies and practices designed to improve the effectiveness of people management in the organization.

Human capital measurement

The role of human capital measurement is to assess the impact of HRM practices and the contribution made by people to organizational performance. Methods of measuring impact and contribution based upon human capital data have therefore to be developed. Human capital measurement is about finding links, correlations and, ideally, causation, between different sets of (HR) data, using statistical techniques.

The need for human capital measurement

There is an overwhelming case for evolving methods of valuing human capital as an aid to people management decision making. This may mean identifying the key people management drivers and modelling the effect of varying them. The need is to develop a framework within which reliable information can be collected and analysed such as added value per employee, productivity and measures of employee behaviour (attrition and absenteeism rates, the frequency/severity rate of accidents, and cost savings resulting from suggestion schemes).

Reasons for the interest in measurement

The recognized importance of achieving human capital advantage has led to an interest in the development of methods of measuring the value and impact of that capital for these reasons:

- People in organizations add value and there is a case for assessing this value to provide a basis for HR planning and for monitoring the effectiveness and impact of HR policies and practices.
- The process of identifying measures and collecting and analysing information relating to them will focus the attention of the organization on what needs to be done to find, keep, develop and make the best use of its human capital.
- Measurements can be used to monitor progress in achieving strategic HR goals and generally to evaluate the effectiveness of HR practices.
- You cannot manage unless you measure.

However, the Institute for Employment Studies (Hartley, 2005) emphasized that reporting on human capital is not simply about measurement. Measures on their own such as those resulting from benchmarking are not enough; they must be clearly linked to business performance. On the basis of their research, it was established by Scarborough and Elias (2002: *x*) that:

> Measures are less important than the activity of measuring – of continuously developing and refining our understanding of the productive role of human capital within particular settings, by embedding such activities in management practices, and linking them to the business strategy of the firm.

Approaches to measurement

Three approaches to measurement are described below.

The human capital index – Watson Wyatt

On the basis of a survey of companies that have linked together HR management practices and market value, Watson Wyatt Worldwide (2002) identified four major categories of HR practice that could be linked to increases in shareholder value creation. These are:

1 total rewards and accountability: 16.5 per cent;
2 collegial, flexible workforce: 9.0 per cent;
3 recruiting and retention excellence: 7.9 per cent;
4 communication integrity: 7.1 per cent.

The organizational performance model – Mercer HR Consulting

As described by Nalbantian *et al* (2004) the organizational performance model developed by Mercer HR Consulting is based on the following elements: people, work processes, management structure, information and knowledge, decision making and rewards, each of which plays out differently within the context of the organization, creating a unique DNA.

The statistical tool, 'Internal Labour Market Analysis' used by Mercer draws on the running record of employee and labour market data to analyse the actual experience of employees rather than stated HR programmes and policies. Thus gaps can be identified between what is required in the workforce to support business goals and what is actually being delivered.

The human capital monitor – Andrew Mayo

Andrew Mayo (2001) has developed the 'human capital monitor' to identify the human value of the enterprise or 'human asset worth', which is equal to 'employment cost × individual asset multiplier'. The latter is a weighted average assessment of capability, potential to grow, personal performance (contribution) and alignment to the organization's values set in the context of the workforce environment (ie how leadership, culture, motivation and learning are driving success). The absolute figure is not important. What does matter is that the process of measurement leads you to consider whether human capital is sufficient, increasing, or decreasing, and highlights issues to address. Mayo advises against using too many measures and instead to concentrate on a few organization-wide measures that are critical in creating shareholder value or achieving current and future organizational goals.

He believes that value added per person is a good measure of the effectiveness of human capital, especially for making inter-firm comparisons. But he considers that the most critical indicator for the value of human capital is the level of expertise possessed by an organization. He suggests that this could be analysed under the headings of identified organizational core competencies. The other criteria he mentions are measures of satisfaction derived from employee opinion surveys and levels of attrition and absenteeism.

Measurement data

The main HCM data used for measurement are:

- Basic workforce data – demographic data (numbers by job category, sex, race, age, disability, working arrangements, absence and sickness, turnover and pay).
- People development and performance data – learning and development programmes, performance management/potential assessments, skills and qualifications.

- Perceptual data – attitude/opinion surveys, focus groups, exit interviews.
- Performance data – financial, operational and customer.

A summary of human capital measures and their possible uses is given in Table 6.1.

Human capital reporting

Internal reporting

Analysing and reporting human capital data to top management and line managers will lead to better informed decision making about what kind of actions or practices will improve business results, an increased ability to recognize problems and take rapid action to deal with them, and the scope to demonstrate the effectiveness of HR solutions and thus support the business case for greater investment in HR practices. The process of reporting the data internally and the inferences obtained from them is therefore a vital part of HCM.

It is necessary to be clear about what data is required and how it will be communicated and used. It is not enough simply to give managers and other stakeholders information on human capital. It must be accompanied by effective analysis and explanation if they are going to understand and act upon it in the interests of maximizing organizational performance.

TABLE 6.1   A summary of human capital measures and their possible uses

Measures	Possible use: analysis leading to action
Workforce composition – gender, race, age, full-time, part-time	• Analyse the extent of diversity • Assess the implications of a preponderance of employees in different age groups, eg extent of loses through retirement • Assess the extent to which the organization is relaying on part-time staff
Length of service distribution	• Indicate level of success in retaining employees • Indicate preponderance of long or short-serving employees • Enable analyses of performance of more experienced employees to be assessed
Skills analysis/assessment – graduates, professionally/technically qualified, skilled workers	• Assess skill levels against requirements • Indicate where steps have to be taken to deal with shortfalls
Attrition – employee turnover rates for different categories of management and employees	• Indicate areas where steps have to be taken to increase retention rates • Provide a basis for assessing levels of commitment
Attrition – cost of	• Support business case for taking steps to reduce attrition
Absenteeism/sickness rates	• Identify problems and need for more effective attendance management policies
Average number of vacancies as a percentage of total workforce	• Identify potential shortfall problem areas
Total pay roll costs (pay and benefits)	• Provide data for productivity analysis

TABLE 6.1   *Continued*

Measures	Possible use: analysis leading to action
Compa-ratio – actual rates of pay as a percentage of policy rates	• Enable control to be exercised over management of pay structure
Percentage of employees in different categories of contingent pay or payment-by-result schemes	• Demonstrate the extent to which the organization believes that pay should be related to contribution
Total pay review increases for different categories of employees as a percentage of pay	• Compare actual with budgeted payroll increase costs • Benchmark pay increases
Average bonuses or contingent pay awards as a % of base pay for different categories of managers and employees	• Analyse cost of contingent pay • Compare actual and budgeted increases • Benchmark increases
Outcome of equal pay reviews	• Reveal pay gap between male and female employees
Personal development plans completed as a percentage of employees	• Indicate level of learning and development activity
Training hours per employee	• Indicate actual amount of training activity (note that this does not reveal the quality of training achieved or its impact)
Percentage of managers taking part in formal management development programmes	• Indicate level of learning and development activity
Internal promotion rate (% of promotions filled from within)	• Indicate extent to which talent management programmes are successful
Succession planning coverage (% of managerial jobs for which successors have been identified)	• Indicate extent to which talent management programmes are successful
Percentage of employees taking part in formal performance reviews	• Indicate level of performance management activity
Distribution of performance ratings by category of staff and department	• Indicate inconsistencies, questionable distributions and trends in assessments
Accident severity and frequency rates	• Assess health and safety programmes
Cost savings/revenue increases resulting from employee suggestion schemes	• Measure the value created by employees

External reporting

The EC Accounts Modernization Directive requires companies to prepare a business review. This has to disclose information that is necessary for understanding the development, performance or position of the business of the company, including the analysis of key financial and other performance indicators, and information relating to environmental and employee matters, social and community issues, and any policies of the company in relation to these matters and their effectiveness.

Introducing HCM

As Baron and Armstrong (2007) observed, it is important to emphasize the notion of HCM as a journey. It is not an all or nothing affair. It does not have to depend on a state-of-the-art HR database or the possession of advanced expertise in statistical analysis. It is not all that difficult to record and report on basic data and, although some degree of analytical ability is required, it is reasonable to assume that any self-respecting HR professional will have that skill.

At the beginning of the journey an organization may do no more than collect basic HR data on, for instance, employee turnover and absence. But anyone who goes a little bit further and analyses that data to draw conclusions on trends and causation leading to proposals on the action required supported by that analysis, is into HCM. Not in a big way perhaps, but it is a beginning. At the other end of the scale there are the highly sophisticated approaches to HCM operated by such organizations as Nationwide and Standard Chartered Bank.

HCM CASE STUDIES ON APPROACHES TO MEASUREMENT

Nationwide Building Society

Nationwide feeds its human capital information into an intranet-based information system that gives users an assessment of how they're doing against a number of indicators. It uses a dashboard of red, amber and green indicators to give each business unit an idea of how they are faring on a number of key drivers of employee commitment. This is backed up with advice on how improvement might be made.

Standard Chartered Bank

Standard Chartered Bank uses a human capital scorecard to analyse its data. This is produced on a quarterly and annual basis with various cuts of the same data produced for different business segments and countries, in addition to a global report. This comprises a series of slides with commentary to enable managers to understand the data.

The data is also included in twice-yearly board reviews on people strategy and forms part of the annual strategy planning process. The scorecard data is reviewed within each global business by a top team 'People Forum'. At country level, each local chief executive and his or her management committee reviews key trends in order to specify areas they need to focus on.

In addition, the Bank uses qualitative analysis to examine trends and this has led it to identify the role of the manager as mediating the relationship between engagement and performance. In turn, this has led to a focus on qualitative research to identify what raises the bank's best managers above the rest. A further example is a qualitative analysis of high performance in selected customer-facing roles to determine the key behaviours that continue to drive customer loyalty.

Key learning points: Human capital management

The concept of human capital

Individuals generate, retain and use knowledge and skill (human capital) and create intellectual capital. Human capital 'defines the link between HR practices and business performance in terms of assets rather than business processes' (Scarborough and Elias, 2002).

Characteristics of human capital

Human capital is non-standardized, tacit, dynamic, context dependent and embodied in people (Scarborough and Elias, 2002).

Constituents of human capital

Human capital consists of intellectual capital, social capital and organizational capital.

Significance of human capital

Human capital theory regards people as assets and stresses that investment by organizations in people will generate worthwhile returns.

Importance of human capital measurement

Measuring and valuing human capital is an aid to people management decision making.

Reasons for interest in human capital measurement

- Human capital constitutes a key element of the market worth of a company.
- People in organizations add value.
- Focus attention on what needs to be done to make the best use of its human capital.

- Monitor progress in achieving strategic HR goals and evaluate HR practices.
- You cannot manage unless you measure.

Approaches to measurement

- The human capital index – Watson Wyatt.
- The organizational performance model – Mercer HR Consulting.
- The human capital monitor – Andrew Mayo.

Measurement elements

Workforce data, people development data, perceptual data and performance data.

Factors affecting choice of measurement

- Type of organization; its business goals and drivers.
- The existing key performance indicators (KPIs).
- Use of balanced scorecard.
- The availability, use and manageability of data.

Criteria for HCM data as a guide to managers

Data will only be useful for managers if:

- it is credible, accurate and trustworthy;
- they understand what it means for them;
- it is accompanied by guidance as to what action can be taken;
- they have the skills and abilities to understand and act upon it.

Questions

1 What is human capital management?
2 What is human capital?
3 What is intellectual capital?
4 What is social capital?
5 What is organizational capital?

6 What is human capital measurement?
7 Why is human capital measurement important?
8 What is the main human capital management data used for measurement?

References

Accounting for People Task Force (2003) *Accounting for People*, London, DTI

Baron, A and Armstrong, M (2007) *Human Capital Management: Achieving added value through people*, London, Kogan Page

Bontis, N, Dragonetti, N C, Jacobsen, K and Roos, G (1999) The knowledge toolbox: a review of the tools available to measure and manage intangible resources, *European Management Journal*, **17** (4), pp 391–402

CFO Research Services (2003) *Human Capital Management: The CFO's perspective*, Boston, MA, CFO Publishing

Davenport, T O (1999) *Human Capital*, San Francisco, CA, Jossey-Bass

Edvinson, L and Malone, M S (1997) *Intellectual Capital: Realizing your company's true value by finding its hidden brainpower*, New York, Harper Business

Hartley, V (2005) *Open for Business: HR and human capital reporting*, Brighton, IES

Kearns, P (2005) *Evaluating the ROI from Learning*, London, CIPD

Mayo, A (2001) *The Human Value of the Enterprise: Valuing people as assets*, London, Nicholas Brealey

Nalbantian, R, Guzzo, R A, Kieffer, D and Doherty, J (2004) *Play to Your Strengths: Managing your internal labour markets for lasting competitive advantage*, New York, McGraw-Hill

Putnam, R D (1996) The strange disappearance of civic America, *The American Prospect*, Winter, pp 34–48

Scarborough, H and Elias, J (2002) *Evaluating Human Capital*, London, CIPD

Schultz, T W (1961) Investment in human capital, *American Economic Review*, **51**, March, pp 1–17

Schultz, T W (1981) *Investing in People: The economics of population quality*, Los Angeles, CA, University of California Press

Watson Wyatt Worldwide (2002) *Human Capital Index: Human capital as a lead indicator of shareholder value*, Washington, DC, Watson Wyatt Worldwide

Wright, P M and McMahan, G C (2011) Exploring human capital: putting human back into strategic human resource management, *Human Resource Management Journal*, **21** (2), pp 93–104

Youndt, M A (2000) Human resource considerations and value creation: the mediating role of intellectual capital, Paper delivered at National Conference of US Academy of Management, Toronto, August

07
Knowledge management

LEARNING OUTCOMES

On completing this chapter you should be able to define these key concepts. You should also know about:

- The purpose and significance of knowledge management
- Knowledge management strategies
- Knowledge management systems
- Knowledge management issues
- The contribution HR can make to knowledge management

Introduction

Knowledge management is concerned with storing and sharing the wisdom, understanding and expertise accumulated in an organization about its processes, techniques and operations. It treats knowledge as a key resource. As Ulrich (1998: 126) remarked: 'Knowledge has become a direct competitive advantage for companies selling ideas and relationships.'

There is nothing new about knowledge management. Hansen *et al* (1999: 106) observed that: 'For hundreds of years, owners of family businesses have passed on their commercial wisdom to children, master craftsmen have painstakingly taught their trades to apprentices, and workers have exchanged ideas and know-how on the job.' But they also commented that: 'As the foundation of industrialized economies has shifted from natural resources to intellectual assets, executives have been compelled to examine the knowledge underlying their business and how that knowledge is used' (*ibid*: 106).

Knowledge management is more concerned with people and how they acquire, exchange and disseminate knowledge than it is about information technology. That is why it has become an important area for HR practitioners, who are in a strong position to exert influence in this aspect of people management. It is associated with intellectual capital theory (see Chapter 6), in that it refers to the notions of human, social and organizational or structural capital. It is also linked to organizational learning (see Chapter 23).

Knowledge management defined

Knowledge management is concerned with storing and sharing the wisdom, understanding and expertise accumulated in an organization about its processes, techniques and operations. It involves transforming knowledge resources by identifying relevant information and then disseminating it so that learning can take place. Knowledge management strategies promote the sharing of knowledge by linking people with people and by linking them to information so that they learn from documented experiences.

Knowledge management was defined by Scarborough *et al* (1999: 1) as 'any process or practice of creating, acquiring, capturing, sharing and using knowledge, wherever it resides, to enhance learning and performance in organizations'. They suggested that it focuses on the development of firm-specific knowledge and skills that are the result of organizational learning processes. Knowledge management is concerned with both stocks and flows of knowledge. Stocks include expertise and encoded knowledge in computer systems. Flows represent the ways in which knowledge is transferred from people to people or from people to a knowledge database. Knowledge management has also been defined by Tan (2000: 10)

as: 'The process of systematically and actively managing and leveraging the stores of knowledge in an organization.'

Knowledge is possessed by organizations and people in organizations. Organizational operational, technical and procedural knowledge can be stored in databanks and found in reports, libraries, policy documents, manuals and presentations. It can also be moved around the organization through information systems and by meetings, workshops, courses, 'master classes', written publications and 'communities of practice', defined by Wenger and Snyder (2000: 139) as 'groups of people informally bound together by shared expertise and a passion for joint enterprise'. The intranet provides an additional and very effective medium.

People in organizations have knowledge acquired through their own experiences at work that will not necessarily be shared formally or even informally with their colleagues. This knowledge may be crucial to the interests of the business and could be lost if it remains locked up in the minds of employees, or taken elsewhere by them if they leave the organization. If this knowledge is important, one of the key issues in knowledge management is how it can be identified and disseminated.

The concept of knowledge

Knowledge is defined as what people understand about things, concepts, ideas, theories, procedures, practices and 'the way we do things around here'. It can be described as know-how or, when it is specific, expertise. A distinction was made by Ryle (1949) between 'knowing how' and 'knowing that'. 'Knowing how' is the ability of a person to perform tasks, and 'knowing that' is holding pieces of knowledge in one's mind. According to Blackler (1995: 1023): 'Rather than regarding *knowledge* as something that people have, it is suggested that *knowing* is better regarded as something that they do.' He also noted that: 'Knowledge is multifaceted and complex, being both situated and abstract, implicit and explicit, distributed and individual, physical and mental, developing and static, verbal and encoded' (*ibid*: 1032–3).

Nonaka (1991) suggested that knowledge is held either by individuals or collectively. In Blackler's (1995) terms, embodied or embraced knowledge is individual and embedded, and cultural knowledge is collective. It can be argued (Scarborough and Carter, 2000) that knowledge emerges from the collective experience of work and is shared between members of a particular group or community.

Explicit and tacit knowledge

Nonaka (1991) and Nonaka and Takeuchi (1995) stated that knowledge is either explicit or tacit. Explicit knowledge can be codified – it is recorded and available and is held in databases, in corporate intranets and intellectual property portfolios. Tacit knowledge exists in people's minds. It is difficult to articulate in writing and is acquired through personal experience. As suggested by Hansen *et al* (1999), it includes scientific or technological expertise, operational know-how, insights about an industry and business judgement. The main challenge in knowledge management is how to turn tacit knowledge into explicit knowledge.

Data, information and knowledge

A distinction can be made between data, information and knowledge:

- *Data* consists of the basic facts – the building blocks – for information and knowledge.
- *Information* is data that have been processed in a way that is meaningful to individuals; it is available to anyone entitled to gain access to it. As Drucker (1988: 46) put it, 'information is data endowed with meaning and purpose'.
- *Knowledge* is information used productively; it is personal and often intangible and it can be elusive – the task of tying it down, encoding it and distributing it is tricky.

The purpose and significance of knowledge management

Knowledge management is about getting knowledge from those who have it to those who need it in order to improve organizational effectiveness. As explained by Blake (1988), the purpose of knowledge management is to capture a company's collective expertise and distribute it to wherever it can achieve the biggest payoff. This is in accordance with the resource-based view of the firm, which suggests that the source of competitive advantage lies within the firm (ie in its people and their knowledge), not in how it positions itself in the market. A successful company is a knowledge-creating company.

In the information age, knowledge rather than physical assets or financial resources is the key to competitiveness. In essence, as pointed out by Mecklenburg *et al* (1999), knowledge management allows companies to make the best use of their employees' creativity and expertise. But, as Boxall and Purcell (2000: 197) noted: 'Managing knowledge inevitably means managing both the company's proprietary technologies and systems (which don't walk out of the door at the end of the day) and the people (who do)'.

Knowledge management strategies

Two approaches to knowledge management strategy have been identified by Hansen *et al* (1999): the codification strategy and the personalization strategy.

The codification strategy

Knowledge is carefully codified and stored in databases where it can be accessed and used easily by anyone in the organization. Knowledge is explicit and is codified using a 'people-to-document' approach. This strategy is therefore document-driven. Knowledge is extracted from the person who developed it, made independent of that person and re-used for various purposes. It will be stored in some form of electronic repository for people to use, and allows many people to search for and retrieve codified knowledge without having to contact the person who originally developed it. This strategy relies largely on information technology to manage databases and also on the use of the intranet.

The personalization strategy

Knowledge is closely tied to the person who has developed it and is shared mainly through direct person-to-person contacts. This is a 'person-to-person' approach that involves ensuring that tacit knowledge is passed on. The exchange is achieved by creating networks and encouraging face-to-face communication between individuals and teams by means of informal conferences, workshops, communities of practice, brainstorming and one-to-one sessions.

Hansen *et al* (1999) proposed that the choice of strategy should be contingent on the organization: what it does and how it does it. Thus consultancies such as Ernst & Young, using knowledge to deal with recurring problems, may rely mainly on codification so that recorded solutions to similar problems are easily retrievable. Strategy consultancy firms such as McKinsey or Bains, however, will rely mainly on a personalization strategy to help them to tackle the high-level strategic problems they are presented with that demand the provision of creative, analytically rigorous advice. They need to channel individual expertise and they find and develop people who are able to use a person-to-person knowledge-sharing approach effectively. In this sort of firm, directors or experts can be established who can be approached by consultants by e-mail, telephone, or personal contact.

The research conducted by Hansen *et al* (1999) established that companies that use knowledge effectively pursue either the codification or the personalization strategy predominantly and use the other strategy to support their first choice. They pointed out that those who try to excel at both strategies risk failing at both.

Knowledge management issues

The various approaches referred to above do not provide easy answers. The issues that need to be addressed in developing knowledge management processes are discussed below.

The pace of change

One of the main issues in knowledge management is how to keep up with the pace of change and identify what knowledge needs to be captured and shared.

Relating knowledge management strategy to business strategy

As Hansen *et al* (1999) showed, it is not knowledge per se but the way it is applied to strategic objectives that is the critical ingredient in competitiveness. They suggested that 'competitive strategy must drive knowledge management strategy' and that management have to answer the question: 'How does knowledge that resides in the company add value for customers?' (*ibid*: 114).

Technology and people

Technology may be central to companies adopting a codification strategy, but for those following a personalization strategy IT is best used in a supportive role. Hansen *et al* (1999: 113) commented that:

> In the codification model, managers need to implement a system that is much like a traditional library – it must contain a large cache of documents and include search engines that allow people to find and use the documents they need. In the personalization model, it's more important to have a system that allows people to find other people.

Scarborough *et al* (1999) suggested that technology should be viewed more as a means of communication and less as a means of storing knowledge. Knowledge management is more about people than technology. Research by Davenport (1996) established that managers get two-thirds of their information from face-to-face or telephone conversations.

There is a limit to how much tacit knowledge can be codified. In organizations relying more on tacit than explicit knowledge, a person-to-person approach works best, and IT can only support this process; it cannot replace it.

The significance of process

Blackler (1995) emphasized that a preoccupation with technology may mean that too little attention is paid to the processes (social, technological and organizational) through which knowledge combines and interacts in different ways. The key processes are the interactions between people. This is the social capital of an organization – 'the network of relationships [that] constitute a valuable resource for the conduct of social affairs' (Nahpiet and Ghoshal, 1998: 243). Social networks can be particularly important in ensuring that knowledge is shared. Trust is also required – people are not willing to share knowledge with those they do not trust.

The culture of the company may inhibit knowledge sharing. The norm may be for people to keep knowledge to themselves as much as they can because 'knowledge is power'. An open culture will encourage people to share their ideas and knowledge.

Knowledge workers

Knowledge workers, as defined by Drucker (1993), are individuals who have high levels of education and specialist skills combined with the ability to apply these skills to identify and solve problems. As Argyris (1991: 100) commented, they are, 'The nuts and bolts of management … increasingly consist of guiding and integrating the autonomous but interconnected work of highly skilled people.' Knowledge management is about the management and motivation of knowledge workers who create knowledge and will be the key players in sharing it.

The contribution of HR to knowledge management

HR can make an important contribution to knowledge management simply because knowledge is shared between people; it is not just a matter of capturing explicit knowledge through the use of IT. The role of HR is to ensure that the organization has the intellectual capital it needs. The resource-based view of the firm emphasizes, in the words of Cappelli and Crocker-Hefter (1996: 7), that 'distinctive human resource practices help to create unique competences that differentiate products and services and, in turn, drive competitiveness'.

HR can contribute by providing advice on culture management, organization design and development and by establishing learning and communication programmes and systems. There are 10 ways of doing this:

1 Help to develop an open culture in which the values and norms emphasize the importance of sharing knowledge.

2 Promote a climate of commitment and trust.

3 Advise on the design and development of organizations that facilitate knowledge sharing through networks, teamwork and communities of practice.

4 Advise on resourcing policies and provide resourcing services that ensure that valued employees who can contribute to knowledge creation and sharing are attracted and retained.

5 Advise on methods of motivating people to share knowledge and rewarding those who do so.

6 Help in the development of performance management processes that focus on the development and sharing of knowledge.

7 Develop processes of organizational and individual learning that will generate and assist in disseminating knowledge.

8 Set up and organize workshops, conferences, seminars, communities of practice and symposia that enable knowledge to be shared on a person-to-person basis.

9 In conjunction with IT, develop systems for capturing and, as far as possible, codifying explicit and tacit knowledge.

10 Generally, promote the cause of knowledge management with senior managers to encourage them to exert leadership and support knowledge management initiatives.

The purpose and significance of knowledge management

Knowledge management is about getting knowledge from those who have it to those who need it in order to improve organizational effectiveness.

Knowledge management strategies

The codification strategy – knowledge is carefully codified and stored in databases where it can be accessed and used easily by anyone in the organization. Knowledge is explicit and is codified using a 'people-to-document' approach.

The personalization strategy – knowledge is closely tied to the person who has developed it and is shared mainly through direct person-to-person contacts. This is a 'person-to-person' approach that involves ensuring that tacit knowledge is passed on.

Knowledge management systems

- **Creating an intranet.**

- **Creating 'data warehouses'.**

- **Using decision support systems.**

- **Using 'groupware', ie information communication technologies such as e-mail or discussion bases.**

- **Creating networks or communities of practice or interest of knowledge workers.**

Knowledge management issues

- **The pace of change.**

- **Relating knowledge management strategy to business strategy.**

- **IT is best used in a supportive role.**

- Attention must be paid to the processes (social, technological and organizational) through which knowledge combines and interacts in different ways.

- The significance of knowledge workers must be appreciated.

The contribution HR can make to knowledge management

- Help to develop an open culture that emphasizes the importance of sharing knowledge.

- Promote a climate of commitment and trust.

- Advise on the design and development of organizations that facilitate knowledge sharing.

- Ensure that valued employees who can contribute to knowledge creation and sharing are attracted and retained.

- Advise on methods of motivating people to share.

- Help in the development of performance management processes that focus on the development and sharing of knowledge.

- Develop processes of organizational and individual learning that will generate and assist in disseminating knowledge.

- Set up and organize workshops, conferences and communities of practice and symposia that enable knowledge to be shared on a person-to-person basis.

- In conjunction with IT, develop systems for capturing and, as far as possible, codifying explicit and tacit knowledge.

- Generally, promote the cause of knowledge management with senior managers.

Questions

1 What is knowledge management?
2 What is knowledge?
3 What is the difference between explicit and tacit knowledge?
4 What is the distinction between data, information and knowledge?
5 What is the purpose of knowledge management?
6 How can HR help to promote knowledge management?

References

Argyris, C (1991) Teaching smart people how to learn, *Harvard Business Review*, May–June, pp 54–62

Blackler, F (1995) Knowledge, knowledge work and experience, *Organization Studies*, **16** (6), pp 16–36

Blake, P (1988) The knowledge management explosion, *Information Today*, **15** (1), pp 12–13

Boxall, P and Purcell, J (2000) Strategic human resource management: where have we come from and where are we going?, *International Journal of Management Reviews*, **2** (2), pp 183–203

Cappelli, P and Crocker-Hefter, A (1996) Distinctive human resources are firms' core competencies, *Organizational Dynamics*, **24** (3), pp 7–22

Davenport, T H (1996) Why re-engineering failed: the fad that forgot people, *Fast Company*, Premier Issue, pp 70–74

Drucker, P (1988) The coming of the new organization, *Harvard Business Review*, January–February, pp 45–53

Drucker, P (1993) *Post-capitalist Society*, Oxford, Butterworth-Heinemann

Hansen, M T, Nohria, N and Tierney, T (1999) What's your strategy for managing knowledge?, *Harvard Business Review*, March–April, pp 106–16

Mecklenberg, S, Deering, A and Sharp, D (1999) Knowledge management: a secret engine of corporate growth, *Executive Agenda*, **2**, pp 5–15

Nahpiet, J and Ghoshal, S (1998) Social capital, intellectual capital and the organizational advantage, *Academy of Management Review*, **23** (2), pp 242–66

Nonaka, I (1991) The knowledge creating company, *Harvard Business Review*, November–December, pp 96–104

Nonaka, I and Takeuchi, H (1995) *The Knowledge Creating Company*, New York, Oxford University Press

Ryle, G (1949) *The Concept of Mind*, Oxford, Oxford University Press

Scarborough, H and Carter, C (2000) *Investigating Knowledge Management*, London, CIPD

Scarborough, H, Swan, J and Preston, J (1999) *Knowledge Management: A literature review*, London, IPD

Tan, J (2000) Knowledge management – just more buzzwords?, *British Journal of Administrative Management*, March/April, pp 10–11

Ulrich, D (1998) A new mandate for human resources, *Harvard Business Review*, January–February, pp 124–34

Wenger, E and Snyder, W M (2000) Communities of practice: the organizational frontier, *Harvard Business Review*, January–February, pp 33–41

TABLE 8.1   Incidence of different competency headings

Competency heading	Summary definition	% used
Team orientation	The ability to work cooperatively and flexibly with other members of the team with a full understanding of the role to be played as a team member.	86
Communication	The ability to communicate clearly and persuasively, orally or in writing.	73
People management	The ability to manage and develop people and gain their trust and cooperation to achieve results.	67
Customer focus	The exercise of unceasing care in looking after the interests of external and internal customers to ensure that their wants, needs and expectations are met or exceeded.	65
Results orientation	The desire to get things done well and the ability to set and meet challenging goals, create own measures of excellence and constantly seek ways of improving performance.	59
Problem solving	The capacity to analyse situations, diagnose problems, identify the key issues, establish and evaluate alternative courses of action and produce a logical, practical and acceptable solution.	57
Planning and organizing	The ability to decide on courses of action, ensuring that the resources required to implement the action will be available and scheduling the programme of work required to achieve a defined end-result.	51
Technical skills	Possession of the knowledge, understanding and expertise required to carry out the work effectively.	49
Leadership	The capacity to inspire individuals to give of their best to achieve a desired result and to maintain effective relationships with individuals and the team as a whole.	43
Business awareness	The capacity continually to identify and explore business opportunities, understand the business needs and priorities of the organization and constantly to seek methods of ensuring that the organization becomes more business-like.	37
Decision making	The capacity to make sound and practical decisions that deal effectively with the issues and are based on thorough analysis and diagnosis.	37

TABLE 8.1 *Continued*

Competency heading	Summary definition	% used
Change orientation	The ability to manage and accept change.	33
Developing others	The desire and capacity to foster the development of members of his or her team, providing feedback, support, encouragement and coaching.	33
Influence and persuasion	The ability to convince others to agree on or to take a course of action.	33
Initiative	The capacity to take action independently and to assume responsibility for one's actions.	29
Interpersonal skills	The ability to create and maintain open and constructive relationships with others, to respond helpfully to their requests and to be sensitive to their needs.	29
Strategic orientation	The capacity to take a long-term and visionary view of the direction to be followed in the future.	29
Creativity	The ability to originate new practices, concepts and ideas.	26
Information management	The capacity to originate and use information effectively.	26
Quality focus	The focus on delivering quality and continuous improvement.	24
Self-confidence and assertiveness	Belief in oneself and standing up for one's own rights.	24
Self-development	Managing one's own learning and development.	22
Managing	Managing resources, people, programmes and projects.	20

The first seven of these were used in over 50 per cent of the respondent organizations.

Examples

The following are two examples of competency frameworks. The first is a fairly simple set of competency headings used in a charity, mainly for recruitment purposes; the second (Table 8.2) is an example of part of a competency framework in a housing association illustrating the use of positive and negative examples for one competency heading. The purpose of these is to extend the broad definition of a competency by providing examples of positive and negative behaviours. The simple definitions in the first examples may not prove sufficient guidance in using the competency framework, especially for performance management.

TABLE 8.2   Example of a competency framework used in a housing association

Competency heading	Manage continuous improvement
Competency definition	Constantly seeking ways of improving the quality of services, the relevance and appeal of those services to the needs of customers and clients, and their effectiveness.
Competency requirement	• Set targets for improvement. • Develop and implement programmes for managing change. • Contribute to the development of quality assurance and control processes and ensure that they are implemented.
Positive indicators	• Encourages the development of new ideas and methods especially those concerned with the provision of quality. • Conscious of the factors that enable change to take place smoothly. • Discusses ideas with colleagues and customers and formulates views on how to improve services and processes.
Negative indicators	• Doesn't try anything that hasn't been done before. • Complacent, believes that there is no room for improvement. • Follows previous practices without considering whether there is any need to change.

Example of a competency framework used in a charity

- *Achievement/results orientation.* The desire to get things done well and the ability to set and meet challenging goals, create own measures of excellence and constantly seek ways of improving performance.
- *Business awareness.* The capacity continually to identify and explore business opportunities, understand the business opportunities and priorities of the organization and constantly to seek methods of ensuring that the organization becomes more business-like.
- *Communication.* The ability to communicate clearly and persuasively, orally or in writing.
- *Customer focus.* The exercise of unceasing care in looking after the interests of external and internal customers to ensure that their wants, needs and expectations are met or exceeded.
- *Developing others.* The desire and capacity to foster the development of members of his or her team, providing feedback, support, encouragement and coaching.
- *Flexibility.* The ability to adapt to and work effectively in different situations and to carry out a variety of tasks.
- *Leadership.* The capacity to inspire individuals to give of their best to achieve a desired result and to maintain effective relationships with individuals and the team as a whole.
- *Planning.* The ability to decide on courses of action, ensuring that the resources required to implement the action will be available and scheduling the programme of work required to achieve a defined end-result.
- *Problem solving.* The capacity to analyse situations, diagnose problems, identify the key issues, establish and evaluate alternative courses of action and produce a logical, practical and acceptable solution.

- *Teamwork.* The ability to work cooperatively and flexibly with other members of the team with a full understanding of the role to be played as a team member.

Using competencies

A number of approaches to using competencies are adopted, as described below.

The 'menu' approach

A 'menu' approach selects competencies that are relevant to generic or individual roles. Some organizations provide guidelines on the number of competencies to be selected (eg four to eight) and others combine their core framework with a menu so that users are required to select the organization-wide core competencies but can add a number of optional ones.

Role-specific competencies

Role-specific competencies are also used by some organizations for generic or individual roles. These may be incorporated in a role profile in addition to a statement of key result areas. This approach is adopted in performance management processes, in recruitment person specifications and in the preparation of individual learning programmes.

Graded competencies

A further, although less common, application of competencies is in graded career or job family structures (career or job families consist of jobs in a function or occupation such as marketing, operations, finance, IT, HR, administration or support services that are related through the activities carried out and the basic knowledge and skills required, but in which the levels of responsibility, knowledge, skill or competence needed differ). In such families, the successive levels in each family are defined in terms of competencies as well as the key activities carried out.

Applications of competency-based HRM

The Competency and Emotional Intelligence 2006/7 survey found that 95 per cent of respondents used behavioural competencies and 66 per cent used technical competencies. It was noted that because the latter deal with specific activities and tasks they inevitably result in different sets of competencies for groups of related roles, functions or activities. The three top areas where competencies were applied are:

1 Learning and development: 82 per cent.
2 Performance management: 76 per cent.
3 Recruitment and selection: 85 per cent.

Only 30 per cent of organizations linked competencies to reward. The ways in which these competencies are used are described below.

Learning and development

Role profiles, which are either generic (covering a range of similar jobs) or individual (role-specific), can include statements of the competencies required. These are used to assess the levels of competency achieved by individuals and so identify their learning and development needs. Learning events can be based on competency analysis related to an organization's competency framework.

Competencies are also used in development centres, which help participants build up their understanding of the competencies they require now and in the future so that they can plan their own self-directed learning programmes.

Recruitment and selection

The language of competencies is used in many organizations as a basis for the person specification that is set out under competency headings developed through role analysis. The competencies defined for a role are used as the framework for recruitment and selection and competency-based interviews are structured around the competencies listed in the specification.

Performance management

Competencies in performance management are used to ensure that performance reviews do not simply focus on outcomes but also consider the behavioural aspects of how the work is carried out that determine those outcomes. Performance reviews conducted on this basis are used to inform personal improvement and development plans and learning programmes.

Reward management

Competency-related pay relates additional awards to assessments of competency but it has never become popular. However, more frequent use is made of contribution-related pay, which provides for people to be rewarded according to both the results they achieve and their level of competence.

Developing a competency framework

A competency framework should be as simple to understand and use as possible. The language should be clear and jargon-free. Without clear language and examples it can be difficult to assess the level of competency achieved. When defining competencies, especially if they are used for performance management or competency-related pay, it is essential to ensure that they can be assessed. They must not be vague or overlap with other competencies and they must specify clearly the sort of behaviour that is expected and the level of technical or functional skills (competencies) required to meet acceptable standards. It is helpful to address the user directly ('you will ...') and give clear and brief examples of how the competency needs to be performed.

Developing a behavioural competency framework that fits the culture and purpose of the organization and provides a sound basis for a number of key HR processes is not to be undertaken lightly. It requires a lot of hard work, much of it concerned with involving staff and communicating with them to achieve understanding and buy-in. The steps required are described below.

Step 1. Programme launch

Decide on the purpose of the framework and the HR processes for which it will be used. Make out a business case for its development, setting out the benefits to the organization in such areas as improved performance, better selection outcomes, more focused performance management, employee development and reward processes. Prepare a project plan that includes an assessment of the resources required and the costs.

Step 2. Involvement and communication

Involve line managers and employees in the design of the framework (Steps 3 and 4) by setting up a task force. Communicate the objectives of the exercise to staff.

Step 3. Framework design – competency list

First, get the task force to draw up a list of the core competencies and values of the business – what it should be good at doing and the values it believes should influence behaviour. This provides a foundation for an analysis of the competencies required by people in the organization. The aim is to identify and define the behaviours that contribute to the achievement of organizational success, and there should be a powerful link between these people competencies and the organization's core competencies (more guidance on defining competencies is provided in Chapter 48).

The list can be drawn up by brainstorming. The list should be compared with examples of other competency frameworks, to avoid replicating other lists. It is essential to produce a competency framework that fits and reflects the organization's own culture, values, core competencies and operations, but referring to other lists will help to clarify the conclusions reached in the initial analysis and serve to check that all relevant areas of competency have been included. When identifying competencies, care must be taken to avoid bias because of sex or race.

Step 4. Framework design – definition of competencies

Care needs to be exercised to ensure that definitions are clear and unambiguous and that they will serve their intended purpose. If, for example, one of the purposes is to provide criteria for conducting performance reviews, then it is necessary to be certain that the way the competency is defined, together with supporting examples, will enable fair assessments to be made. The following four questions have been produced by Mirabile (1998) to test the extent to which a competency is valid and can be used:

1   Can you describe the competency in terms that others understand and agree with?

2   Can you observe it being demonstrated or failing to be demonstrated?

3   Can you measure it?

4   Can you influence it in some way, eg by training, coaching or some other method of development?

It is also important at this stage to ensure that definitions are not biased.

Step 5. Define uses of the competency framework

Define exactly how it is intended the competency framework should be used, covering such applications as performance management, recruitment, learning and development and reward.

Step 6. Test the framework

Test the framework by gauging the reactions of a balanced selection of line managers and other employees to ensure that they understand it and believe that it is relevant to their roles. Also pilot-test the framework in live situations for each of its proposed applications.

Step 7. Finalize the framework

Amend the framework as necessary following the tests and prepare notes for guidance on how it should be used.

Step 8. Communicate

Let everyone know the outcome of the project – what the framework is, how it will be used and how people will benefit. Group briefings and any other suitable means should be used.

Step 9. Train

Give line managers and HR staff training in how to use the framework.

Step 10. Monitor and evaluate

Monitor and evaluate the use of the framework and amend it as required.

Keys to success in using competencies

- The competencies should reflect the organization's values and its needs, as established by analysis, to determine the behaviours that will lead to high performance.
- Frameworks should not be over-complex.
- There should not be too many headings in a framework – seven or eight will often suffice.
- The language used should be clear and jargon-free.
- Competencies must be selected and defined in ways that ensure that they can be assessed by managers – the use of 'behavioural indicators' is helpful.
- Frameworks should be regularly updated.

Competencies and emotional intelligence

Emotional intelligence is a combination of skills and abilities such as self-awareness, self-control, empathy and sensitivity to the feelings of others. It covers many of the interpersonal skills included in competency frameworks.

Dulewicz and Higgs (1999) produced a detailed analysis of how the emotional intelligence elements of self-awareness, emotional management, empathy, relationships, communication and personal style correspond to competencies such as sensitivity, flexibility, adaptability, resilience, impact, listening, leadership, persuasiveness, motivating others, energy, decisiveness and achievement motivation. They conclude that there are distinct associations between competency modes and elements of emotional intelligence.

Key learning points: Competency-based HRM

Competency-based HRM is about using the notion of competency and the results of competency analysis to inform and improve HR processes, especially those concerned with recruitment and selection, learning and development, and performance and reward management.

Competency defined

The term 'competency' refers to an underlying characteristic of a person that results in effective or superior performance.

The different types of competencies

1   Behavioural competencies define behavioural expectations, ie the type of behaviour required to deliver results under such headings as teamworking, communication, leadership and decision making.

2   Technical competencies define what people have to know and be able to do (knowledge and skills) to carry out their roles effectively.

3   NVQ/SNVQ competences specify minimum standards for the achievement of set tasks and activities expressed in ways that can be observed and assessed with a view to certification.

The contents of competency frameworks (the 10 most popular headings)

1	Team orientation	2	Communication
3	People management	4	Customer focus
5	Results orientation	6	Problem solving
7	Planning and organizing	8	Technical skills
9	Leadership	10	Business awareness

Uses of competencies (2006/7)

Learning and development:	82 per cent.
Performance management:	76 per cent.
Selection:	85 per cent.
Recruitment:	55 per cent.
Reward:	30 per cent.

How to develop a competency framework

- Decide on the purpose of the framework and the HR processes for which it will be used.
- Make out a business case for its development, setting out the benefits.
- Prepare a project plan that includes an assessment of the resources required and the costs.
- Involve line managers and employees in the design of the framework.
- Communicate the objectives of the exercise to staff.
- Draw up a list of the core competencies of the business.
- Define the competencies for inclusion in a competency framework.
- Test and finalize and communicate framework.

Keys to success in using competencies

- The competencies should reflect the organization's values and its needs, as established by analysis, to determine the behaviours that will lead to high performance.
- Frameworks should not be over-complex.
- There should not be too many headings in a framework – seven or eight will often suffice.
- The language used should be clear and jargon-free.
- Competencies must be selected and defined in ways that ensure they can be assessed by managers – the use of 'behavioural indicators' is helpful.
- Frameworks should be regularly updated.

Competencies and emotional intelligence

The emotional intelligence elements of self-awareness, emotional management, empathy, relationships, communication and personal style correspond to competencies such as sensitivity, flexibility, adaptability, resilience, impact, listening, leadership, persuasiveness, motivating others, energy, decisiveness and achievement motivation.

Questions

1   What is competency-based HRM?

2   What is a competency?

3   What are behavioural competencies?

4   What are technical competencies?

5   What is the difference between the concepts of competency and competence?

6   What is a competency framework?

7   What are the main ways in which competencies can be used?

References

Boyatzis, R (1982) *The Competent Manager*, New York, Wiley

Competency and Emotional Intelligence (2006/7) *Raising Performance Through Competencies: The annual benchmarking survey*, London, Competency and Emotional Intelligence

Dulewicz, V and Higgs, M (1999) The seven dimensions of emotional intelligence, *People Management*, **28**, October, p 53

Mirabile, R J (1998) Leadership competency development, competitive advantage for the future, *Management Development Forum*, **1** (2), pp 1–15

09
The ethical dimension of HRM

LEARNING OUTCOMES

On completing this chapter you should be able to define these key concepts. You should also understand:

- The meaning of ethics
- The nature of ethical decisions and judgements
- The ethical concepts of deontology, utilitarianism, stakeholder theory and discourse theory
- The significance of the concepts of equity, justice and fair dealing
- The ethical dimension of HRM
- HRM ethical guidelines
- How to resolve ethical dilemmas

Introduction

The theme of this chapter is that there is an ethical dimension to human resource management. As Boxall *et al* (2007: 5) pointed out: 'While HRM does need to support commercial outcomes (often called "the business case"), it also exists to serve organizational needs for social legitimacy.' This means exercising social responsibility, ie being concerned for the interests (wellbeing) of employees and acting ethically with regard to the needs of people in the organization and the community.

To grasp this ethical dimension it is necessary to understand the nature and principles of ethics, the ethical role of HR and the ethical guidelines they can use. It is also necessary to know about approaches to resolving ethical dilemmas.

The meaning and nature of ethics

Ethics is defined by the *Compact Oxford Dictionary* as being 'related to morals, treating of moral questions', and ethical is defined as 'relating to morality'. Morality is defined as 'having moral qualities or endowments' and moral is defined as 'of or pertaining to the distinction between right and wrong'. Petrick and Quinn (1997: 42) wrote that ethics 'is the study of individual and collective moral awareness, judgement, character and conduct'. Hamlin *et al* (2001: 98) noted that ethics is concerned with rules or principles that help us to distinguish right and wrong.

Ethics and morality are sometimes treated as being synonymous, although Beauchamp and Bowie (1983: 1–2) suggested that they are different: 'Whereas morality is a social institution with a history and code of learnable rules, ethical theory refers to the philosophical study of the nature of ethical principles, decisions and problems.' Clearly, ethics is concerned with matters of right and wrong and therefore involves moral judgements. Even if they are not the same, the two are closely linked. As Clegg *et al* (2007: 111) put it: 'We understand ethics as the social organizing of morality.' Simplistically, ethics could be described as being about behaviour while morality is about beliefs.

Ethics is concerned with making decisions and judgements about what is the right course of action to take. It can be described in terms of a framework that sets out different approaches and can be extended to embrace particular concepts that affect and guide ethical behaviour, namely equity, justice and fair dealing. These approaches and concepts are discussed below.

The nature of ethical decisions and judgements

As defined by Jones (1991: 367), an ethical decision is one that is morally acceptable to the larger community. He also noted that: 'A moral issue is present where a person's actions, when freely performed, may harm or benefit others. In other words, the action or decision must have consequences for others and must involve choice, or *volition*, on the part of the actor or decision maker' (*ibid*: 367).

Winstanley and Woodall (2000a: 8–9) observed that:

> Ethics is not about taking statements of morality at face value; it is a critical and challenging tool. There are no universally agreed ethical frameworks ... Different situations require ethical insight and flexibility to enable us to encapsulate the grounds upon which competing claims can be made. Decisions are judgements usually involving choices between alternatives, but rarely is the choice between right and wrong ... Moral disagreement and judgements are concerned with attitudes and feelings, not facts.

Clegg *et al* (2007: 112) emphasized that: 'Ethical decisions emerge out of dilemmas that cannot be managed in advance through rules.' People have to make choices. Foucault (1997: 284) asked: 'What is ethics, if not the practice of freedom?'

Ethical frameworks

The ethical concepts of deontology, utilitarianism, stakeholder theory and discourse theory, as described below, provide frameworks that can be used to evaluate HRM policies and practices.

Deontological theory

Deontological (from the Greek for 'what is right') theory maintains that some actions are right or wrong irrespective of their consequences. It is associated with Kant's notion of the categorical imperative, which contains two main propositions: 1) that one should follow the principle that what is right for one person is right for everyone, and thus you must do to others as you would be done by; and 2) that you should respect all people and treat them as ends in themselves, not as the means to an end.

Utilitarianism

Utilitarianism is the belief that actions are justified when they result in the greatest good to the greatest number. Actions should be judged in terms of their consequences. This is sometimes interpreted as supporting the dubious principle that the end justifies the means. However, the Weberian phenomenon of means subverting ends should be remembered.

Stakeholder theory

In accordance with the ideas of Freeman (1984), stakeholder theory states that the organization should be managed on behalf of its stakeholders: its owners, employees, customers, suppliers and local communities. As Legge (1998: 22) described it, management must act in the interests of the stakeholders as their agent, and also act in the interests of the organization to ensure the survival of the firm, safeguarding the long-term stakes of each group.

Discourse ethics

Foucault (1972) defined discourse as the taken-for-granted ways that people are collectively able to make sense of experience. Discourse ethics, as explained by Winstanley and Woodall (2000a: 14), suggests that 'the role of ethicists is not to provide solutions to ethical problems, but rather to provide a practical process and procedure which is both rational and consensus enhancing, through which issues can be debated and discourse can take place'.

Equity theory

Equity theory, as formulated by Adams (1965), is concerned with the perceptions people have about how they are being treated as compared with others. To be dealt with equitably is to be treated fairly in comparison with another group of people (a reference group) or a relevant other person. Equity involves feelings and perceptions and it is always a comparative process. It is not synonymous with equality, which means treating everyone the same and would be inequitable if they deserve to be treated differently.

Justice

Justice is the process of treating people in a way which is inherently fair, right and proper. An egalitarian theory of justice was proposed by Rawls (2005) which contained two principles: 1) every person has the right to basic liberty compatible with similar liberty for others; and 2) inequalities should be arranged so that they are expected to be to everyone's advantage and attached to positions open to all.

There are four types of justice: social justice, natural justice, procedural justice and distributive justice.

Social justice

Social justice is based on the concepts of human rights and equality. Rawls (2005: 3) rejected the principle of utilitarianism when he asserted that in society: 'Each person possesses an inviolability founded on justice that even the welfare of society as a whole cannot override. For this reason justice denies that the loss of freedom for some is made right by a greater good shared by others.' In organizations, social justice means relating to employees generally in ways that recognize their natural rights to be treated justly, equitably and with respect.

Natural justice

According to the principles of natural justice employees should know the standards they are expected to achieve and the rules to which they are expected to conform. They should be given a clear indication of where they are failing or what rules have been broken and, except in cases of gross misconduct, they should be given a chance to improve before disciplinary action is taken.

Procedural justice

Procedural justice (Adams, 1965; Leventhal, 1980) involves treating people in ways that are fair, consistent, transparent and properly consider their views and needs. It is concerned with fair process and the perceptions employees have about the fairness with which company procedures in such areas as performance appraisal, promotion and discipline are being operated. The five factors that affect perceptions of procedural justice, as identified by Tyler and Bies (1990), are:

1 Adequate consideration of an employee's viewpoint.

2 Suppression of personal bias towards an employee.

3 Applying criteria consistently across employees.

4 Providing early feedback to employees about the outcome of decisions.

5 Providing employees with an adequate explanation of decisions made.

Distributive justice

Distributive justice (Adams, 1965; Leventhal, 1980) means ensuring that people are rewarded equitably in comparison with others in the organization and in accordance with their contribution, and that they receive what was promised to them (management 'delivers the deal').

Ethical HRM

Legge (1998: 20–21) commented that: 'In very general terms I would suggest that the experience of HRM is more likely (but not necessarily) to be viewed positively if its underlying principles are ethical.' HR professionals have a special responsibility for guarding and promoting core values in the organization on how people should be managed and treated. They need to take action to achieve fair dealing. This means treating people according to the principles of social, natural, procedural and distributive justice, and seeing that decisions or policies that affect them are transparent in the sense that they are known, understood, clear and applied consistently.

HR professionals need to take a deontological stance that stresses that some actions are right or wrong irrespective of their consequences and that all people should be respected and treated as ends in themselves, not as the means to an end. This is not easy. Ethical decisions may not be clear cut. Interests conflict. But an ethical approach is a necessary part of a professional approach to HRM.

An important role for HR professionals is to do whatever they can to embed the consistent application of ethical values in the organization so that they can become values in use rather than simply professed values in a code of practice or values statement. As Winstanley and Woodall (2000b: 7) remarked: 'HR professionals have to raise awareness of ethical issues, promote ethical behaviour, disseminate ethical practices widely among line managers, communicate codes of ethical conduct, ensure people learn about what constitutes ethical behaviours, manage compliance and monitor arrangements.'

To do all this HR professionals may sometimes have to nag away without appearing to nag. They need the courage to stand up and be counted as necessary. This calls for determination, persuasive skills and the ability to deal with the ethical dilemmas that they and line managers face in as rational a manner as possible. In the field of organizational ethics, HR people can lead by example. They can handle ethical issues in ways that become part of the organization's culture – 'the way we do things around here'.

The difficulties that HR professionals face in doing all this have been well described by Guest and King (2004: 421) as follows:

> Much management activity is typically messy and ambiguous. This appears to apply more strongly to people management than to most other activities. By implication, the challenge lies not in removing or resolving the ambiguities in the role [of HR professionals] but in learning to live with them. To succeed in this requires skills in influencing, negotiating and learning when to compromise.

For those with a high tolerance of ambiguity, the role of HR specialist, with its distinctive opportunity to contribute to the management of people in organizations, offers unique challenges; for those only comfortable if they can resolve the ambiguities, the role may become a form of purgatory.

HRM ethical guidelines

The guidelines set out below relate to how employees are treated in general and to the major HRM activities of organization development, recruitment and selection, learning and development, performance management, reward management and employee relations. They also relate to employment practices concerning the work environment, employee wellbeing, equal opportunities, managing diversity, handling disciplinary matters and grievances, job security and redundancy.

General guidelines

- Recognize that the strategic goals of the organization should embrace the rights and needs of employees as well as those of the business.
- Recognize that employees are entitled to be treated as full human beings with personal needs, hopes and anxieties.
- Do not treat employees simply as means to an end or mere factors of production.
- Relate to employees generally in ways that recognize their natural rights to be treated justly, equitably and with respect.

Organization development (OD)

- Agree in advance with clients and individuals the goals, content and risks of an OD programme.
- Make explicit any values or assumptions used in the programme.
- Obtain the maximum involvement of all concerned in the programme so that they understand the processes involved and how they can benefit from them.

- Work with clients to plan and implement change to the benefit of all stakeholders.
- Enable individuals to continue with their development on completing the programme.
- Protect confidentiality.

Recruitment and selection

- Treat candidates with consideration – applications should be acknowledged, candidates should be kept informed without undue delay of decisions made about their application, and they should not be kept waiting for the interview.
- Avoid intrusive or hectoring questioning in interviews.
- Do not put candidates under undue stress in interviews.
- Do not criticize any aspect of the candidate's personality or experience.
- Use relevant selection criteria based on a proper analysis of job requirements.
- Give candidates reasonable opportunity to present their case and to ask questions.
- Avoid jumping to conclusions about candidates on inadequate evidence or as a result of prejudice.
- Give accurate and complete information to candidates about the job, prospects, security and terms and conditions of employment.
- Only use properly validated tests administered by trained testers.
- Do not use discriminating or biased tests.
- Monitor tests for impact and unintended bias.
- Ensure that candidates are not unfairly disadvantaged by testing processes.
- Give candidates feedback on test results unless there are compelling reasons why feedback should not be given.
- Ensure that selection decisions are free of discrimination or bias on the grounds of sex, sexual orientation, race, age or disability.
- Give unsuccessful candidates the reason for the decision if they request it.

Learning and development

- Respect individual rights for dignity, self-esteem, privacy and autonomy.

- Recognize that it is necessary and legitimate to provide individuals with learning opportunities that enable them to gain the knowledge and skills required to perform well in their jobs and develop their potential. But note that individuals should still be allowed autonomy to choose the extent to which they pursue learning and development programmes beyond this basic requirement.

- Accept that while the organization has the right to conduct learning and development activities that enhance performance, individuals also have the right to be provided with opportunities to develop their own knowledge, skills and employability.

- Ensure that people taking part in learning events feel 'psychologically safe' in accordance with the view expressed by Schein (1993: 91) that: 'To make people feel safe in learning, they must have a motive, a sense of direction, and the opportunity to try out new things without the fear of punishment.'

- Avoid manipulating people to accept imposed organizational values.

Performance management

Performance management ethical principles have been defined by Winstanley and Stuart-Smith (1996) as follows:

- *Respect for the individual* – people should be treated as 'ends in themselves' and not merely as 'means to other ends'.

- *Mutual respect* – the parties involved in performance management should respect each other's needs and preoccupations.

- *Procedural fairness* – the procedures incorporated in performance management should be operated fairly in accordance with the principles of procedural justice.

- *Transparency* – people affected by decisions emerging from performance management processes should have the opportunity to scrutinize the basis upon which decisions were made.

Reward management

- Generally apply the principles of procedural and distributive justice.

- Ensure that reward policies and practices are fair, equitable and transparent and that they are applied consistently.

- Reward people according to their contribution.

- Ensure that people know in general the basis upon which rewards are provided and in particular how their own reward package is determined.

- Maintain reasonable and defensible pay differentials.

- Ensure that equal pay is provided for work of equal value.

- Base decisions about performance pay or bonuses on fair and equitable criteria.

- Avoid bonus schemes that encourage undesirable behaviour.

Employee relations

- Deliver the deal.

- Be open to employees' input and responsive to justifiable questions and concerns about employment policies and practices.

- Provide genuine opportunities and channels for employees to express their views and influence decisions on matters that affect them.

- Negotiate in good faith.

- Recognize that the interests of management and employees do not necessarily coincide and develop and implement employee relations policies accordingly.

Employment practices

- Create a healthy, safe and fulfilling work environment.

- Promote the wellbeing of employees by improving the quality of working life provided for them, enhancing work–life balance and developing family-friendly policies.

- Provide equal opportunities for all with regard to recruitment and selection, learning and development, talent management, career progression and promotion.

- Manage diversity by recognizing the differences between people and ensuring that everyone feels valued and that the talents of all employees will be properly utilized.

- Handle disciplinary matters according to the principles of natural justice.

- Recognize that people may have legitimate grievances and respond to them promptly, fully and sympathetically.

- Preserve job security as far as possible and take alternative action to avoid compulsory redundancies.

- If compulsory redundancy is unavoidable, do whatever is possible to alleviate the distress by, for example, helping people to find work.

Ethical dilemmas

'Ethics will be enacted in situations of ambiguity where dilemmas and problems will be dealt with without the comfort of consensus or certitude' (Clegg *et al*, 2007: 109). As Baumann, quoted in Bauman and Tester (2001: 44), commented: 'Morality concerns choice first of all – it is the predicament human beings encounter when they must make a selection amongst various possibilities.' And Derrida (1992) observed that ethical responsibility can exceed rational calculation.

Resolving ethical dilemmas

As Adam Smith (1759) wrote in *The Theory of Modern Sentiments* (quoted by Harrison, 2009: 246): 'When ethically perplexed, the question we should always ask is: would a disinterested observer, in full possession of the relevant facts, approve or disapprove of our actions?' This guidance is just as compelling and relevant today.

Woodall and Winstanley (2000: 285) suggested that 'being ethical is not so much about finding one universal principle to govern all action, but more about knowing how to recognize and mediate between often unacknowledged differences of view'. By definition, an ethical dilemma is one that will be difficult to resolve. There may be all sorts of issues surrounding the situation, some of which will be unclear or contentious. The extent to which people react or behave rationally may be limited by their

Checklist – ethical dilemmas

1 What are the known facts about the situation and is it possible that there are facts or circumstances that have not come to light, and if so what can be done to uncover them?

2 In disciplinary or conduct cases, to what extent does the conduct contravene the organization's code of ethical conduct (if one exists) or any other relevant organizational policy guidelines and rules?

3 Have different versions or interpretations of the facts and circumstances been offered and if so, what steps can be taken to obtain the true and full picture?

4 Is the proposed action in line with both the letter and the spirit of the law?

5 Is the proposed action and any investigations leading to it consistent with the principles of natural, procedural or distributive justice?

6 Will the proposed action benefit the organization and if so how?

7 Is there any risk of the proposed action doing harm to the organization's reputation for fair dealing?

8 Will the proposed action be harmful to the individual affected or to employees generally in any way and if so how?

9 Do the facts as established and confirmed justify the proposed action?

10 Are there any mitigating circumstances (in disciplinary cases)?

capacity to understand the complexities of the situation they are in and affected by their emotional reactions to it (the concept of bounded rationality). As Harrison (2009: 331) explained:

> Some of the factors that militate against a purely 'rational' approach include confused, excessive, incomplete or unreliable data, incompetent processing or communicating of information, pressures of time, human emotions, and differences in individuals' cognitive processes, mental maps and reasoning capacity.

Faced with factors such as these the process of ethical dilemma resolution can be hard going.

There is no 'one right way' to deal with an ethical dilemma, but an approach based on systematic questioning, analysis and diagnosis to get at the facts and establish the issues involved is more likely to produce a reasonably satisfactory outcome than one relying purely on 'gut feeling'. The checklist on page 105 – used judiciously and selectively according to the circumstances – can provide a basis for such questioning and analysis.

Key learning points: The ethical dimension of HRM

Ethics and morality defined

Ethics is defined by the *Compact Oxford Dictionary* as being 'related to morals, treating of moral questions', and ethical is defined as 'relating to morality'. Morality is defined as 'having moral qualities or endowments' and moral is defined as 'of or pertaining to the distinction between right and wrong' Simplistically, ethics could be described as being about behaviour while morality is about beliefs.

Ethics is concerned with making ethical decisions and judgements. It can be described in terms of an ethical framework that sets out different approaches and can be extended to embrace particular concepts that affect and guide ethical behaviour, namely equity, justice, and fair dealing. An ethical decision is one that is morally acceptable to the larger community.

Ethical concepts

The ethical concepts of deontology, utilitarianism, stakeholder theory and discourse theory provide frameworks that can be used to evaluate HRM policies and practices.

The role of HR

HR professionals have a special responsibility for guarding and promoting core values in the organization on how people should be managed and treated generally. They are particularly concerned with values relating to just and fair treatment.

An important role for HR professionals is to do whatever they can to embed the consistent application of ethical values in the organization so that they can become values in use rather than simply professed values in a code of practice or values statement.

Ethical guidelines

Ethical guidelines set out how employees are treated in general, and to the major HRM activities of organization development, recruitment and selection, learning and development, performance management, reward management, employee relations, and employment practices concerning the work environment, employee wellbeing, equal opportunities, managing diversity, handling disciplinary matters and grievances, job security and redundancy.

Handling ethical dilemmas

There is no 'one right way' to deal with an ethical dilemma but an approach based on systematic questioning, analysis and diagnosis to get at the facts and establish the issues involved is more likely to produce a reasonably satisfactory outcome than one relying purely on 'gut feeling'. An ethical dilemma is one that will be difficult to resolve. There may be all sorts of issues surrounding the situation, some of which will be unclear or contentious.

Questions

1 What are ethics?

2 What is the nature of ethical judgements?

3 What is the deontological theory of ethics?

4 What is the utilitarian theory of ethics?

5 What is stakeholder theory?

6 What is procedural justice?

7 What is distributive justice?

8 What is the ethical dimension of HRM?

9 What are commonly accepted general guidelines on HR ethical behaviour?

10 How should ethical dilemmas be dealt with?

References

Adams, J S (1965) Injustice in social exchange, in (ed) L Berkowitz, *Advances in Experimental Psychology*, New York, Academic Press

Bauman, Z and Tester, K (2001) *Conversations with Zygmunt Bauman*, Cambridge, Polity Press

Beauchamp, T L and Bowie, N E (1983) *Ethical Theory and Business*, 2nd edn, Englewood Cliffs, NJ, Prentice Hall

Boxall, P F, Purcell, J and Wright, P (2007) Human resource management; scope, analysis and significance, in (eds) P Boxall, J Purcell and P Wright, *The Oxford Handbook of Human Resource Management*, Oxford, Oxford University Press, pp 1–18

Clegg, S, Kornberger, M and Rhodes, C (2007) Business ethics as practice, *British Journal of Management*, **18** (2), pp 107–22

Derrida, J (1992) Forces of law: the mystical foundation of authority, in (eds) D Cornell, M Rosenfeld and D G Carlson, *Deconstruction and the Possibility of Justice*, London, Routledge, pp 3–68

Foucault, M (1972) *The Archaeology of Knowledge and the Discourse on Language*, New York, Pantheon Books

Foucault, M (1997) *Ethics, Subjectivity and Truth. Essential Works of Foucault, 1954–1984*, ed P Rabinow, New York, The New Press

Freeman, R E (1984) *Strategic Management: A stakeholder perspective*, Englewood Cliffs, NJ, Prentice Hall

Guest, D E and King, Z (2004) Power, innovation and problem-solving: the personnel managers' three steps to heaven?, *Journal of Management Studies*, **41** (3), pp 401–23

Hamlin, B, Keep, J and Ash, K (2001) *Organizational Change and Development: A reflective guide for managers*, London, FT Pitman

Harrison, R (2009) *Learning and Development*, 5th edn, London, CIPD

Jones, T M (1991) Ethical decision making by individuals in organizations: An issue-contingent model, *Academy of Management Review*, **16** (2), pp 366–95

Legge, K (1998) The morality of HRM, in (eds) C Mabey, D Skinner and T Clark, *Experiencing Human Resource Management*, London, Sage, pp 14–32

Leventhal, G S (1980) What should be done with equity theory?, in (eds) G K Gergen, M S Greenberg and R H Willis, *Social Exchange: Advances in Theory and Research*, New York, Plenum

Petrick, J A and Quinn, J F (1997) *Management Ethics: Integrity at work*, London, Sage

Rawls, J (2005) *A Theory of Justice*, Cambridge, MA, Harvard University Press

Schein, E (1993) How can organizations learn faster? The challenge of entering the green room, *Sloan Management Review*, **34** (2), pp 85–92

Tyler, T R and Bies, R J (1990) Beyond formal procedures: the interpersonal context of procedural justice, in (ed) J S Carrol, *Applied Social Psychology and Organizational Settings*, Hillsdale, NJ, Lawrence Erlbaum

Winstanley, D and Stuart-Smith, K (1996) Policing performance: the ethics of performance management, *Personnel Review*, **25** (6), pp 66–84

Winstanley, D and Woodall, J (2000a) Introduction, in (eds) D Winstanley and J Woodall, *Ethical Issues in Contemporary Human Resource Management*, Basingstoke, Macmillan, pp 3–22

Winstanley, D and Woodall, J (2000b) The ethical dimension of human resource management, *Human Resource Management Journal*, **10** (2), pp 5–20

Woodall, J and Winstanley, D (2000) Concluding comments: ethical frameworks for action, in (eds) D Winstanley and J Woodall, *Ethical Issues in Contemporary Human Resource Management*, Basingstoke, Macmillan, pp 3–22

10
Corporate social responsibility

LEARNING OUTCOMES

On completing this chapter you should be able to define these key concepts. You should also know about:

- The meaning of corporate social responsibility (CSR)
- CSR activities
- CSR strategy
- Developing a CSR strategy
- The rationale for CSR

Introduction

The notion that businesses should act in a socially responsible way by practising 'corporate social responsibility' (CSR) has been around for some time. JM Keynes wrote in 1923 that: 'The business man is only tolerable so long as his gains can be held to bear some relation to what, roughly and in some sense, his activities have contributed to society.' The aim of this chapter is to explore what it means as a concept and a strategy. The rationale for CSR is also considered – the arguments in favour are overwhelming, but reference is made to powerful opposing views.

HR professionals have an important role to play in furthering CSR because of the ethical dimension of their function, as described in Chapter 9. CSR was justified by the CIPD (2009: 1) as a relevant and important HR activity because:

CSR needs to be embedded in an organization's culture to make a change to actions and attitudes, and the support of the top team is critical to success. HR already works at communicating and implementing ideas, policies, cultural and behavioural change across organizations. Its role in influencing attitudes and links with line managers and the top team means it is ideally placed to do the same with CSR.

HR professionals need to marshal the arguments in favour of CSR, as set out in this chapter, to overcome any overt or covert resistance. They must be able to advise on CSR strategies and how they can be implemented. This is not an easy task and suggestions on the approaches that can be adopted are made in the concluding section of the chapter.

Corporate social responsibility defined

Corporate social responsibility (CSR) is exercised by organizations when they conduct their business in an ethical way, taking account of the social, environmental and economic impact of how they operate, and going beyond compliance. Wood (1991: 695) stated that: 'The basic idea of corporate social responsibility is that business and society are interwoven rather than distinct entities; therefore, society has certain expectations for appropriate business behaviour and outcomes.' As Baron (2001: 11) noted, CSR involves 'providing to others benefits beyond those generated by economic transactions with the firm or required by law'.

McWilliams *et al* (2006: 1) stated that CSR refers to the actions taken by businesses 'that further some social good beyond the interests of the firm and that which is required by law'. CSR has also been described by Husted and Salazar (2006: 76) as being concerned with 'the impact of business behaviour on society' and by Porter and Kramer (2006: 83) as a process of integrating business and society. The latter argued that to advance CSR, 'We must root it in a broad understanding of the interrelationship between a corporation and society while at the same time anchoring it in the strategies and activities of specific companies.'

CSR is concerned generally with how companies function and this includes how they manage their people. The CIPD (2003: 5) emphasized that 'the way a company treats its employees will contribute directly to the picture of a company that is willing to accept its wider responsibilities'.

Strategic CSR defined

Strategic CSR is about deciding initially the degree to which the firm should be involved in social issues and then creating a corporate social agenda – considering what social issues to focus on and to what extent. As Porter and Kramer (2006: 85) observed: 'It is through strategic CSR that the company will make the greatest social impact and reap the greatest business benefits.' They also observed that strategy is always about choice – organizations that 'make the right choices and build focused, proactive and integrated social initiatives in concert with their core strategies will increasingly distance themselves from the pack' (*ibid*: 91).

CSR strategy needs to be integrated with the business strategy but it is also closely associated with HR strategy. This is because it is concerned with socially responsible behaviour both outside and within the firm – with society generally and with the internal community. In the latter case this means creating a working environment where personal and employment rights are upheld and HR policies and practices provide for the fair and ethical treatment of employees.

CSR activities

CSR activities as listed by McWilliams *et al* (2006) include incorporating social characteristics or features into products and manufacturing processes, adopting progressive HRM practices, achieving higher levels of environmental performance through recycling and pollution abatement and advancing the goals of community organizations. The information set out below was obtained by Business in the Community research.

Business in the Community also reported a growing emphasis on responsible business as a source of competitive advantage as firms move beyond minimizing risk to creating opportunities. A survey

Source review

The CSR activities of 120 leading British companies – Business in the Community (2007)

1   *Community* – skills and education, employability and social exclusion were frequently identified as key risks and opportunities. Other major activities were support for local community initiatives and being a responsible and safe neighbour.

2   *Environment* – most companies reported climate change and resource-use as key issues for their business: 85 per cent of them managed their impacts through an environmental management system.

3   *Marketplace* – the issues most frequently mentioned by companies were research and development, procurement and supply chain, responsible selling, responsible marketing and product safety. There was a rising focus on fair treatment of customers, providing appropriate product information and labelling, and on the impacts of products on customer health.

4   *Workplace* – this was the strongest management performing area as most companies have established employment management frameworks that can cater for workplace issues as they emerge. Companies recognized the crucial role of employees to achieve responsible business practices. Increasing emphasis was placed on internal communications and training to raise awareness and understanding of why CSR is relevant to them and valuable for the business. More attention was being paid to health and wellbeing issues as well as the traditional safety agenda. More work was being done on diversity, both to ensure the business attracts a diverse workforce and to communicate the business case for diversity internally.

conducted by Industrial Relations Services (Egan, 2006) found that:

- most employers believe that employment practices designed to ensure the fair and ethical treatment of staff can boost recruitment and retention;
- relatively few employers are strongly convinced of a positive link to business performance or productivity;
- the issue of ethics in employment is often viewed as part of a broader social responsibility package;
- policies on ethical employment most commonly cover HR practice in the areas of recruitment, diversity, redundancy/dismissal proceedings and employee involvement.

The rationale for CSR

Stakeholder theory, as first propounded by Freeman (1984), suggests that managers must satisfy a variety of constituents (eg workers, customers, suppliers, local community organizations) who can influence firm outcomes. According to this view, it is not sufficient for managers to focus exclusively on the needs of stockholders or the owners of the corporation. Stakeholder theory implies that it can be beneficial for the firm to engage in certain CSR activities that non-financial stakeholders perceive to be important.

The rationale for CSR, as defined by Hillman and Keim (2001), is based on two propositions. First, there is a moral imperative for businesses to 'do the right thing' without regard to how such decisions affect firm performance (the social issues argument) and secondly, firms can achieve competitive advantage by tying CSR activities to primary stakeholders (the stakeholders argument). Their research in 500 firms implied that investing in stakeholder management may be complementary to shareholder value creation and could indeed provide a basis for competitive advantage as important resources and capabilities are created that differentiate a firm from its competitors. However, participating in social issues beyond the direct stakeholders may adversely affect a firm's ability to create shareholder wealth. Strong arguments for CSR were made by Porter and Kramer.

Arguments supporting CSR – Porter and Kramer (2006)

1   *The moral appeal* – the argument that companies have a duty to be good citizens. The US business association Business for Social Responsibility (2007) asks its members 'to achieve commercial success in ways that honour ethical values and respect people, communities and the natural environment'.

2   *Sustainability* – an emphasis on environmental and community stewardship. This involves meeting the needs of the present without compromising the ability of future generations to meet their own needs.

3   *Licence to operate* – every company needs tacit or explicit permission from government, communities and other stakeholders to do business.

4   *Reputation* – CSR initiatives can be justified because they improve a company's image, strengthen its brand, enliven morale and even raise the value of its stock.

Moran and Ghoshal (1996: 45) contended 'that what is good for society does not necessarily have to be bad for the firm, and what is good for the firm does not necessarily have to come at a cost to society. Value creation, rather than value appropriation, lies at the heart of effective firm strategies'.

The opposing view

The opposing view is that businesses are there to make a profit, not to exercise social responsibility. The marketing expert Theodore Levitt (1958: 41), in a *Harvard Business Review* article on the dangers of social responsibility, posed the questions: 'Are top executives being taken in by pretty words and soft ideas? Are they letting the country in for a nightmare return to feudalism by forgetting that they must be businessmen first, last and almost always?' He did write that CSR can be used as 'a way of maximizing the lifetime of capitalism by taking the wind out of its critics' sails' (*ibid*: 43). But, writing as an unrestructured capitalist, he suggested that: 'The essence of free enterprise is to go after profit in any way that is consistent with its own survival as an economic system' (*ibid*: 44).

The Chicago monetarist, Milton Friedman (1962: 133–4) questioned the ability of business managers to pursue the social interest. He asked:

> If businessmen do have a social responsibility other than making maximum profits for stockholders, how are they to know what it is? Can self-selected private individuals decide what the social interest is? Can they decide how great a burden they are justified in placing on themselves or their stockholders to serve that social interest?

Later (Friedman, 1970) he stated that the social responsibility of business is to maximize profits within the bounds of the law. He argued that the mere existence of CSR was an agency problem within the firm in that it was a misuse of the resources entrusted to managers by owners, which could be better used on value-added internal projects or returned to the shareholders.

These outspoken views may no longer be supported so openly but they still exist and are still acted on. There is lots of evidence that CSR is not on the agenda – for example, UK banks that made money by selling worthless investments or insurance policies and then failed to respond adequately to complaints. And, less egregiously, a glance at the 'Your Problems' column in the *Observer* reveals plenty of instances of businesses indulging in anti-social behaviour. It is necessary therefore to have a convincing case for the benefits of CSR.

Benefits of CSR

Benefits from CSR listed by the CIPD (2003: 4) include, 'offering distinctive positioning in the market place, protecting reputation, building credibility and trust with customers and employees, redefining corporate purpose or mission and securing the company's licence to operate'.

PART II

People and organizations

PART II CONTENTS

Introduction

Human resource management policies and practices need to be based on an understanding of the factors that affect the behaviour of people in organizations. The purpose of this part of the book is to outline a basic set of concepts and to provide analytical tools that will enable HR specialists to diagnose organizational behaviour and to take appropriate actions.

The part starts in Chapter 11 with a general analysis of the concept of organizational behaviour, the term used to describe how organizations function with regard to their structure, processes and culture and the characteristics of people and how they act in organizations, individually or in groups. Organization behaviour theory is based on the main behavioural science disciplines; like all proven theories it offers significant insights into good practice.

Organization behaviour theory provides guidance on the design of work systems, organizations and jobs, as discussed in Chapter 12, and approaches to organization development (the systematic process of improving organizational capability which is concerned with process – how things get done) in Chapter 13. It also provides the conceptual framework for approaches to achieving the engagement, motivation and commitment of people, as considered in the next three chapters. Employee engagement is what everyone talks about nowadays. It takes place when people are interested in and positive, even excited, about their jobs and are prepared to go the extra mile to get them done to the best of their ability. But it is useful from the viewpoint of developing HR practice to distinguish the associated concepts of:

- Motivation – the strength and direction of behaviour and the factors that influence people to behave in certain ways in carrying out their work.

- Organizational commitment – the strength of an individual's identification with, and involvement in, a particular organization.

- Organizational citizenship – positive behaviour at work that goes beyond role requirements.

11
Organizational behaviour

LEARNING OUTCOMES

On completing this chapter you should be able to define these key concepts. You should also know about:

- What is meant by organizational behaviour
- The sources and applications of organization behaviour theory
- How organizations function
- Organizational culture
- Organizational climate
- Organizational processes
- Characteristics of people
- Implications for HR specialists

Introduction

An understanding of how organizations function and how people behave in them is important to HR professionals, indeed to all managers, as pointed out by Nadler and Tushman.

The significance of organizational behaviour theory – Nadler and Tushman (1980: 30)

Managers perform their jobs within complex social systems called organizations. In many senses, the task of the manager is to influence behaviour in a desired direction, usually towards the accomplishment of a specific task or performance goal. Given this definition of the managerial role, skills in the diagnosis of patterns of organizational behaviour become vital. Specifically, the manager needs to *understand* the patterns of behaviour that are observed, *predict* in what direction behaviour will move (particularly in the light of managerial action), and to use this knowledge to *control* behaviour over the course of time.

Organizational behaviour defined

Organizational behaviour was defined by Huczynski and Buchanan (2007: 843) as the term used to describe 'the study of the structure, functioning, and performance of organizations and the behaviour of groups and individuals within them'. The following are the characteristics of organizational behaviour theory.

Characteristics of organizational behaviour – Ivancevich *et al* (2008: 11)

- It is a way of thinking – about individuals, groups and organizations.

- It is multidisciplinary – it uses principles, models, theories and methods from other disciplines.

- There is a distinctly humanistic orientation – people and their attitudes, perceptions, learning capacities, feelings and goals are of major importance.

- It is performance-orientated – it deals with the factors affecting performance and how it can be improved.

- The use of scientific method is important in studying variables and relationships.

- It is applications-orientated in the sense of being concerned with providing useful answers to questions which arise when managing organizations.

The sources and applications of organizational behaviour theory

Organizational behaviour theory is based on the main behavioural science disciplines. These are defined as the fields of enquiry dedicated to the study of human behaviour through sophisticated and rigorous methods. The ways in which they contribute to different aspects of organization behaviour theory and how they in turn influence HRM practices are summarized in Figure 11.1.

FIGURE 11.1 The sources and applications of organizational behaviour theory

How organizations function

An organization is an entity that exists to achieve a purpose through the collective efforts of the people who work in or for it. Organizing is the process of making arrangements in the form of defined or understood responsibilities and relationships to enable those people to work cooperatively together. Organizations can be described as systems which, as affected by their environment, have a structure that has both formal and informal elements.

Organization structures are frameworks for getting things done. Traditional formal structures were based on laid down hierarchies (lines of command) represented in organization charts, and use was made of closely defined job descriptions. But to varying extents organizations operate informally as well as formally by means of a network of roles and relationships that cut across formal organizational boundaries and lines of command. Organization structures can evolve almost spontaneously as circumstances change and new activities have to be carried out.

The processes that take place in organizations of interaction and networking, leadership, group behaviour, the exercise of power and the use of politics may well have much more effect on how organizations function than a well-defined organization chart supported by elaborate job descriptions and an organization manual. Moreover, the way in which an organization functions will be largely contingent on its purpose, technology, methods of working and external environment. A number of theories have been developed, summarized in Table 11.1, to explain how organizations function, culminating in the contingency and post-bureaucratic schools that now predominate.

The culture of an organization has been described by Deal and Kennedy (2000: 4) as 'the way we do things around here'. It's more complex than that, as other definitions given below indicate. But this simplistic definition at least demonstrates that it is an all-pervading notion that affects the way in which people behave and has to be taken into account as a contingency factor in any programme for developing organizations and HR policies and practices. Organizational culture offers a shared system of meanings that is the basis for communications and mutual understanding. If these functions are not fulfilled in a satisfactory way, culture may significantly reduce the efficiency of an organization. This is why it is important for HR specialists to understand the concept of organizational culture and how it affects organizations.

Organizational culture defined

Organizational or corporate culture is the pattern of values, norms, beliefs, attitudes and assumptions that may not have been articulated but shape the ways in which people in organizations behave and things get done. 'Values' refer to what is believed to be important about how people and organizations behave. 'Norms' are the unwritten rules of behaviour.

This definition emphasizes that organizational culture is concerned with the subjective aspect of what goes on in organizations. It refers to abstractions such as values and norms that pervade the

TABLE 11.1   Schools of organization theory

School	Leading exponents	Summary of theory
The classical school	Taylor (1911), Fayol (1916), Urwick (1947)	Organizations need control, measurement, order and formality to function well. They have to minimize the opportunity for unfortunate and uncontrollable informal relations, leaving room only for the formal ones.
The human relations school	Barnard (1938), Roethlisberger and Dickson (1939)	Barnard emphasized the importance of the informal organization – the network of informal roles and relationships which, for better or worse, strongly influences the way the formal structure operates. In the Hawthorne studies Roethlisberger and Dickson stressed the importance of informal groups and decent, humane leadership.
The behavioural science school	Argyris (1957), Herzberg *et al* (1957), McGregor (1960), Likert (1961), Schein (1965)	A humanistic point of view is adopted which is concerned with what people can contribute and how they can best be motivated.

TABLE 11.1   *Continued*

School	Leading exponents	Summary of theory
The bureaucratic model	Weber (translated in 1946)	Max Weber coined the term 'bureaucracy' as a label for a type of formal organization in which impersonality and rationality are developed to the highest degree. Bureaucracy, as he conceived it, was the most efficient form of organization because it was logical and because personalized relationships and non-rational, emotional considerations do not get in its way.
The socio-technical model	Emery (1959), Trist *et al* (1963)	In any system of organization, technical or task aspects are interrelated with the human or social aspects. The emphasis is on interrelationships between, on the one hand, the technical processes of transformation carried out within the organization and, on the other hand, the organization of work groups and the management structures of the enterprise.
The systems school	Miller and Rice (1967)	Organizations should be treated as open systems which are continually dependent upon and influenced by their environments. The basic characteristic of the enterprise as an open system is that it transforms inputs into outputs within its environment.
The contingency school	Burns and Stalker (1961), Woodward (1965), Lawrence and Lorsch (1969)	Members of the contingency school analysed a variety of organizations and concluded that their structures and methods of operation are a function of the circumstances in which they exist. They do not subscribe to the view that there is one best way of designing an organization or that simplistic classifications of organizations as formal or informal, bureaucratic or non-bureaucratic are helpful.
The post-bureaucratic school	Pascale (1990), Ghoshal and Bartlett (1995)	Rather than seeing organizations as a hierarchy of static roles, members of the post-bureaucratic school think of them as a portfolio of dynamic processes which overlay and often dominate the vertical, authority-based processes of the hierarchical structure. The emphasis is on 'horizontal tasks', collaboration and networking across units rather than on 'vertical tasks' within functional units. Hence the concept of the 'boundaryless organization' popularized by Jack Welch.

whole or part of a business, which may not be defined, discussed or even noticed. Nevertheless, culture can have a significant influence on people's behaviour. The following are some other definitions of organizational culture:

- A strong culture is a system of informal rules that spells out how people are to behave most of the time. (Deal and Kennedy, 2000: 15)
- The culture of an organization refers to the unique configuration of norms, values, beliefs and ways of behaving that characterize the manner in which groups and individuals combine to get things done. (Eldridge and Crombie, 1974: 89)
- Organizational culture offers a shared system of meanings which is the basis for communications and mutual understanding. (Furnham and Gunter, 1993: 70–71)
- Culture is a pattern of basic assumptions – invented, discovered or developed by a given group as it learns to cope with the problems of external adaptation and internal integration – that has worked well enough to be considered valid and, therefore, to be taught to new members as the correct way to perceive, think and feel in relation to these problems. (Schein, 1990: 110)

How organizational culture develops

The values and norms that are the basis of culture are formed in four ways; first, by the leaders in the organization, especially those who have shaped it in the past. Schein (1990) indicates that people identify with visionary leaders – how they behave and what they expect. They note what such leaders pay attention to and treat them as role models. Secondly, as Schein also points out, culture is formed around critical incidents – important events from which lessons are learnt about desirable or undesirable behaviour. Thirdly, culture develops from the need to maintain effective working relationships among organization members that establishes values and expectations. Finally, culture is influenced by the organization's environment, which may be dynamic or unchanging.

Culture evolves over time as a result of shared experiences. Schein (1984) suggested that this is a learning process that takes place either through the trauma model, in which members of the organization learn to cope with some threat by the erection of defence mechanisms, or by means of the positive reinforcement model, where things that seem to work become embedded and entrenched. Learning takes place as people adapt to and cope with external pressures, and as they develop successful approaches and mechanisms to handle the internal challenges, processes and technologies in their organization. Where culture has developed over long periods of time and has become firmly embedded it may be difficult to change quickly, if at all, unless a traumatic event occurs.

The diversity of culture

The development process described above may result in a culture that characterizes the whole organization. But there may be different cultures within organizations. For example, the culture of an outward-looking marketing department may be substantially different from that of an internally-focused manufacturing function. There may be some common organizational values or norms, but in some respects these will vary between different work environments.

The components of culture

Organizational culture can be described in terms of values, norms, artefacts and management or leadership style.

Values

Values are beliefs in what is best or good for the organization and what should or ought to happen. The 'value set' of an organization may only be recognized at top level, or it may be shared throughout the business, in which case it could be described as value-driven.

The stronger the values the more they will influence behaviour. This does not depend upon their having been articulated. Implicit values that are deeply embedded in the culture of an organization and are reinforced by the behaviour of management can be highly influential, while espoused values that are mere rhetoric and are not reflected in managerial behaviour may have little or no effect. When values are acted on they are called 'values in use'.

Areas in which values may be expressed – explicitly or implicitly

- Care and consideration for people.
- Competence.
- Competitiveness.
- Customer service.
- Innovation.
- Performance.
- Quality.
- Teamwork.

Typical norms

- How managers treat the members of their teams (management style) and how the latter relate to their managers.
- The prevailing work ethic, eg 'work hard, play hard', 'come in early, stay late', 'if you cannot finish your work during business hours you are obviously inefficient', 'look busy at all times', 'look relaxed at all times'.
- Status – how much importance is attached to it; the existence or lack of obvious status symbols.
- Ambition – naked ambition is expected and approved of, or a more subtle approach is the norm.
- Performance – exacting performance standards are general; the highest praise that can be given in the organization is to be referred to as 'very professional'.
- Power – recognized as a way of life; executed by political means, dependent on expertise and ability rather than position; concentrated at the top; shared at different levels in different parts of the organization.
- Politics – rife throughout the organization and treated as normal behaviour; not accepted as overt behaviour.
- Loyalty – expected, a cradle-to-grave approach to careers; discounted, the emphasis is on results and contribution in the short term.
- Anger – openly expressed; hidden, but expressed through other, possibly political, means.
- Approachability – managers are expected to be approachable and visible; everything happens behind closed doors.
- Formality – a cool, formal approach is the norm; forenames are/are not used at all levels; there are unwritten but clearly understood rules about dress.

Values are translated into reality through norms and artefacts, as described below. They may also be expressed through the media of language (organizational jargon), rituals, stories and myths.

Norms

Norms are the unwritten rules of behaviour, the 'rules of the game' that provide informal guidelines on how to behave. Norms tell people what they are supposed to be doing, saying, believing, even wearing. They are never expressed in writing – if they were, they would be policies or procedures. They are passed on by word of mouth or behaviour and can be enforced by the reactions of people if they are violated. They can exert very powerful pressure on behaviour because of these reactions – we control others by the way we react to them.

Artefacts

Artefacts are the visible and tangible aspects of an organization that people hear, see or feel and which contribute to their understanding of the organization's culture. Artefacts can include such things as the working environment, the tone and language used in e-mails, letters or memoranda, the manner in which people address each other at meetings or over the telephone, the welcome (or lack of welcome) given to visitors and the way in which receptionists deal with outside calls. Artefacts can be very revealing.

Management style

The approach managers use to deal with people – their management or leadership style – is a significant part of the culture of an organization. Management style can be described in terms of the following extremes:

charismatic	↔	non-charismatic
autocratic	↔	democratic
controller	↔	enabler
transactional	↔	transformational

Most managers adopt an approach somewhere between the extremes. Some will vary it according to the situation or their feelings at the time; others will stick to the same style whatever happens. Every manager has his or her own style but this will be influenced by the organizational culture, which may produce a prevailing management style that represents a behavioural norm for managers that is generally expected and adopted.

Classifying organizational culture

There have been many attempts to classify or categorize organizational cultures as a basis for analysis and for taking action to support or change them. Most of these classifications are expressed in four dimensions; three of the best-known ones are summarized below. Note that following the lead of Harrison (1972), there is much common ground between them.

Harrison (1972) – organization ideologies

Power-orientated – competitive, responsive to personality rather than expertise.

People-orientated – consensual, management control rejected.

Task-orientated – focus on competency, dynamic.

Role-orientated – focus on legality, legitimacy and bureaucracy.

Handy (1981) culture typology

1 *The power culture* is one with a central power source which exercises control. There are few rules or procedures and the atmosphere is competitive, power-orientated and political.

2 *The role culture* in which work is controlled by procedures and rules and the role, or job description, is more important than the person who fills it. Power is associated with positions not people.

3 *The task culture* in which the aim is to bring together the right people and let them get on with it. Influence is based more on expert power than in position or personal power. The culture is adaptable and teamwork is important.

4 *The person culture* in which the individual is the central point. The organization exists only to serve and assist the individuals in it.

Schein (1984)

1 *Power culture* in which leadership resides in a few and rests on their ability and which tends to be entrepreneurial.

2 *Role culture* in which power is balanced between the leader and bureaucratic structure. The environment is likely to be stable and roles and rules are clearly defined.

3 *Achievement culture* in which personal motivation and commitment are stressed and action, excitement and impact are valued.

4 *Support culture* in which people contribute out of a sense of commitment and solidarity.

Appropriate cultures

It is not possible to say that one culture is better than another, only that a culture is to a greater or lesser extent appropriate in the sense that it is relevant to the needs and circumstances of the organization and helps rather than hinders its performance. However, embedded cultures can exert considerable influence on organizational behaviour. If there is an appropriate and effective culture it would therefore be desirable to take steps to support or reinforce it. If the culture is inappropriate attempts should be made to determine what needs to be changed and to develop and implement plans for change. A culture will be more effective if it is consistent in its components and shared amongst organizational members, and if it makes the organization unique, thus differentiating it from other organizations.

Organizational climate

As defined by Harrison and Shirom (1999: 263), organizational climate refers to 'members' perceptions of organizational features such as decision-making, leadership and norms about work'. Ivancevich *et al* (2008: 528) described organizational climate as: 'A set of properties of the work environment, perceived directly or indirectly by the employees, that is assumed to be a major force in influencing employee behaviour.'

The term 'organizational climate' is sometimes confused with 'organizational culture' and there has been much debate on what distinguishes them from one another. In his analysis of this issue, Denison (1996) suggested that 'culture' refers to the deep structure of organizations, which is rooted in the values, beliefs and assumptions held by organizational members. In contrast, 'climate' refers to those aspects of the environment that are consciously perceived by organizational members. Rousseau (1988) stated that climate is a perception and is descriptive. Perceptions are sensations or realizations experienced by an individual. Descriptions are what a person reports of these sensations.

The debate about the meanings of these terms can become academic. It is easiest to regard organizational climate as how people perceive (see and feel about) the culture existing in their organization. French *et al* (1985) distinguish between the actual situation (ie culture) and the perception of it (climate).

Organizational processes

A number of social processes take place in organizations that affect how they function. These are: interaction and networking, communication, group behaviour, leadership, power, politics and conflict.

Interaction and networking

Interactions between people criss-cross the organization, creating networks for getting things done and exchanging information that are not catered for in the formal structure. 'Networking' is an increasingly important process in flexible and delayered organizations where more fluid interactions across the structure are required between individuals and teams. Individuals can often get much more done by networking than by going through formal channels. This means that they can canvass opinion and enlist support to promote their projects or ideas. People also get things done in organizations by creating alliances – getting agreement on a course of action with other people and joining forces to put the proposed action into effect.

Communications

The communications processes used in organizations have a marked effect on how it functions, especially if they take place through the network, which can then turn into the 'grapevine'. E-mails encourage the instant flow of information (and sometimes produce information overload) but may inhibit the face-to-face interactions, which are often the best ways of doing things.

Group behaviour

Organizations consist of groups or teams of people working together. They may be set up formally as part of the structure or they may be informal gatherings. A group can be a permanent or a temporary feature in an organization. Interactions take place within and between groups and the degree to which these processes are formalized varies according to the organizational context.

Formal groups or teams are created by organizations to achieve a defined purpose. People are brought together with the necessary skills to carry out the tasks and a system exists for directing, coordinating and controlling the group's activities. Informal groups are set up by people in organizations who have some affinity for one another. It could be said that formal groups satisfy the needs of the organization while informal groups satisfy the needs of their members.

Groups develop an ideology that affects the attitudes and actions of their members and the degree of satisfaction they feel. If the group ideology is strong and individual members identify closely with the group, it will become increasingly cohesive. Group norms or implicit rules will be evolved that define what is acceptable behaviour and what is not. This is described as a 'reference group', which consists of the group of people with whom an individual identifies. The individual accepts the group's norms and if in doubt about what to do or say, reference is made to these norms or to other group members before action is taken. Most people in organizations belong to a reference group and this can significantly affect the ways in which they behave.

Four stages of group development were identified by Tuckman (1965):

1 *Forming*, when there is anxiety, dependence on the leader and testing to find out the nature of the situation and the task, and what behaviour is acceptable.

2 *Storming*, where there is conflict, emotional resistance to the demands of the task, resistance to control and even rebellion against the leader.

3 *Norming*, when group cohesion is developed, norms emerge, views are exchanged openly, mutual support and cooperation increase and the group acquires a sense of its identity.

4 *Performing*, when interpersonal problems are resolved, roles are flexible and functional, there are constructive attempts to complete tasks and energy is available for effective work.

Leadership

Organizations largely function by means of managers and supervisors who exercise leadership in order to get their teams into action and ensure that they achieve the results expected of them. Goleman (2000) reported that a study by Hay McBer of 3,871 executives, selected from a database of more than 20,000 executives worldwide, established that leadership had a direct impact on organizational climate, and that climate in turn accounted for nearly one-third of the financial results of organizations. The conclusion from research conducted by Higgs (2006) was that leadership behaviour accounts for almost 50 per cent of the difference between change success and failure. Research by Northouse (2006) into 167 US firms in 13 industries established that over a 20-year period leadership accounted for more variations in performance than any other variable.

Power

Organizations exist to get things done and in the process of doing this, people or groups exercise power. Directly or indirectly, the use of power in influencing behaviour is a pervading feature of organizations, whether it is exerted by managers, specialists, informal groups or trade union officials. It is a way of achieving results, but it can be misused.

Politics

Political behaviour is an inevitable feature of organizational life. The aim of organizational politicians is to get their own way by influencing people to accept their point of view without going through the usual channels or relying on their authority. Some individuals genuinely believe that the best way to get something done is by using political means, especially when they are frustrated by the normal decision processes. Others unashamedly pursue their own ends. Political behaviour can be harmful when it is underhand and devious, but it can sometimes help to enlist support and overcome obstacles to getting results. All managers need political skills, as described in Chapter 56, but, because of the nature of their role, such skills are particularly important for HR specialists.

Conflict

Conflict is also inevitable in organizations because they function by means of adjustments and compromises among competitive elements in their structure and membership. Conflict also arises when there is change, because it may be seen as a threat to be challenged or resisted, or when there is frustration. Conflict is not always deplorable. It can be a result of progress and change and it can be used constructively.

Characteristics of people

To manage people effectively, it is necessary to take into account the factors that affect how they behave at work. The development of HR processes and the design of organizations are often predicated on the belief that everyone is the same and will behave rationally when faced with change or other demands. But the behaviour of people differs because of their characteristics and individual differences and it is not always rational.

The management of people would be much easier if everyone were the same, but they aren't. As discussed below, they are, of course, different because of variations in personal characteristics and the influence of their background (the culture in which they were brought up). Sex, race or disability are also considered to be factors by some people, although holding this view readily leads to discrimination. In addition, there will be differences in ability, intelligence and personality.

Variations in personal characteristics

The headings under which personal characteristics can vary have been classified by Mischel as follows.

These are affected by environmental or situational variables, which include the type of work individuals carry out; the culture, climate and management style in the organization; the social group within which they work; and the 'reference groups' individuals use for comparative purposes (eg comparing conditions of work or pay between one category of employee and another).

The personal characteristics that affect people's behaviour at work, as discussed below, are their ability, intelligence, personality, attitudes, emotions and emotional intelligence.

Source review

Variations in personal characteristics – Mischel (1968)

- *Competencies* – abilities and skills.

- *Constructs* – the conceptual framework which governs how people perceive their environment.

- *Expectations* – what people have learnt to expect about their own and others' behaviour.

- *Values* – what people believe to be important.

- *Self-regulatory plans* – the goals people set themselves and the plans they make to achieve them.

Ability

Ability is the quality possessed by people that makes an action possible. Abilities have been analysed by Burt (1954) and Vernon (1961). They classified them into two major groups: *V:ed* – standing for verbal, numerical, memory and reasoning abilities, and *K:m* – standing for spatial and mechanical abilities, as well as perceptual (memory) and motor skills relating to physical operations such as eye/hand coordination and mental dexterity.

They also suggested that overriding these abilities there is general mental ability (GMA), which accounts for most variations in performance. Following a meta-analysis of 85 years of research findings, Schmidt and Hunter (1998) established that the most valid predictor of future performance and learning was GMA for selecting people without previous experience.

Intelligence

Intelligence has been variously defined as:

- The capacity to solve problems, apply principles, make inferences and perceive relationships. (Argyle, 1989: 53)

- The capacity for abstract thinking and reasoning with a range of different contents and media. (Toplis *et al*, 2004: 20)

- What is measured by intelligence tests.
  (Wright and Taylor, 1970: 31)

The last, tautological definition is not facetious. As an operational definition, it can be related to the specific aspects of reasoning, inference, cognition (ie knowing, conceiving) and perception (ie understanding, recognition) which intelligence tests attempt to measure.

General intelligence, as noted above, consists of a number of mental abilities that enable a person to succeed at a wide variety of intellectual tasks that use the faculties of knowing and reasoning. It is measured by an intelligence test and is sometimes expressed as an intelligence quotient (IQ), which is the ratio of an individual's mental age to the individual's actual age as measured by an intelligence test.

The concept of emotional intelligence as described below stresses that emotional maturity in the sense of the ability to identify, assess, and manage the emotions of one's self and others is also important.

Personality

Personality has been defined by Huczynski and Buchanan (2007) as: 'The psychological qualities that influence an individual's characteristic behaviour patterns in a stable and distinctive manner.' As noted by Ivancevich *et al* (2008), personality appears to be organized into patterns which are, to some degree, observable and measurable and involves both common and unique characteristics – every person is different from every other person in some respects but similar to other people in other respects. Personality is a product of both nature (hereditary) and nurture (the pattern of life experience). Personality can be described in terms of traits or types.

Traits

Traits are predispositions to behave in certain ways in a variety of different situations. The leading model of personality traits is the following 'big five' classification (Costa and McRae, 1992; Digman, 1990):

1 *Openness* – inventive/curious or consistent/cautious.

2 *Conscientiousness* – efficient/organized or easy-going/careless.

3 *Extraversion* – outgoing/energetic or solitary/reserved.

4 *Agreeableness* – friendly/compassionate or cold/unkind.

5 *Neuroticism* – sensitive/nervous or secure/confident.

The assumption that people are consistent in the ways they express these traits is the basis for making predictions about their future behaviour. We all attribute traits to people in an attempt to understand why they behave in the way they do. But people do not necessarily express the same trait across different situations or even the same trait in the same situation. Different people may exhibit consistency in some traits and considerable variability in others.

Types

Type theories of personality identify a number of types of personality that can be used to categorize people and may form the basis of a personality test. The types may be linked to descriptions of various traits. One of the most widely used type theories is that of Jung (1923). He identified four major preferences:

1 relating to other people – extraversion or introversion;

2 gathering information – sensing (dealing with facts that can be objectively verified), or intuitive (generating information through insight);

3 using information – thinking (emphasizing logical analysis as the basis for decision making), or feeling (making decisions based on internal values and beliefs);

4 making decisions – perceiving (collecting all the relevant information before making a decision), or judging (resolving the issue without waiting for a large quantity of data).

This theory of personality forms the basis of personality tests such as the Myers-Briggs Types Indicator.

Traits should be distinguished from types. As Huczynski and Buchanan (2007: 142) put it: 'Type approaches fit people into categories possessing common behaviour patterns. A personality trait, on the other hand, is an enduring behaviour that occurs in a variety of settings. While individuals belong to types, traits belong to individuals.'

Attitudes

An attitude can broadly be defined as a settled mode of thinking. Attitudes are evaluative. They are developed through experience but they are less stable than traits and can change as new experiences are gained or influences absorbed. Within organizations they are affected by cultural factors (values and norms), the behaviour of management (management style), policies such as those concerned with pay, recognition, promotion and the quality of working life, and the influence of the 'reference group' (the group with whom people identify). Sometimes there may be a discrepancy between attitudes and behaviour, ie someone may believe in one thing such as being fair to people but act differently. This is called 'cognitive dissonance'.

Emotions

Emotions are feelings such as anger, fear, sadness, joy, anticipation and acceptance that arouse people and therefore influence their behaviour. The mildest forms of emotions are called 'moods', which are low intensity, long-lasting emotional states.

Emotional intelligence

The notion of emotional intelligence was first defined by Salovey and Mayer (1990), who proposed that it involves the capacity to perceive emotion, integrate emotion in thought, understand emotion and manage emotions effectively. Goleman (1995) popularized the concept. He defined emotional intelligence as: 'The capacity for recognizing our own feelings and that of others, for motivating ourselves, for managing emotions well in ourselves as well as others.' He suggested that its four components were:

1 *Self-management* – the ability to control or redirect disruptive impulses and moods and regulate own behaviour coupled with a propensity to pursue goals with energy and persistence. The six competencies associated with this component are self-control, trustworthiness and integrity, initiative, adaptability – comfort with ambiguity, openness to change, and strong desire to achieve.

2 *Self-awareness* – the ability to recognize and understand your moods, emotions and drives as well as their effect on others. This is linked to three competencies: self-confidence, realistic self-assessment, and emotional self-awareness.

3 *Social awareness* – the ability to understand the emotional makeup of other people and skill in treating people according to their emotional reactions. This is linked to six competencies: empathy, expertise in building and retaining talent, organizational awareness, cross-cultural sensitivity, valuing diversity, and service to clients and customers.

4 *Social skills* – proficiency in managing relationships and building networks to get the desired result from others and reach personal goals, and the ability to find common ground and build rapport. The five competencies associated with this component are: leadership, effectiveness in leading change, conflict management, influence/communication, and expertise in building and leading teams.

According to Goleman, it is not enough to have a high IQ; emotional intelligence is also required.

Since Goleman's contribution, three major models of emotional intelligence, as summarized by Clarke (2007), have dominated the writing in this area:

1 *Personality models* have become the most popular theory of emotional intelligence following Goleman. Here, emotional intelligence is viewed as comprising a range of emotional dispositions as well as competences, from individual traits to a number of learnt capabilities. These are all contained within the components of emotional intelligence listed above.

2 *Mixed models:* these comprise aspects of personality as well as abilities to perceive emotional intelligence and manage emotions.

3 *The ability model* views emotional intelligence more narrowly as a set of four cognitive abilities that involve the capacity to identify, reason with, and utilize emotions effectively.

As Clarke comments, the first two models have come under criticism in terms of the ambiguity associated with the areas included and the measurement approaches employed. The ability model has received more positive commentary as possessing greater validity.

Critical evaluation of the concept of emotional intelligence

The notion that there is more to being effective as a manager or working with people than having a high IQ is persuasive. What matters is how that intelligence is used, especially when relating to people. The term 'emotional intelligence' has become a convenient and recognizable label for this requirement: someone who is poor at dealing with people is described as lacking in emotional intelligence.

Instruments are available for measuring emotional intelligence such as the Trait Emotional Intelligence Questionnaire (Petrides and Furnham, 2000). On the basis of such questionnaires, learning and development programmes can be created for individuals or groups which focus on any weaknesses revealed.

But doubts have been expressed about the notion of emotional intelligence. Locke (2005: 426), a well-respected occupational psychologist, made the following observation:

> the concept of emotional intelligence has now become so broad and the components so variegated that no one concept could possibly encompass or integrate all of them, no matter what the concept was called; it is no longer even an intelligible concept. What is the common or integrating element in a concept that includes: introspection about emotions, emotional expression, non-verbal communication with others, empathy, self-regulation, planning, creative thinking and the direction of attention? There is none.

He suggested that emotional intelligence should be renamed as a skill.

Goleman's mixed model of emotional intelligence, although the most popular, has been heavily criticized. Mayer *et al* (2008) described it as mere 'pop psychology'. There is also the question of whether the concept of emotional intelligence adds anything significant to that of behavioural competencies. Dulewicz and Higgs (1999) have produced a detailed analysis of how the emotional intelligence elements of self-awareness, emotional management, empathy, relationships, communication and personal style correspond to competencies such as sensitivity, flexibility, adaptability, resilience, impact, listening, leadership, persuasiveness, motivating others, energy, decisiveness and achievement motivation. They conclude that there are distinct associations between competency modes and elements of emotional intelligence. There is a danger of confusion if emotional intelligence notions and competency frameworks overlap.

Implications for HR specialists

The main implications for HR specialists of organizational behaviour theory are summarized below.

How organizations function

When involved in organization design bear in mind that, while the highly structured classical model with clearly defined roles and lines of control and communication may appear to be the ideal solution, in practice organizations function differently. It is necessary to take into account the post-bureaucratic school and think of the organization as a portfolio of dynamic processes that overlay and often dominate the vertical, authority-based processes of the hierarchical structure. Similarly, organizational development activities should be based on an analysis and understanding of these dynamic processes.

Organizational culture

While it may not be possible to define an ideal culture or to prescribe how it can be developed, it can at least be stated with confidence that embedded cultures exert considerable influence on organizational behaviour and therefore performance. If there is an appropriate and effective culture it is desirable to take steps to support or reinforce it. If the culture is inappropriate, attempts should be made to determine what needs to be changed and to develop and implement plans for change (approaches to culture management are described in Chapter 13). HR innovations need to take account of the culture in which they will operate. They are likely to fail if they are counter-cultural.

Organizational climate

The perceptions of employees about the organization which form the organization climate need to be assessed and understood so that action can be taken to deal with negative factors. Diagnostic tools, as described in Chapter 13, can be used for this purpose.

Organizational processes

The social processes of interaction and networking, communication, group behaviour, leadership, power, politics and conflict need to be understood and considered when considering ways of improving organizational effectiveness (the ability of an organization to achieve its goals by making effective use of the resources available to it). Social and political factors can affect how HR decisions are made and how well they are implemented.

Individual differences

When designing jobs, preparing learning and development programmes, assessing and counselling staff, developing reward systems and dealing with grievances and disciplinary problems, it is necessary to remember that all people are different. What fulfils or motivates one person may not fulfil or motivate another. Abilities, aptitudes and intelligence differ widely and it is necessary to take particular care in fitting the right people in the right jobs and giving them the right training. Personalities, attitudes and emotions also differ. It is important to focus on how to manage diversity. This should take account of individual differences, which will include any issues arising from the employment of women, people from different ethnic groups, those with disabilities and older people. The predictive effectiveness of GMA tests as selection aids should be noted.

Judgements on personality

Personality should not be judged or measured simplistically in terms of stereotyped traits. People are complex and they change, and account has to be taken of this. The problem for HR specialists and managers in general is that, while they have to accept and understand these differences and take full account of them, they have ultimately to proceed on the basis of fitting them to the requirements of the situation, which are essentially what the organization needs to achieve. There is always a limit to the extent to which an organization that relies on collective effort to achieve its goals can adjust itself to the specific needs of individuals. But the organization has to appreciate that the pressures it places on people can result in stress and therefore can become counter-productive.

Key learning points: Organizational behaviour

People perform their roles within complex systems called organizations. The study of organizational behaviour focuses on how this happens.

Organizational behaviour defined

Organizational behaviour was defined by Huczynski and Buchanan (2007) as the term used to describe 'the study of the structure, functioning, and performance of organizations and the behaviour of groups and individuals within them'.

The sources and applications of organization behaviour theory

Organization behaviour theory is based on the main behavioural science disciplines. These are defined as the fields of enquiry dedicated to the study of human behaviour through sophisticated and rigorous methods.

How organizations function

- An organization is an entity that exists to achieve a purpose through the collective efforts of the people who work in or for it.

- Organizing is the process of making arrangements in the form of defined or understood responsibilities and relationships to enable those people to work cooperatively together.

- Organizations can be described as systems which, as affected by their environment, have a structure that has both formal and informal elements.

- Organization structures are frameworks for getting things done.

- Traditional formal structures were based on laid down hierarchies (lines of command) represented in organization charts, and use was made of closely defined job descriptions.
- But to varying extents organizations operate informally as well as formally by means of a network of roles and relationships that cut across formal organizational boundaries and lines of command.

Organizational culture

The culture of an organization has been described by Deal and Kennedy (2000: 4) as 'the way we do things around here'. Organizational or corporate culture is the pattern of values, norms, beliefs, attitudes and assumptions that may not have been articulated but shape the ways in which people in organizations behave and things get done.

How organizational culture develops

The values and norms that are the basis of culture are formed in four ways:

1 By the leaders in the organization, especially those who have shaped it in the past.

2 Around critical incidents – important events from which lessons are learnt about desirable or undesirable behaviour.

3 From the need to maintain effective working relationships among organization members; this establishes values and expectations.

4 Influenced by the organization's environment. The external environment may be relatively dynamic or unchanging.

The components of culture

Organizational culture can be described in terms of values, norms, artefacts and management style.

Classifying organizational culture (Harrison, 1972):

- *Power-orientated* – competitive, responsive to personality rather than expertise.

- *People-orientated* – consensual, management control rejected.
- *Task-orientated* – focus on competency, dynamic.
- *Role-orientated* – focus on legality, legitimacy and bureaucracy.

Appropriate cultures

It is not possible to say that one culture is better than another, only that a culture is to a greater or lesser extent appropriate in the sense that it is relevant to the needs and circumstances of the organization and helps rather than hinders its performance.

Organizational climate

As defined by Harrison and Shirom (1999), organizational climate refers to 'members' perceptions of organizational features such as decision-making, leadership and norms about work'.

Organizational processes

A number of social processes take place in organizations that affect how they function. These are: interaction and networking, communication, group behaviour, leadership, power, politics and conflict.

Personal characteristics

The personal characteristics that affect people's behaviour at work are their ability, intelligence, personality, attitudes, emotions and emotional intelligence.

Emotional intelligence

Emotional intelligence is a combination of skills and abilities such as self-awareness, self-control, empathy and sensitivity to the feelings of others. Someone with high levels of emotional intelligence should be able to relate to people effectively.

Questions

1 What is organizational behaviour?

2 On what is organizational behaviour theory based?

3 What is an organization?

4 What is organization structure?

5 What is generally agreed to be the most realistic theory of organization?

6 What is organizational culture?

7 How does organizational culture develop?

8 What are the components of culture?

9 How can cultures be classified?

10 What is organizational climate?

11 What are the key organizational processes?

12 What is the big five?

13 What is emotional intelligence?

14 What are the implications of organization theory for HR specialists?

References

Argyle, M (1989) *The Social Psychology of Work*, Harmondsworth, Penguin

Argyris, C (1957) *Personality and Organization*, New York, Harper & Row

Barnard, C (1938) *The Functions of an Executive*, Boston, MA, Harvard University Press

Burns, T and Stalker, G (1961) *The Management of Innovation*, London, Tavistock

Burt, C (1954) The differentiation of intellectual ability, *British Journal of Educational Psychology*, **24**, pp 45–67

Clarke, N (2007) Be selective when choosing emotional intelligence training, *People Management*, 3 May, p 47

Costa, P and McRae, R R (1992) *NEO PI-R: Professional manual*, Odessa, FL, Psychological Assessment Resources

Deal, T and Kennedy, A (2000) *Corporate Cultures*, New York, Perseus Books

Denison, D R (1996) What *is* the difference between organizational culture and organizational climate? A native's point of view on a decade of paradigm wars, *Academy of Management Review*, **21** (3), pp 619–54

Digman, J M (1990) Personality structure: emergence of the five-factor model, *Annual Review of Psychology*, **41**, pp 417–40

Dulewicz, V and Higgs, M (1999) The seven dimensions of emotional intelligence, *People Management*, 28 October, p 53

Eldridge, J and Crombie, A (1974) *The Sociology of Organizations*, London, Allen & Unwin

Emery, F E (1959) *Characteristics of Socio-technical Systems*, London, Tavistock Publications

Fayol, H (1916) *Administration Industrielle et General*, trans C Storrs (1949) as *General and Industrial Management*, London, Pitman

French, W L, Kast, F E and Rosenzweig, J E (1985) *Understanding Human Behaviour in Organizations*, Harper & Row, New York

Furnham, A and Gunter, B (1993) *Corporate Assessment*, London, Routledge

Ghoshal, S and Bartlett, C A (1995) Changing the role of top management: beyond structure to process, *Harvard Business Review*, January–February, pp 86–96

Goleman, D (1995) *Emotional Intelligence*, New York, Bantam

Goleman, D (2000) Leadership that gets results, *Harvard Business Review*, March–April, pp 78–90

Handy, C (1981) *Understanding Organizations*, Harmondsworth, Penguin Books

Harrison, R (1972) Understanding your organization's character, *Harvard Business Review*, September–October, pp 119–28

Harrison, M and Shirom, A (1999) *Organizational Diagnosis and Assessment*, Thousand Oaks, CA, Sage

Herzberg, F W, Mausner, B and Snyderman, B (1957) *The Motivation to Work*, New York, Wiley

Higgs, M (2006) *Change and its Leadership*, New York, Rowland, Fisher, Lennox Consulting

Huczynski, A A and Buchanan, D A (2007) *Organizational Behaviour*, 6th edn, Harlow, FT Pitman

Ivancevich, J M, Konopaske, R and Matteson, M T (2008) *Organizational Behaviour and Management*, 8th edn, New York, McGraw-Hill/Irwin

Jung, C (1923) *Psychological Types*, London, Routledge Kegan Paul

Lawrence, P R and Lorsch, J W (1969) *Developing Organizations*, Reading, MA, Addison-Wesley

Likert, R (1961) *New Patterns of Management*, New York, Harper & Row

Locke, E A (2005) Why emotional intelligence is an invalid concept, *Journal of Organizational Behavior*, **26** (4), pp 425–31

Mayer, J D, Salovey, P and Caruso, D R (2008) Emotional intelligence: new ability or eclectic traits?, *American Psychologist*, **63** (6), pp 503–17

McGregor, D (1960) *The Human Side of Enterprise*, New York, McGraw-Hill

Miller, E and Rice, A (1967) *Systems of Organization*, London, Tavistock

Mischel, W (1968) *Personality and Assessment*, New York, Wiley

Nadler, D A and Tushman, M L (1980) A congruence model for diagnosing organizational behaviour, in (ed) R H Miles, *Resource Book in Macro-organizational Behaviour*, Santa Monica, CA, Goodyear Publishing, pp 30–49

Northouse, P G (2006) *Leadership: Theory and practice*, 4th edn, Thousand Oaks, CA, Sage

Pascale, R (1990) *Managing on the Edge*, London, Viking

Petrides, K V and Furnham, A (2000) On the dimensional structure of emotional intelligence, *Personality and Individual Differences*, **29**, pp 313–20

Roethlisberger, F and Dickson, W (1939) *Management and the Worker*, Cambridge, MA, Harvard University Press

Rousseau, D M (1988) The construction of climate in organizational research, in (eds) L C Cooper and I Robertson, *International Review of Industrial and Organizational Psychology*, Chichester, Wiley

Salovey, P and Mayer, J D (1990) *Emotional Intelligence, Imagination, Cognition and Personality*, **9**, pp 185–211

Schein, E H (1965) *Organizational Psychology*, Englewood Cliffs, NJ, Prentice-Hall

Schein, E H (1984) Coming to a new awareness of culture, *Sloan Management Review*, **25** (2), pp 1–15

Schein, E H (1990) Organizational culture, *American Psychologist*, **45**, pp 109–19

Schmidt, F L and Hunter, J E (1998) The validity and utility of selection methods in personnel psychology: practical and theoretical implications of 85 years of research findings, *Psychological Bulletin*, **124** (2), pp 262–74

Taylor, F W (1911) *Principles of Scientific Management*, New York, Harper

Toplis, J, Dulewicz, V and Fletcher, C (2004) *Psychological Testing*, Institute of Personnel Management, London

Trist, E L, Higgin, G W, Murray, H and Pollock, A B (1963) *Organizational Choice*, London, Tavistock Publications

Tuckman, B (1965) Development sequences in small groups, *Psychological Bulletin*, **63**, pp 123–56

Urwick, L F (1947) *Dynamic Administration*, London, Pitman

Vernon, P E (1961) The *Structure of Human Abilities*, London, Methuen

Weber, M (1946) *From Max Weber*, ed H H Gerth and C W Mills, Oxford, Oxford University Press

Woodward, J (1965) *Industrial Organization*, Oxford, Oxford University Press

Wright, D S and Taylor, A (1970) *Introducing Psychology*, Harmondsworth, Penguin

12
Work, organization and job design

LEARNING OUTCOMES

On completing this chapter you should be able to define these key concepts. You should also know about:

- Work design methodology
- Work system design
- Smart working
- High performance working
- Organization design

- Changes in the nature of work
- Process planning
- Flexible working
- Lean manufacturing
- Job design

Introduction

Work, organization, and job design are three distinct but closely associated processes that establish what work is done in organizations and how it is done. *Work design* deals with the ways in which work is carried out in the work system of a business by teams and individuals. *Organization design* is concerned with deciding how organizations should be structured. *Job design* is about establishing what people in individual jobs or roles are there to do. Although these three activities are dealt with separately in this chapter they share one purpose – to ensure that the organization's work systems and structure operate effectively, make the best use of people in their jobs and roles and take account of the needs of people at work.

In theory, to achieve that purpose, work, organization and job design function sequentially. The work system is designed to meet the specific needs of the business and to deliver value to its customers or clients. An organization structure or system (not all organizations are rigidly structured) has to be developed to enable the work system to operate. The structure is made up of jobs or roles (there is a distinction that will be explained later) which have to be designed in ways that will maximize the extent to which they can be carried out effectively and provide intrinsic motivation, ie motivation from the work itself.

In practice the processes involved can run concurrently – the work system will involve deciding how the work should be organized, and both the work system and organization design processes will define what sort of jobs or roles are required. At the same time, job design considerations will affect how the work is organized and how the work system functions. This chapter deals with each aspect of design separately but it should be remembered that the processes interlink and overlap.

Work design

Work design is the creation of systems of work and a working environment that enhance organizational effectiveness and productivity, ensure that the organization becomes 'a great place in which to work' and are conducive to the health, safety and wellbeing of employees. *Work* involves the exertion of effort and the application of knowledge and skills to achieve a purpose. *Systems of work* are the combined processes, methods and techniques used to get work done. *The work environment* comprises the design of jobs, working conditions and the ways in which people are treated at work by their managers and co-workers as well as the work system. Work design is closely associated with organization and job design in that the latter is conducted within the context of the system of work and the work environment.

To understand the meaning of work design it is necessary first to appreciate what is happening to work and next to review its history.

What is happening to work

The key changes in the contextual and external environment surrounding the world of work have been set out clearly by Parker *et al* (2001). They are:

- a shift away from large-scale industrial production, with a dramatic decline in manufacturing jobs and rise in service work;

- partly as a consequence of this, an increase in customer-facing roles involving some form of emotional behaviour – the requirement for employees to express positive emotions in the way in which they interact with customers;

- significant shifts in the demographics of the workforce in the shape of an increased proportion of women, greater ethnic diversity, more educated employees and an ageing workforce;

- growth in the number of employees engaged in 'knowledge work' – for example, professional services and new product and service development;

- the requirement for a greater variety of products and services and flexibility and agility in responding to customer needs and increased global competition;

- developments in technology affecting the degree to which jobs are involved in IT and become dependent on it;

- shifts from traditional, office or factory-based working to more flexible alternatives, including homeworking;
- a significant increase in the number of employers that an individual employee expects to work for during his or her career.

Work design – a short history

Work design began with the concept of the division of labour originated by Adam Smith (1776). Much later came 'Taylorism', the scientific management movement pioneered by Taylor (1911), which was based on the belief that the most efficient way to do tasks was to remove the responsibility for how to do the work from the individual employee to engineers or managers. The next step was 'Fordism', the moving assembly line introduced by Henry Ford in 1914. Thereafter, the practice of work simplification became embedded in organizations and to a large extent still exists.

The first move away from this situation was provided by the concept of job enrichment popularized by Herzberg (1968: 83), who referred to it as 'vertical job loading'. His definition of the principles and motivators involved is set out in Table 12.1.

This was reinforced by job design theory (Hackman and Oldham, 1974). Another approach was provided by socio-technical systems theory (Emery, 1959), which focused on group rather than individual work and gave rise to the idea of autonomous working groups (self-managing teams).

TABLE 12.1 Vertical job loading (job enrichment) principles and motivators involved

Principles	Motivators involved
Removing some controls while retaining accountability	Responsibility and personal achievement
Increasing the accountability of individuals for own work	Responsibility and personal achievement
Giving a person a complete natural unit of work (module, division, area, and so on)	Responsibility and recognition
Granting additional authority to employees in their activity; job freedom	Responsibility, achievement and recognition
Making periodic reports directly available to the workers themselves rather than to supervisors	Internal recognition
Introducing new and more difficult tasks not previously handled	Growth and learning
Assigning individuals specific or specialized tasks, enabling them to become experts	Responsibility, growth and advancement

SOURCE: Herzberg, 1968: 83

More recently, the notion of 'smart working' has emerged. Essentially, this means managing the work environment to release employees' energy and drive business performance. Smart working, as described in detail later, has been the subject of extensive research conducted on behalf of the CIPD by Capgemini (CIPD, 2008).

However, before examining the notion of smart working it is necessary to remember that it takes place within the system of work, and approaches to work system design are therefore examined first.

Work system design

A system is a set of practices or activities that fit together and interact to achieve a purpose. Work system design is concerned with how the various processes required to make a product or provide a service should operate. It deals with the set of related activities that combine to give a result that customers want. The structure of the system describes the relations between different operations.

A work system may be centred on activities such as manufacturing, chemical processing, information processing, supply, distribution, transport, the provision of public services or customer service. There is usually a choice between different processes within the work system. As the design of the work system affects costs, quality and productivity it is important to provide the best match between the product or service and the process used to make or deliver it.

Process-centred organizations

Process-centred organizations avoid focusing too closely on the design of a rigid work system but instead concentrate on the stream of products or services required and the processes required to ensure that work flows smoothly to the ultimate satisfaction of the customer or client. They have the following features:

- The focus is on horizontal processes that cut across organizational boundaries.
- The overriding objective will be to maintain a smooth flow of work between functions and to achieve synergy by pooling resources from different functions in task forces or project teams.

- The organization will not be based on the old hierarchical 'command and control' structure, ie one that consists of a functional structure with a number of different disciplines and a project structure consisting of project teams drawn from the disciplines. Instead it will be a 'matrix' or 'lattice' organization (a matrix organization is one that consists of a functional structure with a number of different disciplines and a project structure consisting of project teams drawn from the disciplines; a lattice organization is one with a non-hierarchical, flat structure where the emphasis is on horizontal processes, the elimination of boundaries between functions and teamwork).
- There may still be designated functions for, say, manufacturing, sales and distribution. but the emphasis will be on how these areas work together on multi-functional projects to deal with demands such as product/market development.
- Belief in and reliance on teamwork.
- Expansion of traditional jobs and increased emphasis on flexible roles, with employees making decisions and dealing with all types of customer issues.
- Access to all types of information and knowledge throughout the organization.
- Quality and continuous improvement will be regarded as a common responsibility shared between managers and staff from each function.

Process planning

Work system design covers the planning of processes such as flexible manufacturing systems (computer numerical control machines controlled by a central computer which allows fast and easy changes between products), and supply chain management (the control of products from the original suppliers of materials through to the final customers). It may involve facility layout – the physical arrangement of equipment, offices, rooms, work stations (including 'hot-desks' – individual desks shared between several people) and other resources.

Process planning may determine how manufacturing or the provision of a service should be divided into a series of stages such as machines in

FIGURE 12.1 Typical structure of a manufacturing process

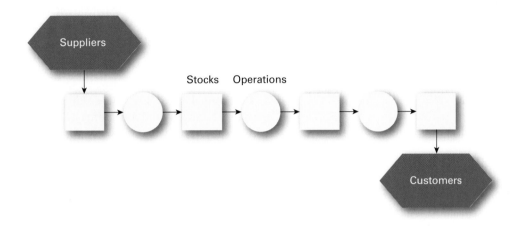

FIGURE 12.2 Customers are more involved in service processes

a production line, each of which uses resources and adds value. Typical process structures are shown in Figures 12.1 and 12.2.

Requirements to be met in work system design

When designing a work system it is necessary to see that it will:

- fit work requirements for efficiency and flexibility;
- ensure the smooth flow of processes or activities, or of materials from supplier to customer;
- facilitate the effective use of resources and the control of waste;
- as far as possible enable employees to gain fulfilment from their work by providing scope for variety, challenge and autonomy;
- encourage cooperative effort through teamworking;
- provide a good work environment in terms of working conditions;
- take account of the need to provide a healthy and safe system of work ('build safety into the system') bearing in mind the need to minimize stress and pay attention to

ergonomic considerations in the design of equipment and work stations to eliminate or at least significantly reduce the risk of such conditions as repetitive strain injury;

- take account of environmental considerations;
- operate generally in accordance with the principles of 'smart working' as described below.

Smart working

As defined by the CIPD (2008: 4), smart working is: 'An approach to organizing work that aims to drive greater efficiency and effectiveness in achieving job outcomes through a combination of flexibility, autonomy and collaboration, in parallel with optimizing tools and working environments for employees.' The characteristics of smart working as established by the CIPD research were:

- self-management – a high degree of autonomy and a philosophy of empowerment;
- the use of virtual teams or work groups;
- focus on outcome-based indicators of performance;
- high-performance working;
- flexibility in work locations and hours;
- use of more advanced communications technology;
- hot-desking and working from home;
- ways of working that are underpinned by or drive high-trust working relationships;
- alignment of smart working with business objectives.

As identified by the CIPD research, typical smart working arrangements include flexible working, high-performance working, 'lean production' and designing jobs in which there is a higher degree of freedom to act. The role of each of those arrangements in work design is described below.

Flexible working

Flexible working is a pattern of working practice or working hours that deviates from the standard or normal arrangement. The aim is to provide for greater operational flexibility, improve the use of employees' skills and capacities, increase productivity and reduce employment costs. Flexible working has become increasingly important as a means of enhancing operational effectiveness.

Flexible working means reconsidering traditional employment patterns. This could include operational flexibility, multi-skilling, the use of sub-contracting and outsourcing, or introducing working arrangements such as flexible hours, job sharing and homeworking.

Forms of operational flexibility

Operational flexibility refers to flexibility in the ways in which work is carried out. The term is sometimes extended to include financial flexibility. The three forms of operational flexibility are:

1 Functional flexibility so that employees can be redeployed quickly and smoothly between activities and tasks. It may require multi-skilling – workers who possess and can apply a number of skills, for example, both mechanical and electrical engineering, or multi-tasking – workers who carry out a number of different tasks in a work team.

2 Structural flexibility in a 'flexible firm' where the core of permanent employees is supplemented by a peripheral group of part-time employees, employees on short- or fixed-term contracts or sub-contracted workers, as described by Doeringer and Priore (1971) and Atkinson (1984).

3 Numerical flexibility, which is associated with structural flexibility and means that the number of employees can be quickly and easily increased or decreased in line with even short-term changes in the level of demand for labour.

Financial flexibility provides for pay levels to reflect the state of supply and demand in the external labour market and also means the use of flexible pay systems that facilitate either functional or numerical flexibility.

Multi-skilling

Multi-skilling takes place when workers acquire through experience and training a range of different skills they can apply when carrying out different tasks (multi-tasking). This means that they can be used flexibly, transferring from one task to another as the occasion demands.

A multi-skilling strategy will mean providing people with a variety of experience through, for example, job rotation and secondments, and by making arrangements for them to acquire new skills through training. It typically includes setting up flexible work teams the members of which can be deployed on all or many of the team's tasks. A flexible employee resourcing policy can then be established that enables the organization to redeploy people rapidly to meet new demands. This implies abandoning the traditional job description which prescribes the tasks to be carried and replacing it with a role profile which specifies the range of knowledge and skills the role holder needs.

Job-sharing

This is an arrangement in which two employees share the work of one full-time position, dividing pay and benefits between them according to the time each works. Job-sharing can mean splitting days or weeks or, less frequently, working alternate weeks. The advantages of job-sharing include reduced employee turnover and absenteeism, because it suits the needs of individuals. Greater continuity results because if one half of the job-sharing team is ill or leaves, the sharer will continue working for at least half the time. Job-sharing also means that a wider employment pool can be tapped for those who cannot work full-time but want permanent employment. The disadvantages are the administrative costs involved and the risk of responsibility being divided.

Hot-desking

Hot-desking means that individual desks are shared between several people who use them at different times. Those involved do not therefore have a permanent work station. This is convenient for the organization but not everyone likes them.

Homeworking

Home-based employees can carry out such roles as consultants, analysts, designers or programmers, or they can undertake administrative work. The advantages are flexibility to respond rapidly to fluctuations in demand, reduced overheads and lower employment costs if the homeworkers are self-employed (care, however, has to be taken to ensure that they are regarded as self-employed for Income Tax and National Insurance purposes).

Flexible hour arrangements

Flexible hour arrangements can be included in a flexibility plan in one or more of the following ways:

- flexible daily hours – these may follow an agreed pattern day by day according to typical or expected workloads (eg flexitime systems);
- flexible weekly hours – providing for longer weekly hours to be worked at certain peak periods during the year;
- flexible daily and weekly hours – varying daily or weekly hours or a combination of both to match the input of hours to the required output. Such working times, unlike daily or weekly arrangements, may fluctuate between a minimum and a maximum;
- compressed working weeks in which employees work fewer than the five standard days;
- annual hours – scheduling employee hours on the basis of the number of hours to be worked, with provisions for the increase or reduction of hours in any given period, according to the demand for goods or services.

High-performance working

High-performance working was defined by Combs *et al* (2006) as the sum of the processes, practices and policies put in place by employers to enable employees to perform to their full potential. They referred to employee participation and flexible working arrangements as examples of such systems that have a direct impact on ways of working and therefore flow through to job design.

Sung and Ashton (2005) defined high-performance work practices as a set or 'bundle' of 35 complementary work practices covering three broad areas:

1 High employee involvement work practices – eg self-directed teams, quality circles and sharing/access to company information.

2 Human resource practices – eg sophisticated recruitment processes, performance appraisals, mentoring and work redesign.

3 Reward and commitment practices – eg various financial rewards, family-friendly policies, job rotation and flexible hours.

Lean manufacturing

Lean manufacturing or lean production, often known simply as 'Lean', is a process improvement methodology developed by Toyota in Japan. Lean focuses on minimizing waste and ensuring the flow of production in order to deliver value to customers. It concentrates initially on the design of the process so that waste can be minimized during manufacture. It then involves paying close attention to operations to identify opportunities to improve the flow of production, remove wasteful practices and engage in continuous improvement. Various tools can be used such as 'FiveS', which is a workplace methodology that uses a list of five words starting with the letter 'S' (sorting, straightening, systematic cleaning, standardizing and sustaining) and reference to these enables a dialogue to take place with employees on how work should be done.

But as noted by the CIPD (2008: 11), the success of Lean depends not so much on the tools but on its approach to work. Lean is implemented by communities of people who carry out and supervise the work and may include stakeholders such as customers. Lean team members will be encouraged to think flexibly and be adaptable to change. Importantly, they will have a sense of ownership of what they do and achieve.

The contribution of job design to smart working

As was noted by the CIPD (2008: 6):

> The term smart work is increasingly being used to refer to the variety of ways in which employers can build autonomy, self-control and development into jobs to pursue an interlinked agenda of employee productivity and business performance ... Many organizations now operate within a flexible environment, but this is not just about the physical work environment. Organizations are providing their people with a greater level of autonomy, choice and freedom than we have seen before.

CASE STUDIES

Work organization: W L Gore

As described by the CIPD (2008: 25–6), W H Gore, which is best known for its GORE-TEX® fabrics, has a non-hierarchical, flat organization structure (a 'lattice' structure). There are no traditional organization charts, no ranks or job titles and no chains of command nor predetermined channels of communication. What is important when recruiting new people is that they have the right fit with Gore's culture. There are no rigid job specifications. Instead, associates make a commitment to contribute individually and collectively to work areas or projects according to their skills. Individuals are encouraged to take an interest in a wide variety of job areas or projects.

Provided the core responsibilities within their role are carried out, associates can then stretch and build on their role to suit their interests, aspirations and the business needs. Gore's 'lattice' structure gives associates the opportunity to use their own judgement, take ownership of work areas and access the resources they need for projects to be successful. Gore's core values and ways of working are built on the principles of 'smart working'. Its unique culture, which fosters creativity, self-motivation, participation and equality, has proved to be a key contributor to associate satisfaction and retention.

Flexible working: B&Q

Flexible working arrangements have been extended at B&Q in association with its diversity strategy. The main components of its flexible working policy are:

- term-time contracts available to parents and grandparents with children/grandchildren up to the age of 16 years (18 if the child is disabled);

- job share for employees who do not want – or are unable – to work full-time; online job-share register available to help individuals find a job-share partner;

- staggered start/finish times, allowing for personal commitments/interests;

- part-time hours;

- split shifts to fit in with employees' personal commitments;

- dual store contracts, allowing employees to work at more than one location;

- one employee/two roles, allowing employees to develop new and different skills, benefit from multi-skilling and work in more than one area of the business;

- home/remote working, allowing employees to work from home or away from their normal workplace on an occasional basis;

- career breaks of three to 12 months can be taken for any reason;

- childcare vouchers available across the organization;

- maternity, paternity and adoption policies enhanced above the statutory minimum;

- shared maternity/paternity leave; unpaid additional leave can be taken by father/partner where both parents work for B&Q and mother returns to work;

- IVF leave: one week paid time off for IVF treatment;

- paid compassionate or carer's leave: one week off per year.

Organization design

Organization design is the process of deciding how organizations should be structured and function. The ways in which work is organized involves all managers when they decide on a day-to-day relatively informal basis how their overall task should be divided between employees. Methods of organizing work can also be determined by more formal organizational reviews, which could focus on a single department or function, a number of departments or the whole business.

In each case, although on differing scales, similar questions arise: 'Who does what?', 'How should activities be grouped together?', 'What lines and means of communication need to be established?', 'Are we doing everything that we ought to be doing and nothing that we ought not to be doing?', 'Have we got too many layers of management or supervision?' These are questions involving people that concern line managers but they also interest HR specialists in their capacity of helping the business to make the best use of its people. HR professionals should be able to contribute to the processes of organization design or redesign because of their understanding of the factors affecting organizational behaviour and because they are in a position to take an overall view of what the business is there to achieve and how it should be organized.

Approaches to organization design today have to take account of the major changes that have been happening to the ways organizations function. As noted by Parker *et al* (2001: 418): 'Organizations … differ from the rather static and inflexible enterprises of earlier times. Greater flexibility is required to enable the rapid delivery of low-cost, high quality and customized products, and to provide increasingly powerful and demanding customers with seamless service.' They also noted that the use of teamworking and other flexible forms of working continues to grow, distinctions between departments are disappearing as organizations become more integrated, and IT has changed the way in which work is conducted.

Aims of organization design

The overall aim of organization design is to *optimize* the arrangements for conducting the affairs of the business or function and thus achieve the 'best fit' between the structure and what the business or function is there to do. The detailed aims of organization design are to:

- clarify the overall purposes of the organization or function – the strategic goals that govern what it does and how it operates;
- define how work should be organized to achieve that purpose, including the use of technology and other work processes;
- ensure that the structure is appropriate to the purpose of the organization or function, the activities it carries out and its work systems;
- define as precisely as possible the key activities involved in carrying out the work;
- group these activities logically together to avoid unnecessary overlap or duplication;
- provide for the integration of activities and the achievement of cooperative effort and teamwork;
- build flexibility into the system so that arrangements can adapt quickly to new situations and challenges;
- provide for the rapid communication of information;
- define the role and function of each organizational or functional unit so that all concerned know how it plays its part in achieving the overall purpose;
- clarify individual roles, accountabilities and authorities;

- take account of individual needs and aspirations;
- decide how to overcome what has been called by Huczynski and Buchanan (2007) 'the organizational dilemma', meaning the question of how to reconcile the potential inconsistency between individual needs and aspirations on the one hand, and the collective purpose of the organization on the other;
- design jobs to make the best use of the skills and capacities of the job holders and to provide them with high levels of motivation from the work itself (intrinsic motivation);
- plan and implement organization development activities to ensure that the various processes operate in a manner that contributes to organizational effectiveness;
- set up teams and project groups as required to be responsible for specific processing, development, professional or administrative activities or for the conduct of projects.

Conducting organization reviews

These aims are achieved through organizational reviews, which can be conducted in the following stages:

1 *An analysis* of the existing arrangements and the factors that may affect the organization now and in the future.

2 *A diagnosis* of the problems and issues facing the organization and what therefore needs to be done to improve the way in which the organization is structured and functions.

3 *The choice* in the light of this analysis and diagnosis of how the business or part of it should be designed or revised.

4 *A plan* to implement any revisions to the structure, possibly in phases.

Organization analysis

The starting point for an organization review is an analysis of the existing circumstances, structure and processes of the organization and an assessment of the strategic issues that might affect it in the future. This covers the following areas.

The external environment

This includes the economic, market, competitive, social and legal matters that may affect the organization. Plans for product/market development will be significant.

The internal environment

This is mission, organization culture and climate, management style, technology, work systems and processes of the organization as they affect the way it functions and should be structured to carry out its function. Technological developments may be particularly important as well as the introduction of processes such as just-in-time or a new computer system.

Strategic issues and objectives

As a background to the study it is necessary to identify the strategic issues facing the organization and its objectives. These may be considered under such headings as growth, competition, and market position and standing. Issues concerning the availability of the required human, financial and physical resources would also have to be considered.

Activities

Activity analysis establishes what work is done and what needs to be done in the organization to achieve its objectives within its environment. The analysis should cover what is and is not being done, who is doing it and where, and how much is being done. An answer is necessary to the key questions: 'Are all the activities required properly catered for?', 'Are there any unnecessary activities being carried out, ie those that do not need to be done at all or which could be conducted more economically and efficiently by external contractors or providers?'

Structure

The analysis of structure covers how activities are grouped together, the number of levels in the hierarchy, the extent to which authority is decentralized to divisions and strategic business units (SBUs), where functions such as finance, HR, IT and research and development are placed in the structure (eg as central functions or integrated into divisions or SBUs) and the relationships that exist between different units and functions (with particular attention being given to the way in which they communicate and cooperate with one another). Attention would be paid to such issues as the logic of the way in which activities are grouped and decentralized, the span of control of managers (the number of separate functions or people they are directly responsible for), any overlap between functions or gaps leading to the neglect of certain activities, and the existence of unnecessary departments, units, functions or layers of management.

It is necessary to bear in mind that structural requirements in organizations or organizational units will vary widely according to what they are there to do and the activities they have to carry out. That is why there are no absolute principles such as the traditional precepts of 'unity of command' (one person, one boss) or the need to limit spans of control (the number of functions or people for which a manager is responsible). It all depends. Burns and Stalker (1961) established in their study of electronic companies in Scotland that in stable conditions a highly structured or 'mechanistic' organization will emerge with specialized functions, clearly defined roles, strict administrative routines and a hierarchical system of exercising control. However, when the environment is volatile, a rigid system of ranks and routine will inhibit the organization's speed and sensitivity of response. In these circumstances the structure is, or should be, 'organic' in the sense that is a function of the situation in which the enterprise finds itself rather than conforming to any predetermined and rigid view of how it should operate.

For example, in a process-based organization there will still be designated functions for, say, manufacturing, sales and distribution. But the emphasis will be on how these areas work together on multi-functional projects to deal with new demands such as product/market development. Teams will jointly consider ways of responding to customer requirements. Quality and continuous improvement will be regarded as a common responsibility shared between managers and staff from each function. The overriding objective will be to maintain a smooth flow of work between functions and to achieve synergy by pooling resources from different functions in task forces or project teams.

Organization diagnosis

The aim of the diagnosis is to establish, on the basis of the analysis, the reasons for any structural problems facing the organization or function.

Organizational choice

There is never one best way of organizing anything. There is always a choice. In a relatively stable manufacturing business, a traditional 'line and staff' structure may be appropriate. This is one consisting of line managers who exist to carry out the primary functions of the organization, and staff functions such as finance and HR that exist to support the line. There may be a choice on how to structure the organization into separate divisions – these could be functions such as manufacturing or research and development, or based on products, regions or markets.

In a consultancy a matrix organization is required. In a process-based organization where the emphasis is on horizontal processes a 'lattice' structure may emerge. A knowledge-based and innovative business will choose not to bother about rigid structures and will instead concentrate on achieving organizational agility – the ability to respond flexibly to new challenges. These are the 'organic structures' described by Burns and Stalker (1961), which evolve to meet the requirements of their processes and environment rather than being specifically designed.

The organizational analysis will help in the evaluation of the alternatives, but the law of the situation, as described originally by Follett (1924), should prevail. This states that the work that people are required to do depends on the objective requirements of the situation. The final choice will depend upon the context and circumstances of the organization – as Lupton (1975) pointed out, it is important to achieve best fit.

The concept of strategic choice, as developed by Child (1972), emphasized the significance of persuading the leadership group (the dominant coalition) to influence the structures of the organizations through an essentially political process. In 1997 Child pointed out that strategic choice analysis regards debate and negotiation in the social networks existing in organizations as integral to decision making on organizational priorities, policies, structures and actions.

Organization structures are generally strongly influenced by personal and human considerations – the inclinations of top management, the strengths and weaknesses of management generally, the availability of people to work in the new organization and the need to take account of the feelings of those who will be exposed to change. Cold logic may sometimes have to override these considerations. If it does, then it needs to be deliberate and the consequences must be appreciated and allowed for when planning the implementation of the new organization. It may have to be accepted that a logical regrouping of activities cannot be introduced in the short term because no one with the experience is available to manage the new activities, or because capable individuals are so firmly entrenched in one area that to uproot them would cause serious damage to their morale and would reduce the overall effectiveness of the new organization.

The worst sin that organization designers can commit is that of imposing their own ideology on the organization. Their job is to be eclectic in their knowledge, sensitive in their analysis of the situation and deliberate in their approach to the evaluation of alternatives.

Implementation

Having made the choice and planned the structures, relationships and roles, it is necessary to consider how the new organization should be implemented. It may be advisable to stage implementation over a number of phases, especially if new people have to be found and trained.

Successful organization design

Research conducted by Whittington and Molloy (2005) indicated that to achieve success in organization design it is necessary to:

- obtain top management support, especially personal commitment and political support;
- avoid piecemeal, uncoordinated change initiatives by making a strategic business case that anticipates implications across the entire organization;
- achieve substantive, rather than tokenistic, employee involvement in the change process,

moving beyond communication to active engagement;

- invest in communications with external stakeholders, including customers, suppliers and financial stakeholders;

- involve HR professionals closely, right from the start – involving HR has been proved to positively impact on a range of performance outcomes;

- maintain effective project management disciplines;

- build skilled change management teams, with the right mix of experience and abilities, that can work together.

An organization design toolkit is provided in Chapter 59.

Job design

Job design specifies the contents of jobs in order to satisfy work requirements and meet the personal needs of the job holder, thus increasing levels of employee engagement. As observed by Wall and Clegg (1998: 265):

> Jobs are created by people for people. Whether deliberately or by default, choices are made about which tasks to group together to form a job, the extent to which job holders should follow prescribed procedures in completing those tasks, how closely the job incumbent will be supervised, and numerous other aspects of the work. Such choices are the essence of job design.

Jobs and roles

A distinction can be made between jobs and roles. A *job* is an organizational unit consisting of a group of defined tasks or activities to be carried out or duties to be performed. A *role* is the part played by individuals and the patterns of behaviour expected of them in fulfilling their work requirements. Jobs are about tasks, roles are about people. This distinction means that while jobs may be designed to fit work requirements, roles are developed as people work flexibly, demonstrate that they can do more and take on different responsibilities.

Factors affecting job design

Deciding on the content of a job starts from work requirements because that is why the job exists. When the tasks to be done have been determined it is then necessary to consider how the jobs can be set up to provide the maximum degree of intrinsic motivation for those who have to carry them out with a view to improving performance and productivity. Consideration has also to be given to another important aim of job design: to fulfil the social responsibilities of the organization to the people who work in it by improving the quality of working life, an aim which, as stated in Wilson's (1973) report on this subject, depends upon both efficiency of performance and satisfaction of the worker.

Clearly, the content of a job depends on the work system in which it exists and the organization structure in which it is placed. Job design therefore happens within the context of work and organization design, as described in this chapter, but it is also affected by the following factors:

- the characteristics of jobs;
- the characteristics of task structure;
- the process of intrinsic motivation;
- the job characteristics model;
- the implications of group activities.

The characteristics of jobs

There are three fundamental characteristics shared by all jobs:

1 Job range – the number of operations a job holder performs to complete a task.

2 Job depth – the amount of discretion a job holder has to decide job activities and job outcomes.

3 Job relationships – the interpersonal relationships between job holders and their managers and co-workers.

Task structure

Job design requires the assembly of a number of tasks into a job or a group of jobs. An individual may carry out one main task that consists of a number of interrelated elements or functions. Or task functions may be allocated to a team working closely together in a manufacturing 'cell' or customer service unit, or strung along an assembly line. In more complex jobs, individuals may carry out a variety of connected tasks (multi-tasking), each with a number of functions, or these tasks may be allocated to a team of workers or divided between them. In the latter case, the tasks may require a variety of skills that have to be possessed by all members of the team (multi-skilling) in order to work flexibly. Complexity in a job may be a reflection of the number and variety of tasks to be carried out, the different skills or competencies to be used, the range and scope of the decisions that have to be made, or the difficulty of predicting the outcome of decisions.

The internal structure of each task consists of three elements: *planning* (deciding on the course of action, its timing and the resources required), *executing* (carrying out the plan), and *controlling* (monitoring performance and progress and taking corrective action when required). A completely integrated job includes all these elements for each of the tasks involved. The worker, or group of workers, having been given objectives in terms of output, quality and cost targets, decides on how the work is to be done, assembles the resources, performs the work, and monitors output, quality and cost standards. Responsibility in a job is measured by the amount of authority someone has to do all these things.

The ideal arrangement from the point of view of engagement and motivation is to provide for fully integrated jobs containing all three task elements. In practice, management and team leaders are often entirely responsible for planning and control, leaving the worker responsible for execution. To a degree, this is inevitable, but one of the aims of job design is often to extend the responsibility of workers into the functions of planning and control. This can involve empowerment – giving individuals and teams more responsibility for decision making and ensuring that they have the training, support and guidance to exercise that responsibility properly.

Intrinsic motivation

The case for using job design techniques is based on the premise that effective performance and genuine satisfaction in work follow mainly from the intrinsic content of the job. This is related to the fundamental concept that people are motivated when they are provided with the means to achieve their goals. Work provides the means to earn money, which as an extrinsic reward satisfies basic needs and is instrumental in providing ways of satisfying higher-level needs. But work also provides intrinsic rewards related to achievement, responsibility and the opportunity to use and develop skills that are more under the control of the worker.

The job characteristics model

The most influential model for job design is the job characteristics model developed by Hackman and Oldham (1974). They identified five core job characteristics:

1 Skill variety: the degree to which a job requires an employee to perform activities that challenge his or her skills and abilities.

2 Task identity: the degree to which the job requires completion of an identifiable piece of work.

3 Task significance: the degree to which the job outcome has a substantial impact on others.

4 Autonomy: the degree to which the job gives an employee freedom and discretion in scheduling work and determining how it is performed.

5 Feedback: the degree to which an employee gets information about the effectiveness of his or her efforts – with particular emphasis on feedback directly related to the work itself rather than from a third party (for example, a manager).

Hackman and Oldham explained that if the design of a job satisfied the core job characteristics the employee would perceive that the work was worthwhile, would feel responsible for the work and would know if the work had been completed satisfactorily. The outcome of this would be high-quality work performance and high job satisfaction as a result of intrinsic motivation.

The implications of group activities

Jobs should never be considered in isolation. All job holders belong to formal or informal groups and the interrelationships that exist in such groups should be considered when looking at the content of an individual job.

Approaches to job design

Job design starts with an analysis of task requirements, using the job analysis techniques described in Chapter 48. These requirements will be a function of the system of work and the organization structure. As described by Robertson and Smith (1985), the method can be based on the job characteristics model as follows:

1 Influence skill variety by providing opportunities for people to do several tasks and by combining tasks.

2 Influence task identity by combining tasks to form natural work units.

3 Influence task significance by forming natural work units and informing people of the importance of their work.

4 Influence autonomy by giving people responsibility for determining their own working systems.

5 Influence feedback by establishing good relationships and opening feedback channels.

These methods influence the five approaches to job design described below.

Job rotation

This is the movement of employees from one task to another to reduce monotony by increasing variety.

Job enlargement

This means combining previously fragmented tasks into one job, again to increase the variety and meaning of repetitive work.

Job enrichment

This goes beyond job enlargement to add greater autonomy and responsibility to a job. Job enrichment aims to maximize the interest and challenge of work by providing the employee with a job that has these characteristics:

- it is a complete piece of work in the sense that the worker can identify a series of tasks or activities that end in a recognizable and definable product;

- it affords the employee as much variety, decision-making responsibility and control as possible in carrying out the work;

- it provides direct feedback through the work itself on how well the employee is doing his or her job.

As described by Herzberg (1968), job enrichment is not just increasing the number or variety of tasks, nor is it the provision of opportunities for job rotation. These approaches may relieve boredom, but they do not result in positive increases in motivation.

Self-managing teams (autonomous work groups)

These are self-regulating teams who work largely without direct supervision. The philosophy on which this technique is based is a logical extension of job enrichment but is strongly influenced by socio-technical systems theory (see Chapter 11). A self-managing team enlarges individual jobs to include a wider range of operative skills (multiskilling), decides on methods of work and the planning, scheduling and control of work, distributes tasks itself among its members, and monitors its own performance, taking corrective action when required.

The advocates of self-managing teams or autonomous work groups claim that this approach offers a more comprehensive view of organizations than the rather simplistic individual motivation theories that underpin job rotation, enlargement and enrichment. Be that as it may, the strength of this system is that it takes account of the social or group factors and the technology as well as the individual motivators.

In a study of customer service representatives in a telecommunications company, Batt (1999) found that work organized into self-managed teams led to better service and sales performance (an increase of 9.2 per cent per employee) than traditional work designs, and that the interactive effect of self-managed teams and new technology raised sales by an additional 17.4 per cent.

Choice of approach

Of the five approaches described above, it is generally recognized that, although job rotation and job enlargement have their uses in developing skills and relieving monotony, they do not go to the root of the requirements for intrinsic motivation and for meeting the various motivating characteristics of jobs. These are best satisfied by using, as appropriate, job enrichment, autonomous work groups, or high-performance work design.

High-performance work design

This concentrates on setting up working groups in environments where high levels of performance can be achieved. As described by Buchanan (1987), this requires management to define what it needs in the form of methods of production and the results expected from its introduction. It involves multi-skilling – job demarcation lines are eliminated as far as possible and encouragement and training

are provided for employees to acquire new skills. Self-managed teams are set up with full responsibility for planning, controlling and monitoring the work.

Role development

Role development is the continuous process through which roles are defined or modified as work proceeds and evolves. Job design as described above takes place when a new job is created or an existing job is changed, often following a reorganization or the introduction of a new work system. But the part people play in carrying out their roles can

---

Key learning points: Work, organization and job design (1)

Work, organization and job design

These are three distinct but closely associated processes that establish what work is done in organizations and how it is done.

Work design

Work design is the creation of systems of work and a working environment that enhance organizational effectiveness and productivity, ensure that the organization becomes 'a great place in which to work' and are conducive to the health, safety and wellbeing of employees.

Work system design

Work system design is concerned with how the processes required to make a product or provide a service should operate. It deals with the set of related activities that combine to give a result that customers want. The structure of the system describes the relations between different operations.

Smart working

The CIPD (2008: 4) defined smart working as: 'An approach to organizing work that aims to drive

greater efficiency and effectiveness in achieving job outcomes through a combination of flexibility, autonomy and collaboration, in parallel with optimizing tools and working environments for employees.'

Flexible working

Flexible working is a pattern of working practice or working hours that deviates from the standard or normal arrangement.

High-performance working

High-performance working was defined by Combs *et al* (2006) as the sum of the processes, practices and policies put in place by employers to enable employees to perform to their full potential.

Lean manufacturing

A process improvement methodology developed by Toyota. 'Lean' focuses on minimizing waste and ensuring the flow of production in order to deliver value to customers.

evolve over time as people grow into them and grow with them and as incremental changes take place in the scope of the work and the degree to which individuals have freedom to act (their autonomy). Roles will be developed as people develop in them – responding to opportunities and changing demands, acquiring new skills and developing competencies.

Role development takes place in the context of day-to-day work and is therefore a matter between managers and the members of their teams. It means agreeing definitions of accountabilities, objectives and competency requirements as they evolve. When these change – as they probably will in all except the most routine jobs – it is desirable to achieve mutual understanding of new expectations.

The process of understanding how roles are developing and agreeing the implications can take place through performance management in which the regularly updated performance agreement spells out agreed outcomes (key result areas) and competency requirements. It is necessary to ensure that managers and team leaders define roles within the performance management framework, taking into account the principles of job design set out above.

Key learning points: Work, organization and job design (2)

Aims of organization design

The overall aim of organization design is to optimize the arrangements for conducting the affairs of the business or function and thus achieve the 'best fit' between the structure and what the business or function is there to do.

Organization analysis

The starting point for an organization review is an analysis of the existing circumstances, structure and processes of the organization and an assessment of the strategic issues that might affect it in the future.

Organization diagnosis

The aim of the diagnosis is to establish, on the basis of the analysis, the reasons for any structural problems facing the organization or function.

Organizational choice

There is never one best way of organizing anything. There is always a choice.

Job design

Job design specifies the contents of jobs in order to satisfy work requirements and meet the personal needs of the job holder, thus increasing levels of employee engagement.

Jobs and roles

A *job* is an organizational unit consisting of a group of defined tasks or activities to be carried out or duties to be performed. A *role* is the part played by individuals and the patterns of behaviour expected of them in fulfilling their work requirements. Jobs are about tasks, roles are about people.

The job characteristics model

The job characteristics model was developed by Hackman and Oldham (1974). They identified five core job characteristics: skill variety, task identity, task significance, autonomy, and feedback.

Approaches to job design

Job design starts with an analysis of task requirements, using job analysis techniques.

Role development

Role development is the continuous process through which roles are defined or modified as work proceeds and evolves.

Questions

1 What is work design?
2 What is work system design?
3 What is smart working?
4 What are the main forms of operational flexibility?
5 What is a flexible firm?
6 What are the overall aims of organization design?
7 What are the stages of an organization review?
8 What is job design?
9 What is the difference between a job and a role?
10 What is the job characteristics model?
11 What is job enrichment?
12 What is role development?

References

Atkinson, J (1984) Manpower strategies for flexible organizations, *Personnel Management*, August, pp 28–31

Batt, R (1999) Work organization, technology and performance in customer service and sales, *Industrial and Labor Relations Review*, **52** (4), pp 539–64

Buchanan, D (1987) Job enrichment is dead: long live high performance work design!, *Personnel Management*, May, pp 40–43

Burns, T and Stalker, G (1961) *The Management of Innovation*, London, Tavistock

Child, J (1972) Organizational structure, environment and performance: the role of strategic choice, *Sociology*, **6** (1), pp 1–22

Child, D (1997) Strategic choice in the analysis of action, structure, organizations and environment: retrospective and prospective, *Organizational Studies*, **18** (1), pp 43–76

CIPD (2008) *Smart Working: How smart is UK PLC? Findings from organizational practice*, London, CIPD

Combs, J, Liu, Y and Hall, A (2006) How much do high-performance work practices matter? A meta-analysis of their effects on organizational performance, *Personnel Psychology*, **59** (3), pp 501–28

Doeringer, P and Priore, M (1971) *Internal Labor Markets and Labor Market Analysis*, Lexington, DC, Heath

Emery, F E (1959) *Characteristics of Socio-technical Systems*, London, Tavistock Publications

Follett, M P (1924) Creative *Experience*, New York, Longmans Green

Hackman, J R and Oldham, G R (1974) Motivation through the design of work: test of a theory, *Organizational Behaviour and Human Performance*, **16** (2), pp 250–79

Herzberg, F (1968) One more time: how do you motivate employees?, *Harvard Business Review*, January–February, pp 109–20

Huczynski, A A and Buchanan, D A (2007) *Organizational Behaviour*, 6th edn, Harlow, FT Prentice Hall

Lupton, T (1975) Best fit in the design of organizations, *Personnel Review*, **4** (1), pp 15–22

Parker, S K, Wall, T D and Cordery, J L (2001) Future work design research and practice: towards an elaborated model of work design, *Journal of Occupational and Organizational Psychology*, **74** (4), pp 413–40

Robertson, I T and Smith, M (1985) *Motivation and Job Design*, London, IPM

Smith, A (1776) *The Wealth of Nations*, Penguin Books, Harmondsworth, 1986

Sung, J and Ashton, D (2005) *High Performance Work Practices: Linking strategy and skills to performance outcomes*, London, DTI

Taylor, F W (1911) *Principles of Scientific Management*, New York, Harper

Wall, T D and Clegg, C (1998) Job design, in (ed) N Nicholson, *Blackwell's Encyclopaedic Dictionary of Organizational Behaviour*, Oxford, Blackwell, pp 265–8

Whittington, R and Molloy, E (2005) *HR's Role in Organizing: Shaping change*, London, CIPD

Wilson, N A B (1973) *On the Quality of Working Life*, London, HMSO

13
Organization development

LEARNING OUTCOMES

On completing this chapter you should be able to define these key concepts. You should also understand:

- The meaning of organization development
- The contents of traditional organization development (OD) programmes
- The criticisms made of the original OD concept
- How OD has moved on since it was first introduced
- The nature of organization development today including the processes of diagnosis and programming

Introduction

Work, organization and job design provide the basic ingredients for operating a business. But is it is necessary to see that the processes involved function well, which is what organization development aims to do. In this chapter, organization development is defined and its somewhat chequered history is described, from its origins as 'OD' to the more focused and business-like approaches adopted today. This leads to a discussion of organization development strategy and an examination of organization development in practice involving the use of diagnostics as the basis for preparing organization development programmes.

Organization development defined

Organization development is a systematic approach to improving organizational capability, which is concerned with process – how things get done. As expressed by Beer (1980: 10), OD operates as 'A system wide process of data collection, diagnosis, action planning, intervention and evaluation.'

Organization development in its traditional form as OD was later defined by Rowlandson (1984: 90) as 'an intervention strategy that uses group processes to focus on the whole culture of an organization in order to bring about planned change'. More recently, the CIPD (2010: 1) defined it broadly as a 'planned and systematic approach to enabling sustained organization performance through the involvement of its people'.

The nature of organization development

Organization development in its original version as OD was based on behavioural science concepts, ie the field of enquiry dedicated to the study of human behaviour through sophisticated and rigorous methods. OD was practised through what were called 'interventions'.

However, during the 1980s and 1990s a number of other approaches were introduced and further changes occurred in the following decade during which a more strategic focus was adopted and more business-focused activities such as smart working and high-performance working came to the fore. It is these changes that led to the broader definition produced by the CIPD.

Organization development used to be the province of specialized consultants who tended to practise it as a mystery, with HR playing a supporting role if it played any role at all. But *HR Magazine* spelt out the close relationship between HR and organization development as follows.

> ### Source review
>
> HR and organization development – *HR Magazine* (2007: 1)
>
> To remain competitive in today's global marketplace, organizations must change. One of the most effective tools to promote successful change is organization development (OD). As HR increasingly focuses on building organizational learning, skills and workforce productivity, the effective use of OD to help achieve company business goals and strategies is becoming a broad HR competency as well as a key strategic HR tool. While there are variations regarding the definition of OD, the basic purpose of organization development is to increase an organization's effectiveness through planned interventions related to the organization's processes (often company-wide), resulting in improvements in productivity, return on investment and employee satisfaction.

The CIPD (2010: 3) stated that: 'We place considerable importance on OD, seeing it as one of the ten professional areas within the HR profession map which emphasizes its importance as a HR skill.' The CIPD also commented that:

> OD is not a new discipline and has always had a focus on people but has only relatively recently become considered as a mainstream discipline of HR. Supporters of OD argue that its strength is its ability to understand the whole organization and

as such it may be inhibiting to root it too firmly in the HR function. However, given the increasing need for the HR profession to act as a business partner, OD and its methods have a part to play in developing HR's strategic role and its involvement in organizational change, organizational culture and employee engagement. (*ibid*: 3)

The strategic nature of organization development as an integral part of HRM arises because it can play a significant role in the implementation of business strategy. For example, a strategy for business model innovation (the process followed by an organization to develop a new business model or change an existing one) could result in the need for new organization structures and processes. This would involve organization development and change management activities. The aim of this chapter is to explain the purpose of organization development in the light of an analysis of the history of the concept and how it can be applied as part of a strategic HRM approach.

The story of organization development

There are three chapters in the story of organizational development: the original version of the 1960s and 70s, the extensions and modifications to the original approach in the 1980s and 90s, and the new look at organization development of the 2000s.

The first chapter – the original version

Organization development emerged as the 'OD' movement in the 1960s. It was based on the strong humanistic values of its early founders, who wanted to improve the conditions of people's lives in organizations by applying behavioural science knowledge. Its origins can be traced to the writings of behavioural scientists such as Lewin (1947, 1951) on group dynamics (the improvement of group processes through various forms of training, eg team building, interactive skills training, T-groups) and change management. Other behavioural scientists included Maslow (1954) who produced his needs theory of motivation, Herzberg *et al* (1957) who wrote about

the motivation to work, and Argyris (1957) who emphasized the need to plan for integration and involvement. McGregor (1960) produced his 'Theory Y', which advocates the recognition of the needs of both the organization and the individual on the basis that given the chance, people will not only accept but seek responsibility. Likert (1961) added his theory of supportive relationships.

The two founders of the organization development movement were Beckhard (1969) who probably coined the term, and Bennis (1969) who, according to Buchanan and Huczynski (2007: 575), described OD as a 'truth, trust, love and collaboration approach'. Ruona and Gibson (2004: 53) explained that:

> Early OD interventions can be categorized as primarily focusing on individuals and interpersonal relations. OD was established as a social philosophy that emphasized a long-term orientation, the applied behavioural sciences, external and process-oriented consultation, change managed from the top, a strong emphasis on action research and a focus on creating change in collaboration with managers.

The objectives, assumptions and values of the original version of OD

As originally conceived, OD programmes aimed to increase the effectiveness of the various processes that take place in organizations, especially those relating to the ways in which people work together. It was also concerned with improving the quality of working life of people. The original OD philosophy was that of humanism – the belief that human factors are paramount in the study of organizational behaviour. This led to an approach that focused on the needs of people as individuals and in groups with an emphasis on process – how people worked together and how this could be improved. The assumptions and values of OD were that:

- Most individuals are driven by the need for personal growth and development as long as their environment is both supportive and challenging.

- The work team, especially at the informal level, has great significance for feelings of satisfaction, and the dynamics of such teams have a powerful effect on the behaviour of their members.

- Organizations can be more effective if they learn to diagnose their own strengths and weaknesses.

- Managers often do not know what is wrong and need special help in diagnosing problems, although the outside 'process consultant' ensures that decision making remains in the hands of the client.

Traditional OD programmes

OD during this time was practised predominantly by external consultants working with senior managers. Personnel specialists were not involved to any great extent. OD programmes consisted then of 'interventions' such as those listed below. In OD jargon an intervention is a planned activity designed to improve organizational effectiveness or manage change. The following are the traditional OD interventions; they can still feature in current programmes:

- *Process consultation* – helping clients to generate and analyse information that they can understand and, following a thorough diagnosis, act upon. The information relates to organizational processes such as inter-group relations, interpersonal relations and communications.

- *Change management* – often using the techniques advocated by Lewin (1951), which consisted of processes of managing change by unfreezing, changing and freezing, and force-field analysis (analysing and dealing with the driving forces that affect transition to a future state).

- *Action research* – collecting data from people about process issues and feeding it back in order to identify problems and their likely causes as a basis for an action plan to deal with the problem.

- *Survey feedback* – a variety of action research in which data is systematically collected about the system through attitude surveys and workshops leading to action plans.

- *Group dynamics* – improving the ways in which people work together by means of programmes that aim to increase the effectiveness of groups through various forms of training, eg team building,

interactive skills training and T-groups ('training groups', which aim to increase sensitivity, diagnostic ability and action skills).

- *Personal interventions* – developing interpersonal skills through such processes as transactional analysis (an approach to understanding how people behave and express themselves through transactions with others), behaviour modelling (the use of positive reinforcement and corrective feedback to change behaviour) and neuro-linguistic programming or NLP (teaching people to programme their reactions to others and develop unconscious strategies for interacting with them).

The second chapter – criticisms of the original version of OD and new approaches

The OD movement as originally conceived and practised was characterized by what Buchanan and Huczynski (2007: 559) called 'quasi-religious values' with some of the features of a religious movement, which, they claimed, is one reason why it has survived as a concept in spite of the criticisms that began to be levelled at it in the 1980s. Weidner (2004: 39) wrote that: 'OD was something that practitioners felt and lived as much as they *believed*' (original emphasis).

One of the earliest critics was McLean (1981: 4) who noted 'the moral and ethical misgivings concerned with the development of what might be regarded as a sophisticated science of manipulation'. He cited a comment by Strauss (1976) that at times OD is little more than abstract moralization and asserted that:

> It is becoming increasingly apparent that there exists a considerable discrepancy between OD as practised and the prescriptive stances taken by many OD writers … The theory of change and change management which is the foundation of most OD programmes is based on over-simplistic generalizations which offer little specific guidance to practitioners faced with the confusing complexity of a real change situation. (*ibid*: 13)

Armstrong (1984: 113) commented that: 'Organization development has lost a degree of credibility in recent years because the messianic zeal displayed by some practitioners has been at variance with the circumstances and real needs of the organization.' Burke (1995: 8) stated that 'in the mid-1970s, OD was still associated with T-groups, participative management and consensus, Theory Y, and self-actualization – the soft human, touchy-feely kinds of activities'.

An even more powerful critic was Legge (1995: 212), who observed that the OD rhetoric fitted the era of 'flower power' and that: 'OD was seen, on the one hand as a form of devious manipulation, and on the other as "wishy-washy" and ineffectual.' She noted 'the relative lack of success of OD initiatives in effecting major and lasting cultural change, with the aim of generating commitment to new values in the relatively small number of organizations in which it was tried' (*ibid*: 213), and produced the following devastating critique.

Source review

A critique of organization development – Legge (1995: 213)

In order to cope with an increasingly complex and changing environment, many of the initiatives were, in retrospect, surprisingly inward looking, involving schemes of management development, work system design, attempts at participation, almost as a good in their own right, without close attention as to how they were to deliver against market-driven organizational success criteria. The long-term nature of OD activities, together with difficulties to clearly establishing to sceptics their contribution to organizational success criteria (and within a UK culture of financial short-termism) rendered the initiatives at best marginal ... and at worst to be treated with a cynical contempt.

The main criticisms of OD, as noted by Marsh *et al* (2010: 143), were that it was 'Orientated to process and tools rather than results ... where techniques are considered to be ends in themselves rather than a means to deliver organizational performance.'

During the 1980s and 90s an alternative approach emerged, that of culture management, which aimed at achieving cultural change as a means of enhancing organizational capability. Culture change or management programmes start with an analysis of the existing culture, which may involve the use of a diagnostic such as the 'Organizational Culture Inventory' devised by Cooke and Lafferty (1989). The desired culture is then defined – one that enables the organization to function effectively and achieve its strategic objectives. As a result, a 'culture gap' is identified, which needs to be filled. This analysis of culture identifies behavioural expectations so that HR processes can be used to develop and reinforce them. This sounds easier than it really is. Culture is a complex and often hard to define notion and it is usually strongly embedded and therefore difficult to change. Anthony (1990: 4) argued that: 'The management of culture ... purports to define the meaning of people's lives so that they become concomitant with the organization's view of itself. [It is] the adjustment of human meaning for organizational ends.' He also observed that: 'Published cases do exist of organizations within which major changes in culture have been successfully accomplished and shown to persist but they are rare' (*ibid*: 5). However, culture management became a process in its own right and OD consultants jumped on the bandwagon.

Culture management involves change management, another important item in the OD toolkit. But as Caldwell (2003: 132) argued: 'It is assumed within most OD models that change can be planned in a "rational" or linear manner, and that the change agent can facilitate this group process, although there is little evidence to support this illusion of "manageability".'

Other movements in this period that could be described as organization development activities but can exist as distinct entities included total quality management (TQM) and quality circles. TQM aims to ensure that all activities within an organization happen in the way they have been planned in order to meet the defined needs of customers. Its approach is holistic – quality management is not a separate function to be treated in isolation, but is an integral part of all operations. Quality circles are groups of volunteers engaged in related work who meet regularly to discuss and propose ways of improving working methods under a trained leader.

Another approach more closely related to OD that emerged at this time was organizational transformation. This was defined by Cummins and

Worley (2005: 752) as 'A process of radically altering the organization's strategic direction, including fundamental changes in structures, processes and behaviours.'

Holistic approaches to improving organizational capability emerging in this period, which were not part of what was conventionally known as OD, included high-performance working, high commitment management, high involvement management and performance management. The development of these systems in the 2000s led to a radically changed view of what constituted organization development.

The third chapter – changing the focus

The most significant change in the 2000s was the shift to a strategic perspective. As noted by Cummins and Worley (2005: 12): 'Change agents have proposed a variety of large-scale or strategic-change models; each of these models recognizes that strategic change involves multiple layers levels of the organization and a change in its culture, is driven from the top by powerful executives, and has important effects on performance.' They also commented that the practice of organization development therefore went far beyond its humanistic origins. Another development was the emergence of the concept of 'smart working', as described in Chapter 12. This could be described as an OD intervention because it involves taking a fundamental look at methods of improving organizational effectiveness.

There was also more emphasis on associating organization design and organization development. Marsh *et al* (2010) suggested that organization design and organization development need to be merged into one HR capability, with organization design taking precedence. They considered that this should all be brought in-house as a necessary part of the business model innovation process. But as they observed: 'We do not believe that the field of organization development has passed its sell-by date. Far from it. It just needs to be repositioned as an HR capability' (*ibid*: 143).

However, Weidner (2004: 37) made the following more pessimistic comment about OD: 'Unfortunately, after sixty years – despite the best efforts and intentions of many talented people – OD finds itself increasingly at the margins of business, academe, and practice. The field continues to affirm its values, yet has no identifiable voice.' OD 'interventions' still have a role to play in improving performance but as part of an integrated business and HR strategy planned and implemented by HR in conjunction with senior management, with or without outside help.

The main change that has taken place in the move from traditional OD to organizational development as practised currently is the focus on improving organizational performance and results through organization-wide initiatives. These do encompass the behaviour of people, especially when this relates to their levels of engagement (the degree to which people are committed to their work and the organization and motivated to achieve high levels of performance). But they are also concerned with the organizational processes that affect behaviour and engagement, namely, strategic HRM, work system design, smart working, high-performance working, organization design and job design.

Organization development strategy

Organization development strategy is founded on the aspiration to improve organizational capability, which is broadly the capacity of an organization to function effectively in order to achieve desired results. It has been defined more specifically by Ulrich and Lake (1990: 40) as 'the ability to manage people for competitive advantage'. It is concerned with mapping out intentions on how the work system should be developed in line with the concept of smart working, on how the organization should be structured to meet new demands, on system-wide change in fields such as reward and performance management, on how change should be managed, on what needs to be done to improve organizational processes involving people such as teamwork, communications and participation, and how the organization can acquire, retain, develop and engage the talent it needs. These intentions will be converted into actions on work systems development, structure design, the redesign of jobs and, possibly, OD-type interventions. The latter could take the form of action research, survey feedback and programmes for improving group processes and interpersonal skills, as described earlier in this chapter. The strategy can involve processes of integrated strategic change, as described below, and will be based on organizational diagnosis leading to the design of an organization development programme, as considered in the following two sections.

Integrated strategic change

The process of integrated strategic change as conceived by Worley *et al* (1996) can be used to formulate and implement organization development strategies. The steps required are:

1 Strategic analysis, a review of the organization's strategic orientation (its strategic intentions within its competitive environment) and a diagnosis of the organization's readiness for change.

2 Develop strategic capability – the ability to implement the strategic plan quickly and effectively.

3 Integrate individuals and groups throughout the organization into the processes of analysis, planning and implementation to maintain the firm's strategic focus, direct attention and resources to the organization's key competencies, improve coordination and integration within the organization and create higher levels of shared ownership and commitment.

4 Create the strategy, gain commitment and support for it and plan its implementation.

5 Implement the strategic change plan, drawing on knowledge of motivation, group dynamics and change processes, dealing with issues such as alignment, adaptability, teamwork and organizational and individual learning.

6 Allocate resources, provide feedback and solve problems as they arise.

Organizational diagnosis

The practice of organization development is based on an analysis and diagnosis of the circumstances of the organization, the strategic, operational or process issues that are affecting the organization and its ability to perform well. As defined by Manzini (1988: *ix*), 'An organizational diagnosis is a systematic process of gathering data about a business organization – its problems, challenges, strengths and limitations – and analysing how such factors influence its ability to interact effectively and profitably with its business environment.' This involves the use of the diagnostic cycle with associated analytical and diagnostic tools, which enable those concerned with development to identify areas of concern that can be dealt with in an organization development programme.

The diagnostic cycle

As described by Manzini (1988: 11), the diagnostic cycle consists of:

1 data gathering;

2 analysis;

3 feedback;

4 action planning;

5 implementation;

6 evaluation.

Analytical tools

The two most used analytical tools are SWOT analysis and PESTLE analysis. A *SWOT analysis* is a 'looking in' and 'looking out' approach that covers the internal organizational factors of strengths and weaknesses and the external factors of opportunities and threats. *PESTLE analysis* is an environmental scanning tool that covers the following factors: political, economic, social, technological, legal and environmental.

Diagnostics

Diagnostics are tools such as a questionnaire or checklist that gather information about a business or the opinions and attitudes of employees in order to identify issues and problems that can be dealt with in an organization development programme. They enable those concerned with organization development to understand what is happening and why it is happening so that they can do something about it. Diagnostics can be used to assess overall organizational effectiveness in the shape of general strategic, business and operational issues, or they can deal with more specific areas of concern such as a review of the organization's ideology, culture or climate, or a survey of levels of engagement or commitment. Examples of the approach used by various diagnostic instruments are given below.

Overall organizational effectiveness (Armstrong, 1994, pp 20–26, modified in 2011)

The basic questions in this organizational effectiveness survey are:

1 How well is the business performing in terms of financial results, growth, innovation, productivity, reputation (views of stakeholders), operational efficiency, social and environmental responsibility?

2 Is the organization delivering quality and value to its clients and customers?

3 Is there a clear and relevant business strategy that is acted upon effectively?

4 Is the business model (the picture of an organization that explains how it achieves competitive advantage and makes money) appropriate, realistic and understood by all concerned?

5 Is there a need and scope for business model innovation (developing a new business model or changing the existing one)?

6 Is there a well-defined and understood set of core values, including an ethical approach to business, which are 'values in use' rather than mere rhetoric?

7 Are the work systems operating effectively?

8 Has a 'smart working' approach been put into operation that incorporates high-performance working and flexibility?

9 Is the organization's structure appropriate and working well?

10 Has the organization got the resources required (including people) and are they being managed and used effectively?

Organizational ideology questionnaire (Harrison, 1972)

This questionnaire deals with the four orientations defined by Harrison (power, role, task and self). The questionnaire is completed by ranking statements according to views on what is closest to the organization's actual position. Statements include:

- a good boss is strong, decisive and firm but fair;

- a good subordinate is compliant, hard-working and loyal;

- people who do well in the organization are shrewd and competitive, with a strong need for power;

- the basis of task assignment is the personal needs and judgements of those in authority;

- decisions are made by people with the most knowledge and expertise about the problem.

Organizational culture inventory (Cooke and Lafferty, 1989)

This instrument assesses organizational culture under 12 headings:

1 *Humanistic-helpful* – organizations managed in a participative and person-centred way.

2 *Affiliative* – organizations that place a high priority on constructive relationships.

3 *Approval* – organizations in which conflicts are avoided and interpersonal relationships are pleasant – at least superficially.

4 *Conventional* – conservative, traditional and bureaucratically controlled organizations.

5 *Dependent* – hierarchically controlled and non-participative organizations.

6 *Avoidance* – organizations that fail to reward success but punish mistakes.

7 *Oppositional* – organizations in which confrontation prevails and negativism is rewarded.

8 *Power* – organizations structured on the basis of the authority inherent in members' positions.

9 *Competitive* – a culture in which winning is valued and members are rewarded for out-performing one another.

10 *Competence/perfectionist* – organizations in which perfectionism, persistence and hard work are valued.

11 *Achievement* – organizations that do things well and value members who set and accomplish challenging but realistic goals.

12 *Self-actualization* – organizations that value creativity, quality over quantity, and both task accomplishment and individual growth.

Typical dimensions of organizational climate questionnaires (Koys and De Cotiis, 1991)

1 *Autonomy* – the perception of self-determination with respect to work procedures, goals and priorities.

2 *Cohesion* – the perception of togetherness or sharing within the organization setting.

3 *Trust* – the perception of freedom to communicate openly with members at higher organizational levels about sensitive or personal issues with the expectation that the integrity of such communications will not be violated.

4 *Resource* – the perception of time demands with respect to task completion and performance standards.

5 *Support* – the perception of the degree to which superiors tolerate members' behaviour, including willingness to let members learn from their mistakes without fear of reprisal.

6 *Recognition* – the perception that members' contributions to the organization are acknowledged.

7 *Fairness* – the perception that organizational policies are non-arbitrary or capricious.

8 *Innovation* – the perception that change and creativity are encouraged, including risk-taking into new areas where the member has little or no prior experience.

Employee attitude or opinion surveys

A number of organizations conduct attitude or opinion surveys on behalf of their clients. Apart from the advantage of being well-tested and professionally administered they also facilitate benchmarking. Surveys provided by such organizations include the CIPD People and Performance employee questionnaire, the IES engagement survey, the Gallop engagement survey and the Saratoga engagement and commitment matrix.

An example of a general attitude survey is given in Table 13.1 and a toolkit for designing and using attitude surveys is provided in Chapter 70 of this handbook.

Organization development programmes

The traditional OD programme was behavioural science-based and almost entirely devoted to interpersonal relationships, organizational processes and culture change in the broadest sense. There may still be a need for such interventions today but organization development is a more eclectic affair – anything can be included under the organization development heading as long as it contributes to organizational effectiveness. The choice is from such activities as high-performance working, lean manufacturing, smart working, and the enhancement of levels of engagement. These have specific and measurable objectives related to performance and capability.

Organization development is no longer the preserve of external process consultants with behavioural science backgrounds. Instead it is a territory inhabited by business-oriented people based in the organization and acting, in effect, as internal consultants. They include HR specialists who are there not just because they know about HRM but because they are familiar with how businesses operate and where people management fits in.

The organization development processes with which internal specialists and their colleagues are concerned will be determined by the outcome of diagnostic reviews. Because these outcomes will always be different, organizational development programmes will always be different. There is no such thing as a standard 'OD' approach, as was formerly the case. A number of approaches are available, but which to use and how to use is a matter of choice depending on the facts of the situation. This is why the initial analysis and diagnosis is so important. An analytical toolkit for organization development is provided in Chapter 60.

TABLE 13.1   Attitude survey

		Strongly agree	Agree	Disagree	Strongly disagree
The organization					
1	I am proud to work for this organization	1	2	3	4
2	I would not encourage anyone else to work here	1	2	3	4
3	I want to go on working for this organization	1	2	3	4
Your job					
4	I like my job	1	2	3	4
5	I am not clear about what I am expected to achieve	1	2	3	4
6	I have plenty of scope to decide how to do my work	1	2	3	4
7	I have to work too hard to achieve the results expected of me	1	2	3	4
8	I am well motivated to do a good job	1	2	3	4
9	The balance between my work and domestic life is unsatisfactory	1	2	3	4
Your boss					
10	My boss does a very good job	1	2	3	4
11	My boss gives me clear direction	1	2	3	4
12	My boss lets me know how I am getting on	1	2	3	4
13	My boss does not support me very well	1	2	3	4
14	My boss helps me to improve my performance	1	2	3	4
15	My boss treats everyone fairly	1	2	3	4
Learning and development					
16	I have been given every opportunity to develop my knowledge and skills	1	2	3	4
17	I am satisfied with the career opportunities provided by the organization	1	2	3	4
18	I am not given much opportunity to discuss my development needs with my boss	1	2	3	4
Your pay					
19	I am fairly paid for the work I do	1	2	3	4
20	I feel that my pay does not reflect my contribution	1	2	3	4
21	My pay compares favourably with what I could get elsewhere	1	2	3	4
Communication					
22	I do not feel that I am fully informed about what the organization is setting out to do	1	2	3	4
23	I am told about the plans for my department/group	1	2	3	4
Teamwork and colleagues					
24	The members of my team work very effectively together	1	2	3	4
25	I get on well with my colleagues	1	2	3	4

Key learning points: Organization development

Organization development defined

Organization development in its traditional form as 'OD' was defined by Rowlandson (1984: 90) as 'an intervention strategy that uses group processes to focus on the whole culture of an organization in order to bring about planned change'. The CIPD (2010: 1) defined organization development as a 'planned and systematic approach to enabling sustained organization performance through the involvement of its people'.

Strategic nature of organization development

The strategic nature of organization development as an integral part of HRM arises because it can play a significant role in the implementation of business strategy.

Assumptions and values of OD

The assumptions and values of OD as originally conceived were that:

- Most individuals are driven by the need for personal growth and development as long as their environment is both supportive and challenging.

- The work team, especially at the informal level, has great significance for feelings of satisfaction and the dynamics of such teams have a powerful effect on the behaviour of their members.

- OD programmes aim to improve the quality of working life of all members of the organization.

- Organizations can be more effective if they learn to diagnose their own strengths and weaknesses.

- Managers often do not know what is wrong and need special help in diagnosing problems, although the outside 'process consultant' ensures that decision making remains in the hands of the client.

OD interventions

OD interventions include process consultation, change management, action research, survey feedback, group dynamics and personal interventions.

Criticisms of OD

The main criticisms of OD, as noted by Marsh *et al* (2010: 143), were that it was 'Orientated to process and tools rather than results ... where techniques are considered to be ends in themselves rather than a means to deliver organizational performance.'

Organization development strategy

Organization development strategy is based on the aspiration to improve organizational capability, which is broadly the capacity of an organization to function effectively in order to achieve desired results.

The practice of organization development

The practice of organization development is based on an analysis and diagnosis of the circumstances of the organization, the strategic, operational or process issues that are affecting the organization and its ability to perform well. This involves the use of diagnostic tools.

Organization development programmes

The traditional OD programme was behavioural science-based and almost entirely devoted to inter-personal relationships, organizational processes and culture change in the broadest sense. There may still be a need for such interventions today but the emphasis now is on much more focused activities to do with high-performance working, lean manufacturing, smart working and the enhancement of levels of engagement.

Questions

1 What was the original concept of organization development?

2 What is an OD intervention?

3 What are the most typical types of interventions?

4 What were the main criticisms made of OD in the 1980s and 1990s?

5 How has the approach to OD altered since then?

References

Argyris, C (1957) *Personality and Organization*, New York, Harper & Row

Anthony, P D (1990) The paradox of managing culture or 'he who leads is lost', *Personnel Review*, **19** (4), pp 3–8

Armstrong, M (1984) *A Handbook of Personnel Management Practice*, 2nd edn, London, Kogan Page

Armstrong, M (1994) *Improving Organizational Effectiveness*, London, Kogan Page

Beckhard, R (1969) *Organization Development: Strategy and models*, Reading, MA, Addison-Wesley

Beer, M (1980) *Organization Change and Development: A systems view*, Santa Monica, CA, Goodyear

Bennis, W G (1969) *Organization Development: Its nature, origin and prospects*, Reading, MA, Addison-Wesley

Buchanan, D and Huczynski, A (2007) *Organizational Behaviour*, Harlow, FT Prentice-Hall

Burke, W W (1995) Organization development: then, now and tomorrow, *Organization Development Journal*, **13** (4), pp 7–17

Caldwell, R (2003) Models of change agency: a fourfold classification, *British Journal of Management*, **14** (2), pp 131–42

CIPD (2010) *Organization Development*, London, CIPD

Cooke, R and Lafferty, J (1989) *Organizational Culture Inventory*, Plymouth, MI, Human Synergistic

Cummins, T G and Worley, C G (2005) *Organization Development and Change*, Mason, OH, South Western

Harrison, R (1972) Understanding your organization's character, *Harvard Business Review*, 5, pp 119–28

HR Magazine (2007) Organization development: a strategic HR tool, **52** (9), pp 1–10

Herzberg, F, Mausner, B and Snyderman, B (1957) *The Motivation to Work*, New York, Wiley

Koys, D and De Cotiis, T (1991) Inductive measures of organizational climate, *Human Relations*, **44**, pp 265–85

Legge, K (1995) *Human Resource Management: Rhetorics and realities*, London, Macmillan

Lewin, K (1947) Frontiers in group dynamics, *Human Relations*, **1** (1), pp 5–42

Lewin, K (1951) *Field Theory in Social Science*, New York, Harper & Row

Likert, R (1961) *New Patterns of Management*, New York, Harper & Row

McGregor, D (1960) *The Human Side of Enterprise*, New York, McGraw-Hill

McLean, A (1981) Organization development: a case of the emperor's new clothes?, *Personnel Review*, **4** (1), pp 3–14

Manzini, A O (1988) *Organizational Diagnosis*, New York, AMACOM

Marsh, C, Sparrow, P and Hird, M (2010) Improving organization design: The new priority for HR directors, in (eds) P Sparrow, A Hesketh, M Hird and C Cooper, *Leading HR*, Basingstoke, Palgrave Macmillan, pp 136–61

Maslow, A (1954) *Motivation and Personality*, New York, Harper & Row

Rowlandson, P (1984) The oddity of OD, *Management Today*, November, pp 91–3

Ruona, W E A and Gibson, S K (2004) The making of twenty-first century HR: the convergence of HRM, HRD and OD, *Human Resource Management*, **43** (1), pp 49–66

Strauss, G (1976) Organization development, in (ed) R Dubin, *Handbook of Work, Organization and Society*, Chicago, IL, Rand MacNally

Ulrich, D and Lake, D (1990) *Organizational Capability: Competing from the inside out*, New York, Wiley

Weidner, C K (2004) A brand in dire straits: organization development at sixty, *Organization Development Journal*, **22** (2), pp 37–47

Worley, C, Hitchin, D and Ross, W (1996) *Integrated Strategic Change: How organization development builds competitive advantage*, Reading, MA, Addison-Wesley

14
Employee engagement

LEARNING OUTCOMES

On completing this chapter you should be able to define these key concepts. You should also know about:

- The meaning of employee engagement
- Organizational engagement
- The drivers of engagement
- Enhancing overall engagement

- Job engagement
- The theory of engagement
- Outcomes of engagement
- Methods of enhancing engagement

Introduction

The concept of employee engagement is often defined as 'willingness to go the extra mile'. It has become a new management mantra. Reilly and Brown (2008) noted that the terms 'job satisfaction', 'motivation' and 'commitment' are generally being replaced now in business by 'engagement' because it appears to have more descriptive force and face validity.

Everyone believes that engagement is a good thing but many, although they think they know it when they see it, are vague about what it really is. Perhaps this is because the concept of engagement is defined in so many different ways. It is often used loosely as a notion that embraces pretty well everything the organization is seeking to do with regard to the contribution and behaviour of its employees in terms of job performance, discretionary effort, organizational citizenship and commitment. Furthermore, it is not clear where the concept of motivation fits in. Is it just an aspect of engagement or is it something that needs to be treated separately?

The vagueness of the term is illustrated by the difficulty of answering the question, 'engagement to what?' Are employees engaged with their job, their career, or their organization, or all three or any two of them? Some definitions avoid this dilemma by referring to engagement as a condition that is solely related to the jobs people do. Others define it as, in effect, identification with the purposes and values of the organization. Only Saks (2006) and, following him, Balain and Sparrow (2009) make a clear distinction between the two. This distinction is important because unless it is made it will be difficult in programmes for enhancing engagement to distinguish between the job aspects and the organizational aspects. Faced with this confusion, Guest (2009) suggested that the concept of employee engagement needed to be more clearly defined or be abandoned.

But the notion of employee engagement seems to excite managers, HR practitioners and academics. It is here to stay. This chapter therefore begins with an attempt to clarify its meaning and define its significance. This leads to an assessment of the drivers of engagement and a discussion of one of the key notions associated with it – that of discretionary effort. The chapter ends with a review of approaches to engaging employees.

The meaning of employee engagement

One of the earliest writers to consider engagement, (Kahn, 1990), regarded it as a psychological state experienced by employees in relation to their work, together with associated behaviours. A definition based on research by Maslach et al (2001: 74) referred to engagement as: 'A positive, fulfilling, work-related state of mind that is characterized by vigour, dedication, and absorption.' Macey et al (2009: 7) produced the following working definition: 'Engagement is an individual's purpose and focused energy, evident to others in the display of personal initiative, adaptability, effort and persistence directed towards organizational goals.'

In their comprehensive study of employee engagement, MacLeod and Clarke (2009: 4) concluded that: 'The way employee engagement operates can take many forms.' So can descriptions of what it means. There are three approaches to definition, as described below.

Job engagement

The term 'engagement' can be used in a specific job-related way to describe what takes place when people are interested in and positive, even excited, about their jobs, exercise discretionary behaviour and are motivated to achieve high levels of performance. Erickson (2005) described the job as the key antecedent of the state of engagement. Truss et al (2006: ix) stated that: 'Put simply, engagement means feeling positive about your job.' They went on to explain that: 'The engaged employee is the passionate employee, the employee who is totally immersed in his or her work, energetic, committed and completely dedicated' (ibid: 1). Gallup, as quoted by Balain and Sparrow (2009: 8), defined engagement as: 'The individual's involvement and satisfaction with as well as enthusiasm for work.'

Other sources have defined engagement on similar lines, often emphasizing the importance of discretionary behaviour as the key outcome or distinguishing feature of an engaged employee. Watkin (2001: 4) defined 'engaged performance' as: 'A result that is achieved by stimulating employees' enthusiasm for their work and directing it towards organizational success. This result can only be achieved when employers offer an implied contract to their employees that elicits specific positive behaviours aligned with the organization's goals.'

Organizational engagement

Organizational engagement focuses on attachment to or identification with the organization as a whole.

The Conference Board (2006) defined employee engagement as the heightened connection that employees feel for their organization. Robinson *et al* (2004: 9) emphasized the organizational aspect of engagement when they referred to it as 'a positive attitude held by the employee towards the organization and its values'. This definition of engagement strongly resembles the traditional notion of commitment, as discussed in Chapter 16.

Analytical definitions

Perhaps the most illuminating and helpful approach to definition is to analyse the concept specifically in terms of both job and organizational engagement. A good example of this is the explanation of the antecedents, types and consequences of engagement shown in Table 14.1, produced by Balain and Sparrow (2009: 17) based on the work of Saks (2006).

Engagement defined

On the basis of the Balain and Sparrow analysis, engagement can be defined as follows:

Engagement happens when people are committed to their work and the organization and motivated to achieve high levels of performance. It has two interrelated aspects: 1) *job engagement*, which takes place when employees exercise discretionary effort because they find their jobs interesting, challenging and rewarding; and 2) *organizational engagement*, when they identify with the values and purpose of their organization and believe that it is a great place in which to work and to continue to work.

The theory of engagement

The variety of definitions quoted above illustrates the elusiveness of the concept of engagement. As Alfes *et al* (2010: 4) commented: 'In theoretical, conceptual and empirical terms, we in fact know relatively little about the concept of employee engagement.' They also noted that most consultancies and survey firms regard engagement as something that is *done* to employees. In contrast, some academics such as May *et al* (2004) suggested that engagement

TABLE 14.1   Antecedents, types and consequences of engagement (Balain and Sparrow, 2009)

Antecedents of engagement	Types of employee engagement	Consequences
Enriched and challenging jobs (job characteristics)	Job engagement	Job satisfaction
Quality of the employee-organization relationship (perceived organizational support)	Organizational engagement	Organizational commitment
Quality of the employee-supervisor relationship (perceived supervisor support)		Level of intention to quit
Rewards and recognition		Organizational citizenship behaviour
Fairness in the processes that allocate resources or resolve disputes (procedural justice)		
What is considered just or right in the allocation of goods in a society (distributive justice)		

is *experienced* by individuals, a state of being that may be affected by management strategies and approaches, but is not in itself, such a strategy. The latter view was the one adopted by Alfes *et al* as the basis for their research.

As discussed below, the concept of engagement has been further explored in terms of its components, its facets, its underpinning theory and the notion of discretionary behaviour.

Components of engagement

The Institute for Employment Studies has modelled the components of engagement as shown in Figure 14.1.

- *Commitment* is the relative strength of the individual's identification with, and involvement in, an organization.

- *Organizational citizenship behaviour*, as defined by Organ (1988), is employee behaviour that goes above and beyond the call of duty and contributes to organizational effectiveness. It is discretionary and not explicitly recognized by the employing organization's formal reward system.

FIGURE 14.1

IES model of employee engagement

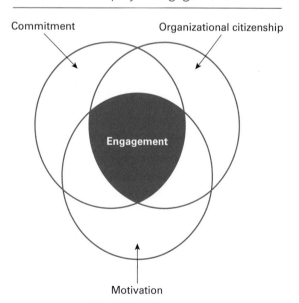

SOURCE: Armstrong *et al*, 2010

- *Motivation* is the force that energizes, directs and sustains behaviour. It can be *intrinsic*, ie behaviour is affected by factors that may arise from the work itself and are self-generated; or *extrinsic*, which occurs when things are done to or for people to motivate them. The motivation element in engagement is intrinsic. As Macey *et al* (2009: 67) observed: 'When the work itself is meaningful it is also said to have intrinsic motivation. This means that it is not the pay or recognition that yields positive feelings of engagement but the work itself.' They also commented that engaged employees 'feel that their jobs are an important part of what they are' (*ibid*: 127).

Facets of engagement

Alfes *et al* (2010: 5) see engagement as having three core facets:

1 *intellectual engagement* – thinking hard about the job and how to do it better;

2 *affective engagement* – feeling positively about doing a good job;

3 *social engagement* – actively taking opportunities to discuss work-related improvements with others at work.

Ultimately, engagement will have behavioural outcomes leading to what can be described as an 'engaged employee'.

Balain and Sparrow (2010: 183) considered that engagement should be seen as a 'belief' and not an attitude, ie it is largely a cognitive construct (intellectual engagement) rather than an affective or behavioural one. They suggested that engagement will have affective and behavioural outcomes but it is necessary to separate the cause from the effect.

Saks (2006) suggested that a strong theoretical rationale for engagement is provided by social exchange theory. As he described it:

> Social exchange theory argues that obligations are generated through a series of interactions between parties who are in a state of reciprocal interdependence. A basic tenet of social exchange theory is that relationships evolve over time into trusting, loyal and mutual commitments as long as the parties abide by certain 'rules' of exchange ...

[These] usually involve reciprocity or repayment rules such that the actions of one party lead to a response or actions by the other party.
(*ibid*: 603)

This is consistent with the description of engagement by Robinson *et al* (2004) as a two-way relationship between the employer and the employee. Balain and Sparrow (2009: 16) concluded that:

To understand what really causes engagement, and what it causes in turn, we need to embed the idea in a well-founded theory. The one that is considered most appropriate is social exchange theory, which sees feelings of loyalty, commitment, discretionary effort as all being forms of social reciprocation by employees to a good employer.

Discretionary behaviour

Employee engagement is associated with the notion of discretionary behaviour or effort. As described by Purcell *et al* (2003), discretionary behaviour refers to the choices that people at work often have about the way they do the job and the amount of effort, care, innovation and productive behaviour they display. It can be positive when people 'go the extra mile' to achieve high levels of performance. It can be negative when they exercise their discretion to slack at their work. Discretionary behaviour is hard for the employer to define, monitor and control. But positive discretionary behaviour can happen when people are engaged with their work.

Drivers of employee engagement

The following drivers of engagement were listed by MacLeod and Clarke (2009):

- Leadership, which ensures a strong, transparent and explicit organizational culture which gives employees a line of sight between their job and the vision and aims of the organization.

- Engaging managers who offer clarity, appreciation of employees' effort and contribution, who treat their people as individuals and who ensure that work is

organized efficiently and effectively so that employees feel they are valued, and equipped and supported to do their job.

- Employees who feel that they are able to voice their ideas and be listened to, both about how they do their job and in decision making in their own department, with joint sharing of problems and challenges and a commitment to arrive at joint solutions.

- A belief among employees that the organization lives its values, and that espoused behavioural norms are adhered to, resulting in trust and a sense of integrity.

Macey *et al* (2009) placed greater emphasis on the work environment and the jobs people do. They noted that: 'Engagement requires a work environment that does not just demand more but promotes information sharing, provides learning opportunities and fosters a balance in people's lives, thereby creating the bases for sustained energy and personal initiative (*ibid*: 11). They also commented that, 'When people have the opportunity to do work in a way that: a) effectively uses their skills; b) fits their values and c) provides them the freedom to exercise choice, they will be fully motivated to engage in their work' (*ibid*: 126). They observed that 'Engaged employees feel that their jobs are an important part of who they are' (*ibid*: 127).

Research conducted by Alfes *et al* (2010: 2) established that the main drivers of engagement are meaningful work (the most important), senior management vision and communication, positive perceptions of one's line manager and employee voice – having a say in matters that concern them. 'HR practices do not impact directly on engagement; the relationship is mediated by person-job fit and line management style.'

Sparrow (2011) attaches importance to job design (the most significant), organizational support, leadership in terms of leader-member exchange (the two-way relationship between leaders and the people they lead), reward and fairness.

Outcomes of engagement

Research conducted by the Institute for Employment Studies (Robinson *et al*, 2004) led to the conclusion that an engaged employee:

- is willing to 'go the extra mile';
- believes in and identifies with the organization;
- wants to work to make things better;
- understands the business context and the 'bigger picture';
- respects and help colleagues.

Guest (2009) explained that the benefits of engagement were as follows:

> Employee engagement will be manifested in positive attitudes (for example job satisfaction, organizational commitment and identification with the organization) and behaviour (low labour turnover and absence and high citizenship behaviour) on the part of employees; and evidence of perceptions of trust, fairness and a positive exchange within a psychological contract where two-way promises and commitments are fulfilled.

Alfes *et al* (2010: 2) concluded that engaged employees perform better, are more innovative than others, are more likely to want to stay with their employers, enjoy greater levels of personal wellbeing and perceive their workload to be more sustainable than others.

Enhancing overall employee engagement

Promoting the engagement of their employees is what all employers want to do. But how can they do it? There are no universal prescriptions and any actions taken should be based on evidence, including measurements of levels of engagement, trends in those levels and benchmarking. This data needs to be analysed and assessed to provide information on what might be done (approaches to measurement are examined in the last section of this chapter).

MacLeod and Clarke (2009: 6) pointed out that: 'Engagement is about establishing mutual respect in the workplace for what people can do and be.' They also observed that: 'Engagement is two way: organizations must work to engage the employee, who in turn has a choice about the level of engagement

to offer the employer. Each reinforces the other' (*ibid*: 9). Following their research, Alfes *et al* (2010: 2) concluded that engagement requires a work environment that does not just demand more but promotes information sharing, provides learning opportunities and fosters a balance in people's lives, thereby creating the bases for sustained energy and personal initiative.

To enhance engagement employers have to address issues concerning both aspects of engagement – job and organizational engagement. These are interrelated and any actions taken to enhance either aspect will be mutually supporting. However, it is useful to consider what can be done specifically in each area, bearing in mind the particular circumstances and needs of the organization.

To summarize, job engagement will be affected by work and job design, the quality of leadership exercised by line managers and the reward system. Organizational engagement will be affected by the quality of life provided by the working environment and by having an employee value proposition that ensures the organization is an employer of choice.

Enhancing job engagement

Job engagement can be enhanced through good job design, learning and development programmes, performance management, and improving the quality of leadership provided by line managers. In addition, rewards in the broadest sense, ie non-financial as well as financial, can play a part.

Job design

Job design has a key role to play in enhancing engagement. Macey *et al* (2009: 69) commented that: 'People come to work for pay but get engaged at work because the work they do is meaningful.' Intrinsic motivation and therefore increased engagement can be generated by the work itself if it provides interest and opportunities for achievement and self-fulfilment.

An early but influential perspective on the factors affecting job design and motivation was provided by Hackman and Oldham (1974), whose job

Key learning points: Employee engagement

The meaning of employee engagement

Engagement happens when people are committed to their work and the organization and motivated to achieve high levels of performance. It has two interrelated aspects: 1) *job engagement*, which takes place when employees exercise discretionary effort because they find their jobs interesting, challenging and rewarding; and 2) *organizational engagement*, when they identify with the values and purpose of their organization and believe that it is a great place in which to work and to continue to work.

Elements of engagement

Commitment, organizational citizenship behaviour and motivation.

Facets of engagement

- Intellectual engagement – thinking hard about the job and how to do it better.

- Affective engagement – feeling positively about doing a good job.

- Social engagement – actively taking opportunities to discuss work-related improvements with others at work.

- Behavioural outcomes.

Theories of engagement

Engagement will have behavioural outcomes leading to what can be described as an 'engaged employee'. Saks (2006) suggested that a strong theoretical rationale for engagement is provided by social exchange theory.

Discretionary behaviour

Discretionary behaviour refers to the choices that people at work often have about the way they do the job and the amount of effort, care, innovation and productive behaviour they display.

Drivers of engagement

Macey *et al* (2009) emphasize the importance of the work environment and the jobs people do. Alfes *et al* (2010) established that the main drivers of engagement are meaningful work (the most important), senior management vision and communication, positive perceptions of one's line manager and employee voice – having a say in matters that concern them.

Enhancing engagement

Job engagement can be enhanced through good job design, learning and development programmes, and improving the quality of leadership provided by line managers. In addition, rewards in the broadest sense, ie non-financial as well as financial, can play a part. It was suggested by Guest (2009) that organizational engagement can be enhanced:

through effective leadership of a strong, positive culture that ensures the enactment of organizational values; through strong management that supports employees' work and wellbeing; through careful design of systems and jobs to enable employees to contribute through full use of their knowledge and skills; through effective employee voice; and through provision of appropriate resources, tools and information to perform effectively.

Questions

1 What is employee engagement?
2 What is job engagement?
3 What is organizational engagement?
4 What are the components of engagement?
5 What is organizational citizenship behaviour?
6 What is the relationship between engagement and commitment?
7 What is the relationship between engagement and motivation?
8 What are the facets of engagement?
9 What are the main outcomes of engagement (name at least four)?
10 What are the main conclusions about engagement reached by the research conducted by Saks (2006)?
11 What are the main conclusions about engagement reached by the research conducted by Balain and Sparrow (2009)?
12 What are the main conclusions about engagement reached by the research conducted by MacLeod and Clarke (2009)?
13 What are the main conclusions about engagement reached by the research conducted by Alfes *et al* (2010)?
14 What is social exchange theory?
15 What is discretionary behaviour?
16 What are the main drivers of engagement as listed by MacLeod and Clarke (name at least three)?
17 How can job engagement be enhanced?
18 What is the role of job design in job engagement?
19 How can organizational engagement be enhanced?
20 What is high-involvement management?

References

Alfes, K, Truss, C, Soane, E C, Rees, C and Gatenby, M (2010) *Creating an Engaged Workforce*, London, CIPD

Armstrong, M, Brown, D and Reilly, P (2010) *Evidence-based Reward Management*, London, Kogan Page

Balain, S and Sparrow, P (2009) *Engaged to Perform: A new perspective on employee engagement*, Lancaster, Lancaster University Management School

Balain, S and Sparrow, P (2010) Understanding the value of engagement, in (eds) P Sparrow, A Hesketh, M Hird and C Cooper, *Leading HR*, Basingstoke, Palgrave Macmillan, pp 162–88

Conference Board (2006) *Employee Engagement: A review of current research and its implications*, New York, Conference Board

Erickson, T J (2005). Testimony submitted before the US Senate Committee on Health, Education, Labor and Pensions, May 26

Guest, D (2009) Review of employee engagement: Notes for a discussion (unpublished), prepared specifically for the MacLeod and Clarke 2009 review of employee engagement

Hackman, J R and Oldham, G R (1974) Motivation through the design of work: test of a theory, *Organizational Behaviour and Human Performance*, **16** (2), pp 250–79

Harter, J K, Schmidt, F L and Hayes, T L (2002) Business-unit-level relationship between employee satisfaction, employee engagement, and business outcomes: A meta-analysis, *Journal of Applied Psychology*, **87**, pp 268–79

Kahn, W A (1990) Psychological conditions of personal engagement and disengagement at work, *Academy of Management Journal*, **33** (4), pp 692–724

Lawler, E E (1986) *High Involvement Management*, San Francisco, CA, Jossey-Bass

Macey, W H, Schneider, B, Barbera, K M and Young, S A (2009) *Employee Engagement*, Malden, MA, Wiley-Blackwell

MacLeod, D and Clarke, N (2009) *Engaging for Success: Enhancing performance through employee engagement*, London, Department for Business Innovation and Skills

Maslach, C, Schaufeli, W B and Leiter, M P (2001) Job burnout, *Annual Review of Psychology*, **52**, pp 397–422

May, D R, Gilson R L and Harter, L M (2004) The psychological conditions of meaningfulness, safety and availability and the engagement of the human spirit at work, *Journal of Occupational & Organizational Psychology*, **77** (1), pp 11–37

Organ, D W (1988) *Organizational Citizenship Behaviour: The good soldier syndrome*, Lexington, MA, Lexington Books

Purcell, J, Kinnie, K, Hutchinson, N, Rayton, B and Swart, J (2003) *People and Performance: How people management impacts on organizational performance*, London, CIPD

Reilly, P and Brown, D (2008) Employee engagement: future focus or fashionable fad for reward management?, *WorldatWork Journal*, **17** (4), pp 37–49

Robertson, I T and Smith, M (1985) *Motivation and Job Design*, London, IPM

Robinson, D, Perryman, S and Hayday, S (2004) *The Drivers of Employee Engagement*, Brighton, Institute for Employment Studies

Saks, A M (2006) Antecedents and consequences of employee engagement, *Journal of Managerial Psychology*, **21** (6), pp 600–619

Sparrow, P (2011) Engagement and Reward, presentation at E-Reward conference, 29 June

Truss, C, Soane, E, Edwards, C, Wisdom, K, Croll, A and Burnett, J (2006) *Working Life: Employee attitudes and engagement*, London, CIPD

Watkin, C (2001) Engage employees to boost performance, *Selection & Development Review*, **18** (2), pp 3–6

15
Motivation

KEY CONCEPTS AND TERMS

Content (needs) motivation theory

Expectancy theory

Goal theory

Instrumentality

Line of sight

Motivation

Reinforcement

Equity theory

Extrinsic motivation

Herzberg's two factor model of motivation

Intrinsic motivation

Management by objectives

Process theory

Self-efficacy

LEARNING OUTCOMES

On completing this chapter you should be able to define these key concepts. You should also understand:

- The meaning of motivation
- Types of motivation
- The process of motivation
- The different motivation theories
- The points that have been made in critically evaluating those theories
- Approaches to developing a motivation strategy

Introduction

Motivation is the force that energizes, directs and sustains behaviour. High performance is achieved by well-motivated people who are prepared to exercise discretionary effort. Even in fairly basic roles, Hunter *et al* (1990) found through their research that the difference in value-added discretionary performance between 'superior' and 'standard' performers was 19 per cent. For highly complex jobs it was 48 per cent.

The meaning of motivation

A motive is a reason for doing something. Motivation is concerned with the strength and direction of behaviour and the factors that influence people to behave in certain ways. The term 'motivation' can refer variously to the goals individuals have, the ways in which individuals chose their goals and the ways in which others try to change their behaviour.

Types of motivation

A distinction is made between extrinsic and intrinsic motivation. *Extrinsic motivation* occurs when things are done to or for people to motivate them, including rewards such as incentives, increased pay, praise, or promotion, and punishments, such as disciplinary action, withholding pay, or criticism. *Intrinsic motivation* is provided by the work itself and is associated with the concept of engagement, as explained in Chapter 14.

The process of motivation

The process of motivation can be modelled in a number of ways. Two of the best known models are provided by content or needs theory and expectancy theory.

Content/needs theory

The theory focuses on the content of motivation in the shape of needs. Its basis is the belief that an unsatisfied need creates tension and a state of disequilibrium. To restore the balance a goal is identified that will satisfy the need, and a behaviour pathway is selected that will lead to the achievement of the goal and the satisfaction of the need. Behaviour is therefore motivated by unsatisfied needs. A content theory model is shown in Figure 15.1. Content theory, as the term implies, defines the components of motivation but it does not explain how motivation affects performance – a necessary requirement if the concept is to provide guidance on HR policy and practice. This is the role of expectancy theory, as described below.

Expectancy theory

Expectancy theory states that motivation to perform will be high when people know what they have to do to get a reward, expect that they will be able to get the reward and expect that the reward will be worthwhile. Motivation is only likely when a clearly perceived and usable relationship exists between performance and outcome, and the outcome is seen as a means of satisfying needs. Porter and Lawler (1968) spelt out that the level of effort was affected by the value of rewards and the probability that reward followed effort, but they pointed out that effort was not enough to achieve high performance. Two additional factors affecting performance had to be taken into account: 1) ability – individual characteristics such as intelligence, knowledge, skills; and 2) role perceptions – what individuals want to do or think they are required to do. A model of their theory is shown in Figure 15.2.

Motivation theories

The main motivation theories, including content and expectancy theory, are summarized in Table 15.1.

FIGURE 15.1   The process of motivation according to content theory

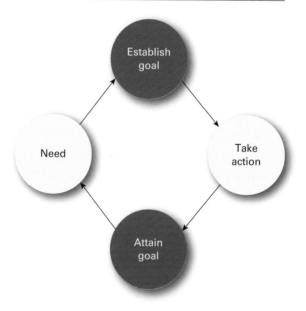

FIGURE 15.2   Motivation model (Porter and Lawler)

Critical evaluation of motivation theories

Instrumentality

This theory emphasized economic outcomes and the need to rationalize work. It assumes that people will be motivated to work if rewards and penalties are tied directly to their performance; thus the awards are contingent upon effective performance. Instrumentality theory has its roots in the scientific management methods of Taylor (1911).

This theory provides a rationale for incentive pay, albeit a dubious one. Motivation using this approach has been and still is widely adopted and can be successful in some circumstances, eg piece work. But it relies exclusively on a system of external controls and does not recognize a number of other human needs. It also fails to appreciate the fact that the formal control system can be seriously affected by the informal relationship existing between workers.

Reinforcement

It has been suggested that behavioural theories based on the principle of reinforcement pay insufficient attention to the influence of expectations, and no indication is given of any means of distinguishing in advance the class of outcomes that would strengthen responses and those that would weaken them. They are limited because they imply, in Allport's (1954) vivid phrase, a 'hedonism of the past'. They assume that the explanation of the present choices of individuals is to be found in an examination of the consequences of their past choices.

Content/needs theory

Content or needs theory has a considerable amount of face validity; it seems almost self-evident that people are motivated by unsatisfied needs. In particular, Maslow's needs hierarchy has an intuitive appeal and has been very popular. But his theory has not been verified by empirical research such as that conducted by Wahba and Bridwell (1979). It has been criticized, first, for its apparent rigidity – different people may have different priorities; secondly, because it is difficult to accept that needs progress steadily up the hierarchy; and thirdly, for the misleading simplicity of Maslow's conceptual language. In fact, Maslow himself expressed doubts about the validity of a strictly ordered hierarchy.

Alderfer (1972) produced his more convincing and simpler ERG theory identifying three primary categories of needs:

1   *Existence needs*, such as hunger and thirst – pay, fringe benefits and working conditions are other types of existence needs.

2   *Relatedness needs*, which acknowledge that people are not self-contained units but must engage in transactions with their human environment – acceptance, understanding, confirmation and influence are elements of the relatedness process.

TABLE 15.1   Summary of motivation theories

Category	Type	Theorist(s)	Summary of theory	Implications
Instrumentality	Taylorism	Taylor (1911)	If we do one thing it leads to another. People will be motivated to work if rewards and punishments are directly related to their performance.	Basis of crude attempts to motivate people by incentives. Often used as the implied rationale for performance-related pay, although this is seldom an effective motivator.
Reinforcement	The motivation process	Hull (1951)	As experience is gained in satisfying needs, people perceive that certain actions help to achieve goals while others are unsuccessful. The successful actions are repeated when a similar need arises.	Provide feedback that positively reinforces effective behaviour.
Content (needs) theory	Hierarchy or sets of needs	Maslow (1954), Alderfer (1972)	People are motivated by their needs, which are translated into goals for them to attain. The content of motivation is therefore those needs and the goals they generate to which people aspire. In Maslow's theory, a hierarchy of needs exists: physiological, safety, social, esteem and self-fulfilment. Needs at a higher level only emerge when a lower need is satisfied. Alderfer produced a simpler three-factor non-hierarchical theory identifying three basic needs.	Focuses attention on the various needs that motivate people and the notion that a satisfied need is no longer a motivator. The concept of a hierarchy has no practical significance.

Theory	Reference	Description	Relevance
Two-factor model / Related to needs theory	Herzberg et al (1957)	Two groups of factors affect job satisfaction: 1) those intrinsic to the work itself; 2) those extrinsic to the job (extrinsic motivators or hygiene factors) such as pay and working conditions.	Identifies a number of fundamental needs within the two-factor model, ie achievement, recognition, advancement, autonomy and the work itself. It also indicates that satisfaction from a pay increase (extrinsic motivation) does not last long. The research methodology has been strongly criticized and the underpinning assumption that everyone has the same needs is invalid. But it has influenced approaches to job design (job enrichment) and it supports the proposition that reward systems should provide for both financial and non-financial rewards.
Process/ cognitive theory			
Expectancy theory	Vroom (1964), Porter and Lawler (1968)	Effort (motivation) depends on the likelihood that rewards will follow effort and that the rewards are worthwhile.	The key theory informing approaches to rewards, ie that there must be a link between effort and reward (line of sight), the reward should be achievable and should be worthwhile.
Goal theory	Latham and Locke (1979)	Motivation will improve if people have demanding but agreed goals and receive feedback.	Influences performance management and learning and development practices.
Equity theory	Adams (1965)	People are better motivated if treated equitably, ie treated fairly in comparison with another group of people (a reference group) or a relevant other person.	Need to have equitable reward and employment practices.

3 *Growth needs*, which involve people in finding the opportunities 'to be what they are most fully and to become what they can'.

The content model of motivation shown in Figure 15.1, coupled with the Alderfer concept, usefully emphasize the significance of needs and goals as factors affecting motivation and how they function. But content or need theory ignores the important factor of expectations covered by expectancy theory. This means that it does not really explain how people make choices about their goals and behaviour.

Herzberg's two-factor model

Herzberg's two-factor theory in effect identifies needs but it has been attacked by, for example, Opsahl and Dunnette (1966). The research method has been criticized because no attempt was made to measure the relationship between satisfaction and performance. It has been claimed that the two-factor nature of the theory is an inevitable result of the questioning method used by the interviewers. It has also been suggested that wide and unwarranted inferences have been drawn from small and specialized samples and that there is no evidence to suggest that the satisfiers do improve productivity. The underpinning assumption that everyone has the same needs is invalid. Rousseau (2006: 263) summed up the views of academics about Herzberg as follows: 'Herzberg's long discredited two-factor theory is typically included in the motivation section of management textbooks, despite the fact that it was discredited over thirty years ago.'

In spite of these criticisms, the Herzberg two-factor theory continues to thrive, partly because it is easy to understand and seems to be based on 'real-life' rather than academic abstractions, and partly because it convincingly emphasizes the positive value of the intrinsic motivating factors. It is also in accord with a fundamental belief in the dignity of labour and the Protestant ethic – that work is good in itself. As a result, Herzberg had immense influence on the job enrichment movement, which sought to design jobs in a way that would maximize the opportunities to obtain intrinsic satisfaction from work and thus improve the quality of working life (Herzberg, 1968).

Expectancy theory

Expectancy theory focuses on how motivation affects performance and describes how people make choices about desired goals. It is generally accepted as the leading theory of motivation and has become an important basis for explaining what motivates people to work. It is used to inform decisions on the design and management of contingent pay schemes and to measure the effectiveness of such schemes.

The theory was developed by Vroom (1964) but has its origins in the ancient Greek principle of hedonism, which assumes that behaviour is directed toward pleasure and away from pain. Individuals will choose from alternative courses of action that behaviour which they think will maximize their pleasure or minimize their pain.

But research has not provided unequivocal backing for the theory. Connolly (1976) noted that: 'The expectancy model appears to have enjoyed substantial if uneven support.' House *et al* (1974) commented that: 'Evidence for the validity of the theory is very mixed.' They also established that there were a number of variables affecting expectations that make it difficult to predict how they function. These are:

- *Leadership behaviour* – the function of the leader in clarifying expectations, guiding, supporting and rewarding subordinates.
- *Individual characteristics* – the subjects' perception of their ability to perform the required task.
- *Nature of the task* – whether accomplishing the task provides the necessary reinforcements and rewards.
- *The practices of the organization* – its reward and control systems and how it functions.

Research conducted by Behling and Starke (1973) established that individuals:

- make crucial personal decisions without clearly understanding the consequences;
- do not in practice consistently evaluate their order of preference for alternative actions;
- have to assign two values when making a decision – its desirability and its achievability, but they tend to be influenced mainly by desirability – they let their tastes influence their beliefs;

- may be able to evaluate the extrinsic rewards they expect but may find it difficult to evaluate the possibility of achieving intrinsic rewards;
- may find it difficult to distinguish the benefits of one possible outcome from another.

They concluded that: 'Expectancy theory can account for some of the variations in work effort but far less than normally attributed to it.'

The findings of research by Reinharth and Wahba (1975) based on a survey of the sales forces of four industrial companies showed no support for either the Vroom expectancy model or its components. As they concluded:

> The findings of the study point to the theory's ability to explain at best a very limited portion of human behavior. It may be that the theory, founded on considerations of rationality, can serve as a useful predictor in situations where contingencies between acts and outcomes and between first-level and second-level outcomes are clearly perceived by the individual, whereas ambiguous situations force the individual to develop a choice mechanism not based on the expectancy variables. In short, the earlier optimism for the universality of the theory appears to have been dashed.

Overall, the outcomes of research suggest that while expectancy theory offers what appears to be a convincing explanation of the factors affecting the motivation to work, it does not provide a universal explanation because of individual differences in the approach to decision making, the circumstances in which the scheme operates and the impact of social forces on individuals. However, when designing an incentive scheme and assessing its effectiveness, expectancy theory has considerable face-validity as a commonsense explanation of the factors affecting motivation and what makes incentive schemes work, ie the incentive has to be worthwhile and attainable. It provides the theoretical basis for the concept of 'line of sight' developed by Lawler (1988), which states that for a scheme to be effective there has to be a clear and easily perceived link between effort and reward.

Goal theory

Goal theory provides the rationale for performance management, goal setting and feedback. But its universality has been questioned. For example, Pintrich (2000) noted that people have different goals in different circumstances and that it is hard to justify the assumption that goals are always accessible and conscious. And Harackiewicz *et al* (2002) warned that goals are only effective when they are consistent with and match the general context in which they are pursued. But support for goal theory was provided by Bandura and Cervone (1983), who emphasized the importance of self-evaluation and self-efficacy (a belief in one's ability to accomplish goals).

Goal theory is in line with the 1960s concept of management by objectives or MBO (a process of managing, motivating and appraising people by setting objectives or goals and measuring performance against those objectives). But MBO fell into disrepute because it was tackled bureaucratically without gaining the real support of those involved and, importantly, without ensuring that managers were aware of the significance of the processes of agreement, reinforcement and feedback, and were also skilled in practising them. Goal theory, however, plays a key part in performance management.

Equity theory

Equity theory has been criticized because it is oversimplified and is based on laboratory rather than real-life research (Huseman *et al*, 1982). It has also been suggested by Carrell and Dittrich (1978) that equity can be perceived not only on a person-to-person basis as the theory posits, but also by reference to the fairness of processes in the organization as a whole. But the need to have equitable reward and employment practices that are supported by equity theory cannot be questioned. The problem is how to achieve equity.

Conclusions

In a sense, all the theories referred to above make a contribution to an understanding of the processes that affect motivation. But some, such as reinforcement and instrumentality, have considerable limitations, as do the needs hierarchy and two-factor theories of Maslow and Herzberg. Gerhart and Rynes (2003: 50) pointed out that: 'Although Maslow's and Herzberg's theories were intuitively appealing to many people, research has not supported either theory to any great extent.' In fact, people are far more varied and complex than these theories suggest. To state that there are strong similarities between people leads to the conclusion that there is 'one best way' to motivate and reward them, which is simply not true.

Process theories concerned with expectancy, goal setting and equity are based on more realistic ideas and are much more relevant than the theories of Maslow and Herzberg. Expectancy theory is particularly appropriate when dealing with contingent pay (incentive schemes) but it is still dangerous to generalize that everyone is motivated in the same way by the same pattern of expectations.

Motivation and money

Money, in the form of pay or some other sort of remuneration, is the most obvious extrinsic reward. Money seems to provide the carrot most people want.

Doubts were cast on the effectiveness of money by Herzberg *et al* (1957) because, they claimed, while the lack of it can cause dissatisfaction, its provision does not result in lasting satisfaction. There is something in this, especially for people on fixed salaries or rates of pay who do not benefit directly from an incentive scheme. They may feel good when they get an increase; apart from the extra money, it is a highly tangible form of recognition and an effective means of helping people to feel that they are valued. But this feeling of euphoria can rapidly die away. Other dissatisfactions from Herzberg's list of hygiene factors, such as working conditions or the quality of management, can loom larger in some people's minds when they fail to get the satisfaction they need from the work itself. However, different people have different needs and wants. Some will be much more motivated by money than others. What cannot be assumed is that money motivates everyone in the same way and to the same extent. Thus it is naive to think that the introduction of a performance-related pay scheme will miraculously transform everyone overnight into well-motivated, high-performing individuals.

Nevertheless, money is a powerful force because it is linked directly or indirectly to the satisfaction of many needs. Money may in itself have no intrinsic meaning, but it acquires significant motivating power because it comes to symbolize so many intangible goals. It acts as a symbol in different ways for different people, and for the same person at different times.

But do financial incentives motivate people? The answer is yes, for those people who are strongly motivated by money and whose expectations that they will receive a financial reward are high. But less confident employees may not respond to incentives they do not expect to achieve. Motivation may also take place when there is a very clear line of sight between effort and reward, as in some forms of piecework.

However, it can be argued that extrinsic rewards may erode intrinsic interest – people who work just for money could find their tasks less pleasurable and may not, therefore, do them so well. What we do know is that a multiplicity of factors is involved in performance improvements and many of those factors are interdependent.

Money can therefore provide positive motivation in the right circumstances not only because people need and want money but also because it serves as a highly tangible means of recognition. But badly designed and managed pay systems can demotivate. Another researcher in this area was Jaques (1961), who emphasized the need for such systems to be perceived as being fair and equitable. In other words, the reward should be clearly related to effort or level of responsibility and people should not receive less money than they deserve compared with their fellow workers. Jaques called this the 'felt-fair' principle.

Motivation strategies

Motivation strategies aim to create a working environment and to develop policies and practices that will provide for higher levels of performance from employees. The factors affecting them and the HR contribution are summarized in Table 15.2.

TABLE 15.2   Factors affecting motivation strategies and the HR contribution

Factors affecting motivation strategies	The HR contribution
The complexity of the process of motivation means that simplistic approaches based on instrumentality or needs theory are unlikely to be successful.	Avoid the trap of developing or supporting strategies that offer prescriptions for motivation based on a simplistic view of the process or fail to recognize individual differences.
People are more likely to be motivated if they work in an environment in which they are valued for what they are and what they do. This means paying attention to the basic need for recognition.	Encourage the development of performance management processes that provide opportunities to agree expectations and to recognize accomplishments.
Extrinsic motivators such as incentive pay can have an immediate and powerful effect, but it will not necessarily last long. The intrinsic motivators, which are concerned with the 'quality of working life' (a phrase and movement that emerged from this concept), are likely to have a deeper and longer-term effect because they are inherent in individuals and the work they do and not imposed from outside in such forms as performance-related pay.	Develop total reward systems that provide opportunities for both financial and non-financial rewards to recognize achievements. Bear in mind, however, that financial rewards systems are not necessarily appropriate and the lessons of expectancy, goal and equity theory need to be taken into account in designing and operating them. Pay particular attention to recognition as a means of motivation and developing intrinsic motivation through job design.
Some people will be much more motivated by money than others. It cannot be assumed that money motivates everyone in the same way and to the same extent.	Avoid the introduction of a performance-related pay scheme in the belief that it will miraculously transform everyone overnight into well-motivated, high-performing individuals.
Recognition should be given to the need for work that provides people with the means to achieve their goals, a reasonable degree of autonomy, and scope for the use of skills and competences.	Advise on processes for the design of jobs that take account of the factors affecting the motivation to work, providing for job enrichment in the shape of variety, decision-making responsibility and as much control as possible in carrying out the work.
The need for the opportunity to grow by developing abilities and careers.	Provide facilities and opportunities for learning through such means as personal development planning processes as well as more formal training. Develop career planning processes.
The cultural environment of the organization in the shape of its values and norms will influence the impact of any attempts to motivate people by direct or indirect means.	Advise on the development of a culture that supports processes of valuing and rewarding employees.
Motivation will be enhanced by leadership that sets the direction, encourages and stimulates achievement and provides support to employees in their efforts to reach goals and improve their performance generally.	Devise competency frameworks which focus on leadership qualities and the behaviours expected of managers and team leaders. Ensure that leadership potential is identified through performance management and assessment centres. Conduct leadership development programmes.

Key learning points: Motivation

The process of motivation

Motivation is goal-directed behaviour. People are motivated when they expect that a course of action is likely to lead to the attainment of a goal and a valued reward – one that satisfies their needs and wants.

Types of motivation

The two basic types are intrinsic and extrinsic motivation.

Motivation theories

There are a number of motivation theories which, in the main, are complementary to one another.

The most significant theories are those concerned with expectancy, goal setting and equity, which are classified as process or cognitive theories.

Motivation strategies

Motivation strategies aim to create a working environment and to develop policies and practices that will provide for higher levels of performance from employees. They include the development of total reward systems and performance management processes, the design of intrinsically motivating jobs and leadership development programmes.

Questions

1 What is motivation?

2 What is the difference between extrinsic and intrinsic motivation?

3 What is instrumentality?

4 What is reinforcement?

5 What is content or needs theory?

6 How valid is Maslow's concept of the hierarchy of human needs?

7 How valid is Herzberg's two-factor theory of motivation?

8 What is expectancy theory?

9 What is goal theory?

10 What is equity theory?

11 Which motivation theory provides the best guide on the principles of performance-related pay and why?

12 What message for HR policy is provided by the belief that motivation is a highly complex process?

13 Why is recognition so important as a means of motivation?

14 Why are there limitations in the power of money to motivate?

15 Why is intrinsic motivation through the work itself likely to be more effective in the longer term than extrinsic motivation?

References

Adams, J S (1965) Injustice in social exchange, in (ed) L Berkowitz, *Advances in Experimental Psychology*, New York, Academic Press

Alderfer, C (1972) *Existence, Relatedness and Growth*, New York, The Free Press

Allport, G (1954) The historical background of modern social psychology, in (ed) G Lindzey, *Theoretical Models and Personality*, Cambridge, MA, Addison-Wesley

Bandura, A and Cervone, D (1983) Self-evaluation and self-efficacy mechanisms governing the motivational effects of goal systems, *Journal of Personality and Social Psychology*, 45 (5), pp 1017–28

Behling, O and Starke, F A (1973) The postulates of expectancy theory, *Academy of Management Journal*, **16** (3), pp 375–88

Carrell, M R and Dittrich, J E (1978) Equity theory: the recent literature, methodological considerations and new directions, *Academy of Management Review*, **3** (2), pp 202–10

Connolly, T (1976) Some contested and methodological issues in expectancy models of work performance motivation, *Academy of Management Review*, **1** (4), pp 32–47

Gerhart, B and Rynes, S L (2003) *Compensation: Theory, evidence and strategic implications*, Thousand Oaks, CA, Sage

Harackiewicz, J M, Barron, P R, Pintrich, P R, Elliot, A J and Thrash, T M (2002) Revision of goal theory: necessary and illuminating, *Journal of Educational Psychology*, **94** (3), pp 638–45

Herzberg, F (1968) One more time: how do you motivate employees?, *Harvard Business Review*, January–February, pp 109–20

Herzberg, F W, Mausner, B and Snyderman, B (1957) *The Motivation to Work*, New York, Wiley

House, R J, Shapiro, H J and Wahba, M A (1974) Expectancy theory as a predictor of work behaviour and attitude: a re-evaluation of empirical evidence, *Decision Science*, **5** (3), pp 481–506

Hull, C (1951) *Essentials of Behaviour*, New Haven, CT, Yale University Press

Hunter, J E, Schmidt, F L and Judiesch, M K (1990) Individual differences in output variability as a function of job complexity, *Journal of Applied Psychology*, **75** (1), pp 28–42

Huseman, R C, Hatfield, J D and Milis, E W (1982) A new perception on equity theory: the equity sensitivity constant, *Academy of Management Review*, **12** (2), pp 222–34

Jaques, E (1961) *Equitable Payment*, London, Heinemann

Latham, G and Locke, R (1979) Goal setting – a motivational technique that works, *Organizational Dynamics*, Autumn, pp 68–80

Lawler, E E (1988) Pay for performance: making it work, *Personnel*, October, pp 25–9

Maslow, A (1954) *Motivation and Personality*, New York, Harper & Row

Opsahl, R C and Dunnette, M D (1966) The role of financial compensation in individual motivation, *Psychological Bulletin*, **56**, pp 94–118

Pintrich, P R (2000) An achievement goal perspective on issues in motivation technology, theory and research, *Contemporary Educational Psychology*, **25**, pp 92–104

Porter, L W and Lawler, E E (1968) *Managerial Attitudes and Performance*, Homewood, IL, Irwin-Dorsey

Reinharth, L and Wahba, M A (1975) Expectancy theory as a predictor of work motivation, effort expenditure and job performance, *Academy of Management Journal*, **18** (3), pp 520–37

Rousseau, D M (2006) Is there such a thing as evidence-based management?, *Academy of Management Review*, **31** (2), pp 256–69

Taylor, F W (1911) *Principles of Scientific Management*, New York, Harper

Vroom, V (1964) *Work and Motivation*, New York, Wiley

Wahba, M A and Bridwell, L G (1979) Maslow reconsidered: a review of research on the need hierarchy theory, in (eds) R M Sters and L W Porter, *Motivation and Work Behaviour*, New York, McGraw-Hill

16
Commitment

Introduction

Commitment represents the strength of an individual's identification with, and involvement in, an organization. It is a concept that has played an important part in HRM philosophy. As Guest (1987: 503) suggested, HRM policies are designed to 'maximize organizational integration, employee commitment, flexibility and quality of work'. Beer *et al* (1984: 20) identified commitment in their concept of HRM as a key dimension because it 'can result not only in more loyalty and better performance for the organization, but also in self-worth, dignity, psychological involvement, and identity for the individual'.

The meaning of organizational commitment

Commitment refers to attachment and loyalty. It is associated with the feelings of individuals about their organization. The three characteristics of commitment identified by Mowday *et al* (1982) are:

1 A strong desire to remain a member of the organization.

2 A strong belief in and acceptance of the values and goals of the organization.

3 A readiness to exert considerable effort on behalf of the organization.

Appelbaum *et al* (2000: 183) rephrased this definition as: 'Organizational commitment is a multi-dimensional construct that reflects a worker's: identification with the organization (loyalty), attachment to the organization (intention to stay), and willingness to expend effort on the organization's behalf (discretionary effort).' An alternative, although closely related definition of commitment emphasizes the importance of behaviour in creating commitment. Three features of behaviour are important in binding individuals to their acts: the visibility of the acts, the extent to which the outcomes are irrevocable, and the degree to which the person undertakes the action voluntarily. Commitment, according to Salancik (1977) can be increased and harnessed to obtain support for organizational ends and interests through such ploys as participation in decisions about actions.

The importance of commitment

The importance of commitment was highlighted by Walton (1985a). His theme was that improved performance would result if the organization moved away from the traditional control-oriented approach to workforce management, which relies upon establishing order, exercising control and achieving efficiency. He proposed that this approach should be replaced by a commitment strategy that would enable workers 'to respond best – and most creatively – not when they are tightly controlled by management, placed in narrowly defined jobs, and

treated like an unwelcome necessity, but, instead, when they are given broader responsibilities, encouraged to contribute and helped to achieve satisfaction in their work' (*ibid*: 77). He described the commitment-based approach as follows.

Source review

Richard Walton on commitment – Walton (1985a: 79)

Jobs are designed to be broader than before, to combine planning and implementation, and to include efforts to upgrade operations, not just to maintain them. Individual responsibilities are expected to change as conditions change, and teams, not individuals, often are the organizational units accountable for performance. With management hierarchies relatively flat and differences in status minimized, control and lateral coordination depend on shared goals. And expertise rather than formal position determines influence.

Expressed like this, a commitment strategy sounds idealistic ('the American dream' as Guest, 1990, put it) but it does not appear to be a crude attempt to manipulate people to accept management's values and goals, as some have suggested. In fact, Walton did not describe it as being instrumental in this manner. His prescription was for a broad HRM approach to the ways in which people are treated, jobs are designed and organizations are managed. He believed that the aim should be to develop 'mutuality', a state that exists when management and employees are interdependent and both benefit from this interdependency. The importance of and its relationship to commitment was spelt out by Walton (1985b: 64) as follows:

The new HRM model is composed of policies that promote mutuality – mutual goals, mutual influence, mutual respect, mutual rewards, mutual responsibility. The theory is that policies of mutuality will elicit commitment which in turn will yield both better economic performance and greater human development.

But a review by Guest (1991), of the mainly North American literature, reinforced by the limited UK research available, led him to the conclusion that: 'High organizational commitment is associated with lower labour turnover and absence, but there is no clear link to performance.' Swailes (2002: 164) confirmed that: 'Despite the best efforts of researchers … the evidence for a strong positive link between commitment and performance remains patchy.'

It is probably unwise to expect too much from commitment as a means of making a direct and immediate impact on performance. It is not the same as motivation. It is possible to be dissatisfied with a particular feature of a job while retaining a fairly high level of commitment to the organization as a whole. But it is reasonable to believe that strong commitment to work may result in conscientious and self-directed application to do the job, regular attendance, the need for less supervision and a high level of discretionary effort. Commitment to the organization will certainly be related to the intention to stay there.

Commitment and engagement

The notion of commitment as described above appears to be very similar if not identical to that of organizational engagement which, as defined in Chapter 14, focuses on attachment to, or identification with, the organization as a whole. Are there any differences?

Some commentators have asserted that commitment is a distinct although closely linked entity. As cited by Buchanan (2004: 19), the US Corporate Executive Board divides engagement into two aspects of commitment: 1) *rational commitment*, which occurs when a job serves employees' financial, developmental, or professional self-interest; and 2) *emotional commitment*, which arises when workers value, enjoy and believe in what they do and has four times the power to affect performance as its more pragmatic counterpart. The Corporate Executive Board (2004: 1) indicated that engagement is 'the extent to which employees commit to someone or something in their organization, how hard they work, and how long they stay as a result of that commitment'. Wellins and Concelman (2005: 1)

suggested that 'to be engaged is to be actively committed'. And Macey and Schneider (2008: 8–9) observed that:

> Organizational commitment is an important facet of the state of engagement when it is conceptualized as positive attachment to the larger organizational entity and measured as a willingness to exert energy in support of the organization, to feel pride as an organizational member, and to have personal identification with the organization.

Clearly organizational engagement and commitment are closely associated, and commitment was included by the Institute for Employment Studies in its model (see Chapter 14) as an element of engagement. Appelbaum *et al* (2000: 183) noted that: 'The willingness to exert extra effort is the aspect of organizational commitment that has been shown to be most closely related to an employee's job performance.' Robinson *et al* (2004: 7) suggested that the closest relationship of commitment to engagement was 'affective commitment, ie the satisfaction people get from their jobs and their colleagues and their willingness to go beyond the call of duty for the sake of the organization'. Salanova *et al* (2005) saw commitment as part of engagement but not equivalent to it.

The analysis of the concept of commitment as undertaken in this chapter is based on a considerable body of work exploring its nature and significance, and therefore helps to illuminate the somewhat elusive notion of engagement. But there are problems with commitment, as discussed below.

Critical evaluation of the concept of commitment

A number of commentators have raised questions about the concept of commitment. These relate to three main problem areas: 1) the imprecise nature of the term, 2) its unitary frame of reference, and 3) commitment as an inhibitor of flexibility.

The imprecise nature of the term

Guest (1987: 513) raised the question of what commitment really means as follows:

The case for seeking high commitment among employees seems plausible but the burgeoning research on the topic has identified a number of problems. One of these concerns the definition of the concept. The first issue is – commitment to what? Most writers are interested in commitment to the organization, but others have examined career commitment and job commitment. Once the general concept of commitment is utilized, then union commitment, workgroup commitment and family commitment should also be considered. The possibility of multiple and perhaps competing commitments creates a more complex set of issues.

Unitary frame of reference

The concept of commitment, especially as put forward by Walton, can be criticized as being simplistic, even misguided, in adopting a unitary frame of reference which assumes that organizations consist of people with shared interests. It has been suggested by people like Cyert and March (1963), Mangham (1979) and Mintzberg (1983) that an organization is really a coalition of interest groups where political processes are an inevitable part of everyday life.

Legge (1989: 38) also raised this question in her discussion of strong culture as a key requirement of HRM, which she criticized because it implies 'a shared set of managerially sanctioned values ... that assumes an identification of employee and employer interests'. As Coopey and Hartley (1991: 21) put it: 'Commitment is not an all-or-nothing affair (though many managers might like it to be) but a question of multiple or competing commitments for the individual.' A pluralist perspective recognizes the legitimacy of different interests and is more realistic.

It could be argued that values concerned with performance, quality, service, equal opportunity and innovation are not necessarily wrong *because* they are managerial values. But pursuing a value such as innovation could work against the interests of employees by, for example, resulting in redundancies. And flexibility may sound a good idea but, beyond the rhetoric, as Sisson (1994: 5) observed, the reality may mean that management can do what it wants. It would be quite reasonable for any employee encouraged to behave in accordance with a value supported by management to ask, 'What's in it for me?' It can also be argued that the imposition from above of management's values on employees with-

out their having any part to play in discussing and agreeing them is a form of coercion.

Commitment and flexibility

It was pointed out by Coopey and Hartley (1991: 22) that: 'The problem for a unitarist notion of organizational commitment is that it fosters a conformist approach which not only fails to reflect organizational reality, but can be narrowing and limiting for the organization.' They argued that if employees are expected and encouraged to commit themselves tightly to a single set of values and goals they will not be able to cope with the ambiguities and uncertainties that are endemic in organizational life in times of change. Conformity to 'imposed' values will inhibit creative problem solving, and high commitment to present courses of action will increase both resistance to change and the stress that invariably occurs when change takes place.

If commitment is related to tightly defined plans, this will become a real problem. To avoid it, the emphasis should be on overall strategic directions. These would be communicated to employees with the proviso that changing circumstances will require their amendment. In the meantime, however, everyone can at least be informed in general terms where the organization is heading and, more specifically, the part they are expected to play in helping the organization to get there and, if they can be involved in the decision-making processes on matters that affect them (including management's values for performance, quality and customer service), so much the better.

Values need not necessarily be restrictive. They can be defined in ways that allow for freedom of choice within broad guidelines. In fact, the values themselves can refer to such processes as flexibility, innovation and responsiveness to change. Thus, far from inhibiting creative problem solving, they can encourage it. But they will not do so if they are imposed from above. Employees need to have a say in defining the values they are expected to support.

Factors affecting commitment

Kochan and Dyer (1993) indicated that the factors affecting the level of commitment in what they called 'mutual commitment firms' were as follows:

1 *Strategic level*: supportive business strategies, top management value commitment and effective voice for HR in strategy making and governance.

2 *Functional (human resource policy) level*: staffing based on employment stabilization, investment in training and development and contingent compensation that reinforces cooperation, participation and contribution.

3 *Workplace level*: selection based on high standards, broad task design and teamwork, employee involvement in problem solving and a climate of cooperation and trust.

The research conducted by Purcell *et al* (2003) identified the following key policy and practice factors that influence levels of commitment:

● Received training last year.

● Satisfied with career opportunities.

● Satisfied with the performance appraisal system.

● Think managers are good in people management (leadership).

● Find their work challenging.

● Think their firm helps them achieve a work–life balance.

● Satisfied with communication or company performance.

Developing a commitment strategy

A commitment strategy can be based on the high-commitment model incorporating policies and practices in areas of HR such as job design, learning and development, career planning, performance management, reward management, participation, communication and employee wellbeing. HR should play a major part in developing a high-commitment organization. The 10 steps it can take are:

1 Advise on methods of communicating the values and aims of management and the achievements of the organization so that employees are more likely to identify with it as one they are proud to work for.

2 Emphasize to management that commitment is a two-way process; employees cannot be expected to be committed to the organization unless management demonstrates that it is committed to them and recognizes their contribution as stakeholders.

3 Impress on management the need to develop a climate of trust by being honest with people, treating them fairly, justly and consistently, keeping its word, and showing willingness to listen to the comments and suggestions made by employees during processes of consultation and participation.

4 Develop a positive psychological contract (the set of reciprocal but unwritten expectations that exist between individual employees and their employers) by treating people as stakeholders, relying on consensus and cooperation rather than control and coercion, and focusing on the provision of opportunities for learning, development and career progression.

5 Advise on the establishment of partnership agreements with trade unions that emphasize unity of purpose, common approaches to working together and the importance of giving employees a voice in matters that concern them.

6 Recommend and take part in the achievement of single status for all employees (often included in a partnership agreement) so that there is no longer an 'us and them' culture.

7 Encourage management to declare a policy of employment security and ensure that steps are taken to avoid involuntary redundancies.

8 Develop performance management processes that provide for the alignment of organizational and individual objectives.

9 Advise on means of increasing employee identification with the company through rewards related to organizational performance (profit sharing or gainsharing) or employee share ownership schemes.

10 Enhance employee job engagement, ie identification of employees with the job they are doing, through job design processes that aim to create higher levels of job satisfaction (job enrichment).

Key learning points: Commitment

The meaning of commitment

Commitment refers to attachment and loyalty. It is associated with the feelings of individuals about their organization. The three characteristics of commitment identified by Mowday *et al* (1982) are:

1 A strong desire to remain a member of the organization.

2 A strong belief in and acceptance of the values and goals of the organization.

3 A readiness to exert considerable effort on behalf of the organization.

The impact of high commitment

In his seminal *Harvard Business Review* article, Richard Walton (1985a) stated that 'eliciting employee commitment will lead to enhanced performance [and] the evidence shows this belief to be well founded'. The importance of commitment was highlighted by Walton. His theme was that improved performance would result if the organization moved away from the traditional control-oriented approach to workforce management, which relies upon establishing order, exercising control and achieving efficiency. He proposed that this approach should be replaced by a commitment strategy.

Problems with the concept of commitment

There are four main problem areas: 1) the imprecise nature of the term, 2) its unitary frame of reference, 3) commitment as an inhibitor of flexibility, and 4) the extent to which high commitment does in practice result in improved organizational performance.

Engagement and commitment

Organizational engagement and commitment are closely associated. Commitment was included by the IES in its model as an element of engagement. But commitment is a somewhat wider concept in that it is concerned with both job engagement and organizational engagement.

The factors affecting the level of commitment (Kochan and Dyer, 1993)

- *Strategic level*: supportive business strategies, top management value commitment and effective voice for HR in strategy making and governance.

- *Functional (human resource policy) level*: staffing based on employment stabilization, investment in training and development and contingent compensation that reinforces cooperation, participation and contribution.

- *Workplace level*: selection based on high standards, broad task design and teamwork, employee involvement in problem solving and a climate of cooperation and trust.

HR's role in enhancing commitment

HR should play a major part in developing a high-commitment organization. The 10 steps it can take are:

1 Advise on methods of communicating the values and aims of management.

2 Emphasize to management that commitment is a two-way process.

3 Impress on management the need to develop a climate of trust.

4 Develop a positive psychological contract.

5 Advise on the establishment of partnership agreements with trade unions.

6 Recommend and take part in the achievement of single status for all employees.

7 Encourage management to declare a policy of employment security.

8 Develop performance management processes.

9 Advise on means of increasing employee identification with the company.

10 Enhance employee job engagement through job design processes.

Questions

1   What is commitment?

2   What is mutuality?

3   What are the three characteristics of commitment?

4   Why is commitment important?

5   What impact can high levels of commitment have on performance?

6   What is the relationship between commitment and engagement?

7   What did the research conducted by Purcell *et al* (2003) tell us about the factors affecting commitment?

8   Is a belief in the virtues of commitment based on an unrealistic unitary view of employment relationships?

9   Do high levels of commitment result in lack of flexibility and if so, what can be done about it?

10   What are the essential features of a commitment strategy?

References

Appelbaum, E, Bailey, T, Berg, P and Kalleberg, A L (2000) *Manufacturing Advantage: Why high performance work systems pay off*, Ithaca, NY, ILR Press

Beer, M, Spector, B, Lawrence, P, Quinn Mills, D and Walton, R (1984) *Managing Human Assets*, New York, The Free Press

Buchanan, L (2004) The things they do for love, *Harvard Business Review*, December, pp 19–20

Coopey, J and Hartley, J (1991) Reconsidering the case for organizational commitment, *Human Resource Management Journal*, 1 (3), pp 18–31

Corporate Executive Board (2004) *Driving Performance and Retention through Employee Engagement*, www.corporateleadershipcouncil.com/Images/CLC/PDF/CLC12KADBP.pdf, accessed 13 September 2005

Cyert, R M and March, J G (1963) *A Behavioural Theory of the Firm*, Englewood Cliffs, NJ, Prentice-Hall

Guest, D E (1987) Human resource management and industrial relations, *Journal of Management Studies*, 24 (5), pp 503–21

Guest, D E (1990) HRM and the American dream, *Journal of Management Studies*, 27 (4), pp 377–97

Guest, D E (1991) Personnel management: the end of orthodoxy, *British Journal of Industrial Relations*, 29 (2), pp 149–76

Kochan, T A and Dyer, L (1993) Managing transformational change: the role of human resource professionals, *International Journal of Human Resource Management*, 4 (3), pp 569–90

Legge, K (1989) Human resource management: a critical analysis, in (ed) J Storey, *New Perspectives in Human Resource Management*, London, Routledge, pp 19–40

Macey, W H and Schneider, B (2008) The meaning of employee engagement, *Industrial and Organizational Psychology*, 1, pp 3–30

Mangham, L L (1979) *The Politics of Organizational Change*, London, Associated Business Press

Mintzberg, H (1983) *Power in and around Organizations*, Englewood Cliffs, NJ, Prentice-Hall

Mowday, R, Porter, L and Steers, R (1982) *Employee-organization Linkages: The psychology of commitment, absenteeism and turnover*, London, Academic Press

Purcell, J, Kinnie, K, Hutchinson, R, Rayton, B and Swart, J (2003) *Understanding the People and Performance Link: Unlocking the black box*, London, CIPD

Robinson, D, Perryman, S and Hayday, S (2004) *The Drivers of Employee Engagement*, Brighton, Institute for Employment Studies

Salancik, G R (1977) Commitment and the control of organizational behaviour and belief, in (eds) B M Straw and G R Salancik, *New Directions in Organizational Behaviour*, Chicago, IL, St Clair Press

Salanova, M, Agut, S and Peiro, J M (2005) Linking organizational resources and work engagement to employee performance and customer loyalty: the mediation of service climate, *Journal of Applied Psychology*, 90, pp 1217–27

Sisson, K (1994) Personnel management: paradigms, practice and prospects, in (ed) K Sisson, *Personnel Management*, 2nd edn, Oxford, Blackwell, pp 3–50

Swailes, S (2002) Organizational commitment; a critique of the construct and measures, *International Journal of Management Reviews*, **4** (2), pp 155–78

Walton, R E (1985a) From control to commitment in the workplace, *Harvard Business Review*, March–April, pp 77–84

Walton, R E (1985b) Towards a strategy of eliciting employee commitment based on principles of mutuality, in (eds) R E Walton and P R Lawrence, *HRM Trends and Challenges*, Boston, MA, Harvard Business School Press, pp 35–65

Wellins, R and Concelman, J (2005) *Personal Engagement: Driving growth at the see-level*, www.ddiworld.com/pdf/ ddipersonalengagement.ar.pdf, accessed 29 April 2005

PART III

People resourcing

PART III CONTENTS

Introduction

People resourcing, often called 'employee resourcing' or simply 'resourcing' is the term used to cover employment activities that ensure the organization has the people it needs, and deals with employee turnover and absenteeism issues. The employment activities comprise workforce planning, recruitment and selection, attracting and retaining people, managing employee turnover, absence management, and talent management. It is associated with learning and development programmes that provide for the organization to have the skills and talented people it requires.

Resourcing is a vital organizational activity that recognizes that the strategic capability of a firm depends on its resource capability in the shape of people (the resource-based view). This is the strategic approach to resourcing, as explained in Chapter 17. From this emerges the workforce planning aspect of resourcing covered in Chapter 18, which deals with what sort of workforce the organization requires now and in the future and what steps should be taken to meet those requirements.

The core resourcing activities of recruitment and selection and handling employment issues discussed in the next two chapters are transactional. There are some who are rather dismissive about them, implying that HR is primarily a transformational activity and that recruitment, while necessary, is inferior and best left to the sidelined inhabitants of shared service centres so that business partners can get on with their essential work. They could not be more wrong. If HR does not deliver the transactional services expected of it no amount of strategizing will save the function from being dismissed as a luxury.

However, talent management as described in the last chapter of this part contains both transformational and transactional elements. It recognizes that businesses with the best people win and that the way to transform the organization is to identify and develop those with talent, but it also involves transactional activities such as recruitment and the administration of learning and development events.

17
Strategic resourcing

LEARNING OUTCOMES

On completing this chapter you should be able to define these key concepts. You should also know about:

- The meaning of strategic resourcing
- The objective of strategic resourcing
- The strategic HRM approach to resourcing
- Strategic fit in resourcing
- Integrating business and resourcing strategies
- The components of resourcing strategy

Introduction

Strategic resourcing is a key part of strategic human resource management ie, matching human resources to the strategic and operational requirements of the organization and ensuring the full utilization of those resources. It is concerned not only with obtaining and keeping the number and quality of staff required but also with selecting and promoting people who 'fit' the culture and the strategic requirements of the organization.

The objective of strategic resourcing

Strategic resourcing aims to ensure that the organization has the people it needs to achieve its business goals. Like strategic HRM, strategic resourcing is essentially about the integration of business and employee resourcing strategies so that the latter contribute to the achievement of the former.

The concept that the strategic capability of a firm depends on its resource capability in the shape of people (the resource-based view) provides the rationale for strategic resourcing. The objective is therefore to ensure that a firm achieves competitive advantage by recruiting, retaining and developing more capable people than its rivals. The organization attracts such people by being 'the employer of choice'. It retains them by providing better opportunities and rewards than others and by developing a positive psychological contract (the set of reciprocal but unwritten expectations that exist between individual employees and their employers), which increases engagement and commitment and creates mutual trust. Furthermore, the organization deploys its people in ways that maximize the added value they supply and develops their talents and skills.

The strategic HRM approach to resourcing

The philosophy behind the strategic approach to resourcing is that it is people who implement the strategic plan. As Quinn Mills (1983) put it, the process is one of 'planning with people in mind'.

The integration of business and resourcing strategies is based on an understanding of the direction in which the organization is going and the determination of:

- the numbers of people required to meet business needs;
- the skills and behaviour required to support the achievement of business strategies;
- the impact of organizational restructuring as a result of rationalization, decentralization, delayering, acquisitions, mergers, product or market development, or the introduction of new technology – for example, cellular manufacturing;
- plans for changing the culture of the organization in such areas as ability to deliver, performance standards, quality, customer service, teamworking and flexibility, which indicate the need for people with different attitudes, beliefs and personal characteristics.

These factors will be strongly influenced by the type of business strategies adopted by the organization and the sort of business it is in. These may be expressed in such terms as Miles and Snow's (1978) typology of defender, prospector and analyser organizations.

Strategic HRM places more emphasis than traditional personnel management on finding people whose attitudes and behaviour are likely to fit what management believes to be appropriate and conducive to success. Townley (1989) commented that organizations are concentrating more on the attitudinal and behavioural characteristics of employees. This tendency has its dangers. Innovative and adaptive organizations need non-conformists, even mavericks, who can 'buck the system'. If managers recruit people 'in their own image' there is the risk of staffing the organization with conformist clones and of perpetuating a dysfunctional culture – one that may have been successful in the past but is no longer appropriate in the face of new challenges.

The resourcing strategies that emerge from the process of strategic resourcing exist to provide the people and skills required to support the business strategy, but they should also contribute to the formulation of that strategy. HR directors have an obligation to point out to their colleagues the human resource opportunities and constraints that will affect the achievement of strategic plans. In mergers or acquisitions, for example, the ability of management within the company to handle the new situation and the quality of management in the new business will be important considerations.

Strategic fit in resourcing

Strategic resourcing places more emphasis than traditional personnel management on finding people whose attitudes and behaviour are likely to fit what management believes to be appropriate and conducive to success. As mentioned above, Townley (1989) felt that organizations are concentrating more on the attitudinal and behavioural characteristics of employees, a tendency that has its dangers.

Bundling resourcing strategies and activities

Employee resourcing is not just about recruitment and selection. It is concerned with any means available to meet the firm's need for certain skills and behaviours. A strategy to ensure the organization has the talented people it needs (a talent management strategy) may start with recruitment and selection but would extend into learning and development to enhance abilities and skills and modify behaviours and succession planning. Performance management processes can be used to identify development needs (skills and behaviours) and motivate people to make the most effective use of their abilities. Competency frameworks and profiles can be prepared to define the skills and behaviours required and used in selection, employee development and employee reward processes. The aim should be to develop a reinforcing bundle of strategies along these lines.

The components of strategic employee resourcing

The overarching component of strategic resourcing is the integration of resourcing and business plans. Within this framework strategic resourcing includes specific strategies for:

- *Workforce planning, alternatively called human resource planning* – assessing future business needs and deciding on the numbers and types of people required.
- *Developing the organization's employee value proposition and its employer brand* – the employee value proposition is what an organization has to offer, which prospective or existing employees would value and which would help to persuade them to join or remain with the business; employer brand is the image presented by an organization as a good employer.
- *Resourcing plans* – preparing plans for finding people from within the organization and/or for learning and development programmes to help people learn new skills. If needs cannot be satisfied from within the organization, it involves preparing longer-term plans for ensuring that recruitment and selection processes will satisfy them.
- *Retention* – preparing plans for retaining the people the organization needs.
- *Flexibility* – planning for increased flexibility in the use of human resources to enable the organization to make the best use of people and adapt swiftly to changing circumstances.
- *Talent management* – ensuring that the organization has the talented people it requires to provide for management succession and meet present and future business needs.

CASE STUDY

Recruitment and retention strategy at Buckingham County Council

Attracting and retaining high-quality staff is considered key to the corporate strategy of Buckingham County Council, which employs around 14,000 people. Resourcing is one of the most important things the Council does to improve performance.

Resourcing and people strategy

The resourcing strategy complements and reinforces the people strategy, which has five targets:

1   being the best employer;

2   bringing in additional talent;

3   developing existing talent;

4   championing diversity;

5   transforming the organization.

The people strategy dashboard

A people strategy dashboard has been created to ensure that human resources are managed more effectively. This extends the people strategy targets and is used to monitor progress in achieving them.

Improving recruitment and selection

This involved:

- strengthening the employer brand;
- developing a better recruitment website;
- developing a talent bank to ensure that vacancies were filled quickly;
- streamlining processes to reduce the time to fill vacancies;
- the development of a competency framework used for competency-based selection.

Retaining talent

An holistic approach is adopted to retaining talent. This involves paying attention to every aspect of the employment relationship and setting a best-employer target. A staff survey is used to measure employee engagement.

Total reward strategy

A total reward approach is adopted, including the use of total reward statements.

Talent management

A talent management toolkit is used to identify and develop potential high performers at every level in the organization.

Key learning points: Strategic resourcing

- Employee resourcing, generally known simply as 'resourcing' is the term used to describe activities concerned with the acquisition, retention and development of human resources.

- Strategic resourcing is concerned with ensuring that the organization obtains and retains the people it needs and employs them effectively. It is a key part of the strategic HRM process, which is fundamentally about matching human resources to the strategic and operational needs of the organization and ensuring the full utilization of those resources.

- The aim of strategic resourcing is therefore to ensure that a firm achieves competitive advantage by employing more capable people than its rivals. These people will have a wider and deeper range of skills and will behave in ways that will maximize their contribution.

- Strategic resourcing places more emphasis than traditional personnel management on finding people whose attitudes and behaviour are likely to be congruent with what management believes to be appropriate and conducive to success.

- The philosophy behind the strategic HRM approach to resourcing is that it is people who implement the strategic plan. Resourcing strategies exist to provide the people and skills required to support the business strategy, but they should also contribute to the formulation of that strategy.

- Strategic resourcing is not just about recruitment and selection. It is concerned with any means available to meet the needs of the firm for certain skills and behaviours.

- The overarching component of strategic resourcing is the integration of resourcing and business plans. Within this framework strategic resourcing includes specific strategies for:

  - workforce planning;
  - developing the organization's employee value proposition and its employer brand;
  - resourcing plans;
  - retention;
  - flexibility;
  - talent management.

Questions

1 What is resourcing?

2 What is strategic resourcing?

3 What is the essential nature of strategic resourcing?

4 What is the strategic HRM approach to resourcing?

5 What is meant by integrating business and resourcing strategies?

6 What are the components of resourcing strategy?

References

Miles, R E and Snow, C C (1978) *Organizational Strategy: Structure and process*, New York, McGraw-Hill

Quinn Mills, D (1983) Planning with people in mind, *Harvard Business Review*, November–December, pp 97–105

Townley, B (1989) Selection and appraisal: reconstructing social relations?, in (ed) J Storey, *New Perspectives in Human Resource Management*, London, Routledge

18
Workforce planning

KEY CONCEPTS AND TERMS

Demand forecasting

Human resources planning

Ratio-trend analysis

Soft human resources planning

SWOT analysis

Hard human resources planning

PESTLE analysis

Scenario planning

Supply forecasting

LEARNING OUTCOMES

On completing this chapter you should be able to define these key concepts. You should also know about:

- The nature of workforce planning
- The link between workforce and business planning
- The rationale for workforce planning
- Workforce planning issues
- Approaches to workforce planning

Introduction

Organizations need to know how many people and what sort of people they should have to meet present and future business requirements. This is the function of workforce planning, the term which increasingly is replacing 'human resource planning'.

The purpose of this chapter is to describe how workforce planning functions, bearing in mind that

it is not as straightforward as it was presented when the notion of 'manpower planning' became popular in the 1960s and 70s. Workforce or human resource planning may be well established in the HRM vocabulary but it does not seem to be embedded as a key HR activity.

This chapter starts with a definition of workforce planning and continues with a discussion of its aims and the issues involved, including its link with business planning. The final section of the chapter describes the processes used, namely scenario planning, demand and supply forecasting and action planning.

Workforce planning defined

The following definition of workplace planning was produced by the CIPD (2010a: 4): 'Workforce planning is a core process of human resource management that is shaped by the organizational strategy and ensures the right number of people with the right skills, in the right place at the right time to deliver short- and long-term organizational objectives.'

Workforce planning may be conducted as an overall approach to establishing and satisfying people requirements covering all major employee categories and skills. However, it frequently concentrates on key categories of staff, for example, doctors, nurses and other health workers in the National Health Service, skilled operatives in a manufacturing company, sales staff in a retail store or drivers in a transport company.

Rothwell (1995: 194) distinguished between HR planning in the hard sense – 'to serve as an indicator of the likely match or mismatch of the supply and demand for the right number of people with appropriate skills' – and HR planning in the soft sense – 'to alert the organization to the implications of business strategy for people development, culture and attitudes as well as numbers and skills'. The CIPD (2010a: 4) made a similar distinction between 'hard' and 'soft' workforce planning. As the report on their research commented:

> Hard workforce planning is about numbers. In the past this often revolved around using past trends to predict the future, matching supply and demand for labour with the result that plans were often out of date before the ink was dry. Now there is more emphasis on management information that can help understand cause and effect of certain phenomena.

Soft workplace planning focuses on general issues relating to the supply of and demand for people and how they are deployed.

The precursor to workforce planning – manpower planning as conceived in the 1960s – was almost entirely about numbers in the shape of quantitative demand and supply forecasts. It was the failure in many organizations to produce accurate forecasts and therefore prepare meaningful plans that led to its decline if not fall. Workforce planning today covers a wider range of activities such as succession planning, smart working, flexible working and talent planning, and is not such a numbers game.

Incidence of workforce planning

The CIPD *Annual Survey of Resourcing and Talent Planning* (2010b) found that 61 per cent of organizations conducted workforce planning, although it was most common in the public services sector and in larger organizations. Twenty per cent of organizations planned for less than one year, 41 per cent for one to two years and only 2 per cent for more than five years. The CIPD (2010a) research established that the top five planning activities were:

1 succession planning – 62 per cent;
2 flexible working – 53 per cent;
3 demand/supply forecasting – 53 per cent;
4 skills audit/gap analysis – 49 per cent;
5 talent management – 42 per cent.

The link between workforce and business planning

Workforce planning is an integral part of business planning. The strategic planning process defines projected changes in the types of activities carried out by the organization and the scale of those activities. It identifies the core competencies the organization needs to achieve its goals and therefore its skill and behavioural requirements.

Workforce planning interprets these plans in terms of people requirements. But it may influence the business strategy by drawing attention to ways in which people could be developed and deployed more effectively to further the achievement of business goals as well as focusing on any problems that might have to be resolved to ensure that the people required will be available and will be capable of making the necessary contribution.

The rationale for workforce planning

Workforce planning provides the basis for a systematic approach to assessing the number and type of people needed by an organization and ensuring that people considerations are taken into account in business plans. Having obtained information on the supply of people, and from environmental scanning, it leads to the preparation of recruitment, retention, management succession and talent management plans. It is important because it encourages employers to develop clear and explicit links between their business and HR plans and to integrate the two more effectively. It allows for better control over staffing costs and numbers employed, and it enables employers to make more informed judgements about the skills mix in their organizations.

Research conducted by the Institute for Employment Studies (Reilly, 1999) established that there were three main reasons why organizations engaged in workforce planning:

1   *Planning for substantive reasons*, that is, to have a practical effect by optimizing the use of resources and/or making them more flexible, acquiring and nurturing skills that take time to develop, identifying potential problems and minimizing the chances of making a bad decision.

2   *Planning because of the process benefits*, which involves understanding the present in order to confront the future, challenging assumptions and liberating thinking, making explicit decisions that can later be challenged, standing back and providing an overview and ensuring that long-term thinking is not driven out by short-term focus.

3   *Planning for organizational reasons*, which involves communicating plans so as to obtain support/adherence to them, linking HR plans to business plans so as to influence them, (re)gaining corporate control over operating units and coordinating and integrating organizational decision making and actions.

Workforce planning issues

The main difficulties faced by those involved in quantitative (hard) workforce planning are the impact of change and trying to predict the future. It can be very hard to forecast the demand for or supply of people with any accuracy. The tendency in many organizations is therefore to adopt a short-term approach and deal with deficits or surpluses of people as they arise. This problem is compounded by what Rothwell (1995) referred to as the shifting kaleidoscope of policy priorities and strategies within organizations. It sounds like a good idea to adopt an integrated approach to workforce and business planning but it won't work well if business plans are volatile, vague, misleading or non-existent, as they easily can be. Cappelli (2009: 10) noted that: 'The competitive environment for businesses is so changeable, and firms adjust their own strategies and practices so frequently that these estimates [of the demand for talent] are rarely accurate and they get much worse the farther out one goes.'

This problem will not be so acute in a stable market place, with largely passive (and static) customers, and with scope for long-term forecasting. But these are rare conditions today, even in the public sector where for a long time workplace planning has thrived.

It can be said that workforce planning is more art than science. Perhaps the accuracy of demand and supply forecasts is less important than the overall understanding of what the organization needs in the way of people, which can be generated by the systematic approach described below.

Approaches to workforce planning

A flowchart of the process of workforce planning is shown in Figure 18.1. This identifies the main planning activities described below. Although these are referred to as separate areas, they are closely

FIGURE 18.1   Workforce planning flowchart

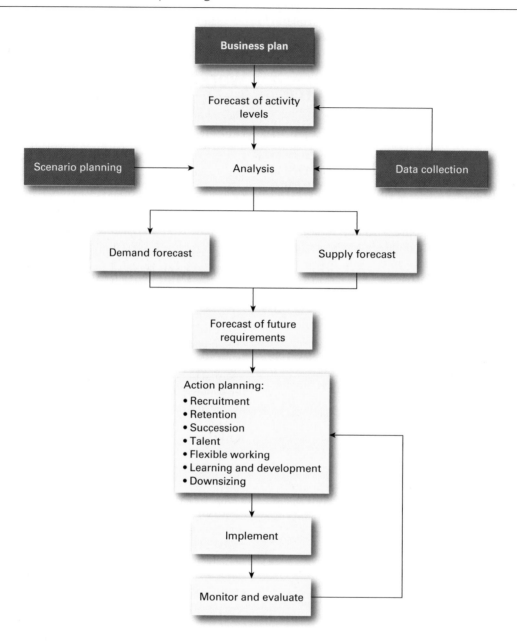

interrelated and often overlap. For example, demand forecasts are estimates of future requirements, and these may be prepared on the basis of assumptions about the productivity of employees. But a forecast of the supply of suitable people will also have to consider productivity trends and how they might affect the supply.

Business planning

The business plan provides the basis for the workforce plan insofar as it sets out what the organization intends to do in terms of activities and the scale of those activities.

Forecast activity levels

Forecasts of future activity levels flow from the business plan, which will have implications for the demand for people. Activity level forecasts will also be affected by external factors, for example demographic and political policy trends, especially in the public sector. Data will need to be collected and analysed for this purpose.

Scenario planning

Scenario planning is an assessment of the environmental changes that are likely to affect the organization so that a prediction can be made of the possible situations that may have to be dealt with in the future. The scenario may list a range of predictions so that different responses can be considered. The scenario is best based on systematic environmental scanning, possibly using the PESTLE approach (an assessment of the political, economic, social, legal, technological and economic factors that might affect the organization). The implications of these factors on the organization's labour markets and what can be done about any human resource issues can then be considered.

Data collection

The information used in workforce planning can be collected under the following headings:

- *Qualitative internal data*: business information on product/market developments, proposed work system and organizational changes; HR information on people (skills, performance, etc).
- *Quantitative internal data*: workforce data on turnover, absence, demographics, skills audits, etc.
- *Qualitative external data*: PESTLE analysis covering the following factors: political, economic, social, technological, legal and environmental.
- *Quantitative external data*: labour market – demographics, skills availability.

Analysis

The analysis stage brings all the information together from the business plan, the activity forecast, scenarios and internal and external data to provide the basis for demand and supply forecasts.

Demand forecasting

Demand forecasting is the process of estimating the future numbers of people required and the likely skills and competences they will need. The basis of the forecast is the annual budget and longer-term business plan, translated into activity levels for each function and department. In a manufacturing company the sales budget would be translated into a manufacturing plan, giving the numbers and types of products to be made in each period. From this information the number of hours to be worked by each skill category to make the quota for each period would be computed.

Details are required of any organizational and work plans that would result in increased or decreased demands for employees. Examples are setting up a new regional organization, creating a new sales department, decentralizing a head office function to the regions, plans for new methods of working, additional outsourcing, increasing productivity and reducing employment costs. The demand forecasting methods for estimating the numbers of people required are described below.

Managerial judgement

The most typical method of forecasting used is managerial judgement. This simply requires managers to sit down, think about their future workloads, and decide how many people they need. It may be quite unscientific.

Forecasting might be done on a 'bottom-up' basis with line managers submitting proposals for agreement by senior management. Alternatively, a 'top-down' approach can be used, in which company and departmental forecasts are prepared by top management, possibly acting on advice from the personnel departments. These forecasts are reviewed and agreed with departmental managers. A less directive approach is for top management to prepare planning guidelines for departmental managers setting out the planning assumptions and the targets they should try to meet.

Perhaps the best way of using managerial judgement is to adopt both the 'bottom-up' and 'top-down' approaches. Guidelines for departmental managers should be prepared indicating broad company assumptions about future activity levels that will affect their departments. Targets are also set where necessary. Armed with these guidelines, departmental managers prepare their forecasts to a laid-down format. They are encouraged to seek help at this stage from the personnel or work study departments. Meanwhile, the HR department, in conjunction as necessary with planning and work study departments, prepares a company forecast. The two sets of forecasts can then be reviewed by a human resource planning committee consisting of functional heads. This committee reconciles with departmental managers any discrepancies between the two forecasts and submits the final amended forecast to top management for approval. This is sometimes called the 'right-angle method'.

Ratio-trend analysis

Ratio-trend analysis is carried out by analysing existing ratios between an activity level and the number of employees working on that activity. The ratio is applied to forecast activity levels to determine an adjusted number of people required. Account can be taken of possible improvements in productivity that would affect the ratio. The analysis may be extended to cover employees connected to but not directly involved in the activity – the indirect workers who provide support to the direct workers responsible for carrying out the activity. The existing ratio of directs to indirects would be applied to the forecast number of directs needed to deal with the new activity levels to forecast the number of indirects needed.

Work study techniques

Work study techniques are used in association with activity level forecasts to calculate how long operations should take and the number of people required. Work study techniques for direct workers can be combined with ratio-trend analysis to calculate the number of indirect workers needed.

Forecasting skill and competence requirements

Forecasting skill and competence requirements is largely a matter of managerial judgement. This judgement should, however, be exercised on the basis of an analysis of the impact of projected product/market developments and the introduction of new technology, either information technology or computerized manufacturing.

Supply forecasting

Supply forecasting measures the number of people likely to be available from within the organization, having allowed for wastage or attrition. The supply analysis covers the following areas:

- existing number of people employed by occupation, skill and potential;
- potential losses to existing resources through attrition (employee turnover);
- sources of supply from within the organization – existing employees and the outputs of talent management or training programmes.

Although supply forecasting may focus on what is available from within the organization it will also take account of environmental changes as revealed by scenario planning. Other issues will need to be considered such as changes to the organization structure, new methods of working (including flexible working; see Chapter 12), more part-time working and different working hours.

Forecast of future requirements

To forecast future requirements it is necessary to analyse the demand and supply forecasts to identify any deficits or surpluses. The analysis can be made with the help of spreadsheets. The basic data can be set out as follows:

1 Current number employed   70
2 Annual level of turnover   10 per cent
3 Expected losses during year   7
4 Balance at end year   63
5 Number required at end year   75
6 Number to be obtained   (4 – 3) = 12
   during year

The data on the number of employees required may be modified by reference to the impact of any productivity plans, organizational changes, new methods of working or revision of role responsibilities.

Action planning

Action plans are derived from the broad resourcing strategies and the more detailed analysis of demand and supply factors. However, the plans often have to be short term and flexible because of the difficulty of making firm predictions about workforce requirements in times of rapid change. The planning activities start with the identification of internal resources available now or which could be made available through learning and development programmes. They continue with plans for recruitment and retention, succession and talent management, the reduction of employee turnover and absenteeism, flexible working, outsourcing, productivity improvement and the revision of role responsibilities. Learning and development programmes may be prepared to provide for future skill requirements. Regrettably, but sometimes inevitably, plans for downsizing may be necessary, but these can aim to avoid compulsory redundancies by such means as recruitment freezes.

Implementation

The implementation of the action plans will provide a challenge. A flexible approach involving quick responses is needed to cope with unforeseeable changes in people requirements.

Monitoring and evaluation

Because of unpredictable events, the implementation of action plans does not always run smoothly. It is necessary to monitor progress carefully, evaluate the effects and, as required, amend the action plan.

CASE STUDIES

Buckinghamshire County Council

Business need drove the workforce planning project at Buckinghamshire County Council. This recognized that current workforce planning practices would not meet the challenge of the Care Standards Act 2000, or of future service delivery. One of the main issues in working with children and families was recruiting and retaining qualified social workers. There were insufficient numbers of social workers in post. Turnover levels among established and new employees were high.

The Council therefore decided to align strategy and workforce planning in social care for children and families. The workforce plan was developed with the input of a team of representatives from social care for children and families. It was recognized that workforce planning was essential to anticipate future areas of skills shortages. This council is now in a position to anticipate skills shortages and has dealt with them innovatively and immediately.

The workforce plan looked at short- and long-term planning. Short-term planning covered immediate action on recruitment and promotion. Long-term planning covered activities that may span the next five years. Workforce planning allowed for an assessment of skills and an exploration of the levels employees need to work at.

Plymouth Primary Care Trust

The Trust set up a multidisciplinary team drawn from the workforce planning and development department, finance, and public health teams within the organization to introduce workforce planning across the whole organization.

The Trust's 230 managers and budget holders were then invited to an awareness programme to introduce the Six Steps Workforce Planning Methodology developed by the NHS Workforce Projects Team (2009). The steps are:

1 Define the plan.

2 Map service change.

3 Define the required workforce.

4 Understand workforce availability.

5 Plan to deliver the required workforce.

6 Implement, monitor and refresh.

Managers were informed that, using this framework, they would be required to produce plans over a one-year, two-year and five-year timescale.

The guide was applied by asking each manager to define their workforce plan, outline forces for change, assess demand, assess supply, undertake a gap analysis and subsequent action planning and carry out implementation and a review of the plans.

It was found that while some managers were skilled in workforce planning, the majority needed support to link together the financial, workforce and planning elements of the process.

The outcomes were:

- trust-wide workforce planning, using electronic staff record and planning tools;

- workforce planning is now part of day-to-day trust business;

- detailed workforce plans across clinical and non-clinical directorates;

- increased awareness of financial position, age profiles, and workforce risk assessment;

- the development of a more efficient workforce by reviewing skill mix and succession planning;

- integration of workforce planning into the corporate management programme.

Reference

Workforce Projects Team (2009) Skills for Health, available at http://www.healthcareworkforce.nhs.uk/resource/latest _resources/introduction_to_workforce_planning.html, accessed 29 July 2011

Siemens (UK)

Workforce planning at Siemens (UK), the engineering and technology services company, (as reported by the CIPD, 2010a), involves obtaining answers to three fundamental questions: What do we have? What do we want? How do we fill the gap?

At the highest level, the corporate people strategy gives the context for workforce planning, the key objective of which is to ensure that Siemens has the right level of capability to execute business strategy. In essence, the process of workforce planning is one in which the business strategy converges with the people strategy.

The workforce planning process starts with a review of the current workforce derived from SAP data [SAP is a business software system] and onto this is overlaid the likely attrition. Future requirements are identified by means of a dialogue between HR business partners and business unit managers. This enables the skills in each job family to be matched to business initiatives and provides the basis for the workforce forecast.

Key learning points: Workforce planning

Workforce planning defined

The following definition of workplace planning was produced by the CIPD (2010a: 4): 'Workforce planning is a core process of human resource management that is shaped by the organizational strategy and ensures the right number of people with the right skills, in the right place at the right time to deliver short- and long-term organizational objectives.'

Incidence of workforce planning

The CIPD (2010a) research revealed that workforce planning in one form or another is taking place in many organizations.

Link to business planning

Workforce planning is an integral part of business planning.

The rationale for workforce planning

Workforce planning provides a basis for a systematic approach to assessing the number and type of people needed and, having taken into account information on the supply of labour and environmental scanning, for the preparation of recruitment, retention, management succession and talent management plans. Workforce planning is important because it encourages employers to develop clear and explicit links between their business and HR plans and to integrate the two more effectively.

Workforce planning issues

The main difficulties faced by those involved in workforce planning are the impact of change and predicting the future.

Approaches to workforce planning

- Business planning.
- Forecast activity levels.
- Scenario planning.
- Data collection.
- Analysis.
- Demand forecasting.
- Supply forecasting.
- Forecast of future requirements.
- Action planning.
- Implementation.
- Monitoring and evaluation.

Questions

1 What is workforce planning?
2 What is the link between business and workforce planning?
3 What is the rationale for workforce planning?
4 What are the main approaches to workforce planning?

References

Cappelli, P (2009) A supply chain approach to workforce planning, *Organizational Dynamics*, **38** (1), pp 8–15

CIPD (2010a) *Workforce Planning: Right people, right time, right skills*, London, CIPD

CIPD (2010b) *Annual Survey of Resourcing and Talent Planning*, London, CIPD

Reilly, P (1999) *The Human Resource Planning Audit*, Cambridge, Cambridge Strategy Publications

Rothwell, S (1995) Human resource planning, in (ed) J Storey, *Human Resource Management: A critical text*, London, Routledge

19
Recruitment and selection

LEARNING OUTCOMES

On completing this chapter you should be able to define these key concepts. You should also know about:

- The recruitment and selection process
- Defining requirements
- Attracting candidates
- Processing applications
- Selection methods – interviewing and tests
- References and offers
- Dealing with recruitment problems

Introduction

Recruitment is the process of finding and engaging the people the organization needs. Selection is that part of the recruitment process concerned with deciding which applicants or candidates should be appointed to jobs. Recruitment can be costly. The 2011 CIPD survey of resourcing and talent planning found that the average recruitment cost of filling a vacancy for a director or senior manager was £7,500 while for other employees it was £2,500.

The recruitment and selection process

The stages of recruitment and selection are:

1 Defining requirements.
2 Attracting candidates.
3 Sifting applications.
4 Interviewing.
5 Testing.
6 Assessing candidates.
7 Obtaining references.
8 Checking applications.
9 Offering employment.
10 Following up.

Defining requirements

The number and categories of people required may be set out in formal workforce plans from which are derived detailed recruitment plans. More typically, requirements are expressed as ad hoc demands for people because of the creation of new posts, expansion into new activities or areas, or the need for a replacement. These short-term demands may put HR under pressure to deliver candidates quickly.

Requirements are set out in the form of role profiles and person specifications. These provide the information required to post vacancies on the company's website or the internet, draft advertisements, brief agencies or recruitment consultants and assess candidates by means of interviews and selection tests.

Role profiles

Role profiles define the overall purpose of the role, its reporting relationships and the key result areas. For recruiting purposes, the profile is extended to include information on terms and conditions (pay, benefits and hours of work), special requirements such as mobility, travelling or unsocial hours, and learning, development and career opportunities. The recruitment role profile provides the basis for a person specification.

Person specification

A person specification, also known as a recruitment or job specification, defines the knowledge, skills and abilities (KSAs) required to carry out the role, the types of behaviour expected from role holders (behavioural competencies) and the education, qualifications, training and experience needed to acquire the necessary KSAs. The specification is set out under the following headings:

- *Knowledge* – what the individual needs to know to carry out the role.
- *Skills and abilities* – what the individual has to be able to do to carry out the role.
- *Behavioural competencies* – the types of behaviour required for successful performance of the role. These should be role-specific, ideally based on an analysis of employees who are carrying out their roles effectively. The behaviours should also be linked to the core values and competency framework of the organization to help in ensuring that candidates will fit and support the organization's culture.
- *Qualifications and training* – the professional, technical or academic qualifications required or the training that the candidate should have undertaken.
- *Experience* – the types of achievements and activities that would be likely to predict success.
- *Specific demands* – anything that the role holder will be expected to achieve in specified areas, eg develop new markets or products, improve sales, productivity or levels of customer service, introduce new systems or processes.

● *Special requirements* – travelling, unsocial hours, mobility, etc.

It is advisable not to overstate the requirements. Perhaps it is natural to go for the best, but setting an unrealistically high level for candidates increases the problems of attracting applicants and results in dissatisfaction among recruits when they find their talents are not being used. Understating requirements can, of course, be equally dangerous, but it happens less frequently.

The KSAs and competencies defined in the role profile form a fundamental feature of the selection process which, rightly, becomes more of a person-based than a job-based approach. They are used as the basis for structured interviews and provide guidance on which selection techniques such as psychological testing or assessment centres are most likely to be useful.

The following is an example of the key KSA and competencies parts of a person specification for an HR recruitment adviser.

KSA and competency requirements for a recruitment adviser

1. Knowledge of

● all aspects of recruitment;

● sources of recruits;

● different media for use in recruiting;

● relevant test instruments (OPQ qualified).

2. Skills and abilities in

● interviewing techniques;

● test administration;

● role analysis.

3. Behavioural competencies

● able to relate well to others and use interpersonal skills to achieve desired objectives;

● able to influence the behaviour and decisions of people on matters concerning recruitment and other HR or individual issues;

● able to cope with change, to be flexible and to handle uncertainty;

● able to make sense of issues, identify and solve problems and 'think on one's feet';

● focus on achieving results;

● able to maintain appropriately directed energy and stamina, to exercise self-control and to learn new behaviours;

● able to communicate well, orally and on paper.

Attracting candidates

The following steps are required when planning how to attract candidates:

1 Analyse recruitment strengths and weaknesses – the outcome of this analysis can be used to develop an employee value proposition and employer brand.

2 Analyse the requirement: what sort of person is needed.

3 Identify potential sources of candidates.

Analyse recruitment strengths and weaknesses

Attracting candidates is primarily a matter of identifying, evaluating and using the most appropriate sources of applicants. However, in cases where difficulties in attracting or retaining candidates are being met or anticipated, it may be necessary to carry out a study of the factors that are likely to attract or repel candidates – the strengths and weaknesses of the organization as an employer. The study could make use of an attitude survey to obtain the views of existing employees.

The analysis of strengths and weaknesses should cover such matters as the national or local reputation of the organization, pay, employee benefits and working conditions, the intrinsic interest of the job, security of employment, opportunities for education and training, career prospects, and the location of the office or plant. These need to be compared with the competition so that a list of what are, in effect, selling points, can be drawn up as in a marketing exercise in which the preferences of potential customers are compared with the features of the product so that those aspects likely to provide the most appeal to the customers can be emphasized. The analysis can show where the organization needs to improve as an employer if it is to attract more or better candidates *and* to retain those selected.

Candidates are, in a sense, selling themselves, but they are also buying what the organization has to offer. If, in the latter sense, the labour market is a buyer's market, then the company selling itself to candidates must study their wants and needs in relation to what it can provide. The study can be used to develop an employee value proposition and an employee brand incorporating the features set out above. They can help in the preparation of a better image of the organization for use on corporate websites and in advertisements, brochures or interviews.

Analyse the requirement

First it is necessary to establish how many jobs have to be filled and by when. Then turn to an existing role profile and person specification or, if not available or out of date, draw up new ones that set out information on responsibilities and competency requirements. This information can be analysed to determine the required education, qualifications and experience.

The next step is to consider where suitable candidates are likely to come from: the companies, jobs or education establishments they are in, and the parts of the country where they can be found. Next, define the terms and conditions of the job (pay and benefits).

Finally, refer to the analysis of strengths and weaknesses to assess what it is about the job or the organization that is likely to attract good candidates so the most can be made of these factors when advertising the vacancy or reaching potential applicants in other ways. Consider also what might put them off, for example the location of the job, so that objections can be anticipated. Analyse previous successes or failures to establish what does or does not work.

Identify sources of candidates

First consideration should be given to internal candidates. In addition, it is always worth trying to persuade former employees to return to the organization or obtain suggestions from existing employees (referrals). Talent banks that record candidate details electronically can be maintained and referred to at this stage.

If these approaches do not work, the sources of candidates are online recruiting, advertising, recruitment agencies, job centres, consultants, recruitment process outsourcing providers and direct approaches to educational establishments. The main sources used by employers, as established by the 2011 CIPD survey, were:

- own corporate website – 59 per cent;
- recruitment agencies – 54 per cent;
- local newspaper advertisements – 36 per cent;
- employee referral scheme – 35 per cent;
- commercial job boards – 33 per cent;
- specialist journals – 27 per cent;
- Jobcentre Plus – 25 per cent;
- search consultants – 15 per cent;
- links with educational establishments – 13 per cent;
- national newspaper advertisements – 11 per cent;
- social networking sites – 4 per cent.

There is usually a choice between different methods or combinations of them. The criteria to use when making the choice are: 1) the likelihood that it will produce good candidates, 2) the speed with which the choice enables recruitment to be completed, and 3) the costs involved, bearing in mind that there may be direct advertising costs or consultants' fees.

Online recruitment

Online or e-recruitment uses the internet to advertise or 'post' vacancies, provides information about jobs and the organization and enables e-mail communications to take place between employers and candidates. The latter can apply for jobs online and can e-mail application forms and CVs to employers or agencies. Tests can be completed online.

Organizations are using Web 2.0 technologies to search for recruits and find out more about them online through social networking sites such as the Linkedin corporate recruiter tool and Facebook. They sometimes provide 'blogs' from existing employees covering their experiences in working for the organization. The main types of online recruitment sites are corporate websites, job boards and agency sites.

Corporate websites may simply list vacancies and contact details. A more elaborate approach would consist of a dedicated website area that gives details of vacancies, person specifications, benefits and how to apply for jobs by, for example completing online application forms and tests. Such areas may be linked directly to an organization's home page so that general browsers can access them. An intranet link may be available to enable internal staff to access the website. Some organizations are building their own professional communities or talent networks. The management of websites can be outsourced to recruitment consultants or specialized web agencies.

Job boards are operated by specialized firms such as Monster.co.uk and Fish4jobs.com and consist of large databanks of vacancies. Companies pay to have their jobs listed on the sites. Information about vacancies may reproduce an advertisement so that the site is simply an additional form of communication, but some vacancies are only found online. Links may be provided to the organization's website.

Agency sites are run by established recruitment agencies. Candidates register online but may be expected to discuss their details in person before these are forwarded to a prospective employer.

The advantages of online recruiting are that it can reach a wider range of possible applicants, and it is quicker and cheaper than traditional methods of advertising. More details of jobs and firms can be supplied on the site and CVs can be matched and applications can be submitted electronically. The disadvantages are that it may produce too many irrelevant or poor applications and it is still not the first choice of many job seekers.

Making the best use of online recruiting

- Consider using it in conjunction with other recruitment methods to maximize response.
- Keep the content of the site up to date.
- Ensure the site is accessible directly or through search engines.
- Provide contact numbers for those with technical problems.
- Take care over the wording of online copy – the criteria for good copy in conventional advertisements apply.

Advertising

Advertising has traditionally been the most obvious method of attracting candidates and it is still fairly important, especially at local level and in specialized journals. However, as the CIPD 2011 survey revealed, many organizations now prefer to use online recruitment, agencies or consultants. A conventional advertisement will have the following aims.

Aims of an advertisement

- *Generate candidates* – attract a sufficient number of good candidates at minimum cost.
- *Attract attention* – it must compete for the attention of potential candidates against other employees.
- *Create and maintain interest* – it has to communicate, in an attractive and interesting way, information about the job, the company and the terms and conditions of employment.
- *Stimulate action* – the message needs to be conveyed in a way that will prompt a sufficient number of replies from candidates with the right qualifications for the job.

To achieve these aims, it is necessary to carry out the actions set out below. A recruitment advertisement should start with a compelling headline and then contain information on the following.

Information in a recruitment advertisement

- The organization.
- The job.
- The person required – qualifications, experience, etc.
- The pay and benefits offered.
- The location.
- The action to be taken.

The headline is all-important. The simplest and most obvious approach is to set out the job title in bold type. To gain attention, it is advisable to quote the rate of pay and key benefits such as a company car. Applicants are suspicious of clauses such as 'salary will be commensurate with age and experience' or 'salary negotiable'. This often means either that the salary is so low that the company is afraid to reveal it, or that pay policies are so incoherent that the company has no idea what to offer until someone tells them what he or she wants.

The name of the company should be given. Do not use box numbers – if you want to be anonymous, use a consultant. Add any selling points, such as growth or diversification, and any other areas of interest to potential candidates, such as career prospects. The essential features of the job should be conveyed by giving a brief description of what the job holder will do and, as far as space permits, the scope and scale of activities. Create interest in the job but do not oversell it.

The qualifications and experience required should be stated as factually as possible. There is no point in overstating requirements and seldom any point in specifying exactly how much experience is wanted. Be careful about including a string of personal qualities such as drive, determination and initiative. These have no real meaning to candidates. Phrases such as 'proven track record' and 'successful experience' are equally meaningless. No one will admit to not having either of them.

The advertisement should end with information on how the candidate should apply. 'Brief but comprehensive details' is a good phrase. Candidates can be asked to write or e-mail their response, but useful alternatives are to ask them to telephone or to come along for an informal chat at a suitable venue.

Remember the anti-discrimination legislation set out in the Equality Act (2010). This makes it unlawful to discriminate in an advertisement by favouring either sex, the only exceptions being a few jobs that can be done only by one sex. Advertisements must therefore avoid sexist job titles such as 'salesman' or 'stewardess'. They must refer to a neutral title such as 'sales representative', or amplify the description to cover both sexes by stating 'steward or stewardess'. Potential respondents should be referred to only as the 'candidate' or the 'applicant', otherwise you must specify 'man or woman' or 'he or she'. It is accepted, however, that certain job titles are unisex and therefore non-discriminatory, including director, manager, executive and officer.

It is also unlawful to place an advertisement that discriminates against any particular race. As long as race is never mentioned or even implied in an advertisement, you should have no problem in keeping within the law. The Equality Act make it unlawful to discriminate against employees on account of their age. Age limits should therefore not be included in advertisements and the wording should not indicate that people below or above a certain age are not wanted.

It is essential to measure the response to advertisements to provide guidance on the relative cost-effectiveness of different media. Cost per reply is the best ratio.

Recruitment agencies

Most recruitment agencies deal with secretarial and office staff who are registered with them. They are usually quick and effective but quite expensive. Agencies can charge a fee of 15 per cent or more of the first year's salary for finding someone. It can be cheaper to advertise or use the internet, especially when the company is in a buyer's market. Shop around to find the agency that suits the organization's needs at a reasonable cost.

Agencies should be briefed carefully on what is wanted. They can produce unsuitable candidates but the risk is reduced if they are clear about the requirements.

Jobcentre plus

The job centres operated by the Government are mainly useful for manual and clerical workers and sales or call centre assistants.

Recruitment consultants

Recruitment consultants advertise, interview and produce a shortlist. They provide expertise and reduce workload. The organization can be anonymous if it wishes. Most recruitment consultants charge a fee based on a percentage of the basic salary for the job, usually ranging from 15 to 20 per cent.

When choosing a recruitment consultant check their reputation and expertise, compare fees and meet the person who will work on the assignment to assess his or her quality. To use them effectively:

- Agree terms of reference.
- Brief them on the organization, where the job fits in, why the appointment is to be made, terms and conditions and any special requirements.
- Give them every assistance in defining the job and the person specification – they will do much better if they have comprehensive knowledge of what is required and what type of person is most likely to fit into the organization well.
- Check carefully the proposed programme and the draft text of the advertisement.
- Clarify the arrangements for interviewing and shortlisting.
- Clarify the basis upon which fees and expenses will be charged.
- Ensure that arrangements are made to deal directly with the consultant who will handle the assignment.

Executive search consultants

Use an executive search consultant or 'head hunter' for senior jobs where there is only a limited number of suitable people and a direct lead to them is wanted. They are not cheap. Head hunters charge a fee of 30 to 50 per cent or so of the first year's salary, but they can be quite cost-effective.

Executive search consultants first approach their own contacts in the industry or profession concerned. The good ones have an extensive range of contacts and their own data bank. They will also have researchers who will identify suitable people who may fit the specification or can provide a lead to someone else who may be suitable. The more numerous the contacts, the better the executive search consultant. When a number of potentially suitable and interested people have been assembled, a fairly relaxed and informal meeting takes place and the consultant forwards a shortlist with full reports on candidates to the client.

There are some good and some not so good executive search consultants. Do not use one unless a reliable recommendation is obtained.

Recruitment process outsourcing

Recruitment process outsourcing (RPO) is the term used when an organization commissions a provider to take responsibility for the end-to-end delivery of the recruitment process, covering all vacancies or a selection of them. This involves liaising with hiring managers to define requirements and specifications, deciding on the best ways to attract candidates, processing applications, and setting up and facilitating interviews. Some companies do not hand over all recruitment, using RPO only for high-volume vacancies. They may retain responsibility for senior and specialist jobs.

The advantage of RPO is that it can save time, bring outside expertise to bear on recruitment problems and free up HR for more value-adding activities. The disadvantage is the perception by some HR people and line managers that the provider is too remote to deal with the real issues and that there is a danger of losing control.

Educational and training establishments

Many jobs can, of course, be filled by school leavers. For some organizations the main source of recruits for training schemes will be universities and colleges as well as schools. Graduate recruitment is a major annual exercise for some companies, which go to great efforts to produce glossy brochures, visit campuses on the 'milk run' and use elaborate sifting and selection procedures to vet candidates, including 'biodata' and assessment centres.

Comparison of sources

A summary of sources and an analysis of their advantages and disadvantages is given in Table 19.1.

TABLE 19.1   Summary of sources of candidates

Source	Description	Advantages	Disadvantages
Online recruitment	Company websites, job boards, social media.	• Generally, can reach a wider range of possible applicants, and it is quicker and cheaper than traditional methods of advertising. More details of jobs and firms can be supplied on the site and CVs can be matched and applications can be submitted electronically. • Websites can use an organization's brand to attract candidates. • Job boards are keyword searchable. Job details can be changed and CVs managed electronically. • Social media are good for reach – Linkedin currently has 100 million members worldwide.	• Generally, may produce too many irrelevant or poor applications and it is still not the first choice of many job seekers. • Websites are expensive and still need other media to drive traffic to the site. • Job boards are bad for 'passive seekers'. • Social media – employer/recruiter has to manage own profile.
Advertising	Display or classified advertisements in national or local newspapers or journals.	Attract 'passing trade' – people who are not actively looking for a job.	Soon become irrelevant.
Recruitment agencies	Mainly recruit office and sales staff who are registered with them.	Convenient, save time and trouble, draw on an established pool of candidates.	Can produce unsuitable candidates. Pool may be limited.
Job centres	Mainly for manual workers and clerical and sales staff.	No cost; usually plenty of choice	Limited to relatively routine jobs.
Recruitment consultants	Advertise, interview and produce a shortlist.	Provide expertise and reduce workload.	Can be expensive.
Executive search consultants	Conduct searches for senior executives	Can find top level people who might not otherwise be interested.	Expensive, limited to top jobs.
Recruitment process outsourcing	Deliver complete recruiting process.	Save time, bring outside expertise to bear on recruitment problems and free up HR for more value-adding activities.	Feeling that provider is too remote to deal with the real issues and that there is a danger of losing control.
Educational establishments	Universities, colleges and schools.	Major source of future talent.	Recruitment campaigns can be costly.

Dealing with applications

If recruitment agencies or consultants are used they will deliver their client a shortlist of candidates for interview. If not, the organization has to sift the applications itself. This means examining the information supplied by applicants, sorting them and drawing up a shortlist of applicants to be interviewed.

Examining information from candidates

Candidates may respond to an online notice or an advertisement with a written application (by e-mail or letter), usually supported by a CV. The applicant may be asked to complete and return an application form by post or by e-mail to supplement the letter and CV. An application form, as illustrated in Figure 19.1 sets out the information on a candidate in a standardized format and provides a structured basis for drawing up shortlists, the interview itself and for the subsequent actions in offering an appointment and in setting up records. This ensures that all applicants are considered on the same basis – it can be very difficult to plough through a pile of letters or CVs that may be badly organized or ill-written. The following suggestions have been made by Pioro and Baum (2005) on how to use application forms more effectively:

- Decide what the criteria for selection are and how these will be assessed by use of the application form.
- Keep questions clear, relevant and non-discriminatory.
- Ask for only the bare minimum of personal details.
- Widen your pool of applicants by offering different options and guidance for completing and viewing application forms.

However, to save time and trouble, recruiters may prefer to make a decision on the initial letter plus CV where it is quite clear that an applicant meets or does not meet the specification, rather than ask for a form.

Employers may also refer for further information to social networks or the candidate's own blog.

Processing applications

When the vacancy or vacancies have been posted or advertised and a fair number of replies received, the initial step is to list the applications on the recruitment database setting out name, date application received and actions taken (reject, hold, interview, shortlist, offer). A standard acknowledgement letter should be sent to each applicant unless an instant decision can be made to interview or reject. The next steps are to sift applications prior to drawing up a shortlist and arranging interviews.

Sorting applications

Applications are sifted by comparing the information available about them with the key criteria in the person specification. The criteria should be analysed with care so that they are fully understood. The criteria can be classified under the following three headings so that they can be applied consistently to guide sifting decisions:

1 *Essential* – applicants will not be considered unless this criterion is satisfied.

2 *Very desirable* – preference will be given to applicants who meet this criterion.

3 *Desirable* – applicants who meet this criterion will be given favourable consideration but it is not an essential requirement. However, if a number of applicants meet the first two criteria, satisfying desirable criteria would be a factor in making a choice.

A highly structured method of sifting applications is provided by the use of biodata. These are items of biographical data that are criterion-based (ie they relate to established criteria in such terms as qualifications and experience which indicate that individuals are likely to be suitable). These are objectively scored and, by measurements of past achievements, predict future behaviour.

Following the analysis, applicants can be sorted initially into three categories: possible, marginal and unsuitable. The more information made available and the clearer the criteria the easier this process is. When there is a large field of applicants with many 'possibles', sifting may have to be repeated against more stringent criteria until a shortlist for interview is identified.

FIGURE 19.1   Example of application form (compressed)

APPLICATION FORM

Surname:	First name:

Address:

Tel. (home)	Tel. (work)	e-mail (personal)

Position applied for:

Education

Dates		Name of secondary school, college or university	Main subjects taken	Qualifications
From	To			

Specialized training received

Other qualifications and skills (including languages, keyboard skills, current driving licence, etc)

Employment history

(Give details of all positions held since completing full-time education; start with your present or most recent position and work back)

Dates		Name of employer, address and nature of business including any service in the Armed Forces	Position and summary of main duties	Starting and leaving rate of pay	Reasons for leaving or wanting to leave
From	To				

Add any comments you wish to make to support your application

I confirm that the information given on this application form is correct

Signature of applicant...**Date**......................

Ideally, the numbers on the shortlist should be between four and eight. Fewer than four leaves relatively little choice (although such a limitation may be forced on the recruiter if an insufficient number of good applications have been received). More than eight will mean that too much time is spent on interviewing and there is a danger of diminishing returns setting in.

Draw up an interviewing programme

The time allowed for an interview will vary according to the complexity of the job. For a fairly routine job, 30 minutes or so should suffice. For a more senior job, 60 minutes or more is required. It is best not to schedule too many interviews for more senior jobs in a day – interviewers who try to conduct more than five or six exacting interviews will quickly run out of steam and do neither the interviewee nor the organization any justice. It is advisable to leave about 15 minutes between interviews to write up notes and prepare for the next one.

Administering the selection programme

When the interviewing programme has been drawn up shortlisted candidates can be invited for interview, using a standard letter where large numbers are involved. Candidates should be asked to complete an application form if they have not already done so. There is much to be said at this stage for sending candidates more details of the organization and the job so that too much time is not spent in going through this information at the interview.

Review the remaining 'possibles' and 'marginals' and decide if any are to be held in reserve. Send reserves a standard 'holding' letter and send the others a standard rejection letter. The latter should thank candidates for the interest shown and inform them briefly, but not too brusquely, that they have not been successful. A typical reject letter might read as follows.

> Since writing to you on … we have given careful consideration to your application for the above position. I regret to inform you, however, that we have decided not to ask you to attend for an interview. We should like to thank you for the interest you have shown.

Selection methods

The aim of selection is to assess the suitability of candidates by predicting the extent to which they will be able to carry out a role successfully. It involves deciding on the degree to which the characteristics of applicants in terms of their KSAs, competencies, experience, qualifications, education and training match the person specification and then using this assessment to make a choice between candidates. The so-called 'classic trio' of selection methods consists of application forms, interviews and references. To these should be added selection tests and assessment centres.

Interviewing

The interview is the most familiar method of selection. The aim is to elicit information about candidates that will enable a prediction to be made about how well they will do the job and thus lead to a selection decision.

An interview involves face-to-face discussion. When it is an individual rather than a panel interview, it provides the best opportunity for the establishment of close contact – rapport – between the interviewer and the candidate, thus facilitating the acquisition of the required information about the candidate's suitability and how he or she would fit into the organization. As described below, interviews should be structured (detailed consideration of selection interviewing skills is given in Chapter 47). The advantages and disadvantages of interviews are set out in the panel overleaf.

These disadvantages are most common when unstructured interviews are used, but they can be alleviated, first, using a structured approach as also described below, and secondly, by training interviewers. The use of other opinions can also help to reduce bias, especially if the same structured approach is adopted by all the interviewers. Finally, selection tests, especially those measuring intelligence or general ability, can provide valuable information that supplements the interview.

Interviews are frequently conducted on a one-to-one basis but there is a case for using a second interviewer to avoid a biased or superficial decision. The alternative is a selection board or panel, which is often used in the public sector. This brings

> ## Advantages and disadvantages of interviews as a method of selection
>
> ### Advantages
>
> - Provide opportunities for interviewers to ask probing questions about the candidate's experience and to explore the extent to which the candidate's competencies match those specified for the job.
>
> - Enable interviewers to describe the job (a 'realistic job preview') and the organization in more detail, providing some indication of the terms of the psychological contract.
>
> - Provide opportunities for candidates to ask questions about the job and to clarify issues concerning training, career prospects, the organization and terms and conditions of employment.
>
> - Enable a face-to-face encounter to take place so that the interviewer can make an assessment of how the candidate would fit into the organization and what he or she would be like to work with.
>
> - Give the candidate the same opportunity to assess the organization, the interviewer and the job.
>
> ### Disadvantages
>
> - Can lack validity as a means of making sound predictions of performance, and lack reliability in the sense of measuring the same things for different candidates.
>
> - Rely on the skill of the interviewer – many people are poor at interviewing, although most think that they are good at it.
>
> - Do not necessarily assess competence in meeting the demands of the particular job.
>
> - Can lead to biased and subjective judgements by interviewers.

together a number of parties interested in the selection decision. But the drawbacks are that questions tend to be unplanned and delivered at random and the candidates are unable to do justice to themselves because they may not be allowed to expand.

Unstructured interviews

Unstructured interviews are essentially a general discussion during which the interviewer asks a few questions that are relevant to what he or she is looking for but without any specific aim in mind other than getting an overall picture of the candidate as an individual. Questions are often random and non-specific. Candidates are judged on the general impression they make and the process is likely to be quite subjective. Research quoted later in this chapter has shown that the predictive validity (the extent to which it predicts performance in a job) of an unstructured interview is fairly low. The preferred method is a structured interview which, when conducted well, has a higher level of predictive validity.

Structured interviews

A structured interview is one based on a defined framework. Within the framework there may be a set of predetermined questions. All candidates are asked the same questions and the answers may be scored through a rating system.

The most typical framework is the person specification. Interview questions aim to establish the extent to which a candidate has the required knowledge, skills and abilities and the right level of desirable behavioural competencies. This may be referred to as a 'competency-based interview', especially if the focus is on assessing the level of the behavioural competencies possessed by candidates. However, most interviewers are also seeking information on knowledge, skills and capabilities (KSAs as required for the job rather than simply behavioural competencies).

A framework for an interview can be provided by the candidate's CV or application form. This was used by 63 per cent of the respondents to the CIPD 2011 survey. But within this framework a properly structured interview will be based on questions prepared in advance to find out if the qualifications and experience described in the CV match the specification.

Competency-based interviews

In its purest form, a competency-based interview is a structured interview that focuses on the required behavioural competencies as set out in the person specification. The questions will be designed to establish the typical behaviour of a candidate in work situations and each question will target a specific competency or skill. Candidates are required to back up their answers with concrete examples.

The aim is to select people who will behave in accordance with the values of the business. However, an interview could be described as competency-based if it also covers technical competencies (what people have to know and be able to do in terms of knowledge and skills to carry out their roles effectively). If both types of competency are included, as is desirable in most situations, then a competency-based interview is in effect one based on the person specification.

The CIPD 2011 survey found that competency-based interviews were the most common approach (70 per cent of the respondents claimed they used them). However, it is possible that some respondents were referring to interviews structured by reference to KSAs, in other words, referring to technical as well as behavioural competencies.

The advantage of basing interviews on behavioural competencies is that information will be obtained on how candidates will behave at work. This is particularly important in jobs such as sales staff where certain types of behaviour are crucial to success. For example, Selfridges, the department store, takes great care to develop specifications that define the behaviours required and to use selection techniques that provide for cultural fit between the individual and the organization.

It is relevant to know how people are likely to behave but it is also necessary to extend the area covered to knowledge, skills and abilities with the aim of finding out what people know and are able to do. The ultimate purpose of an interview is to establish the degree to which a candidate is up to the job, not just how they are going to behave. Appropriate behaviour is important but so is the ability to do the work. Basing an interview on a person specification covering all these points is the best approach.

Selection testing

Selection tests are used to provide valid and reliable evidence of levels of abilities, intelligence, personality characteristics, aptitudes and attainments. Psychological or psychometric tests assess intelligence or personality. They use systematic and standardized procedures to measure differences in individual characteristics, thus enabling selectors to gain a greater understanding of candidates to help in predicting the extent to which they will be successful in a job. Psychological tests are measuring instruments, which is why they are often referred to as psychometric tests: 'psychometric' means mental measurement.

Intelligence tests

Intelligence tests measure a range of mental abilities that enable a person to succeed at a variety of intellectual tasks using the faculties of abstract thinking and reasoning. They are concerned with general intelligence (termed 'g' by Spearman, 1927, one of the pioneers of intelligence testing) and are sometimes called 'general mental ability' (GMA) tests. Intelligence tests measure abilities while cognitive tests measure an individual's learning in a specific subject area. They contain questions, problems and tasks. The meta-analysis conducted by Schmidt and Hunter (1998) showed that intelligence tests had high predictive validity.

The outcome of a test can be expressed as a score that can be compared with the scores of members of the population as a whole, or the population of all or part of the organization using the test (norms). An intelligence test may be recorded as an intelligence quotient (IQ), which is the ratio of an individual's mental age to the individual's actual age as measured by an intelligence test. When the mental and actual age correspond, the IQ is 100. Scores above 100 indicate that the individual's level of average is above the norm for his or her age, and vice versa. It is usual now for IQs to be directly computed as an IQ test score. It is assumed that intelligence is distributed normally throughout the population; that is, the frequency distribution of intelligence corresponds with the normal curve shown in Figure 19.2.

The normal curve is a way of expressing how scores will typically be distributed; for example,

FIGURE 19.2   A normal curve

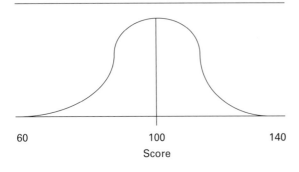

60   100   140
Score

that 60 per cent of the population are likely to get scores between x and y, 20 per cent are likely to get scores below x and 20 per cent are likely to get more than y. Intelligence tests can be administered to a single individual or to a group. They can also be completed online.

Ability tests

Ability tests establish what people are capable of knowing or doing. They measure the capacity for:

- *verbal reasoning* – the ability to comprehend, interpret and draw conclusions from oral or written language;
- *numerical reasoning* – the ability to comprehend, interpret and draw conclusions from numerical information;
- *spatial reasoning* – the ability to understand and interpret spatial relations between objects;
- *mechanical reasoning* – understanding of everyday physical laws such as force and leverage.

Personality tests

Personality tests attempt to assess the personality of candidates in order to make predictions about their likely behaviour in a role. There are many different theories of personality and, consequently, many different types of personality tests. These include self-report personality questionnaires and other questionnaires that measure interests, values or work behaviour.

Personality tests can provide interesting supplementary information about candidates that is free from the biased reactions that frequently occur in face-to-face interviews, but they have to be used with great care. The tests should have been developed by a reputable psychologist or test agency on the basis of extensive research and field testing, and they must meet the specific needs of the user.

Aptitude tests

Aptitude tests are occupational or job-related tests that assess the extent to which people can do the work. They typically take the form of work sample tests, which replicate an important aspect of the actual work the candidate will have to do, such as using a keyboard or carrying out a skilled task such as repair work. Work sample tests can be used only with applicants who are already familiar with the task through experience or training.

Characteristics of a good test

A good test is one that provides data that enables reliable predictions of behaviour or performance to be made and therefore assists in the process of making objective and reasoned decisions when selecting people for jobs. It will be based on research that has produced standardized criteria derived by using the same measure to test a number of representative people to produce a set of 'norms' for comparison purposes. The test should be capable of being objectively scored by reference to the normal or average performance of the group.

The two key characteristics of a good test are that, 1) it is reliable in the sense that it always measures the same thing: a test aimed at measuring a particular characteristic, such as intelligence, should measure the same characteristic when applied to different people at the same or a different time or to the same person at different times; and 2) it is valid in the sense that it measures the characteristic the test is intended to measure. Thus, an intelligence test should measure intelligence (however defined) and not simply verbal facility. A test meant to predict success in a job or in passing examinations should produce reasonably convincing (statistically significant) predictions.

A criterion-related approach is used to assess validity. This means selecting criteria against which the validity of the test can be measured. These criteria must reflect 'true' performance at work as accurately as possible. A single criterion is inadequate: multiple criteria should be used. The extent to which criteria can be contaminated by other factors should also be considered and it should be remembered that criteria are dynamic – they will change over time.

Interpreting test results

Test results can be interpreted by the use of norms or through criterion scores.

Norms

An individual's score in a test is not meaningful on its own. It needs to be compared with the scores achieved by the population on whom the test was standardized – the norm or reference group. A normative score is read from a norms table and might, for example, indicate that someone has performed the test at a level equivalent to the top 30 per cent of the relevant population.

Criterion scores

Norms simply tell us how someone has performed a test relative to other people. A more powerful approach is to use the relationship between test scores and an indication of what the test is designed to measure, such as job success. This is described as a criterion measure.

The use of tests in a selection procedure

While validated intelligence and personality tests can produce useful data, they should not be relied on entirely. It is best to combine them in a selection procedure with structured interviews.

Tests are often used as part of a selection procedure for occupations where a large number of recruits are required, and where it is not possible to rely entirely on examination results or information about previous experience as the basis for predicting future performance. In these circumstances it is economical to develop and administer the tests, and a sufficient number of cases can be built up for the essential validation exercise. Tests usually form part of an assessment centre programme.

Intelligence tests are particularly helpful in situations where intelligence is a key factor and there is no other reliable method of measuring it. Aptitude tests are most useful for jobs where specific and measurable skills are required, such as word-processing and skilled repair work. Personality tests can complement structured interviews and intelligence and aptitude tests. Some organizations use them for jobs such as selling, where they believe that 'personality' is important and where it is not too difficult to obtain quantifiable criteria for validation purposes. They may be used to assess integrity and conscientiousness where these characteristics are deemed to be important.

In some situations a battery of tests may be used, including various types of intelligence, personality and aptitude tests. These may be a standard battery supplied by a test agency, or a custom-built battery may be developed. The biggest pitfall to avoid is adding extra tests just for the sake of it, without ensuring that they make a proper contribution to the success of the predictions for which the battery is being used.

Tests should be administered only by people who have been trained in what the tests are measuring, how they should be used, and how they should be interpreted. Also, it is essential to evaluate all tests by comparing the results at the interview stage with later achievements. To be statistically significant, these evaluations should be carried out over a reasonable period of time and cover as large a number of candidates as possible.

Assessment centres

Assessment centres assemble a group of candidates and use a range of assessment techniques over a concentrated period (one or two days) with the aim of providing a more comprehensive and balanced view of the suitability of individual members of the group. The main features of assessment centres are that:

- exercises are used to capture and simulate the key dimensions of the job; these may include one-to-one role-plays and group exercises; it is assumed that performance in these simulations predicts behaviour on the job;
- candidates are interviewed and tested;
- performance is measured in several dimensions in terms of the competencies required to achieve the target level of

performance in a particular job or at a particular level in the organization;

- several candidates or participants are assessed together to allow interaction and to make the experience more open and participative;

- several trained assessors or observers are used in order to increase the objectivity of assessments.

The case for assessment centres is that they obtain much more information about candidates than conventional interviews, even when these are supplemented by tests. But research by Schmidt and Hunter (1998) has shown that on their own, the ability of assessment centres to predict how well someone will perform (predictive validity) is lower than that of intelligence tests combined with structured interviews. Assessment centres are expensive and time-consuming and their use tends to be restricted to large organizations for managerial positions or for graduates.

Choice of selection methods

There is a choice between the selection methods. The most important criterion is the ability of a selection method or combination of methods to predict future performance. Predictive ability is expressed as a coefficient – complete validity would be 1.0; no validity would be 0.0.

The meta-analysis on the validity of different selection methods conducted by Schmidt and Hunter (1998: 265), which covered 85 years of research findings, produced the following predictive validity coefficients:

Intelligence tests and structured interviews	.63
Intelligence tests and unstructured interviews	.55
Assessment centres and structured interviews	.53
Intelligence tests only	.51
Structured interviews only	.51
Unstructured interviews only	.38
Assessment centres only	.37
Graphology only	.02

Robertson and Smith (2001) added personality assessments to this list with a validity coefficient of .37.

Schmidt and Hunter (1998) established that the reason why intelligence (GMA) is such a good predictor of job performance is that more intelligent people acquire job knowledge more rapidly and acquire more of it, and it is this knowledge of how to perform the job that causes their job performance to be higher. Their research clearly indicates that the combination of structured interviews and intelligence tests is the most effective in terms of predictive validity. Graphology is useless.

Provisional offers and obtaining references

After the interviewing and testing procedure has been completed, a provisional decision to make an offer by telephone or in writing can be made. This is normally 'subject to satisfactory references' and the candidate should, of course, be told that these will be taken up. If there is more than one eligible candidate for a job it may be advisable to hold one or two people in reserve. Applicants often withdraw, especially those whose only purpose in applying for the job was to carry out a 'test marketing' operation, or to obtain a lever with which to persuade their present employers to value them more highly.

The main purpose of a reference is to obtain in confidence factual information about a prospective employee. This information is straightforward and essential. It is necessary to confirm the nature of the previous job, the period of time in employment, the reason for leaving (if relevant), the salary or rate of pay and, possibly, the attendance record.

Opinions about character, competence, performance and suitability are unreliable. Referees are reluctant to commit themselves and they are not in any position to assess suitability – only the prospective employer can do that. Personal referees are, of course, entirely useless. All they prove is that the applicant has at least one or two friends.

A written request for a reference could simply ask the previous employer to confirm the candidate's employment record. More precise answers may be obtained if a standard form is provided for the employer to complete. The questions asked on this form should be limited to the following:

- What was the period of employment?
- What was the job title?
- What work was carried out?
- What was the rate of pay or salary?
- How many days' absence were there over the last 12 months?
- Would you re-employ (if not, why not)?

The last question is important, if it is answered honestly or at all.

Telephone references may save time and may be more reliable. They can be used as an alternative or in addition to written references. Ask factual questions only and keep a record of the conversation.

References – legal aspects

The key legal points that should be considered when asking for or giving references are:

- Once the decision has been made to make an offer, the letter should state that 'this is a provisional offer subject to the receipt of satisfactory references'.

- It has been generally held that there is no common law duty on an employer to provide references for a serving or past employee unless there is a term to that effect in the employment contract. But it has been ruled (*Spring* v. *Guardian Assurance* 1994) that there might be a moral duty to provide a reference where it is 'natural practice' to require a reference from a previous employer before offering employment, and where the employee could not expect to enter that type of employment without a reference.

- If a reference contains a false or unsubstantiated statement that damages the reputation of the individual, action for damages may result.

- It is possible to succeed in a claim for damages if it can be shown that the reference provided was negligent because reasonable care had not been taken in preparing it, which includes ensuring that it is factually correct.

Checking applications

It is a sad fact that applicants all too often misinform their prospective employers about their education, qualifications and employment record. This was confirmed by a survey carried out by the CIPD (2008), which found that 25 per cent of employers had to withdraw their offers because applicants had lied or misrepresented their application. It is always advisable to check with universities, professional institutes and previous employers that the facts given by applicants are correct. Other checks can be made such as:

- interview questions about actual (not hypothetical) experiences, with deep probing to ascertain the extent of the individual's personal involvement, decision making and contribution;
- detailed application forms with open-ended questions about specific learning related to the skills, knowledge and competencies required for the vacancies under consideration;
- identification check;
- electoral register check;
- credit reference agency check (especially appropriate for positions in the financial services sector);
- confirmation of previous employment with HM Revenue and Customs or through the Department of Work and Pensions;
- Criminal Records Bureau check;
- Companies House check (for directors); and
- fraud prevention check, including Cifas staff fraud database check (to prevent an employer unwittingly employing people previously dismissed for fraud somewhere else). Cifas is a not-for-profit fraud prevention service.

Offering employment

The final stage in the selection procedure is to confirm the offer of employment after satisfactory references have been obtained, and the applicant has passed the medical examination required for pension and life assurance purposes or because a certain standard of physical fitness is required for the work. The contract of employment should also be prepared at this stage.

Following up

It is essential to follow up newly engaged employees to ensure that they have settled in and to check on how well they are doing. If there are any problems it is much better to identify them at an early stage rather than allowing them to fester.

Following up is also important as a means of checking on the selection procedure. If by any chance a mistake has been made, it is useful to find out how it happened so that the procedure can be improved. Misfits can be attributed to a number of causes; for example: inadequate person specification, poor sourcing of candidates, weak advertising, poor interviewing techniques, inappropriate or invalidated tests, or prejudice on the part of the selector.

Dealing with recruitment problems

Every experienced HR professional who is responsible for recruitment and selection will occasionally come across a vacancy that is particularly difficult to fill. In this situation any compromise that involves appointing someone who does not meet the specification must be avoided. To deal with the problem constructively it is necessary to take the following actions.

Dealing with recruitment problems

- Ensure that all the possible sources of candidates have been used.

- Consider any ways in which the advertisement or website entry could be made more attractive.

- Check that the person specification is realistic – that the requirements have not been overstated.

- Consider whether it might be necessary to improve the package offered to candidates – check market rates to ensure that the level of pay and benefits are competitive.

- In discussion with the line manager, examine the possibility of reshaping the role to increase its attractiveness.

- If the worst comes to the worst, discuss with the manager alternative ways of carrying out the work with existing staff.

CASE STUDIES

Recruitment assessment processes at Embarq

Embarq is the largest independent local telecoms provider in the United States. It suffered catastrophic rates of staff turnover in its call centres; then a new assessment process designed by PreVisor reduced turnover from 33.5 per cent in the first 90 days to 12.5 per cent.

The new process begins with an online screening tool that identifies characteristics and motivations that define long-term success in the roles, such as 'customer focus' and 'persistence'. There follows a behaviour-based structured interview and a sales-based role-play exercise. This exercise takes place over the phone, which tests candidates in the most realistic way possible, and is more convenient and cost-effective.

Sales have since increased by 24 per cent, and customer service has also improved.

Recruitment and retention at Paul UK

Paul UK operates a chain of 22 retail patisserie and bakery shops employing 400 people. Its staff turnover rate of 168 per cent was below the sector's average but still too high. The steps taken to overcome this problem were as follows:

- a robust recruitment process was introduced using branded application forms and centralized recruiting;

- role descriptions and skills specifications were created for posts;

- a competency-based approach to recruitment was introduced – the competencies are closely linked to the company's values and defined the behaviours and attitudes required;

- recruitment literature was professionally designed by an agency;

- an employer brand was built – the promotional leaflet highlights the benefits of working for the company;

- an employee referral scheme was introduced (helped by the employer brand);

- a resource centre for recruitment and training was established;

- a rolling induction training programme was introduced;

- a career progression framework was developed.

The outcome was that within two years staff turnover had dropped by 30 per cent and retention rates had doubled.

Key learning points: Recruitment and selection

Define requirements

Requirements are set out in the form of job descriptions or role profiles and person specifications. These provide the information required to draft advertisements, post vacancies on the internet, brief agencies or recruitment consultants and assess candidates by means of interviews and selection tests.

Analyse recruitment strengths and weaknesses

The analysis should cover such matters as the national or local reputation of the organization, pay, employee benefits and working conditions, the intrinsic interest of the job, security of employment, opportunities for education and training, career prospects, and the location of the office or plant.

Analyse the requirement

- Establish how many jobs have to be filled and by when.

- Set out information on responsibilities and competency requirements.

- Consider where suitable candidates are likely to come from.

- Define the terms and conditions of the job (pay and benefits).

- Consider what is likely to attract good candidates.

Identify sources of candidates

Initially, consideration should be given to internal candidates. An attempt can be made to persuade former employees to return to the organization or obtain suggestions from existing employees (referrals). If these approaches do not work the main sources of candidates are online recruiting, advertising, agencies and job centres, consultants, recruitment process outsourcing providers and direct approaches to educational establishments.

Selection methods

The aim is to assess the suitability of candidates by predicting the extent to which they will be able to carry out a role successfully. It involves deciding on the degree to which the characteristics of applicants match the person specification and using this assessment to make a choice between candidates. The interview is the most familiar method of selection. The aim is to elicit information about candidates that will enable a prediction to be made about how well they will do the job and thus lead to a selection decision.

Structured interviews

A structured interview is one based on a defined framework. Within the framework there may be a set of predetermined questions. All candidates are asked the same questions and the answers may be scored through a rating system.

Competency-based interviews

In its purest form, a competency-based interview is a structured interview that focuses on the required behavioural competencies as set out in the person specification. The questions will be designed to establish the typical behaviour of a candidate in work situations.

Selection tests

Selection tests are used to provide valid and reliable evidence of levels of abilities, intelligence, personality characteristics, aptitudes and attainments.

Choice of selection methods

There is a choice between the selection methods. The most important criterion is the predictive validity of the method or combination of methods. Schmidt and Hunter (1998) found that the best results were obtained by combining intelligence tests with structured interviews.

References and offers

After the interviewing and testing procedure has been completed, a provisional offer by telephone or in writing can be made. This is normally 'subject to satisfactory references'. It is essential to check the information provided by candidates on qualifications and their work experience.

Questions

1 What is the difference between recruitment and selection?

2 What are the main stages of recruitment and selection?

3 What is a person specification?

4 How should recruitment strengths and weaknesses be analysed?

5 What are the main sources of candidates?

6 What is a structured interview?

7 What is a competency-based interview?

8 What are the main types of selection tests?

9 What are the main criteria for a good test?

10 How should tests be used in a selection procedure?

References

CIPD (2011) *Survey of Resourcing and Talent Planning*, London, CIPD

Pioro, I and Baum, N (2005) How to design better job application forms, *People Management*, 16 June, pp 42–3

Robertson, I T and Smith, M (2001) Personnel selection, *Journal of Occupational and Organizational Psychology*, 74 (4), pp 441–72

Schmidt, F L and Hunter, J E (1998) The validity and utility of selection methods in personnel psychology: practical and theoretical implications of 85 years of research findings, *Psychological Bulletin*, 124 (2), pp 262–74

Spearman, C (1927) *The Abilities of Man*, New York, Macmillan

20
Resourcing practice

LEARNING OUTCOMES

On completing this chapter you should be able to define these key concepts. You should also know about:

- Employee value propositions
- Measuring employee turnover
- Retention planning
- Absence management
- Creating an employer brand
- Estimating the cost of employee turnover
- Risk of leaving analysis
- Flexibility planning

Introduction

This chapter deals with general resourcing practice in the shape of developing an employee value proposition, creating an employer brand, analysing employee turnover, tackling retention problems, absence or attendance management, introducing people to the organization and releasing them from it.

Employee value proposition

An organization's employee value proposition consists of what it offers to prospective or existing employees that they will value and persuade them to join or remain with the business. It will include remuneration – which is important but can be over-emphasized compared with non-financial factors.

The latter may be crucial in attracting and retaining people and include the attractiveness of the organization, the degree to which it acts responsibly, respects diversity and inclusion, work–life balance and opportunities for personal and professional growth. The aim is to become 'an employer of choice', a firm people want to work for and stay with. The conclusions of Purcell *et al* on the basis of their research were as follows.

Source review

On being an employer of choice – Purcell *et al* (2003)

What seems to be happening is that successful firms are able to meet people's needs both for a good job and to work 'in a great place.' They create good work and a conducive working environment. In this way they become an 'employer of choice'. People will want to work there because their individual needs are met – for a good job with prospects linked to training, appraisal and working with a good boss who listens and gives some autonomy but helps with coaching and guidance.

To develop an employee value proposition it is necessary first to analyse what the organization has to offer people by reference to:

- its reputation as a business and as an employer;
- its working environment;
- its location;
- the career opportunities available;
- the scope for learning new skills it provides;
- the terms and conditions of employment it offers.

The next step is to decide how this proposition can be conveyed to potential applicants on the organization's website or by other means.

Employer brand

The employee value proposition can be expressed as an employer brand – the image presented by an organization as a good employer. An employer brand was defined by Walker (2007: 44) as 'a set of attributes and qualities – often intangible – that make an organization distinctive, promise a particular kind of employment experience and appeal to people who will thrive and perform their best in its culture'. Employer branding is the creation of a brand image of the organization for prospective employees.

Creating an employer brand

- Analyse what the best candidates need and want and take this into account in deciding what should be offered and how it should be offered.

- Establish how far the core values of the organization support the creation of an attractive brand and ensure that these are incorporated in the presentation of the brand, as long as they are 'values in use' (lived by members of the organization) rather than simply espoused.

- Define the features of the brand on the basis of an examination and review of each of the areas that affect people's perceptions of the organization as 'a great place to work' – the way people are treated, the provision of a fair deal, opportunities for growth, work–life balance, leadership, the quality of management, involvement with colleagues and how and why the organization is successful.

- Benchmark the approaches of other organizations (the *Sunday Times* list of the 100 best companies to work for is useful) to obtain ideas about what can be done to enhance the brand.

- Be honest and realistic.

CASE STUDY

Developing an employer brand at the Ordnance Survey

The Ordnance Survey was finding it difficult to recruit technological and commercial staff of the right calibre and it was therefore decided to deal with the problem by conducting an employer branding exercise.

Objectives

The objectives of the exercise were to:

- improve external perceptions of Ordnance Survey as an employer;
- get recruitment campaigns 'right first time';
- reduce recruitment costs;
- attract and recruit high quality people, especially in technology and commercial areas;
- unlock people's potential to deliver great performance;
- match the employee experience to the organization's strong corporate brand.

The research programme

The employee-research company ORC was engaged to conduct internal and external research and consultation. The external research covered four other large employers with which Ordnance Survey compared well. It also included in-depth interviews with recruitment consultants, short-service leavers and those who had been offered a post but not taken it up. Internal research took the form of focus groups, interviews and consultation with recent joiners. The key messages from this external and internal research were fed into the brand development workshop.

The brand development workshop

The workshop consisted of a cross-section of staff who discussed the attributes of Ordnance Survey and the ways in which it presented them. Action groups met to consider particular aspects of the organization and its policies and how the brand could be developed. The focus was on the 'touch points' at which existing and potential employees engaged with the organization. The aim was to create something compelling and achievable with regard to each of these key elements. A leadership development programme was conducted that included looking at the employer brand.

Outcome

The employer brand created by this process was used as a centre point to inform and shape the people strategy and is aligned to the business strategy.

Employee turnover

Employee turnover (sometimes known as 'labour turnover', 'wastage' or 'attrition') is the rate at which people leave an organization. It can be disruptive and costly. The CIPD (2011) survey of resourcing and talent planning found that the average rate of turnover (the number leaving as a percentage of the number employed) in the UK was 12.5 per cent.

It is necessary to measure employee turnover and calculate its costs in order to forecast future losses for planning purposes and to identify the reasons that people leave the organization. Plans can then be made to attack the problems causing unnecessary turnover and to reduce costs. There are a number of different methods of measuring turnover.

Employee turnover index

The employee turnover index as set out below (sometimes referred to as the employee or labour wastage index) is the traditional formula for measuring turnover:

$$\frac{\text{Number of leavers in a specified}}{\text{Average number of employees}} \times 100$$
$$\frac{\text{period (usually 1 year)}}{\text{during the same period}}$$

This method is in common use because it is easy to calculate and to understand. It is a simple matter to work out that, if last year 30 out of an average force of 150 employees left (20 per cent turnover) and this trend continues, then the company will have to recruit 108 employees during the following year to increase and to hold the workforce at 200 in that year (50 extra employees, plus 40 to replace the 20 per cent wastage of the average 200 employees employed, plus 18 to replace wastage of the 90 recruits).

This formula may be simple to use, but it can be misleading. The main objection is that the percentage may be inflated by the high turnover of a relatively small proportion of the workforce, especially in times of heavy recruitment. Thus, a company employing 1,000 people might have had an annual wastage rate of 20 per cent, meaning that 200 jobs had become vacant during the year. But this could have been spread throughout the company, covering all occupations and long- as well as short-service employees. Alternatively, it could have been restricted to a small sector of the workforce – only 20 jobs might have been affected although each of these had to be filled 10 times during the year. These are totally different situations and unless they are understood, inaccurate forecasts would be made of future requirements and inappropriate actions would be taken to deal with the problem. The turnover index is also suspect if the average number of employees upon which the percentage is based is unrepresentative of recent trends because of considerable increases or decreases during the period in the numbers employed.

Stability index

The stability index is considered by many to be an improvement on the turnover index. The formula is:

$$\frac{\text{Number with 1 year's service or more}}{\text{Number employed 1 year ago}} \times 100$$

This index provides an indication of the tendency for longer-service employees to remain with the company, and therefore shows the degree to which there is continuity of employment. But this too can be misleading because the index will not reveal the different situations that exist in an organization with a high proportion of long-serving employees in comparison with one where the majority of employees are short service. Other forms of stability measures are the survival rate and half-life index, as described below.

Survival rate

The survival rate is the proportion of employees who are engaged within a certain period who remain with the organization after so many months or years of service. Thus, an analysis of a cohort of 20 trainees who have completed their training might show that after two years, 10 of the original trainees were still with the company, a survival rate of 50 per cent. The distribution of losses for each entry group, or cohort, can be plotted in the form of a survival curve, as shown in Figure 20.1.

FIGURE 20.1   A survival curve

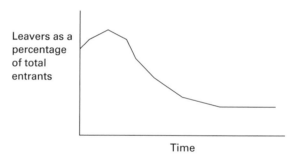

The basic shape of this curve has been found to be similar in many situations, although the peak of the curve may occur further along the time scale and/or may be lower when it relates to more highly skilled or trained entry cohorts. An example of a survival rate analysis is shown in Table 20.1. This indicates that half the number of recruits in any one year may be lost over the next five years, unless something can be done about the factors causing wastage.

The survival rate is useful as a means of tracking a 'cohort' of recruits, eg graduates, to assess the effectiveness of recruitment and retention policies. But it cannot be used as a means of measuring the turnover rates of whole populations in order to allow for future wastage when making supply forecasts.

TABLE 20.1   A survival rate analysis

Entry cohort	Original number	Number surviving to end of year after engagement				
		Year 1	Year 2	Year 3	Year 4	Year 5
A	40	35	28	26	22	20
B	32	25	24	19	18	17
C	48	39	33	30	25	23
D	38	32	27	24	22	19
E	42	36	30	26	23	21
Total	200	167	142	125	110	100
Average survival rate	100%	83%	71%	62%	55%	50%

Half-life index

A simpler concept derived from survival rate analysis is that of the half-life index, which is defined as the time taken for a group or cohort of starters to reduce to half its original size through the wastage process (five years in the above example). Comparisons can then be made for successive entry years or between different groups of employees to show where action may have to be taken to counter undesirable wastage trends.

Leavers' length of service analysis

The information from measures of stability can be enhanced if an analysis is also made of the average length of service of people who leave, as in Table 20.2. This analysis is still fairly crude, because it deals only with those who leave. A more refined analysis would compare for each designated length of service the numbers leaving with the numbers employed. If, in the example shown, the total number employed with less than three months' service was 80 and the total with more than five years' was 80, the proportion

of leavers in each category would be, respectively, 35 per cent and 14 per cent – more revealing figures.

Choice of measurement

It is difficult to avoid using the conventional employee (labour) turnover index as the easiest and most familiar of all methods of measurement. It provides the simplest basis for assessing future levels of supply by allowing for wastage. But it can usefully be supplemented with some measure of stability (eg survival rate or the length of service of leavers) to identify recruitment or retention problems.

The cost of employee turnover

The cost of employee turnover can be considerable. The CIPD 2008 survey established that the average cost per employee was £5,800, rising to £20,000 for senior managers or directors. Cost estimates are useful as means of backing up a business case for taking action to reduce turnover. The following factors should be considered when calculating costs.

TABLE 20.2   Leavers' length of service analysis

Occupation	Leavers by length of service						Total number leaving	Average number employed	Index of employee turnover %
	Less than 3 months	3–6 months	6 months– 1 year	1–2 years	3–5 years	5 or more years			
A	5	4	3	3	2	3	20	220	9
B	15	12	10	6	3	4	50	250	20
C	8	6	5	4	3	4	30	100	30
Totals	28	22	18	13	8	11	100	570	18

Factors affecting the cost of employee turnover

- Direct cost of recruiting replacements (advertising, interviewing, testing, etc).
- Direct cost of introducing replacements (induction cost).
- Direct cost of training replacements in necessary skills.
- Leaving costs – payroll and HR administration.
- Opportunity cost of time spent by HR and line managers in recruitment, induction and training.
- Loss of output from those leaving before they are replaced.
- Loss of output because of delays in obtaining replacements.
- Loss of output while new starters are on their learning curves acquiring the necessary knowledge and skills.

Research by Phillips (1990) found that the 'visible', ie direct, costs of recruitment accounted for only 10 to 15 per cent of total costs. By far the highest costs were associated with the inefficiencies arising while the post was vacant (33 per cent) and the inefficiency of new workers (32 per cent). On average, 12.5 months were required for executives to be comfortable in a new position and 13.5 months were required for a new employee to achieve maximum efficiency.

Retention planning

The turnover of key employees can have a disproportionate impact on the business. The people organizations wish to retain are often the ones most likely to leave. It was claimed by Reed (2001) that every worker is five minutes away from handing in his or her notice, and 150 working hours away from walking out of the door to a better offer. There is no such thing as a job for life and today's workers have few qualms about leaving employers for greener pastures. Concerted action is required to retain talented people, but there are limits to what any organization can do. It is also necessary to encourage the greatest contribution from existing talent and to value them accordingly.

Factors affecting retention

Retention strategies should be based on an under-standing of the factors that affect whether or not employees leave or stay. For early-career employees (30 years old and under) career advancement is significant. For mid-career employees (age 31–50) the ability to manage their careers and satisfaction from their work are important. Late-career employees (aged over 50) will be more interested in security. It is also the case that a younger workforce will change jobs and employers more often than an older workforce, and workforces with a lot of part-timers are less stable than those with predominately full-time staff. The other factors that affect reten-tion are:

● company image;
● recruitment, selection and deployment;
● leadership – 'employees join companies and leave managers';
● learning opportunities;
● performance recognition and rewards.

A study by Holbeche (1998) of high flyers found that the factors that aided the retention and motivation of high performers included providing challenge and achievement opportunities (eg assignments), mentors, realistic self-assessment and feedback.

Basis of the retention strategy

A retention strategy takes into account the retention issues the organization is facing and sets out ways in which these issues can be dealt with. This may mean accepting the following argument offered by Cappelli (2000: 104):

> To adopt the new strategy you have to accept the new reality: the market, not your company, will ultimately determine the movement of your employees. Yes, you can make your organization as pleasant and rewarding a place in which to work in as possible – you can fix problems that might push people towards the exits. But you can't counter the pull of the market; you can't shield your people from attractive opportunities and aggressive recruiters. The old goal of HR – to minimize overall employee turnover – needs to be replaced by a new goal: to influence who leaves and when.

Bevan *et al* (1997) proposed the use of risk analysis to quantify the seriousness of losing key people or of key posts becoming vacant.

Risk of leaving analysis

Risk analysis can be carried out by initially identify-ing potential risk areas – the key people who may leave and, for each of them, as individuals or groups, estimate:

1 the likelihood of this occurring;
2 how serious the effects of a loss would be on the business;
3 the ease with which a replacement could be made and the replacement costs.

Each of the estimates could be expressed on a scale, say: very high, high, medium, low, very low. An overview of the ratings under each heading could then indicate where action may need to be taken to retain key people or groups of people.

The analysis provides specific information on areas for concern. Reasons for leaving can be amongst the following:

● more pay;
● better prospects (career move);
● more security;
● more opportunity to develop skills;
● unable to cope with job;
● better working conditions;
● poor relationships with manager/team leader;
● poor relationships with colleagues;
● bullying or harassment;
● personal – pregnancy, illness, moving away from area, etc.

Some indication of the reasons for leaving, and therefore where action needs to be taken, can be provided by exit interviews, but they are fallible. More reliance can be placed on the results of attitude or opinion surveys to identify any areas of dissatisfaction. The retention plan should propose actions that would focus on each of the areas in which lack of commitment and dissatisfaction can arise.

Areas for action

Depending on the outcome of the risk analysis and the overall assessment of reasons for leaving, the possible actions that can be taken are as follows:

- Ensure that selection and promotion procedures match the capacities of individuals to the demands of the work they have to do. Rapid turnover can result simply from poor selection or promotion decisions.

- Develop commitment to the work (job engagement) not only through job design but also by organizing work around projects with which people can identify more readily than the company as a whole.

- Reduce the losses of people who cannot adjust to their new job – the 'induction crisis' – by giving them proper training and support when they join the organization.

- Deal with uncompetitive, inequitable or unfair pay systems. But as Cappelli (2000) pointed out, there is a limit to the extent to which people can be bribed to stay.

- Design jobs to maximize skill variety, task significance, autonomy, control over work and feedback, and ensure that they provide opportunities for learning and growth. Some roles can be 'customized' to meet the needs of particular individuals.

- Encourage the development of social ties within the company. In the words of Cappelli (2000: 108), 'loyalty to companies may be disappearing but loyalty to colleagues is not'.

- Take steps to improve work–life balance by developing policies, including flexible working, that recognize the needs of employees outside work.

- Eliminate as far as possible unpleasant working conditions or the imposition of too much stress on employees.

- Select, brief and train managers and team leaders so that they appreciate the positive contribution they can make to improving retention by the ways in which they lead their teams. Bear in mind that people often leave their managers rather than their organization.

- Ensure that policies for controlling bullying and harassment are in place and are applied.

Absence management

Absence or attendance management is the development and application of policies and procedures designed to reduce levels of absenteeism. The CIPD (2010) report on absence management revealed that:

- the average length of employee absence was 7.7 days per employee per year;

- absence is highest in the public sector at 9.6 days per employee per year;

- absence is also relatively high in the non-profit sector at an average of 8.3 days per employee per year;

- absence is lowest in the private sector; manufacturing organizations reported an average of 6.9 days lost per employee per year, while private sector services organizations reported an average absence of 6.6 days per employee per year;

- larger organizations have higher average levels of absence than smaller organizations;

- on average, two-thirds of working time lost to absence is accounted for by short-term absences of up to seven days; absences of between eight days and four weeks account for 16 per cent of short-term absence, and a similar proportion is caused by absences of four weeks or longer;

- the median cost of absence was £600 per employee per year;

- the average cost of absence is much higher in the public sector (£889) than in private sector organizations (£600).

Something has to be done about it. This means understanding the causes of absence, adopting comprehensive absence management (or more positively, attendance management) policies, measuring absence and implementing procedures for the management of short- and long-term absence.

Causes of absence

The causes of absence have been analysed by Huczynski and Fitzpatrick (1989) under three headings: job situation factors, personal factors and attendance factors.

Job situation factors

- Job scope – a high degree of task repetitiveness is associated with absenteeism, although job satisfaction itself is a contributory rather than a primary cause of absence.

- Stress – it is estimated that 40 million working days are lost each year in the UK through stress. This can be attributed to work load, poor working conditions, shift work, role ambiguity or conflict, relationships and organizational climate.

- Frequent job transfers increase absenteeism.

- Management style – the quality of management, especially that of immediate supervisors, affects the level of absenteeism.

- Physical working conditions.

- Work group size – the larger the organization the higher the absence rate.

Personal factors

- Employee values – for some workers, doing less work for the same reward improves the deal made with the employer (the effort-reward bargain). The following positive outcomes of absence have been shown by research to be particularly important to employees: break from routine, leisure time, dealing with personal business and a break from co-workers.

- Age – younger employees are more frequently absent than older ones.

- Personality – some people are absence-prone (studies have noted that between 5 and 10 per cent of workers account for about half of the total absence, while a few are never absent at all).

Attendance factors

- Reward systems – as pay increases attendance improves.

- Sick-pay schemes may increase absenteeism.

- Work group norms can exert pressure for or against attendance.

Absence policies

Absence policies should cover:

- methods of measuring absence;

- setting targets for the level of absence;

- deciding on the level of short-term absence that would trigger action, possibly using the Bradford Factor, as explained below;

- the circumstances in which disciplinary action might be taken;

- what employees must do if they are unable to attend work;

- sick-pay arrangements;

- provisions for the reduction and control of absence such as return-to-work interviews;

- other steps that can be taken to reduce absence, such as flexible working patterns.

The skills required to manage absenteeism are examined in Chapter 54.

Recording and measuring absence

As a basis for action, absence levels need to be recorded so that they can be measured and monitored against targets for maintaining absence at a certain level, or reducing absenteeism.

An HR information system (HRIS) can provide the best means of recording absenteeism. If a self-service approach is in place, managers and team leaders have direct access to absence records showing the incidence of absenteeism (number and lengths of absence). This data can be consolidated for use by HR in compiling absence statistics and monitoring against targets. The most common measurement is the percentage of time available that has been lost due to absence.

The Bradford Factor

The Bradford Factor provides a useful measure. This index identifies persistent short-term absence by measuring the number and duration of spells of absence. Its exact origin is a mystery, although IDS (2007) believes that it has some connection with Bradford University's School of Management. It is calculated using the formula $S \times S \times D$ = Bradford points score, where S is the number of occasions of absence in the last 52 weeks and D is the total number of days' absence in the last 52 weeks. Thus, for employees with a total of 14 days' absence in a 52-week period, the Bradford score can vary enormously depending on the number of occasions involved. For example:

one absence of 14 days is 14 points: $1 \times 1 \times 14$

seven absences of two days each is 686 points: $7 \times 7 \times 14$

14 absences of one day each is 2,744 points: $14 \times 14 \times 14$

The Bradford index can be used as a trigger to initiate action. It is typically set at 250 points so that action would be triggered if, for example, there had been 10 days absence over five spells.

Controlling short-term absence

Short-term absence can be controlled by the following:

- Return-to-work interviews conducted by line managers, which can identify problems at an early stage and provide an opportunity for a discussion on ways of reducing absence.
- Use of trigger mechanisms such as the Bradford Factor to review attendance.
- Invoking disciplinary procedures for unacceptable absence levels.
- Training line managers in methods of controlling absence, including return-to-work interviews.
- Extending the scope for flexible working.

Managing long-term absence

The best way to manage long-term absence is to keep in contact with employees by letter, telephone or visits to discuss the situation and, where possible, plan the return to work. This plan may include modified working hours or a modified role for a period.

CASE STUDIES

Controlling sickness absence at Wincanton

Distribution company Wincanton had a problem controlling sickness absence because its large workforce is spread over 285 sites. The solution was to outsource absence management to Active Health Partners, which operates a call centre staffed by nurses – employees must report their absences and can receive medical advice. An online absence recording system is also provided, which provides line managers with information on absences and access to absence statistics.

As soon as an employee calls Active Health Partners an e-mail or text is sent to the employee's line manager via an automated system, informing him or her of the absence and the reason for it and giving an approximate return-to-work date. The system also provides various triggers to line managers. For example, once an employee has been away for more than 15 days the manager receives a message indicating that contact needs to be made. Managers are expected to conduct return-to-work interviews and have more formal discussions when an absence exceeds 15 days. They will explore why there has been this amount of time off, if there is an underlying health issue, if an employee should be referred to Occupational Health and if the disciplinary process should be started.

As a result, Wincanton reduced sickness absence by 10,000 days in six months.

Absence management at Westminster City Council

Monitoring

Sickness absence is recorded by line managers on the intranet system.

Return-to-work interviews

A return-to-work interview is held between the manager and the employee after any length of absence, even one day, although this may only take a couple of minutes. Employees are required to complete a self-certification/return to work form. Employees who have been absent for eight days or more are informed that they will be referred to Occupational Health.

Absence trigger points

An employee who has had more than seven days' sickness absence in any rolling 365-day period is dealt with through the 'enhanced sickness management procedure'. If sickness absence exceeds 20 days, the long-term sickness procedure is applied.

The enhanced sickness management procedure

- Line managers complete a referral form which is forwarded to Occupational Health staff who decide to conduct a face-to-face consultation or make a desktop assessment and in either case provide any advice necessary to the manager or the individual and send a report to the manager and HR.
- Within 10 days of receiving the report the manager meets the employee to review the sickness record, consider any further explanations for the absence, discuss the report from Occupational Health and agree action to improve attendance and minimize sickness.
- As necessary, especially in cases of disability, Occupational Health will discuss with the manager and the employee any reasonable adaptations to the work environment that may be helpful.

Long-term sickness absence management

- Every four weeks managers review cases of long-term absence with the Occupational Health service and also contact the employee.
- If an employee has been off work the managers and Occupational Health hold a case conference to assess the situation. The employee is required to meet Occupational Health if this is possible.
- The manager makes an assessment following the case conference covering the nature and likely length of the illness, the impact of the absence on the work and how any impact will be managed.
- Following this assessment a face-to-face meeting is held with the employee to ensure that other relevant factors and personal circumstances are taken into account.
- A sickness absence hearing may be called as a result of this meeting and the case conference.

Employee assistance programme

An EAP is available through an external provider. Employees can raise problems with helpline staff, and face-to-face counselling can be made available.

Induction

Induction is the process of receiving and welcoming employees when they first join a company and giving them the basic information they need to settle down quickly and happily and start work. The aims are to:

- smooth the preliminary stages when everything is likely to be strange and unfamiliar to the starter;
- establish quickly a favourable attitude to the organization in the mind of new employees so that they are more likely to stay;
- obtain effective output from the new employee in the shortest possible time;
- reduce the likelihood of the employee leaving quickly.

Introduction to the organization

New starters will be concerned about who they are going to work for (their immediate manager or team leader), who they are going to work with, what work they are going to do on their first day and the geographical layout of their place of work (location of entrances, exits, lavatories, restrooms and the canteen).

Some of this information may be provided by a member of the HR department, or an assistant in the new employee's place of work. But the most important source of information is the immediate manager, supervisor or team leader.

Departmental induction

The departmental induction programme should, wherever possible, start with the departmental manager, not the immediate team leader. The manager may give only a general welcome and a brief description of the work of the department before handing new employees over to their team leaders for the more detailed induction. But it is important for the manager to be involved at this stage so that he or she is not seen as a remote figure by the new employee. At least this means that the starter will not be simply a name or a number to the manager.

The detailed induction in the workplace is probably best carried out by the immediate team leader.

Induction to the workplace

The team leader should introduce new starters to their fellow team members. It is best to get one member of the team to act as a guide or 'starter's friend'. There is much to be said for these initial guides being people who have not been long with the organization. As relative newcomers they are likely to remember all the small points that were a source of worry to them when they started work, and so help new employees to settle in quickly.

On-the-job induction training

Most new starters other than those on formal training schemes will learn on-the-job, although this may be supplemented with special off-the-job courses to develop particular skills or knowledge. But on-the-job training can be haphazard, inefficient and wasteful. A planned, systematic approach is desirable. This can incorporate an assessment of what the new starter needs to learn, the use of designated and trained colleagues to act as guides and mentors, and coaching by team leaders or specially appointed and trained departmental trainers.

These on-the-job arrangements can be supplemented by self-managed learning arrangements, offering access to flexible learning packages or providing advice on learning opportunities.

Release from the organization

One of the most demanding areas of human resource management in organizations is that of handling arrangements for releasing people through redundancy, dismissal or retirement.

Redundancy

Redundancy takes place when the organization as a whole is going through a downsizing exercise, when structural changes are being made following mergers and acquisitions, and when individual jobs are no longer needed. If, unfortunately, redundancy has to take place, it is necessary to plan ahead – seeking and implementing methods of avoiding redundancy as far as possible, making arrangements for voluntary redundancy and helping people to find jobs (outplacement). HR usually has the onerous responsibility of handling the redundancy itself.

Planning ahead

Planning ahead means that future reductions in people needs are anticipated and steps are taken to minimize compulsory redundancies. This can be done by freezing recruitment and allowing the normal flow of leavers (natural wastage) to reduce or even eliminate the need for redundancy, calling in outsourced work, reducing or eliminating overtime, reducing the number of part-timers and temporary staff, work-sharing (two people splitting one job between them) or, more reluctantly, temporary layoffs.

Voluntary redundancy

Asking for volunteers – with a suitable payoff – is another way of reducing compulsory redundancies. The disadvantage is that the wrong people might go, ie the good workers who find it easy to get other work. It is sometimes necessary to go into reverse and offer such people a special loyalty bonus if they stay on.

Outplacement

Outplacement is about helping redundant employees to find other work. It means helping them to cope with the trauma of redundancy through specialized outplacement consultants and counselling or by setting up 'job shops'.

Outplacement consultants provide counselling on how people can make the best use of what they can offer to other employers. They can be helped to identify their strengths and achievements, the type of job they are qualified to do and the sort of employer that is most likely to want people with their experience and qualifications. Assistance can be provided in preparing what is sometimes called an 'achievement CV', which spells out what the individual has been successful in and prompts the thought in the employer's mind: 'What the individual has done for them he or she can do for us.'

Counselling involves help and advice in identifying possible moves, preparing CVs and how to make the best impression in interviews. Counselling may be provided by HR staff, but there is much to be said for using specialized outplacement consultants.

Help may be provided on an individual basis through counselling or outplacement consultants, but in larger scale redundancies *job shops* can be set up. The staff of the job shop, who may be from HR or are sometimes members of a specialized outplacement consultancy, scour the travel-to-work area seeking job opportunities, match people to jobs and arrange interviews.

Dismissal

Dismissal takes place when an employer terminates the employment of someone with or without notice. A contract can be terminated as a result of demotion or transfer, as well as dismissal. People can be 'constructively dismissed' if they resign because of their employer's unreasonable behaviour.

Approach to dismissal

Dismissals should be handled in accordance with the following principles of natural justice:

- Individuals should know the standards of performance they are expected to meet and the rules to which they are expected to conform.

- They should be given a clear indication of where they are failing or what rules they have broken.

- Except in cases of gross misconduct, they should be given an opportunity to improve before disciplinary action is taken.

Disciplinary procedure

These principles should form the basis of a disciplinary procedure, which is staged as follows:

1 An informal discussion on the problem.
2 A first written warning.
3 A final written warning.
4 Dismissal or action short of dismissal such as loss of pay or demotion.

Employees should be reminded of their right to be accompanied by a colleague or employee representative in disciplinary hearings. (An example of a full disciplinary procedure incorporating the stages listed above is given in Chapter 39.)

Managers and team leaders should be made aware of the procedure and told what authority they have to take action. It is advisable to have all written warnings and any final action approved by a higher authority. In cases of gross misconduct, managers and team leaders should be given the right to suspend if higher authority is not available, but not to dismiss. The importance of obtaining and recording the facts should be emphasized. Managers should always have a colleague with them when issuing a final warning and should make a note to file of what was said on the spot.

Retirement

Retirement is a major change and should be prepared for. Retirement policies need to specify:

- when people are due to retire;

- the circumstances, if any, in which they can work beyond their normal retirement date;

- the provision of pre-retirement training on such matters as finance, insurance, state pension rights and other benefits, health, working either for money or for a voluntary organization, and sources of advice and help;

- the provision of advice to people about to retire.

Employee value proposition

An organization's employee value proposition consists of what it offers to prospective or existing employees that they will value and will persuade them to join or remain with the business. It can be developed by analysing everything that the organization has to offer potential employees and then conveying that offer to them on the organization's website or by other means.

Employer brand

The employee value proposition can be expressed as an employer brand – the image presented by an organization as a good employer. To create an employer brand:

- analyse what the best candidates need and want;
- establish how far the core values of the organization support the creation of an attractive brand;
- define the features of the brand on the basis of an examination and review of each of the areas that affect the perceptions of people about the organization as 'a great place to work';
- benchmark the approaches of other organizations;
- be honest and realistic.

Measuring employee turnover

It is necessary to measure employee turnover and calculate its costs in order to forecast future losses for planning purposes and to identify the reasons that people leave the organization. Plans can then be made to attack the problems causing unnecessary turnover and to reduce costs. The methods available are: employee turnover index, half-life index, length of service analysis, stability index and survival rate.

Estimating the cost of employee turnover

- Direct cost of recruiting replacements.
- Direct cost of introducing replacements.
- Direct cost of training replacements.
- Leaving costs.
- Opportunity cost of time spent by HR and line managers in recruitment, etc.
- Loss of output.

Retention planning

Retention strategies should be based on an understanding of the factors that affect whether or not employees leave or stay.

Risk of leaving analysis

- More pay.
- Better prospects (career move).
- More security.
- More opportunity to develop skills.
- Unable to cope with job.
- Better working conditions.
- Poor relationships with manager/team leader.
- Poor relationships with colleagues.
- Bullying or harassment.
- Personal – pregnancy, illness, moving away from area, etc.

Absence policies

Areas:

- methods of measuring absence;
- setting targets for the level of absence;
- deciding on the level of short-term absence that would trigger action, possibly using the Bradford Factor;
- the circumstances in which disciplinary action might be taken;
- what employees must do if they are unable to attend work;
- sick-pay arrangements;
- provisions for the reduction and control of absence such as return-to-work interviews;
- other steps that can be taken to reduce absence such as flexible working patterns.

Induction

Induction is the process of receiving and welcoming employees when they first join a company and giving them the basic information they need to settle down quickly and happily and start work.

Release from the organization

One of the most demanding areas of HRM in organizations is in handling arrangements for releasing people through redundancy, dismissal or retirement.

Questions

1 What is an employee value proposition?

2 What is an employer brand?

3 What is the employee turnover index and why can it be misleading?

4 What factors affect employee retention?

5 What should absence policies cover?

6 What are the principles of natural justice?

References

Bevan, S, Barber, I and Robinson, D (1997) *Keeping the Best: A practical guide to retaining key employees*, Brighton, Institute for Employment Studies

Cappelli, P (2000) A market-driven approach to retaining talent, *Harvard Business Review*, January–February, pp 103–11

CIPD (2008) *Survey of Recruitment, Retention and Turnover*, London, CIPD

CIPD (2010) *Survey of Absence Management*, London, CIPD

CIPD (2011) *Survey of Resourcing and Talent Planning*, London, CIPD

Holbeche, L (1998) *Motivating People in Lean Organizations*, Oxford, Butterworth-Heinemann

Huczynski, A and Fitzpatrick, M J (1989) *Managing Employee Absence for a Competitive Edge*, London, Pitman

IDS (2007) *Absence Management, HR Study 810*, London, IDS

Phillips, J D (1990) The price tag of turnover, *Personnel Journal*, December, pp 58–61

Purcell, J, Kinnie, K, Hutchinson, S, Rayton, B and Swart, J (2003) *People and Performance: How people management impacts on organizational performance*, London, CIPD

Reed, A (2001) *Innovation in Human Resource Management*, London, CIPD

Walker, P (2007) Develop an effective employer brand, *People Management*, 18 October, pp 44–5

21
Talent management

LEARNING OUTCOMES

On completing this chapter you should be able to define these key concepts. You should also know about:

- The meaning of talent management
- The process of talent management
- Developing a talent management strategy
- Management succession planning
- Career management

Introduction

The notion of talent management is based on the proposition that 'those with the best people win'. It emerged in the late 1990s when McKinsey and Company coined the phrase 'the war for talent'. It has now been recognized as a major resourcing activity, although its elements are all familiar. Guest, cited by Warren (2006: 29), commented that:

Organizations espouse a lot of notions about talent management and give it a lot of emphasis, but in practical terms it doesn't have a very different meaning to what most organizations have always done. Talent management is an idea that has been around a long time. It's been relabelled.

Iles and Preece (2010: 244–5) commented that:

Many current ideas in talent management, now often presented as novel and best practice, such as assessing potential, 360-degree feedback, assessment centres and coaching, come from the 1950s era of large stable bureaucracies and sophisticated succession planning as part of more general 'manpower planning'.

There are many versions of talent management but in one way or another most incorporate familiar activities such as potential assessment, leadership and management development, succession planning and career planning. But as Guest also noted, it brings together some old ideas and gives them a freshness. It can also provide a means of integrating these practices so that a coherent approach is adopted by the use of mutually supportive practices. The fundamental concept of talent management – that the need to engage in talent planning to build a talent pool by means of a talent pipeline – is a key concern of human resource management.

This chapter covers the meaning and process of talent management and talent management strategy. Two important aspects of talent management – management succession planning and career management – are dealt with at the end of the chapter.

Talent management defined

Talent management is the process of ensuring that the organization has the talented people it needs to attain its business goals. It involves the strategic management of the flow of talent through an organization by creating and maintaining a talent pipeline. As suggested by Younger et al (2007), the approaches required include emphasizing 'growth from within', regarding talent development as a key element of the business strategy, being clear about the competencies and qualities that matter, maintaining well-defined career paths, taking management development, coaching and mentoring seriously, and demanding high performance.

The term 'talent management' may refer simply to management succession planning and/or management development activities, although this notion does not really add anything to these familiar processes except a new name; admittedly quite an evocative one. It is better to regard talent management as a more comprehensive and integrated bundle of activities, the aim of which is to create a pool of talent in an organization, bearing in mind that talent is a major corporate resource.

Iles *et al* (2010: 127) identified three broad strands of thought about talent management:

1 It is not essentially different from HRM or HRD. Both involve the right people in the right job at the right time and managing the supply and development of people throughout the organization.

2 It is simply integrated HRD with a selective focus on a small 'talented' section of the workforce (a 'talent pool').

3 It involves organizationally-focused competence development through managing and developing flows of talent through the organization. The focus is on the talent pipeline rather than the talent pool. This strand is closely related to succession and human resource planning.

Before describing the process of talent management it is necessary to answer three questions:

1 What does it mean when reference is made to 'the war for talent'?

2 What is talent?

3 Who is covered by talent management programmes?

The war for talent

Following the McKinsey lead, the phrase 'the war for talent' has become a familiar metaphor for talent management. Michaels, of McKinsey and Co, and his colleagues (2001) identified five imperatives that companies need to act on if they are going to win what they called the 'war for managerial talent':

1 Creating a winning employee value proposition that will make your company uniquely attractive to talent.

2 Moving beyond recruiting hype to build a long-term recruiting strategy.

3 Using job experience, coaching and mentoring to cultivate the potential in managers.

4 Strengthening the talent pool by investing in A players, developing B players and acting decisively on C players.

5 Central to this approach is a pervasive mindset – a deep conviction shared by

leaders throughout the company that competitive advantage comes from having better talent at all levels.

But Pfeffer (2001: 258) expressed doubts about the war for talent concept, which he believed was the wrong metaphor for organizational success. He argued that:

> Fighting the war for talent can readily create self-fulfilling prophesies that leave a large portion of the workforce demotivated or ready to quit, and produce an arrogant attitude that makes it hard to learn or listen. It can cause the company to focus always on getting better people, mainly from outside, instead of fixing the culture and system of management practices that research has shown are consequential for performance.

He suggested (*ibid*: 249) that perceiving talent management as a 'war' leads to:

- an invariable emphasis on individual performance thereby damaging team work;
- a tendency to glorify the talents of those outside the company and downplay the skills and abilities of insiders;
- those labelled as less able *becoming* less able because they are asked to do less and given fewer resources and training;
- a de-emphasis on fixing the systemic, cultural and business issues that are invariably more important for enhancing performance;
- the development of an elitist, arrogant attitude (*cf* Enron).

What talent is

Talent is what people have when they possess the skills, abilities and aptitudes that enable them to perform effectively in their roles. They make a difference to organizational performance through their immediate efforts and they have the potential to make an important contribution in the future. Talent management aims to identify, obtain, keep and develop those talented people.

The people involved

The McKinsey prescription has often been misinterpreted to mean that talent management is only about obtaining, identifying and nurturing high-flyers, ignoring the point made by Michaels *et al* (2001) that competitive advantage comes from having better talent at all levels.

But many organizations focus on the elite. For example, Microsoft UK is most concerned with its 'A list', the top 10 per cent of performers, regardless of role and level, whilst Six Continents targets executives below board level and high-potential individuals, as the two cadres are likely to provide their leaders of tomorrow. Huselid *et al* (2005) argued that talent management policies should concentrate on what they called 'A positions'. Iles and Preece (2010: 248) have identified three main perspectives:

1 *Exclusive people* – key people with high performance and/or potential irrespective of position.

2 *Exclusive position* – the right people in the strategically critical jobs.

3 *Inclusive people* – everyone in the organization is seen as actually or potentially talented, given opportunity and direction.

The first two perspectives, or a combination of the two, are the most common. According to Clarke and Winkler (2006), the third approach is comparatively rare in practice, although there have been strong advocates of it such as Buckingham and Vosburgh (2001: 18), who wrote that the talent is inherent in each person: 'HR's most basic challenge is to help one particular person increase his or her performance; to be successful in the future we must restore our focus on the unique talents of each individual employee, and on the right way to transfer those talents into lasting performance.'

If the other approaches are adopted there is a danger of talent management being perceived as an exclusive and elitist approach. As the CIPD (2010a: 1) observed: 'Talent management and diversity need to be interlinked. Diversity should be threaded through all talent management activities and strategies to ensure that organizations make the best use of the talent and skills of all their employees in ways that are aligned to business objectives.'

HR people have different views, which state on the one hand that everyone has talent and it is not just about the favoured few, and on the other that you need to pay most attention to the best. Thorne and Pellant (2007: 9) argued that: 'No organization should focus all its attention on development of only part of its human capital. What is important, however, is recognizing the needs of different individuals within its community.'

The general consensus seems to be that the main concerns of talent management are obtaining, identifying and developing people with high potential. This is to be expected, although it should not be at the expense of the development needs of people generally. Organizations that simply cater for the high-flyers and ignore the rest do so at their peril. The latter are the people in the engine room on whom the organization depends.

The process of talent management

Talent management takes the form of a 'bundle' of interrelated processes, as shown in Figure 21.1.

Talent management starts with the business strategy and what it signifies in terms of the talented people required by the organization. This provides the basis for talent planning. Ultimately, the aim is to develop and maintain a pool of talented people. This is done through the talent pipeline, which consists of the processes of resourcing, retention planning, succession and career planning and learning and development (especially leadership and management development) that maintain the flow of talent needed by the organization. Its elements are described below.

Talent planning

Talent planning is the process of establishing how many and what sort of talented people are needed now and in the future. It is a sub-set of workforce planning, as described in Chapter 18, and uses the same techniques. It leads to the development of policies for attracting and retaining talent and the

FIGURE 21.1   The elements of talent management

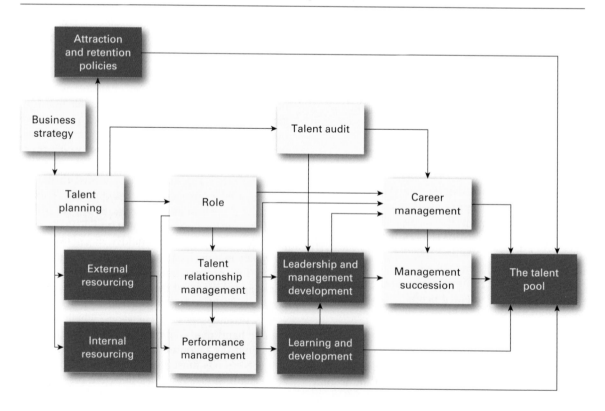

determination of future requirements as monitored by talent audits. It also influences the development of the roles talented people carry out.

Resourcing

The outcomes of talent planning are programmes for obtaining people from within and outside the organization (internal and external resourcing). They involve the implementation of policies for attracting high-quality people.

Attraction and retention policies and programmes

These policies and programmes describe the approach to ensuring that the organization gets and keeps the talent it needs. Attraction policies influence programmes for external resourcing. Retention policies are designed to ensure that people remain as engaged and committed members of the organization. Line managers can be asked to carry out separate risk analyses for any key staff to assess the likelihood of their leaving so that steps can be taken to encourage them to stay. The outcome of these policies is a talent flow that creates and maintains the talent pool.

Talent audit

A talent audit identifies those with potential, often through a performance management assessment. It provides the basis for career planning and development – ensuring that talented people have the sequence of experience supplemented by coaching, mentoring and learning programmes that will equip them for carrying out more demanding roles in the future. Talent audits can also be used to indicate the possible danger of talented people leaving (risk analysis) and what action may need to be taken to retain them.

Role development

Talent management is concerned with the roles people carry out. This involves role development – ensuring that roles provide the responsibility, challenge and autonomy required to create role engagement and motivation. It also means taking steps to ensure that people have the opportunity and are given the encouragement to learn and develop in their roles. Talent management policies focus on role flexibility – giving people the chance to expand their roles by making better and extended use of their talents.

Talent relationship management

Talent relationship management is about building effective relationships with people in their roles. It is better to build on an existing relationship than try to create a new one when someone leaves. The aims are to recognize the value of individual employees, provide opportunities for growth, treat them fairly and achieve 'talent engagement', ensuring that people are committed to their work and the organization.

Performance management

Performance management processes, including 360-degree feedback, provide ways of building relationships with people, identifying talent and potential, planning learning and development activities and making the most of the talent possessed by the organization. Properly carried out, performance management is a means of increasing the engagement and motivation of people by providing positive feedback and recognition. This is part of a total reward system.

Learning and development

Learning and development policies and programmes are essential components in the process of talent management – ensuring that people acquire and enhance the skills and competencies they need. Policies should be formulated by reference to 'employee success profiles', which are described in terms of competencies and define the qualities that need to be developed. Employee success profiles can be incorporated in role profiles.

Leadership and management development

The research conducted by the CIPD (2010b: 11) found that there was a considerable emphasis on leadership and management development in the talent management programmes of respondents. Many of them referred to the introduction of a variety of management and leadership development interventions to properly equip managers. While some spoke in general terms – 'launching leadership and management development programmes' – respondents also referred to specific training and development around particular themes, including:

- change management;
- talent management and development;
- people and performance management;
- decision making and difficult conversations.

Management succession planning

Management succession planning takes place to ensure that, as far as possible, the organization has the managers it requires to meet future business needs. It is considered in detail later in this chapter.

Career management

Career management, also discussed later in this chapter, is concerned with the provision of opportunities for people to develop their abilities and their careers so that the organization has the flow of talent it needs and they can satisfy their own aspirations.

Developing a talent management strategy

A talent management strategy consists of a view on how the processes described above should mesh together with an overall objective – to acquire and nurture talent wherever it is and wherever it is needed by using a number of interdependent policies and practices. Talent management is the notion of 'bundling' in action. The strategy should be based on definitions of what is meant by talent in terms of competencies and potential, who the talent management programme should cover, and the future talent requirements of the organization. The aims should be to:

- develop the organization as an 'employer of choice';

- plan and implement recruitment and selection programmes that ensure good-quality people are recruited who are likely to thrive in the organization and stay with it for a reasonable length of time (but not necessarily for life);
- introduce reward policies that help to attract and retain high-quality staff;
- design jobs and develop roles that give people opportunities to apply and grow their skills and provide them with autonomy, interest and challenge;
- provide talented staff with opportunities for career development and growth;
- recognize those with talent by rewarding excellence, enterprise and achievement;
- provide for management succession.

It can be difficult to introduce comprehensive talent management processes covering all the activities referred to earlier. A phased approach may be best. Resourcing activities take place anyhow, although the advantages of planning them on the basis of assessments of talent requirements are considerable; and it makes sense to devote energies to retaining key staff. But beyond that, the starting point in practice for an extended talent management programme could be a process of identifying people with talent through a performance management system. It would then be possible to concentrate on leadership and management development programmes. Sophisticated approaches to succession and career planning could be introduced later.

What is happening in talent management

A study by CIPD (2007) of nine UK private and public sector organizations found that:

- What is seen as talent and how it is developed is highly varied.
- There is no one definition of talent management.
- There was little evidence of employers adopting a formal talent management strategy.
- Talent management programmes varied in terms of who they were aimed at and how.

- There were issues relating to the demotivation of individuals not selected for talent management, especially if this meant that they had fewer resources and opportunities for progression.
- There was often a lack of integration with other HR programmes.

The CIPD 2011 learning and talent development survey revealed that the proportion of employers involved in talent management was 61 per cent. Organizations operating in the private sector are significantly more likely to undertake such activities (70 per cent), as are those with a specific training budget (64 per cent). The likelihood of organizations having talent management activities is also related to their size. Three-quarters of very large organizations (5,000+ employees) undertake talent management activities compared with two-fifths of organizations with fewer than 50 employees. Talent management activities were most commonly concerned with high-potential employees (77 per cent). The top three aims of talent management quoted by respondents were developing high-potential employees, growing future managers/leaders and retaining key staff.

Management succession planning

Management succession planning is the process of assessing and auditing the talent in the organization in order to answer three fundamental questions: first, are there enough potential successors available – a supply of people coming through who can take key roles in the longer term? Second, are they good enough? Third, do they have the right skills and competencies for the future? At different stages in their careers, managers may be categorized as being ready to do the next job now, or being ready for a specified higher-grade position in, say, two years' time, or as a high-flyer on the 'A list' who has senior management potential. Such assessments generate development plans such as leadership and development programmes, special assignments and job rotation.

As noted by Iles and Preece (2010: 256), succession planning can be seen in terms of identifying successors for key posts and then planning career moves and/or development activities for these potential successors. They suggested that:

> Processes need to be designed round purpose, population, principles, process and players, with senior management engagement and HR championing. The highest potential employees are thus offered accelerated development and career paths. Of course, the downside is that non-selected employees may feel that they are less valued and have less access to development opportunities.

They also commented that in reality few companies have such programmes and that some are critical of attempts to equate succession planning with talent management, arguing instead for a 'talent on demand' framework, 'based on managing risk (not overestimating the places to be filled) and using talent pools to span functions' (*ibid*: 256). They reported that some people are more positive about the value of 'leadership pipelines', which enable the organization to:

- focus on development;
- identify critical 'lynchpin' roles;
- create transparent succession management systems;
- regularly measure progress;
- ensure flexibility.

Succession planning is based on the information about managers in supply and demand forecasts, talent audits and performance and potential reviews. In some large organizations where demand and supply forecasts can be made accurately, there are highly formalized succession planning processes based on the sort of management succession schedule illustrated in Figure 21.2.

However, the scope for formal succession planning may be limited in today's more flexible and rapidly changing organizations where elaborate succession plans could be out of date as soon as they are made. In these circumstances, the most that can be done is to use talent management and management development processes to ensure that there are plenty of talented people around in 'talent pools' to fill vacancies as they arise on the basis of 'talent on demand', bearing in mind that the most talented or ambitious individuals may not want to wait very long.

FIGURE 21.2   Management succession schedule

MANAGEMENT SUCCESSION SCHEDULE						Department:		Director/manager:		
Existing managers							Potential successors			
Name	Position	Due for replacement	Rating		If promotable, to what position and when?		Names: 1st and 2nd choice	Positions	When	
			Performance	Potential						

Career management

Career management is complementary to management succession planning in that it aims to ensure that the organization has the flow of talent it needs. But it is also concerned with the provision of opportunities for people to develop their abilities and their careers in order to satisfy their own aspirations. It is about integrating the needs of the organization with the needs of the individual.

An important part of career management is career planning, which shapes the progression of individuals within an organization in accordance with assessments of organizational needs, defined employee success profiles and the performance, potential and preferences of individual members of the enterprise. Career management also involves career counselling to help people develop their careers to their advantage as well as that of the organization.

Aims

For the organization, the aim of career management is to meet the objectives of its talent management policies, which are to ensure that there is a talent flow that creates and maintains the required talent pool. For employees, the aims of career management

policies are, 1) to give them the guidance, support and encouragement they need to fulfil their potential and achieve a successful career with the organization in tune with their talents and ambitions; and 2) to provide those with promise a sequence of experience and learning activities that will equip them for whatever level of responsibility they have the ability to reach.

Career management calls for an approach that explicitly takes into account both organizational needs and employee interests. It calls for creativity in identifying ways to provide development opportunities. Career management policies and practices are best based on an understanding of the stages through which careers progress in organizations.

Career stages

The stages of a career within an organization can be described as a career lifecycle. Hall (1984) set this out as follows:

1 *Entry to the organization*, when the individual can begin the process of self-directed career planning.

2 *Progress within particular areas of work*, where skills and potential are developed

FIGURE 21.3 Career progression curves

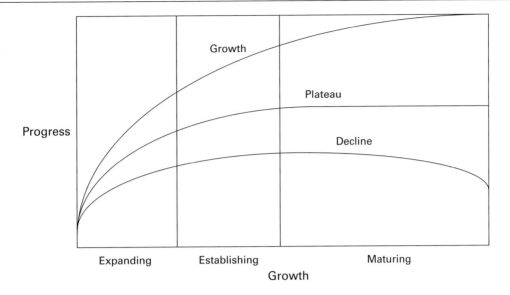

through experience, training, coaching, mentoring and performance management.

3 *Mid-career*, when some people will still have good career prospects while others may have got as far as they are going to get, or at least feel that they have. It is necessary to ensure that these 'plateaued' people do not lose interest at this stage by taking such steps as providing them with cross-functional moves, job rotation, special assignments, recognition and rewards for effective performance, etc.

4 *Later career*, when individuals may have settled down at whatever level they have reached but are beginning to be concerned about the future. They need to be treated with respect as people who are still making a contribution and given opportunities to take on new challenges wherever this is possible. They may also need reassurance about their future with the organization and what is to happen to them when they leave.

5 *End of career with the organization*, the possibility of phasing disengagement by being given the chance to work part-time for a period before they finally have to go, should be considered at this stage.

Career dynamics

Career management should be based on an understanding of career dynamics. This is concerned with how careers progress – the ways in which people move through their careers either upwards when they are promoted, or by enlarging or enriching their roles to take on greater responsibilities or make more use of their skills and abilities. The three stages of career progression – expanding, establishing and maturing – are illustrated in Figure 21.3. This also shows how individuals progress or fail to progress at different rates through these stages.

Career development strategy

A career development strategy might include the following activities:

- a policy of promoting from within wherever possible;

- career routes enabling talented people to move upwards or laterally in the organization as their development and job opportunities take them;

- personal development planning as a major part of the performance management process, to develop each individual's knowledge and skills;

- systems and processes to achieve sharing and development of knowledge (especially tacit) across the firm;
- multidisciplinary project teams, with a shifting membership, to offer developmental opportunities for as wide a range of employees as possible.

Career management activities

As described by Hirsh and Carter (2002), career management encompasses recruitment, personal development plans, lateral moves, special assignments at home or abroad, development positions, career bridges, lateral moves and support for employees who want to develop.

Baruch and Peiperl (2000) identified 17 career management practices, and their survey of 194 UK companies established a rank order for their use. The practices are listed below in order, from most frequent to least frequent use:

1 Postings regarding internal job openings.
2 Formal education as part of career development.
3 Performance appraisal as a basis for career planning.
4 Career counselling by manager.
5 Lateral moves to create cross-functional experience.

6 Career counselling by HR department.
7 Retirement preparation programmes.
8 Succession planning.
9 Formal mentoring.
10 Common career paths.
11 Dual ladder career paths (parallel hierarchy for professional staff).
12 Books and/or pamphlets on career issues.
13 Written personal career planning (as done by the organization or personally).
14 Assessment centres.
15 Peer appraisal.
16 Career workshops.
17 Upward (subordinate) appraisal.

The process of career management is illustrated in Figure 21.4.

Career management policies

The organization needs to decide on the degree to which it 'makes or buys' talented people, which means answering the questions: To what extent should it grow its own talent (a promotion from within policy)? How much should it rely on external recruitment (bringing 'fresh blood' into the organization)? The policy may be to recruit potentially high performers who will be good at their present

FIGURE 21.4   The process of career management

job and are rewarded accordingly. If they are really good, they will be promoted and the enterprise will get what it wants. Deliberately training managers for a future that will never happen is a waste of time.

In contrast, and much less frequently, employers who believe in long-term career planning develop structured approaches to career management. These include elaborate reviews of performance and potential, assessment centres to identify talent or confirm that it is there, high-flyer schemes and planned job moves in line with a predetermined programme.

There may also be policies for dealing with the 'plateaued' manager who has got so far but will get no further. Some managers in this position may be reconciled to reaching that level but continue to work effectively. Others will become bored, frustrated and unproductive, especially rising stars on the wane. The steps that can be taken to deal with this problem include:

- lateral moves into different functional areas or specialized subsidiaries, to provide new challenges and career breadth;

- temporary assignments and secondments outside the organization;

- appointments as leaders of project teams set up to deal with performance barriers inside the organization such as the slowness of responses to customer complaints.

Career planning

Career planning involves the definition of career paths – the routes people can take to advance their careers within an organization. It uses all the information provided by the organization's assessments of requirements, the assessments of performance and potential and management succession plans, and translates it into the form of individual career development programmes and general arrangements for management development, career counselling and mentoring.

It is possible to define career progression in terms of what people are required to know and be able to do to carry out work to progress up the 'career ladder' (the sequence of jobs at increasing levels of responsibility that constitutes a career). These levels can be described as 'competency bands'. For each band, the competencies needed to achieve a move to that level would be defined in order to produce a career map incorporating 'aiming points' for individuals, as illustrated in Figure 21.5. People would be made aware of the competency levels they must reach to achieve progress in their careers. This would help them to plan their own development, although support and guidance should be provided by their managers, HR specialists and, if they exist, management development advisers or mentors. The provision of additional experience and training could be arranged as appropriate, but it would be important

FIGURE 21.5   Competency band career progression system

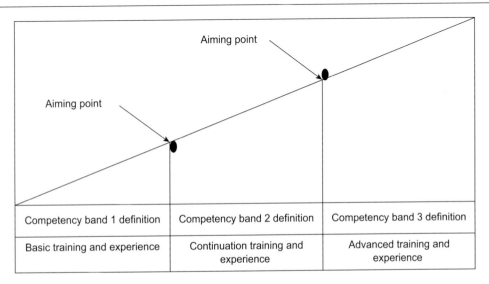

to clarify what individual employees need to do for themselves if they want to progress within the organization. At Procter & Gamble, for example, 'destination jobs' are identified for rising stars, which are attainable only if the employee continues to perform, impress and demonstrate growth potential.

Career family grade structures, as described in Chapter 29, can define levels of competency in each career family and show career paths upwards within families or between families. This is illustrated in Figure 21.6.

FIGURE 21.6   Career paths in a career family structure

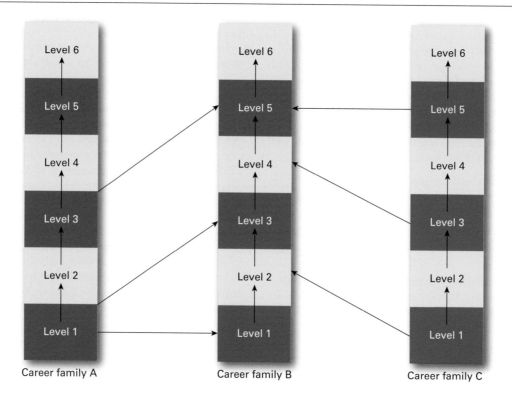

Formal career planning may be the ideal but, as noted by Hirsh *et al* (2000), there has been a shift from managed career moves to more open internal job markets. The process of internal job application has become the main way in which employees progress their careers.

Self-managed careers

The organization may need to manage careers as part of its talent management and management succession programmes and can provide support and guidance to people with potential. Ultimately, however, it is up to individuals to manage their own careers within and beyond their present organization.

Handy (1984) used the term 'portfolio career' to describe his forecast that people will increasingly change the direction of their careers during the course of their working life. Hall (1996) coined the phrase the 'protean career' in which individuals take responsibility for transforming their career path (the name comes from the Greek god Proteus, who could change his shape at will).

Schein (1978) originated the notion of 'career anchors'. He defined them as the self-concept of people, consisting of self-perceived talents and abilities, basic values and a sense of motives and needs relating to their careers. As people gain work experience, career anchors evolve and function as stabilizing forces, hence the metaphor of 'anchor'.

CASE STUDIES

BT

BT's approach to investing in its talent is primarily focused on responding to individual needs in line with a BT-wide 'Talent Deal'. This is a set of commitments made to individuals in BT's talent pool on the support they can expect in areas such as career planning and movement, opportunities for networking and meeting top executives and mentoring. It also specifies the commitments expected of BT's talent pool members, such as the contribution they make to supporting the development of other colleagues.

Cargill

The Cargill food business operates a global, corporate-level labour and talent management process. This is structured on the lines of 'food platforms' (collections of around eight business units that operate in the food businesses) and has representatives from Latin America, Europe, Asia, etc meeting twice a year. They look at the work of the businesses and consider how talent might be managed and succession planned in those businesses. A workable model exists to look at talent management and succession planning at a platform level and at a practical level. Consideration is being given to how to integrate talent management and succession planning on a global basis and a start has been made on highlighting positive and negative aspects of talent management and succession planning. These will be discussed at corporate level by the board to ensure that Cargill values are embedded in future talent management and succession planning strategy, policies and practices.

GlaxoSmithKline

GlaxoSmithKline is identifying those positions, at both the corporate and business-unit levels, that are critical to the company's success in a rapidly changing competitive environment. As part of that initiative, the company developed a statement of its workforce philosophy and management guidelines. One of these explicitly addresses 'workforce differentiation' and reads, in part: 'It is essential that we have key talent in critical positions and that the careers of these individuals are managed centrally.'

HSBC

As reported by Ready and Conger (2007: 72–3), HSBC has created a system of talent pools that track and manage the careers of employees with high potential. Employees in these pools are selected initially for new assignments within their region or line of business and, over time, are given positions that cross boundaries in order to demonstrate that they have the potential to reach a senior management role. They can then be placed in the group talent pool, which means that they have the potential to reach the senior executive level in three to five years and top management in the longer term. Leaders conduct talent relationship dialogues with members of each pool to address their development needs and concerns.

IBM

The overall aim of talent management within IBM is 'to develop the leaders of tomorrow'. Part of what makes it a global company is the importance it places on high-potential people gaining international experience. For employees, being identified as talent therefore drives many opportunities in the company.

Every leader in the company has responsibility for identifying and nurturing talent. The areas for them to look for are aptitude, potential and the ability to grow and develop. The identification of talented individuals is based on their performance against 10 leadership competencies, which are consistent globally. The leadership competencies are used as a development tool for employees at all levels in IBM, not just those already highlighted as having potential.

Readiness for promotion to executive roles is linked to competencies. For example, if an individual needs to get client relationship-building skills – then his or her next job has to include that. Readiness is categorized in terms of 'next job' or 'two jobs away' rather than a number of years.

Standard Chartered Bank

As reported by the CIPD (2010c), Standard Chartered was looking closely at its existing approach to talent management. This has involved:

- re-examining the processes, to ensure that there is greater transparency, education and understanding about the importance of robust talent identification and development;

- embedding talent processes to establish clearer links between our talent processes and other global people processes around performance management and engagement;

- encouraging more experiential-based learning centred more on on-the-job learning and learning from others;

- providing support to help our managers and leaders engage and motivate their teams;

- ensuring that talented staff continue to perform above their peer group, are highly engaged and that they are retained.

Key learning points: Talent management

The meaning of talent management

Talented people possess special gifts, abilities and aptitudes that enable them to perform effectively. Talent management is the process of identifying, developing, recruiting, retaining and deploying those talented people.

The process of talent management

Talent management starts with the business strategy and what it signifies in terms of the talented people required by the organization. Ultimately, its aim is to develop and maintain a pool of talented people. Its elements are talent planning, resourcing strategies, attraction and retention programmes, role design, talent relationship management, performance management, learning and development, management succession planning and career management.

Developing a talent management strategy

A talent management strategy consists of a view on how the processes should mesh together with an overall objective – to acquire and nurture talent wherever it is and wherever it is needed by using a number of interdependent policies and practices. Talent management is the notion of 'bundling' in action.

Management succession planning

Management succession planning is the process of assessing and auditing the talent in the organization in order to answer three fundamental questions: 1) are there enough potential successors available – a supply of people coming through who can take key roles in the longer term, 2) are they good enough, and 3) do they have the right skills and competencies for the future?

Career planning

Career planning involves the definition of career paths – the routes people can take to advance their careers within an organization. It uses all the information provided by the organization's assessments of requirements, the assessments of performance and potential and management succession plans, and translates it into the form of individual career development programmes and general arrangements for management development, career counselling and mentoring.

Questions

1 What is talent management?

2 What is talent?

3 What are the elements of a talent management programme?

4 What is management succession planning?

5 What is career management?

References

Baruch, Y and Peiperl, M (2000) Career management practices: an empirical survey and explanations, *Human Resource Management*, **39** (4), pp 347–66

Buckingham, M and Vosburgh, R (2001) The 21st century human resources function: it's the talent, stupid, *Human Resource Planning*, **24** (4), pp 17–23

CIPD (2007) *Talent: Strategy, management, measurement*, London, CIPD

CIPD (2010a) *Opening up Talent for Business Success*, London, CIPD

CIPD (2010b) *War on Talent? Talent management under threat in uncertain times, Part 1*, London, CIPD

CIPD (2010c) *Fighting Back through Talent Innovation: Talent management under threat in uncertain times, Part 2*, London, CIPD

CIPD (2011) *Learning and Talent Development Survey*, London, CIPD

Clarke, R and Winkler, V (2006) *Reflections on Talent Management*, London, CIPD

Hall, D T (1984) Human resource development and organizational effectiveness, in (eds) D Fombrun, M A Tichy and M A Devanna, *Strategic Human Resource Management*, New York, Wiley

Hall, D T (1996) *The Career is Dead: Long Live the Career*, San Francisco, CA, Jossey-Bass

Handy, C (1984) *The Future of Work*, Oxford, Blackwell

Hirsh, W and Carter, A (2002) *New Directions in Management Development*, Paper 387, London, Institute for Employment Studies

Hirsh, W, Pollard, E and Tamkin, P (2000) Management development, *IRS Employee Development Bulletin*, November, pp 8–12

Huselid, M A, Beatty, R W and Becker, B E (2005) A-players or A-positions? The strategic logic of workforce management, *Harvard Business Review*, December, pp 110–17

Iles, P and Preece, D (2010) Talent management and career development, in (eds) J Gold, R Thorpe and A Mumford, *Gower Handbook of Leadership and Management Development*, Farnham, Gower, pp 243–60

Iles, P, Preece, D and Chuai, X (2010) Talent management as a management fashion in HRD: towards a research agenda, *Human Resource Development International*, **13** (2), pp 125–45

Michaels, E G, Handfield-Jones, H and Axelrod, B (2001) *The War for Talent*, Boston, MA, Harvard Business School Press

Pfeffer, J (2001) Fighting the war for talent is hazardous to your organization's health, *Organizational Dynamics*, **29** (4), pp 248–59

Ready, D A and Conger, J A (2007) Make your company a talent factory, *Harvard Business Review*, June, pp 68–77

Schein, E H (1978) *Career Dynamics: Matching individual and organizational needs*, Reading, MA, Addison-Wesley

Thorne, K and Pellant, A (2007) *The Essential Guide to Managing Talent*, London, Kogan Page

Warren, C (2006) Curtain call, *People Management*, 23 March, pp 24–29

Younger, J, Smallwood, N and Ulrich, D (2007) Developing your organization's brand as a talent developer, *Human Resource Planning*, **30** (2), pp 21–9

PART IV

Learning and development

PART IV CONTENTS

Introduction

Learning and development strategies and practices, as described in this part, aim to ensure that people in the organization acquire and develop the knowledge, skills and competencies they need to carry out their work effectively and advance their careers to their own benefit and that of the organization. As Harrison (2009: 5) observed:

> The term human resource development retains its popularity among academics but it has never been attractive to practitioners. They tend to dislike it because they see its reference to people as a 'resource' to be demeaning. Putting people on a par with money, materials and equipment creates the impression of 'development' as an unfeeling, manipulative activity.

The term 'learning and development' (L&D) has largely replaced that of 'human resource development' (HRD), at least for practitioners, although the two terms are almost indistinguishable. They are indeed often used interchangeably by commentators and practitioners although the introduction of 'learning' has emphasized the belief that what matters for individuals is that they are given the opportunity to learn, often for themselves, with guidance and support, rather than just being on the receiving end of what the organization provides.

The following definition of strategic HRD, produced by Walton (1999: 82), could serve equally well as a definition of strategic L&D:

> Strategic human resource development involves introducing, eliminating, modifying, directing, and guiding processes in such a way that all individuals and teams are equipped with the skills, knowledge and competences they require to undertake current and future tasks required by the organization.

This part deals with L&D under the following headings:

- strategic learning and development – how L&D is aligned to the business strategy and the characteristics of L&D strategy;

- the process of learning and development – how people and organizations learn, the concept of the learning organization, the different forms of L&D activities;

- the practice of learning and development – identifying L&D needs, encouraging and supporting workplace learning, planning and implementing learning programmes and events, evaluating L&D;

- leadership and management development – the planning and implementation of processes and programmes for developing leadership qualities and for developing managers generally.

References

Harrison, R (2009) *Learning and Development*, 5th edn, London, CIPD
Walton, J (1999) *Strategic Human Resource Development*, Harlow, FT Prentice Hall

22
Strategic learning and development

LEARNING OUTCOMES

On completing this chapter you should be able to define these key concepts. You should also know about:

- The meaning of learning and development (L&D)
- The meaning and aims of strategic L&D
- The basic philosophies that underpin L&D strategy and practice
- How to create a learning culture
- The nature of strategies for promoting individual learning

Introduction

Organizations need people with high levels of knowledge, skills and abilities. It is necessary to ensure that any steps taken to satisfy this need are business-led in the sense that they are based on an understanding of the strategic imperatives of the business and support the achievement of its goals. But organizations also need to take account of the personal needs of those they employ for development and growth. This is a good in itself but it means that the organization will be a more fulfilling and therefore attractive place in which to work.

This chapter starts with a definition of the process of learning and development and its elements, which leads to a definition of strategic learning and development (L&D) and its aims. Consideration is then given to the philosophy of L&D before examining strategies for creating a learning culture and for promoting organizational and individual learning.

Learning and development defined

Learning and development is defined as the process of ensuring that the organization has the knowledgeable, skilled and engaged workforce it needs. It involves facilitating the acquisition by individuals and teams of knowledge and skills through experience, learning events and programmes provided by the organization, guidance and coaching provided by line managers and others, and self-directed learning activities carried out by individuals. Harrison (2009: 8) defined learning and development more broadly as follows:

> The primary purpose of learning and development as an organizational process is to aid collective progress through the collaborative, expert and ethical stimulation and facilitation of learning and knowledge that support business goals, develop individual potential, and respect and build on diversity.

The constituents of L&D are:

- *Learning* – the process by which a person acquires and develops knowledge, skills, capabilities, behaviours and attitudes. It involves the modification of behaviour through experience as well as more formal methods of helping people to learn within or outside the workplace.

- *Development* – the growth or realization of a person's ability and potential through the provision of learning and educational experiences.

- *Training* – the systematic application of formal processes to impart knowledge and help people to acquire the skills necessary for them to perform their jobs satisfactorily.

- *Education* – the development of the knowledge, values and understanding required in all aspects of life rather than the knowledge and skills relating to particular areas of activity.

Learning should be distinguished from training. 'Learning is the process by which a person constructs new knowledge, skills and capabilities, whereas training is one of several responses an organization can undertake to promote learning' (Reynolds *et al*, 2002: 9). Learning is what individuals do; training is what organizations do to individuals. The components of learning and development are shown in Figure 22.1.

Strategic L&D defined

Strategic L&D is an approach to helping people to learn and develop that is concerned with how the organization's goals will be achieved through its human resources by means of integrated L&D strategies, policies and practices. Like strategic HRM, it is based on the fundamental proposition that the human resources of an organization play a strategic role in its success. Strategic L&D policies are closely associated with that aspect of strategic HRM concerned with investing in people and developing the organization's human capital.

Aims of strategic L&D

Strategic L&D aims to produce a coherent and comprehensive framework for developing people through

FIGURE 22.1   Components of learning and development

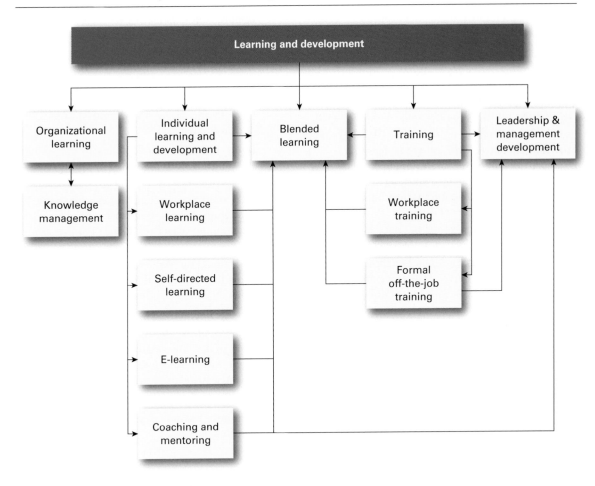

the creation of a learning culture and the formulation of organizational and individual learning strategies. It exists to enhance resource capability in accordance with the belief that a firm's human resources are a major source of competitive advantage. It is therefore about developing the intellectual capital required by the organization as well as ensuring that people of the right quality are available to meet present and future needs.

The main thrust of strategic L&D is to provide an environment in which people are encouraged to learn and develop. Although it is business-led, its strategies have to take into account the needs of individual employees. The importance of increasing employability outside as well as within the organization is also a concern.

Learning and development philosophy

The philosophy underpinning strategic L&D is as follows:

- Learning and development activities make a major contribution to the successful attainment of the organization's objectives and investment in it benefits all the stakeholders of the organization.

- Learning and development plans and programmes should be integrated with and support the achievement of business and human resource strategies.

- Learning and development should be performance-related – designed to achieve specified improvements in corporate, functional, team and individual performance and make a major contribution to bottom-line results.

- Everyone in the organization should be encouraged and given the opportunity to learn – to develop their skills and knowledge to the maximum of their capacity.

- The framework for individual learning is provided by personal development plans that focus on self-managed learning and are supported by coaching, mentoring and formal training.

- The organization needs to invest in learning and development by providing appropriate learning opportunities and facilities, but the prime responsibility for learning and development rests with individuals, who will be given the guidance and support of their managers and, as necessary, members of the HR department.

The business case for L&D

The business case for learning and development should demonstrate how L&D programmes will meet business needs. Kearns and Miller (1997) go as far as to claim that if a business objective cannot be cited as a basis for designing training and development, then no training and development should be offered.

A cost/benefit analysis is required comparing the benefits expressed in quantified terms as far as possible that will result from the learning activity. The business case has to convince management that there will be an acceptable return on the investment (RoI) in learning and training programmes and events. It can be difficult to produce realistic figures, although the attempt is worth making with the help of finance specialists. The case for investing in L&D can refer to all or any of the following potential benefits:

- Improve individual, team and corporate performance in terms of output, quality, speed and overall productivity.

- Attract high-quality employees by offering them learning and development opportunities, increasing their levels of competence and enhancing their skills, thus enabling them to obtain more job satisfaction, to gain higher rewards and to progress within the organization.

- Provide additional non-financial rewards (growth and career opportunities) as part of a total reward policy.

- Improve operational flexibility by extending the range of skills possessed by employees (multi-skilling).

- Increase the commitment of employees by encouraging them to identify with the mission and objectives of the organization.

- Help to manage change by increasing understanding of the reasons for change and providing people with the knowledge and skills they need to adjust to new situations.

- Provide line managers with the skills required to manage and develop their people.

- Help to develop a positive culture in the organization, one, for example, that is oriented towards performance improvement.

- Provide higher levels of service to customers.

- Minimize learning costs (reduce the length of learning curves).

Learning and development strategies

Learning and development strategies are the active components of an overall approach to strategic L&D. They express the organization's intentions on how L&D activities will take place and provide guidance on how these activities should be planned and implemented. L&D strategies should be business-led in the sense that they are designed to support the achievement of business goals by promoting human capital advantage, but they should also be people-led, which means taking into account the needs and aspirations of people to grow and develop. Achieving the latter aim, of course, supports the achievement of the former. The strategies ensure that an L&D philosophy as set out above is acted upon. They are concerned with developing a learning culture, promoting organizational learning and providing for individual learning.

Strategies for creating a learning culture

A learning culture is one in which learning is recognized by top management, line managers and employees generally as an essential organizational process to which they are committed and in which they engage continuously. The characteristics of a learning culture are self-managed learning not instruction, long-term capacity-building not short-term fixes, and empowerment not supervision.

Reynolds (2004: 9) described a learning culture as a 'growth medium', in which 'employees will commit to a range of positive discretionary behaviours, including learning'. He suggested that to create a learning culture it is necessary to develop organizational practices that 'give employees a sense of purpose in the workplace, grant employees opportunities to act upon their commitment, and offer practical support to learning'.

The steps required to create a learning culture as proposed by Reynolds (2004) are:

1 Develop and share the vision – belief in a desired and emerging future.

2 Empower employees – provide 'supported autonomy'; freedom for employees to manage their work within certain boundaries (policies and expected behaviours) but with support available as required. Adopt a facilitative style of management in which responsibility for decision making is ceded as far as possible to employees.

3 Provide employees with a supportive learning environment where learning capabilities can be discovered and applied, eg peer networks, supportive policies and systems, and protected time for learning.

4 Use coaching techniques to draw out the talents of others by encouraging employees to identify options and seek their own solutions to problems.

5 Guide employees through their work challenges and provide them with time, resources and, crucially, feedback.

6 Recognize the importance of managers acting as role models.

7 Encourage networks – communities of practice.

8 Align systems to vision – get rid of bureaucratic systems that produce problems rather than facilitate work.

Organizational learning strategies

Organizational learning strategies aim to improve organizational effectiveness through the development and acquisition of knowledge, understanding, insights, techniques and practices. This is in accordance with one of the basic principles of HRM, namely that it is necessary to invest in people in order to develop the human capital required by the organization and to increase its stock of knowledge and skills. As stated by Ehrenberg and Smith (1994: 279–80), human capital theory indicates that: 'The knowledge and skills a worker has – which comes from education and training, including the training that experience brings – generate productive capital.'

Individual learning strategies

Individual learning comprises the processes and programmes used to ensure that individual employees acquire and develop the new knowledge, skills, capabilities, behaviours and attitudes required to perform their roles effectively and to develop their potential. The individual learning strategies of an organization are driven by its human resource requirements, the latter being expressed in terms of the sort of skills and behaviours that will be required to achieve business goals. The strategies should cover:

● how learning needs will be identified;

● the role of self-managed learning;

● the facilitation of workplace learning;

● the support that should be provided for individual learning in the form of guidance, coaching, mentoring, learning resource centres and internal or external training programmes and courses.

Key learning points: Strategic learning and development

Learning and development

Learning and development is the process of acquiring and developing knowledge, skills capabilities, behaviours and attitudes through learning or developmental experiences.

Strategic L&D

Strategic L&D is an approach to helping people to learn and develop that is concerned with how the organization's goals will be achieved through its human resources by means of integrated L&D strategies, policies and practices. Strategic L&D aims to produce a coherent and comprehensive framework for developing people through the creation of a learning culture and the formulation of organizational and individual learning strategies.

Learning and development strategies

Learning and development strategies are the active components of an overall approach to strategic L&D. They express the organization's intentions on how L&D activities will take place in the organization and provide guidance on how these activities should be planned and implemented.

Learning culture

A learning culture is one in which learning is recognized by top management, line managers and employees generally as an essential organizational process to which they are committed and in which they engage continuously.

Organizational learning strategies

Organizational learning strategies aim to develop a firm's resource-based capability.

Individual learning strategies

The individual learning strategies of an organization are driven by its human resource requirements, the latter being expressed in terms of the sort of skills and behaviours that will be required to achieve business goals.

Questions

1 What is learning and development (L&D)?
2 What is learning?
3 What is training?
4 What is development?
5 What is education?

6 What is strategic L&D?
7 What are the aims of strategic L&D?
8 What is a learning culture?
9 What is organizational learning strategy?
10 What is individual learning strategy?

References

Ehrenberg, R G and Smith, R S (1994) *Modern Labor Economics*, New York, Harper Collins
Harrison, R (2009) *Learning and Development*, 5th edn, London, CIPD
Kearns, P and Miller, T (1997) Measuring the impact of training and development on the bottom line, *FT Management Briefings*, London, Pitman

Reynolds, J (2004) *Helping People Learn*, London, CIPD
Reynolds, J, Caley, L and Mason, R (2002) *How Do People Learn?*, London, CIPD

23

The process of learning and development

KEY CONCEPTS AND TERMS

Cognitive learning theory

Double-loop learning

Experiential learning

Operant conditioning

Progressive parts method of training

Self-directed (self-managed) learning

Social learning theory

Discretionary learning

Experienced workers standard (EWS)

Learning organization

Organizational learning

Reinforcement theory

Single-loop learning

LEARNING OUTCOMES

On completing this chapter you should be able to define these key concepts. You should also know about:

- How people learn
- Learning theory
- The motivation to learn
- Learning styles
- Learning to learn
- The learning curve
- The implications of learning theory and concepts
- Organizational learning
- The learning organization
- Self-directed learning

Introduction

The practice of learning and development should be based on an understanding of the processes involved in learning and development as described in this chapter. These processes are complex and varied. They consist of the ways in which individuals and organizations learn, as explained by learning theory, the concept of organizational learning, the dubious idea of the learning organization, and the contribution made by individuals to their own learning and development (self-directed or self-managed learning).

How people learn

Individuals learn for themselves and learn from other people. They learn as members of teams and by interaction with their managers, co-workers and people outside the organization (social learning). People learn by doing (experiential learning) and by instruction. The ways in which individuals learn will differ and the extent to which they learn will depend largely on how well they are motivated or self-motivated. Discretionary learning can take place when individuals of their own volition actively seek to acquire the knowledge and skills they need to carry out their work effectively. It should be encouraged and supported.

How people learn is explained by learning theory, as described below. It depends on how well they are motivated to learn, their learning styles, the extent to which they are capable of 'learning to learn' and the phenomenon of the learning curve.

Learning theory

The key learning theories are:

- *Reinforcement theory* – based on the work of Skinner (1974) this expresses the belief that changes in behaviour take place as a result of an individual's response to events or stimuli and the ensuing consequences (rewards or punishments). Individuals can be 'conditioned' to repeat the behaviour by positive reinforcement in the form of feedback and knowledge of results. This is known as 'operant conditioning'.

- *Cognitive learning theory* – learning involves gaining knowledge and understanding by absorbing information in the form of principles, concepts and facts and then internalizing it. Learners can be regarded as powerful information-processing machines.

- *Experiential learning theory* – experiential learning takes place when people learn from their experience by absorbing and reflecting on it so that it can be understood and applied. Thus people become active agents of their own learning.

- *Social learning theory* – this states that effective learning requires social interaction. Wenger (1998) suggested that we all participate in 'communities of practice' (groups of people with shared expertise who work together) and that these are our primary sources of learning. Bandura (1977) viewed learning as a series of information-processing steps set in train by social interactions.

The motivation to learn

People will learn more effectively if they are motivated to learn. As Reynolds *et al* (2002: 34) commented: 'The disposition and commitment of the learner – their motivation to learn – is one of the most critical factors affecting training effectiveness. Under the right conditions, a strong disposition to learn, enhanced by solid experience and a positive attitude, can lead to exceptional performance.'

Two motivation theories are particularly relevant to learning. *Expectancy theory* states that goal-directed behaviour is driven by the expectation of achieving something the individual regards as desirable. If individuals feel that the outcome of learning is likely to benefit them they will be more inclined to pursue it. When they find that their expectations have been fulfilled, their belief that learning is worthwhile will be reinforced.

Goal theory states that motivation is higher when individuals aim to achieve specific goals, when these goals are accepted and, although difficult, are achievable, and when there is feedback on performance. Learning goals may be set for individuals (but to be effective as motivators they must be agreed) or individuals may set their own goals (self-directed learning).

Learning styles

Learning theories describe in general terms how people learn, but individual learners will have different styles – a preference for a particular approach to learning. The two most familiar classifications of learning styles are those produced by Kolb *et al* and by Honey and Mumford.

Kolb *et al*'s learning style inventory

Kolb *et al* (1974) identified a learning cycle consisting of four stages, as shown in Figure 23.1.

FIGURE 23.1   The Kolb learning cycle

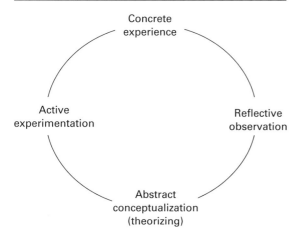

These stages were defined as follows:

1 *Concrete experience* – this can be planned or accidental.

2 *Reflective observation* – this involves actively thinking about the experience and its significance.

3 *Abstract conceptualization (theorizing)* – generalizing from experience to develop various concepts and ideas that can be applied when similar situations are encountered.

4 *Active experimentation* – testing the concepts or ideas in new situations. This gives rise to a new concrete experience and the cycle begins again.

The key to this model is that it is a simple description of how experience is translated into concepts that are then used to guide the choice of new experiences. To learn effectively, individuals must shift from being observers to participants, from direct involvement to a more objective analytical detachment. Every person has his or her own learning style and one of the most important arts that trainers have to develop is to adjust their approaches to the learning styles of trainees. Trainers must acknowledge these learning styles rather than their own preferred approach.

The Honey and Mumford learning styles

Another analysis of learning styles was made by Honey and Mumford (1996). They identified the following four styles:

1 *Activists*, who involve themselves fully without bias in new experiences and revel in new challenges.

2 *Reflectors*, who stand back and observe new experiences from different angles. They collect data, reflect on it and then come to a conclusion.

3 *Theorists*, who adapt and apply their observations in the form of logical theories. They tend to be perfectionists.

4 *Pragmatists*, who are keen to try out new ideas, approaches and concepts to see if they work.

However, none of these four learning styles is exclusive. It is quite possible that one person could be both a reflector and a theorist and someone else could be an activist/pragmatist, a reflector/pragmatist or even a theorist/pragmatist.

Use of learning style theory

Learning style theory can be used in the design and conduct of learning events or personal development programmes. Learning situations can be set up to fit the learning style of participants. The problem is that people do not necessarily have a single learning style and there will certainly be a large range of styles in any learning group. It may therefore be difficult to fit the approach to the style.

Learning to learn

People learn all the time and through doing so acquire knowledge, skills and insight. But they will learn more effectively if they 'learn how to learn'. As defined by Honey (1998), the process of learning to learn is the acquisition of knowledge, skills and insights about the learning process itself. The aims are to:

- provide a basis for organizing and planning learning;
- pinpoint precisely what has been learnt and what to do better or differently as a consequence;
- share what has been learnt with other people so that they benefit;
- check on the quality of what has been learnt;
- transfer what has been learnt and apply it in different circumstances;
- improve the learning process itself so that how people learn, not just what people learn, is given constant attention.

The learning curve

The concept of the learning curve refers to the time it takes an inexperienced person to reach the required level of performance in a job or a task, which is sometimes called the experienced worker's standard (EWS). The existence of the learning curve needs to be taken into account when planning and implementing training or instruction programmes. The standard learning curve is illustrated in Figure 23.2.

But rates of learning vary, depending on the effectiveness of the training, the experience and natural aptitude of the learner and the latter's interest in learning. Both the time taken to reach the EWS and the variable speed with which learning takes place at different times affect the shape of the curve, as shown in Figure 23.3.

Learning is often stepped, with one or more plateaus while further progress is halted. This may be because learners cannot continually increase their skills or speeds of work and need a pause to consolidate what they have already learnt. The existence of steps such as those shown in Figure 23.4 can be used when planning skills training to provide deliberate reinforcement periods when newly acquired skills are practised in order to achieve the expected standards.

When a training module is being prepared that describes what has to be learnt and the training needed to achieve the required levels of skill and speed, it is often desirable to proceed step-by-step, taking one task or part of a task at a time, reinforcing it and then progressively adding other parts, consoli-

FIGURE 23.2   A standard learning curve

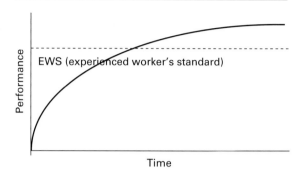

FIGURE 23.3   Different rates of learning

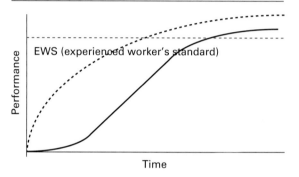

FIGURE 23.4   A stepped learning curve

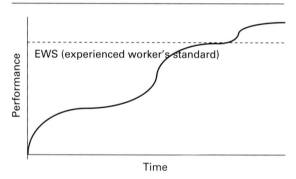

dating at each stage. This is called the 'progressive parts method' of training.

The implications of learning theory and concepts

The practical implications of the learning theories described above are summarized in Table 23.1.

TABLE 23.1   The practical implications of learning theory and concepts

Theory/concept	Content	Practical implications
The process of learning	• Learning is complex and is achieved in many different ways. • The context is important.	• Different learning needs require different learning methods, often in combination. • Learning effectiveness depends on the extent to which the organization believes in learning and supports it.
Reinforcement theory	Behaviours can be strengthened by reinforcing them with positive feedback (conditioning).	Reinforcement theory underpins training programmes concerned with developing skills through instruction. In these, the learner is conditioned to make a response and receives immediate feedback and progress is made in incremental steps, each directed to a positive outcome.
Cognitive learning theory	Learners acquire understanding which they internalize by being exposed to learning materials and by solving problems.	The knowledge and understanding of learners can be enriched and internalized by presenting them with learning materials (eg e-learning). Case studies, projects and problem-solving activities can also be used for this purpose. Self-directed learning, personal development planning activities and discovery learning processes with help from facilitators, coaches or mentors are underpinned by cognitive learning theory.
Experiential learning theory	People learn by constructing meaning and developing their skills through experience.	Learning through experience can be enhanced by encouraging learners to reflect on and make better use of what they learn through their own work and from other people. Self-directed learning and personal development planning activities with help from facilitators, coaches or mentors are also underpinned by experiential learning theory, as is action learning.
Social learning theory	Learning is most effective in a social setting. Individual understanding is shaped by active participation in real situations.	Learning can be encouraged in communities of practice and in project teams and networks.

TABLE 23.1   *Continued*

Theory/ concept	Content	Practical implications
Learning styles	Every person has their own learning style.	Learning programmes need to be adjusted to cope with different learning styles. Trainers have also to flex their methods. People will learn more effectively if they are helped to 'learn how to learn' by making the best use of their own style but also by experimenting with other styles.
The motivation to learn	People need to be motivated to learn effectively.	Learners should be helped to develop learning goals and to understand the benefits to them of achieving them. Performance management processes leading to personal development plans can provide a means of doing this.
The learning curve	The time required to reach an acceptable standard of skill or competence, which varies between people. Learning may proceed in steps with plateaus rather than being a continuous process.	Recognize that progress may vary and may not be continuous. Enable learners to consolidate their learning and introduce reinforcement periods in training programmes to recognize the existence of learning steps and plateaus.

Organizational learning

Organizational learning theory is concerned with how learning takes place in organizations. It focuses on collective learning but takes into account the proposition made by Argyris (1992) that organizations do not perform the actions that produce the learning; it is individual members of the organization who behave in ways that lead to it, although organizations can create conditions that facilitate such learning. The concept of organizational learning recognizes that the way in which this takes place is affected by the context of the organization and its culture.

Organizational learning defined

Organizational learning is about the development and acquisition in organizations of knowledge, understanding, insights, techniques and practices in order to improve organizational effectiveness. It is concerned with the methods adopted by organizations to promote learning; it is not simply the sum of all the learning and development activities that are carried out in an organization.

The process of organizational learning

Organizational learning can be characterized as an intricate three-stage process consisting of knowledge acquisition, dissemination and shared implementation. As such it is closely related to knowledge management. Knowledge may be acquired from direct experience, the experience of others or organizational memory.

Argyris (1992) suggested that organizational learning occurs under two conditions: first, when an organization achieves what is intended and, secondly, when a mismatch between intentions and outcomes is identified and corrected. He distinguished between single-loop and double-loop learning. These two types of learning have been described as adaptive or generative learning.

Single-loop or adaptive learning is incremental learning that does no more than correct deviations from the norm by making small changes and improvements without challenging assumptions, beliefs or decisions. Organizations where single-loop learning is the norm define what Argyris calls the 'governing variables', ie what they expect to achieve in terms of targets and standards and then monitor and review achievements, and take corrective action as necessary, thus completing the loop.

Double-loop or generative learning involves challenging assumptions, beliefs, norms and decisions rather than accepting them. On this basis, learning takes place through the examination of the root causes of problems so that a new learning loop is established that goes far deeper than the traditional learning loop provided by single-loop or instrumental learning. It occurs when the monitoring process initiates action to redefine the governing variables to meet the new situation, which may be imposed by the external environment. The organization has learnt something new about what has to be achieved in the light of changed circumstances and can then decide how this should be done. This learning is converted into action. The process is illustrated in Figure 23.5.

FIGURE 23.5
Single- and double-loop learning

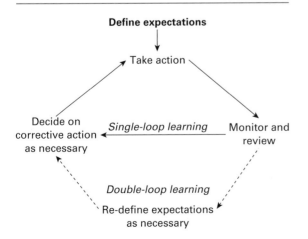

As Easterby-Smith and Araujo (1999) commented, single-loop learning could be linked to incremental change. In contrast, double-loop learning is associated with radical change, which may involve a major change in strategic direction. It is generally assumed that double-loop learning is superior, but there are situations when single-loop learning may be more appropriate.

The notion of the learning organization

A learning organization was described by Senge (1990: 3), who originated the idea, as one 'where people continually expand their capacity to create the results they truly desire, where new and expansive patterns of thinking are nurtured, where collective aspiration is set free, and where people are continually learning how to learn together'. Further definitions of a learning organization were provided by Wick and Leon (1995: 299), who stated that it was one that 'continually improves by rapidly creating and refining the capabilities required for future success', and by Pedler *et al* (1997: 3), who referred to it as an organization that 'facilitates the learning of all its members and continually transforms itself'. Garvin (1993) suggested that learning organizations are good at doing five things:

1 *Systematic problem solving* – which rests heavily on the philosophy and methods of the quality movement. Its underlying ideas include relying on scientific method rather than guesswork, for diagnosing problems – what Deming (1986) called the 'plan-do-check-act' cycle and others refer to as 'hypothesis-generating, hypothesis-testing' techniques. Data rather than assumptions are required as the background to decision making – what quality practitioners call 'fact-based management', and simple statistical tools such as histograms, Pareto charts and cause-and-effect diagrams are used to organize data and draw inferences.

2 *Experimentation* – this activity involves the systematic search for and testing of new knowledge. Continuous improvement programmes – 'kaizen' – are an important feature in a learning organization.

3 *Learning from past experience* – learning organizations review their successes and failures, assess them systematically and record the lessons learnt in a way that employees find open and accessible. This process has been called the 'Santayana principle', quoting the philosopher George Santayana who coined the phrase: 'Those who cannot remember the past are condemned to repeat it.'

4 *Learning from others* – sometimes the most powerful insights come from looking outside one's immediate environment to gain a new perspective. This process has been called SIS, for 'steal ideas shamelessly'. Another more acceptable word for it is 'benchmarking' – a disciplined process of identifying best practice organizations and analysing the extent to which what they are doing can be transferred, with suitable modifications, to one's own environment.

5 *Transferring knowledge quickly and efficiently throughout the organization* – by seconding people with new expertise, or by education and training programmes, as long as the latter are linked explicitly with implementation.

Critical evaluation of the learning organization notion

The notion of the learning organization is persuasive because it provides a rationale for comprehensive learning and development programmes. However, Scarborough *et al* (1999) argued that the learning organization concept is over-concerned with organization systems and design. Little attention seems to be paid to what individuals want to learn or how they learn. The idea that individuals should be enabled to invest in their own development seems to have escaped learning organization theorists, who are more inclined to focus on the imposition of learning by the organization, rather than creating a climate conducive to learning.

Viewing organizations as learning systems is a limited notion. Argyris and Schon (1996) explained that organizations are products of visions, ideas, norms and beliefs so that their shape is much more fragile than the organization's material structure. People act as learning agents for the organization in ways that cannot easily be systematized. They are not only individual learners but also have the capacity to learn collaboratively. This is described by organization learning theory and leads to the belief that it is the culture and environment that are important, not the systems approach implied by the concept of the learning organization.

The notion of a learning organization is rather nebulous. It incorporates miscellaneous ideas about human resource development, systematic training, action learning, organizational development and knowledge management, with an infusion of the precepts of total quality management. But they do not add up to a convincing whole. Easterby-Smith (1997) contended that attempts to create a single best-practice framework for understanding the learning organization are fundamentally flawed. There are other problems with the concept: it is idealistic, knowledge management models are beginning to supersede it, few organizations can meet the criteria, and there is little evidence of successful learning organizations.

Burgoyne (1999), one of the earlier exponents of the learning organization, has admitted that there has been some confusion about it and that there have been substantial naiveties in most of the early thinking. He believes that the concept should be integrated with knowledge management initiatives so that different forms of knowledge can be linked, fed by organizational learning and used in adding value.

The learning organization and organizational learning

The notion of the learning organization is often associated with the concept of organizational learning. But they are different. Easterby-Smith and Araujo (1999) explained that the literature on organizational learning focuses on the observation and analysis of the processes of individual and collective learning in organizations, whereas the learning organization literature is concerned with using specific diagnostic and evaluative tools that can help to identify, promote and evaluate the quality of the learning processes inside organizations. In other words, organizational learning is about *how* people learn in organizations, and the learning organization notion attempts to explain *what* organizations should do to facilitate the learning of their members.

However, as explained above, learning organization theory provides a dubious base for action. The idea of a learning culture supported by the understanding of how organizations learn provided by organizational learning theory and knowledge management initiatives, has more to offer.

Self-directed learning

Self-directed or self-managed learning involves encouraging individuals to take responsibility for their own learning needs, either to improve performance in their present job or to develop their potential and satisfy their career aspirations. It can also be described as 'self-reflective learning' (Mezirow, 1985), which is the kind of learning that involves encouraging individuals to develop new patterns of understanding, thinking and behaving.

Key learning points: The process of learning and development

The processes of L&D

The processes of learning and development are complex and varied. They consist of the ways in which individuals and organizations learn as explained by learning theory, the concept of organizational learning, the dubious notion of the learning organization, and the contribution made by individuals to their own learning and development (self-directed or self-managed learning).

How people learn

Individuals learn for themselves and from other people. They learn as members of teams and by interaction with their managers, co-workers and people outside the organization (social learning). People learn by doing and by instruction. The ways in which individuals learn will differ and the extent to which they learn will depend largely on how well they are motivated or self-motivated:

- The key learning theories are reinforcement theory, cognitive learning theory, experiential learning theory and social learning theory.

- People will learn more effectively if they are motivated to learn.

- Learning theories describe in general terms how people learn but individual learners will have different styles – a preference for a particular approach to learning. The two most familiar classifications of learning styles are those produced by Kolb and by Honey and Mumford.

- People learn all the time and through doing so acquire knowledge, skills and insight. But they will learn more effectively if they 'learn how to learn'.

- The concept of the learning curve refers to the time it takes an inexperienced person to reach the required level of performance in a job or a task.

Organizational learning

Organizational learning is about the development and acquisition in organizations of knowledge, understanding, insights, techniques and practices in order to improve organizational effectiveness. It is concerned with the processes adopted by organizations in promoting learning; it is not simply the sum of all the learning and development activities that are carried out in an organization.

The learning organization

Defined by Pedler *et al* (1997) as an organization that 'facilitates the learning of all its members and continually transforms itself'. Learning organization theory provides a dubious base for action. The idea of a learning culture, supported by the understanding of how organizations learn provided by organizational learning theory and knowledge management initiatives, has more to offer.

Self-directed learning

Self-directed or self-managed learning involves encouraging individuals to take responsibility for their own learning needs, either to improve performance in their present job or to develop their potential and satisfy their career aspirations.

Questions

1 How do people learn?

2 What are the key learning theories?

3 How are people motivated to learn?

4 What is the learning curve and what is its significance?

5 What is organizational learning?

6 What is the notion of a learning organization and how valid is it?

7 Is there any difference between the concepts of organizational learning and the learning organization? If so, what is it?

8 What is self-directed learning?

References

Argyris, C (1992) *On Organizational Learning*, Cambridge, MA, Blackwell

Argyris, C and Schon, D A (1996) *Organizational Learning: A theory of action perspective*, Reading, MA, Addison Wesley

Bandura, A (1977) *Social Learning Theory*, Englewood Cliffs, NJ, Prentice Hall

Burgoyne, J (1999) Design of the times, *People Management*, 3 June, pp 39–44

Deming, W E (1986) *Out of the Crisis*, Cambridge, MA, Massachusetts Institute of Technology Center for Advanced Engineering Studies

Easterby-Smith, M (1997) Disciplines of organizational learning: contributions and critiques, *Human Relations*, 50 (9), pp 1085–113

Easterby-Smith, M and Araujo, J (1999) Organizational learning: current debates and opportunities, in (eds) M Easterby-Smith, J Burgoyne and L Araujo, *Organizational Learning and the Learning Organization*, London, Sage

Garvin, D A (1993) Building a learning organization, *Harvard Business Review*, July–August, pp 78–91

Honey, P (1998) The debate starts here, *People Management*, 1 October, pp 28–9

Honey, P and Mumford, A (1996) *The Manual of Learning Styles*, 3rd edn, Maidenhead, Honey Publications

Kolb, D A, Rubin, I M and McIntyre, J M (1974) *Organizational Psychology: An experimental approach*, Englewood Cliffs, NJ, Prentice Hall

Mezirow, J A (1985) A critical theory of self-directed learning, in (ed) S Brookfield, *Self-directed Learning: From theory to practice*, San Francisco, CA, Jossey-Bass

Pedler, M, Burgoyne, J and Boydell, T (1997) *The Learning Company: A strategy for sustainable development*, 2nd edn, Maidenhead, McGraw-Hill

Reynolds, J, Caley, L and Mason, R (2002) *How Do People Learn?*, London, CIPD

Scarborough, H, Swan, J and Preston, J (1999) *Knowledge Management: A literature review*, London, IPM

Senge, P (1990) *The Fifth Discipline: The art and practice of the learning organization*, London, Doubleday

Skinner, B F (1974) *About Behaviourism*, London, Cape

Wenger, E (1998) *Communities of Practice: Learning, meaning and identity*, Cambridge, Cambridge University Press

Wick, C W and Leon, L S (1995) Creating a learning organization: from ideas to action, *Human Resource Management*, 34 (2), pp 299–311

25
Leadership and management development

KEY CONCEPTS AND TERMS

Action learning

Leadership

Leadership development

Management development

Outdoor learning

Development centre

Leadership and management development

Management

Management succession planning

LEARNING OUTCOMES

On completing this chapter you should be able to define these key concepts. You should also know about:

- The nature of leadership and management development
- The nature of leadership and management
- Leadership and management development compared
- Leadership development
- Management development
- Formal approaches to management development
- Informal approaches to management development
- The role of the organization
- The role of the individual
- The role of HR and L&D specialists
- The criteria for leadership and management development

Introduction

This chapter is about what organizations can do to develop effective leaders and managers, bearing in mind the point made by Drucker (1955: 158) that: 'The prosperity if not the survival of any business depends on the performance of its managers of tomorrow.'

The chapter starts with a definition of leadership and management development. This leads to a discussion of the nature of leadership and management as a basis for an analysis of what leadership and management development programmes might cover and an examination of the extent, if at all, to which leadership development and management development programmes are different. The conclusion is reached that while they are closely associated, and indeed may be conducted jointly, they are sufficiently different to justify being examined separately, which is undertaken in the next two sections of the chapter.

Leadership and management development defined

Leadership and management development programmes provide for managers to have the leadership and managerial qualities required to achieve success. They form a vital ingredient in talent management, in association with the career planning and career management activities described in Chapter 21. A blended learning approach is used, which combines a number of learning activities such as planned experience, self-directed learning, coaching, mentoring, action learning, outdoor learning and formal education and training in programmes based on an analysis of learning needs.

The nature of leadership and management

There has been much debate on how leadership differs from management. The problem is that leadership involves management and management involves leadership so that it may be difficult to separate the two. There is some consensus on the essential nature of both and the skills involved, as set out below, but there is more disagreement on which is the most important.

Leadership

Leadership means inspiring people to do their best to achieve a desired result. It involves developing and communicating a vision for the future, motivating people and securing their engagement. As defined by Dixon (1994: 214): 'Leadership is no more than exercising such an influence upon others that they tend to act in concert towards achieving a goal which they might not have achieved so readily had they been left to their own devices.' Leadership skills include the ability to:

- inspire others;
- persuade others willingly to behave differently;
- clarify what needs to be done and why;
- communicate a sense of purpose to their team;
- understand, as established by research conducted by Tamkin *et al* (2010), that they cannot create performance themselves but are conduits for performance through their influence on others;
- get their team into action so that the task is achieved.

Management

The word 'management' is derived from the Italian verb *maneggiare*, which means 'to handle a horse'. This definition at least states that to manage is to have charge of or responsibility for something, but there is clearly more to it than that. Management has often been defined as 'getting things done through people' thus emphasizing its leadership component. But managers are also responsible for guiding and controlling the business or their part of it by managing their other resources – finance, work systems and technology. Management could therefore be defined as deciding what to do and then getting it done through the effective use of resources.

Research by Tamkin *et al* (2003) established that the abilities managers need are to:

- empower and develop people – understand and practise the process of delivering through the capability of others;

- manage people and performance – managers increasingly need to maintain morale while also maximizing performance;

- work across boundaries, engaging with others, working as a member of a team, thinking differently about problems and their solutions;

- develop relationships and a focus on the customer, building partnerships with both internal and external customers;

- balance technical and generic skills – the technical aspects of management and the management of human relationships.

This list emphasizes the leadership component of management. However, managers are primarily there to get results by ensuring that their function, unit or department operates effectively. They manage people and their other resources, which include time and themselves. They are accountable for attaining goals, having been given authority over those working in their unit or department.

The traditional model of what managers do is that it is a logical and systematic process of planning, organizing, motivating and controlling. But this is misleading. Managers often carry out their work on a day-to-day basis in conditions of variety, turbulence and unpredictability. Managers may have to be specialists in ambiguity, with the ability to cope with conflicting and unclear requirements.

Managers are doers. They deal with events as they occur. But they must also be concerned with where they are going. This requires strategic thinking, especially at higher levels. As strategic thinkers, managers develop a sense of purpose and frameworks for defining intentions and future directions. They are engaged in the process of strategic management.

What are the differences?

Are leadership and management the same or different? Some commentators regard leadership as synonymous with management; others see them as distinct but closely linked and equally necessary activities; others consider management a subset of leadership; and yet others praise leadership and demonize management. Bennis (1989) viewed managers as those who promote efficiency, follow the rules and accept the status quo, while leaders focus on challenging the rules and promoting effectiveness. Kotter (1991) saw managers as being the ones who plan, budget, organize and control, while leaders set direction, manage change and motivate people. Hersey and Blanchard (1998) claimed that management merely consists of leadership applied to business situations; or in other words, management forms a sub-set of the broader process of leadership.

But as Birkinshaw (2010: 23) commented: 'By dichotomizing the work of executives in this way, Kotter, Bennis and others squeezed out the essence of what managers do and basically left them with the boring work that "leaders" don't want.' His view on the leadership-versus-management debate was that: 'Leadership is a process of social influence, concerned with the traits, styles and behaviours of individuals that cause others to follow them. Management is the act of getting people together to accomplish desired goals. To put it simply, we all need to be both leaders and managers' (*ibid*: 23). Burgoyne (2010: 42) observed that: 'Both [management and leadership] are needed and need to work closely together, often through the same person or team.' Earlier, Mintzberg (2004: 22) summed it all up (as he often did) when he wrote: 'Let's stop the dysfunctional separation of leadership from management. We all know that managers who don't lead are boring, dispiriting. Well, leaders who don't manage are distant, disconnected.'

Leadership and management development compared

In some quarters the term 'leadership development' has replaced 'management development', perhaps because the importance of ensuring that people have leadership qualities has been recognized, while it is believed that they can be safely left to acquire management skills in other ways, eg experience.

However, the two are different even though they are closely associated.

A rather simplistic way of differentiating the two is that leadership development tends to be concerned with nurturing the softer skills of leadership through various educational processes, including formal learning events and programmes and coaching. This is illustrated in the three case studies at the end of the next section of this chapter. In contrast, management development relies more on ensuring that managers have the right sequence of experience, which may be supplemented by self-directed learning and courses on management techniques. Further guidance may be provided by coaching and from mentors. But management development programmes traditionally also cover leadership skills.

Leadership development

It is sometimes said that leaders are born not made. This is a rather discouraging statement for those who are not leaders by birth-right. It may be true to the extent that some exceptional people seem to be visionaries, have built-in charisma and a natural ability to impose their personality on others. However, even they probably have to develop and hone these qualities when confronted with a situation demanding leadership. Ordinary mortals need not despair: they too can build on their natural capacities and develop their leadership abilities. As Burgoyne (2010: 42) observed: 'The will to lead is largely innate but the ability to do it well is largely learnt.'

As defined by Burgoyne (2010: 43): 'Leadership development in the widest sense involves the acquisition, development and utilization of leadership capability or the potential for it.' Leadership development programmes prepare people for leadership roles and situations beyond their current experience. The essential elements of leadership development, as suggested by Bolden (2010: 129), are reflection, practice, self-awareness, personal support, opportunities to apply learning and relevance to work.

Burgoyne (2010: 44) identified the following leadership development activities:

- job/work placements with leadership capability development as one of the purposes;
- education, training and development of individuals including the 'context sensitive' methods of coaching, mentoring and more formal education, training and development programmes;
- 'soft' organization development processes including culture change, team building and 'hearts and minds' collective mission/values-creating initiatives.

Yukl (2006) proposed the following conditions for successful leadership development:

- clear learning objectives;
- clear, meaningful content;
- appropriate sequencing of content;
- appropriate mix of training methods;
- opportunity for active practice;
- relevant, timely feedback;
- high trainee confidence;
- appropriate follow-up activities.

But it is not all about subjecting leaders to development programmes. The organization has to play its part in ensuring that leaders are provided with the support and the working conditions they need to carry out their role properly. As Fiedler (1967: 276) emphasized: 'If we wish to increase organizational and group effectiveness we must learn not only to train leaders more effectively but also to build an organizational environment in which the leaders can perform well.'

Leadership development

Leadership development programmes prepare people for leadership roles and situations beyond their current experience.

Management development

- Management development is concerned with improving the performance of managers in their present roles, preparing them to take on greater responsibilities in the future and also developing their leadership skills.

- Formal approaches to management development consist of processes and events planned and provided by the organization. They include planned experience, coaching and mentoring, action learning, outdoor learning, performance management, formal training and structured self-development.

- Informal approaches to management development make use of the learning experiences managers encounter during the course of their everyday work.

Responsibility for management development

Individual managers are largely responsible for their own development but need guidance, support and encouragement from their own managers and the HR function.

Questions

1 What is the aim of leadership and management development?

2 What is leadership?

3 What is management?

4 What is the difference between leadership development and management development?

5 What is leadership development?

6 What are the main features of a leadership development programme?

7 What is management development?

8 What formal approaches can be adopted to management development?

9 What is action learning?

10 What informal approaches can be adopted to management development?

References

Baldwin, T T and Patgett, M Y (1994) Management development: a review and a commentary, in (eds) C L Cooper and J T Robertson, *Key Reviews in Management Development*, New York, Wiley

Bennis, W G (1989) *On Becoming a Leader*, New York, Addison Wesley

Birkinshaw, J (2010) An experiment in reinvention, *People Management*, 15 July, pp 22–4

Bolden, R (2010) Leadership, management and organizational development, in (eds) J Gold, R Thorpe and A Mumford, *Gower Handbook of Leadership and Management Development*, Gower, Farnham, pp 118–32

Burgoyne J (2010) Crafting a leadership and management development strategy, in (eds) J Gold, R Thorpe and A Mumford, *Gower Handbook of Leadership and Management Development*, Farnham, Gower, pp 42–55

Dixon, N F (1994) *On the Psychology of Military Incompetence*, London, Pimlico

Drucker, P (1955) *The Practice of Management*, Oxford, Heinemann

Fiedler, F E (1967) *A Theory of Leadership Effectiveness*, New York, McGraw-Hill

Hersey, P and Blanchard, K H (1998) *Management of Organizational Behaviour*, Englewood Cliffs, NJ, Prentice Hall

Kotter, J P (1991) Power, dependence and effective management, in (ed) J Gabarro, *Managing People and Organizations*, Boston, MA, Harvard Business School Publications

McGregor, D (1960) *The Human Side of Enterprise*, New York, McGraw-Hill

Mintzberg, H (2004) Enough leadership, *Harvard Business Review*, November, p 22

Peters, K (2010) National and international developments in leadership and management development, in (eds) J Gold, R Thorpe and A Mumford, *Gower Handbook of Leadership and Management Development*, Gower, Farnham, pp 23–38

Spackman, T (2010) Crafting a leadership and management development strategy 2, in (eds) J Gold, R Thorpe and A Mumford, *Gower Handbook of Leadership and Management Development*, Gower, Farnham, pp 57–81

Tamkin, P, Hirsh, W and Tyers, C (2003) *Chore to Champion: The making of better people managers*, Report 389, Brighton, Institute for Employment Studies

Tamkin, P, Pearson, G, Hirsh, W and Constable, S (2010) *Exceeding Expectation: The principles of outstanding leadership*, London, The Work Foundation

Yukl, G (2006) *Leadership in Organizations*, 6th edn, Upper Saddle River, NJ, Prentice-Hall

PART V

Performance and reward

PART V CONTENTS

Introduction

One of the most important functions of HR is to advise management on the development of a high-performance strategy supported by performance and reward management initiatives. This is understood by the CIPD, which in its profession map (2009) defines what an HR or reward professional needs to do about performance and reward as follows: 'Builds a high performance culture by delivering programmes that recognize and reward critical skills, capabilities, experience and performance, and ensures that reward systems are market-based, equitable and cost-effective.'

The aim of this part is to explore the relationship between performance and reward and how in consort they contribute to the achievement of business goals. It starts with an examination of the basics of performance and reward and continues with descriptions of how performance management operates in practice, the role of strategic reward management and the practice of reward management, covering the main reward activities of market pricing, job evaluation, base pay management, and the administration of contingent pay and employee benefits.

Reference

CIPD (2009) *HR Profession Map: Strategy, insights and solutions*, http://www.cipd.co.uk/binaries/HR-Profession-Map, accessed 16 July 2011

26
Performance and reward basics

KEY CONCEPTS AND TERMS

Control theory

Performance

Reward

Self-efficacy

Total rewards

Goal theory

Performance management

Reward management

Social cognitive theory

LEARNING OUTCOMES

On completing this chapter you should be able to define these key concepts. You should also know about:

- The meaning of performance
- The meaning of reward
- The basics of performance management
- The basics of reward management

Introduction

Performance is concerned with how well something is done and reward is with how people should be recognized for doing it. They are therefore closely associated topics that play an important part in achieving one of the key goals of HRM – to contribute to the development of a high-performance culture. The aim of this chapter is to provide a foundation for the examination of how this is achieved through performance and reward management.

Performance and reward systems need to be based on an understanding of the meaning of performance and reward as considered in the first section of this chapter. The rest of the chapter is devoted to preliminary descriptions of performance management and reward management systems, which are enlarged on in the next three chapters.

The meaning of performance

The *Oxford English Dictionary* defines performance as: 'The accomplishment, execution, carrying out, working out of anything ordered or undertaken.' This refers to outputs/outcomes (accomplishment) but also states that performance is about doing the work as well as being about the results achieved.

Performance was regarded by Bernadin *et al* (1995) and Kane (1996) as simply the outcomes of work; a record of a person's accomplishments. But performance could be seen as behaviour – the ways in which organizations, teams and individuals get work done. This was argued by Campbell (1990), who defined performance as behaviour and stated that it should be distinguished from the outcomes because they can be contaminated by systems factors.

A more comprehensive view of performance is achieved if it is defined as embracing both outcomes and behaviour. This was well put by Brumbach (1988: 387):

> Performance means both behaviours and results. Behaviours emanate from the performer and transform performance from abstraction to action. Not just the instruments for results, behaviours are also outcomes in their own right – the product of mental and physical effort applied to tasks – and can be judged apart from results.

He observed that because of the significance of behaviour there was more to success or failure than whether results were achieved: 'Success is not always positive nor failure always negative' (*ibid*: 388). This concept of performance leads to the conclusion that when rewarding the performance of individuals and teams a number of factors have to be considered including both outputs (results) and inputs (behaviour).

Any attempt to manage performance should bear in mind that it is a complicated notion. Bates and Holton (1995) emphasized that it is a multi-dimensional construct. It has been pointed out by Campbell *et al* (1993) that the components of performance are: 1) job-specific task proficiency; 2) non-job-specific proficiency (eg organizational citizenship behaviour); 3) written and oral communication proficiency; 4) demonstration of effort; 5) maintenance of personal discipline; 6) facilitation of peer and team performance; 7) supervision/leadership; and 8) management/administration.

The meaning of reward

A reward recognizes a person's contribution. People are rewarded financially for the job they are in (base pay) and may receive additional rewards related to the level of their performance, competence or skill (contingent or variable pay), or their service in the job (service-related pay). They can also receive non-financial rewards such as recognition, praise or the opportunity to develop and learn new skills.

Performance management

Performance management is a systematic process for improving individual, team and organizational performance. Strategic performance management focuses on what needs to be done to help the organization achieve its business goals. The management of performance is clearly a major preoccupation in any business and ways of doing it are considered in Chapter 27. However, performance management systems are usually treated as a matter for individuals and to a more limited degree, teams (team performance management is also dealt with in Chapter 27).

At the individual level, performance management is a means of getting better results by understanding and managing performance within an agreed framework of planned goals, standards and competency requirements. It involves developing a shared understanding about what is to be achieved and how it is to be achieved. Brumbach (1988: 389) suggested that 'human performance is managed in order to achieve positive successes, avoid negative successes and failures and be hospitable to positive failures'. For individuals, performance management:

- aligns their objectives to organizational objectives and encourages them to uphold corporate core values;
- enables expectations to be defined and agreed in terms of role responsibilities and accountabilities (expected to do), skills (expected to have) and behaviours (expected to be);
- provides opportunities for them to identify their own goals and develop their skills and competencies.

Performance management is often seen as primarily a developmental process and may therefore be referred to as 'performance and development management'. It can also be used to generate ratings that inform performance pay decisions.

Underpinning theories

The following three theories underpinning performance management for individuals have been identified by Buchner (2007).

Goal theory

Goal theory, as developed by Latham and Locke (1979), highlights four mechanisms that connect goals to performance outcomes: 1) they direct attention to priorities; 2) they stimulate effort; 3) they challenge people to bring their knowledge and skills to bear to increase their chances of success; and 4) the more challenging the goal, the more people will draw on their full repertoire of skills. This theory supports the emphasis in performance management on setting and agreeing objectives against which performance can be measured and managed.

Control theory

Control theory focuses attention on feedback as a means of shaping behaviour. As people receive feedback on their behaviour they appreciate the discrepancy between what they are doing and what they are expected to do and take corrective action to overcome the discrepancy. Feedback is recognized as a crucial part of performance management processes.

Social cognitive theory

Social cognitive theory was developed by Bandura (1986). It is based on his central concept of self-efficacy. This suggests that what people believe they can or cannot do powerfully impacts on their performance. Developing and strengthening positive self-belief in employees is therefore an important performance management objective.

Objectives of performance management for individuals

The main objective of performance management for individuals is to develop the capacity of people to meet and exceed expectations and to achieve their full potential to the benefit of themselves and the organization. Performance management provides the basis for self-development but, importantly, it is also about ensuring that the support and guidance people need to develop and improve are readily available. Performance management can play an important role in rewarding employees by providing them with positive feedback and the recognition of their accomplishments.

Shields (2007: 24) explained that a performance management system has a four-fold purpose:

1 *Strategic communication* – convey to people what doing a good job means and entails.

2 *Relationship-building* – create stronger work relationships by bringing managers and those they manage together regularly to review performance achievements.

3 *Employee development* – provide performance feedback as a basis for the joint analysis of strengths, weaknesses and areas for improvement and an agreement on a personal development plan and learning contract.

4 *Employee evaluation* – assess the performance of employees (performance appraisal) as a basis for making decisions on job reassignment, promotion or performance-related reward.

Shields noted that, 'the relationship between the developmental and evaluative purposes is frequently a troubled one and maintaining a harmonious relationship between the two is undoubtedly one of the greatest challenges that awaits the unsuspecting human resource manager' (*ibid*: 25).

Respondents to an e-reward survey in 2005 identified the following performance management objectives:

- Align individual and organizational objectives – 64 per cent.
- Improve organizational performance – 63 per cent.
- Improve individual performance – 46 per cent.
- Provide the basis for personal development – 37 per cent.
- Develop a performance culture – 32 per cent.
- Inform contribution/performance pay decisions – 21 per cent.

The following is a statement of objectives from one respondent to the e-reward survey: 'To support culture change by creating a performance culture and reinforcing the values of the organization with an emphasis on the importance of these in getting a balance between "what" is delivered and "how" it is delivered.' The operation of a performance management system for individuals is covered in Chapter 27.

Reward management

Reward management is about deciding how people should be rewarded and ensuring that reward policies and practices are implemented. Strategic reward aligns reward strategies, systems and processes with the fundamental need of the business for high performance. It involves developing total reward strategies, which provide for both financial and non-financial rewards, determining levels of pay, base pay management, the management of contingent pay schemes and the provision of employee benefits. Its aim is to make an impact on performance, but in doing so a stakeholder approach is required.

How reward makes an impact on performance

Reward makes a positive impact on performance when it contributes to the development of a high-performance culture, one in which the values, norms and HR practices of an organization combine to create a climate in which the achievement of high levels of performance is a way of life. Such a culture can be manifested in a high-performance work system. Within the high-performance culture and work system, reward impacts on individual and organizational performance by:

- focusing attention on the values of the organization for high performance and the behaviours required to achieve it;
- ensuring that performance expectations are defined and understood;
- providing the means to encourage and recognize high performance;
- enhancing engagement and promoting positive discretionary effort;
- persuading talented people to join and stay with the organization.

A stakeholder approach to reward management

Reward management shares the purpose of HRM, which is to meet the needs of all the stakeholders in the business – employees, customers, suppliers and the public at large as well as management and shareholders. Reward management can make a significant contribution to meeting the varied needs of stakeholders successfully. It is concerned with improving business performance, shaping the behaviour of employees and developing a climate of trust.

There is also an ethical dimension. Reward management policies in association with HR policies can help to create a working environment that provides for the just, fair and ethical treatment of employees. They are about treating people right and avoiding the creation of unacceptable reward practices that reflect badly on the organization. The bonus schemes for top management operated in the banks and elsewhere in the financial services sector are good examples of where reward policy and practice went wrong. They were against the interests of every stakeholder except the recipients of the huge sums of money involved.

Key learning points: Performance and reward basics

Performance and reward

Performance is concerned with how well something is done and reward with how people should be recognized for doing it. They are therefore closely associated topics that play an important part in achieving one of the key goals of HRM – to contribute to the development of a high-performance culture.

The meaning of performance

Performance is defined as embracing both outcomes and behaviour.

The meaning of reward

A reward recognizes a person's contribution. People are rewarded financially for the job they are in (base pay) and, often for the level of their performance, competence or skill (contingent or variable pay), or for their service in the job (service-related pay). They can also receive non-financial rewards such as recognition, praise or the opportunity to develop and learn new skills.

Performance management

Performance management is a systematic process for improving organizational performance by developing the performance of individuals and teams. The objective of performance management is to develop the capacity of people to meet and exceed expectations and to achieve their full potential to the benefit of themselves and the organization. The underpinning theories of performance management are:

- Goal theory, which supports the emphasis in performance management on setting and agreeing objectives against which performance can be measured and managed.

- Control theory, which focuses attention on feedback as a means of shaping behaviour.

- Social cognitive theory, which suggests that what people believe they can or cannot do powerfully impacts on their performance.

Reward management

Reward management is about deciding how people should be rewarded and ensuring that reward policies and practices are implemented. It aims to make an impact on performance, but in doing so a stakeholder approach is required.

Reward management makes a positive impact on performance when it contributes to the development of a high-performance culture, one in which the values, norms and HR practices of an organization combine to create a climate in which the achievement of high levels of performance is a way of life.

It shares the purpose of HRM, which is to meet the needs of all the stakeholders in the business – employees, customers, suppliers and the public at large as well as management and shareholders.

Questions

1 What is performance?

2 What is performance management?

3 What are the three main theories underpinning performance management?

4 What is reward management?

5 How does reward impact on performance?

References

Bandura, A (1986) Social *Boundaries of Thought and Action*, Englewood Cliffs, NJ, Prentice-Hall

Bates, R A and Holton, E F (1995) Computerized performance monitoring: a review of human resource issues, *Human Resource Management Review*, Winter, pp 267–88

Bernadin, H K, Kane, J S, Ross, S, Spina, J D and Johnson, D L (1995) Performance appraisal design, development and implementation, in (eds) G R Ferris, S D Rosen and D J Barnum, *Handbook of Human Resource Management*, Cambridge, MA, Blackwell

Brumbach, G B (1988) Some ideas, issues and predictions about performance management, *Public Personnel Management*, **17** (4), pp 387–402

Buchner, T W (2007) Performance management theory: a look from the performer's perspective with implications for HRD, *Human Resource Development International*, **10** (1), pp 59–73

Campbell, J P (1990) Modelling the performance prediction problem in industrial and organizational psychology, in (eds) M P Dunnette and L M Hugh, *Handbook of Industrial and Organizational Psychology*, Cambridge, MA, Blackwell

Campbell, J P, McCloy, R A, Oppler, S H and Sager, C E (1993) A theory of performance, in (eds) N Schmitt and W Borman, *Personnel Selection in Organizations*, San Francisco, CA, Jossey-Bass

e-reward (2005) *Survey of Performance Management Practice*, Stockport, e-reward

Kane, J S (1996) The conceptualization and representation of total performance effectiveness, *Human Resource Management Review*, Summer, pp 123–45

Latham, G P and Locke, E A (1979) Goal setting – a motivational technique that works, *Organizational Dynamics*, Autumn, pp 442–7

Shields, J (2007) *Managing Employee Performance and Reward*, Port Melbourne, Cambridge University Press

27

The practice of performance management

LEARNING OUTCOMES

On completing this chapter you should be able to define these key concepts. You should also know about:

- Managing organizational performance
- Managing team performance
- Characteristics of performance management
- The performance management cycle
- Performance and development agreements
- Types of objectives
- Performance planning
- Managing performance throughout the year
- Reviewing performance
- Assessing performance
- Dealing with under-performers
- Introducing performance management
- Line managers and performance management

Introduction

Clearly, the aim of performance management is to improve performance; but whose performance? Its scope is sometimes perceived as only extending to individuals and their managers. This is often described as a 'performance management system'. However, while it may be assumed that using performance management processes to improve individual performance will inevitably improve team and organizational performance, this cannot be left to chance. Performance management processes should also be applied to teams and organizations. Shields (2007: 21) observed that: 'Individual results flow into group results, which in turn contribute to organization-wide results.' But he also pointed out that collective behaviour both arises from and shapes individual behaviour. In this chapter, therefore, organizational, team and individual performance management practices are considered separately although they are clearly interconnected. The chapter ends with a description of a special type of performance management: 360-degree feedback.

Managing organizational performance

The management of organizational performance is the prime responsibility of top management who plan, organize, monitor and control activities and provide leadership to achieve strategic objectives and satisfy the needs and requirements of stakeholders. As Gheorghe and Hack (2007: 19) noted: 'Actively managing performance is simply running a business – running the entire business as one entity. It's a continuous cycle of planning, executing, measuring results and planning the next actions. In the context of a larger strategic initiative, that means continuous improvement.'

Aim

The aim of managing organizational performance is to increase organizational capability – the capacity of an organization to function effectively. It is about the ability of an organization to guarantee high levels of performance, achieve its purpose (sustained competitive advantage in a commercial business), deliver results and, importantly, meet the needs of its stakeholders. It is concerned with the organization as a system and is in line with the belief expressed by Coens and Jenkins (2002) that to focus on the overall 'system' of the organization yields better results than trying to get individual employees to improve their performance.

The prime longer-term aim of organizational performance management is to develop a high-performance culture by means of high-performance work systems, as described in Chapter 4. On a day-to-day basis, however, the aim is to manage the normal processes of setting business goals, monitoring progress towards their achievement and taking steps to improve performance and remedy problems.

This has to take place in a context in which organizations are increasingly embracing a new management culture based on inclusion, involvement and participation, rather than on the traditional command, control and compliance approaches. As a new management paradigm this requires the development of a high-performance work environment through management practices that value and support achievement, growth and learning. It also calls for facilitative behaviours that focus on employee empowerment, learning and development. In other words, it needs performance management.

The dimensions of managing organizational performance

Sink and Tuttle (1990) stated that managing organizational performance has five dimensions:

1 Creating visions for the future.

2 Planning – determining the present organizational state, and developing strategies to improve that state.

3 Designing, developing and implementing improvement interventions.

4 Designing, redesigning, developing and implementing measurement and evaluation systems.

5 Putting cultural support systems in place to reward and reinforce progress.

A strategic approach to managing organizational performance means taking a broad and long-term view of where the business is going and managing performance in ways that ensure this strategic thrust is maintained. Organizational performance management systems are strategic in the sense that they are aligned to the business strategy of the organization and support the achievement of its strategic goals. The objective is to provide a sense of direction in an often turbulent environment so that the business needs of the organization and the individual and collective needs of its employees can be met by the development and implementation of integrated systems for managing and developing performance, which can be illustrated in strategy maps, as described below.

Mapping business strategy

To develop these systems and make them function effectively it is necessary to ensure that the business strategy is understood by all concerned. This includes paying attention, as expressed by Kaplan and Norton (2000: 167), 'to the crucial but perplexing processes by which intangible assets will be converted into tangible outcomes'. The notion of mapping strategy was a development of their concept of the balanced scorecard (assessing performance from different perspectives).

Strategy maps show the cause-and-effect links by which specific improvements create desired outcomes. They describe the elements of the organization's systems and their interrelationships and so provide a route map for systems improvement leading to performance improvement. In addition, they give employees a clear line of sight into how their jobs are linked to the overall objectives of the organization and provide a visual representation of a company's critical objectives and the relationships between them that drive organizational performance. Bourne et al (2003) called them 'success maps', which they describe as diagrams that show the logic of how the objectives of the organization interact to deliver overall performance. An example of an organizational performance strategy map is given in Figure 27.1.

This map shows an overall objective to improve profitability as measured by return on capital employed. In the next line the map indicates that the main contributors to increased profitability are increases to the gross margin (the difference between the value of sales and the cost of sales), improvements to operational capability and better cost

management. At the next level down the objective is to increase sales turnover in order to increase the gross margin. How this is to be achieved is set out in the next group of objectives and their interconnections, comprising increases in customer satisfaction and sales force effectiveness, innovations in product/market development and marketing, and improvements in customer service and quality levels. The key objective of improving operational capability is underpinned by developments in high-performance working and the contribution of the organization's human capital. The latter is supported by HRM objectives in the fields of performance management, reward management, talent management, levels of employee engagement, and learning and development.

The overall objective of increasing profitability in this example addresses the concerns of only one section of the stakeholders of an organization: the investors. This need would probably be given precedence by many quoted companies. But there are other objectives they could and should have that relate to their other stakeholders, for example those concerned with corporate social responsibility. These could be catered for in separate strategy maps. Better still, they could be linked to their commercial objectives. Public and voluntary sector organizations will certainly have objectives that relate to all their stakeholders as well as their overall purpose. A stakeholder approach to strategic performance management is required.

The performance prism

A multiple stakeholder framework for organizational performance management – the performance prism – was formulated by Neely et al (2002). This framework is based on the proposition that organizations exist to satisfy their stakeholders and their wants and needs should be considered first. Neely et al contend that companies in particular must assume a broader role than simply delivering value to their shareholders. To be successful over time, even for and on behalf of shareholders, businesses must address multiple stakeholders. If companies do not give each of their stakeholders the right level of focus, both their corporate reputation and their market capitalization – and therefore shareholder value – are likely to suffer in one way or another. They suggest that the performance prism

FIGURE 27.1   Strategy map – organizational performance

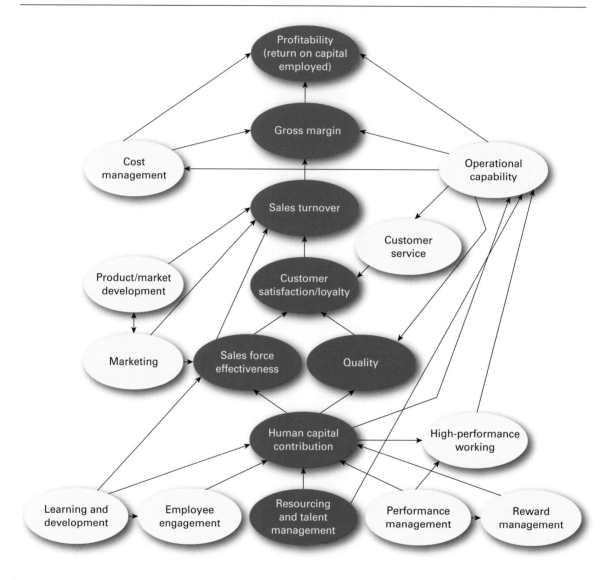

can facilitate or structure the analysis of multiple stakeholders in preparation for applying performance measurement criteria.

They explained the term 'performance prism' as follows. A prism refracts light; it illustrates the hidden complexity of something as apparently simple as white light. So it is with the performance prism: it illustrates the true complexity of performance measurement and management. It is a thinking aid that seeks to integrate five related perspectives and provide a structure that allows

executives to think through the answers to five fundamental questions:

1 *Stakeholder satisfaction:* Who are our stakeholders and what do they want and need?

2 *Stakeholder contribution:* What do we want and need from our stakeholders?

3 *Strategies:* What strategies do we need to put in place to satisfy these wants and needs?

4 *Processes:* What processes do we need to put in place to satisfy these wants and needs?

5 *Capabilities:* What capabilities – people, practices, technology and infrastructure – do we need to put in place to allow us to operate our processes more effectively and efficiently?

Managing team performance

As Purcell *et al* (1998: 8) pointed out, teams supply the elusive bridge between the aims of the individual employee and the objectives of the organization. They can provide the medium for linking employee performance targets to the factors critical to the success of the business. Managing team performance involves setting work and process objectives and conducting team reviews, as described below.

Setting performance objectives

Performance objectives for teams are based on an analysis of the purpose of the team and the results for which it is accountable. Targets and standards of performance should be discussed and agreed by the team as a whole. These may specify what individual members are expected to contribute. Project teams will agree project plans that define what has to be done, who does it, the standards expected and the timescale.

Setting process objectives

Process objectives are defined by the team, getting together and agreeing how they should conduct themselves as a team in terms of team competencies such as:

- interpersonal relationships;
- the quality of participation and collaborative effort and decision making;
- the team's relationships with internal and external customers;
- the capacity of the team to plan and control its activities;
- the ability of the team and its members to adapt to new demands and situations;
- the flexibility with which the team operates;
- the effectiveness with which individual skills are used;

- the quality of communications within the team and between the team and other teams or individuals.

Team performance reviews

Team performance review meetings analyse and assess feedback and control information on their joint achievements against objectives and project plans. The agenda for such meetings could be as follows:

1 *General feedback review:*
   - progress of the team as a whole;
   - problems encountered by the team that have caused difficulties or hampered progress;
   - helps and hindrances to the operation of the team.

2 *Work reviews:*
   - how well the team has functioned;
   - review of the individual contribution made by each team member – ie peer review (see below);
   - discussion of any new problems encountered by individual team members.

3 *Group problem solving:*
   - analysis of reasons for any shortfalls or other problems;
   - agreement on what needs to be done to solve them and prevent their reoccurrence.

4 *Update objectives:*
   - review of new requirements, opportunities or threats;
   - amendment and updating of objectives and project plans.

Managing individual performance

Individual performance is developed through performance management systems that provide the framework for improving performance through the agreement of performance expectations and the formulation and implementation of performance improvement and personal development plans. As vehicles for feedback, recognition and development and by providing motivation, they have a major role in a performance and reward system. They can also inform contingent pay decisions. The importance of the developmental aspect of performance management is often recognized by calling it 'performance and development management'.

This section starts by considering the characteristics and principles of individual performance management. Summaries of the processes involved follow, and the section ends with notes on recording the information and the use of web-enabled performance management systems.

Characteristics of individual performance management

Individual performance management is a planned process of which the five primary elements are agreement, measurement, feedback, positive reinforcement and dialogue. It is concerned with measuring outcomes in the shape of delivered performance compared with expectations expressed as objectives. In this respect, it focuses on targets, standards and performance measures or indicators. It is based on the agreement of role requirements, objectives and performance improvement and personal development plans. It provides the setting for ongoing dialogues about performance, which involves the joint and continuing review of achievements against objectives, requirements and plans. The four main characteristics of performance management are that:

1 It is concerned with both what people achieve, and how they achieve it, ie outputs and inputs. The latter are often expressed as behavioural competency requirements, which have been set out generally in a competency framework and specifically in role profiles. Developmental needs are identified by defining these requirements and assessing the extent to which the expected levels of performance have been met by meeting behavioural standards.

2 It is not just a top-down affair in which managers tell their subordinates what they think about them, set objectives and institute performance improvement plans, which is what performance appraisal used to be like.

It is not something that is done *to* people. As Buchner (2007) emphasizes, performance management should be something which is done *for* people and in partnership with them.

3 It is continuous and flexible. It involves managers and those whom they manage acting as partners within a framework that sets out how they can best work together to achieve the required results. It is based on the principle of management by contract and agreement rather than management by command. It relies on consensus and cooperation rather than control or coercion.

4 It focuses on future performance planning and improvement and personal development rather than on retrospective performance appraisal. It functions as a continuous and evolutionary process, in which performance improves over time. It provides the basis for regular and frequent dialogues between managers and individuals about performance and development needs based on feedback and self-assessment. The emphasis is on development, although performance management is an important part of the reward system through the provision of feedback and recognition and the identification of opportunities for growth. It may be associated with performance or contribution-related pay but its developmental aspects are more important.

Principles of performance management

The extensive research conducted by the CIPD (Armstrong and Baron, 1998; 2004) identified the following 10 principles of performance management as stated by practitioners.

1 'A management tool which helps managers to manage.'

2 'Driven by corporate purpose and values.'

3 'To obtain solutions that work.'

4 'Only interested in things you can do something about and get a visible improvement.'

5 'Focus on changing behaviour rather than paperwork.'

6 'It's about how we manage people – it's not a system.'

7 'Performance management is what managers do: a natural process of management.'

8 'Based on accepted principle but operates flexibly.'

9 'Focus on development not pay.'

10 'Success depends on what the organization is and needs to be in its performance culture.'

The performance management cycle

Performance management is a natural process of management: it is not an HRM technique or tool. As a natural process of management the performance management cycle, as shown in Figure 27.2, corresponds with Deming's (1986) plan-do-check-act model.

The performance management processes taking place in this cycle are:

- *Plan*: agree objectives and competency requirements as expressed in role profiles; identify the required behaviours; produce plans expressed in performance agreements for meeting objectives and improving performance; prepare personal development plans to enhance knowledge, skills and competence and reinforce the desired behaviours.

- *Act*: carry out the work required to achieve objectives by reference to the plans and in response to new demands.

- *Monitor*: check on progress in achieving objectives and responding to new demands; treat performance management as a continuous process – 'managing performance all the year round' – rather than an annual appraisal.

FIGURE 27.2   The performance management cycle

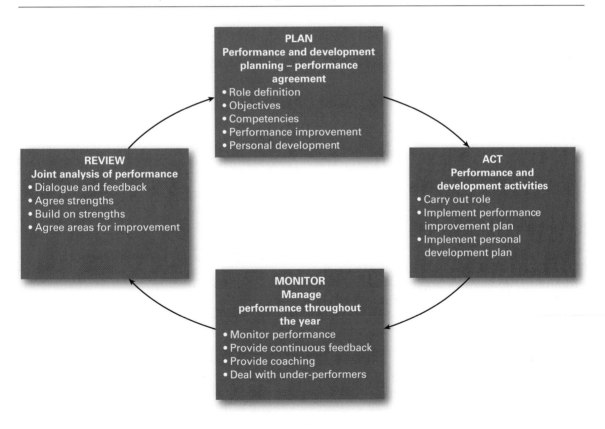

- *Review*: a 'stocktaking' discussion of progress and achievements held in a review meeting and identifying where action is required to develop performance as a basis for completing the cycle by continuing into the planning stage.

The processes involved during the cycle as described below are: concluding performance and development agreements, performance planning, personal development planning, managing performance throughout the year, conducting performance reviews and assessing performance. The outcomes of the planning and review activities may be recorded on a performance management form.

Performance and development agreements

Performance and development agreements form the basis for development, assessment and feedback in the performance management process. Expectations are defined in a role profile, which specifies key result areas and the knowledge, skills and abilities (KSAs) required and sets out what has to be accomplished in the form of objectives. The criteria for an objective can be expressed in the form of the 'SMART' mnemonic:

S = *Specific/stretching* – clear, unambiguous, straightforward, understandable and challenging.

M = *Measurable* – quantity, quality, time, money.

A = *Achievable* – challenging but within the reach of a competent and committed person.

R = *Relevant* – relevant to the objectives of the organization so that the goal of the individual is aligned to corporate goals.

T = *Time framed* – to be completed within an agreed timescale.

Performance agreements emerge from the analysis of role requirements and the performance review. An assessment of past performance leads to an analysis of future requirements. The two processes can take place at the same meeting.

Agreement is also reached at this stage on how performance will be measured and the evidence that will be used to establish levels of competence. It is important that these measures and evidence

requirements should be identified and fully agreed now because they will be used by individuals as well as managers to demonstrate and monitor achievements.

Performance planning

The performance planning part of the performance management sequence involves agreement between the manager and the individual on what the latter needs to do to achieve objectives, raise standards and improve performance.

Personal development planning

A personal development plan provides a learning action plan for which individuals are responsible with the support of their managers and the organization. It may include formal training but, more importantly, it will incorporate a wider set of learning and development activities such as self-managed learning, coaching, mentoring, project work, job enlargement and job enrichment. If multi-source assessment (360-degree feedback) is practised in the organization this will be used to discuss development needs.

Managing performance throughout the year

Perhaps one of the most important features of performance management is that it is a continuous process that reflects normal good management practices of setting direction, monitoring and measuring performance and taking action accordingly. Performance management should not be imposed on managers as something 'special' they have to do. It should instead be treated as a natural function that all good managers carry out.

This approach contrasts with that used in conventional performance appraisal systems, which were usually built around an annual event – the formal review – which tended to dwell on the past. This was carried out at the behest of the personnel department, often perfunctorily, and then forgotten. Managers proceeded to manage without any further reference to the outcome of the review, and the appraisal form was buried in the personnel record system.

Reviewing performance

Although performance management is a continuous process it is still necessary to have a formal review once or twice a year. This provides a focal point for the consideration of key performance and development issues. The performance review meeting is the means through which the five primary performance management elements of agreement, measurement, feedback, positive reinforcement and dialogue can be put to good use. It leads to the completion of the performance management cycle by informing performance and development agreements. It involves some form of assessment, as considered in the next section of this chapter.

The review should be rooted in the reality of the individual's performance. It is concrete, not abstract and it allows managers and individuals to take a positive look together at how performance can become better in the future and how any problems in meeting performance standards and achieving objectives can be resolved. Individuals should be encouraged to assess their own performance and become active agents for change in improving their results. Managers should be encouraged to adopt their proper enabling role: coaching and providing support and guidance.

There should be no surprises in a formal review if performance issues have been dealt with as they should have been – as they arise during the year. Traditional appraisals are often no more than an analysis of where those involved are now, and where they have come from. This static and historical approach is not what performance management is about. The true role of performance management is to look forward to what needs to be done by people to achieve the purpose of the job, to meet new challenges, to make even better use of their knowledge, skills and abilities, to develop their capabilities by establishing a self-managed learning agenda and to reach agreement on any areas where performance needs to be improved and how that improvement should take place. This process also helps managers to improve their ability to lead, guide and develop the individuals and teams for whom they are responsible.

There are 12 golden rules for conducting performance review meetings:

1   *Be prepared.* Managers should prepare by referring to a list of agreed objectives and their notes on performance throughout the year. They should form views about the reasons for success or failure and decide where to give praise, which performance problems should be mentioned and what steps might be undertaken to overcome them. Thought should also be given to any changes that have taken place or are contemplated in the individual's role and to work and personal objectives for the next period. Individuals should also prepare in order to identify achievements and problems, and to be ready to assess their own performance at the meeting. They should also note any points they wish to raise about their work and prospects.

2   *Work to a clear structure.* The meeting should be planned to cover all the points identified during preparation. Sufficient time should be allowed for a full discussion – hurried meetings will be ineffective. An hour or two is usually necessary to get maximum value from the review.

3   *Create the right atmosphere.* A successful meeting depends on creating an informal environment in which a full, frank but friendly exchange of views can take place. It is best to start with a fairly general discussion before getting into any detail.

4   *Provide good feedback.* Individuals need to know how they are getting on. Feedback should be based on factual evidence. It refers to results, events, critical incidents and significant behaviours that have affected performance in specific ways. The feedback should be presented in a manner that enables individuals to recognize and accept its factual nature – it should be a description of what has happened, not a judgement. Positive feedback should be given on the things that the individual did well in addition to areas for improvement. People are more likely to work at improving their performance and developing their skills if they feel empowered by the process.

5   *Use time productively.* The reviewer should test understanding, obtain information, and seek proposals and support. Time should be allowed for the individual to express his or her views fully and to respond to any

comments made by the manager. The meeting should take the form of a dialogue between two interested and involved parties, both of whom are seeking a positive conclusion.

6 *Use praise.* If possible, managers should begin with praise for some specific achievement, but this should be sincere and deserved. Praise helps people to relax – everyone needs encouragement and appreciation.

7 *Let individuals do most of the talking.* This enables them to get things off their chest and helps them to feel that they are getting a fair hearing. Use open-ended questions (ie questions that invite the individual to think about what to reply rather than indicating the expected answer). This is to encourage people to expand.

8 *Invite self-assessment.* This is to see how things look from the individual's point of view and to provide a basis for discussion – many people underestimate themselves.

9 *Discuss performance not personality.* Discussions on performance should be based on factual evidence, not opinion. Always refer to actual events or behaviour and to results compared with agreed performance measures. Individuals should be given plenty of scope to explain why something did or did not happen.

10 *Encourage analysis of performance.* Don't just hand out praise or blame. Analyse jointly and objectively why things went well or badly and what can be done to maintain a high standard or to avoid problems in the future.

11 *Don't deliver unexpected criticisms.* There should be no surprises. The discussion should only be concerned with events or behaviours that have been noted at the time they took place. Feedback on performance should be immediate; it should not wait until the end of the year. The purpose of the formal review is to reflect briefly on experiences during the review period and, on this basis, to look ahead.

12 *Agree measurable objectives and a plan of action.* The aim should be to end the review meeting on a positive note.

These golden rules may sound straightforward and obvious enough but they will only function properly in a culture that supports this type of approach. This emphasizes the importance of getting and keeping top management support and the need to take special care in developing and introducing the system and in training managers *and* their staff.

Assessing performance

Most performance management schemes include some form of appraisal, which is usually carried out during or after a performance review meeting. This may be carried out by overall assessment, rating or visual assessment, as described below.

Overall assessment

Overall assessment is based on a general analysis of performance under the headings of the performance agreement. The aim is to reach agreement about future action rather than to produce a summarized and potentially superficial judgement. Managers are expected to reach an understanding with their team members as a result of the analysis, which will ensure that the latter will appreciate how well or not so well they are doing. The analysis should also identify the high-flyers and those who are failing to meet acceptable standards. An overall assessment is recorded in a narrative consisting of a written summary of views about the level of performance achieved. This at least ensures that managers have to collect their thoughts together and put them down on paper. But different people will consider different aspects of performance and there will be no consistency in the criteria used for assessment, so it is necessary to have a framework for the analysis. This could be provided on a 'what' and 'how' basis. The 'what' is the achievement of previously agreed objectives related to the headings on a role profile. The 'how' is behaviour in relating to competency framework headings. The results for each what and how heading could be recorded following a joint analysis during a review meeting.

One problem with this form of assessment, indeed any form of assessment, is that we can recognize people at either extreme (top performers and inadequate performers) but cannot accurately distinguish performance differences in the bulk of people lying between those extremes. What managers can do is to tell an individual that she has done exceptionally well and that she will therefore be included in the talent management programme, or they can inform another individual that he has not done very well and that they must discuss what needs to be done about it. The others can be told that they are doing a perfectly good job and discussions can take place on how they can build on their strengths or on any learning activity (preferably self-directed) that might help them to do even better. Another problem with overall assessments is that they can be bland, superficial and over-generalized. This is why many schemes use rating.

Rating

Rating summarizes on a scale the views of the rater on the level of performance achieved. A rating scale is supposed to assist in making judgements and it enables those judgements to be categorized to inform performance- or contribution-pay decisions, or simply to produce an instant summary for the record of how well or not so well someone is doing.

Rating scales can be defined alphabetically (a, b, c, etc), or numerically (1, 2, 3, etc). Initials (ex for excellent, etc) are sometimes used in an attempt to disguise the hierarchical nature of the scale. The alphabetical or numerical points scale points may be described adjectivally, for example, a = excellent, b = good, c = satisfactory and d = unsatisfactory. Alternatively, scale levels may be described verbally, as in the following example:

- *Exceptional performance*: Exceeds expectations and consistently makes an outstanding contribution that significantly extends the impact and influence of the role.

- *Well-balanced performance*: Meets objectives and requirements of the role, consistently performs in a thoroughly proficient manner.

- *Barely effective performance*: Does not meet all objectives or role requirements of the role; significant performance improvements are needed.

- *Unacceptable performance*: fails to meet most objectives or requirements of the role; shows a lack of commitment to performance improvement or a lack of ability, which has been discussed prior to the performance review.

The e-reward 2005 survey of performance management found that overall ratings were used by 70 per cent of respondents. The most popular number of levels was five (43 per cent of respondents). However, some organizations are settling for three levels. There is no evidence that any single approach is clearly superior to another, although the greater the number of levels the more is being asked of managers in the shape of discriminatory judgement. It is, however, preferable for level definitions to be positive rather than negative and for them to provide as much guidance as possible on the choice of ratings. It is equally important to ensure that level definitions are compatible with the culture of the organization and that close attention is given to ensuring that managers use them as consistently as possible.

The main problem with ratings is that they are largely subjective and it is difficult to achieve consistency between the ratings given by different managers. Because the notion of 'performance' is often unclear, subjectivity can increase. Even if objectivity is achieved, to sum up the total performance of a person with a single rating is a gross over-simplification of what may be a complex set of factors influencing that performance – to do this after a detailed discussion of strengths and weaknesses suggests that the rating will be a superficial and arbitrary judgement. To label people as 'average' or 'below average', or whatever equivalent terms are used, is both demeaning and demotivating.

The whole performance review session may be dominated by the fact that it will end with a rating, thus severely limiting the forward-looking and developmental focus of the meeting, which is all-important. This is particularly the case if the rating governs performance- or contribution-pay increases.

Another problem is that managers may inflate ratings to avoid confrontation with the individuals concerned. Some organizations (8 per cent of the respondents to the CIPD performance management survey) (Armstrong and Baron, 2004) attempt to counter this by using forced distribution, which requires conforming to a laid down distribution of ratings between different levels, for example: A = 5 per cent, B = 15 per cent, C = 60 per cent, D = 15 per cent and E = 5 per cent. This achieves consistency of a sort but managers and staff rightly resent being forced into this sort of straitjacket.

An alternative to forced distribution is forced ranking. It is more common in the United States than in the UK. Managers are required to place their staff in order from best to worst. The problem with forced ranking, as with forced distribution, is that the notion of performance may not be defined and is therefore unmeasurable. In the case of ranking it is therefore unclear what the resulting order of employees truly represents.

Some organizations, mainly in the United States, have gone as far as adopting the practice of annually terminating the employment of 5 to 10 per cent of the consistently lowest performers. It is claimed that this practice 'raises the bar', ie it is said that it improves the overall level of performance in the business. There is no evidence that this is the case.

Visual assessment

An alternative to rating is to use a visual method of assessment. This takes the form of an agreement between the manager and the individual on where the latter should be placed on a matrix or grid, as illustrated in Figure 27.3. The vertical axis of the grid in this example assesses the behavioural style adopted by the individual in carrying out the role, ie inputs. The elements of behaviour to be assessed would be defined in a competency framework and this would be amplified in schedules of what would be regarded as acceptable or unacceptable behaviour

FIGURE 27.3   Visual performance assessment matrix

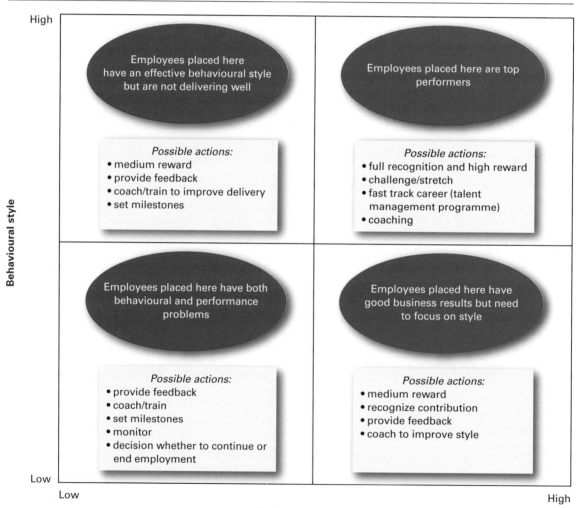

TABLE 27.1   Example of competency definition with behavioural indicators

Competency heading	Leadership
Competency definition	The capacity to inspire individuals to give of their best to achieve a clearly defined result and to maintain effective relationships with individuals and the team as a whole.
Competency requirement	• Accepted by team as an effective and approachable leader • Give clear direction and guidance • Agree objectives and competency requirements • Motivate and coach team members • Take a close interest in the wellbeing of team members
Positive indicators	• Leadership qualities recognized by team • Establishes clear team goals and inspires team to achieve them • Maintains firm support and guidance • Is considerate when dealing with people • Lets people know that they are valued
Negative indicators	• Not respected by team • Doesn't explain why things need to be done • Fails to allocate tasks clearly • Ignores contribution of individuals • Not really interested in people

for each area of competency (an example is given in Table 27.1). The horizontal axis measures the level of business performance, ie outputs or what the individual delivers. The assessment can place someone anywhere in one of the four quadrants according to behavioural style and delivery. Examples of possible actions are provided. A picture is thus provided of the individual's overall contribution which is presented visually and as such provides a better basis for analysis and discussion than a mechanistic rating.

Recording the performance agreement and review

The performance agreement and outcomes of a review can usefully be recorded on a performance management form. This should serve as a working document. It should be regularly used by managers and individuals as a reference document on objectives and plans when reviewing progress. It is a means of recording agreements on performance achievements and actions to be taken to improve performance or develop competence and skills. It should be dog-eared from much use – it should not be condemned to moulder away in a file. Examples of forms are given in Figures 27.4a and 27.4b.

Web-enabled performance management

Web-enabled or online performance management makes it easier for managers and employees to record role profiles and performance agreements, monitor progress against the plans, access performance documents, and gather multi-source (360-degree appraisal) comments. All this data can be used to assist in performance reviews and record further agreements emerging from the reviews. The aim is to reduce paperwork and simplify the process.

FIGURE 27.4a   Performance management form (part 1)

PERFORMANCE AND DEVELOPMENT: AGREEMENT AND PERSONAL DEVELOPMENT PLAN	
Name:	Forename(s):
Job title:	Department:
Reviewer's name:	Job title:
PERFORMANCE AND DEVELOPMENT AGREEMENT	
Objectives	Performance measures
Competencies	Agreed actions

PERSONAL DEVELOPMENT PLAN			
Development need	How it is to be met	Action by whom	Target completion date

FIGURE 27.4b   Performance management form (part 2)

PERFORMANCE AND DEVELOPMENT REVIEW	
Objectives	Achievements
Competencies	Actions taken
Development needs	Actions taken
Comments by reviewer:	
Signed: Date:	
Comments by person reviewed:	
Signed: Date:	

Line managers and performance management

Line managers are crucial to the success of performance management. But there are problems. The e-reward 2005 survey of performance management established that the top four issues concerning respondents about their performance management processes were:

1 Line managers do not have the skills required – 88 per cent.

2 Line managers do not discriminate sufficiently when assessing performance – 84 per cent.

3 Line managers are not committed to performance management – 75 per cent.

4 Line managers are reluctant to conduct performance management reviews – 74 per cent.

When asked how they coped with these problems, respondents emphasized the importance of doing the following:

- Involve line managers in the development and introduction of performance management.

- Train and coach line managers – existing managers and, importantly, potential and newly appointed managers.

- Get top management to stress the importance they attach to performance management – by example as well as exhortation.

- Keep it simple – do not impose a bureaucratic system.

- Emphasize whenever possible that performance management is a normal process of management and that one of the criteria for assessing the performance of managers is how well they do it.

- Do whatever can be done to persuade line managers that formal performance reviews need not be stressful occasions if they are conducted properly, but that they can in fact provide 'quality time' for the two parties to engage in a dialogue about performance and development opportunities (eliminating formal ratings helps).

Performance management as a rewarding process

Performance management, if carried out properly, can reward people by recognition through feedback, the provision of opportunities to achieve, the scope to develop skills, and guidance on career paths. All these are non-financial rewards that can encourage job and organizational engagement and make a longer-lasting and more powerful impact than financial rewards such as performance-related pay.

Performance management is, of course, also associated with pay by generating the information required to decide on pay increases or bonuses related to performance, competence or contribution. In some organizations this is its main purpose, but performance management is, or should be, much more about developing people and rewarding them in the broadest sense.

360-degree feedback

360-degree feedback, also known as multi-source feedback, is a process in which someone's performance is assessed and feedback is given by a number of people who may include their manager, subordinates, colleagues and customers. Assessments take the form of ratings against various performance dimensions. The term '360-degree feedback' is sometimes used loosely to describe upward feedback where this is given by subordinates to their managers. This is the most common approach and is more properly described as 180-degree feedback. Feedback may be presented direct to individuals, or to their managers, or both. Expert counselling and coaching for individuals as a result of the feedback may be provided by a member of the HR department or an outside consultant. 360-degree feedback or a variant of it was used by 30 per cent of the respondents to the 2005 e-reward survey.

Data from questionnaires forms the basis of 360-degree feedback, which measure from different perspectives the behaviours of individuals against a list of competencies. In effect, they ask for an evaluation: 'How well does ... do ...?' The competency model may be one developed within the organization or the competency headings may be provided by the supplier of a questionnaire. A typical questionnaire may cover aspects of performance such as leadership, teamwork, communication, organizational skills, decisiveness, drive and adaptability. Questionnaires are normally processed with the help of software developed within the organization or, most commonly, provided by external suppliers.

Feedback is presented to individuals, often anonymously but sometimes by their manager. If the purpose of the system is primarily developmental, as is most frequently the case, the action may be left to individuals as part of their personal development plans, but the planning process may be shared between individuals and their managers if they both have access to the information. Even if the data only goes to the individual it can be discussed in a performance review meeting so that joint plans can be made, and there is much to be said for adopting this approach.

The disadvantages can all be minimized if not avoided completely by careful design, communication, training and follow-up. But it is still possible to argue, as did Grint (1995: 68–9), that 360-degree feedback 'merely replaces single-assessor subjectivity with multi-assessor subjectivity'.

> ## The advantages and disadvantages of 360-degree feedback
>
> ### Advantages
>
> - Individuals get a broader perspective of how they are perceived by others than previously possible.
> - It gives people a more rounded view of their performance.
> - Increased awareness of and relevance of competencies.
> - Feedback is perceived as more valid and objective because it is from a number of sources rather than a single, possibly prejudiced manager, leading to acceptance of results and actions required.
>
> ### Disadvantages
>
> - People do not always give frank or honest feedback.
> - People may be put under stress in receiving or giving feedback.
> - Lack of action following feedback.
> - Over-reliance on technology.
> - Too much bureaucracy.

CASE STUDIES

Performance management at CEMEX UK

CEMEX UK is a supplier of cement, ready-mixed concrete and aggregates, with 4,000 employees. It is a subsidiary of the Mexican company CEMEX.

Aims

The aims of the Performance and Potential Assessment scheme at CEMEX UK are to:

- promote strategic alignment and respond to business needs;
- facilitate clear communication and understanding of standards;
- ensure objective grading and differentiation of potential levels;
- promote continuous feedback and development;
- reinforce high-performance attitudes.

The annual cycle

Cemex's performance management scheme runs over the calendar year as follows:

- The company's overall budget is set in January and from this the most senior managers' objectives are established, which are then cascaded down the organization.

- Around July, there is a mid-year review of initial objectives set and discussions on how the individual is progressing over the first part of the year.

- Finally, between November and January an ultimate meeting takes place where line managers and individuals meet and staff are rated between one and five by their line managers.

Performance management at DHL

DHL is a global market leader in the international express and logistics industry, with 45,000 staff in Europe.

DHL's annual performance management process begins in August when the bonus framework and core elements of the scheme are designed at the top level. Following this, in mid-November, based on the aims decided upon in August, targets are set for the year by a panel of senior staff. Once devised, these targets are cascaded down the organization into individual personal objectives following discussions between line managers and HR.

The cascading process is designed to ensure that targets are refined and altered to align with each individual's actual job. Further discussions then take place to decide what each target means for employees in practice and their implications for competencies. Around the same time, attainment levels and scoring based on the previous year's performance take place to determine bonus levels and salary rises. Following this, with targets already set, around the middle of January an outline for recording performance targets for personal and financial performance for the coming year is designed, and in mid-February the company's financial results become known. This makes it possible to determine the pot available for bonus payments and salary increases relating to the previous year. Bonuses are paid in either March or April while salary reviews take place in April.

The initial stage of establishing overall objectives and the target-setting framework sets the tone for the year. From year to year, conditions change, with the priorities of senior management reflecting the current state of affairs. As a result, each year there are a number of overarching themes such as serving customers, for example, or health and safety. These core individual key objectives (IKOs) are strictly adhered to, although local managers can determine themselves how to manage their attainment. In contrast, more flexibility exists for other objectives, with managers at lower levels able to alter them to align with their particular needs. There is further flexibility in the system with regard to its timing.

Performance management tools

To ensure the smooth running of the system, managers and staff alike are provided with a number of tools to help them during the performance management process. These include:

- A performance evaluation template: this template enables the appropriate competency model to be reviewed and evaluated.

- An objective agreement template: this template is located within the performance evaluation template and is used to capture both performance and personal objectives.

- Competency models: are available as support tools for personal development planning.

- Technical competencies: these represent a support framework for identifying core technical competencies for key operational roles.

- Development guides: guidelines for use in the support of developing a personal development plan.

- Personal development plan (PDP): a template for assessing an individual against management competencies and developing actions for them to progress their career.

- Career ladder: a guide to support the development of a personal development plan.

- Passport of success: a small booklet retained by the individual (non-management) that identifies completed training.

- Site succession plan: a plan developed utilizing information from the performance review and PDP process.

The annual face-to-face meeting

A key element of the performance management cycle is the face-to-face meeting between line managers and each member of their teams. For operational employees (non-management) the company recommends, as a minimum, this should be a discussion of around 30 minutes, while for managers, a one-hour meeting is suggested. During the meeting, the managers and their direct reports examine performance over the last 12 months with reference to the previous year's objectives. Discussions cover what was achieved, whether support provided was sufficient and, if relevant, what could have been done differently for a more effective result.

Following this they agree performance objectives for the coming year, along with any support in the form of training and development that can be offered. Objectives are documented in a 'target agreement form', information on levels of attainment captured on the 'performance evaluation tool', while training and support needs are recorded in the 'performance development plan'. In addition, as mentioned, further support tools used include competency models, development guides, technical competencies and career ladders.

Unlike performance objectives, development objectives are primarily the individual's responsibility to identify, with support provided by managers via the supply of appropriate resources and by contributing objectivity in discussions on staff potential. In some circumstances, DHL guidance says that it may be appropriate to develop a full performance development action plan, while in others this may not be necessary. In either case though, the tools mentioned above are available to assist. DHL says it is committed to personal development planning because it supports the growth of individuals across the organization, stating that 'growing its people develops talent to meet the organization's future management and leadership requirements'. Further, it is a 'motivator for the individual and allows development priorities to be clearly identified, creating opportunities to fully achieve their potential'.

Competencies

Closely linked to objectives, competencies play an important part throughout DHL's performance management process. In addition to the management of performance, they are used for recruitment, selection, induction and job sizing and feed into decisions on pay increases. There are different competencies for different roles.

Progress meetings

In addition to the main performance management meetings, managers are advised to arrange progress meetings throughout the year. The number will depend on the individual in question, but the company suggests that there should be at least one every 12 months. In this meeting, discussions cover how attainment against objectives and competencies is progressing, whether training and development support aligns with expectations and whether additional support can be provided. Moreover, in some cases, certain senior employees are consulted on their own aspirations, and questions, such as whether they want to move upwards or into a different role or perhaps to change location, are asked.

Performance measurement/scoring

At the end of the year in the subsequent annual meeting the process begins again while, at the same time, ratings for the last 12 months are given based on performance against objectives and the individual's competencies. To aid in the evaluation process, the 'performance evaluation tool' is used, which includes a competency and development needs assessment. Using this, progress against last year's performance evaluation is discussed, particularly drawing on successes during the year. Individual achievement is based on a combination of two ratings. First, there is a measure of achievement against personal objectives – also known as personal targets or individual key objectives (IKOs). This concentrates on *what* is achieved, as distinct from a second rating which examines *how* things are achieved, drawing on competencies. While there is no particular formula, both ratings are taken into account when making decisions on pay, bonuses and career progression. Under the first measure, target achievement level is linked to IKOs and scores are on a scale of 0 to 133.33 per cent. On-target performance gives a score of 100 per cent. Competency ratings are on a scale of 1 to 5 where 5 is exceptional and 1 unsatisfactory, as follows:

1 *Far exceeds*: Consistently demonstrating the competency behaviours effectively, role model.

2 *Exceeds*: Demonstrates the competency behaviours beyond what is expected.

3 *Fully meets*: Behaviours fully correspond with what is expected in the current role.

4 *Partially meets*: Demonstrates minor deficiencies (coachable) in the behaviour.

5 *Does not meet*: Does not demonstrate behaviours expected in the current role.

When it comes to decisions on salary increases, ratings are moderated by employees' positions in their pay bands, local budget constraints and the market. Ratings are used to determine bonus levels and they also tie in to decisions on promotion and succession planning.

Succession planning

Following the evaluation and rating stage, the line manager's immediate superior reviews the results and, in the light of them, considers, among other things, succession and career planning. By using the overall results, senior managers can determine where there are skills gaps or other deficiencies. In addition, it enables them to take a closer look at individual employees to consider whether they might be more suited to be employed elsewhere in the organization. Similarly, managers can examine strengths and weaknesses, which might flag up a shortage of certain abilities, such as commercial acumen, for example. Such issues can therefore be addressed and recruitment can be directed appropriately. Moreover, it also helps when employees leave the organization, making it simple to determine the corresponding skills and behaviours that go from the organization with that individual. To aid with this task, managers are also able to draw on an additional rating for certain senior staff, termed 'potential for job'. This gauges potential for the future and helps by feeding into future decisions on promotion and succession planning.

Key learning points: The practice of performance management

The nature of performance management

Performance management is sometimes perceived as being simply a matter that concerns individuals and their manager, but performance management processes should also be applied to teams and organizations.

Managing organizational performance

- The management of organizational performance is the prime responsibility of top management who plan, organize, monitor and control activities and provide leadership to achieve strategic objectives and satisfy the needs and requirements of stakeholders.

- The aim is to increase organizational capability – the capacity of an organization to function effectively.

- Organizational performance management involves the development of high-performance work systems and the working environment as well as the normal processes of setting business goals, monitoring progress towards their achievement and taking any necessary steps to improve performance and remedy problems.

Managing team performance

Managing team performance involves the key activities of setting work and process objectives and conducting team and individual reviews.

Managing individual performance

- Individual performance is developed through performance management systems, which provide the framework for improving performance through the agreement of performance expectations and the formulation of performance development plans.

- Performance management is a planned process of which the five primary elements are agreement, measurement, feedback, positive reinforcement and dialogue.

- The performance management cycle involves planning, acting, monitoring and reviewing, in sequence.

- The key processes involved during the cycle are concluding performance and development agreements, performance planning, personal development planning, managing performance throughout the year, conducting performance reviews and assessing performance.

- Performance management, if carried out properly, can reward people by recognition through feedback, the provision of opportunities to achieve, the scope to develop skills, and guidance on career paths.

360-degree feedback

360-degree feedback, also known as multi-source feedback, is a process in which someone's performance is assessed and feedback is given by a number of people who may include their manager, subordinates, colleagues and customers.

Questions

1 What is the aim of managing organizational performance?

2 What are the key features of a process for managing organizational performance?

3 What are the actions required to manage team performance?

4 What are the primary elements of individual performance management?

5 What are the key processes in the performance management cycle?

6 What is 360-degree feedback?

References

Armstrong, M and Baron, A (1998) *Performance Management: The new realities*, London, CIPD

Armstrong, M and Baron, A (2004) *Managing Performance: Performance management in action*, CIPD, London

Bourne, M, Franco, M and Wilkes, J (2003) Corporate performance management, *Measuring Business Excellence*, 7 (3), pp 15–21

Buchner, T W (2007) Performance management theory: a look from the performer's perspective with implications for HRD, *Human Resource Development International*, 10 (1), pp 59–73

Coens, T and Jenkins, M (2002) *Abolishing Performance Appraisals: Why they backfire and what to do instead*, San Francisco, CA, Berrett-Koehler

Deming, W E (1986) *Out of the Crisis*, Cambridge, MA, Massachusetts Institute of Technology Centre for Advanced Engineering Studies

e-reward (2005) *Survey of Performance Management Practice*, Stockport, e-reward

Gheorghe, C and Hack, J (2007) Unified performance management: how one company can tame its many processes, *Business Performance Management*, November, pp 17–19

Grint, K (1995) *Management: A sociological introduction*, Cambridge, Polity Press

Kaplan, R S and Norton, D P (2000) Having trouble with your strategy? Then map it, *Harvard Business Review*, September–October, pp 167–76

Neely, A, Adams, C and Kennerley, M (2002) *The Performance Prism: The scorecard for measuring and managing business success*, Harlow, Pearson Education

Purcell, J, Hutchinson, S and Kinnie, N (1998) *The Lean Organization*, London, IPD

Shields, J (2007) *Managing Employee Performance and Reward*, Port Melbourne, Cambridge University Press

Sink, D S and Tuttle, T C (1990) The performance management question in the organization of the future, *Industrial Management*, 32 (1), pp 4–12

Questions

1 What is strategic reward?

2 What is the main characteristic of strategic reward?

3 What are the limitations to the concept of strategic reward?

4 What is reward strategy?

5 What are the main objectives of reward strategy?

6 What are the main arguments in favour of having a reward strategy?

7 What are the principal areas covered by a reward strategy?

8 What is reward philosophy?

9 What is the typical approach to formulating reward strategy?

10 What are the main problems organizations meet in implementing reward strategy and how can they be overcome?

References

Armstrong, M and Brown, D (2006) *Strategic Reward: Making it happen*, London, Kogan Page

Armstrong, M and Murlis, H (2007) *Reward Management*, revised 5th edn, London, Kogan Page

Brown, D (2001) *Reward Strategies: From intent to impact*, London, CIPD

e-reward (2004) *Survey of Grade and Pay Structures*, Stockport, e-reward

Kanter, R M (1984) *The Change Masters*, London, Allen & Unwin

Lawler, E E (1990) *Strategic Pay*, San Francisco, CA, Jossey-Bass

Legge, K (1995) *Human Resource Management: Rhetorics and realities*, London, Macmillan

Mabey, C, Salaman, G and Storey, J (1998) *Human Resource Management: A strategic introduction*, Oxford, Blackwell

Schuster, J R and Zingheim, P K (1992) *The New Pay*, New York, Lexington Books

Thompson, M (1998) Trust and reward, in (eds) S Perkins and St J Sandringham, *Trust, Motivation and Commitment: A reader*, Faringdon, Strategic Remuneration Research Centre

Trevor, J (2011) *Can Pay be Strategic?*, Basingstoke, Palgrave Macmillan

Wright, P M and Nishii, L H (2004) Strategic HRM and organizational behaviour: Integrating multiple levels of analysis, Erasmus University Conference, HRM: What's Next

29
The practice of reward management

LEARNING OUTCOMES

On completing this chapter you should be able to define these key concepts. You should also know about:

- The meaning and aims of reward management
- Total rewards
- Market pricing
- Base pay management
- Recognition schemes
- The evaluation of reward systems

- The reward system and its components
- Financial and non-financial rewards
- Job evaluation
- Contingent pay
- Employee benefits
- The administration of reward

Introduction

The aim of this chapter is to describe how reward management works in practice. It starts with definitions of what reward management is and what it aims to do. Reward management is conducted by means of the reward system and this is explained in the next section. The following sections describe the framework provided by the concept of total rewards and the considerations affecting financial and non-financial rewards. The next five sections deal with the components of the reward system – pay determination, base pay management, contingent pay, recognition and the provision of employee benefits, including pensions. The chapter ends with two sections dealing respectively with the evaluation and management of reward.

Reward management defined

Reward management is concerned with the strategies, policies and processes required to ensure that the value of people and the contribution they make to achieving organizational, departmental and team goals is recognized and rewarded. It is about the design, implementation and maintenance of reward systems that aim to satisfy the needs of both the organization and its stakeholders and to operate fairly, equitably and consistently.

Reward management is not just about pay and employee benefits. It is equally concerned with non-financial rewards such as recognition, learning and development opportunities and increased job responsibility.

Aims of reward management

As Ghoshal and Bartlett (1995) pointed out, reward management is there to add value to people. It is not just about attaching value to them. Its aims are to:

- *Support the achievement of business goals* by helping to ensure that the organization has the talented and engaged people it needs.
- *Promote high performance* by ensuring that the reward system recognizes and encourages it.

- *Support and develop the organization's culture* by linking rewards to behaviour that is in line with core values.
- *Define the right behaviours and outcomes* by defining expectations through performance management and contingent pay schemes.
- *Reward people according to the value they create* by providing for people to be rewarded in line with the degree to which they meet expectations.
- *Align reward practices with employee needs* by paying people fairly for what they do and recognizing their contribution.
- *Help to attract and retain high quality people* by providing competitive pay.

The reward system

A reward system consists of the interrelated processes and practices that combine to ensure that reward management is carried out effectively to the benefit of the organization and the people who work there.

Components of the reward system

The reward system covers all forms of financial rewards or remuneration (the pay, benefits and allowances provided to employees) as described below. It also covers non-financial rewards. Coupling financial rewards with non-financial rewards produces total rewards.

Base pay or base rate

This is the amount of pay that constitutes the rate for the job or the person. It is the fundamental component of the reward system.

Job-based or position-based pay is related solely to the perceived value of the job carried out (job worth, or in an analytical job evaluation scheme, job size – the points score attached to the job).

Person-based pay is related to the level of performance, competence or skill possessed by the person, or the length of time an individual is in a job, rather than just the value or size of the job. The rate for the job is represented by a pay range in a graded pay structure and pay progresses within a range according to performance, competence, skill or time served.

Time-based wages for manual workers are based on a fixed rate per hour, standard day or standard week. Salaries are based on annualized pay and paid to executives, managers and other staff.

Contingent pay

Contingent pay is related to performance, contribution, contribution, competence or skill. It may be consolidated into base pay in a pay progression system or it may be paid as an unconsolidated 'lump sum' in the form of a bonus (cash or shares). In the latter case it is sometimes known as 'variable pay', although this term is also used as an alternative to contingent pay. Contingent pay can be based on individual, team or organizational performance.

Employee benefits

Employee benefits are elements of remuneration such as pensions, sick pay, insurance cover and company cars additional to the various forms of cash pay. They also include provisions for employees that are not strictly remuneration, such as annual holidays.

Reward system processes

The processes in a reward system and their inter-relationships are shown in Figure 29.1. These are summarized below and described in detail in the next sections of this chapter.

Total rewards

Total rewards are the combination of financial and non-financial rewards available to employees. Each aspect of reward, namely base pay, contingent pay, employee benefits and non-financial rewards, which include intrinsic rewards from the work itself, are linked together and treated as an integrated and coherent whole.

Financial rewards

Financial rewards consist of job-based pay, which provides pay related to the value of the job, and person-based pay, which provides rewards that recognize the individual's contribution, competence or skill. They also include employee benefits and pensions and financial recognition schemes.

Non-financial rewards

These are rewards that do not involve the payment of salaries, wages or cash. They include extrinsic rewards such as recognition and praise, opportunities to develop new skills, and the work environment, and intrinsic rewards arising from the work itself (the ways in which jobs are designed).

Pay determination

Pay determination involves making decisions on the value of jobs by means of market pricing and job evaluation.

Performance management

The role of performance management in the reward system is to contribute to improving performance by providing a means of recognition, influencing job design when reviewing role responsibilities, setting up personal development plans and, when appropriate, informing contingent pay decisions.

Total rewards

The concept of total rewards describes an approach to reward management that emphasizes the need to consider all aspects of the work experience of value to employees, not just a few such as pay and employee benefits. It aims to blend the financial and non-financial elements of reward into a cohesive whole. A total rewards approach recognizes that it is necessary to get financial rewards (pay and benefits) right. But it also appreciates the importance of providing people with rewarding experiences that arise from their work environment (the job they do and how they are managed) and the opportunity to develop their skills and careers. It contributes to the production of an employee value proposition that provides a clear, compelling reason why talented people should work for a company.

It is a holistic view of reward that looks at the entire reward system to determine how its elements should be integrated so that they provide mutual support in contributing to the overall effectiveness of the system. Reliance is not placed on one or two reward mechanisms operating in isolation, instead account is taken of every way in which people can be rewarded and obtain satisfaction through their

FIGURE 29.1   A reward system

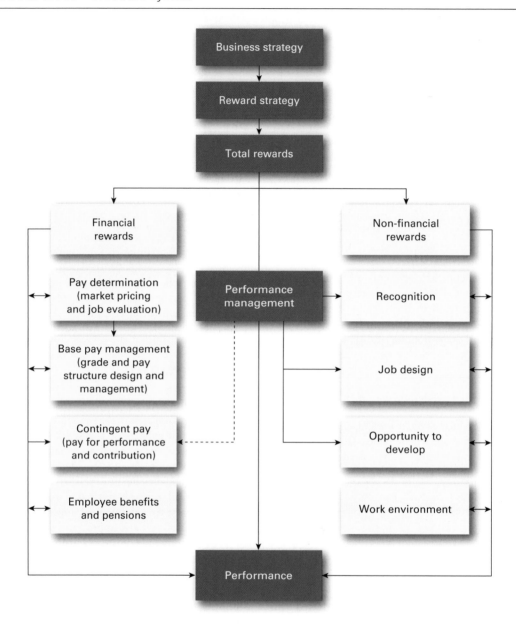

work. The whole is greater than the sum of its parts. The aim is to maximize the combined impact of a wide range of reward initiatives on motivation, commitment and job engagement. The elements of total rewards are modelled in Figure 29.2.

The Towers Perrin model shown in Figure 29.3 is frequently used as the basis for planning a total rewards approach. It consists of a matrix with four quadrants. The upper two quadrants – pay and benefits – represent transactional or tangible rewards. These are financial in nature and are essential to recruit and retain staff but can be easily copied by competitors. By contrast, the relational or intangible non-financial rewards represented in the lower two quadrants cannot be imitated so readily and therefore create both human capital and human process

FIGURE 29.2   The elements of total rewards

FIGURE 29.3   Model of total rewards: Towers Perrin

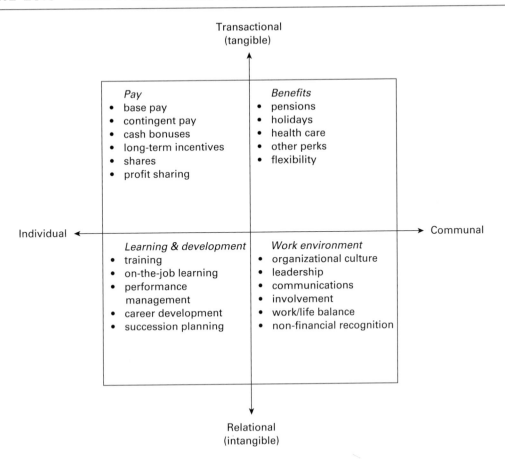

advantage. They are essential to enhancing the value of the upper two quadrants. The real power comes when organizations combine relational and trans-actional rewards. The model also makes a useful distinction between individual and communal rewards, particularly, in the latter case, those provided by the work environment.

The total rewards concept emphasizes the importance of both financial and non-financial rewards. The considerations affecting them are discussed below.

Financial rewards

Financial rewards comprise all rewards that have a monetary value and add up to total remuneration – base pay, pay contingent on performance, contribution, competency or skill, pay related to service, financial recognition schemes, and benefits such as pensions, sick pay and health insurance. They are the core elements in total rewards.

The management of a reward system requires decisions on levels of pay, how jobs should be valued, the design and operation of grade and pay structures and the choice of benefits. Such decisions can be complex and difficult but the problems pale by comparison with the issues surrounding the use of contingent financial rewards.

Labour economists distinguish between the incentive effect of financial rewards (generating more engagement and effort) and the sorting effect (attracting better quality employees). The fundamental issue is the extent to which financial rewards provide an incentive effect. The sorting effect is important but creates less controversy, perhaps because it is more difficult to pin down.

A vociferous chorus of disapproval has been heard on the incentive effect. One of the best known and most influential voices was that of Kohn (1993: 63) who stated in the *Harvard Business Review* that: 'bribes in the workplace simply can't work'. He asserted that: 'Rewards, like punishment, may actually undermine the intrinsic motivation that results in optimal performance. The more a manager stresses what an employee can earn for good work, the less interested that employee will be in the work itself.' Pfeffer (1998: 114) concluded in his equally influential *Harvard Business Review* article, 'Six dangerous myths about pay' that: 'Most merit-pay

systems share two attributes: they absorb vast amounts of management time and make everybody unhappy.'

There is a strong body of opinion, at least in academic circles, that financial rewards are bad – because they don't work and indeed are harmful, while non-financial rewards are good, at least when they provide intrinsic motivation, ie motivation by the work itself. But the critics are mainly referring to financial *incentives*. They do not appear to recognize that incentives are not the same as rewards. They can be distinguished as follows.

Rewards offer tangible recognition to people for their achievements and contribution. Financial rewards consist of job-based pay, which provides base pay related to the value of the job, and person-based pay, which provides rewards that recognize the individual's performance, contribution, competence or skill. Rewards can also be non-financial, for example recognition. If rewards are worth having and attainable and people know how they can attain them, they can act as motivators.

Incentives are intended to encourage people to work harder and achieve more. They are supposed to provide direct motivation: 'Do this and we will make it worth your while.' Incentives are generally financial but they can take the form of non-financial rewards such as promotion or a particularly interesting assignment.

If this distinction is not made it may be assumed that financial rewards only exist to provide an incentive. They may do this or, as the nay-sayers contend, they may not. But financial rewards can be justified because they are a form of tangible recognition – they are a means of informing people that they have done well and they accord with the reasonable and generally accepted belief that people who do better should be valued more highly. However, the use of financial rewards in the shape of contingent pay has aroused strong feelings amongst those who support and those who oppose them. The arguments for and against are set out below.

Arguments for financial rewards

The most powerful argument advanced for financial rewards is that those who contribute more should be paid more. It is right and proper to recognize achievement with a financial and therefore tangible reward. This is in accordance with the principle of distributive justice which, while it states that rewards should be provided equitably, does not require them to be equal except when the value of contribution is equal. Financial rewards can also be used to highlight key performance areas, to indicate the behaviours that are valued and generally to emphasize the importance of high performance.

Arguments against

The main arguments against financial rewards are that:

- the extent to which contingent pay schemes motivate is questionable – the amounts available for distribution are usually so small that they cannot act as an incentive;
- the requirements for success are exacting and difficult to achieve;
- money by itself will not result in sustained motivation: intrinsic motivation provided by the work itself goes deeper and lasts longer;
- people react in widely different ways to any form of motivation – it cannot be assumed that money will motivate all people equally yet that is the premise on which contingent pay schemes are based;
- financial rewards may possibly motivate those who receive them but they can demotivate those that don't, and the numbers who are demotivated could be much higher than those who are motivated;
- contingent pay schemes can create more dissatisfaction than satisfaction if they are perceived to be unfair, inadequate or badly managed;
- employees can be suspicious of schemes because they fear that performance bars will be continuously raised; a scheme may therefore only operate successfully for a limited period;
- schemes depend on the existence of accurate and reliable methods of measuring performance, contribution, competence, or skill, which might not exist;
- individuals are encouraged to emphasize only those aspects of performance that are rewarded;

- contingent pay decisions depend on the judgement of managers which, in the absence of reliable criteria, can be partial, prejudiced, inconsistent or ill-informed;
- the concept of contingent pay is based on the assumption that performance is completely under the control of individuals when in fact it is affected by the system in which they work;
- contingent pay, especially performance-related pay, can militate against quality and teamwork.

Another powerful argument against contingent pay is that it has proved difficult to manage. Organizations, including the UK Civil Service, rushed into performance-related pay in the 1980s without really understanding how to make it work. Inevitably problems of implementation arose. Studies such as those conducted by Bowey and Thorpe (1982), Kessler and Purcell (1992), Marsden and Richardson (1994) and Thompson (1992a; 1992b) have all revealed these difficulties. Failures may arise because insufficient attention has been paid to fitting schemes to the context and culture of the organization, but they are often rooted in implementation and operating difficulties, especially those of inadequate performance management processes, the lack of effective communication and involvement, and line managers who are not capable of or interested in carrying out the actions involved properly. Vicky Wright (1991: 82) remarked that: 'Even the most ardent supporters of performance-related pay recognize that it is difficult to manage well'; Trevor (2011: 201) also questioned the extent to which such systems are manageable.

Criteria for effectiveness

The effectiveness of financial rewards in the shape of contingent pay depends on the following factors:

- the accurate, consistent and fair assessment of performance or contribution;
- pay differences can be related to performance or contribution differences and can be seen to be related;
- the principles of procedural and distributive justice are upheld;
- there is a climate of trust in the organization – Thompson (1992b: 33) noted that 'PRP

schemes work when there is trust, involvement and a commitment to fairness';

- performance management systems function well;
- line managers have the necessary skills and commitment;
- stakeholders, including line managers, employees and employee representatives, have been involved in the design of the scheme;
- the scheme is appropriate to the context and culture of the organization;
- the scheme is not unduly complex;
- the purpose, methodology and effect of the scheme have been communicated and understood;
- there is a clear line of sight between effort and reward;
- rewards are attainable and worth attaining.

These are demanding criteria and difficult to meet. It may be right to reward people for their contribution and there is plenty of research evidence that financial rewards can improve performance. For example, in the UK this was established by Booth and Frank (1999), Marsden (2004), Prentice *et al* (2007) and Thompson (1998). In the United States, Gupta and Shaw (1998), Jenkins *et al* (1998), Lazear (1999) and Prendergast (1999), amongst others, all found positive relationships between financial incentives and performance. But the arguments against financial incentives are very convincing and anyone planning to introduce performance pay should take heed of them and only continue if they have a reasonable chance of meeting the effectiveness criteria.

Critical evaluation of financial rewards

The argument that people should be rewarded in accordance with the value of their contribution is a powerful one, but it stands alone. The evidence that incentives improve performance is conflicting. In some circumstances, as demonstrated by a number of research projects, it works, but in others it doesn't. Certainly, typical performance-related pay schemes are unlikely to provide a direct incentive simply because they do not match the demanding

requirements, eg line of sight, worthwhile reward, for this to happen. Their main purpose is to recognize the level of contribution and even this is questionable because of the difficulty of making fair and consistent assessments of performance as a basis for pay decisions. Such schemes can demotivate more people than they motivate.

But what's the alternative? Should everyone be paid the same rate in a job however well they perform? Or should pay be progressed in line with length of service – paying people for being there? For all its problems, the balance of the argument is in favour of some scheme for relating pay to contribution. But the difficulties of doing this should be recognized and every attempt should be made to ensure that pay decisions are fair, consistent and transparent. Involving staff in the development and monitoring of contribution pay schemes can be a great help.

Non-financial rewards

Non-financial rewards are those that focus on the needs people have to varying degrees for recognition, achievement, responsibility, autonomy, influence and personal growth. They incorporate the notion of relational rewards, which are the intangible rewards concerned with the work environment (quality of working life, the work itself, work–life balance), recognition, performance management and learning and development. Non-financial rewards can be extrinsic, such as praise or recognition, or intrinsic, associated with job challenge and interest and feelings that the work is worthwhile.

It can be said that money will motivate some of the people all of the time and, perhaps, all of the people some of the time. But it cannot be relied on to motivate all of the people all of the time. To rely on it as the sole motivator is misguided. Money has to be reinforced by non-financial rewards, especially those that provide intrinsic motivation. When motivation is achieved by such means it can have a more powerful and longer-lasting effect on people, and financial and non-financial rewards can be mutually reinforcing.

Reward systems should therefore be designed and managed is such a way as provide the best mix of all kinds of motivators according to the needs of the organization and its members. This is the essence of the total rewards philosophy.

Pay determination

Pay determination is the process of deciding on the level of pay for jobs or people. Its two aims, which often conflict, are 1) to be externally competitive to attract, engage and retain the people required by the organization, and 2) to be internally equitable in the sense that rates of pay correctly reflect the relativities between jobs.

Competitive pay

Pay is by no means the only factor that influences people to join or remain with an organization, but it is important. The most significant influence on pay levels is the law of supply and demand. If the demand for labour exceeds supply, pay levels will be higher and vice versa. Organizations pay more to attract and retain high quality employees in critical positions.

The need to be competitive means that organizations have to take account of market rates when deciding on the level of pay for a job. They bear in mind the saying: 'A job is worth what the market says it's worth.' Consequently, establishing market rates through what is termed 'market pricing' as described in the next section of this chapter is a vital step in deciding on levels of pay.

Internally equitable pay

Internally equitable pay is fair pay. This means providing equal pay for work of equal value as required by the Equality Act (2010) and supporting case law, and ensuring that the rates of pay for jobs at different levels properly reflect relative values. Internal relativities are established by job evaluation. But there is a tension between external competitiveness and internal equity. Some adopt the slogan, 'the market rules ok' – internal equity considerations are secondary. But if this policy is pursued too vigorously there is a risk of alienating existing employees and contravening the provisions of equal pay legislation. This risk should be assessed.

Market pricing

Market pricing is the process of making decisions on pay structures and individual rates of pay and obtaining information on market rates (market rate analysis). A policy decision is required on the relationship between market rate levels and levels of pay within the organization. This is called the 'pay stance', which may be expressed in such terms as matching median (average) rates or paying upper quartile rates (loosely, the top 25 per cent).

Use of market pricing

Market rate analysis may be associated with formal job evaluation. The latter establishes internal relativities and the grade structure, and market pricing is used to develop the pay structure – the pay ranges attached to grades. Information on market rates may lead to the introduction of market supplements for individual jobs or the creation of separate pay structures (market groups) to cater for particular market rate pressures. It is referred to as 'extreme market pricing' when market rates are the sole means of deciding on internal rates of pay and relativities, and conventional job evaluation is not used. An organization that adopts this method is said to be 'market-driven'.

Acceptability of market pricing

The acceptability of either form of market pricing is dependent on the availability of robust market data and, when looking at external rates, the quality of the job-to-job matching process, ie comparing like with like. It can therefore vary from analysis of data by job titles to detailed matched analysis collected through bespoke surveys focused on real market equivalence. Extreme market pricing can provide guidance on internal relativities even if these are market-driven. But it can lead to pay discrimination against women where the market has traditionally been discriminatory, and it does not satisfy UK equal pay legislation.

The concept of a market rate

Market pricing attempts to establish the market rate for jobs, but the notion of a market rate is a more elusive concept than it seems. There is no such thing as a definitive market rate for any job, even when comparing identically sized organizations in the same industry and location. Different market information sources for the same types of jobs produce different results because of variations in the sample, the difficulty of obtaining precise matches between jobs in the organization and jobs elsewhere (job matching), and timing (the dates on which the data is collected may differ).

This means that market rate analysis is most unlikely to produce definite information on the rate for the job. The possibly incomplete data from a number of sources, some more reliable than others, has to be interpreted to indicate what the organization should do about it. This may be expressed as a 'derived market rate', which is a sort of average of a range of pay information – a dubious notion. Data may be available for some jobs but not for others that are unique to the organization.

Market rate analysis

Market rate analysis involves the following steps:

1 Identify and define the jobs for which market rate data is required. These are benchmark jobs that are representative of different levels and occupations and can be compared with similar jobs. In conducting the survey the aim will be to 'match' these jobs as closely as possible with jobs elsewhere.

2 Identify the sources of information. These can include published surveys conducted by a pay consultancy or research organization, surveys conducted specially by the organization, 'pay clubs' (groups of employers who exchange pay information) and advertisements. Published surveys are likely to provide the most convenient source of robust information. Special surveys and pay clubs can produce useful data but they are time-consuming. More than one source should be used if possible. Advertisements are useless.

3 Collect, analyse and interpret the information. The pay data for jobs may be presented in the form of a range of pay from lowest to highest, the median rate (the midpoint in a distribution of rates of pay) and the upper and lower quartiles (the values

which, respectively, are exceeded by a quarter of the values in the distribution or below which a quarter of the values in a distribution occur). Interpreting the data may mean producing a derived market rate from the different sources.

4 Apply the information in line with a policy decision on market stance – the pay levels required to be competitive and affordable.

Job evaluation

Job evaluation is a systematic and formal process for defining the relative worth or size of jobs within an organization in order to establish internal relativities. It is carried out through either an analytical or a non-analytical scheme.

Analytical job evaluation schemes

Analytical job evaluation is based on a process of breaking down whole jobs into a number of defined elements or factors such as responsibility, decisions and the knowledge and skill required. These are assumed to be present in all the jobs to be evaluated but to different degrees. In point-factor and fully analytical matching schemes, jobs are then compared factor by factor either with a graduated scale of points attached to a set of factors or with grade or role profiles analysed under the same factor headings.

The advantages of an analytical approach are that first, evaluators have to consider each of the characteristics of the job separately before forming a conclusion about its relative value and secondly, evaluators are provided with defined yardsticks or guidelines that help to increase the objectivity and consistency of judgements. It can also provide a defence in the UK against an equal pay claim. The main analytical schemes, as described below, are point-factor rating and analytical matching.

Point-factor rating

Point-factor schemes are the most common forms of analytical job evaluation. They were used by 70 per cent of the respondents with job evaluation schemes in the e-reward 2003 job evaluation survey.

The basic methodology is to break down jobs into factors. These are the elements in a job such as the level of responsibility, knowledge and skill or decision making that represent the demands made by the job on job holders. For job evaluation purposes it is assumed that each of the factors will contribute to the value of the job and is an aspect of all the jobs to be evaluated, but to different degrees.

Each factor is divided into a hierarchy of levels, typically five or six. Definitions of these levels are produced to provide guidance on deciding the degree to which the factor applies in the job to be evaluated. A maximum points score is allocated to each factor. The scores available may vary between different factors in accordance with beliefs about their relative significance. This is termed 'explicit weighting'. If the number of levels varies between factors this means that they are implicitly weighted because the range of scores available will be greater in the factors with more levels.

The total score for a factor is divided between the levels to produce the numerical factor scale. The complete scheme consists of the factor and level definitions and the scoring system (the total score available for each factor and distributed to the factor levels). This comprises the 'factor plan'.

Jobs are 'scored' (ie allocated points) under each factor heading on the basis of the level of the factor in the job. This is done by comparing the features of the job with regard to that factor with the factor level definitions to find out which definition provides the best fit. The separate factor scores are then added together to give a total score, which indicates the relative value of each job and can be used to place the jobs in rank order or allocate them into grades in a graded pay structure that have been defined in terms of job evaluation points.

Analytical job matching

Like point-factor job evaluation, analytical job matching is based on the analysis of a number of defined factors. Profiles of roles to be evaluated that have been analysed and described in terms of job evaluation factors are compared with grade, band or level profiles that have been analysed and described in terms of the same job evaluation factors. The role profiles are then 'matched' with the range of grade or level profiles to establish the best fit and thus grade the job.

Analytical matching can be used to grade jobs or place them in levels following the initial evaluation

of a sufficiently large sample of benchmark jobs, ie representative jobs that provide a valid basis for comparisons. This can happen in big organizations when it is believed that it is not necessary to go through the whole process of point-factor evaluation for every job, especially where 'generic' roles are concerned. It takes much less time than using a point-factor scheme and the results can be just as accurate.

A toolkit for designing an analytical job evaluation scheme is provided in Chapter 68.

Non-analytical job evaluation

Non-analytical job evaluation schemes enable whole jobs to be compared in order to place them in a grade or a rank order – they are not analysed by reference to their elements or factors. They can operate on a *job-to-job* basis in which a job is compared with another job to decide whether it should be valued more, less, or the same (ranking and 'internal benchmarking' processes). Alternatively, they may function on a *job-to-grade* basis in which judgements are made by comparing a whole job with a defined hierarchy of job grades (job classification) – this involves matching a job description to a grade description. Non-analytical schemes are simple to introduce and operate but provide no defined standards of judgement. Differences between jobs are not measured and they do not provide a defence in an equal pay case.

Base pay management

The management of base pay uses the information from market pricing and job evaluation to design and operate grade and pay structures that cater for job-based pay and allow scope for pay to progress within the structure through person-based pay.

Grade and pay structures

Grade and pay structures provide the framework for base pay management as a means of implementing an organization's pay policies. They enable the organization to determine where jobs should be placed in a hierarchy, define pay levels and the scope for pay progression, and provide the basis upon which relativities can be managed, equal pay achieved and the processes of monitoring and controlling the implementation of pay practices can take place. Grade and pay structures also enable organizations to communicate the career and pay opportunities available to employees.

Grade structures

A grade structure consists of a sequence or hierarchy of grades, bands or levels into which groups of jobs that are broadly comparable in size are placed. Narrow-graded structures tend to have 10 or more grades, broad-graded structures have six to eight grades, and broad-banded structures have fewer than six 'bands'. There may be a single structure defined by the number of grades or bands it contains; alternatively the structure may be divided into a number of career or job families consisting of groups of jobs where the essential nature and purpose of the work are similar but it is carried out at different levels.

Pay structures

A pay structure consists of pay ranges, brackets or scales that are attached to each grade, band or level in a grade structure. Pay structures are defined by the number of grades they contain and, especially in narrow- or broad-graded structures, the span or width of the pay ranges attached to each grade. 'Span' is the scope the grade provides for pay progression and is usually measured as the difference between the lowest and the highest point in the range as a percentage of the lowest point. Thus a range of £20,000 to £30,000 would have a span of 50 per cent.

Pay can progress within the grades in a narrow- or broad-graded structure on the basis of performance, contribution or time served in the grade. Broad-banded structures in theory allow more flexibility but they often contain pay zones that provide an indication of the extent to which the pay of individuals in a particular role or cluster of roles can vary around what is known as an 'anchor point' – the rate for a fully competent person in a role that is aligned to market rates. Another form of pay structure is a pay spine (found mainly in the public and voluntary sectors) consisting of a number of pay points that mark progression on the basis of time served.

Guiding principles for grade and pay structures

Grade and pay structures should:

- be appropriate to the culture, characteristics and needs of the organization and its employees;
- facilitate the management of relativities and the achievement of equity, fairness, consistency and transparency in managing gradings and pay;
- enable jobs to be graded appropriately and not be subject to grade drift (unjustified upgradings);
- be flexible enough to adapt to pressures arising from market rate changes and skill shortages;
- facilitate operational flexibility and continuous development;
- provide scope as required for rewarding performance, contribution and increases in skill and competence;
- clarify reward, lateral development and career opportunities;
- be constructed logically and clearly so that the basis upon which they operate can readily be communicated to employees;
- enable the organization to exercise control over the implementation of pay policies and budgets.

Types of grade and pay structures

The main types of grade and pay structures and their advantages and disadvantages are summarized in Table 29.1.

Criteria for choice

There is always a choice of structures, and the criteria are given in Table 29.2.

Pay progression

Pay progression takes place when base pay advances through pay ranges or brackets in a grade and pay structure, or through promotions or upgradings. The alternative is a spot rate system, which allows for

TABLE 29.1   Summary description of different grade and pay structures

Type of structure	Features	Advantages	Disadvantages
Narrow-graded	• A sequence of job grades – 10 or more • Narrow pay ranges, eg 20–40% • Progression usually linked to performance	• Clearly indicate pay relativities • Facilitate control • Easy to understand	• Create hierarchical rigidity • Prone to grade drift • Inappropriate in a delayered organization
Broad-graded	• A sequence of between 6 and 9 grades • Fairly broad pay ranges, eg 40–50% • Progression linked to contribution and may be controlled by thresholds or zones	As for narrow-graded structures but in addition: • the broader grades can be defined more clearly • better control can be exercised over grade drift	• Too much scope for pay progression • Control mechanisms can be provided but they can be difficult to manage • May be costly
Broad-banded	• A series of, often, 5 or 6 'broad' bands • Wide pay bands – typically between 50 and 80% • Progression linked to contribution and competence	• More flexible • Reward lateral development and growth in competence • Fit new style organizations	• Create unrealistic expectations of scope for pay rises • Seem to restrict scope for promotion • Difficult to understand • Equal pay problems
Career family	• Career families identified and defined • Career paths defined for each family in terms of key activities and competence requirements • Same grade and pay structure for each family	• Clarify career paths within and between families • Facilitate the achievement of equity between families and therefore equal pay • Facilitate level definitions	• Could be difficult to manage • May *appear* to be divisive if 'silos' emerge
Job family	• Separate grade and pay structures for job families containing similar jobs • Progression linked to competence and/or contribution	• Facilitate pay differentiation between market groups • Define career paths against clear criteria	• Can appear to be divisive • May inhibit lateral career development • May be difficult to maintain internal equity between job families unless underpinned by job evaluation
Pay spine	• A series of incremental pay points covering all jobs • Grades may be superimposed • Progression linked to service	• Easy to manage • Pay progression not based on managerial judgement	• No scope for differentiating rewards according to performance • May be costly as staff drift up the spine

TABLE 29.2   Grade and pay structures: criteria for choice

Type of structure	Criteria for choice: the structure may be considered more appropriate when:
Narrow-graded	• the organization is large and bureaucratic with well-defined and extended hierarchies; • pay progression is expected to occur in small but relatively frequent steps; • the culture is one in which much significance is attached to status as indicated by gradings; • when some but not too much scope for pay progression is wanted.
Broad-graded	• it is believed that if there is a relatively limited number of grades it will be possible to define and therefore differentiate them more accurately as an aid to better precision when grading jobs; • an existing narrow-graded structure is the main cause of grade drift; • it is considered that pay progression through grades can be related to contribution and that it is possible to introduce effective control mechanisms.
Broad-banded	• greater flexibility in pay determination and management is required; • it is believed that job evaluation should no longer drive grading decisions; • the focus is on rewarding people for lateral development; • the organization has been delayered.
Career family	• there are distinct families and different career paths within and between families can be identified and defined; • there is a strong emphasis on career development in the organization; • robust methods of defining competencies exist.
Job family	• there are distinct market groups that need to be rewarded differently; • the range of responsibility and the basis upon which levels exist vary between families; • it is believed that career paths need to be defined in terms of competence requirements.
Pay spine	• this is the traditional approach in public or voluntary sector organizations and it fits the culture; • it is believed to be impossible to measure different levels of contribution fairly and consistently; • ease of administration is an important consideration.

no progression and is entirely job-based. Progression through pay brackets in a person-based approach may be determined formally by means of an individual contingent pay scheme (pay for performance or contribution) or by fixed increments. Informal progression takes place when there is no contingent or incremental pay scheme and increases are not based on a systematic process.

A decision has to be made on whether an individual contingent pay scheme should be used, taking into account the arguments for and against financial rewards set out earlier in this chapter. The alternatives are to use service-related fixed increments, spot rates or some form of bonus scheme based on team or organizational performance (the latter can be offered in addition to individual or team pay).

Contingent pay

Contingent pay provides financial rewards that are related to individual, team or organizational performance or a combination of these.

For salary earners, individual contingent pay can take the form of consolidated increases to base pay that provide for pay progression, or cash bonuses (or both). The CIPD 2011 reward survey found that 90 per cent or more of the respondents provided 65.9 per cent of their employees with performance pay. Policy decisions have to be made on the rate of pay progression or the pay mix – the proportion of bonus payments to the base or consolidated rate. Research by Trevor (2011) found that the proportion for junior and middle management was 10–25 per cent of base pay in the case study companies.

Wage earners may receive unconsolidated cash payments in addition to their base pay through an incentive scheme.

Individual contingent pay for salaried employees

If a decision is made to have individual contingent pay for salaried employees, there is a choice between types of scheme. A segmented approach might be adopted, ie the schemes vary for different categories of staff. Typically, directors and senior executives may have separate schemes. The features, advantages and disadvantages and the appropriateness of individual contingent pay schemes are set out in Table 29.3.

In making the choice and then designing and managing the scheme, account should be taken of the following five criteria for effective individual contingent pay:

1 Individuals have a clear line of sight between what they do and what they will get for doing it.

2 Rewards are worth having.

3 Fair and consistent means are available for measuring or assessing performance, competence, contribution or skill.

4 People are able to influence their performance by changing their behaviour and developing their competencies and skills.

5 The reward follows as closely as possible the accomplishment that generated it.

These requirements are exacting and few schemes meet them in full. That is why contingent pay arrangements can often promise more than they deliver. Research conducted by Thompson (1992b: *ix*) led to the conclusion that:

> The benefits most often claimed for PRP (performance-related pay) are not met in practice. Firstly, PRP does not serve to motivate (even those with high performance ratings) and may do more to demotivate employees. Secondly, there was little evidence to suggest that PRP could help to retain high performers and no evidence to point to poor performers seeking to leave the organizations. Thirdly, employees are negative or broadly neutral on its impact on organizational culture even in schemes that had been in operation for three or more years. Lastly, employees are unclear whether PRP rewards fairly (neither agreeing nor disagreeing).

No research conducted since then has contradicted these findings.

Incentive pay for manual workers

Incentive schemes for manual workers consist of:

- *Payment-by-result* (PBR) schemes, which pay for output and include piece work, work measured schemes and measured day work.

- *Contingent pay schemes*, which relate pay to performance or skill (performance-related pay and skill-based pay). Increases may be consolidated or paid as lump sum bonuses.

TABLE 29.3 Summary of individual contingent pay schemes

Type of scheme	Main features	Advantages	Disadvantages	When appropriate
Performance-related pay	Increases to basic pay or bonuses are related to assessment of performance	• May motivate (but this is uncertain) • Links rewards to objectives • Meets the need to be rewarded for achievement • Delivers message that good performance is important and will be rewarded	• May *not* motivate • Relies on judgements of performance, which may be subjective • Prejudicial to teamwork • Focuses on outputs, not quality • Relies on good performance management processes • Difficult to manage well	• For people who are likely to be motivated by money • In organizations with a performance-oriented culture • When performance can be measured objectively
Competency-related pay	Pay increases are related to the level of competency	• Focus attention on need to achieve higher levels of competency • Encourages competency development • Can be integrated with other applications of competency-based HR management	• Assessment of competency levels may be difficult • Ignores outputs – danger of paying for competencies that will not be used • Relies on well-trained and committed line managers	• As part of an integrated approach to HRM where competencies are used across a number of activities • Where competency is a key factor where it may be inappropriate or hard to measure outputs • Where well-established competency frameworks exist
Contribution-related pay	Increases in pay or bonuses are related both to inputs (competency) and outputs (performance)	• Rewards people not only for what they do but how they do it	As for both PRP and competence-related pay – it may be hard to measure contribution and it is difficult to manage well	When it is believed that a well-rounded approach covering both inputs and outputs is appropriate
Skill-based pay	Increments related to the acquisition of skills	• Encourages and rewards the acquisition of skills	Can be expensive when people are paid for skills they don't use	On the shop floor or in retail organizations

● *Collective schemes*, which pay bonuses related to either team or plant performance.

Team pay

Team pay links payments to members of a formally established team to the performance of that team. The rewards are shared among the members of the team in accordance with a published formula, or on an ad hoc basis in the case of exceptional achievements. Rewards for individuals may also be influenced by assessments of their contribution to team results. Team pay can:

● encourage teamworking and cooperative behaviour;

● enhance flexible working within teams and encourage multi-skilling, clarify team goals and priorities and provide for the integration of organizational and team objectives;

● encourage less effective performers to improve in order to meet team standards;

● serve as a means of developing self-managed or self-directed teams.

But:

● The effectiveness of team pay depends on the existence of well-defined and mature teams and they may be difficult to identify and, even if they can be, do they need to be motivated by a purely financial reward?

● Team pay may seem unfair to individuals who could feel that their own efforts are unrewarded.

● Pressure to conform, which is accentuated by team pay, could result in the team maintaining its output at lowest common denominator levels – sufficient to gain what is thought collectively to be a reasonable reward but no more.

● It can be difficult to develop performance measures and methods of rating team performance that are seen to be fair – team pay formulae may well be based on arbitrary assumptions about the correct relationship between effort and reward.

● There may be pressure from employees to migrate from poorly performing teams to highly performing teams which, if allowed, could cause disruption and stigmatize the teams from which individuals transfer, or if refused, could leave dissatisfied employees in the inadequate teams, making them even worse.

For many organizations, the disadvantages outweigh the advantages.

Pay for organizational performance

Many organizations believe that their financial reward systems should extend beyond individual contingent pay, which does not recognize collective effort, or team pay, which is difficult. They believe that their system should help to enhance engagement and commitment and convince employees that they have a stake in the business as well as providing them with additional pay. The response to this belief is to offer financial rewards that are related to business or organizational performance (sometimes known as 'company-wide' or 'factory-wide' schemes).

The three types of formal business performance schemes are:

1 *Profit-sharing* – the payment of sums in cash or shares related to the profits of the business; 13.7 per cent of the respondents to the 2011 CIPD reward survey had such schemes.

2 *Share schemes* – employees are given the opportunity to take out share options or participate in a save-as-you-earn scheme of a share incentive plan; 33.3 per cent of the respondents to the 2011 CIPD survey had such schemes.

3 *Gain-sharing* – the payment of cash sums to employees related to the financial gains made by the company because of its improved performance; only 3.6 per cent of the CIPD 2011 respondents had such schemes.

Recognition schemes

Recognition schemes as part of a total reward package enable appreciation to be shown to individuals for their achievements either informally on a day-to day basis or through formal recognition arrangements. They can take place quietly between managers and individuals in their teams or be visible celebrations of success.

A recognition scheme can be formal and organization-wide, providing scope to recognize achievements by gifts or treats or by public applause. Typically, the awards are non-financial but some organizations provide cash awards. Importantly, recognition is also given less formally when managers simply say, 'Well done', 'Thank you', or 'Congratulations' face-to-face or in a brief note of appreciation.

Employee benefits

Employee benefits consist of arrangements made by employers for their employees that enhance the latter's wellbeing. They are provided in addition to pay and form important parts of the total reward package. As part of total remuneration, they may be deferred or contingent like a pension scheme, insurance cover or sick pay, or they may be immediate like a company car or a loan. Employee benefits also include holidays and leave arrangements, which are not strictly remuneration. Benefits are sometimes referred to dismissively as 'perks' (perquisites) or 'fringe benefits', but when they cater for personal security or personal needs they could hardly be described as 'fringe'. Flexible benefit schemes give employees a choice, within limits, of the type or scale of benefits offered to them by their employers.

Pension provision has undergone considerable change recently. The traditional defined benefit scheme, which provides a pension based on final salary, is disappearing rapidly (too costly) and is being replaced by defined contribution schemes where the retirement pension is whatever annual payment can be purchased with the money accumulated in the fund for a member (cheaper).

Employee benefits are a costly part of the remuneration package. They can amount to one third or more of basic pay costs and therefore have to be planned and managed with care.

Evaluating reward

Reward evaluation uses information obtained from reward reviews and reward measurements to assess the level of effectiveness achieved by existing or new reward policies and practices. In essence, it is the comparison of reward outcomes with reward objectives to answer the question of how far the reward system has achieved its purpose. The aims are to:

- find out how well established reward policies and practices are working and identify any problems;
- establish whether reward innovations are functioning as planned and achieving the objectives set for them;
- ensure that value for money is obtained from the different parts of the reward system;
- provide the evidence required to indicate what needs to be done to improve reward effectiveness.

A failure to evaluate pay and reward practices is a critical blind-spot for many of those involved in reward management. This was noted by Pfeffer (1998: 213), who wrote that: 'Little evidence demonstrates the efficacy of rewards, although much evidence indicates that rewards and their design loom large in management attention.' Gerhart and Rynes (2003: 1) commented that:

> Compensation is a complex and often confusing topic. Although compensation costs comprise, on average, 65 per cent to 70 per cent of total costs in the US economy and are likewise substantial elsewhere, most managers are not sure of the likely consequences of spending either more, or less on employees or of paying employees in different ways.

Reward evaluation is a necessary way of improving reward management effectiveness. It is a way of thinking based upon obtaining answers to the following questions posed by Armstrong et al (2010: 101):

- What are we trying to do here, what's important to this organization, how do we measure that?

- How are current reward practices helping or hindering what we are trying to do and what evidence do we have of this?

- How might reward changes improve the delivery of the desired outcomes?

- How can we best implement improvements and how can we show ourselves that they are working?

Use of an evidence-based management approach

An evidence-based management approach is required to provide a systematic basis for evaluating reward. As Pfeffer (1998: 196) pointed out: 'Thinking about pay ought to be based on logic and evidence, not on belief or ideology.' Rousseau (2006: 256) explained that: 'Evidence-based management means translating principles based on best evidence into organizational practices.'

Research conducted by Armstrong *et al* (2011) concluded that there are a number of common components to a process of evidence-based reward management, namely: setting strategic objectives,

conducting reward reviews of current policies and practices, measuring reward effectiveness, and using the data generated by reviews and measurements to evaluate reward outcomes as a basis for introducing new or improved reward practices. But these are applied in all sorts of ways; sometimes sequentially, sometimes not, depending on the needs of the situation. A model of how the components function in practice is shown in Figure 29.4. It appears to describe a sequential progress in the form of a continuous cycle from setting objectives and success criteria, through review, measurement, evaluation, and development activities to implementation and further review. This can happen in some circumstances, for example a review by outside consultants. But,

FIGURE 29.4   A model of the interrelationships between the components of evidence-based reward management

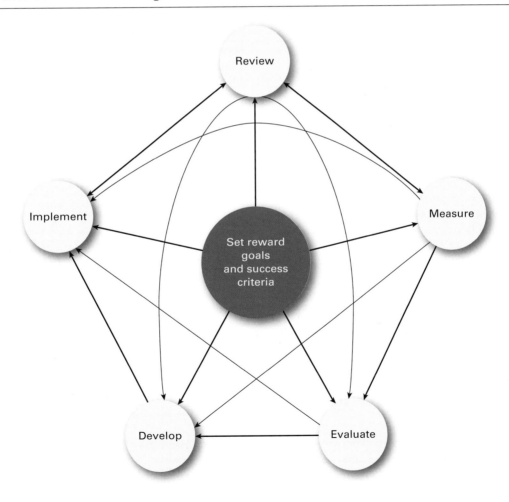

as was established from the research case studies, in practice the components are not necessarily specified or managed in an orderly sequence. They are closely interlinked and they may overlap. Objective setting, review and measurement affect all the other components, as does evaluation. They can take place at any time (or all at once) and they all directly influence the ultimate activities of development and implementation.

Advice on reward evaluation

The following advice on reward evaluation was given by a senior reward practitioner in one of the Armstrong *et al* (2011) case study companies:

- The best starting point before setting any targets or measuring anything is to decide what the organization wants to achieve.

- Once this has been decided, you should use as much data as you can and benchmark this against the market, before deciding where the company should be positioned.

- Take care when interpreting data such as high staff satisfaction scores and other perception-related measures – they could simply be reflecting generous, rather than effective, rewards.

- In some cases evaluation is not necessary – it is plain to see when certain elements of the reward system are working or not.

- It is your job to place evidence in context and try to interpret what is really happening and why.

- Some of the reward evaluation software packages available, although clever, tend only to use quantitative measures, so they don't take account of some of the other factors that might be at work. This is where you come in – to interpret and make sense of the grey as well as black and white areas.

Administering reward management

The administration of reward management is conducted through three main activities: base pay

management through compa-ratio analysis, conducting general pay reviews and conducting individual pay reviews.

Base pay management through compa-ratio analysis

A compa-ratio (short for 'comparative ratio') measures the relationship in a graded pay structure between actual and policy rates of pay as a percentage. The policy value used is the mid-point or reference point in a pay range, which represents the 'target rate' for a fully competent individual in any job in the grade. This point is aligned with market rates in accordance with the organization's market stance.

Compa-ratios can be used to define the extent to which pay policy is achieved (the relationship between the policy and actual rates of pay). The analysis of compa-ratios indicates what action may have to be taken to slow down or accelerate increases if compa-ratios are too high or too low compared with the policy level. This is sometimes called 'mid-point management'. Compa-ratios can also be used to measure where an individual is placed in a pay range and therefore provide information on the size of pay increases when a pay matrix is used, as described later in this chapter. Compa-ratios are calculated as follows:

$$\frac{\text{actual rate of pay}}{\text{mid or reference point of range}} \times 100$$

A compa-ratio of 100 per cent means that actual pay and policy pay are the same. Compa-ratios higher or lower than 100 per cent mean that, respectively, pay is above or below the policy target rate. For example, if the target (policy) rate in a range were £20,000 and the average pay of all the individuals in the grade were £18,000, the compa-ratio would be 90 per cent. Compa-ratios establish differences between policy and practice. The reasons for such differences need to be established.

General pay reviews

General reviews take place when employees are given an increase in response to general market rate movements, increases in the cost of living, or union negotiations. General reviews are often combined with individual reviews, but employees are usually informed of both the general and individual components of any increase they receive. Alternatively the general review may be conducted separately to enable better control to be achieved over costs and to focus employees' attention on the performance-related aspect of their remuneration.

Some organizations have completely abandoned the use of across-the-board reviews. They argue that the decision on what people should be paid should be an individual matter, taking into account the personal contribution people are making and their 'market worth' – how they as individuals are valued in the market place. This enables the organization to adopt a more flexible approach to allocating pay increases in accordance with the perceived value of individuals to the organization.

The steps required to conduct a general review are:

1   Decide on the budget.

2   Analyse data on pay settlements made by comparable organizations and rates of inflation.

3   Conduct negotiations with trade unions as required.

4   Calculate costs.

5   Adjust the pay structure – by either increasing the pay brackets of each grade by the percentage general increase or by increasing pay reference points by the overall percentage and applying different increases to the upper or lower limits of the bracket, thus altering the shape of the structure.

6   Inform employees.

Individual pay reviews

Individual pay reviews determine contingent pay increases or bonuses. The e-reward 2009 survey of contribution pay found that the average size of the contingent pay awards made by respondents was 3.3 per cent. Individual awards may be based on ratings, an overall assessment that does not depend on ratings, or ranking, as discussed below.

Individual pay reviews based on ratings

Managers propose increases on the basis of their performance management ratings within a given pay review budget and in accordance with pay review guidelines. Forty-two per cent of the respondents to the CIPD performance management survey (Armstrong and Baron, 2004) used ratings to inform contingent pay decisions.

There is a choice of methods. The simplest way is to have a direct link between the rating and the pay increase, for example:

Rating	% Increase
A	6
B	4
C	3
D	2
E	0

A more sophisticated approach is to use a pay matrix, as illustrated in Table 29.4. This indicates the percentage increase payable for different performance ratings according to the position of the individual's pay in the pay range. This is sometimes referred to as an individual 'compa-ratio' and expresses pay as a percentage of the mid-point in a range. A compa-ratio of 100 per cent means that the salary would be at the mid-point.

Many people argue that linking performance management too explicitly to pay prejudices the essential developmental nature of performance management. However, realistically, it is accepted that decisions on performance-related or contribution-related increases have to be based on some form of assessment. One solution is to 'decouple' performance management and the pay review by holding them several months apart; 45 per cent of the respondents to the CIPD survey (Armstrong and Baron, 2004) separated performance management reviews from pay reviews (43 per cent of the respondents to the e-reward 2005 survey separated the review). There is still a read-across but it is not so immediate. Some try to do without formulaic approaches (ratings and pay matrices) altogether, although it is impossible to dissociate contingent pay completely from some form of assessment.

TABLE 29.4   A pay matrix

Rating	Percentage pay increase according to performance rating and position in pay range (compa-ratio)			
	Position in pay range			
	80–90%	91–100%	101–110%	111–120%
Excellent	12%	10%	8%	6%
Very effective	10%	8%	6%	4%
Effective	6%	4%	3%	0
Developing	4%	3%	0	0
Ineligible	0	0	0	0

Guidelines to managers on conducting individual pay reviews

Guidelines have to be issued to managers on how they should conduct reviews. The guidelines will stipulate that they must keep within their budgets and may indicate the maximum and minimum increases that can be awarded, with an indication of how awards could be distributed, eg, when the budget is 4 per cent overall, it might be suggested that a 3 per cent increase should be given to the majority of their staff and the others given higher or lower increases as long as the total percentage increase does not exceed the budget. Managers in some companies are instructed that they must follow a forced pattern of distribution (a forced choice system), but only 8 per cent of the respondents to the CIPD survey (Armstrong and Baron, 2004) used this method.

Steps required

The steps required to conduct an individual pay review are:

1 Agree budget.

2 Prepare and issue guidelines on the size, range and distribution of awards and on methods of conducting the review.

3 Provide advice and support.

4 Review proposals against budget and guidelines and agree modifications to them if necessary.

5 Summarize and cost proposals and obtain approval.

6 Update payroll.

7 Inform employees.

CASE STUDIES

Kent County Council: successful reward

The Council attributes success in its reward policies to a strong and united political direction from the top; a long-term consistency of purpose, but with the appropriate phasing of changes and with adaptation to local circumstances; and a high involvement approach.

McDonald's: demonstrating reward effectiveness

McDonald's is a company with a strong culture of measurement and has built its own people-profit chain methodology to produce impressive evidence that demonstrates how rewards can enhance employee engagement and thereby business performance. The operational and cost focus in the business means that reward arrangements are reviewed regularly and changed if they are not found to be delivering. But the subtler processes of consultation and change management are equally vital in maintaining and strengthening reward effectiveness.

The NSPCC: approaches to achieving reward effectiveness

The experience of the NSPCC was that while measures of organizational and reward effectiveness may differ, the delivery of them is every bit as critical, if not more so, in voluntary organizations. It also shows that limited resources need not be a barrier to assessing and demonstrating effectiveness. Establishing links to the core purpose of the organization was the major driver behind the extensive research undertaken into effectiveness. The culture of the organization and its values were important considerations as was ensuring that the values of the people in the organization were aligned to them.

Changing the pay structure at Marks & Spencer

Prior to 2005 there were 429 different rates for customer assistants, ranging from £4.94 an hour for new staff, up to £10 an hour for long-serving employees. In May 2005, M&S announced it would reduce these to four standard rates for customer assistants (with regional variations), which would be tied to specific roles – trainee and qualified, which already existed, and two newly created positions: coach and section coordinator. The move was designed to give staff better career progression opportunities.

Key learning points: The practice of reward management (1)

Reward management defined

Reward management is concerned with the strategies, policies and processes required to ensure that the value of people and the contribution they make to achieving organizational, departmental and team goals is recognized and rewarded.

The reward system

A reward system consists of the interrelated processes and practices that combine to ensure reward management is carried out effectively to the benefit of the organization and the people who work there.

Total rewards

The concept of total rewards describes an approach to reward management that emphasizes the need to consider all aspects of the work experience of value to employees, not just a few such as pay and employee benefits.

Financial rewards

Financial rewards comprise all rewards that have a monetary value and add up to total remuneration – base pay, pay contingent on performance, contribution, competency or skill, pay related to service, financial recognition schemes, and benefits such as pensions, sick pay and health insurance.

Non-financial rewards

Non-financial rewards are those which focus on the needs people have to varying degrees for recognition, achievement, responsibility, autonomy, influence and personal growth.

Pay determination

Pay determination is the process of deciding on the level of pay for jobs or people. The two aims of pay determination, which frequently conflict, are, 1) to be externally competitive in order to attract, engage and retain the people required by the organization, and 2) to be internally equitable in the sense that rates of pay correctly reflect the relativities between jobs.

Market pricing

Market pricing is the process of making decisions on pay structures and individual rates of pay and obtaining information on market rates (market rate analysis). Market rate analysis may be associated with formal job evaluation. The latter establishes internal relativities and the grade structure, and market pricing is used to develop the pay structure – the pay ranges attached to grades. Information on market rates may lead to the introduction of market supplements for individual jobs or the creation of separate pay structures (market groups) to cater for particular market rate pressures.

Job evaluation

Job evaluation is a systematic and formal process for defining the relative worth or size of jobs within an organization in order to establish internal relativities. It is carried out through either an analytical or a non-analytical scheme. *Analytical* job evaluation is based on a process of breaking down whole jobs into a number of defined elements or factors such as responsibility, decisions and the knowledge and skill required. *Non-analytical* job evaluation schemes enable whole jobs to be compared in order to place them in a grade or a rank order – they are not analysed by reference to their elements or factors.

Base pay management

The management of base pay uses the information from market pricing and job evaluation to design and operate grade and pay structures that cater for job-based pay and allow scope for pay to progress within the structure through person-based pay.

Key learning points: The practice of reward management (2)

Grade and pay structures

Grade and pay structures provide a framework within which an organization's pay policies can be implemented. They enable the organization to determine where jobs should be placed in a hierarchy, define pay levels and the scope for pay progression, and provide the basis upon which relativities can be managed, equal pay achieved and the processes of monitoring and controlling the implementation of pay practices can take place.

A grade structure consists of a sequence or hierarchy of grades, bands or levels into which groups of jobs that are broadly comparable in size are placed. A grade structure becomes a pay structure when pay ranges, brackets or scales are attached to each grade, band or level. The main types of grade and pay structures are narrow-graded, broad-graded, broad-banded and pay spines.

Pay progression

Pay progression takes place when base pay advances through pay ranges or brackets in a grade and pay structure, or through promotions or upgradings.

Contingent pay

Contingent pay can be related to individual, team or organizational performance or a combination of these.

For salary earners, individual contingent pay can take the form of consolidated increases to base pay that provide for pay progression, or cash bonuses (or both). Wage earners may receive unconsolidated cash payments in addition to their base pay through an incentive scheme.

Team pay

Team pay links payments to members of a formally established team to the performance of that team.

This is a popular form of reward – the 2009 e-reward reward survey found that 59 per cent of respondents had such schemes.

Pay for organizational performance

The provision of financial rewards that are related to business or organizational performance (sometimes known as 'company-wide' or 'factory-wide' schemes). They include profit-sharing, share schemes and gain-sharing.

Recognition schemes

Recognition schemes as part of a total reward package enable appreciation to be shown to individuals for their achievements, informally on a day-to day basis or through formal recognition arrangements.

Employee benefits

Employee benefits consist of arrangements made by employers for their employees that enhance the latter's wellbeing. They are provided in addition to pay and form important parts of the total reward package.

Evaluating reward

Reward evaluation uses information obtained from reward reviews and reward measurements to assess the level of effectiveness achieved by existing or new reward policies and practices.

Administering reward management

The administration of reward management is conducted through three main activities: base pay management through compa-ratio analysis, conducting general pay reviews and conducting individual pay reviews.

Questions

1   What is reward management?

2   What are the main aims of reward management?

3   What is a reward system?

4   What is base pay?

5   What is contingent pay?

6   What are financial rewards?

7   What are the main arguments in favour of financial rewards?

8   What are the main arguments against financial rewards?

9   What is a total rewards approach?

10   What is market pricing?

11   What is job evaluation?

12   What are the main types of job evaluation schemes?

13   What is base pay management?

14   What is a grade structure?

15   What is a pay structure?

16   What are the main types of grade and pay structures?

17   What are the guiding principles for grade and pay structures?

18   What is contingent pay?

19   What are the main types of contingent pay?

20   What are the main types of individual contingent pay schemes?

21   What is team pay?

22   What are the main schemes relating rewards to organizational performance?

23   What is evidence-based reward management?

24   What is a compa-ratio and how is it used?

25   What are the steps needed to conduct an individual pay review?

References

Armstrong, M and Baron, A (2004) *Managing Performance: Performance management in action*, London, CIPD

Armstrong, M, Brown, D and O'Reilly, P (2010) *Evidence-based Reward*, London, Kogan Page

Armstrong, M, Brown, D and O'Reilly, P (2011) Increasing the effectiveness of reward; an evidence-based approach, *Employee Relations*, **33** (2), pp 106–20

Booth, A L and Frank, J (1999) Earnings, productivity and performance related pay, *Journal of Labor Economics*, **17** (3), pp 447–63

Bowey, A and Thorpe, R (1982) *The Effects of Incentive Pay Systems*, London, Department of Employment

CIPD (2011) *Reward Management Annual Survey Report*, London, CIPD

e-reward (2003) *Survey of Job Evaluation*, Stockport, e-reward

e-reward (2005) *Survey of Performance Management Practice*, Stockport, e-reward

e-reward (2009) *Survey of Contingent Pay*, Stockport, e-reward

Gerhart, B and Rynes, S L (2003) *Compensation: Theory, evidence and strategic implications*, Thousand Oaks, CA, Sage

Ghoshal, S and Bartlett, C A (1995) Changing the role of top management: beyond structure to process, *Harvard Business Review*, January–February, pp 86–96

Gupta, N and Shaw, J D (1998) Financial incentives, *Compensation & Benefits Review*, March/April, pp 26, 28–32

Jenkins, D G, Mitra, A, Gupta, N and Shaw, J D (1998) Are financial incentives related to performance? A meta-analytic review of empirical research, *Journal of Applied Psychology*, **3**, pp 777–87

Kessler, I and Purcell, J (1992) Performance-related pay: objectives and application, *Human Resource Management Journal*, **2** (3), pp 16–33

Kohn, A (1993) Why incentive plans cannot work, *Harvard Business Review*, September–October, pp 54–63

Lazear, E P (1999) Performance pay and productivity, *American Economic Review*, 90, pp 1346–61

Marsden, D (2004) The role of performance-related pay in renegotiating the 'effort bargain': the case of the British public service, *Industrial and Labor Relations Review*, **57** (3), pp 350–70

Marsden, D and Richardson, R (1994) Performing for pay? The effects of 'merit pay' on motivation in a public service, *British Journal of Industrial Relations*, **32** (2), pp 243–61

Pfeffer, J (1998) Six dangerous myths about pay, *Harvard Business Review*, May–June, pp 109–19

Prendergast, C (1999) The provision of financial incentives in firms, *Journal of Economic Literature*, **37**, pp 7–63

Prentice, G, Burgess, S and Propper, C (2007) *Performance Pay in the Public Sector: A review of the issues and evidence*, London, Office of Manpower Economics

Rousseau, D M (2006) Is there such a thing as evidence-based management?, *Academy of Management Review*, **31** (2), pp 256–69

Thompson, M (1992a) *Pay and Performance: The employer experience*, Brighton, IMS

Thompson, M (1992b) *Pay and Performance: The employee experience*, Brighton, IMS

Thompson, M (1998) HR and the bottom line, *People Management*, 16 April, pp 38–41

Trevor, J (2011) *Can Pay be Strategic?*, Basingstoke, Palgrave Macmillan

Wright, V (1991) Performance-related pay, in (ed) E Neale, *The Performance Management Handbook*, London, Institute of Personnel Management

PART VI

Employee relations

PART VI CONTENTS

Introduction

Employee relations are concerned with managing the employment relationship and the psychological contract. They consist of the approaches and methods adopted by employers to deal with employees either collectively through their trade unions or individually. This includes providing employees with a voice and developing communications between them and management.

Employee relations cover a wider spectrum of the employment relationship than industrial relations, which are essentially about what goes on between management and trade union representatives and officials involving collective agreements, collective bargaining and disputes resolution. This wider definition recognizes the move away from collectivism towards individualism in the ways in which employees relate to their employers.

30
Strategic employee relations

KEY CONCEPTS AND TERMS

Collectivism

Employee relations

Individualism

Mutuality

Pluralist viewpoint

Union recognition

De-recognition

Employee relations climate

Industrial relations

Pay-work bargain

Single-table bargaining

LEARNING OUTCOMES

On completing this chapter you should be able to define these key concepts. You should also know about:

- The process of employee relations
- Employee relations policies
- The employee relations climate
- The basis of employee relations
- Employee relations strategies
- Managing with and without unions

Introduction

Strategic employee relations is concerned with the development of strategies designed to create a situation that satisfies the needs of the business for harmonious and productive relationships and the needs of employees to be treated justly and well. These strategies will be based on the fundamental policies an organization adopts to managing the way in which it relates to employees and their unions.

Against the background of definitions of the process and basis of employee relations, this chapter examines in turn employee relations policies and strategies, the development of a satisfactory employee relations climate and what happens when organizations work with or without unions.

The process of employee relations

Employee relations are concerned with managing and maintaining the employment relationship taking into account the implications of the notion of the psychological contract (these concepts are discussed in the next two chapters). This means dealing with employees either collectively through their trade unions or individually, handling employment practices, terms and conditions of employment and issues arising from employment, providing employees with a voice and communicating with employees.

The basis of employee relations

Employee relations are basically about how managements and employees live together and what can be done to make that work. There are two views about the relationship. The unitary viewpoint is the belief that management and employees share the same concerns and it is therefore in both their interests to cooperate. This was expressed by Walton (1985: 64) as the principle of mutuality. A similar belief is expressed in the idea of social partnership, which states that as stakeholders, the parties involved in employee relations should aim to work together to the greater good of all. Partnership agreements, as described in Chapter 33, try to put this idea into practice.

In contrast, the pluralist viewpoint is that the interests of employees will not necessarily coincide with their employers and that the unitary view is naive, unrealistic and against the interests of employees. People of this persuasion don't believe that partnership agreements can work.

The basis of employee relations can be described somewhat simplistically in terms of the pay-work bargain – the agreement made between employers and employees whereby the former undertakes to pay for the work done by the latter. According to this notion, many employers simply want employees who will do what they are told without costing too much. They want engagement and commitment but on their own terms. But employees want a 'fair day's pay for a fair day's work' and a say in their terms and conditions of employment and the way in which their work is organized. They want good working conditions, security of employment, a healthy and safe working environment and the scope to raise and resolve grievances. Conflicts of interest can arise between employers and employees on these issues, and where there are unions these conflicts are resolved by the various industrial relations procedures described in Chapter 33. Because of this, employee relations need to be managed by reference to understood and communicated policies and strategies.

Employee relations policies

Employee relations policies express the philosophy of the organization on what sort of relationships between management and employees and, where necessary, their unions, is wanted, and how the pay-work bargain should be managed. A social partnership policy will aim to develop and maintain a positive, productive, cooperative and trusting climate of employee relations.

Approaches

There are four approaches to employee relations:

1 *Adversarial*: the organization decides what it wants to do, and employees are expected to fit in. Employees only exercise power by refusing to cooperate.

2 *Traditional*: a reasonably good day-to-day working relationship but management proposes and the workforce reacts through its elected representatives, if there are any; if not, employees just accept the situation or walk.

3 *Partnership*: the organization involves employees in the drawing up and execution of organization policies, but retains the right to manage.

4 *Power sharing*: employees are involved in both day-to-day and strategic decision making.

Adversarial approaches are less common now than in the 1960s and 1970s. The traditional approach is still the most typical but more interest is being expressed in partnership. Power sharing is rare.

Objectives of employee relations policies

The objectives of employee relations policies may include maintaining good relations with employees and their unions, developing a cooperative and constructive employee relations climate, the effective management of the work process, the control of labour costs, and the development of an engaged and committed workforce. When they are articulated, policies provide guidelines for taking action on employee relations issues and can help to ensure that these issues are dealt with consistently. They provide the basis for defining management's intentions (its employee relations strategy) on key matters such as union recognition and collective bargaining.

Employee relations policy areas

The areas covered by employee relations policies are:

- *Trade union recognition* – whether trade unions should be recognized or de-recognized, which union or unions the organization would prefer to deal with, and whether or not it is desirable to recognize only one union for collective bargaining and/or employee representational purposes. The policy will have to consider the factors affecting managing with or without unions, as discussed later in this chapter.
- *Collective bargaining* – the extent to which it should be centralized or decentralized and the scope of areas to be covered by collective bargaining.
- *Employee relations procedures* – the nature and scope of procedures for redundancy, grievance handling and discipline.
- *Participation and involvement* – how far the organization is prepared to go in giving employees a voice on matters that concern them.
- *Partnership* – the extent to which a partnership approach is thought to be desirable.
- *The employment relationship* – the extent to which terms and conditions of employment should be governed by collective agreements or based on individual contracts of employment (ie collectivism *versus* individualism).

- *Harmonization* of terms and conditions of employment for staff and manual workers.
- *Working arrangements* – the degree to which management has the prerogative to determine working arrangements without reference to trade unions or employees (this includes job-based or functional flexibility).

Policy choices

The following four policy options for organizations on industrial relations and HRM have been described by Guest (1995):

1 *The new realism – a high emphasis on HRM and industrial relations.* The aim is to integrate HRM and industrial relations.

2 *Traditional collectivism – priority to industrial relations without HRM.* This involves retaining the traditional industrial relations arrangements within an unchanged industrial relations system. Management may take the view in these circumstances that it is easier to continue to operate with a union, since it provides a useful, well-established channel for communication and for the handling of grievance, discipline and safety issues.

3 *Individualized HRM – high priority to HRM with no industrial relations.* According to Guest, this approach is not very common, except in North American-owned firms. It is, he believes, essentially piecemeal and opportunistic.

4 *The black hole – no industrial relations.* This option is becoming more prevalent in organizations in which HRM is not a policy priority for managements but where they do not see that there is a compelling reason to operate within a traditional industrial relations system. When such organizations are facing a decision on whether or not to recognize a union, they are increasingly deciding not to do so.

Employee relations strategies

Employee relations strategies set out how employee relations policy objectives are to be achieved. The intentions expressed by employee relations strategies may direct the organization towards any of the following:

- Altering the forms of recognition, including single union recognition, or de-recognition.
- Changes in the form and content of procedural agreements.
- New bargaining structures, including decentralization or single-table bargaining (ie bringing all the unions in an organization together as a single bargaining unit).
- The achievement of increased levels of commitment through involvement or participation.
- Deliberately by-passing trade union representatives to communicate directly with employees.
- Increasing the extent to which management controls operations in such areas as flexibility.
- Developing a 'partnership' with trade unions, recognizing that employees are stakeholders and that it is to the advantage of both parties to work together.
- Generally improving the employee relations climate, as discussed below, to produce more harmonious and cooperative relationships.

Employee relations climate

The employee relations climate of an organization refers to the perceptions of management, employees and their representatives about the ways in which employee relations are conducted and how the various parties (managers, employees and trade unions) behave when dealing with one another. An employee relations climate may be created by the management style adopted by management (see below) or by the behaviour of the trade unions or employee representatives (cooperative, hostile, militant, etc) or by the two interacting with one another. It can be good, bad or indifferent according to perceptions about the extent to which:

- management and employees trust one another;
- management treats employees fairly and with consideration;

- management is open about its actions and intentions – employee relations policies and procedures are transparent;
- harmonious relationships are generally maintained on a day-to-day basis that result in willing cooperation rather than grudging submission;
- conflict, when it does arise, is resolved without resort to industrial action and resolution is achieved by integrative processes that result in a 'win-win' solution;
- employees are generally committed to the interests of the organization and, equally, management treat them as stakeholders whose interests should be protected as far as possible.

Management style in employee relations

The term 'management style' refers to the overall approach the management of an organization adopts to the conduct of employee relations. Purcell and Sisson (1983) identified five typical styles:

1 *Authoritarian* – employee relations are not regarded as important and people issues are not attended to unless something goes wrong.

2 *Paternalistic* – in some ways this resembles the authoritarian style but a more positive attitude to employees is adopted.

3 *Consultative* – trade unions are welcomed and employee consultation is a high priority.

4 *Constitutional* – there is a trade union presence but the management style tends to be adversarial.

5 *Opportunistic* – management style is determined by local circumstances, which in turn determine whether or not unions are recognized and the extent to which employee involvement is encouraged.

Purcell (1987: 535) defined management style as 'a guiding set of principles which delineate the boundaries and direction of acceptable management action in dealing with employees'. He described two major dimensions: 1) *individualism*, which refers to the extent to which personnel policies are focused on the rights and capabilities of individual workers, and 2) *collectivism*, which is concerned with the extent to which management policy is directed towards inhibiting or encouraging the development of collective representation by employees and allowing employees a collective voice in management decision making. According to Purcell, style is a deliberate choice linked to business policy. Organizations may choose to focus on one or both aspects. Not all firms have a distinctive preferred management style.

Improving the climate

Improvements to the climate can be attained by developing fair employee relations policies and procedures and implementing them consistently. Line managers and team leaders who are largely responsible for the day-to-day conduct of employee relations need to be educated and trained on the approaches they should adopt. Transparency should be achieved by communicating policies to employees, and commitment increased by involvement and participation processes. Problems that need to be resolved can be identified by simply talking to employees, their representatives and their trade union officials. Importantly, as discussed below, the organization can address its obligations to the employees as stakeholders and take steps to build trust.

An ethical approach

Businesses aim to achieve prosperity, growth and survival. Ideally, success should benefit all the stakeholders in the organization – owners, management, employees, customers and suppliers. However, the single-minded pursuit of business objectives can act to the detriment of employees' wellbeing and security. There may be a tension between accomplishing business purposes and the social and ethical obligations of an organization to its employees. But the chances of attaining a good climate of employee relations are slight if no attempt is made to recognize and act on an organization's obligations to its members.

An ethical approach will be based on high-commitment and high-involvement policies. The commitment will be mutual and the arrangements for involvement will be genuine, ie management will be prepared not only to listen but to act on the views expressed by employees or at least, if it cannot take action, the reasons will be explained. It will also be transparent and, although the concept of a 'job for life' may no longer be valid in many organizations, an attempt will be made to maintain full employment policies.

Managing with unions

Ideally, managements and trade unions learn to live together, often on a give-and-take basis, the presumption being that neither would benefit from a climate of hostility or by generating constant confrontation. It would be assumed in this ideal situation that mutual advantage would come from acting in accordance with the spirit as well as the letter of agreed joint regulatory procedures. However, both parties would probably adopt a realistic pluralist viewpoint. This means recognizing the inevitability of differences of opinion, even disputes, but believing that with goodwill on both sides they could be settled without resource to industrial action.

Of course, the reality in the 1960s and 1970s was often different. In certain businesses, for example in the motor and shipbuilding industries, hostility and confrontation were rife, and newspaper proprietors tended to let their unions hold sway in the interests of peace and profit. Times have changed. Trade union power has diminished in the private sector if not in the public sector. Managements in the private sector have tended to seize the initiative. They may be content to live with trade unions but they give industrial relations lower priority. They may feel that it is easier to continue to operate with a union because it provides a useful, well-established channel for communication and for the handling of grievance, discipline and safety issues. In the absence of a union, management would need to develop its own alternatives, which would be costly and difficult to operate effectively. The management perspective may be that it is safer to marginalize the unions than formally to de-recognize them and risk provoking a confrontation.

The pattern varies considerably but there is general agreement based on studies such as the Workplace Employee Relations Survey (2004) that employers have been able to assert their prerogative – 'management must manage' in the workplace.

They seem generally to have regained control over how they organize work, especially with regard to the flexible use of labour and multi-skilling. The 'status quo' clause, typical of many agreements in the engineering industry, whereby management could not change working arrangements without union agreement, has virtually disappeared in the private sector.

Four types of industrial relations managements have been identified by Purcell and Sisson (1983):

1   *Traditionalists*, who have unitary beliefs and are anti-union with forceful management.

2   *Sophisticated paternalists*, who are essentially unitary but they do not take it for granted that their employees accept the organization's objectives or automatically legitimize management decision making. They spend considerable time and resources in ensuring that their employees adopt the right approach.

3   *Sophisticated moderns*, who are either constitutionalists, where the limits of collective bargaining are codified in an agreement but management is free to take decisions on matters that are not the subject of such an agreement; or consulters, who accept collective bargaining but do not want to codify everything in a collective agreement, and instead aim to minimize the amount of joint regulation and emphasize joint consultation with 'problems' having to be solved rather than 'disputes' settled.

4   *Standard moderns*, who are pragmatic or opportunist. Trade unions are recognized, but industrial relations are seen as primarily fire-fighting and are assumed to be non-problematic unless events prove otherwise. This is by far the most typical approach.

On the whole, pluralism prevails and management and unions will inevitably disagree from time to time on employment issues. The aim is to resolve these issues before they become disputes. This means adopting a more positive partnership approach. Where collective agreements are being made, a cooperative or integrative bargaining philosophy can be adopted, based on perceptions about the mutual interdependence of management and employees and the recognition by both parties that this is a means to achieve more for themselves.

Managing without unions

Some firms, especially larger ones, manage without trade unions by adopting a union substitution policy that offers employment policies and pay packages that employees will see as an attractive alternative to trade union membership. They may focus on communications and information sharing but they will basically deal with people individually rather than collectively. Others, especially smaller firms, simply deal with employees individually, sometimes well, sometimes not, and make no attempt to provide substitute arrangements.

Implementing employee relations strategy

The implementation of employee relations strategy needs to take account of the concepts of the employment relationship and the psychological contract as considered in the next two chapters. The issues involved in implementing strategy in a unionized environment are discussed in Chapter 33, which deals with the practice of industrial relations. Chapters 34 and 35 are concerned with the implementation of employee voice and communications strategy, which are general employee relations matters that affect organizations whether or not they recognize trade unions.

Key learning points: Strategic employee relations

Strategic employee relations

Strategic employee relations is concerned with the policies an organization adopts to managing how it relates to employees and their unions and the strategies it develops to create a situation in which the needs of the business for harmonious and productive relationships and the needs of employees to be treated justly and well are satisfied.

Employee relations

Employee relations are concerned with managing and maintaining the employment relationship, taking into account the implications of the concept of the psychological contract. Employee relations are basically about how managements and employees live together and what can be done to make that work.

Employee relations policies

Employee relations policies express the philosophy of the organization on what sort of relationships between management and employees and their unions is wanted, and how the pay-work bargain should be managed. The areas covered by employee relations policies are trade union recognition, collective bargaining, employee relations procedures, participation and involvement, partnership harmonization and working arrangements.

Employee relations strategies

Employee relations strategies set out how employee relations policy objectives are to be achieved. The intentions expressed by employee relations strategies may direct the organization towards any of the following:

- Altering the forms of recognition, including single union recognition, or de-recognition.

- Changes in the form and content of procedural agreements.

- New bargaining structures, including decentralization or single-table bargaining (ie bringing all the unions in an organization together as a single bargaining unit).

- The achievement of increased levels of commitment through involvement or participation.

- Deliberately by-passing trade union representatives to communicate directly with employees.

- Increasing the extent to which management controls operations in such areas as flexibility.

- Developing a 'partnership' with trade unions, recognizing that employees are stakeholders and that it is to the advantage of both parties to work together.

- Generally improving the employee relations climate to produce more harmonious and cooperative relationships.

Employee relations climate

The employee relations climate of an organization refers to the perceptions of management, employees and their representatives about the ways in which employee relations are conducted and how the various parties (managers, employees and trade unions) behave when dealing with one another. An employee relations climate may be created by the management style adopted by management or by the behaviour of the trade unions or employee representatives (cooperative, hostile, militant, etc) or by the two interacting with one another.

Managing with unions

Ideally, managements and trade unions learn to live together, often on a give-and-take basis, the presumption being that neither would benefit from a climate of hostility or by generating constant confrontation. It would be assumed in this ideal situation that mutual advantage would come from acting in accordance with the spirit as well as the letter of agreed joint regulatory procedures. However, both parties would probably adopt a realistic pluralist viewpoint. This means recognizing the inevitability of differences of opinion, even disputes, but believing that with goodwill on both sides they could be settled without resource to industrial action.

Managing without trade unions

Some firms, especially larger ones, manage without trade unions by adopting a union substitution policy that offers employment policies and pay packages employees will see as an attractive alternative to trade union membership. They may focus on communications and information sharing but they will basically deal with people individually rather than collectively. Others, especially smaller firms, simply deal with employees individually, sometimes well, sometimes not and make no attempt to provide substitute arrangements.

Questions

1 What are strategic employee relations?

2 What are employee relations?

3 What are industrial relations?

4 What is the unitary viewpoint?

5 What is the pluralism viewpoint?

6 What are the main areas covered by employee relations policies?

7 What are employee relations strategies?

8 What areas are covered by employee relations strategies?

9 What is an employee relations climate?

References

Guest, D E (1995) Human resource management: trade unions and industrial relations, in (ed) J Storey, *Human Resource Management: A critical text*, London, Routledge

Purcell, J (1987) Mapping management styles in employee relations, *Journal of Management Studies*, **24** (5), pp 78–91

Purcell, J and Sisson, K (1983) Strategies and practice in the management of industrial relations, in (ed) G Bain, *Industrial Relations in Britain*, Oxford, Blackwell

Walton, R E (1985) From control to commitment in the workplace, *Harvard Business Review*, March–April, pp 77–84

Workplace Employee Relations Survey (2004) HMSO, Norwich

31

The employment relationship

LEARNING OUTCOMES

On completing this chapter you should be able to define these key concepts. You should also understand:

● The nature of the employment relationship

● Employment relationship contracts

● Managing the employment relationship

● Developing a high-trust organization

Introduction

The employment relationship describes how employers and employees work together. A positive employment relationship is, ideally, one in which management and employees are interdependent and both benefit from this interdependency, and where there is mutual trust. Such a relationship provides a foundation for employment and employee relations policies. This chapter describes the employment relationship, how it is managed and how a climate of trust can be created.

The nature of the employment relationship

The employment relationship can be expressed formally by what Rubery *et al* (2002) regarded as the

FIGURE 31.1   Dimensions of the employment relationship

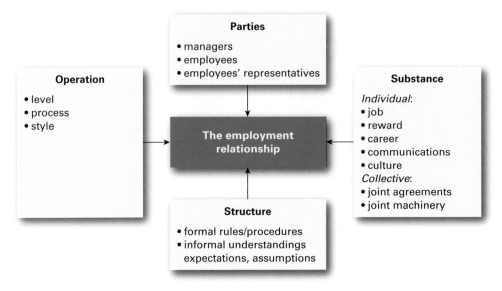

SOURCE: Kessler and Undy, 1996

cornerstone of the employment relationship, namely the contract of employment. The employment relationship can additionally be defined by such means as procedure agreements and work rules.

But the employment relationship is essentially an informal and constant process that happens whenever an employer has dealings with an employee, and vice versa. Underpinning the employment relationship is the psychological contract, which expresses certain assumptions and expectations about what managers and employees have to offer and are willing to deliver. The dimensions of the employment relationship as described by Kessler and Undy (1996) are shown in Figure 31.1.

The basis of the employment relationship

The starting point of the employment relationship is an undertaking by an employee to provide skill and effort to the employer in return for which the employer provides the employee with a salary or a wage (the pay-work bargain). Initially the relationship is founded on a legal contract. This may be a written contract,

but the absence of such a contract does not mean that no contractual relationship exists. Employers and employees still have certain implied legal rights and obligations. The employer's obligations include the duty to pay salary or wages, provide a safe workplace, to act in good faith towards the employee and not to act in such a way as to undermine the trust and confidence of the employment relationship. The employee has corresponding obligations, which include obedience, competence, honesty and loyalty. As Marsden (2007: 1263) observed:

> At the heart of the employment relationship lies a 'zone of acceptance' within which employees agree to let management direct their labour. This may relate to the range of tasks that employees are willing to undertake at management's direction, but it may also include the priority to be accorded to different types of work, and the willingness to vary working time according to management's requirements. Depending on how large this zone is, and how its boundaries are drawn, it provides organizations with varying degrees of flexibility to respond to changing production and market requirements.

Marsden and Canibano (2010) referred to this as the 'frontier of control'.

The employment relationship exists at different levels in the organization (management to employees generally, and managers to individual employees and their representatives or groups of people). The operation of the relationship will also be affected by processes such as communications and consultation, and by the management style prevailing throughout the organization or adopted by individual managers.

An important point to remember about the employment relationship is that, generally, it is the employer who has the power to dictate the contractual terms unless they have been fixed by collective bargaining. Individuals, except when they are in demand, have little scope to vary the terms of the contract imposed upon them by employers. Inevitably there are conflicts of interest between employers who want to control compliant and high-performing employees and the employees who want to maintain their rights to 'a fair day's pay for a fair day's work'.

Labour process theory and the employment relationship

The employment relationship is sometimes explained by labour process theory. In its original form, as defined by Braverman (1974), this stated that the application of modern management techniques in combination with mechanization and automation, secures the real subordination of labour and de-skilling of work in the office as well as the shop floor. Thompson and Harley (2007: 149) noted that: 'The notion of the workplace as contested terrain is a central motif of labour process theory.' They pointed out that what is happening is a process of 'capitalizing on humanity' rather than investing in human capital. However, they did comment that, 'In the employment relationship there will always be (actual and potential) conflict, but simultaneously there will be shared interests' (*ibid*: 156). And they suggested that, 'In an environment where employee skills and commitment are central to organizational success, it is precisely by giving more that organizations will gain more' (*ibid*: 149).

Employment relationship contracts

Two types of contracts defining the employment relationship have been distinguished by Rousseau and Wade-Benzoni (1994), namely transactional contracts and relational contracts. *Transactional contracts* are formal contracts that have well-described terms of exchange between employer and employees, often expressed financially. They contain specified performance requirements. *Relational contracts* are largely informal contracts with more abstract terms and refer to an open-ended membership of the organization. Performance requirements attached to this continuing membership are incomplete or ambiguous. There is also the psychological contract, which is implied rather than stated.

More specifically, the employment relationship is governed by express agreements between employers and employees. These consist of written contracts of employment but they may be conveyed orally at an interview or even set out in an advertisement. In addition, express terms may be included in collective agreements or works rules. The employment relationship is also affected by the terms implied by common law and statutory requirements.

Managing the employment relationship

The dynamic and often nebulous nature of the employment relationship increases the difficulty of managing it. The problem is compounded by the multiplicity of factors that influence the contract – the culture of the organization, the prevailing management style, the values (espoused and practised) of top management, the existence or non-existence of a climate of trust, day-to-day interactions between employees and line managers, and the HR policies and practices of the business.

The latter are particularly important. The nature of the employment relationship is strongly influenced by HR actions. These cover all aspects of HRM. How people are treated in such areas as recruitment, performance reviews, promotion, career development, reward, involvement and participation, grievance handling, disciplinary procedures and redundancy will be particularly important. The ways in which people are required to carry out their work (including flexibility and multi-skilling), how performance expectations are expressed and communicated, how work is organized and how people are managed will also make a significant impact on the employment relationship. HR specialists can contribute to the development of a positive and productive employment relationship in the following ways:

- during *recruitment interviews* – presenting the unfavourable as well as the favourable aspects of a job in a 'realistic job preview';

- in *induction programmes* – communicating to new starters the organization's HR policies and procedures and its core values, indicating to them the standards of performance expected in such areas as quality and customer service, and spelling out requirements for flexibility;

- by encouraging the maximum amount of *contact* between managers and team leaders and their team members to achieve mutual understanding of expectations and to provide a means of two-way communications;

- by adopting a general policy of *transparency* – ensuring that on all matters affecting them, employees know what is happening, why it is happening and the impact it will make on their employment, development and prospects.

These approaches to managing the employment relationship cover all aspects of people management. It is important to remember, however, that this is a continuous process. The effective management of the relationship means ensuring that values are upheld and that a transparent, consistent and fair approach is adopted in dealing with all aspects of employment. It is also important to remember that perhaps the best way of improving the employment relationship is to develop a high-trust organization.

High-trust organizations

A high-trust organization is one in which high levels of trust exist between employees and management.

A climate of trust is an essential ingredient in a positive employment relationship. Trust, as defined by the *Oxford English Dictionary*, is a firm belief that a person may be relied on. It has been suggested by Herriot *et al* (1988) that trust should be regarded as social capital – the fund of goodwill in any social group that enables people within it to collaborate with one another.

Developing a high-trust organization

This ideal state may seldom, if ever, be attained, but it does represent a picture of an effective organization in which, as Thompson (1998: 69) noted, trust is an outcome of good management. He also commented that a number of writers have generally concluded that trust is 'not something that can, or should, be directly managed'. He cites Sako (1994) who wrote that: 'Trust is a cultural norm which can rarely be created intentionally because attempts to create trust in a calculative manner would destroy the effective basis of trust.'

In the end trust is not to do with managing people or processes but is more about relationships and mutual support. Trust is created and maintained by managerial behaviour and by the development of better mutual understanding of expectations – employers of employees, and employees of employers.

Clearly, the sort of behaviour that is most likely to engender trust is when management is honest with people, keeps its word (delivers the deal) and practises what it preaches. Organizations that espouse core values ('people are our greatest asset') and then proceed to ignore them will be low trust organizations. More specifically, trust will be developed if management acts fairly, equitably and consistently, if a policy of transparency is implemented, if intentions and the reasons for proposals or decisions are communicated both to employees generally and to individuals, if there is full involvement in developing reward processes, and if mutual expectations are agreed through performance management.

Renewing trust

As suggested by Herriot *et al* (1988), if trust is lost, a four-step programme is required to renew it:

1   Admission by top management that it has paid insufficient attention in the past to employees' diverse needs.

2   A limited process of contracting whereby a particular transition to a different way of working for a group of employees is done in a form that takes individual needs into account.

3   Establishing 'knowledge-based' trust, which is based not on a specific transactional deal but on a developing perception of trustworthiness.

4   Achieving trust based on identification in which each party empathizes with each other's needs and therefore takes them on board themselves (although this final state is seldom reached in practice).

Key learning points: The employment relationship

The employment relationship

The employment relationship describes how employers and employees work together and relate to one another.

Basis of the employment relationship

The basis of the employment relationship is an undertaking by an employee to provide skill and effort to the employer in return for which the employer provides the employee with a salary or a wage. The employer's obligations also include the duty to provide a safe workplace, to act in good faith towards the employee and not to act in such a way as to undermine the trust and confidence of the employment relationship. The employee has corresponding obligations, which include obedience, competence, honesty and loyalty.

Employment relationship contracts

The three types of employment relationship contracts are transactional, relational and psychological.

Managing the employment relationship

The nature of the employment relationship is strongly influenced by HR actions. These cover all aspects of HRM. How people are treated in such areas as recruitment, performance reviews, promotion, career development, reward, involvement and participation, grievance handling, disciplinary procedures and redundancy will be particularly important. The ways in which people are required to carry out their work (including flexibility and multi-skilling), how performance expectations are expressed and communicated, how work is organized and how people are managed will also make a significant impact on the employment relationship.

Developing a high-trust organization

A high-trust organization exists when management is honest with people, keeps its word (delivers the deal) and practises what it preaches. Trust is created and maintained by managerial behaviour and by the development of better mutual understanding of expectations – employers of employees, and employees of employers.

Questions

1   What is the employment relationship?
2   What is the basis of the employment relationship?

3   How can the employment relationship be managed?
4   How can trust between employers and employees be developed in an organization?

References

Braverman, H (1974) *Labour and Monopoly Capital*, New York, Monthly Review Press

Herriot, P, Hirsh, W and Riley, P (1988) *Trust and Transition: Managing the employment relationship*, Chichester, Wiley

Kessler, S and Undy, R (1996) *The New Employment Relationship: Examining the psychological contract*, London, IPM

Marsden, D (2007) Individual employee voice: renegotiation and performance management in public services, *International Journal of Human Resource Management*, **18** (7), pp 1263–78

Marsden, D and Canibano, A (2010) An economic perspective on employee participation, in (eds) A Wilkinson, P J Gollan, M Marchington and D Lewins, *The Oxford Handbook of Participation in Organizations*, Oxford, Oxford University Press, pp 131–63

Rousseau, D M and Wade-Benzoni, K A (1994) Linking strategy and human resource practices: how employee and customer contracts are created, *Human Resource Management*, **33** (3), pp 463–89

Rubery, J, Earnshaw, J, Marchington, M, Cooke, F L and Vincent, S (2002) Changing organizational forms and the employment relationship, *Journal of Management Studies*, **39** (5), pp 645–72

Sako, M (1994) The informational requirement of trust in supplier relations: evidence from Japan, the UK and the USA, unpublished

Thompson, M (1998) Trust and reward, in (eds) S Perkins and St John Sandringham, *Trust, Motivation and Commitment: A reader*, Faringdon, Strategic Remuneration Research Centre, pp 66–71

Thompson, P and Harley, B (2007) HRM and the worker: labour process perspectives, in (eds) P Boxall, J Purcell and P Wright, *Oxford Handbook of Human Resource Management*, Oxford, Oxford University Press, pp 147–65

32
The psychological contract

KEY CONCEPTS AND TERMS

Employability

The psychological contract

Realistic job preview

LEARNING OUTCOMES

On completing this chapter you should be able to define these key concepts. You should also know about:

- The psychological contract defined
- The significance of the psychological contract
- The psychological contract and the employment relationship
- The problem with the psychological contract
- Developing a positive psychological contract

Introduction

The psychological contract underpins the employment relationship. This chapter defines the psychological contract, explains its significance and describes how a positive contract can be developed.

The psychological contract defined

A psychological contract is a set of unwritten expectations that exist between individual employees and their employers. As Guest (2007: 133) explained, it is concerned with: 'The perceptions of both parties to the employment relationship, organization and individual, of the reciprocal promises and obligations implied in that relationship.' A psychological contract is a system of beliefs that encompasses the actions employees believe are expected of them and what response they expect in return from their employer, and, reciprocally, the actions employers believe are expected of them and what response they expect in return from their employees.

An expanded definition was produced by Rousseau and Wade-Benzoni (1994: 464) as follows:

> Psychological contracts refer to beliefs that individuals hold regarding promises made, accepted and relied upon between themselves and another. (In the case of organizations, these parties include an employee, client, manager, and/or organization as a whole.) Because psychological contracts represent how people *interpret* promises and commitments, both parties in the same employment relationship (employer and employee) can have different views regarding specific terms.

Within organizations, as Katz and Kahn (1966) pointed out, every role is basically a set of behavioural expectations. These expectations are often implicit – they are not defined in the employment contract. Basic models of motivation such as expectancy theory (Vroom, 1964) and operant conditioning (Skinner, 1974) maintain that employees behave in ways they expect will produce positive outcomes. But they do not necessarily know what to expect.

Employees may expect to be treated fairly as human beings, to be provided with work that uses their abilities, to be rewarded equitably in accordance with their contribution, to be able to display competence, to have opportunities for further growth, to know what is required of them and to be given feedback (preferably positive) on how they are doing. Employers may expect employees to do their best on behalf of the organization – 'to put themselves out for the company' – to be fully committed to its values, to be compliant and loyal, and to enhance the image of the organization with its customers and suppliers. Sometimes these assumptions are justified – often they are not. Mutual misunderstandings can cause friction and stress and lead to recriminations and poor performance, or to a termination of the employment relationship. As Guest and Conway (1998: ix) commented, the psychological contract lacks many of the characteristics of the formal contract: 'It is not generally written down, it is somewhat blurred at the edges, and it cannot be enforced in a court or tribunal.'

The significance of the psychological contract

The concept of the psychological contract highlights the fact that employee/employer expectations take the form of unarticulated assumptions. Disappointments on the part of management as well as employees may therefore be inevitable. These disappointments can, however, be alleviated if managements appreciate that one of their key roles is to manage expectations, which means clarifying what they believe employees should achieve, the competencies they should possess and the values they should uphold. This is a matter not just of articulating and stipulating these requirements but of discussing and agreeing them with individuals and teams.

The psychological contract and the employment relationship

As described by Guest *et al* (1996), the psychological contract may provide some indication of the answers to the two fundamental employment relationship questions which individuals pose: 'What can I reasonably expect from the organization?' and, 'What should I reasonably be expected to contribute in return?' But it is unlikely that the psychological contract and therefore the employment relationship will ever be fully understood by either party.

The aspects of the employment relationship covered by the psychological contact will include, from the employees' point of view:

- how they are treated in terms of fairness, equity and consistency;
- security of employment;
- scope to demonstrate competence;

- career expectations and the opportunity to develop skills;
- involvement and influence;
- trust in the management of the organization to keep their promises.

From the employer's point of view, the psychological contract covers such aspects of the employment relationship as competence, effort, compliance, commitment and loyalty. The research conducted by Guest and Conway (2002: 22) led to the conclusion that:

> The management of the psychological contract is a core task of management and acknowledged as such by many senior HR and employment relations managers, and shows that it has a positive association with a range of outcomes within the employment relationship and is a useful way of conceptualizing that relationship.

How psychological contracts develop

Psychological contracts are not developed by means of a single transaction; they evolve over time and can be multi-faceted. There are many contract makers who exert influence over the whole duration of an employee's involvement with an organization. Spindler (1994: 326) observed that:

> Every day we create relationships by means other than formal contracts … As individuals form relationships they necessarily bring their accumulated experience and developed personalities with them. In ways unknown to them what they expect from the relationship reflects the sum total of their conscious and unconscious learning to date.

The problem with psychological contracts

The problem with psychological contracts is that employees are often unclear about what they want from the organization or what they can contribute to it. Some employers are equally unclear about what they expect from their employees.

Because of these factors, and because a psychological contract is essentially implicit, it is likely to develop in an unplanned way with unforeseen consequences. Anything that management does or is perceived as doing that affects the interests of employees will modify the psychological contract. Similarly, the actual or perceived behaviour of employees, individually or collectively, will affect an employer's concept of the contract.

Developing and maintaining a positive psychological contract

As Guest *et al* (1996: *v*) explained: 'A positive psychological contract is worth taking seriously because it is strongly linked to higher commitment to the organization, higher employee satisfaction and better employment relations. Again this reinforces the benefits of pursuing a set of progressive HRM practices.' They also emphasized the importance of a high-involvement climate and suggest in particular that HRM practices such as the provision of opportunities for learning, training and development, focus on job security, promotion and careers, minimizing status differentials, fair reward systems and comprehensive communication and involvement processes will all contribute to a positive psychological contract. The steps required to develop such a contract are:

1 Define expectations during recruitment and induction programmes.

2 Communicate and agree expectations as part of the continuing dialogue implicit in good performance management practices.

3 Adopt a policy of transparency on company policies and procedures and on management's proposals and decisions as they affect people.

4 Generally treat people as stakeholders, relying on consensus and cooperation rather than control and coercion.

On the basis of their research, Guest and Conway (2002) emphasized the importance of communications in shaping the psychological contract, especially at the recruitment and induction stage when promises and commitments can be made by employers on such matters as interesting work, learning and development opportunities, not making unreasonable demands on employees, feedback on performance, fair treatment, work–life balance, a reasonable degree of security and a safe working environment. At this stage it is advisable to provide what is called a 'realistic job preview', which means communicating to candidates any special demands that will be made on them in the job for which they are applying such as the standards they will be expected to achieve, the working conditions, the hours they may have to work, the travelling they have to do and any requirement for mobility in the UK or abroad.

Guest and Conway concluded that following the recruitment and induction stage, communications are most effective if they are personal and job-related. Top-down communications are less important. They also stressed that a positive psychological contract can only be achieved if management keeps its word – if it does not breach the contract.

Key learning points: The psychological contract

The psychological contract defined

A psychological contract is a set of unwritten expectations that exist between individual employees and their employers. It is a system of beliefs encompassing the actions employees believe are expected of them and the response they expect in return from their employer, and, reciprocally, the actions employers believe are expected of them and the response they expect in return from their employees.

The significance of the psychological contract

The concept of the psychological contract highlights the fact that employee/employer expectations take the form of unarticulated assumptions. Disappointments on the part of management as well as employees may therefore be inevitable.

The psychological contract and the employment relationship

The aspects of the employment relationship covered by the psychological contract will include, from the employees' point of view:

- how they are treated in terms of fairness, equity and consistency;
- security of employment;
- scope to demonstrate competence;
- career expectations and the opportunity to develop skills;
- involvement and influence;
- trust in the management of the organization to keep their promises.

From the employer's point of view, the psychological contract covers such aspects of the employment relationship as competence, effort, compliance, commitment and loyalty.

How psychological contracts develop

Psychological contracts are not developed by means of a single transaction; they evolve over time and can be multi-faceted.

Steps required to develop a positive psychological contract

1 Define expectations during recruitment and induction programmes.
2 Communicate and agree expectations as part of the continuing dialogue implicit in good performance management practices.
3 Adopt a policy of transparency on company policies and procedures and on management's proposals and decisions as they affect people.
4 Generally treat people as stakeholders, relying on consensus and cooperation rather than control and coercion.

Questions

1 What is the psychological contract?

2 What is the significance of the psychological contract?

3 What is the link between the psychological contract and the employment relationship?

4 How do psychological contracts develop?

5 How can a positive psychological contract be developed?

References

Guest, D (2007) HRM and the worker: Towards a new psychological contract, in (eds) P Boxall, J Purcell and P Wright, *Oxford Handbook of Human Resource Management*, Oxford, Oxford University Press, pp 128–46

Guest, D E and Conway, N (1998) *Fairness at Work and the Psychological Contract*, London, IPD

Guest, D E and Conway, N (2002) Communicating the psychological contract: an employee perspective, *Human Resource Management Journal*, 12 (2), pp 22–39

Guest, D E, Conway, N and Briner, T (1996) *The State of the Psychological Contract in Employment*, London, IPD

Katz, D and Kahn, R (1966) *The Social Psychology of Organizations*, New York, John Wiley

Rousseau, D M and Wade-Benzoni, K A (1994) Linking strategy and human resource practices: how employee and customer contracts are created, *Human Resource Management*, 33 (3), pp 463–89

Skinner, B F (1974) *About Behaviourism*, London, Cape

Spindler, G S (1994) Psychological contracts in the workplace: a lawyer's view, *Human Resource Management*, 33 (3), pp 325–33

Vroom, V (1964) *Work and Motivation*, New York, Wiley

34
Employee voice

KEY CONCEPTS AND TERMS

Employee voice

Joint consultation

Involvement

Participation

LEARNING OUTCOMES

On completing this chapter you should be able to define these key concepts. You should also know about:

- The meaning of employee voice
- Categorization of employee voice
- Levels of employee voice
- Effectiveness of employee voice
- The elements of employee voice
- Expression of employee voice
- Stages of employee voice
- Planning for voice

Introduction

The term 'employee voice' refers to the say employees have in matters of concern to them in their organization. Participation and involvement in this chapter are treated as aspects of employee voice although, as Wilkinson and Dundon (2010: 168) noted: 'Employee participation, involvement and voice are somewhat elastic terms with considerable width in the range of definitions.'

The meaning of employee voice

As defined by Boxall and Purcell (2003: 162), 'Employee voice is the term increasingly used to cover a whole variety of processes and structures which enable, and sometimes empower employees, directly and indirectly, to contribute to decision making in the firm.' They declared that employee voice was important because 'it was necessary to recognize a plurality of interests and interest groups which would need to learn to live together and resolve their differences without the use of force' (*ibid*: 164).

Employee voice describes arrangements for a two-way dialogue to take place that allows employees to influence events at work and includes the processes of involvement, participation, upward problem solving and upward communication. It covers the provision of opportunities for employees to register discontent, express complaints or grievances, and modify the power of management. Direct employee voice takes the form of contacts between management and employees without the involvement of trade unions. Union voice is expressed through representatives and can be power-based.

The elements of employee voice

The elements of employee voice are participation and involvement. *Participation* takes place when employees play a greater part in the decision-making process by being given the opportunity to influence management decisions and to contribute to the improvement of organizational performance. As Williams and Adam-Smith (2006) explain, the term 'participation' refers to arrangements that give workers some influence over organizational and workplace decisions. *Involvement* takes place when employees are able to discuss issues that affect them with management. Williams and Adam-Smith (2006) suggest that this term is most usefully applied to management initiatives that are designed to further the flow of communication at work as a means of enhancing the organizational commitment of employees.

The difference between participation and involvement was explained by Brewster *et al* (2007: 1248) as follows: 'At the most modest level involvement entails consultation, or soliciting of opinions that may or may not be acted on, rather than bargaining. In contrast, participation accords employees a genuine – clearly demarcated – input into how the firm is governed, even if this input is limited.' Wood (2010: 554) declared that:

> *Participation* takes place when employees are accorded some say in the running of the enterprise; in other words, they may make decisions which

are likely to be implemented – not merely considered – by management ... Employers may seek to *involve* employees, through regular communication and through soliciting their views on a number of issues, which, however, the employer has no obligation to act on.

Categorization of employee voice

Marchington *et al* (2001) suggested that the elements of employee voice could be categorized as representative participation and upward problem solving.

Representative participation

- *Joint consultation* – a formal mechanism that provides the means for management to consult employee representatives on matters of mutual interest.
- *Collective representation* – the role of trade unions or other forms of staff association in collective bargaining and representing the interests of individual employees and groups of employees. This includes the operation of grievance procedures.
- *Partnership schemes* – these emphasize mutual gains and tackling issues in a spirit of cooperation rather than through traditional, adversarial relationships.
- *European Works Councils* – these may be set up across European sites as required by EC legislation.

Upward problem solving

- *Upward communication*, which is any means through which employees can make representations to management about their concerns through their representatives, through established channels (consultative committees, grievance procedures, 'speak-up' programmes, etc) or informally.
- *Attitude surveys* – seeking the opinions of staff through questionnaires.

- *Suggestion schemes* – the encouragement of employees to make suggestions, often accompanied by rewards for accepted ideas.
- *Project teams* – getting groups of employees together with line managers to develop new ideas, processes, services or products or to solve problems (quality circles and improvement groups come into this category, although the former have often failed to survive as a specific method of involvement).

Expression of employee voice

The degree to which employees have a voice will vary considerably. At one end of the scale there will be unilateral management and employees will have no voice at all. At the other end, employees might have complete self-management and control as in a cooperative, although this is very rare. In between, the steps in the degree to which employees have voice, as defined by Boxall and Purcell (2003: 167), are as follows:

- little voice – information provided;
- downward – right to be told;
- some – opportunity to make suggestions;
- two-way – consulted during decision making;
- two-way plus – consulted at all stages of decision making and implementation;
- a lot – the right to delay a decision;
- power to affect outcome – the right to veto a decision;
- substantial – equality or co-determination in decision making.

Levels of employee voice

Involvement and participation take various forms at different levels in an enterprise, as described below:

- *The job level*, at which team leaders and their teams get together to communicate information about work and exchange ideas about how the work should be done. These processes are informal.

- *The management level*, where information can be shared and joint decisions made about working arrangements and conditions. There are limits. Management as a whole, and individual managers, want to retain authority to do what their function requires. Involvement does not imply anarchy, but it does require some degree of willingness on the part of management to share its decision-making powers. At this level, involvement and participation may become more formalized, through consultative committees, briefing groups or other joint bodies involving management and employees or their representatives.
- *The policy-making level*, where the direction in which the business is going is determined and total participation would imply sharing the power to make key decisions. This is seldom practiced in the UK, although there may be processes for communicating information on proposed plans (which would almost certainly not reveal proposals for acquisitions or disinvestments or anything else where commercial security is vital) and discussing the implications of those plans.
- *The ownership level*, where participation implies a share in the equity, which is not meaningful unless the workers have sufficient control through voting rights to determine the composition of the board. This is not a feature of British employee relations.

Stages of employee voice

The stages of employee voice are shown in Figure 34.1. At one end of the scale, management makes decisions unilaterally and exercises its full prerogative; at the other end, decisions are made jointly. Between these extremes there are two intermediate points. The point on this scale at which participation should or can take place at any level in an organization depends on the attitudes, willingness and enthusiasm of both management and employees. Management may be reluctant to give up too much of its authority except under pressure from the unions (which is less likely today), or from European Commission directives on worker consultation.

FIGURE 34.1   Stages of employee voice

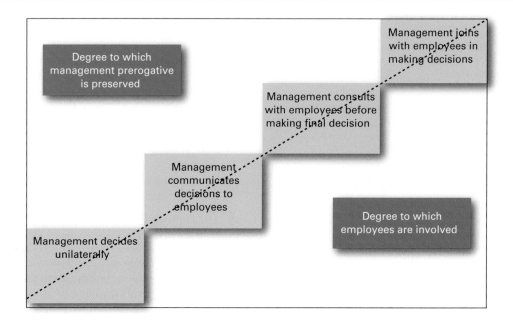

Effectiveness of employee voice

Research by Dundon and Gollan (2007: 9) showed that:

> an integrated approach to employee participation in which such participation is accompanied by related initiatives in employment security, selective employee hiring, variable compensation, extensive training and information sharing with employees is most likely to lead to higher levels of performance.

Later research by Dundon (2009) established that voice could have a positive effect in three ways:

1. valuing employee contributions;
2. improved performance;
3. improved management systems (tapping into employees' ideas).

Research conducted by Cox *et al* (2006) indicated that to be effective, employee involvement and participation mechanisms had to be embedded in the organization – well-established and part of everyday working life. Combinations of involvement and participation practices worked best. The main barriers to effective employee voice appear to be a partial lack of employee enthusiasm, absence of necessary skills to implement and manage employee voice programmes, and issues concerning line managers – such as middle managers acting as blockers through choice or ignorance. Making employee voice effective requires top management support, good leadership skills and finding the right mechanisms for involvement and participation.

Planning for voice

The forms of voice appropriate for an organization depend upon the values and attitudes of management and, if they exist, trade unions, and the current climate of employee relations. Attention has also to be paid to the EC directives on European Works Councils and Information and Consultation of Employees.

Planning should be based on a review of the existing forms of voice, which would include discussions with stakeholders (line managers, employees and trade union representatives) on the effectiveness of existing arrangements and any improvements required. In the light of these discussions, new or revised approaches can be developed, but it is necessary to brief and train those involved on the part they should play.

CASE STUDIES

Employee involvement at Harrod

Harrod UK is a manufacturer of sport equipment. It has adopted the following approach to employee involvement:

- the whole workforce is involved in business planning;

- company-wide meetings are held to plan and review corporate strategy;

- the HR processes of a company training plan and profit-related pay based on the achievement of continuous improvement measures support the consultative culture.

Involving unions in outsourcing decisions at Co-operative Financial Services

When Co-operative Financial Services (CFS) began thinking of outsourcing its life and savings administration business it decided to bring the unions in right at the start of the process. A 'pre-consultation period' enabled Amicus, the National Association of Co-operative Officials and the Transport and General Workers' Union, which between them represent an estimated 70–80 per cent of the CFS workforce, to understand what was being contemplated and to talk to shortlisted outsourcing providers before the company made its final decisions on which ones to choose.

CFS was able to bring one of the outsourcing firms together with its potential new employees to discuss terms and conditions, organizational culture and other issues that mattered to both parties.

Following the success of this process, CFS agreed with the unions a set of principles that would govern any future outsourcing deals between CFS and external partners.

Key learning points: Employee voice

The meaning of employee voice

'Employee voice is the term increasingly used to cover a whole variety of processes and structures which enable, and sometimes empower employees, directly and indirectly, to contribute to decision-making in the firm' Boxall and Purcell (2003).

The forms of employee voice

The basic elements of employee voice are participation and involvement. These take the forms of joint consultation, participation, collective representation, upward communication (consultative committees, etc), attitude surveys, suggestion schemes and project teams (quality circles or improvement groups).

Expression of employee voice

The degree to which employees have voice will vary considerably.

Effectiveness of employee involvement and participation

To be effective, employee involvement and participation mechanisms have to be embedded in the organization – well-established and part of everyday working life. Combinations of involvement and participation practices worked best, according to Cox et al (2006).

Planning for voice

Planning should be based on a review of the existing forms of voice, which would include discussions with stakeholders (line managers, employees and trade union representatives) on the effectiveness of existing arrangements and any improvements required. In the light of these discussions, new or revised approaches can be developed, but it is necessary to brief and train those involved on the part they should play.

Questions

1 What is employee voice?

2 What is participation?

3 What is involvement?

4 How can employee voice be categorized?

5 How is employee voice expressed?

6 What are the levels of employee voice?

References

Boxall, P F and Purcell, J (2003) *Strategy and Human Resource Management*, Basingstoke, Palgrave Macmillan

Brewster, C, Croucher, R, Wood, G and Brookes, M (2007) Collective and individual voice: convergence in Europe?, *International Journal of Human Resource Management*, **18** (7), pp 1246–62

Cox, A, Zagelmeyer, S and Marchington, M (2006) Embedding employee involvement and participation at work, *Human Resource Management Journal*, **16** (3), pp 250–67

Dundon, T (2009) Employee participation, in (eds) T Redman and A Wilkinson, *Contemporary Human Resource Management*, London, Pearson

Dundon, T and Gollan, P J (2007) Re-conceptualising voice in the non-union workshop, *International Journal of Human Resource Management*, **18** (7), pp 1182–98

Marchington, M, Wilkinson, A, Ackers, P and Dundon, A (2001) *Management Choice and Employee Voice*, London, CIPD

Wilkinson, A and Dundon, T (2010) Direct employee participation, in (eds) A Wilkinson, P J Gollan, M Marchington and D Lewins, *The Oxford Handbook of Participation in Organizations*, Oxford, Oxford University Press, pp 167–85

Williams, S and Adam-Smith, D (2006) *Contemporary Employment Relations: A critical introduction*, Oxford, Oxford University Press

Wood, G (2010) Participation in developing countries, in (eds) A Wilkinson, P J Gollan, M Marchington and D Lewins, *The Oxford Handbook of Participation in Organizations*, Oxford, Oxford University Press, pp 552–69

36
The practice of employee wellbeing

KEY CONCEPTS AND TERMS

Employee assistance programme (EAP)   Family-friendly policies

Flexible working   Flexitime

Quality of working life   Work environment

Work–life balance

LEARNING OUTCOMES

On completing this chapter you should be able to define these key concepts. You should also know about:

- Reasons for concern with employee wellbeing
- The significance of the work environment
- Managerial behaviour and wellbeing
- The achievement of work–life balance
- Managing stress
- Sexual harassment
- Bullying
- Services for individuals
- Group employee services

Introduction

For the reasons given below, employers need to be concerned with the wellbeing of their employees. The practice of employee wellbeing as examined in this chapter deals with creating a satisfactory work environment, managing stress, attending to work–life balance issues, dealing with sexual harassment and bullying problems, providing services for individuals including employee assistance programmes, and providing group services such as restaurants and social/sporting facilities.

Reasons for concern

The reasons for being concerned about employee wellbeing are as follows:

- Employers have a duty of care and this means adopting a socially responsible approach to looking after their people.
- Employers are responsible for creating a good work environment not only because it is their duty to do so but also as part of the total reward system.
- It is in the interests of employers to do so because this will increase the likelihood of their employees being committed to the organization and help to establish it as a 'best place to work'.

The work environment

The work environment consists of the system of work, the design of jobs, working conditions and the ways in which people are treated at work by their managers and co-workers. Wellbeing is achieved when account is taken in designing the work system and the jobs in it of the needs of the people concerned. Working conditions need to meet health and safety requirements. The way people are treated is a matter of managerial behaviour, achieving work–life balance and dealing with issues such as stress, harassment and bullying.

Managerial behaviour

Lawler (2003) suggests that what managers have to do is 'treat people right'. This means recognizing them as individuals with different needs and wants, rewarding their achievements, helping them to develop and treating them with consideration as human beings.

Work–life balance

Work–life balance employment practices are concerned with providing scope for employees to balance what they do at work with the responsibilities and interests they have outside work and so reconcile the competing claims of work and home by meeting their own needs as well as those of their employers. The term 'work–life balance' has largely replaced 'family-friendly policy'. As Kodz *et al* (2002) explain, the principle of work–life balance is that: 'There should be a balance between an individual's work and their life outside work, and that this balance should be healthy.'

The concept of work–life balance is about the achievement by employees of a satisfactory equilibrium between work and non-work activities (eg parental responsibilities and wider caring duties, as well as other activities and interests). Practical day-to-day business and related needs should be considered when organizations set about selecting the range of work–life options that should be made available to staff, whether on a collective basis (eg flexible hours) or on an individual level (eg allowing someone to work only during term time). Individual requests for a particular working arrangement generally need to be considered on a case-by-case basis, but it is important for there to be a culture that does not discourage employees from making such requests. In addition to fearing the reaction of line managers, the risk of career-damage is a common reason for poor take-up of work–life balance arrangements. Line management will need to be convinced that work–life balance measures are important and pay off in terms of increased engagement.

Work–life balance can be enhanced by what are sometimes called 'family-friendly' policies that facilitate flexible working. This covers homeworking, part-time working, compressed working weeks, annualized hours, job sharing, term-time only working and 'flexitime' (an arrangement for providing flexible hours in which employees are contracted to work for a weekly or monthly number of hours; within limits, they may vary their start or finish times as long as they work the hours required during the defined period). It can also involve special leave schemes that provide employees with the freedom to respond to a domestic crisis or to take a career break without jeopardizing their employment status.

Work–life balance policies can lower absence and help to tackle the low morale and high degrees of stress that can lead to retention problems as employees tire of juggling work and life responsibilities. The research conducted by the Institute for Employment Studies (Kodz *et al*, 2002) identified employees who were staying longer with their firms because of access to flexible working arrangements.

Managing stress

There are four main reasons why organizations should be concerned about stress and do something about it. First, they should act in a socially responsible way to provide a good quality of working life; secondly, because excessive stress causes illness; thirdly, because it can result in inability to cope with the demands of the job which, of course, creates more stress; and finally, because excessive stress can reduce employee effectiveness and therefore organizational performance. The ways in which stress can be managed by an organization include the following.

Ways of managing stress

- *Job design* – clarifying roles, reducing the danger of role ambiguity and conflict and giving people more autonomy within a defined structure to manage their responsibilities.

- *Targets and performance standards* – setting reasonable and achievable targets that may stretch people but do not place impossible burdens on them.

- *Job placement* – taking care to place people in jobs that are within their capabilities.

- *Career development* – planning careers and promoting staff in accordance with their capabilities, taking care not to over- or under-promote.

- *Performance management processes,* which allow a dialogue to take place between managers and individuals about the latter's work problems and ambitions.

- *Counselling* – giving individuals the opportunity to talk about their problems with a member of the HR department, or through an employee assistance programme, as described later in this chapter.

- *Anti-bullying campaigns* – bullying at work is a major cause of stress.

- *Management training* in what managers can do to alleviate their own stress and reduce it in others.

Sexual harassment

Sadly, sexual harassment has always been a feature of life at work. Perhaps it is not always quite as blatant today as it has been in the past, but it is still there, in more or less subtle forms, and it is just as unpleasant. People subject to sexual harassment can take legal action, but it must be the policy of the organization to make it clear that it will not be tolerated and this policy should be backed up by procedures and practices for dealing with harassment.

Problems of dealing with harassment

There are three problems in dealing with harassment. First, it can be difficult to make a clear-cut case. An accusation of harassment can be hard to prove unless there are witnesses, and those who indulge in this practice usually take care to carry it out on a one-to-one basis. In this situation, it may be a case of one person's word against another's. The harasser, almost inevitably a man, resorts to two defences: one, that it did not take place ('it was all in her mind'); and two, that if anything did take place it was provoked by the behaviour of the female. When this happens, whoever deals with the case has to exercise judgement and attempt, difficult though it may be, to remove any prejudice in favour of the word of the man, the woman, the boss or the subordinate.

The second problem is that victims of sexual harassment are often unwilling to take action and in practice seldom do so. This is because of the actual or perceived difficulty of proving their case. But they may also feel that they will not get a fair hearing and are worried about the effect making such accusations will have on how they are treated by their boss or their colleagues in the future, whether or not they have substantiated their accusation.

The third, and perhaps the most deep-rooted and difficult problem is that sexual harassment may be part of the culture of the organization – 'the way we do things around here'; a norm, practised at all levels.

Solutions

There are no easy solutions to these problems. It may be very hard to eradicate sexual harassment completely. But the effort must be made, along the following lines.

Bullying

Bullying is a form of harassment and can be very unpleasant. It is perhaps one of the most difficult aspects of employee relationships to control. Like sexual harassment, it can be hard to prove that bullying has taken place and employees may be reluctant to complain about a bullying boss, simply because he or she *is* a bully. But this does not mean that an organization can ignore the problem. A policy should be published stating that bullying is unacceptable behaviour. People who feel that they are being bullied should have the right to discuss the problem with someone in the HR department or a trained counsellor. Bullies should not be punished automatically. They should initially be helped to acknowledge the impact of their behaviours, and to

---

Dealing with sexual harassment

1   Issue a clear statement by the chief executive that sexual harassment will not be tolerated.

2   Back up the statement with a policy directive that spells out in more detail that the organization deplores it, why it is not acceptable and what people who believe they are being subjected to harassment can do about it.

3   Reinforce the policy statement by behaviour at senior level that demonstrates that it is not merely words but that these exhortations have meaning.

4   Ensure that the sexual harassment policy is stated clearly in induction courses and is conveyed to everyone on promotion. Reinforce this message by regular reminders.

5   Make arrangements for employees subjected to sexual harassment to seek advice, support and counselling without any obligation to take a complaint forward. They could talk informally with someone in HR. Alternatively, a counsellor (possibly engaged as part of an employee assistance programme) can usefully offer guidance on harassment problems; assist in resolving them informally by seeking, with the agreement of the complainant, a confidential and voluntary interview with the person complained against to achieve a solution without recourse to a formal disciplinary procedure; assist in submitting a complaint if the employee wishes to raise it formally; and counselling the parties on their future conduct.

6   Create a special procedure for hearing complaints about sexual harassment. The normal procedure may not be suitable because the harasser could be the employee's line manager.

7   The procedure should provide for employees to bring their complaint to someone of their own sex, should they so choose.

8   Handle complaints about harassment with sensitivity and due respect for the rights of both the complainant and the accused. Ensure that hearings are conducted fairly and both parties are given an equal opportunity to put their case.

9   Where sexual harassment has taken place, crack down on it. It should be stated in the policy that it is regarded as gross misconduct and, if it is proved, makes the individual liable to instant dismissal. Less severe penalties may be reserved for minor cases, but there should always be a warning that repetition will result in dismissal.

10 Ensure that everyone is aware that the organization does take action when required to punish those who indulge in sexual harassment.

11 Provide training to line managers and team leaders to ensure that the policy is properly implemented and to make them aware of their direct responsibility to prevent harassment taking place and to take action if it does.

change. Punishment should be reserved for those who persist in spite of this guidance.

Services for individuals

Services may be provided for individuals to help them deal with their problems. This may involve counselling or personal case work where the aim is, as far as possible, to get individuals to help themselves. The areas where counselling and other forms of help may be provided are:

- *Sickness* – the provision of help and advice to employees absent from work for long periods due to illness; this may include sick visits.

- *Bereavement* – advice on how to cope with the death of a partner or close relative.

- *Domestic problems* – normally they should not be the concern of the employer, but if someone is very distressed, help can be offered through a counselling service.

- *Retirement* – advice can be made available to employees who are about to retire to prepare them for their new circumstances; continued counselling and visiting services may be provided for retired employees.

Counselling is a skilled business, and is best carried out by trained people. This is where employee assistance programmes (EAPs) can be useful. EAP services are provided by external agencies that enable employees to access counselling through a phone service, although face-to-face counselling may also be offered. Employers can refer employees to the service, which is confidential between the agency and the individual.

CASE STUDY

B&Q's employee assistance programme

The aims of the B&Q employee assistance programme are to:

- Support employees of all ages and backgrounds through the full spectrum of life experiences by offering advice, information, practical help and emotional support free of charge and in confidence.

- Support carers of the chronically sick, disabled or elderly by offering advice and information. Locating care options and community resources.

- Save time for working parents by helping them find and arrange good quality, affordable and reliable care arrangements for children of all ages.

- Support parents through a wide range of parenting issues including understanding and choosing education options and understanding and monitoring behaviour of children.

- Reduce unplanned absence by encouraging employees with personal, practical, emotional and financial problems to seek early help and advice.

- Offer information and support to managers and HR staff with their personal issues, and issues facing their staff.

- Raise employee morale and commitment by showing the caring face of the employer.

- Improve customer service and productivity by saving employees' time and solving and avoiding work–life conflicts.

Group employee services

Group employee services mainly consist of subsidized restaurants, sports and social clubs and child care facilities.

Restaurant facilities are desirable in any large establishment where local facilities are limited. Sports or social clubs should not be laid on because they are 'good for morale' – there is no evidence that they are. They should only be provided if there is a real need for them arising from a lack of local facilities. In the latter case the facilities should be shared with the local community. Child care facilities are one of the most popular forms of group services if they fill a need that cannot be met easily elsewhere.

Key learning points: The practice of employee wellbeing

Reasons for concern with wellbeing

Employers have a duty of care and this means adopting a socially responsible approach to looking after their people.

Employers are responsible for creating a good work environment not only because it is their duty to do so but also as part of the total reward system. It is in the interests of employers to do so because this will increase the likelihood of their employees being committed to the organization and help to establish it as a 'best place to work'.

The significance of the work environment

The work environment consists of the system of work, the design of jobs, working conditions and the ways in which people are treated at work by their managers and co-workers. Wellbeing is achieved when account is taken in designing the work system and the jobs in it of the needs of the people concerned. Working conditions need to meet health and safety requirements. The way people are treated is a matter of managerial behaviour, achieving work–life balance and dealing with issues such as stress, harassment and bullying.

The achievement of work–life balance

Flexible working is the most practical solution to establishing an effective work–life balance. This covers flexitime, homeworking, part-time working, compressed working weeks, annualized hours, job sharing and term-time only working. It also refers to special leave schemes, which provide employees with the freedom to respond to a domestic crisis or to take a career break without jeopardizing their employment status.

Managing stress

Employers have the social responsibility to provide a good quality of working life. Stress can result in inability to cope with the demands of the job, which creates more stress. Excessive stress causes illness and can reduce employee effectiveness and therefore organizational performance.

Sexual harassment

Sexual harassment is difficult to deal with but it is important to make a determined attempt to minimize it through policy statements backed up by special procedures for seeking help and making complaints.

Bullying

A policy should be published stating that bullying is unacceptable behaviour. People who feel that they are being bullied should have the right to discuss the problem with someone in the HR department or a trained counsellor.

Services for individuals

Counselling, possibly through EAP programmes, can be provided for sickness, bereavement, domestic problems and retirement.

Group employee services

These mainly consist of subsidized restaurants, sports and social clubs and child care facilities.

Questions

1 What does employee wellbeing mean?

2 What is work–life balance and what can be done about it?

3 How can stress be managed?

4 What are employee assistance programmes (EAPs)?

References

Kodz, J, Harper, H and Dench, S (2002) *Work–life Balance: Beyond the rhetoric*, Report 384, Brighton, Institute for Employment Studies

Lawler E E (2003) *Treat People Right! How organizations and individuals can propel each other into a virtuous spiral of success*, San Francisco, CA, Jossey-Bass

They are also directly responsible for ensuring that employees are conscious of health and safety hazards and do not take risks.

- *Employees* should be aware of what constitute safe working practices as they affect them and their fellow workers. While management and managers have the duty to communicate and train, individuals also have the duty to take account of what they have heard and learnt in the ways they carry out their work.

- *Health and safety advisers* advise on policies and procedures and on healthy and safe methods of working. They conduct risk assessments, safety audits and investigations into accidents in conjunction with managers and health and safety representatives, maintain statistics and report on trends and necessary actions.

- *Health and safety representatives* deal with health and safety issues in their areas and are members of health and safety committees.

- *Medical advisers* have two functions: preventative and clinical. The preventative function is most important, especially on occupational health matters. The clinical function is to deal with industrial accidents and diseases and to advise on the steps necessary to recover from injury or illness arising from work. They do not usurp the role of the family doctor in non-work-related illnesses.

- *Safety committees* consisting of health and safety representatives advise on health and safety policies and procedures, help in conducting risk assessments and safety audits, and make suggestions on improving health and safety performance.

Key learning points: Health and safety

Managing health and safety at work

The achievement of a healthy and safe place of work and the elimination to the maximum extent possible of hazards to health and safety is the responsibility of everyone employed in an organization, as well as those working there under contract. But the onus is on management to achieve and indeed go beyond the high standard in health and safety matters required by the legislation – the Health and Safety at Work, etc Act 1974 and the various regulations laid down in the Codes of Practice.

Health and safety policies

Written health and safety policies are required to demonstrate that top management is concerned about the protection of the organization's employees from hazards at work and to indicate how this protection will be provided.

Risk assessments

Risk assessments are concerned with the identification of hazards and the analysis of the risks attached to them. The purpose is to initiate preventative action.

Health and safety audits

Health and safety audits provide for a much more comprehensive review of all aspects of health and safety policies, procedures and practices.

Health and safety inspections

Health and safety inspections should be carried out on a regular and systematic basis by line managers and supervisors, with the advice and help of health and safety advisers.

Accident prevention

- Identify the causes of accidents.
- Take account of safety factors at the design stage.
- Design safety equipment and protective devices and provide protective clothing.
- Carry out regular risk assessments audits and inspections and take action to eliminate risks.
- Investigate all accidents.
- Maintain good records and statistics in order to identify problem areas and unsatisfactory trends.

- Conduct a continuous programme of education and training on safe working habits.

Occupational health programmes

- Eliminate the hazard at source through design and process engineering.

- Isolate hazardous processes and substances so that workers do not come into contact with them.

- Change the processes or substances used to promote better protection or eliminate the risk.

- Provide protective equipment, but only if changes to the design, process or specification cannot completely remove the hazard.

- Train workers to avoid risk.

Measuring health and safety performance

This is important as a guide to action using the standard measures of frequency, incidence and severity rate.

Communicating the need for better health and safety practices

It is necessary to deliver the message that health and safety is important as long as this supplements rather than replaces other initiatives.

Health and safety training

Health and safety training is a key part of the preventative programme. It should start as part of the induction course. It should also take place following a transfer to a new job or a change in working methods.

Organizing health and safety

Health and safety concerns everyone in an establishment, although the main responsibility lies with management in general and individual managers in particular. The specific roles should be defined for managers and employees, health and safety advisers, medical advisers and the health and safety committee.

Questions

1 What are health and safety and occupational health programmes?

2 What is the purpose of health and safety policies?

3 What is the distinction between risk assessments, health and safety audits and health and safety inspections?

4 What steps need to be taken to prevent accidents?

5 How are occupational health problems controlled?

PART VIII

HR policies, procedures and systems

Introduction

The HR function is responsible for ensuring that a consistent, fair and thorough approach is adopted to dealing with HRM issues, that systems are in place that provide for the efficient administration of HR matters, and that information is available that guides decisions on HR strategy and practice. As described in this part, these responsibilities are fulfilled by the development and administration of:

- HR policies that set out the approaches used by the organization to deal with key aspects of HRM and provide guidelines to ensure the consistent application of these approaches;

- HR procedures that are formalized ways of dealing with specific employment matters such as discipline, redundancy and grievance handling;

- HR systems that are computer-based processes for managing the HRM and providing HR information, also known as e-HRM.

38
HR policies

KEY CONCEPTS AND TERMS

Diversity   Equal opportunities

LEARNING OUTCOMES

On completing this chapter you should know about:

- The reasons for having HR policies
- Overall HR policy
- Specific HR policies
- Formulating HR policies
- Implementing HR policies

Introduction

HR policies set out the approaches the organization adopts to dealing with key aspects of HRM and provide continuing guidelines on how these approaches should be applied. They define the philosophies and values of the organization on how people should be treated, and from these are derived the principles upon which managers are expected to act when dealing with HR matters.

HR policies should be distinguished from procedures. A policy provides generalized guidance on how HR issues should be dealt with. A procedure spells out precisely what steps should be taken to deal with major employment issues such as grievances, discipline, capability and redundancy.

Why have HR policies?

HR policies define how the organization wants to handle key aspects of people management. As guidelines the aim is to ensure that any HR issues are dealt with consistently in accordance with the values of the organization and in line with certain defined principles. All organizations have HR policies. Some, however, exist implicitly as a philosophy of management and an attitude to employees that is expressed in the way in which HR issues are handled; for example, the introduction of a new grade and pay structure. The advantage of explicit policies in terms of consistency and understanding may appear to be obvious, but there are disadvantages: written policies can be inflexible, constrictive, platitudinous, or all three. To a degree, policies have often to be expressed in abstract terms and managers do not care for abstractions. But they do prefer to know where they stand – people like structure – and formalized HR policies can provide the guidelines they need.

Formalized HR policies can be used in induction, team leader and management training to help participants understand the philosophies and values of the organization and how they are expected to behave within that context. They are a means for defining the employment relationship and the psychological contract. HR policies can be expressed formally as overall statements of the values of the organization or in specific areas, as discussed in this chapter.

Overall HR policy

The overall HR policy defines how the organization fulfils its social responsibilities for its employees and sets out its attitudes towards them. It is an expression of its values or beliefs about how people should be treated. The values expressed in an overall statement of HR policies may explicitly or implicitly refer to the following concepts.

These values are espoused by many organizations in one form or another. But to what extent are they practised when making 'business-led' decisions, which can, of course be highly detrimental to employees if, for example, they lead to redundancy? One of the dilemmas facing all those who formulate HR policies is: 'How can we pursue policies focusing on business success *and* fulfil our obligations to employees in such terms as equity, consideration, quality of working life, security and working conditions?' To argue, as some do, that HR policies should be entirely business-led implies that human considerations are unimportant. Organizations have obligations to all their stakeholders, not just their owners.

It may be difficult to express these overall policies in anything but generalized terms but employers increasingly have to recognize that they are subject to external as well as internal pressures and moral imperatives that act as constraints on the extent to which they can disregard the higher standards of behaviour towards their employees that are expected of them. What needs to be done to avoid

Values expressed in overall HR policy

- *Equity* – treating employees fairly and justly by adopting an 'even-handed' approach. This includes protecting individuals from any unfair decisions made by their managers, providing equal opportunities for employment and promotion, and operating an equitable payment system.

- *Consideration* – taking account of individual circumstances when making decisions that affect the prospects, security or self-respect of employees.

- *Organizational learning* – a belief in the need to promote the learning and development of all the members of the organization by providing the processes and support required.

- *Performance through people* – the importance attached to developing a performance culture and to continuous improvement; the significance of performance management as a means of defining and agreeing mutual expectations; the provision of fair feedback to people on how well they are performing.

- *Quality of working life* – consciously and continually aiming to improve the quality of working life. This involves increasing the sense of satisfaction people obtain from their work by, so far as possible, reducing monotony, increasing variety, autonomy and responsibility, avoiding placing people under too much stress and providing for an acceptable balance between work and life outside work.

- *Working conditions* – providing healthy, safe and, so far as practicable, pleasant working conditions.

accusations that general HR policy statements are mere rhetoric is to convert them into reality through specific HR policies and rigorously enforce their application.

Specific HR policies

The most common areas in which specific HR policies exist are age and employment, AIDS, bullying, discipline, e-mails and the internet, employee development, employee relations, employee voice, employment, equal opportunity, grievances, health and safety, managing diversity, promotion, redundancy, reward, sexual harassment, substance abuse and work–life balance.

Age and employment

The policy on age and employment should take into account the UK legislation on age discrimination and the following facts:

- age is a poor predictor of job performance;
- it is misleading to equate physical and mental ability with age;
- more of the population are living active, healthy lives as they get older.

AIDS

An AIDS policy could include the following points:

- The risk through infection in the workplace is negligible.
- Where the occupation does involve blood contact, as in hospitals, doctors' surgeries and laboratories, the special precautions advised by the Health and Safety Commission will be implemented.
- Employees who know that they are infected with AIDS will not be obliged to disclose the fact to the company, but if they do, it will remain completely confidential.
- There will be no discrimination against anyone with or at risk of acquiring AIDS.
- Employees infected by HIV or suffering from AIDS will be treated no differently from anyone else suffering a severe illness.

Bullying

An anti-bullying policy will state that bullying will not be tolerated by the organization and that those who persist in bullying staff will be subject to disciplinary action, which could be severe in particularly bad cases. The policy will make it clear that individuals who are being bullied should have the right to discuss the problem with another person, a representative or a member of the HR function, and to

make a complaint. The policy should emphasize that if a complaint is received it will be thoroughly investigated.

Discipline

The disciplinary policy should state that employees have the right to know what is expected of them and what could happen if they infringe the organization's rules. It should also make the point that, in handling disciplinary cases, the organization will treat employees in accordance with the principles of natural justice. It should be supported by a disciplinary procedure (see Chapter 39).

Diversity management

A policy on managing diversity recognizes that there are differences among employees and that these differences, if properly managed, will enable work to be done more efficiently and effectively. It does not focus exclusively on issues of discrimination but instead concentrates on recognizing the differences between people.

Managing diversity is a concept that recognizes the benefits to be gained from differences. It is not the same as equal opportunity, which aims to legislate against discrimination, assumes that people should be assimilated into the organization and, often, relies on affirmative action. A management of diversity policy could:

- acknowledge cultural and individual differences in the workplace;
- state that the organization values the different qualities that people bring to their jobs;
- emphasize the need to eliminate bias in such areas as selection, promotion, performance assessment, pay and learning opportunities;
- focus attention on individual differences rather than group differences.

e-mails and use of the internet

The policy on e-mails could state that the sending or downloading of offensive e-mails is prohibited and that the senders or downloaders of such messages are subject to normal disciplinary procedures. The policy may also prohibit any internet browsing or downloading of material not related to the business, although this can be difficult to enforce. Some companies have always believed that reasonable use of the telephone is acceptable and that policy may be extended to the internet.

If it is decided that employees' e-mails should be monitored to check on excessive or unacceptable use, this should be included in an e-mail policy, which would therefore be part of the contractual arrangements. A policy statement could be included to the effect that: 'The company reserves the right to access and monitor all e-mail messages created, sent, received or stored on the company's system.'

Employee development

The employee development policy could express the organization's commitment to the continuous development of the skills and abilities of employees in order to maximize their contribution and to give them the opportunity to enhance their skills, realize their potential, advance their careers and increase their employability, both within and outside the organization.

Employee relations

The employee relations policy will set out the organization's approach to the rights of employees to have their interests represented to management through trade unions, staff associations or some other form of representative system. It will also cover the basis upon which the organization works with trade unions, eg emphasizing that this should be regarded as a partnership.

Employee voice

The employee voice policy should spell out the organization's belief in giving employees an opportunity to have a say in matters that affect them. It should define the mechanisms for employee voice such as joint consultation and suggestion schemes.

Employment

Employment policies should be concerned with fundamental aspects of the employment relationship. They should take account of the requirements of relevant UK and European legislation and case law, which is beyond the scope of this handbook to cover in detail. Recent important Acts and Regulations include those concerning the minimum wage, working time and part-time workers. The latter is especially significant because it requires that part-time workers should be entitled to the same terms and conditions as full-time workers, including *pro rata* pay. Note should also be taken of the UK Human Rights Act (1998), which gave further effect to rights and freedoms guaranteed under the European Convention on Human Rights. The rights are essentially civil and political rather than economic or social rights, and they only apply to a narrow range of employment. Moreover, they are not directly enforceable against an employer unless it is an 'obvious' public authority. It has, however, been held by the European Court of Human Rights that statutory rights not to be unlawfully dismissed or discriminated against can be regarded as 'civil rights'. Provisions inserted into the Employment Rights Act must be interpreted by employment tribunals in a way that is compatible with the European Convention's right to freedom of expression. This could apply to whistle-blowing.

Equal opportunity

The equal opportunity policy should spell out the organization's determination to give equal opportunities to all, irrespective of sex, sexual orientation, race, creed, disability, age or marital status. The policy should also deal with the extent to which the organization wants to take 'affirmative action' to redress imbalances between the numbers employed according to sex or race or to differences in the levels of qualifications and skills they have achieved. The policy could be set out as follows:

1   We are an equal opportunity employer. This means that we do not permit direct or indirect discrimination against any employee on the grounds of race, nationality, sex, sexual orientation, disability, religion, marital status or age.

2   Direct discrimination takes place when a person is treated less favourably than others are, or would be, treated in similar circumstances.

3   Indirect discrimination takes place when, whether intentional or not, a condition is applied that adversely affects a considerable proportion of people of one race, nationality, sex, sexual orientation, religion or marital status, or those with disabilities or older employees.

4   The firm will ensure that equal opportunity principles are applied in all its HR policies and in particular to the procedures relating to the recruitment, training, development and promotion of its employees.

5   Where appropriate and where permissible under the relevant legislation and codes of practice, employees of under-represented groups will be given positive training and encouragement to achieve equal opportunity.

Grievances

The policy on grievances could state that employees have the right to raise their grievances with their manager, to be accompanied by a representative if they so wish, and to appeal to a higher level if they feel that their grievance has not been resolved satisfactorily. The policy should be supported by a grievance procedure (see Chapter 39).

Health and safety

Health and safety policies cover how the organization intends to provide healthy and safe places and systems of work (see Chapter 37).

New technology

A new technology policy statement could state that there will be consultation about the introduction of new technology and the steps that would be taken by the organization to minimize the risk of compulsory redundancy or adverse effects on other terms and conditions or working arrangements.

Promotion

A promotion policy could state the organization's intention to promote from within wherever this is appropriate as a means of satisfying its requirements for high quality staff. The policy could, however, recognize that there will be occasions when the organization's present and future needs can only be met by recruitment from outside. The point could be made that a vigorous organization needs infusions of fresh blood from time to time if it is not to stagnate. In addition, the policy might state that employees will be encouraged to apply for internally advertised jobs and will not be held back from promotion by their managers, however reluctant the latter may be to lose them. The policy should define the approach the organization adopts to engaging, promoting and training older employees. It should emphasize that the only criterion for selection or promotion should be ability to do the job, and for training, the belief, irrespective of age, that the employee will benefit.

Redundancy

The redundancy policy should state that the aim of the organization is to provide for employment security. It is the organization's intention to use its best endeavours to avoid involuntary redundancy through its redeployment and retraining programmes. However, if redundancy is unavoidable, those affected will be given fair and equitable treatment, the maximum amount of warning and every help that can be provided to obtain suitable alternative employment. The policy should be supported by a redundancy procedure (see Chapter 39).

Reward

The reward policy could cover such matters as:

- providing an equitable pay system;
- equal pay for work of equal value;
- paying for performance, competence, skill or contribution;
- sharing in the success of the organization (gain sharing or profit sharing);
- the relationship between levels of pay in the organization and market rates;
- the provision of employee benefits, including flexible benefits, if appropriate;
- the importance attached to the non-financial rewards resulting from recognition, accomplishment, autonomy, and the opportunity to develop.

Sexual harassment

The sexual harassment policy should state that:

- Sexual harassment will not be tolerated.
- Employees subjected to sexual harassment will be given advice, support and counselling as required.
- Every attempt will be made to resolve the problem informally with the person complained against.
- Assistance will be given to the employee to complain formally if informal discussions fail.
- A special process will be available for hearing complaints about sexual harassment. This will provide for employees to bring their complaint to someone of their own sex if they so wish.
- Complaints will be handled sensitively and with due respect for the rights of both the complainant and the accused.
- Sexual harassment is regarded as gross misconduct and, if proved, makes the individual liable for instant dismissal. Less severe penalties may be reserved for minor cases, but there will always be a warning that repetition will result in dismissal.

Substance abuse

A substance abuse policy could include assurances that:

- employees identified as having substance abuse problems will be offered advice and help;
- any reasonable absence from work necessary to receive treatment will be granted under the organization's sickness scheme, provided there is full cooperation from the employee;
- an opportunity will be given to discuss the matter once it has become evident or suspected that work performance is being affected by substance-related problems;

- the right to be accompanied by a friend or employee representative in any such discussion;
- agencies will be recommended to which the employee can go for help if necessary;
- employment rights will be safeguarded during any reasonable period of treatment.

Work–life balance

Work–life balance policies define how the organization intends to allow employees greater flexibility in their working patterns so that they can balance what they do at work with the responsibilities and interests they have outside work. The policy will indicate how flexible work practices can be developed and implemented. It will emphasize that the numbers of hours worked must not be treated as a criterion for assessing performance. It will set out guidelines on the specific arrangements that can be made, such as flexible hours, compressed working week, term-time working contracts, working at home, special leave for parents and carers, career breaks and various kinds of child care.

A flexibility policy will need to take account of the Work and Families Act 2006, an extension of which gives carers the right to request flexible working to care for an elderly or sick relative. This provides for the following actions: 1) the request must be acknowledged in writing; 2) the employee must be notified if not all the required information is provided, so that he or she can resubmit the application properly completed; 3) if the employee unreasonably refuses to provide the additional information needed, the employer can treat the application as withdrawn; 4) a meeting has to be arranged with the employee within 28 days to discuss the desired work pattern and consider if it might be accommodated; 5) if the request cannot be accommodated, alternative working arrangements may be discussed and a trial period agreed; 6) in certain circumstances, a solution might be to develop an informal arrangement, outside the legislation, to allow flexible working for a limited period.

Formulating HR policies

HR policies need to address the key HR issues that have been identified in the organization. They must also take account of external factors such as legislation. The maximum amount of consultation should take place with managers, employees and their representatives and the policies should be communicated widely with guidelines on their application. The following steps should be taken when formulating HR policies.

Formulating HR policies

1 Gain understanding of the corporate culture and its shared values.

2 Analyse existing policies – written and unwritten. HR policies will exist in any organization, even if they are implicit rather than expressed formally.

3 Analyse external factors. HR policies are subject to the requirements of UK employment legislation, European Commission employment regulations, and the official Codes of Practice issued by bodies in the UK, such as ACAS (the Advisory, Conciliation and Arbitration Service), the Commission for Equality and Human Rights and the Health and Safety Executive. The Codes of Practice issued by relevant professional institutions, such as the CIPD, should also be consulted.

4 Assess any areas where new policies are needed or existing policies are inadequate.

5 Check with managers, preferably starting at the top, on their views about HR policies and where they think they could be improved.

6 Seek the views of employees about the HR policies, especially the extent to which they are inherently fair and equitable and are implemented fairly and consistently. Consider doing this through an attitude survey.

7 Seek the views of union representatives.

8 Analyse the information obtained in the first seven steps and prepare draft policies.

9 Consult, discuss and agree policies with management and union representatives.

10 Communicate the policies with guidance notes on their implementation as required (although they should be as self-explanatory as possible). Supplement this communication with training.

Implementing HR policies

The aim will be to implement policies fairly and consistently. Line managers have an important role in doing this. It is they who will be largely responsible for policy implementation. Members of the HR function can give guidance, but it is line managers who are on the spot and have to make decisions about people. The role of HR is to communicate and interpret the policies, convince line managers that they are necessary, and provide training and support that will equip managers to implement them. As Purcell *et al* (2003) emphasized, it is line managers who bring HR policies to life.

Key learning points: HR policies

The reasons for having HR policies

HR policies provide guidelines on how key aspects of people management should be handled. The aim is to ensure that any HR issues are dealt with consistently in accordance with the values of the organization and in line with certain defined principles.

Overall HR policy

The overall HR policy defines how the organization fulfils its social responsibilities for its employees and sets out its attitudes towards them. It is an expression of its values or beliefs about how people should be treated.

Specific HR policies

Specific HR policies cover age and employment, AIDS, bullying, discipline, e-mails and the internet, employee development, employee relations, employee voice, employment, equal opportunity, grievances, health and safety, managing diversity, promotion, redundancy, reward, sexual harassment, substance abuse and work–life balance.

Formulating HR policies

HR policies need to address the key HR issues that have been identified in the organization. They must also take account of external factors such as legislation. The maximum amount of consultation should take place with managers, employees and their representatives, and the policies should be communicated widely with guidelines on their application.

Implementing HR policies

The aim will be to implement policies fairly and consistently. Line managers have a key role in doing this.

Questions

1 What are HR policies?

2 Why have HR policies?

3 What values may be expressed in overall HR policy?

4 What are the areas in which specific HR policies may be required?

5 How should HR policies be formulated?

Reference

Purcell, J, Kinnie, K, Hutchinson, Rayton, B and Swart, J (2003) *Understanding the People and Performance Link: Unlocking the black box*, London, CIPD

39
HR procedures

What are HR procedures?

HR procedures set out the ways in which certain actions concerning people should be carried out by the management or individual managers. In effect they constitute a formalized approach to dealing with specific matters of policy and practice.

They should be distinguished from HR policies, as described in Chapter 38, which serve as guidelines on people management practices but do not necessarily lay down precisely the steps that should be taken in particular situations. Procedures are more exacting. They state what *must* be done as well as spelling out how to do it.

It is desirable to have the key HR procedures written down to ensure that HR policies are applied consistently and in accordance with both legal requirements and ethical considerations. The existence of a written and well-publicized procedure ensures that everyone knows precisely what steps need to be taken when dealing with certain significant and possibly recurring employment issues.

The introduction or development of HR procedures should be carried out in consultation with employees and, where appropriate, their representatives. It is essential to brief everyone on how the procedures operate and they should be published either in an employee handbook or as a separate document. Line managers may need special training on how they should apply the procedures, and the HR department should provide guidance wherever necessary. HR will normally have the responsibility of ensuring that procedures are followed consistently.

Procedures are required to deal with capability and disciplinary issues, grievances and redundancy, discussed below.

Capability procedure

Some organizations deal with matters of capability under a disciplinary procedure, but there is a good case to be made for dealing with poor performance issues separately, leaving the disciplinary procedure to be invoked for situations such as poor timekeeping. An example of a capability procedure is given below.

CAPABILITY PROCEDURE

Policy

The company aims are to ensure that performance expectations and standards are defined, performance is monitored and employees are given appropriate feedback, training and support to meet these standards.

Procedure

1   If a manager/team leader believes that an employee's performance is not up to standard an informal discussion will be held with the employee to try to establish the reason and to agree the actions required to improve performance by the employee and/or the manager/team leader. If, however:

a   it is agreed that the established standards are not reasonably attainable, they will be reviewed;

b   it is established that the performance problems are related to the employee's personal life, the necessary counselling/support will be provided;

c   it is decided that the poor performance emanates from a change in the organization's standards, those standards will be explained to the employee and help will be offered to obtain conformity with the standards;

d   it is apparent that the poor performance constitutes misconduct, the disciplinary procedure will be invoked.

2   Should the employee show no (or insufficient) improvement over a defined period (weeks/months), a formal interview will be arranged between the employee (together with a representative if so desired). The aims of this interview will be to:

a   explain clearly the shortfall between the employee's performance and the required standard;

b   identify the cause(s) of the unsatisfactory performance and to determine what – if any – remedial treatment (training, retraining, support, etc) can be given;

c   obtain the employee's commitment to reaching that standard;

d   set a reasonable period for the employee to reach the standard and agree on a monitoring system during that period; and

e   tell the employee what will happen if that standard is not met.

3   The outcome of this interview will be recorded in writing and a copy will be given to the employee.

4   At the end of the review period a further formal interview will be held, at which time:

a   if the required improvement has been made, the employee will be told of this and encouraged to maintain the improvement;

b   if some improvement has been made but the standard has not yet been met, the review period will be extended;

c   if there has been no discernible improvement and performance is still well below an acceptable standard this will be indicated to the employee and consideration will be given to whether there are alternative vacancies which the employee would be competent to fill; if there are, the employee will be given the option of accepting such a vacancy or being considered for dismissal;

d   if such vacancies are available, the employee will be given full details of them in writing before being required to make a decision;

e   in the absence of suitable alternative work, the employee will be informed and invited to give his or her views on this before the final decision is taken.

5   Employees may appeal against their dismissal. The appeal must be made within three working days.

Disciplinary procedure

A disciplinary procedure sets out the stages through which any disciplinary action should proceed. An example is given below.

DISCIPLINARY PROCEDURE (PART 1)

Policy

It is the policy of the company that if disciplinary action has to be taken against employees it should:

- be undertaken only in cases where good reason and clear evidence exists;

- be appropriate to the nature of the offence that has been committed;

- be demonstrably fair and consistent with previous action in similar circumstances;

- take place only when employees are aware of the standards that are expected of them or the rules with which they are required to conform;

- allow employees the right to be represented by a representative or colleague during any formal proceedings;

- allow employees the right to know exactly what charges are being made against them and to respond to those charges;

- allow employees the right of appeal against any disciplinary action.

Disciplinary rules

The company is responsible for ensuring that up-to-date disciplinary rules are published and available to all employees. These will set out the circumstances in which an employee could be dismissed for gross misconduct.

Procedure

The procedure is carried out in the following stages:

1 *Informal warning.* A verbal or informal warning is given to the employee in the first instance or instances of minor offences. The warning is administered by the employee's immediate team leader or manager.

2 *Formal warning.* A written formal warning is given to the employee in the first instance of more serious offences or after repeated instances of minor offences. The warning is administered by the employee's immediate team leader or manager – it states the exact nature of the offence and indicates any future disciplinary action that will be taken against the employee if the offence is repeated within a specified time limit. A copy of the written warning is placed in the employee's personal record file but is destroyed 12 months after the date on which it was given, if the intervening service has been satisfactory. The employee is required to read and sign the formal warning and has the right to appeal to higher management if he or she thinks the warning is unjustified. The HR manager should be asked to advise on the text of the written warning.

3 *Further disciplinary action.* If, despite previous warnings, an employee still fails to reach the required standards in a reasonable period of time, it may become necessary to consider further disciplinary action. The action taken may be up to three days' suspension without pay, or dismissal. In either case the departmental manager should discuss the matter with the HR manager before taking action. Staff below the rank of departmental manager may only recommend disciplinary action to higher management, except when their manager is not present (for example, on night-shift), when they may suspend the employee for up to one day pending an inquiry on the following day. Disciplinary action should not be confirmed until the appeal procedure has been carried out.

DISCIPLINARY PROCEDURE (PART 2)

Summary dismissal

An employee may be summarily dismissed (ie given instant dismissal without notice) only in the event of gross misconduct, as defined in company rules. Only departmental managers and above can recommend summary dismissal, and the action should not be finalized until the case has been discussed with the HR manager and the appeal procedure has been carried out. To enable this review to take place, employees should be suspended pending further investigation, which must take place within 24 hours.

Appeals

In all circumstances, an employee may appeal against suspension, dismissal with notice, or summary dismissal.

The appeal is conducted by a member of management who is more senior than the manager who initially administered the disciplinary action. The HR manager should also be present at the hearing. If he or she wishes, the employee may be represented at the appeal by a fellow employee of his or her own choice. Appeal against summary dismissal or suspension should be heard immediately. Appeals against dismissal with notice should be held within two days. No disciplinary action that is subject to appeal is confirmed until the outcome of the appeal.

If an appeal against dismissal (but not suspension) is rejected at this level, the employee has the right to appeal to the chief executive. The head of HR and, if required, the employee's representative should be present at this appeal.

Grievance procedure

A grievance procedure spells out the policy on handling grievances and the approach to dealing with them. An example of a grievance procedure is given below.

GRIEVANCE PROCEDURE

Policy

It is the policy of the company that employees should:

- be given a fair hearing by their immediate supervisor or manager concerning any grievances they may wish to raise;
- have the right to appeal to a more senior manager against a decision made by their immediate supervisor or manager;
- have the right to be accompanied by a fellow employee of their own choice when raising a grievance or appealing against a decision.

The aim of the procedure is to settle the grievance as nearly as possible to its point of origin.

Procedure

The main stages through which a grievance may be raised are as follows:

1   The employee raises the matter with his or her immediate team leader or manager and may be accompanied by a fellow employee of his or her own choice.

2   If the employee is not satisfied with the decision, the employee requests a meeting with a member of management who is more senior than the team leader or manager who initially heard the grievance. This meeting takes place within five working days of the request and is attended by the manager, a HR manager or business partner, the employee appealing against

the decision, and, if desired, his or her representative. The HR manager records the results of the meeting in writing and issues copies to all concerned.

3 If the employee is still not satisfied with the decision, he or she may appeal to the appropriate director. The meeting to hear this appeal is held within five working days of the request and is attended by the director, the head of HR, the employee making the appeal and, if desired, his or her representative. The manager responsible for HR records the result of this meeting in writing and issues copies to all concerned.

Redundancy procedure

A redundancy procedure aims to meet statutory, ethical and practical considerations when dealing with this painful process. An example of a procedure is given below.

REDUNDANCY PROCEDURE (PART 1)

Definition

Redundancy is defined as the situation in which management decides that an employee or employees are surplus to requirements in a particular occupation and cannot be offered suitable alternative work.

Employees may be surplus to requirements because changes in the economic circumstances of the company mean that fewer employees are required, or because changes in methods of working mean that a job no longer exists in its previous form. An employee who is given notice because he or she is unsuitable or inefficient is not regarded as redundant and would be dealt with in accordance with the usual disciplinary or capability procedure.

Objectives

The objectives of the procedure are to ensure that:

- employees who may be affected by the discontinuance of their work are given fair and equitable treatment;

- the minimum disruption is caused to employees and the company;

- as far as possible, changes are effected with the understanding and agreement of the unions and employees concerned.

Principles

The principles governing the procedure are as follows:

- The trade unions concerned will be informed as soon as the possibility of redundancy is foreseen.

- Every attempt will be made to:
  - absorb redundancy by the natural wastage of employees;
  - find suitable alternative employment within the company for employees who might be affected, and provide training if this is necessary;
  - give individuals reasonable warning of pending redundancy in addition to the statutory period of notice.

- If alternative employment in the company is not available and more than one individual is affected, the factors to be taken into consideration in deciding who should be made redundant will be:
  - length of service with the company;
  - value to the company;
  - other things being equal, length of service should be the determining factor.

- The company will make every endeavour to help employees find alternative work if that is necessary.

REDUNDANCY PROCEDURE (PART 2)

The procedure for dealing with employees who are surplus to requirements is set out below.

Review of employee requirements

Management will continuously keep under review possible future developments that might affect the number of employees required, and will prepare overall plans for dealing with possible redundancies.

Measures to avoid redundancies

If the likelihood of redundancy is foreseen, the company will inform the union(s), explaining the reasons, and in consultation with the union(s) will give consideration to taking appropriate measures to prevent redundancy.

Departmental managers will be warned by the management of future developments that might affect them so that detailed plans can be made for running down the numbers of employees by allowing natural wastage to take place without replacements, retraining, or transfers.

Departmental managers will be expected to keep under review the work situation in their departments so that contingency plans can be prepared and the HR manager is informed of any likely surpluses.

Consultation on redundancies

If all measures to avoid redundancy fail, the company will consult the union(s) at the earliest opportunity in order to reach agreement.

Selection of redundant employees

In the event of impending redundancy, the individuals who might be surplus to requirements should be selected by the departmental manager with the advice of the HR manager on the principles that should be adopted.

The HR manager should explore the possibilities of transferring affected employees to alternative work. The HR manager should inform management of proposed action (either redundancy or transfer) to obtain approval.

The union(s) will be informed of the numbers affected, but not of individual names.

The departmental manager and the HR manager will jointly interview the employees affected either to offer a transfer or, if a suitable alternative is not available, to inform them they will be redundant. At this interview, full information should be available to give to the employee on, as appropriate:

- the reasons for being surplus;
- the alternative jobs that are available;
- the date when the employee will become surplus (that is, the period of notice);
- the entitlement to redundancy pay;
- the employee's right to appeal to an appropriate director;
- the help the company will provide.

REDUNDANCY PROCEDURE (PART 3)

An appropriate director will hear any appeals with the manager responsible for personnel.

The HR manager will ensure that all the required administrative arrangements are made.

If the union(s) have any points to raise about the selection of employees or the actions taken by the company, these should be discussed in the first place with the HR manager.

If the results of these discussions are unsatisfactory, a meeting will be arranged with an appropriate director.

Alternative work within the company

If an employee is offered and accepts suitable alternative work within the company, it will take effect without a break from the previous employment and will be confirmed in writing. Employees will receive appropriate training and will be entitled to a four-week trial period to see if the work is suitable. This trial period may be extended by mutual agreement to provide additional training. During this period, employees are free to terminate their employment and if they do, would be treated as if they had been made redundant on the day the old job

ended. They would then receive any redundancy pay to which they are entitled.

Alternative employment

Employees for whom no suitable work is available in the company will be given reasonable opportunities to look for alternative employment.

Key learning points: HR procedures

- HR procedures set out the ways in which certain actions concerning people should be carried out by the management or individual managers. In effect they constitute a formalized approach to dealing with specific matters of policy and practice.

- They should be distinguished from HR policies, which serve as guidelines on people management practices but do not necessarily lay down precisely the steps that should be taken in particular situations. Procedures are more exacting: they state what *must* be done as well as spelling out how to do it.

- It is desirable to have the key HR procedures written down to ensure that HR policies are applied consistently and in accordance with both legal requirements and ethical considerations.

- The existence of a written and well-publicized procedure ensures that everyone knows precisely what steps need to be taken when dealing with

certain significant and possibly recurring employment issues.

- The introduction or development of HR procedures should be carried out in consultation with employees and, where appropriate, their representatives.

- It is essential to brief everyone on how the procedures operate, and they should be published either in an employee handbook or as a separate document.

- Line managers may need special training on how they should apply the procedures and the HR department should provide guidance wherever necessary. HR will normally have the responsibility of ensuring that procedures are followed consistently.

- Procedures are required to deal with capability and disciplinary issues, grievances and redundancy.

Questions

1 What are HR procedures?

2 What are the characteristics of a good procedure?

3 What would you expect a capability procedure to cover?

4 What would you expect a disciplinary procedure to cover?

5 What would you expect a grievance procedure to cover?

6 What would you expect a redundancy procedure to cover?

40
HR information systems

LEARNING OUTCOMES

On completing this chapter you should be able to define these key concepts. You should also know about:

- Reasons for using an HRIS
- Features of an HRIS
- Functions of an HRIS
- Introducing an HRIS

Introduction

An HR information system (HRIS) is a computer-based information system for managing the administration of HR processes and procedures. 'e-HRM' is an alternative term for the use of computer technology within the HR function. Parry and Tyson (2011: 335) defined it as: 'A way of implementing HR strategies, policies and practices in organizations through a conscious and directed support of and/or with the full use of web technology-based channels.' They listed five goals for e-HRM: efficiency, service delivery, strategic orientation, manager empowerment and standardization (*ibid*: 335).

Reasons for introducing an HRIS

The CIPD (2007) survey established that the top 10 reasons for introducing an HRIS were:

1 To improve quality of information available.
2 To reduce administrative burden on the HR department.
3 To improve speed at which information is available.
4 To improve flexibility of information to support business planning.
5 To improve services to employees.
6 To produce HR metrics.
7 To aid human capital reporting.
8 To improve productivity.
9 To reduce operational costs.
10 To manage people's working time more effectively.

The functions of an HRIS

The functions that an HRIS can perform (its 'functionality') are set out below. They cover almost every aspect of HRM.

The 2007 CIPD survey found that the 10 most popular uses to which respondents put their HRIS were:

1 Absence management.
2 Training and development.
3 Rewards.
4 Managing diversity.
5 Recruitment and selection.
6 Other (usually payroll).
7 Appraisal/performance management.
8 HR planning.
9 Knowledge management.
10 Expenses.

Features of an HRIS

The features of particular interest in an HRIS system are the use of software, integration with other IT systems in the organization, use of the intranet, and provisions for self-service.

Use of software

It is customary to buy software from an external supplier. There is a choice between buying a 'vanilla system' (ie an 'off-the-shelf' system without any

---

The functions that an HRIS can perform

absence recording and management	employee records
employee surveys	employee turnover analysis
e-learning	equal opportunity modelling
expenses	HR planning and forecasting
job evaluation	knowledge management
intranet	manage diversity
manager and employee self-service	metrics and human capital reporting
online recruitment	online performance management systems and 360-degree feedback
payroll administration	pay reviews
pensions and benefits administration	reward modelling
total reward statements	

upgrades) or customizing the supplier's system to meet specified business requirements. Extensive customization can make future upgrades problematic and expensive, so it is important to limit it to what is absolutely necessary.

If an external supplier is used the choice should be made as follows:

- research HR software market through trade exhibitions and publications;
- review HR processes and existing systems;
- produce a specification of system requirements;
- send an invitation to tender to several suppliers;
- invite suppliers to demonstrate their products;
- obtain references from existing customers, including site visits;
- analyse and score the product against the specification.

Alternative approaches

There are ways of providing IT services other than doing it yourself. It is possible to choose 'cloud computing' (the provision of services via an external network or across the internet). 'Software as a service' (SaaS) is an on-demand software delivery model in which users are charged for accessing and managing HR IT provision via a network.

Integration

Enterprise resource planning (ERP) systems integrate all data and processes of an organization into a unified system with the same database. HR systems are not frequently integrated to this extent although they often link payroll administration with other HR functions. Integration of the HR system with IT systems in the wider organization so that they can 'talk to one another' will enable the more effective management of HR data. However, many HR functions retain stand-alone systems, because they believe integration would compromise their own system, potential lack of confidentiality, and the cost and perceived risks involved.

Intranet

An intranet system is one where computer terminals are linked so that they can share information within an organization or within part of an organization. The scope of the information that can be shared across terminals can be limited to preserve confidentiality and this security can be enhanced by using passwords. HR intranet systems can be used for purposes such as updating personal details, applications for internal jobs online, requests for training, access to e-learning, administration of queries and communications.

Self-service

A human resource self-service system (HRSS) allows managers and employees access to information and the facility to interact with the system to input information or make choices of their own. This can operate through an HR portal (a site that functions as a point of access to information on the intranet), which may be specially designed to produce a brand image of the HR function. This is sometimes referred to as a 'business-to-employees' (B2E) portal.

For managers, self-service means that they can access information immediately. This might be HR metrics (human capital reporting measures) in such areas as absenteeism, personal details, performance management data, learning and development progress, and pay (as a basis for pay reviews). They can also input data on their staff. This facilitates the devolution of responsibility to line managers and reduces the administrative burden on HR.

Employees can also access information, input data about themselves, request training and apply for jobs online.

Introducing an HRIS

The steps required are illustrated in Figure 40.1.

The points to consider when introducing an HRIS are set out below.

FIGURE 40.1   Introducing an HRIS

e-HRM achievements

Research conducted by Parry and Tyson (2011) in 10 case study organizations established that efficiency goals were achieved by most of the organizations. Service delivery improvements were generally achieved, supporting improved effectiveness of the HR function. The findings showed that a potential goal for e-HRM is to standardize operational procedures across an organization, but they noted that: 'The realization of improved efficiency and effectiveness is dependent on the design and implementation of the system, and increased effectiveness and involvement in delivering the business strategy may depend on appropriate redeployment and up-skilling of HR staff' (*ibid*: 352).

Below are some case studies, as reported by Parry and Tyson (2011: 341).

Points to consider when introducing an HRIS

- Make sure you really know what you need now and what you are likely to need in the near future so that you can give clear guidelines to the software provider.

- Involve end-users and other stakeholders in the decision-making process.

- It's useful to include a member of staff with IT expertise on the decision-making team, even if they're not HR professionals.

- Go for something clear and straightforward that adds value. Don't go for all the 'bells and whistles': they may cost more, take more time to administer and you will probably end up not using them anyway.

- Evaluate the range of systems on offer in terms of how they report, and how easy and quick it is to produce the types of report you need on a regular basis. Look at how reports are presented: can you download them into an Excel spreadsheet or into Access so that you can manipulate the data yourself? How easy is it to do mail merge with the information reported?

- When buying an off-the-shelf system, don't customize it unless it's critical. Each time the system is upgraded, it's these modifications that may cause you difficulties. If you do have modifications, budget for these to be managed on an ongoing basis.

CASE STUDIES

AVISA

An Oracle HR system is used with extensive management self-service for performing salary changes, cost centre and allowance changes, processing leavers, updating and reporting absence, processing overtime payments and comparing performance ratings. Employee self-service is available to maintain personal details, look at payslips, request holidays and record absence. In addition, an Ask-Jeeves system to answer generic HR queries has been introduced.

BOC

BOC has used a SAP HR system since 1999 to hold HR data and allow managers to access this data via their desktop to record absence and enter bonus ratings salary review details. The system drove the payroll process. An e-recruitment system was introduced in 2003 with a recruitment database that sat centrally and was connected to a number of different career centres. The HR intranet has also recently been relaunched.

Marks & Spencer

The range of technological HRM tools include main HRIS plus payroll and personnel data, pensions and absence management systems and an HR portal for information on policies and practices.

Key learning points: HR information systems

Reasons for using an HRIS

Top five reasons are (CIPD, 2007): to improve quality of information available, to reduce administrative burden on the HR department, to improve speed at which information is available, to improve flexibility of information to support business planning, and to improve services to employees.

Functions of an HRIS

Top five uses of an HRIS (CIPD, 2007): absence management, training and development, rewards, managing diversity, and recruitment and selection.

Features of an HRIS

The features of particular interest in an HRIS system are the use of software, integration with other IT systems in the organization, use of the intranet, and provisions for self-service.

Introducing an HRIS

See Figure 40.1.

Questions

1 What are the main reasons for having a comprehensive human resource information system?

2 What are the five most popular applications of an HRIS?

3 What is self-service and why is it important?

References

CIPD (2007) *HR and Technology: Impact and advantages*, London, CIPD

Parry, E and Tyson, S (2011) Desired goals and actual outcomes of e-HRM, *Human Resource Management Journal*, **21** (3), pp 335–54

PART IX

HR skills

PART IX CONTENTS

Introduction

It can be argued that fully fledged HR professionals have to be able to deploy a range of skills supported by knowledge that is wider than that required by any other professional working in organizations. Even if this claim cannot be substantiated, it is incontrovertible that a very wide variety of skills have to be used by HR specialists on a day-to-day basis.

As business partners they need strategic and business skills. As professionals constantly faced with the need to gain insight into the organizational and business issues they have to address, they need problem-solving, analytical and critical skills. HR professionals need to know about research methodology to understand the contribution of HR research and, increasingly, to take part in research projects. They must be able to analyse and present information on what is happening in their organizations by using statistical skills.

Another major group of skills HR professionals need to have are those concerned with HRM practices, especially selection interviewing, job and competency analysis, learning and development techniques and negotiating. Then there are the skills they need because they have a complex role to play within their organizations. They are involved in leading change and exercising leadership in their own functions and, indirectly, in their dealings with line managers – providing guidance and advice. They have to exert influence, not just by using the authority of their position but by the effective exercise of skills in persuading managers to agree to innovations or adopt different courses of action in people management. They will be constantly involved in handling people problems and, from time to time, in managing conflict. Politics is a feature of life in organizations and HR people must know how to cope with political situations.

The purpose of this part is to provide guidance on the application of all the skills mentioned together with any supporting knowledge required.

41
Strategic HRM skills

LEARNING OUTCOMES

On completing this chapter you should be able to define these key concepts. You should also know about:

- The strategic role of the HR professional
- The strategic business partner model
- The strategic role of HR directors
- The strategic role of heads of HR functions
- The strategic role of HR business partners
- The strategic contribution of HR advisers or assistants
- The strategic skills required
- HR strategic skills as defined by the CIPD

Introduction

HR professionals are constantly being urged to be strategic. This chapter examines what this means and describes the knowledge and skills required.

The strategic role of the HR professional

HR strategic activities support the achievement of the organization's goals and values by aligning HR strategies with business strategies. HR professionals are involved in the development and implementation of forward-looking HR strategies that are integrated with one another. Importantly, they work with their line management colleagues in the continuous formulation and execution of the business strategy.

HR professionals, especially at the highest level, make a strategic contribution that ensures that the organization has the quality of skilled and engaged people it needs. Sparrow *et al* (2010: 88) observed that: 'HR must be fully responsive to the strategy and business model of the business. HR is not a rule to itself. It is not "HR for HR", but HR (as broadly defined across the competing stakeholders whom HR has to satisfy) for the business.' The strategic nature of HR has been expressed in the strategic business partner model, as described below.

The strategic business partner model

HR professionals as strategic business partners work closely with management, influencing the business strategy and contributing to its implementation. They share responsibility with their line management colleagues for the success of the enterprise. Ulrich (1998: 127) remarked that: 'To be full-fledged strategic partners with senior management HR executives should impel and guide serious discussion of how the company should be organized to carry out its strategy.'

In 1985, Tyson, anticipating Ulrich, described HR professionals as business managers who have the capacity to identify business opportunities, to see the broad picture, and to understand how their role can help to achieve the company's business objectives. They integrate their activities closely with top management and ensure that they serve a long-term strategic purpose. They anticipate needs, act flexibly and are proactive.

The notion of strategic partner was introduced by Dyer and Holder, not Ulrich, as is generally assumed. Their description of the role is set out in the source review on this page.

Ulrich and Lake (1990) popularized the idea. They argued that:

> To ensure that management practices become a means for gaining a sustained competitive advantage, human resource professionals need to become strategic business partners and gear their activities to improving business performance. To do this they require a good working knowledge of the organization and its strategies. In assessing the role of human resources in an organization,

Source review

The strategic partner role for HR – Dyer and Holder (1988: 31–2)

The recommended role for the HR function is that of 'strategic partner'. This role typically has four aspects: (1) top HR executives cooperate with their line counterparts in formulating HR strategies, (2) top HR executives fully participate in all business strategy sessions as equals to CFOs and other top executives thus permitting early evaluation of proposals from an HR perspective, (3) HR executives work closely with line managers on an ongoing basis to ensure that all components of the business strategies are adequately implemented, and (4) the HR function itself is managed strategically.

management needs to determine the extent to which these professionals meet the following criteria:

1 Spend time with customers and clients – diagnosing, discussing and responding to needs.

2 Actively participate in business planning meetings and offer informed insights on strategic, technological and financial capabilities.

3 Understand business conditions.

4 Demonstrate competence in business knowledge, particularly customer relations, delivery of world-class management practices and management of change.

Schuler and Jackson (2007: *xiv*) made a similar point when they wrote: 'Today, human resource professionals are being challenged to learn more about the business, its strategy, its environment, its customers, and its competitors.'

Note that none of these comments indicated that HR should be aware of ethical as well as business considerations and act accordingly. However, to do Ulrich justice, he did write later that HR professionals should 'represent both employee needs and implement management agendas' (Ulrich, 1997: 5).

The term 'strategic business partner' has been shortened in common parlance to 'business partner', a term that has been taken up enthusiastically within the HR profession and its professional body – the CIPD. HR business partners work closely with line managers and enable them to achieve their objectives through their people.

The strategic role of HR professionals varies in accordance with their level or function as HR directors, heads of HR functions, business partners, or HR advisers and assistants.

The strategic role of HR directors

The strategic role of HR directors is to promote the achievement of the organization's goals and values by, 1) developing and implementing HR strategies that are integrated with the business strategy and are coherent and mutually supportive, 2) ensuring that a strategic approach is adopted that provides that HR activities support the business and add value, and 3) taking into account the ethical dimension of HRM. To carry out this role HR directors need to:

- understand the strategic goals of the organization;

- appreciate the business imperatives and performance drivers relative to these goals;

- understand the business model of the organization (how it makes money) and play a part in business model innovation;

- comprehend how sustainable competitive advantage can be obtained through the human capital of the organization and know how HR practices can contribute to the achievement of strategic goals;

- contribute to the development of the business strategy on an 'outside-in' basis (Wright *et al*, 2004), starting from an analysis of the customer, competitor and business issues the organization faces – the HR strategy then derives directly from these challenges to create solutions, add value and ensure that the organization has the distinctive human capital required to make an impact;

- contribute to the development for the business of a clear vision and a set of integrated values;

- ensure that senior management understands the HR implications of its business strategy;

- see the big picture, including the broader context (the competitive environment and the business, economic, social, legal factors that affect it) in which the organization operates;

- think in longer terms of where HR should go and how to get there;

- understand the kinds of employee behaviour required to execute the business strategy successfully;

- believe in and practise evidence-based management;

- be capable of making a powerful business case for any proposals on the development of HR strategies;

- fully embrace ethical considerations when developing and implementing HR strategy.

The strategic role of heads of HR functions

The strategic role of heads of HR functions is fundamentally the same for their function as that of HR directors for the whole organization. They promote the achievement of the organization's business goals by developing and implementing functional strategies that are aligned with the business strategy and integrated with the strategies for other HR functions, and adopt a strategic approach in the sense of ensuring that HR activities support the business, add value and are ethical. To carry out this role heads of HR functions should:

- understand the strategic goals of the organization as they affect their function;

- appreciate the business imperatives and performance drivers relative to these goals;

- help senior management to understand the implications of its strategy for the HR function;

- know how HR practices in the function can contribute to the achievement of the strategic goals;

- ensure that their activities provide added value for the organization;

- be aware of the broader context (the competitive environment and the business, economic, social and legal factors that affect it) in which the function operates;
- think in terms of the bigger and longer-term picture of where HR strategies for the function should go and how to get there;
- believe in and practise evidence-based management;
- be capable of making a powerful business case for any proposals on the development of HR strategies for the function;
- fully embrace ethical considerations when developing and implementing HR strategy for their function.

The strategic role of HR business partners

The strategic role of HR business partners is to promote the achievement of the business goals of the organizational unit or function in which they operate. To carry out this role they should:

- understand the business and its competitive environment;
- understand the goals of their part of the business and its plans to attain them;
- ensure that their activities provide added value for the unit or function;
- build relationships founded on trust with their line management clients;
- provide support to the strategic activities of their colleagues;
- align their activities with business requirements;
- believe in and practise evidence-based management;
- be proactive, anticipating requirements, identifying problems and producing innovative and evidence-based solutions to them;
- see the broad picture and rise above the day-to-day detail;
- fully take into account ethical considerations when performing their business partner role.

The strategic contribution of HR advisers or assistants

The role of HR advisers or assistants is primarily that of delivering effective HR services within their function or as a member of an HR service centre. While they are unlikely to be responsible for the formulation of HR strategies they may contribute to them within their own speciality. They will need to understand the business goals of the departments or managers for whom they provide services in order to ensure that these services support the achievement of those goals. They should also fully take into account ethical considerations when performing their role.

The strategic skills required

HR professionals who act strategically will think about what the organization wants to be and become and what they can do to ensure this happens. They will have insight into the real needs of the business and its people and will take a broad view of where the business is going. They will be capable of seeing 'the big picture', looking beyond the confines of the immediate problems they and the business face to what lies ahead, how these problems can be solved and what they can do to support the efforts of other people. This means that they need business, analytical and problem-solving skills, as described in the next three chapters of this book.

The HR Profession Map produced by the CIPD in 2009 sets out what HR professionals do and need to know in the area of 'strategy, insights and solutions'. The CIPD (2010) expanded on what it meant by the need for HR professionals to be insightful; see below.

HR strategic skills as defined by the CIPD

In general, according to the CIPD (2009: 2), an HR professional:

uses deep understanding of the business activities, strategies and plans and underlying drivers of and barriers to sustainable performance, and needs of customers and employees – and unique insights to drive business performance through the creation and delivery of human resources strategy and solutions.

In particular, the CIPD states that in using strategic skills, the HR professional:

● shows a bias towards considering the bigger picture at all times, observing connections and drawing conclusions about the impact of events and activities on each other;

● offers unique insights into the organization borne out of a deep understanding of the business and the market;

● sets out to be observant and to notice events that are out of the ordinary, makes connections and draws conclusions;

● creates meaning out of apparently unconnected ideas or events and uses insights to shape the views of managers;

● uses insights to lead and influence change at a strategic, tactical, team and individual level across the organization.

The CIPD also states that to exercise these skills effectively, HR professionals in their strategic role:

● know the way the organization is structured and how its teams work together;

● understand the product or service the organization provides;

● understand the organization's strategy, performance goals and drivers;

● understand the sector in which the organization operates and the market factors that impact performance;

● know how the organization makes money;

● understand and speak the 'language of the business' and how to translate the organization plan into a people plan;

● understand the capability and skills requirements for the organization to perform.

HR as an insight-driven discipline

The CIPD (2010: 4) expanded on what it meant by the use of 'insight' as follows:

The best HR functions understand exactly how their organization in their market facing their specific challenges can respond in a way unique to it. Indeed in the same way as marketing has become a consumer *insight-driven* function, so some HR functions are delivering unique *organization insight*, helping organizations to find new ways of meeting current and future challenges. In these functions, there is a new relationship to data-gathering and analysis – generating true insight.

Ten things to do if you want to be strategic

1 Exercise insight – understand the business and its competitive environment, what makes it successful and the external and internal political, social, competitive and economic factors that affect its performance.

2 Be aware of the goals of the business and its plans to attain them and understand the business model – 'how it makes money'.

3 Align what you are doing with the organization's business strategy.

4 Know where you are going and how you are going to get there.

5 Remember that formal strategic plans do not guarantee success; it is the implementation of the plans that delivers results.

6 Know how to plan the use of resources to make the best use of business opportunities.

7 Understand how you can contribute to the achievement of the objectives of the key functions in the business and support the strategic activities of your colleagues.

8 Be able to foresee longer-term developments, envisage options and their probable consequences, and select sound courses of action.

9 Rise above the day-to-day detail and see the broad picture.

10 Challenge the status quo.

Key learning points: Strategic HRM skills

The strategic role of the HR professional

HR strategic activities support the achievement of the organization's goals and values by aligning HR strategies to business strategies. HR professionals are involved in the development and implementation of forward-looking HR strategies that are integrated with one another. Importantly, they work with their line management colleagues in the continuous formulation and execution of the business strategy.

The strategic business partner model

HR practitioners share responsibility with their line management colleagues for the success of the enterprise. In 1985, Tyson described them as business managers who have the capacity to identify business opportunities, to see the broad picture and to understand how their role can help to achieve the company's business objectives. They integrate their activities closely with top management and ensure that they serve a long-term strategic purpose. They anticipate needs, act flexibly and are proactive.

The strategic role of HR directors

The strategic role of HR directors is to promote the achievement of the organization's goals and values by, 1) developing and implementing HR strategies that are integrated with the business strategy and are coherent and mutually supportive, 2) ensuring that a strategic approach is adopted that provides that HR activities support the business and add value, and 3) taking into account the ethical dimension of HRM.

The strategic role of heads of HR functions

The strategic role of heads of HR functions is fundamentally the same for their function as that of HR directors for the whole organization. They promote the achievement of the organization's business goals by developing and implementing functional strategies that are aligned with the business strategy and integrated with the strategies for other HR functions, and adopt a strategic approach in the sense of ensuring that HR activities support the business, add value and are ethical.

The strategic role of HR business partners

The strategic role of HR business partners is to promote the achievement of the business goals of the organizational unit or function in which they operate.

The strategic contribution of HR advisers or assistants

The role of HR advisers or assistants is primarily that of delivering effective HR services within their function or as a member of an HR service centre. While they will not be responsible for formulating HR strategies, they may contribute to them within their own specialty.

The strategic skills required

HR professionals who act strategically will think about what the organization wants to be and become and what they can do to ensure this happens. They will have insight into the real needs of the business and its people and will take a broad view of where the business is going. They will be capable of seeing 'the big picture', looking beyond the confines of the immediate problems they and the business face to what lies ahead, how these problems can be solved and what they can do to support the efforts of other people.

Questions

1   What is the strategic role of HR professionals?

2   What is the strategic business partner model?

3   What is the strategic role of HR directors?

4   What are the main strategic skills required?

References

CIPD (2009) *HR Profession Map: Strategy, insights and solutions*, http://www.cipd.co.uk/binaries/HR-Profession-Map, accessed 16 July 2011

CIPD (2010) *CIPD Next Generation*, London, CIPD

Dyer, L and Holder, G W (1988) Strategic human resource management and planning, in (ed) L Dyer, *Human Resource Management: Evolving roles and responsibilities*, Washington, DC, Bureau of National Affairs, pp 1–46

Schuler, R S and Jackson, S E (2007) *Strategic Human Resource Management*, 2nd edn, Oxford, Blackwell

Sparrow, P, Hesketh, A, Hird, M, Marsh, C and Balain, S (2010) Using business model change to tie HR into strategy: reversing the arrow, in (eds) P Sparrow, A Hesketh, M Hird and C Cooper, *Leading HR*, Basingstoke, Palgrave Macmillan, pp 68–89

Tyson, S (1985) Is this the very model of a modern personnel manager?, *Personnel Management*, May, pp 22–5

Ulrich, D (1997) *Human Resource Champions*, Boston, MA, Harvard Business School Press

Ulrich, D (1998) A new mandate for human resources, *Harvard Business Review*, January–February, pp 124–34

Ulrich, D and Lake, D (1990) *Organizational Capability: Competing from the inside out*, New York, Wiley

Wright, P M, Snell, S A and Jacobsen, H H (2004) Current approaches to HR strategies: inside-out versus outside-in, *Human Resource Planning*, 27 (4), pp 36–46

43
Problem-solving skills

LEARNING OUTCOMES

On completing this chapter you should be able to define these key concepts. You should also understand:

- How to improve problem-solving skills
- How to solve a problem

Introduction

Problem solving is a constant feature of life in organizations and elsewhere. A logical approach is desirable but this is not easy – the situations where problems have to be solved are often messy, with conflicting evidence, lack of data and political and emotional issues affecting those involved. But even if it is not possible to apply neat, logical and sequential methods, the principles of getting and analysing what information is available, considering alternatives and making the best choice based on the evidence, an analysis of the context and an assessment of the possible consequences, remain the same.

Problem solving

Problem solving is the process of analysing and understanding a problem, diagnosing its cause and deciding on a solution that solves the problem and prevents it being repeated. You will often have to react to problems as they arise, but as far as possible a proactive approach is desirable, involving anticipating potential problems and dealing with them in advance by taking preventative action using the normal approaches to problem solving set out below. Proactive problem solving may require creative thinking.

Problems and opportunities

It is often said that 'there are no problems, only opportunities'. This is not universally true, of course, but it does emphasize the point that a problem should lead to positive thinking about what is to be done now, rather than to recriminations. If a mistake has been made, the reasons for it should be analysed to ensure that it does not happen again.

Improving your skills

How can you improve your ability to solve problems? There are a few basic approaches you should use, discussed below.

Improve your analytical ability

A complicated situation can often be resolved by separating the whole into its component parts. Such an analysis should relate to facts, although, as Drucker (1955) points out, when trying to understand the root causes of a problem you may have to start with an opinion. Even if you ask people to search for the facts first, they will probably look for those facts that fit the conclusion they have already reached.

Opinions are a perfectly good starting point as long as they are brought out into the open at once and then tested against reality. Analyse each hypothesis and pick out the parts that need to be studied and tested. (Analytical skills are covered in Chapter 44.) Follett's (1924) 'law of the situation' – the logic of facts and events – should rule in the end.

Being creative

A strictly logical answer to the problem may not be the best one. Use creative thinking to get off your tramlines and dream up an entirely new approach.

Keep it simple

One of the basic principles of problem solving is known as Occam's razor. It states that: 'entities are not to be multiplied without necessity'. That is, always believe the simplest of several explanations.

Focus on implementation

A problem has not been solved until the decision has been implemented. Think carefully not only about how a thing is to be done (by whom, with what resources and by when) but also about its likely consequences – its impact on the organization and the people concerned and the extent to which they will cooperate. You will get less cooperation if you impose a solution. The best method is to arrange things so that everyone arrives jointly at a solution, freely agreed to be the one best suited to the situation (the law of the situation again).

Further consideration of the processes of evaluating evidence and options and to the consulting skills used in problem solving is given in the next chapter.

Twelve problem-solving steps

The 12 steps of problem solving are:

1 *Define the situation* – establish what has gone wrong or is about to go wrong.

2 *Specify objectives* – define what is to be achieved now or in the future to deal with an actual or potential problem or a change in circumstances.

3 *Develop hypotheses* – develop hypotheses about what has caused the problem.

4 *Get the facts* – find out what has actually happened and contrast this with an assessment of what ought to have happened. This is easier said than done. Insidious political factors may have contributed to the problem and could be difficult to identify and deal with. The facts may not be clear cut. They could be obscured by a mass of conflicting material. There may be lots of opinions but few verifiable facts. Remember that people will see what has happened in terms of their own position and feelings (their framework of reference). Try to understand the political climate and the attitudes and motivation of those concerned. Bear in mind that, as Pfeffer (1996: 36) commented, 'smart organizations occasionally do dumb things'. Obtain information about internal or external constraints that affect the situation.

5 *Analyse the facts* – determine what is relevant and what is irrelevant. Diagnose the likely cause or causes of the problem. Do not be tempted to focus on symptoms rather than root causes. Test any assumptions. Distinguish between opinions and facts. Dig into what lies behind the problem.

6 *Identify possible courses of action* – spell out what each involves.

7 *Evaluate alternative courses of action* – assess the extent to which they are likely to achieve the objectives, the cost of implementation, any practical difficulties that might emerge and the possible reactions of stakeholders. Critical evaluation techniques, as described in Chapter 44, can be used for this purpose.

8 *Weigh and decide* – determine which alternative is likely to result in the most practical and acceptable solution to the problem. This is often a balanced judgement.

9 *Decide on the objective* – set out goals for implementation of the decision.

10 *Adopt a 'means-end' approach where appropriate* – in complicated situations with long-term implications it may be useful to identify the steps required and select an action at each step that will move the process closer to the goal.

11 *Plan implementation* – prepare a timetable and identify and assemble the resources required.

12 *Implement* – monitor progress and evaluate success. Remember that a problem has not been solved until the decision has been implemented. Always work out the solution to a problem with implementation in mind.

Key learning points: Problem-solving skills

Problem solving is a constant feature of life in organizations and elsewhere. It is the process of analysing and understanding a problem, diagnosing its cause and deciding on a solution that solves the problem and prevents it being repeated.

To improve problem-solving skills it is necessary to: improve your analytical ability, be creative, keep it simple and focus on implementation.

The 12 steps of problem solving are:

1 Define the situation.

2 Specify objectives.

3 Develop hypotheses.

4 Get the facts.

5 Analyse the facts.

6 Identify possible courses of action.

7 Evaluate alternative courses of action.

8 Weigh and decide.

9 Decide on the objective.

10 Adopt a 'means-end' approach where appropriate.

11 Plan implementation.

12 Implement.

Questions

1 What is the nature of problem solving?

2 What is the purpose of analysis in problem solving?

3 What are the key steps that should be taken in problem solving?

References

Drucker, P (1955) *The Practice of Management*, London, Heinemann

Follett, M P (1924) *Creative Experience*, New York, Longmans Green

Pfeffer, J (1996) When it comes to 'best practices', why do smart organizations occasionally do dumb things?, *Organizational Dynamics*, Summer, pp 33–44

44
Analytical and critical skills

KEY CONCEPTS AND TERMS

Analysis

Critical thinking

Fallacy

Critical evaluation

Evidence-based management

Logical reasoning

LEARNING OUTCOMES

On completing this chapter you should be able to define these key concepts. You should also understand:

● The meaning of evidence-based management

● The nature of critical evaluation

● The nature of critical thinking

● The nature of logical reasoning

● The use of analytical skills

Introduction

Rousseau and Barends (2011: 221) remarked that 'Blind faith has no place in professional practice.' The effectiveness of HR initiatives and the processes of problem solving and decision making in which HR practitioners are constantly involved depend largely on thorough analysis and critical thinking, as covered in this chapter. The basis of all these is provided by evidence-based management, as discussed below.

Evidence-based management

Evidence-based management is a method of informing decision making by making use of appropriate information derived from the analysis of policy and practices and surveys of employee opinion within the organization, systematic benchmarking, and the messages delivered by relevant research. It was defined by Rousseau and Barends (2011: 221) as: 'A decision-making process combining critical thinking with the use of the best available scientific evidence and business information.'

The following comments on evidence-based management were made by Pfeffer and Sutton (2006: 70):

Nurture an evidence-based approach immediately by doing a few simple things that reflect the proper mindset. If you ask for evidence of efficacy every time a change is proposed, people will sit up and take notice. If you take the time to pursue the logic behind that evidence, people will become more disciplined in their own thinking. If you treat the organization like an unfinished prototype and encourage trial programs, pilot studies, and experimentation – and reward learning from these activities, even when something new fails – your organization will begin to develop its own evidence base.

The need for evidence-based management

Rousseau and Barends (2011: 221) observed that:

Evidence-based HR is motivated by a basic fact: faulty practices and decision-making abound in HR. Companies persist in using unstructured interviews to assess a job candidate's fit even though there is little evidence to support that. HR departments often pursue one-size-fits-all standardization in their policies, despite considerable evidence that programmes promoting flexibility benefit. In all honesty, can you answer 'yes' to the question, 'Do you know the scientific evidence for ANY of the HR practices your company uses?' Recent surveys of HR practitioners lead us to suspect that the frank response from many readers is 'no'.

The approach to evidence-based management

Rousseau (2006: 2012) suggested that at its core, evidence-based management combines four fundamental features in everyday management practice and decision making:

1 Use of the best-available evidence from peer-reviewed sources.

2 Systematic gathering of organizational facts, indicators and metrics to better act on the evidence.

3 Practitioner judgement assisted by procedures, practices and framework that reduce bias, improve decision quality and create more vivid learning over time.

4 Ethical considerations weighing the short- and long-term impacts of decisions on stakeholders and society.

A five-step approach was recommended by Briner et al (2009: 23):

1 Practitioners or managers gain understanding of the problem or issue.

2 Internal evidence is gathered about the issue or problem leading, possibly, to a reformulation of the problem to make it more specific.

3 External evidence is gathered from published research.

4 The views of stakeholders are obtained.

5 All the sources of information are examined and critically appraised.

It should be emphasized that what is done in organizations with the evidence depends largely on the context in which it is done. Cultural, social and political factors influence perceptions and judgements, and the extent to which people behave rationally is limited by their capacity to understand the complexities of the situation they are in and by their emotional reactions to it – the concept of bounded rationality, as expressed by Simon (1957).

But we need to understand the context – its impact on what is happening and how things are done. We need then to understand what actions can be taken to address the issues emerging from the situation. We need evidence that tells us what is going on within the organization, what has worked well elsewhere that might fit our requirements and what research has revealed about policies and practices that will guide us in making our decisions. And we need to use that evidence as the basis for our choice of the actions we intend to take. In other words, we need to practice evidence-based management using the analytical, logical reasoning and critical thinking skills described in the rest of this chapter.

Analytical skills

Analysis is the process of breaking down a condition or state of affairs into its constituent parts and establishing the relationships between them. In the Aristotelian sense, analysis involves discerning the particular features of a situation.

Analytical skills are used to gain a better understanding of a complex situation or problem. They involve the ability to visualize, articulate and solve complex problems and concepts and make decisions based on available information. Analytical skills include the capacity to evaluate that information to assess its significance, and the ability to apply logical and critical thinking to the situation. They provide the basis for a diagnosis of the cause or causes of a problem and therefore for its solution. Importantly, they are a means of gaining insight into issues that affect the success of the business and which influence business and HR strategy.

Logical reasoning

If you say people are logical, you mean that they draw reasonable inferences – their conclusions can be proved by reference to the facts used to support them – and they avoid ill-founded and tendentious arguments, generalizations and irrelevancies. Logical reasoning is the basis of critical thinking and evaluation. It takes place when there is a clear relationship (a line of reasoning) between the premise (the original proposition) and the conclusion, which is supported by valid and reliable evidence and does not rely on fallacious or misleading argument. Logical reasoning is what Stebbing (1959) called, 'Thinking to some purpose.' Clear thinking is required to establish the validity of a proposition, concept or idea.

It is necessary to question assumptions especially when a belief is expressed as a fact. You need to ask yourself – and others – 'What's the evidence for that?' You have to spot fallacious and misleading arguments. A fallacy is an unsound form of argument leading to an error in reasoning or a misleading impression. The most common form of fallacies that need to be discerned in other people's arguments or avoided in one's own are summarized below:

- *Affirming the consequent* – leaping to the conclusion that a hypothesis is true because a single cause of the consequence has been observed.

- *Begging the question* – taking for granted what has yet to be proved.

- *Chop logic* – 'Contrarywise', said Tweedledee, 'if it was so, it might be, and if it were so, it would be; but as it isn't it ain't. That's logic'. Chop logic may not always be as bad as that, but it is about drawing false conclusions and using dubious methods of argument. For example: selecting instances favourable to a contention while ignoring those that are counter to it, twisting an argument used by an opponent to mean something quite different from what was intended, diverting opponents by throwing on them the burden of proof for something they have not maintained, ignoring the point in dispute, changing the question to one that is less awkward to answer, and reiterating what has been denied and ignoring what has been asserted. Politicians know all about chop logic.

- *Confusing correlation with causation* – assuming that because A is associated with B it has caused B. It may or may not.

- *False choice* – a situation in which only two alternatives are considered, when in fact there are additional options.

- *Potted thinking* – using slogans and catchphrases to extend an assertion in an unwarrantable fashion.

- *Reaching false conclusions* – forming the view that because some are, then all are. An assertion about several cases is twisted into an assertion about all cases. The conclusion does not follow the premise. This is what logicians call the 'undistributed middle'.

- *Selective reasoning* – selecting instances favourable to a contention while ignoring those that conflict with it.

- *Sweeping statements* – over-simplifying the facts.

- *Special pleading* – focusing too much on one's own case and failing to see that there may be other points of view.

Critical thinking

Critical thinking is the process of analysing and evaluating the quality of ideas, theories and concepts to establish the degree to which they are valid and supported by the evidence and the extent to which they are biased. It involves reflecting on and interpreting data, drawing warranted conclusions and recognizing ill-defined assumptions.

'Critical' in this context does not mean disapproval or being negative. There are many positive uses of critical thinking, for example testing a hypothesis, proving a proposition or evaluating a concept, theory or argument. Critical thinking can occur whenever people weigh up evidence and make a judgement, solve a problem or reach a decision. The aim is to come to well-reasoned conclusions and solutions and to test them against relevant criteria and standards. Critical thinking calls for the ability to:

- recognize problems and establish ways of dealing with them;
- gather and marshal pertinent (relevant) information;
- identify unstated assumptions and values;
- interpret data, to appraise evidence and evaluate arguments;
- recognize the existence (or non-existence) of logical relationships between propositions;
- draw warranted conclusions and make valid generalizations;
- test assertions, conclusions and generalizations;
- reconstruct ideas or beliefs by examining and analysing relevant evidence.

Critical evaluation

Critical evaluation is the process of making informed judgements about the validity, relevance and usefulness of ideas and arguments. Critical evaluation means not taking anything for granted and, where necessary, challenging propositions.

It involves making informed judgements about the value of ideas and arguments. It uses critical thinking by analysing and evaluating the quality of theories and concepts to establish the degree to which they are valid and supported by the evidence (evidence-based) and the extent to which they are biased. The arguments for and against are weighed and the strength of the evidence on both sides is assessed. On the basis of this assessment, a conclusion is reached on which proposition or argument is to be preferred. Critical evaluation is required when testing propositions and evaluating the outcomes of research.

Testing propositions

Propositions based on research investigations and evidence can be tested by using the following checklist.

Checklist

- Was the scope of the investigation sufficiently comprehensive?
- Are the instances representative or are they selected simply to support a point of view?
- Are there contradictory instances that have not been looked for?
- Does the proposition conflict with other propositions for which there are equally good grounds?
- If there are any conflicting beliefs or contradictory items of evidence, have they been put to the test against the original proposition?
- Could the evidence lead to other equally valid conclusions?
- Are there any other factors that have not been taken into account that may have influenced the evidence and, therefore, the conclusion?

Critically evaluating research

Putting the outcomes of research, for example material published in academic journals, to the test requires critical evaluation and the following checklist can be used.

Checklist

- Is the research methodology sufficiently rigorous and appropriate?
- Are the results and conclusions consistent with the methodology used and its outcomes?
- Is the perspective adopted by the researchers stated clearly?
- Have hypotheses been stated clearly and tested thoroughly?
- Do there appear to be any misleading errors of omission or bias?
- Are any of the arguments tendentious?
- Are inferences, findings and conclusions derived from reliable and convincing evidence?
- Has a balanced approach been adopted?
- Have any underlying assumptions been identified and justified?
- Have the component parts been covered in terms of their interrelationships and their relationship with the whole?
- Have these component parts been disaggregated for close examination?
- Have they been reconstructed into a coherent whole based on underlying principles?

It is worth repeating that critical evaluation does not necessarily mean negative criticism; it means reaching a judgement based on analysis and evidence, and the judgement can be positive as well as negative.

Developing and justifying original arguments

An argument as an aspect of critical thinking consists of a presentation of reasons that support a contention. It consists of:

- a proposition or statement that expresses a point of view or belief;
- the reasoning that makes a case for the proposition or point of view;
- a discussion, the aim of which is to get the reader or listener to agree with the case that has been made;
- a conclusion that sums up the argument and its significance.

Developing an argument

An argument is based (predicated) on a premise (the proposition) that sets out the underpinning assumption. There may be more than one proposition or assumption. It could be phrased something like this: 'The argument is that A is the case. It is predicated on the assumption that B and C apply.' In a sense this suggests what conclusion the argument is intended to reach but it also indicates that this conclusion depends on the validity of the assumptions, which will have to be proved (there are such things as false premises).

Justifying an argument

The argument continues by supplying reasons to accept the proposition or point of view. These reasons have to be supported by evidence, which should be based on valid research, rigorous observation, or relevant and verifiable experience, not on hearsay. It involves logical reasoning, which avoids the fallacies referred to earlier and requires critical thinking, which means coming to well-reasoned conclusions and solutions and testing them against relevant criteria and standards. It also demands critical evaluation, which means reflecting on and interpreting data, drawing warranted conclusions and identifying faulty reasoning, assumptions and biases. Assumptions have to be tested rigorously and research evidence has to be evaluated. The checklists set out above can be used for this purpose.

Key learning points: Analytical and critical skills

Basis of the processes of problem solving and decision making

The processes of problem solving and decision making depend largely on effective analysis, critical thinking and evaluation.

Evidence-based management

Evidence-based management is a method of informing decision making by making use of appropriate information derived from the analysis of HR policy and practices and surveys of employee opinion within the organization, systematic benchmarking, and the messages delivered by relevant research.

Analytical skills

Analysis is the process of gaining a better understanding of a complex situation or problem by breaking it down into its constituent parts and establishing the relationships between them.

Logical reasoning

Logical reasoning involves clear thinking to establish the validity of a proposition, concept or idea.

Critical thinking

Critical thinking clarifies goals, examines assumptions, discerns hidden values, evaluates evidence, accomplishes actions and assesses conclusions.

Critical evaluation

Critical evaluation involves making informed judgements about the value of ideas and arguments.

Developing and justifying original arguments

An argument as an aspect of critical thinking consists of a presentation of reasons that support a contention.

Questions

1 What is evidence-based management?
2 What does analysis involve?
3 What is logical reasoning?
4 What is a fallacy (give examples of three typical fallacies)?
5 What does critical thinking involve?
6 What is critical evaluation?
7 What approaches can be used to test propositions?
8 How do you critically evaluate research?
9 What does argument consist of?
10 How do you develop an argument?
11 How do you justify an argument?

References

Briner, R B, Denyer, D and Rousseau, D M (2009) Evidence-based management: concept clean-up time?, *Academy of Management Perspectives*, September, pp 19–32

Pfeffer, J and Sutton, R I (2006) Evidence-based management, *Harvard Business Review*, January, pp 62–74

Rousseau, D M (2006) Is there such a thing as evidence-based management?, *Academy of Management Review*, **31** (2), pp 256–69

Rousseau, D M and Barends, E G (2011) Becoming an evidence-based HR practitioner, *Human Resource Management Journal*, **21** (3), pp 221–35

Simon, H (1957) *Administrative Behaviour*, New York, Macmillan

Stebbing, S (1959) *Thinking to Some Purpose*, Harmondsworth, Penguin Books

45
Research skills

KEY CONCEPTS AND TERMS

Critical evaluation	Deduction
Evidence-based	Experimental design
Falsification	Grounded theory
Hypothesis	Induction
Likert scale	Multivariate analysis
Paradigm	Phenomenology
Positivism	Proposition
Qualitative research	Quantitative research
Reductionism	The research question
Theory	Triangulation

LEARNING OUTCOMES

On completing this chapter you should be able to define these key concepts. You should also know about:

- Approaches to research
- The basics of statistical analysis
- Literature reviews
- Methods of collecting data
- The nature of research
- Planning and conducting research programmes
- Research philosophy

Introduction

HRM specialists and those studying for HR professional qualifications may be involved in conducting or taking part in research projects. Postgraduate students will almost certainly do so. Qualified HR specialists should keep up to date as part of their continuous professional development by studying publications that present research findings, such as those produced by the CIPD, or by reading articles in academic journals or those based on research in HR journals such as *PM* (*People Management*). Students must extend their understanding of HRM through reading about research findings.

The purpose of this chapter is to describe the skills and techniques used in research and explain what is involved in planning and conducting research projects. This will be done against the background of a brief review of the nature and philosophy of research.

The nature of research

Research is concerned with establishing what is and from this predicting what will be. It does not decide what ought to be; that is for people interpreting the lessons from research in their own context. Research is about the conception and testing of ideas and hypotheses. This is a creative and imaginative process, although new information is normally obtained within the framework of existing theory and knowledge. Logic and rational argument are methods of testing ideas after they have been created.

What emerges from research is a theory – a well-established explanatory principle that has been tested and can be used to make predictions of future developments. A theory is produced by clear, logical and linear development of argument with a close relationship between information, hypothesis and conclusion. Quality of information is a criterion for good research, as is the use of critical evaluation techniques.

The production of narratives that depict events (case studies) or the collection of data through surveys are elements in research programmes, but they can stand alone as useful pieces of information that illustrate practice. Research can be based on a philosophy of positivism or phenomenology.

Positivism

Positivism is the belief that researchers should focus on facts (observable reality), look for causality and fundamental laws, reduce phenomena to their simplest elements (reductionism), formulate hypotheses and then test them. Researchers are objective analysts. The emphasis in positivism is on quantifiable observations that lend themselves to statistical analysis. It tends to be deductive.

Phenomenology

Phenomenology focuses more on the meaning of phenomena than on the facts associated with them. Researchers adopting this philosophy try to understand what is happening. Their approach is holistic, covering the complete picture, rather than reductionist. Researchers collect and analyse evidence, but their purpose is to use this data to develop ideas that explain the meaning of things. They believe that reality is socially constructed rather than objectively determined. Using a phenomenological approach means that the research unfolds as it proceeds – early evidence is used to indicate how to move on to the next stage of evidence collection and analysis, and so on. It tends to be inductive.

Planning and conducting research programmes

Against this background, the steps required to plan and conduct a research programme are:

1 *Define research area.* This should be one that interests the researcher and has a clear link to an accepted theory or an important issue worth exploring. The research should generate fresh insights into the topic. It is necessary to undertake background reading at this stage by means of a preliminary review of the literature (particularly academic journals but also books, especially those based on research) to identify what has already been achieved in this area and any gaps (academic articles often include proposals on further research). The context within which the research is to be carried out needs to be explained and justified.

2 *Formulate initial research question.* This provides a rationale for the research. It is in effect a statement that answers the questions: 'What is this research project intended to address and what is its potential contribution to increasing knowledge?' At this stage it is based on the outcome of the initial work carried out in step 1, but it will be refined and reformulated at a later stage when more information about the research has been made available.

3 *Review literature.* A literature review will focus mainly on academic journals. The aim is to establish what is already known about the topic, identify existing theoretical frameworks and find out what other relevant research has been carried out.

4 *Develop theoretical framework.* It is necessary to conduct the research within a clear theoretical framework. This will set out the models, concepts and theories that can be drawn on and developed to provide an answer to the research question. If an appropriate framework does not exist, a grounded theory approach may be required in which the researcher uses empirical evidence directly to establish the concepts and relationships that will be contained in the theory adopted as the research framework. It is important to be clear about the assumptions, conditions and limitations that impinge on the investigation.

5 *Finalize the research question.* The initial research question needs to be finalized in the light of the outcome of the earlier steps. The final research question will identify the issues to be explored and the problems to be investigated. It will include a statement of intent, which will set out what the research is to achieve. This statement leads to the formulation of the hypotheses or propositions that will be tested by survey or experiment during the research programme.

6 *Formulate hypotheses or propositions.* A hypothesis provisionally states a relationship between two concepts in such a way that the consequences of the statement being true can be tested. Hypotheses (there may be more than one) indicate the form the research project will take in the shape of obtaining and analysing the evidence required to test them. Hypotheses may be attached to the statement of the research question. A proposition is a proposal put forward as an explanation of an event, a possible situation or a form of behaviour that will be tested by the research.

7 *Design the research.* This means considering initially what research philosophy will be adopted. Is it to be positivist, phenomenological, or both? It is then necessary to establish the methodology. A decision will need to be made as to the extent to which the research will be quantitative, qualitative or, again, a combination of the two. Methods of collecting and analysing evidence and testing hypotheses or propositions will be described. The sources of evidence and how they will be accessed will be identified. This will include the analysis of primary and secondary source documents, further literature reviews, interviews, surveys and field work. Consideration is given to the extent to which triangulation (comparing the information obtained from different sources) is desirable (it usually is) and possible. The design must clearly indicate how it will address the research question and be consistent with the theoretical framework. If at a later stage this is shown not to be the case, then the design will have to be amended.

8 *Draw up research programme.* This will cover how the research will be conducted, the timetable and the resources (funding, people, software, etc) required. Careful project planning is essential.

9 *Prepare and submit proposal.* This will justify the research by setting out the research question, the proposed methodology, and how the research is intended to increase knowledge and understanding. It will also describe the programme and the resources required.

10 *Conduct the research project.* This includes obtaining and analysing the evidence from the various sources needed to answer the research question and prove or disprove hypotheses. The significance of the findings in relation to the research question and the

hypotheses will be discussed and reference will be made to relevant information provided in the literature. This involves an extended literary review, data collection, the use of logical, analytical and critical thinking processes and the use of statistical analysis where relevant.

11   *Develop conclusions.* These draw together all the evidence. They provide the answer to the research question and explain why hypotheses have been accepted or rejected. The significance of the findings will also be assessed in terms of how they contribute to the development of existing knowledge and understanding. Any limitations to the study should also be mentioned.

12   *Make recommendations.* These set out any guidelines emerging from the research. They may also indicate any follow-up actions required if the research has been conducted within an organization.

Quantitative and qualitative methods of research

One of the key decisions to be made in planning and conducting a research programme is the extent to which quantitative methods (which broadly follow the positivist philosophy) or qualitative methods (which broadly follow the phenomenological philosophy) are used.

Quantitative research

Quantitative research is empirical – based on the collection of factual data, which is measured and quantified. It answers research questions from the viewpoint of the researcher. It may involve a considerable amount of statistical analysis, using methods for collecting the data through questionnaires, surveys, observation and experiment. The collection of data is distinct from its analysis.

Qualitative research

Qualitative research aims to generate insights into situations and behaviour so that the meaning of what

is happening can be understood. It emphasizes the interpretation of behaviour from the viewpoint of the participants. It is based on evidence that may not be easily reduced to numbers. It makes use of interviews, case studies and observation but it may also draw on the information obtained from surveys. It may produce narratives or 'stories' describing situations, events or processes.

Methods of collecting data

The main methods of collecting data are interviews, questionnaires, surveys, case studies, observation, diaries and experimental designs.

Interviews

Interviews are an important research method. They obtain factual data and insights into attitudes and feelings and can take three forms:

1   *Structured*, which means that they are entirely concerned with obtaining answers to a pre-prepared set of questions. This ensures that every topic is covered and minimizes variations between respondents. But they may be too rigid and inhibit spontaneous and revealing reactions.

2   *Unstructured*, which means that no questions have been prepared in advance and the person being interviewed is left free to talk about the subject without interruption or intervention. Such 'non-directive' interviews are intended to provide greater insight into the interviewee's perspective, avoid fitting respondents into pre-determined categories and enable interviewers to explore issues as they arise. But they can be inconsequential and lead to poor data that is difficult to analyse.

3   *Semi-structured*, which means that the areas of interest have been pre-determined and the key questions to be asked or information to be obtained have been identified. The interviewer may have a checklist but does not follow this rigidly. This approach enables the interviewer to phrase questions and vary their order to suit the special characteristics of each interviewee. It may avoid the

problems of the completely structured or unstructured interview but it does require a considerable degree of skill on the part of the interviewer.

Interviews are basically qualitative but they can become more quantitative by the use of content analysis. This records the number of times reference is made in an interview to the key issues or areas of interest it was intended to cover.

The advantages of interviews are that they obtain information directly from people involved in the area being researched and can provide insights into attitudes and perspectives that questionnaires and surveys will not reveal, thus promoting in-depth understanding. They enable the interviewer to probe answers and check that questions had been understood. But the disadvantages are that:

- the construction of the interview questions may result in leading questions or bland answers;
- interviewers may influence the interviewees' reactions by imposing their own reference frame;
- respondents may tell interviewers what they want to hear;
- they are time-consuming – to set up, to conduct and to analyse;
- they require considerable interviewing skills, including the abilities to recognize what is important and relevant, to probe when necessary, to listen and to control the interview so that it covers the ground it was intended to cover.

Questionnaires

Questionnaires collect data systematically by obtaining answers on the key issues and opinions that need to be explored in a research project. They are frequently used as a means of gathering information on matters of fact or opinion. They use a variety of methods, namely: closed questions that require a yes or no answer, ranking in order of importance or value, or Likert scales. The latter, named after Rensis Likert, the American sociologist who invented them, ask respondents to indicate the extent to which they agree or disagree with a statement. For example, in response to a statement such as, 'I like my job' the choice may be 1 strongly agree, 2 agree, 3 disagree, 4 strongly disagree. Alternatively, an extended scale may be used and respondents asked to ring round the number that reflects their view about the statement (the higher the number the greater the agreement), for example:

My contribution is fully recognized 1 2 3 4 5 6 7

Extended scales facilitate the quantitative analysis of responses to questionnaires.

To construct and use a questionnaire effectively it is necessary to:

1 Identify the key issues and potential questions.

2 Ensure questions are clear.

3 Avoid asking two questions in one item.

4 Avoid leading questions that supply their own answers.

5 Decide on the structure of the questionnaire including its length (not too many items) and the choice of scale.

6 Code questions for ease of analysis.

7 Start with simple factual questions, moving on later to items of opinion or values.

8 Add variety and the opportunity to check consistency by interspersing positive statements such as, 'I like working for my boss' with occasional associated negative ones such as, 'I do not get adequate support from my boss.'

9 Pilot test the questionnaire.

10 Code results and analyse. Where rating scales have been used the analysis can be quantified for comparison purposes. Content analysis can be used to analyse narrative answers to open-ended questions.

Questionnaires can effectively gather factual evidence but are not so useful for researchers who are investigating how or why things are happening. It is also impossible to assess the degree of subjectivity that has crept in when expressing opinions. For example, HR managers may give an opinion of the extent to which a performance-related pay scheme has in fact improved performance but the evidence to support that opinion will be lacking. This is where interviews can be much more informative.

Surveys

Surveys obtain information from a defined population of people. Typically, they are based on questionnaires but they can provide more powerful data than other methods by using a combination of questionnaires and interviews and, possibly, focus groups (groups of people gathered together to answer and discuss specific questions). When developing and administering surveys the issues are:

1 The definition of the purpose of the survey and the outcomes hoped for – these must be as precise as possible.

2 The population to be covered – this may involve a census of the whole population. Alternatively, if the population is large, sampling will be necessary (see below).

3 The choice of methods – relying entirely on questionnaires may limit the validity of the findings. It is better, if time and the availability of finance permit, to complement them with interviews and, possibly, focus groups. Consideration has to be give to the extent to which triangulation (comparing the information obtained from different sources) is appropriate.

4 The questions to which answers are required, whichever method is used.

5 The design of questionnaires and the ways in which interview or focus groups, if used, should be structured.

6 How the outcome of the survey will be analysed and presented, including the use of case studies.

Sampling

In using surveys, and possibly other methods, it may not be feasible to cover the whole population (the sampling frame) and sampling will therefore be necessary. Sampling means that a proportion of the total population is selected for study and the aim is to see that this proportion represents the characteristics of the whole population. The sample must not be biased and that is why in large-scale surveys use is made of random sampling, ie the individuals covered by a survey are not selected in accordance with any criteria except that they exist in the population and can be reached by the survey. It is the equivalent of drawing numbers out of a hat. However, if the sample frame is considered to be already arranged randomly as in the electoral roll, then structured sampling, that is, sampling at regular intervals, can be employed.

Sampling can produce varying degrees of error depending on the size of the sample. Statistical techniques can be used to establish sample errors and confidence limits. For example, they might establish that a sampling error is 3 per cent and the confidence limit is 95 per cent. This could be reasonably satisfactory, depending on the nature of the research (medical research aims to achieve 100 per cent confidence).

Case studies

A case study is a description or history of an event or sequence of events in a real-life setting. In learning and development, case studies are analysed by those involved to learn something by diagnosing the causes of a problem and working out how to solve it.

Case studies are used extensively in HRM research as a means of collecting empirical evidence in a real-life context. Information is obtained about an event or a set of events that establishes what has happened, how it happened and why. Case studies provide information that contributes to the creation of a theory as part of a grounded theory approach or the validation of an established theory. In addition, they can take the form of stories or narratives that illuminate a decision or a set of decisions, why they were taken, how they were implemented and with what result. They can illustrate a total situation and describe the processes involved and how individuals and groups behave in a social setting.

Case study protocol sets out the objectives of the research, how the case study will support the achievement of those objectives, including the evidence required, and how the work of producing the case study will be conducted. The methodology covers:

- sources of evidence – interviews, observation, documents and records;

- the need to use multiple sources of evidence (triangulation) so far as possible;

- the questions to which answers need to be obtained;

- how the case study should be set up, including informing those involved of what is taking place and enlisting their support;

- the schedule of interviews and other evidence collection activities;

- how the case study database recording the evidence will be set up and maintained;

- how the case study will be presented – including the chain of evidence so that the reader can follow the argument and trace the development of events, the headings and report guidelines (these may be finalized during the course of the exercise) and whether or not the name of the organization will be revealed on publication (named cases studies are more convincing than anonymous ones);

- how approval will be sought for the publication of the case study, especially if it reveals the name of the organization.

Case studies are useful ways of collecting information on the reality of organizational life and processes. But there is a danger of them being no more than a story or an anecdote that does not contribute to greater knowledge or understanding. Quite a lot of skill and persistence are required from the researcher in gaining support, ensuring that relevant and revealing information is obtained and presenting the case study as a convincing narrative from which valid and interesting conclusions can be derived. All this must be done without taking a biased view, which can be difficult.

Observation

Observation of individuals or groups at work is a method of getting a direct and realistic impression of what is happening. It can be done by a detached or an involved observer, or by participant observation.

Detached observers who simply study what is going on without getting involved with the people concerned may only get a superficial impression of what is happening and may be resented by the people under observation as 'eaves-dropping'. Involved observers work closely with employees and can move around, observe and participate as appropriate. This means that they can get closer to

events and are more likely to be accepted, especially if the objectives and methods have been agreed in advance.

Participant observation in the fullest sense means that the researcher becomes an employee and experiences the work and the social processes that take place at first hand. This can provide powerful insights but is time-consuming and requires considerable skill and persistence.

The issues with any form of observation are getting close enough to events to understand their significance and then analysing the mass of information that might be produced in order to come up with findings that contribute to answering the research question.

Diaries

Getting people to complete diaries of what they do is a method of building a realistic picture of how people, especially managers, spend their time.

Experimental designs

Experimental designs involve setting up an experimental group and a control group and then placing subjects at random in one or other group. The conditions under which the experimental group functions are then manipulated and the outcomes compared with the control group, whose conditions remain unchanged. The classic case of an experimental design was the Hawthorne experiment, the results of which had a major impact on thinking about how groups function and on the human relations movement. But this was exceptional. It is much easier to use experiments in a laboratory setting which has been done many times with students. But there is always the feeling that such experiments do not reflect real-life conditions.

Processes involved in research

This section describes the logical, analytical and critical thinking processes that are used in research: deduction, induction, hypothesis testing, grounded theory, paradigms and critical evaluation.

Deduction

Research involves deduction, which is the process of using logical reasoning to reach a conclusion that necessarily follows from general or universal premises. If the premises are correct, so is the deduction. The conclusion is therefore contained within the evidence. It is not a creative or imaginative argument that produces new ideas.

Induction

Research can also be based on induction, which is the process of reaching generalized conclusions from the observation of particular instances. In contrast to deduction, inductive conclusions may be tentative but they contain new ideas. In research, both deductive and inductive reasoning can be used in hypothesis testing.

Hypothesis testing

Formulating a hypothesis is an important element in a research project in that it provides a basis for the development of theory and the collection and analysis of data. A hypothesis is a supposition – a tentative explanation of something. It is a provisional statement that is taken to be true for the purpose of argument or a study and usually relates to an existing wider body of knowledge or theory. A hypothesis has to be tested and should be distinguished from a theory which, by definition, has been tested. A good hypothesis contains two concepts and proposes a relationship between the two. A working hypothesis is a general hypothesis that has been operationalized so that it can be tested.

Hypothesis formulation and testing uses the strengths of both deductive and inductive argument; the former entirely conclusive but unimaginative, the latter tentative but creative. Induction produces ideas and deduction tests them.

To test a hypothesis, data has to be obtained that will demonstrate that its predicted consequences are true or false. Simply leaping to the conclusion that a hypothesis is true because a single cause of the consequence has been observed falls into the trap of what logicians call the 'fallacy of affirming the consequent'. There may be alternative and more valid causes. The preferred method of testing is that of denying the consequent. This is 'falsification' as advocated by Popper (1959). His view was that however much data may be assembled to support a hypothesis, it is not possible to reach a conclusive proof of the truth of that hypothesis. Popper therefore proposed that it was insufficient simply to assemble confirmatory evidence: what must also be obtained is evidence that refutes the hypothesis. Only one instance of refutation is needed to falsify a theory, whereas however many confirmations of the theory exist it will still not be proved conclusively.

Grounded theory

Grounded theory is an inductive method of developing the general features of a theory by grounding the account in empirical observations or evidence. The researcher uses empirical evidence directly to establish the concepts and relationships that will be contained in the theory. Evidence is collected from both primary sources (ie obtained directly by the researcher from the originator of the evidence) and secondary sources (ie information that is already available in the literature or on the internet). Use is made of triangulation.

Paradigm

The term 'paradigm' has become popularized as meaning a way of looking at things. It is often used loosely, but properly it means the philosophical and theoretical framework of a scientific school or discipline within which theories, laws and generalizations and the experiments performed in support of them, are formulated. In other words, it is a common perspective that underpins the work of theorists so that they use the same approach to conducting research.

Critical evaluation

Critical evaluation involves making informed judgements about the value of ideas and arguments. It uses critical thinking, which is the process of analysing and evaluating the quality of ideas, theories and concepts to establish the degree to which they are valid and supported by the evidence (evidence-based) and the extent to which they are biased. It means reflecting on and interpreting data, drawing warranted conclusions and identifying faulty reasoning, assumptions and biases. A creative leap may be required to reach a judgement; it was described fully in Chapter 43.

Key learning points: Research skills

The nature of research

Research is concerned with establishing what is and from this predicting what will be. It is about the conception and testing of ideas.

Research philosophy

Research design can be based on a philosophy of positivism or phenomenology. *Positivism* is the belief that researchers should focus on facts (observable reality), look for causality and fundamental laws. *Phenomenology* is concerned more with the meaning of phenomena than the facts associated with them.

Planning and conducting research programmes

1   Define research area.

2   Formulate initial research question.

3   Review literature.

4   Assess existing theoretical frameworks.

5   Formalize the research question.

6   Formulate hypotheses.

7   Establish the methodology.

8   Draw up research programme.

9   Prepare and submit proposal.

10   Collect and analyse evidence.

11   Develop conclusions.

Approaches to research

- Research can be quantitative or qualitative.

- It can use inductive or deductive methods.

- It involves the testing of hypotheses and may adopt a grounded theory approach, ie an inductive method of developing the general features of a theory by grounding the account in empirical observations or evidence.

- Use may be made of paradigms – common perspectives that underpin the work of theorists so that they use the same approach to conducting research.

- Informed judgements about the value of ideas and arguments are made through critical evaluation.

- It makes use of critical thinking, which is the process of analysing and evaluating the quality of ideas, theories and concepts to establish the degree to which they are valid and supported by the evidence.

Methods of collecting data

- Interviews obtain factual data and insights into attitudes and feelings and can be structured, unstructured or semi-structured.

- Questionnaires collect data systematically by obtaining answers on the key issues and opinions that need to be explored in a research project.

- Surveys obtain information from a defined population of people.

- Case studies collect empirical evidence in a real-life context.

Questions

1 What is the nature of research?

2 What are the steps required to conduct a research project?

3 What are the advantages and disadvantages of interviews as a research technique?

4 What are the advantages and disadvantages of case studies as a research technique?

5 What is induction?

6 What is deduction?

7 What is grounded theory?

8 What is triangulation?

9 What is the difference between a hypothesis and a theory?

10 What is a paradigm?

Reference

Popper, K (1959) *The Logic of Scientific Discovery*, London, Hutchinson

Key learning points: Statistical skills

Use of statistics

Statistics are used to describe and summarize data relating to a 'population', ie a homogeneous set of items with variable individual values. This involves measuring frequencies, central tendencies and dispersion.

They are also used, to measure the relationships between variables (correlation and regression) to establish the relation between cause and effect (causality) and to assess the degree of confidence that can be attached to conclusions (tests of significance) and to test hypotheses (the chi-squared test and null-hypothesis testing).

Statistics are used extensively in HRM to analyse and present quantitative information that can be used to guide decisions and monitor outcomes.

Measures of central tendency

Measures of central tendency identify the middle or centre of a set of data. There are three types: arithmetic average or mean, median and mode.

Measures of dispersion

It is useful to measure the extent to which the items in a set are dispersed or spread over a range of data.

Correlation

Correlation represents the relationship between two variables. If they are highly correlated they are strongly connected to one another, and vice versa.

Regression

Regression is another way of looking at the relationship between variables. It expresses how changes in levels of one item relate to changes in levels of another.

Causality

Determining the link between independent and dependent variables (cause and effect) – is a major issue in research, especially in the HRM field. It may be relatively easy to establish correlations in the shape of a demonstration that X is associated with Y; it is much more difficult and sometimes impossible to prove that X causes Y.

Tests of significance

Significance as a statistical concept refers to the degree to which an event could have occurred by chance.

Questions

1 How are statistics used?
2 What use is made by HR specialists of statistics?
3 What is frequency in statistics?
4 What are the three measures of central tendency?
5 What is dispersion and how is it measured?
6 What is correlation?
7 What is regression?
8 What is causality?
9 What are the problems of establishing causation?
10 What is a test of significance?
11 How can hypotheses be tested?

47
Selection interviewing skills

LEARNING OUTCOMES

On completing this chapter you should be able to define these key concepts. You should also know about:

- Selection interviewing skills
- Planning the interview
- Coming to a conclusion
- Preparing for the interview
- Questioning techniques
- Dos and don'ts of selection interviewing

Introduction

The purpose of a selection interview is to establish the extent to which a candidate will be able to do the job. This means finding out how well a candidate's levels of skill, knowledge, abilities and competency fit a person specification for the job that sets out these requirements. Selection interviewing is a skilled process, and this chapter starts with a description of the basic skills required. It then deals with the three areas in which these skills are applied: preparing for the interview, conducting the interview and reaching a conclusion.

Selection interviewing skills

An interview is a conversation with a purpose. It is a conversation because candidates should be given the opportunity to talk freely about themselves and their careers. But the conversation has to be planned, directed and controlled to achieve your aims in the time available. Overall, an effective approach to interviewing can be summed up as the three Cs:

- *Content* – the information you want and the questions you ask to get it.
- *Contact* – your ability to make and maintain good contact with candidates; to establish the sort of rapport that will encourage them to talk freely, thus revealing their strengths *and* their weaknesses.
- *Control* – your ability to control the interview so that you get the information you want.

This involves using the following interviewing skills: establishing rapport, questioning, listening, maintaining continuity, keeping control and note taking.

Establishing rapport

Establishing rapport means establishing a good relationship with candidates – getting on their wavelength, putting them at ease, encouraging them to respond and generally being friendly. This is not just a question of being 'nice' to candidates. If you achieve rapport you are more likely to get them to talk freely about both their strengths and weaknesses.

Good rapport is created by the way in which you greet candidates, how you start the interview and how you put your questions and respond to replies. Questions should not be posed aggressively or imply that you are criticizing some aspect of the candidate's career. Some people like the idea of 'stress' interviews but they are counter-productive. Candidates clam up and gain a negative impression of you and the organization.

When responding to answers you should be appreciative, not critical: 'Thank you, that was very helpful; now can we go on to …?' not, 'Well, it seems to me that things did not go according to plan.'

Body language can also be important. If you maintain natural eye contact, avoid slumping in your seat, nod and make encouraging comments when appropriate, you will establish better rapport and get more out of the interview.

Questioning

Questioning is the key skill interviewers need to possess. Their purpose is to draw candidates out and elicit the information the interviewer has decided must be obtained to reach a conclusion. Questioning is a fundamental part of a structured interview. There are a number of different types of questions, described later in the section on questioning techniques.

Listening

If an interview is a conversation with a purpose, listening skills are important. You need not only to hear but also to understand what candidates are saying. When interviewing you must concentrate on what candidates are telling you. Summarizing at regular intervals forces you to listen because you have to pay attention to what they have been saying in order to get the gist of their replies. If you play back to candidates your understanding of what they have told you for them to confirm or amend, it will ensure that you have fully comprehended the messages they are delivering.

Maintaining continuity

So far as possible link your questions to a candidate's last reply so that the interview progresses logically and a cumulative set of data is built up. You can put bridging questions to candidates such as: 'Thank you, that was an interesting summary of what you have been doing in this aspect of your work. Now, could you tell me something about your other key responsibilities?'

Keeping control

You want candidates to talk, but not too much. When preparing for the interview you should have drawn up an agenda and you must try to stick to it. Don't cut candidates short too brutally but say something like: 'Thank you, I've got a good picture of that, now what about …?'

Focus on specifics as much as you can. If candidates ramble on a bit, ask a pointed question (a 'probe' question) that asks for an example illustrating the particular aspect of their work that you are considering.

Note taking

You won't remember everything that candidates tell you. It is useful to take notes of the key points they make, discreetly, but not surreptitiously. However, don't put candidates off by frowning or tut-tutting when you are making a negative note. It may be helpful to ask candidates if they would mind if you take notes. They can't really object, but will appreciate the fact that they have been asked.

Preparing for the interview

Your first step in preparing for an interview is to familiarize or re-familiarize yourself with the person specification which, as mentioned in Chapter 19, should be set out under the following headings:

- *Knowledge* – what the individual needs to know to carry out the role.
- *Skills and abilities* – what the individual has to be able to do to carry out the role.
- *Behavioural competencies* – the types of behaviour required for successful performance of the role. These should be role-specific, ideally based on an analysis of employees who are carrying out their roles effectively. The behaviours should also be linked to the core values and competency framework of the organization to help in ensuring that candidates will fit and support the organization's culture.
- *Qualifications and training* – the professional, technical or academic qualifications required or the training that the candidate should have undertaken.
- *Experience* – the types of achievements and activities likely to predict success.
- *Specific demands* – anything that the role holder will be expected to achieve in specified areas, eg develop new markets or products, improve sales, productivity or levels of customer service, introduce new systems or processes.
- *Special requirements* – travelling, unsocial hours, mobility, etc.

You should then read the candidates' CVs and application forms or letters and refer to any other information about them obtained from the internet. This will identify any special questions you should ask about their career. For example, it may be necessary to fill in any gaps: 'What does this gap between jobs C and D signify?' (although you would not put the question as baldly as that; it would be better to say something like this: 'I see there was a gap of six months between when you left your job in C and started in D. Would you mind telling me what you were doing during this time?')

Finally, you should consider how you will structure and plan the interview.

Structuring the interview

A structured interview is one that is based on a defined framework within which there is a set of predetermined questions. All candidates are asked the same questions and the answers may be scored through a rating system. The most typical framework is the person specification, which means that the questions focus on the KSAs (knowledge, skills and abilities) required and the type and level of behavioural competencies expected.

Interviews can be competency-based, which means that they are structured by reference to the competencies required for effective performance in the job. These could be just behavioural competencies, which specify behaviour requirements, or they could be technical competencies – what people have to know and be able to do in terms of knowledge and skills to carry out their roles effectively. If both types of competency are included, as is desirable in most situations, then a competency-based interview is in effect one based on the person specification.

Planning the interview

Structured interviews need to be planned in terms of their three main parts, the questions to be put to candidates and how the questions will be sequenced.

The parts of an interview

The content of an interview can be analysed into three parts: its beginning, middle and end.

Beginning

At the start of the interview you should put candidates at their ease. You want them to talk freely in response to your questions. They won't do this if you plunge in too abruptly. Welcome them and thank them for coming to the interview, expressing genuine pleasure about the meeting. But don't waste too much time talking about their journey or the weather.

Some interviewers start by describing the company and the job. Wherever possible it is best to eliminate this part of the interview by sending candidates a brief job description and something about the organization.

If you are not careful you will spend far too much time at this stage, especially if the candidate later turns out to be clearly unsuitable. A brief reference to the job should suffice, and this can be extended at the end of the interview.

Middle

This is when you ask questions designed to provide information on the extent to which the knowledge, skills, capabilities and personal qualities of candidates meet the person specification, and the career history and ambitions of candidates and, sometimes, on certain aspects of their behaviour at work such as sickness and absenteeism.

This part should take at least 80 per cent of the time, leaving, say, 5 per cent at the beginning and 15 per cent at the end.

End

At the end of the interview you should give candidates the opportunity to ask about the job and the company. How they do this can often give you clues as to the degree to which applicants are interested and their ability to ask pertinent questions.

You may want to expand a little on the job. If candidates are promising, some interviewers at this stage extol the attractive features of the job. This is fine as long as these are not exaggerated. To give a 'realistic preview', the possible downsides should be mentioned, for example the need to travel or unsocial working hours. If candidates are clearly unsuitable you can tactfully help them to de-select themselves by referring to aspects of the work that may not appeal to them, or for which they are not really qualified. It is best not to spell out these points too strongly. It is often sufficient simply to put the question: 'This is a key requirement of the job, how do you feel about it?' You can follow up this general question by more specific questions: 'Do you feel you have the right sort of experience?', 'Are you happy about (this aspect of the job)?'

At this stage you should ask final questions about the availability of candidates, as long as they are promising. You can ask when they would be able to start and about any holiday arrangements to which they are committed.

You should also ask their permission to obtain references from their present and previous employers. They might not want you to approach their present employer. But you should tell them that if they are made an offer of employment it would be conditional on a satisfactory reference from that employer. It is useful to ensure that you have the names of people you can approach.

Finally, you inform candidates of what happens next. If some time could elapse before they hear from you, they should be told that you will be writing as soon as possible but that there will be some delay (don't make a promise you will be unable to keep).

It is not normally good practice to inform candidates of your decision at the end of the interview. You should take time to reflect on their suitability and you don't want to give them the impression that you are making a snap judgement.

Deciding on the questions

The key questions in structured interviews should be planned in advance. This particularly applies to behavioural event questions, which are designed to reveal how a candidate would behave in a typical situation and therefore reveal information about the level of behavioural competency. Such questions are linked to the behavioural competencies required in the role.

Capability questions can be planned to establish what candidates know, the skills they possess and what they are capable of doing. Situation-based questions ask candidates how they would deal with a typical problem.

Sequencing the questions

When planning interviews you should give some thought to how you are going to sequence your questions, especially in the middle part. There are two basic approaches, as described below.

Biographical approach

The biographical approach is probably the most popular because it is simple to use and appears to be logical. The interview can be sequenced chronologically, starting with the first job or even before that at school and, if appropriate, college or university. The succeeding jobs, if any, are then dealt with in turn, ending with the present job to which most attention is given if the candidate has been in it for some time.

However, if you are not careful, using the chronological method for someone who has had a number of jobs can mean spending too much time on the earlier jobs, leaving insufficient time for the most important recent experience. To overcome this problem, an alternative biographical approach is to start with the present job, which is discussed in some depth. The interviewer then works backwards, job by job, but only concentrating on particularly interesting or relevant experience in earlier jobs.

The problem with the biographical approach is that it is predictable. Experienced candidates are familiar with it and have their story ready, glossing over any weak points. It can also be unreliable. You can easily miss an important piece of information by concentrating on a succession of jobs rather than focusing on key aspects of the candidates' experience that illustrate their capabilities. This is why the alternative targeted approach may be preferred.

Targeted or criteria-based approach

A target-based interview is a form of structured interview. It is based on an analysis of the person specification from which criteria are identified for judging the suitability of the candidate. Interview questions can then 'target' these criteria by asking for specific information on what candidates know, what they can do and how they would typically behave in certain situations. They would be asked to support their answers with evidence from their practical experience and their education or training. Responses can be compared with the criteria to assess the extent to which candidates meet the specification. This is probably the best way of focusing your interview to ensure that you get all the information you require about candidates for comparison with the person specification.

Questioning techniques

As mentioned earlier, an interview is a conversation with a purpose. The interviewer's job is to draw the candidate out, at the same time ensuring that the information required is obtained. To this end it is desirable to ask a number of open-ended questions – questions that cannot be answered by 'yes' or 'no' and which promote a full response. But a good interviewer will have an armoury of other types of questions to be asked when appropriate, as described below.

Open questions

Open questions are phrased generally, give no indication of the expected reply and cannot be answered by 'yes' or 'no'. They encourage candidates to talk – drawing them out and obtaining a full response. Single-word answers are seldom illuminating. It is a good idea to begin the interview with some open questions to obtain a general picture of candidates, thus helping them to settle in. Open questions or phrases inviting a response can be phrased as follows.

Open questions can give you a lot of useful information, but you may not get exactly what you want and answers can go into too much detail. For example, the question: 'What has been the main feature of your work in recent months?' may result in a one-word reply – 'marketing'. Or it may produce a lengthy explanation that takes up too much time. Replies to open questions can get bogged down in too much detail, or miss out some key points. They can come to a sudden halt or lose their way. You need to ensure that you get all the facts, keep the flow going and maintain control. Remember that you are in charge. Hence the value of probing, closed and the other types of questions.

Open questions or phrases inviting a response

- I'd like you to tell me about the sort of work you are doing in your present job.

- What do you know about …?

- Could you give me some examples of …?

- In what ways do you think your experience fits you to do the job for which you have applied?

- How have you tackled …?

- What have been the most challenging aspects of your job?

- Please tell me about some of the interesting things you have been doing at work recently.

Closed questions

Closed questions aim to clarify a point of fact. The expected reply will be an explicit single word or brief sentence. A closed question aims to produce a succinct factual statement without going into detail. When you ask a closed question you intend to find out the following.

Subjects for closed questions

- What the candidate has or has not done – 'What did you do then?'

- Why something took place – 'Why did that happen?'

- When something took place – 'When did that happen?'

- How something happened – 'How did that situation arise?'

- Where something happened – 'Where were you at the time?'

- Who took part – 'Who else was involved?'

Probing questions

Probing questions ask for further details and explanations to ensure that you are getting all the facts. You ask them when answers have been too generalized or when you suspect that there may be some more relevant information that candidates have not disclosed. A candidate may claim to have done something and it may be useful to find out more about exactly what contribution was made. Poor interviewers tend to let general and uninformative answers pass by without probing for further details, simply because they are sticking rigidly to a predetermined list of open questions. Skilled interviewers are able to flex their approach to ensure they get the facts while still keeping control to ensure that the interview is completed on time.

A candidate could say to you something like: 'I was involved in a major exercise that produced significant improvements in the flow of work through the factory.' This statement conveys nothing about what the candidate actually did. You have to ask probing questions, such as the examples below.

Probing questions

- You've informed me that you have had experience in …. Could you tell me more about what you did?

- What sort of targets or standards have you been expected to achieve?

- How successful have you been in achieving those targets or standards? Please give examples.

- Could you give an example of any project you have undertaken?

- What was your precise role in this project?

- What exactly was the contribution you made to its success?

- What knowledge and skills were you able to apply to the project?

- Were you responsible for monitoring progress?

- Did you prepare the final recommendations in full or in part? If in part, which part?

- Could you describe in more detail the equipment you used?

Situation-based questions

Situation-based questions are hypothetical questions used in structured interviews. They describe a situation to candidates who are asked how they would deal with it. Situation-based questions can be prepared in advance to test how candidates would approach a typical problem or issue they might meet in the job for which they are being considered. Such questions may be phrased: 'What do you think you would do if ...?' When such questions lie well within the candidate's expertise and experience the answers can be illuminating. But it could be unfair to ask candidates to say how they would deal with a problem without knowing more about the context in which the problem arose. It can also be argued that what candidates say they would do and what they actually do could be quite different. Hypothetical questions can produce hypothetical answers. The best data upon which judgements about candidates can be made are what they have actually done or achieved. You need to find out if they have successfully dealt with the sort of issues and problems they may be faced with if they join your organization.

Behavioural event questions

Behavioural event questions as used in behaviour-based structured interviews aim to get candidates to tell you how they would behave in situations that have been identified as critical to successful job performance. The assumption upon which such questions are based is that past behaviour in dealing with or reacting to events is the best predictor of future behaviour.

Capability questions

Capability questions aim to establish what candidates know, the skills they possess and what they are capable of doing. They can be open, probing or closed, but they will always be focused as precisely as possible on the contents of the person specification, referring to knowledge, skills and competences.

Capability questions should therefore be explicit – focused on what candidates must know and be able to do. Their purpose is to obtain evidence from candidates that shows the extent to which they meet the specification in each of its key areas. Because time is always limited it is best to concentrate on the most important aspects of the work, and it is always best to prepare the questions in advance. The sort of capability questions you can ask are set out below.

Behavioural event questions

- Could you give an instance of when you persuaded others to take an unusual course of action?

- Could you describe an occasion when you completed a project or task in the face of great difficulties?

- Could you describe any contribution you have made as a member of a team in achieving an unusually successful result?

- Could you give an instance of when you took the lead in a difficult situation in getting something worthwhile done?

Capability questions

- What do you know about ...?

- How did you gain this knowledge?

- What are the key skills you are expected to use in your work?

- How would your present employer rate the level of skill you have reached in ...?

- Could you please tell me exactly what sort and how much experience you have had in ...?

- Could you tell me more about what you have actually been doing in this aspect of your work?

- Can you give me any examples of the sort of work you have done that would qualify you to do this job?

- What are the most typical problems you have to deal with?

- Would you tell me about any instances when you have had to deal with an unexpected problem or a crisis?

Motivation questions

The degree to which candidates are motivated is a personal quality to which it is necessary to give special attention if it is to be properly assessed. This is usually achieved by inference rather than direct questions. 'How well are you motivated?' is a leading question that will usually produce the response: 'Highly.' You can make inferences about the level of motivation of candidates by asking questions on the following subjects.

Subjects for motivation questions

- *Their career* – replies to such questions as: 'Why did you decide to move on from there?' can give an indication of the extent to which they have been well-motivated in progressing their career.

- *Achievements* – not just, 'What did you achieve?' but, 'How did you achieve it?' and, 'What difficulties did you overcome?'

- *Triumphing over disadvantages* – candidates who have done well in spite of an unpromising upbringing and relatively poor education may be more highly motivated than those with all the advantages that upbringing and education can bestow, but who have not made good use of these advantages.

- *Spare time interests* – don't accept at its face value a reply to a question about spare time interests which, for example, reveals that a candidate collects stamps. Find out if the candidate is well-motivated enough to pursue the interest with determination and to achieve something in the process.

Continuity questions

Continuity questions aim to keep the flow going in an interview and encourage candidates to enlarge on what they have told you, within limits. Here are some examples.

Continuity questions

- What happened next?
- What did you do then?
- Can we talk about your next job?
- Can we move on now to …?
- Could you tell me more about …?

It has been said that to keep the conversation going during an interview the best thing an interviewer can do is to make encouraging grunts at appropriate moments. There is more to interviewing than that, but single words or phrases like, 'good', 'fine', 'that's interesting', 'carry on' can help things along.

Play-back questions

Play-back questions test your understanding of what candidates have said by putting to them a statement of what it appears they have told you, and asking them if they agree or disagree with your version. For example, you could say: 'As I understand it, you resigned from your last position because you disagreed with your boss on a number of fundamental issues – have I got that right?' The answer might simply be 'yes' to this closed question, in which case you might probe to find out more about what happened. Or the candidate may reply 'Not exactly', in which case you ask for the full story.

Career questions

As mentioned earlier, questions about the career history of candidates can provide some insight into motivation as well as establishing how they have progressed in acquiring useful and relevant knowledge, skills and experience. You can ask questions such as those given below.

Focused work questions

These are questions designed to tell you more about particular aspects of the candidate's work history, such as those shown below.

Career questions

- What did you learn from that new job?
- What different skills did you have to use when you were promoted?
- Why did you leave that job?
- What happened after you left that job?
- In what ways do you think this job will advance your career?

Focused work questions

- How many days absence from work did you have last year?
- How many times were you late last year?
- Have you been absent from work for any medical reason not shown on your application form?
- Do you have a clean driving licence (for those whose work will involve driving)?

Unhelpful questions

- *Multiple questions* such as 'What skills do you use most frequently in your job? Are they technical skills, leadership skills, teamworking skills or communicating skills?' will only confuse candidates. You will probably get a partial or misleading reply. Ask only one question at a time.
- *Leading questions,* which indicate the reply you expect are also unhelpful. If you ask a question such as: 'That's what you think, isn't it?' you will get the reply: 'Yes, I do.' If you ask a question such as: 'I take it that you don't really believe that …?' you will get the reply: 'No, I don't.' Neither of these replies will get you anywhere.

Questions to be avoided

Avoid any questions such as those given below that could be construed as being biased on the grounds of sex, race, disability or age.

Don't ask

- Who is going to look after the children?
- Are you planning to have any more children?
- Are you concerned at all about racial prejudice?
- Would it worry you being the only immigrant around here?
- With your disability, do you think you can cope with the job?
- Do you think that at your time of life you will be able to learn the new skills associated with this job?

Useful questions

Ten useful questions

1. What are the most important aspects of your present job?
2. What do you think have been your most notable achievements in your career to date?
3. What sort of problems have you successfully solved recently in your job?
4. What have you learnt from your present job?
5. What has been your experience in …?
6. What do you know about …?
7. What particularly interests you in this job and why?
8. Now you have heard more about the job, would you please tell me which aspects of your experience are most relevant?
9. What do you think you can bring to this job?
10. Is there anything else about your career that hasn't come out yet in this interview but you think I ought to hear?

Coming to a conclusion

It is essential not to be beguiled by a pleasant, articulate and confident interviewee who is all surface and no substance. Beware of the 'halo' effect, which occurs when one or two good points are seized upon, leading to the neglect of negative indicators. The opposite 'horns' effect of focusing on the negatives should also be avoided.

Individual candidates should be assessed against the criteria. These could be set out under the headings of knowledge and skills, competencies, education, qualifications, training, experience and overall suitability. Ratings can be given against each heading, for example: very acceptable, acceptable, marginally acceptable, unacceptable. If you have used situational or behaviourally based questions you can indicate against each question whether the reply was good, just acceptable or poor. These assessments can inform your overall assessment of knowledge and skills and competencies.

Next, compare your assessment of each of the candidates against one another. You can then make a conclusion on those preferred by reference to their assessments under each heading.

In the end, your decision between qualified candidates may well be judgemental. There may be one suitable candidate but there could be two or three (although sometimes there may be none at all). Where there is a choice you have to come to a balanced view by reference to your notes and ratings on which particular candidate is more likely to fit the job and the organization *and* have potential for a long-term career, if this is possible. Don't, however, settle for second best in desperation. It is better to try again.

Remember to make and keep notes of the reasons for your choice and why candidates have been rejected. These, together with the applications, should be kept for at least six months just in case your decision is challenged as being discriminatory. An example of an interview rating form is given in Table 47.1.

TABLE 47.1   Example of an interview rating form

	Very acceptable	Acceptable	Marginally acceptable	Unacceptable	Comments
Knowledge and skills					
Competencies					
Education and qualifications					
Training					
Experience					
Overall suitability					

Dos and don'ts of selection interviewing

Do
• Plan the interview.
• Give yourself sufficient time.
• Use a structured interview approach whenever possible.
• Create the right atmosphere.
• Establish an easy and informal relationship – start with open questions.
• Encourage the candidate to talk.
• Cover the ground as planned, ensuring that you complete a prepared agenda and maintain continuity.
• Analyse the candidate's career to reveal strengths, weaknesses and patterns of interest.
• Make use of open questions that invite people to talk.
• Ensure that questions are clear and unambiguous.
• Get examples and instances of the successful application of knowledge, skills and the effective use of capabilities.
• Make judgements on the basis of the factual information you have obtained about candidates' experience and attributes in relation to the person specification.
• Keep control over the content and timing of the interview.

Don't
• Start the interview unprepared.
• Plunge too quickly into demanding (probe) questions.
• Ask multiple or leading questions.
• Pay too much attention to isolated strengths or weaknesses.
• Allow candidates to gloss over important facts.
• Talk too much or allow candidates to ramble on.
• Allow your prejudices to get the better of your capacity to make objective judgements.
• Fall into the 'halo' effect trap, ie drawing conclusions about a person on the basis of one or two good points, leading to the neglect of negative indicators; or into the 'horns' trap – focusing too much on one or two weak points.
• Ask questions or make remarks that could be construed as in any way discriminatory.
• Attempt too many interviews in a row.

Key learning points: Selection interviewing skills (1)

Purpose of an interview

The purpose of a selection interview is to establish the extent to which a candidate will be able to do the job. This means finding out how well a candidate's levels of skill, knowledge, abilities and competency fit a person specification for the job that sets out these requirements.

Nature of an interview

An interview is a conversation with a purpose. It is a conversation because candidates should be given the opportunity to talk freely about themselves and their careers. But the conversation has to be planned, directed and controlled to achieve your aims in the time available.

Interviewing skills

- Establishing rapport – creating a good relationship with candidates – getting on their wavelength, putting them at ease, encouraging them to respond and generally being friendly.

- Questioning is the key skill interviewers need to possess. Their purpose is to draw candidates out and elicit the information the interviewer has decided must be obtained to reach a conclusion.

- If an interview is a conversation with a purpose, listening skills are important. You need not only to hear but also to understand what candidates are saying. When interviewing you must concentrate on what candidates are telling you.

- So far as possible link your questions to a candidate's last reply so that the interview progresses logically and a cumulative set of data is built up.

- You want candidates to talk, but not too much.

- It is useful to take notes of the key points they make, discreetly, but not surreptitiously.

Preparing for the interview

Your first step in preparing for an interview is to familiarize or re-familiarize yourself with the person specification.

Planning the interview

Interviews need to be planned in terms of their three main parts, the structure of questions and how the questions will be sequenced.

The parts of an interview

The content of an interview is in three parts: its beginning, middle and end.

Structuring the interview

A structured interview is one based on a defined framework within which there is a set of predetermined questions. All candidates are asked the same questions and the answers may be scored through a rating system. The most typical framework is the person specification.

Sequencing the interview

When planning interviews you should give some thought to how you are going to sequence your questions, especially in the middle part. There are two basic approaches. The *biographical approach* is probably the most popular because it is simple to use and appears to be logical. This approach is often referred to as a 'structured interview'. The *targeted approach* is based on an analysis of the person specification from which criteria are identified for judging the suitability of the candidate. Interview questions can then 'target' these criteria by asking for specific information on what candidates know, what they can do and how they would typically behave in certain situations.

Questions

1 What is the purpose of a selection interview?

2 Why is an interview described as 'a conversation with a purpose'?

3 What are the main interviewing skills?

4 How should interviews be planned?

5 What is a structured interview?

6 What is a biographical interview?

7 What is a targeted interview?

8 What is an open question?

9 What is a closed question?

10 What questions should be avoided?

48
Job, role, competency and skills analysis

LEARNING OUTCOMES

On completing this chapter you should be able to define these key concepts. You should also know about:

- Job analysis methodology and techniques
- Job descriptions
- Role analysis methodology
- Analysing behavioural competencies
- Analysing technical competencies

Introduction

The analysis of jobs, roles, competencies and skills is one of the key techniques in human resource management. It provides the information required to produce job descriptions, role profiles, and person and learning specifications. It is of fundamental importance in organization and job design, recruitment and selection, performance management, learning and development, management development, career management, job evaluation and the design of grade and pay structures. These constitute most of the key HRM activities.

This chapter starts with definitions of the terms used in job and role analysis and then deals with the skills required to analyse jobs, roles, competencies and skills and to produce job descriptions and role profiles.

Definitions

Jobs and roles

The terms 'job' and 'role' are often used interchangeably, but they are different. A *job* is an organizational unit consisting of a group of defined tasks or activities to be carried out or duties to be performed. A *role* is the part people play in their work – the emphasis is on the expected patterns of behaviour to achieve agreed outcomes. Roles are about people. Jobs are about tasks and duties.

Job description

A job description defines what job holders are required to do in terms of activities, duties or tasks. It is prescriptive and inflexible, giving people the opportunity to say: 'It's not in my job description', meaning that they only need to do the tasks listed there. A job description is more concerned with tasks than outcomes, and with the duties to be performed than the competencies required to perform them (technical competencies covering knowledge and skills, and behavioural competencies).

Job analysis

Job analysis is the process of collecting, analysing and setting out information about jobs in order to provide the basis for a job description and data for recruitment, training, job evaluation and performance management. Job analysis concentrates on what job holders do and achieve. It identifies the tasks job holders undertake and the outcomes and outputs they are expected to produce. Outcomes are the results of performance expressed as something that has been attained, such as a task or a project. Outputs are the results of performance expressed in quantified terms such as sales volume, income generated or units of production.

Role profile

A role profile defines key result areas, accountabilities and competencies for an individual role. It concentrates on outcomes rather than duties and therefore provides better guidance than a job description on expectations. It does not constrain people by prescribing their tasks. Outcomes may be expressed as 'key result areas' – elements of the role for which clear outputs and standards can be defined, each of which makes a significant contribution to achieving its overall purpose. Alternatively, they may be termed 'accountabilities' – areas of the role for which role holders are responsible in the form of being held to account for what they do and what they achieve.

A role profile does not prescribe in detail what has to be done to achieve the required outcomes. It therefore allows for greater flexibility than a job description and is more easily updated to reflect changing demands.

Role profiles are person-oriented. A role can be described in behavioural terms – given certain expectations, this is how the person needs to behave to meet them. Because it identifies knowledge, skill and competency requirements it also provides a better basis for recruitment and selection, performance management and learning and development purposes.

Accountability profile

An accountability profile is a type of role profile that focuses on what role holders will be held to account for in terms of what they do and what they achieve. It may be set out as a list of main accountabilities.

Generic role

A generic role is a role in which essentially similar activities are carried out by a number of people, for example a team leader or a call centre agent. In effect, it covers an occupation rather than a single role. It is described in a generic role profile.

Role analysis

Role analysis finds out what people are expected to achieve when carrying out their work and the competencies and skills required to meet those expectations. Role analysis uses similar techniques to job analysis, although the objective of the analysis will be different.

Competency analysis

Competency analysis is concerned with behavioural analysis to establish the behavioural dimensions that affect job performance, and functional analysis to determine technical or work-based competencies. Behavioural or personal competencies are the personal characteristics of individuals they bring to their work roles. Technical or work-based competencies refer to expectations of workplace performance and the standards and outputs that people carrying out specified roles are expected to attain. They are also described as competences.

Skills analysis

Skills analysis determines the skills required to achieve an acceptable level of performance.

Person specification

A person specification, also known as a job or role specification, defines the knowledge, skills and abilities (KSAs) required to carry out a role and the education, training, qualifications and experience needed to acquire the necessary KSAs. It may also refer specifically to the competencies required for effective job performance.

Learning specification

A learning specification defines the knowledge and skills needed to achieve an acceptable level of performance. It is used as the basis for devising learning and development programmes. Learning specifications may be drawn up on the basis of competency and skills analysis.

Job analysis

Job analysis produces the following information about a job:

- *Overall purpose* – why the job exists and, in essence, what the job holder is expected to contribute.
- *Organization* – to whom the job holder reports and who reports to the job holder.
- *Content* – the nature and scope of the job in terms of the tasks and operations to be performed and duties to be carried out.

If the outcome of the job analysis is to be used for job evaluation purposes, the job will also be analysed in terms of the factors or criteria used in the job evaluation scheme.

Job analysis methodology

The essence of job analysis is the application of systematic methods to the collection of information about job content. It is essentially about data collection and the basic steps are:

- obtain documents such as existing organization, procedure or training manuals that give information about the job;
- obtain from managers fundamental information concerning the job;
- obtain from job holders similar information about their jobs.

There are a number of job analysis techniques used for data collection, described below.

Interviews

The full flavour of a job is best obtained by interviewing job holders and checking findings with their managers or team leaders. The aim of the interview should be to obtain the relevant facts about the job, namely the job title, organizational details (reporting relationships as described in an organization chart) and a list of the tasks or duties performed by the job holder. The interview should also establish outcomes and outputs.

For recruitment, training or job evaluation purposes these basic details can be supplemented by questions designed to elicit from the job holders more information about the level of their responsibilities and the demands made upon them by the job. These can cover the amount of supervision received, the degree of discretion allowed in making decisions, the typical problems to be solved, the amount of guidance available when solving the problems, the relative difficulty of the tasks to be performed and the qualifications and skills required to carry out the work.

Conducting a job analysis interview

- Work to a logical sequence of questions that help interviewees to order their thoughts about the job.

- Probe as necessary to establish what people really do in terms of outputs and outcomes – answers to questions are often vague and information may be given by means of untypical instances.

- Ensure that job holders are not allowed to get away with vague or inflated descriptions of their work – if, for example, the interview is part of a job evaluation exercise, they would not be human if they did not present the job in the best possible light.

- Sort out the wheat from the chaff; answers to questions may produce a lot of irrelevant data that must be sifted before preparing the job description.

- Obtain a clear statement from job holders about their authority to make decisions and the amount of guidance they receive from their manager or team leader. This is not easy: if asked what decisions they are authorized to make, most people look blank because they think about their job in terms of duties and tasks rather than abstract decisions.

- Avoid asking leading questions that make the expected answer obvious.

- Allow the job holder ample opportunity to talk by creating an atmosphere of trust.

It is helpful to use a checklist when conducting the interview. Elaborate checklists are not necessary; they only confuse people. The basic questions to be answered are as follows.

Job analysis interview checklist

1   What is the title of your job?

2   To whom are you responsible?

3   Who is responsible to you? An organization chart is helpful.

4   What is the main purpose of your job in overall terms, ie what are you expected to do?

5   What are the key activities you have to carry out in your role? Try to group them under no more than 10 headings.

6   What are the results you are expected to achieve in each of those key activities?

7   What are you expected to know to be able to carry out your job?

8   What skills should you have to carry out your job?

The answers to these questions may need to be sorted out – they can often result in a mass of jumbled information that has to be analysed so that the various activities can be distinguished and refined to seven or eight key areas.

The advantages of the interviewing method are that it is flexible, can provide in-depth information and is easy to organize and prepare. It is therefore the most common approach. But interviewing can be time-consuming, which is why in large job analysis exercises, questionnaires may be used to provide advance information about the job. This speeds up the interviewing process or even replaces the interview altogether, although this means that much of the 'flavour' of the job – ie what it is really like – may be lost.

Questionnaires

Questionnaires about their roles can be completed by role holders and approved by the role holder's manager or team leader. They are helpful when a large number of roles have to be covered. They can also save interviewing time by recording purely factual information and by enabling the analyst to structure questions in advance to cover areas that need to be explored in greater depth. The simpler the questionnaire the better: it need only cover the eight questions listed above.

The advantage of questionnaires is that they can produce information quickly and cheaply for a large number of jobs. But a substantial sample is needed and the construction of a questionnaire is a skilled job, which should only be carried out on the basis of some preliminary fieldwork. It is highly advisable to pilot test questionnaires before launching into a full-scale exercise. The accuracy of the results also depends on the willingness and ability of job holders to complete questionnaires. Many people find it difficult to express themselves in writing about their work.

Observation

Observation means studying role holders at work, noting what they do, how they do it, and how much time it takes. This method is most appropriate for routine administrative or manual roles but it is seldom used because of the time it takes.

Job descriptions

Job descriptions should be based on the job analysis and should be as brief and factual as possible. The headings under which the job description should be written and notes for guidance on completing each section are set out below.

Job title

The existing or proposed job title should indicate as clearly as possible the function in which the job is carried out and the level of the job within that function. The use of terms such as 'manager', 'assistant manager' or 'senior' to describe job levels should be reasonably consistent between functions with regard to grading of the jobs.

Reporting to

The job title of the manager or team leader to whom the job holder is directly responsible should be given under this heading. No attempt should be made to indicate here any functional relationships the job holder might have to other people.

Reporting to job holder

The job titles of all the posts directly reporting to the job holder should be given under this heading. Again, no attempt should be made here to indicate any functional relationships that might exist between the job holder and other employees.

Overall purpose

This section should describe as concisely as possible the overall purpose of the job. The aim should be to convey in one sentence a broad picture of the job that will clearly distinguish it from other jobs and establish the role of job holders and the contribution they should make towards achieving the objectives of the company and their own function or unit. No attempt should be made to describe the activities carried out under this heading, but the overall summary should lead naturally to the analysis of activities in the next section. When preparing the job description, it is often best to defer writing down the definition of overall responsibilities until the activities have been analysed and described.

Main activities, tasks or duties

The following method of describing activities, tasks or duties should be adopted:

1 Group the various activities identified by the job analysis together so that no more than seven or eight areas remain. If the number is extended much beyond that, the job description will become over-complex and it will be difficult to be specific about tasks or duties.

2 Define each activity in one sentence, starting with a verb in the active voice, to provide a positive indication of what has to be done and eliminate unnecessary wording. Examples are: plan, prepare, produce, implement, process, provide, schedule, complete, dispatch, maintain, liaises with, and collaborates with.

3 Describe what is done as succinctly as possible, for example: test new systems, post cash to the nominal and sales ledgers, dispatch packed output to the warehouse, schedule production, ensure that management accounts are produced, prepare marketing plans.

4 State briefly the purpose of the activity in terms of outcomes, outputs or standards to be achieved. For example: test new systems to ensure they meet agreed systems specifications; post cash to the nominal and sales ledgers in order to provide up-to-date and accurate financial information; dispatch to the warehouse planned output so that all items are removed by carriers on the same day they are packed; schedule production to meet laid-down output and delivery targets; ensure that management accounts are produced that provide the required level of information to management and individual managers on financial performance against budget and on any variances; prepare marketing plans that support the achievement of the marketing strategies of the enterprise, are realistic, and provide clear guidance on the actions to be taken by the development, production, marketing and sales departments; plan and implement sales campaigns to meet sales targets.

An example of a job description is given in Figure 48.1.

Role analysis and role profiles

Role analysis uses the same techniques as job analysis but the focus is on identifying inputs – KSAs (knowledge, skill and abilities), competency requirements and required outcomes (key result areas or accountabilities) rather than simply listing the tasks to be carried out. A role profile is initially set out under the same headings as a job description, ie role title, responsible to, responsible to role holder and the purpose of the role, but it then focuses on the following aspects of the role.

Key result areas

A key result area is an element of a role for which clear outputs and outcomes can be defined, each of which makes a significant contribution to achieving the overall purpose of the role. It may be described as an 'accountability' – an aspect of the role for which the role holder is responsible (held to account for).

The number of key result areas is unlikely to be more than seven or eight, certainly not more than 10. The basic structure of a key result area definition

FIGURE 48.1 Example of job description

Job title:	HR Adviser; Recruitment
Reports to:	HR Service Centre Manager
Reports to job holder:	none
Overall purpose:	To provide recruitment services to line managers for jobs below management level

Main activities:

1 Respond promptly to requests from line managers to assist in recruiting staff.

2 Produce person specifications that clearly indicate requirements for recruitment purposes.

3 Agree on the use of sources of applicants such as web-based recruitment, agencies or media advertisements that will generate high calibre candidates at a reasonable cost.

4 Brief and liaise with agencies and/or draft advertisements for jobs for approval by line managers and place advertisements or information on vacancies using the media and/or the internet.

5 Process replies and draw up shortlists that enable a choice to be made between well-qualified candidates.

6 Conduct preliminary interviews independently or conduct shortlist interviews with line managers that identify candidates who meet the specification.

7 Agree offer terms with line manager, take up references and confirm the offer.

8 Review and evaluate sources of candidates and analyse recruitment costs.

should resemble that of a job description task definition, ie it should be expressed in one sentence starting with an active verb. However, the content of the definition should focus more on the specific purpose of the activity in terms of outputs or standards to be achieved than on describing in detail the duties involved.

Knowledge, skills and abilities required

Knowledge, skills and abilities should be expressed in terms of 'need to know' – the required knowledge of techniques, processes, procedures, systems and the business generally (its products or services and its competitors and customers), and 'need to be able to do' – the skills required in each area of activity. These are the technical competencies required by the job.

Behavioural competencies

Behavioural competencies describe how the role holder is expected to behave when carrying out the role. They may be linked to the organization's competency framework and cover such areas as teamworking, communication, people management and development, and customer relations. An example of a role profile is given in Figure 48.2.

Generic role profiles

Generic role profiles cover occupations rather than individual roles. They tend to be more generalized and may be somewhat simpler than individual role profiles, for example by restricting the profile to lists of key result areas and competency dimensions. An example of a generic role profile is given in Figure 48.3.

Behavioural competency analysis

Competency analysis, sometimes known as 'behavioural competency modelling', is the method used to identify, analyse and describe behavioural com-

petencies. These define the behaviours that organizations expect their employees to practise in their work in order to reach an acceptable level of performance. They have an important part to play in providing information that contributes to a number of HRM activities, for example, recruitment, learning and development, and performance management. Examples of competencies and competency frameworks were given in Chapter 8, and suggestions were made about how a competency framework should be constructed. Table 48.1 shows guidance on the criteria for a fully rigorous competency definition produced by Shippmann *et al* (2000).

These are exacting criteria. The emphasis is on the systematic collection and analysis of data. There are five approaches to behavioural competency analysis: in ascending order of complexity these are:

- expert opinion;
- structured interview;
- workshops;
- critical-incident technique;
- repertory grid analysis.

Expert opinion

The basic, crudest and least satisfactory method is for an 'expert' member of the HR department, possibly in discussion with other 'experts' from the same department to draw up a list from their own understanding of 'what counts', coupled with an analysis of other published lists. This is unsatisfactory because the likelihood of the competencies being appropriate, realistic and measurable in the absence of detailed analysis, is fairly remote. The list tends to be bland and, because line managers and job holders have not been involved, unacceptable.

Structured interview

This method begins with a list of competencies drawn up by 'experts' and proceeds by subjecting a number of role holders to a structured interview. The interviewer starts by identifying the key result areas of the role and goes on to analyse the behavioural characteristics that distinguish performers at different levels of competence. The basic question is: 'What are the positive or negative indicators of

FIGURE 48.2 Example of a role profile

Role title: Database administrator

Department: Information systems

Purpose of role: Responsible for the development and support of databases and their underlying environment.

Key result areas

- Identify database requirements for all projects that require data management, to meet the needs of internal customers.
- Develop project plans collaboratively with colleagues to deliver against their database needs.
- Support underlying database infrastructure.
- Liaise with system and software providers to obtain product information and support.
- Manage project resources (people and equipment) within predefined budget and criteria, as agree with line manager and originating department.
- Allocate work to and supervise contractors on day-to-day basis.
- Ensure security of the underlying database infrastructure through adherence to established protocols and develop additional security protocols where needed.

Need to know

- Oracle database administration.
- Operation of Designer 2000 and oracle forms SQL/PLSQL, Unix administration, shell programming.

Able to

- Analyse and choose between options where the solution is not always obvious.
- Develop project plans and organize own workload on a timescale of 1–2 months.
- Adapt to rapidly changing needs and priorities without losing sight of overall plans and priorities.
- Interpret budgets in order to manage resources effectively within them.
- Negotiate with suppliers.
- Keep abreast of technical developments and trends, bring these into day-to-day work when feasible and build them into new project developments.

Behavioural competencies

- Aim to get things done well and set and meet challenging goals, create own measures of excellence and constantly seek ways of improving performance.
- Analyse information from range of sources and develop effective solutions/recommendations.
- Communicate clearly and persuasively, orally or in writing, dealing with technical issues in a non-technical manner.
- Work participatively on projects with technical and non-technical colleagues.
- Develop positive relationships with colleagues as the supplier of an internal service.

FIGURE 48.3   Example of a generic role profile

Generic role title: Team leader

Overall purpose of role: To lead teams in order to attain team goals and further the achievement of the organization's objectives.

Key result areas:

1   Agree targets and standards with team members that support the attainment of the organization's objectives.

2   Plan with team members work schedules and resource requirements that will ensure that team targets will be reached, indeed exceeded.

3   Agree performance measures and quality assurance processes with team members that will clarify output and quality expectations.

4   Agree with team members the allocation of tasks, rotating responsibilities as appropriate to achieve flexibility and the best use of the skills and capabilities of team members.

5   Coordinate the work of the team to ensure that team goals are achieved.

6   Ensure that the team members collectively monitor the team's performance in terms of achieving output, speed of response and quality targets and standards, and agree with team members any corrective action required to ensure that team goals are achieved.

7   Conduct team reviews of performance to agree areas for improvement and actions required.

Competencies:

- Build effective team relationships, ensuring that team members are committed to the common purpose.
- Encourage self-direction amongst team members but provide guidance and clear direction as required.
- Share information with team members.
- Trust team members to get on with things – not continually checking.
- Treat team members fairly and consistently.
- Support and guide team members to make the best use of their capabilities.
- Encourage self-development by example.
- Actively offer constructive feedback to team members and positively seek and be open to constructive feedback from them.
- Contribute to the development of team members, encouraging the acquisition of additional skills and providing opportunities for them to be used effectively.

---

behaviour conducive or non-conducive to achieving high levels of performance?' These may be analysed under the headings set out overleaf. Under each heading instances will be sought that illustrate effective or less effective behaviour.

One of the problems with this approach is that it relies too much on the ability of the expert to draw out information from interviewees. It is also undesirable to use a deductive approach that pre-empts the analysis with a prepared list of competency headings. It is better to do this by means of an inductive approach, which starts from specific types of behaviour and then groups them under competence headings. This can be done in a workshop by analysing positive and negative indicators to gain an understanding of the competence dimensions of an occupation or job, as described below.

TABLE 48.1   Criteria for a fully rigorous competency definition

Variable	Conditions required to meet high rigorous criteria
Method of investigation	A logically selected mix of multiple methods are used to obtain information, eg interviews, focus groups, questionnaires.
Type of descriptor content collected	Variable combinations of multiple types of information are collected, eg work activities, KSAs (knowledge, skills and abilities statements) and performance standards.
Procedures for developing descriptors	Information collected from content experts using a structured protocol and a representative sample.
Detail of descriptor content	Use of a number of labels representing discrete categories of content which operationally define each category and leave no room for misinterpretation.
Link to business goals and strategies	Steps taken to ensure that results are aligned with the broader goals and longer-term strategies of the organization.
Content review	Formal review takes place to ensure that: • item level descriptions are clear; • content categories do not overlap, content categories are internally consistent; • items represent measurable content appropriate for the intended application.
Ranking descriptor content	The set of descriptors are prioritized and ranked.
Assessment of reliability	Content category labels are matched with item-level descriptors and rated according to their relative importance for successful job performance.
Item retention criteria	Multiple, clear, logical criteria are consistently applied to items to determine whether content is retained or deleted.
Documentation	Clear definitions are made of the procedures to be employed in applying the competency framework.

Behavioural headings

- Personal drive (achievement motivation).
- Impact on results.
- Analytical power.
- Strategic thinking.
- Creative thinking (ability to innovate).
- Decisiveness.
- Commercial judgement.
- Team management and leadership.
- Interpersonal relationships.
- Ability to communicate.
- Ability to adapt and cope with change and pressure.
- Ability to plan and control projects.

Workshops

Workshops bring a group of people together who have 'expert' knowledge or experience of the role – managers and role holders as appropriate – with a facilitator, usually but not necessarily a member of the HR department or an outside consultant.

The members of the workshop begin by getting agreement to the overall purpose of the role and its key result areas. They then develop examples of effective and less effective behaviour for each area, which are recorded on flipcharts. For example, one of the key result areas for a divisional HR director might be workforce planning, defined as:

> Prepares forecasts of human resource requirements and plans for the acquisition, retention and effective utilization of employees, which ensure that the company's needs for people are met.

The positive indicators for this competency area could include:

- seeks involvement in business strategy formulation;
- contributes to business planning by taking a strategic view of longer-term human resource issues that are likely to affect business strategy;

- networks with senior management colleagues to understand and respond to the human resource planning issues they raise;
- suggests practical ways to improve the use of human resources, for example, the introduction of annual hours.

Negative indicators could include:

- takes a narrow view of HR planning – does not seem to be interested in or understand the wider business context;
- lacks the determination to overcome problems and deliver forecasts;
- fails to anticipate skills shortages; for example, unable to meet the multi-skilling requirements implicit in the new computer-integrated manufacturing system;
- does not seem to talk the same language as line management colleagues – fails to understand their requirements;
- slow in responding to requests for help.

When the positive and negative indicators have been agreed, the next step is to distil the competency dimensions that can be inferred from the lists. In this example they could be:

- strategic capability;
- business understanding;
- achievement motivation;
- interpersonal skills;
- communication skills;
- consultancy skills.

These dimensions might also be reflected in the analysis of other areas of competency so that, progressively, a picture of the competencies is built up, which is linked to actual behaviour in the workplace.

The facilitator's job is to prompt, help the group to analyse its findings and assist generally in the production of a set of competence dimensions that can be illustrated by behaviour-based examples. The facilitator may have some ideas about the sort of headings that may emerge from this process but should not try to influence the group to come to a conclusion it has not worked out for itself, albeit with some assistance from the facilitator.

Workshops can use the critical-incident or repertory grid techniques, as described below.

Critical-incident technique

The critical-incident technique is a means of eliciting data about effective or less effective behaviour related to examples of actual events – critical incidents. The technique is used with groups of job holders and/or their managers or other 'experts' (sometimes, less effectively, with individuals) as follows:

- Explain what the technique is and what it is used for, ie 'to assess what constitutes good or poor performance by analysing events that have been observed to have a noticeably successful or unsuccessful outcome, thus providing more factual and "real" information than by simply listing tasks and guessing performance requirements'.

- Agree and list the key results in the role to be analysed. To save time, the analyst can establish these prior to the meeting but it is necessary to ensure that they are agreed provisionally by the group, which can be told that the list may well be amended in the light of the forthcoming analysis.

- Take each area of the role in turn and ask the group for examples of critical incidents. If, for instance, one of the job responsibilities is dealing with customers, the following request could be made: 'I want you to tell me about a particular occasion at work which involved you – or that you observed – in dealing with a customer. Think about what the circumstances were, eg who took part, what the customer asked for, what you or the other member of the staff did and what the outcome was.'

- Collect information about the critical incident under the following headings:
  - what the circumstances were;
  - what the individual did;
  - the outcome of what the individual did.

- Record this information on a flipchart.

- Continue this process for each key result area.

- Refer to the flipchart and analyse each incident by obtaining ratings of the recorded behaviour on a scale such as 1 for least effective to 5 for most effective.

- Discuss these ratings to get initial definitions of effective and ineffective performance for each of the key result areas.

- Refine these definitions as necessary after the meeting – it can be difficult to get a group to produce finished definitions.

- Produce the final analysis, which can list the competencies required and include performance indicators or standards of performance for each key result area.

Repertory grid

Like the critical-incident technique, the repertory grid can be used to identify the dimensions that distinguish good from poor standards of performance. The technique is based on Kelly's (1955) personal construct theory. Personal constructs are the ways in which we view the world. They are personal because they are highly individual and they influence the way we behave or view other people's behaviour. The aspects of the role to which these 'constructs' or judgements apply are called 'elements'.

To elicit judgements, a group of people are asked to concentrate on certain elements, which are the tasks carried out by role holders, and develop constructs about these elements. This enables them to define the qualities that indicate the essential requirements for successful performance.

The procedure followed by the analyst is known as the 'triadic method of elicitation' (a sort of three-card trick) and involves the following steps:

1 Identify the tasks or elements of the role to be subjected to repertory grid analysis. This is done by one of the other forms of job analysis, eg interviewing.

2 List the tasks on cards.

3 Draw three cards at random from the pack and ask the members of the group to nominate which of these tasks is the odd one out from the point of view of the qualities and characteristics needed to perform it.

4 Probe to obtain more specific definitions of these qualities or characteristics in the form of expected behaviour. If, for example, a characteristic has been described as the 'ability to plan and organize', ask questions such as: 'What sort of behaviour or actions indicate that someone is planning effectively?'

or, 'How can we tell if someone is not organizing his or her work particularly well?'

5 Draw three more cards from the pack and repeat steps 3 and 4.

6 Repeat this process until all the cards have been analysed and there are no more constructs to be identified.

7 List the constructs and ask the group members to rate each task on every quality, using a six- or seven-point scale.

8 Collect and analyse the scores to assess their relative importance.

Like the critical-incident technique, repertory grid analysis helps people to articulate their views by reference to specific examples. An additional advantage is that the repertory grid makes it easier for them to identify the behavioural characteristics or competencies required in a job by limiting the area of comparison through the triadic technique. Although a full statistical analysis of the outcome of a repertory grid exercise is helpful, the most important results that can be obtained are the descriptions of what constitute good or poor performance in each element of the job.

Both the repertory grid and the critical-incident techniques require a skilled analyst who can probe and draw out the descriptions of job characteristics. They are quite detailed and time-consuming, but even if the full process is not followed much of the methodology is of use in a less elaborate approach to competency analysis.

Choice of approach

Workshops are probably the best approach, although they can be time-consuming. They get people involved and do not rely on 'expert' opinion. Critical-incident or repertory grid techniques are more sophisticated but they are even more time-consuming and considerable expertise is required to run them.

Technical competencies analysis

Technical competencies or competences can be analysed through the process of functional analysis, which is used to produce definitions of the competences contained in NVQ (National Vocational Qualification) frameworks. Functional analysis focuses on the *outcomes* of work performance. Note that the analysis is not simply concerned with *outputs* in the form of quantifiable results but deals with the broader results that have to be achieved by role holders. An outcome could be a satisfied customer, a more highly motivated subordinate or a better-functioning team.

Functional analysis deals with processes such as developing staff, providing feedback and monitoring performance as well as tasks. It starts with an analysis of the roles fulfilled by an individual in order to arrive at a description of the separate components or 'units' of performance that make up that role. The resulting units consist of performance criteria, described in terms of outcomes, and a description of the knowledge and skill requirements that underpin successful performance. The techniques used in functional analysis are similar to those used in job analysis, described earlier in this chapter.

Skills analysis

Skills analysis determines the skills required to achieve an acceptable standard of performance. It is mainly used for technical, craft, manual and office jobs to provide the basis for devising learning and training programmes. Skills analysis starts from a broad job analysis but goes into details of not only what job holders have to do but also the particular abilities and skills they need to do it. Skills analysis techniques are described below.

Job breakdown

The job breakdown technique analyses a job into separate operations, processes, or tasks that can be used as the elements of an instruction sequence. A job breakdown analysis is recorded in a standard format of three columns:

1 *The stage column*, in which the different steps in the job are described – most semiskilled jobs can easily be broken down into their constituent parts.

2 *The instruction column*, in which a note is made against each step of how the task should be done. This, in effect, describes what has to be learnt by the trainee.

3 *The key points column*, in which any special points such as quality standards or safety instructions are noted against each step so that they can be emphasized to a trainee learning the job.

Manual skills analysis

Manual skills analysis is a technique developed from work study. It isolates for instructional purposes the skills and knowledge employed by experienced workers in performing tasks that require manual dexterity. It is used to analyse short-cycle, repetitive operations such as assembly tasks and other similar factory work.

The hand, finger and other body movements of experienced operatives are observed and recorded in detail as they carry out their work. The analysis concentrates on the tricky parts of the job which, while presenting no difficulty to the experienced operative, have to be analysed in depth before they can be taught to trainees. Not only are the hand movements recorded, but particulars are also noted of the cues (visual and other senses) that the operative absorbs when performing the tasks. Explanatory comments are added when necessary.

Task analysis

Task analysis is a systematic analysis of the behaviour required to carry out a task with a view to identifying areas of difficulty and the appropriate training techniques and learning aids necessary for successful instruction. It can be used for all types of jobs but is specifically relevant to administrative tasks.

The analytical approach used in task analysis is similar to those adopted in the job breakdown and manual skills analysis techniques. The results of the analysis are usually recorded in a standard format of four columns, as follows:

1 *Task* – a brief description of each element.
2 *Level of importance* – the relative significance of each task to the successful performance of the role.

3 *Degree of difficulty* – the level of skill or knowledge required to perform each task.

4 *Training method* – the instructional techniques, practice and experience required.

Faults analysis

Faults analysis is the process of analysing the typical faults that occur when performing a task, especially the more costly faults. It is carried out when the incidence of faults is high. A study is made of the job and, by questioning workers and team leaders, the most commonly occurring faults are identified. A faults specification is then produced, which provides trainees with information on what faults can occur, how they can be recognized, what causes them, what effect they have, who is responsible for them, what action the trainees should take when a particular fault occurs, and how a fault can be prevented from recurring.

Job learning analysis

Job learning analysis, as described by Pearn and Kandola (1993), concentrates on the inputs and process rather than the content of the job. It analyses nine learning skills that contribute to satisfactory performance. A learning skill is one used to increase other skills or knowledge and represents broad categories of job behaviour which need to be learnt. The learning skills are the following:

1 physical skills requiring practice and repetition to get right;

2 complex procedures or sequences of activity that are memorized or followed with the aid of written material such as manuals;

3 non-verbal information such as sight, sound, smell, taste and touch, used to check, assess or discriminate, and which usually takes practice to get right;

4 memorizing facts or information;

5 ordering, prioritizing and planning, which refer to the degree to which a role holder has any responsibility for and flexibility in, determining the way a particular activity is performed;

6 looking ahead and anticipating;

7   diagnosing, analysing and problem solving, with or without help;

8   interpreting or using written manuals and other sources of information such as diagrams or charts;

9   adapting to new ideas and systems.

In conducting a job learning analysis interview, the interviewer obtains information on the main aims and principal activities of the job and then, using question cards for each of the nine learning skills, analyses each activity in more depth, recording responses and obtaining as many examples as possible under each heading.

Key learning points: Job, role, competency and skills analysis

Job analysis methodology and techniques

The essence of job analysis is the application of systematic methods to the collection of information about job content. It is essentially about data collection and the basic steps are:

- obtain documents such as existing organization, procedure or training manuals that give information about the job;

- obtain from managers fundamental information concerning the job;

- obtain from job holders similar information about their jobs.

Job descriptions

Job descriptions should be based on the job analysis and should be as brief and factual as possible. The headings should be: job title, reporting to, reporting to job holder, main purpose of job, main activities, tasks or duties.

Role analysis methodology

Role analysis uses the same techniques as job analysis but the focus is on identifying inputs (knowledge, skill and competency requirements) and required outcomes (key result areas) rather than simply listing the tasks to be carried out.

Behavioural competency modelling

Behavioural competency modelling is used for identifying, analysing and describing behavioural competencies that define the behaviours that organizations expect their staff to practise in their work in order to reach an acceptable level of performance. The emphasis is on the systematic collection and analysis of data. There are five approaches to behavioural competency analysis. In ascending order of complexity these are: expert opinion, structured interview, workshops, critical-incident technique, and repertory grid analysis.

Analysing technical competencies

Functional analysis starts with an analysis of the roles fulfilled by an individual in order to arrive at a description of the separate components or 'units' of performance that make up that role. The resulting units consist of performance criteria, described in terms of outcomes, and a description of the knowledge and skill requirements that underpin successful performance.

Skills analysis

Skills analysis determines the skills required to achieve an acceptable standard of performance. It is mainly used for technical, craft, manual and office jobs to provide the basis for devising learning and training programmes. Skills analysis starts from a broad job analysis but goes into details of what job holders have to do and the particular abilities and skills they need to do it. Skills analysis techniques include job breakdown, manual skills analysis, faults analysis and job learning analysis.

Questions

1 What is the difference between a job and a role?

2 What is a job description?

3 What is a role profile?

4 What is a generic role profile?

5 How should a job analysis interview be conducted?

6 What are the advantages and disadvantages of questionnaires as a method of analysing jobs?

References

Kelly, G (1955) *The Psychology of Personal Constructs*, New York, Norton

Pearn, K and Kandola, R (1993) *Job Analysis: A manager's guide*, London, IPM

Shippmann, J S, Ash, R A and Battista, M (2000) The practice of competency modelling, *Personnel Psychology*, 53 (3), pp 703–40

49
Learning and development skills

LEARNING OUTCOMES

On completing this chapter you should be able to define these key concepts. You should also know about coaching, mentoring and job instruction skills.

Introduction

HR professionals need skills in coaching and mentoring to fulfil their important responsibilities for enhancing the knowledge and skills of employees and for providing guidance to line managers on conducting their learning and development activities.

Coaching

Coaching is a personal (usually one-to-one) approach that enables people to develop their skills and knowledge and improve their performance. As Whitmore (2002: 8) suggested: 'Coaching is unlocking a person's potential to maximize their own performance. It is helping them to learn rather than teaching them.' Clutterbuck (2004: 23) noted that: 'Coaching is primarily focused on performance within the current job and emphasizes the development of skills.'

Coaching is often provided by specialists from inside or outside the organization who concentrate on specific areas of skills or behaviour, for example leadership. But it is also something that HR professionals have to be prepared to do as part of their normal learning and development duties, and this means deploying the skills described below.

The approach to coaching

To succeed in coaching you need to understand that your role is to help people to learn and see that they are motivated to learn. They should be aware of the advantages to them as well as the organization of developing their present level of knowledge or skill or modifying their behaviour. Individuals should be given guidance on what they should be learning and feedback on how they are doing and, because learning is an active not a passive process, they should be actively involved with their coach.

Coaching is sometimes informal but it has to be planned. It is not simply checking from time to time on what people are doing and then advising them on how to do it better. Nor is it occasionally telling people where they have gone wrong and throwing in a lecture for good measure. As far as possible, coaching should take place within the framework of a general plan of the areas and direction in which individuals will benefit from further development. Coaching plans should be incorporated into the personal development plans set out in a performance agreement.

Coaching should provide motivation, structure and effective feedback. As a coach, you should believe that people can succeed and that they can contribute to their own success.

Coaching styles

Clutterbuck and Megginson (2005: 52) identified four coaching styles:

1 *Assessor* – this is akin to instruction and involves telling people the way to do something.

2 *Demonstrator* – this is less directive than the assessor style. It involves showing learners how to do something and then getting them to do it with guidance and comments from the coach as required.

3 *Tutor* – this involves encouraging learners to find out how to do things for themselves. It is still relatively directive as it is the coach who suggests what learners should look for.

4 *Stimulator* – this helps learners to teach themselves by guiding their thinking through the use of insight-provoking questions.

Criteria for effectiveness

The following criteria for evaluating the performance of a coach were listed by Gray (2010: 379):

- establishes rapport;
- creates trust and respect;
- demonstrates effective communication skills;
- promotes self-awareness and self-knowledge;
- uses active listening and questioning techniques;
- assists goal development and setting;
- motivates;
- encourages alternative perspectives;
- assists in making sense of a situation;
- identifies significant patterns of thinking and behaving;
- provides an appropriate mix of challenge and support;
- facilitates depth of understanding;
- shows compassion;
- acts ethically;
- inspires curiosity;
- acts as a role model;
- values diversity and difference;
- promotes action and reflection.

Mentoring

Mentors offer guidance, pragmatic advice and continuing support to help those allocated to them to learn and develop. It is a method of helping people to learn as distinct from coaching, which can be a relatively directive means of increasing people's competence. Mentors may be line managers. They are often appointed and trained by learning and development specialists who therefore need to be aware of the skills required. L&D professionals may act as mentors themselves, although experienced managers are best if they have the skills and enthusiasm required.

Mentors provide people with:

- advice in drawing up self-development programmes or learning contracts;
- general help with learning programmes;
- guidance on how to acquire the necessary knowledge and skills to do a new job;

- advice on dealing with any administrative, technical or people problems individuals meet, especially in the early stages of their careers;
- information on 'the way things are done around here' – the corporate culture in terms of expected behaviour;
- coaching in specific skills;
- help in tackling projects – not by doing it for them but by pointing them in the right direction, helping people to help themselves;
- a parental figure with whom individuals can discuss their aspirations and concerns and who will lend a sympathetic ear to their problems.

Mentors need to adopt a non-directive but supportive approach to helping the person or persons they are dealing with.

Job instruction

When people learn specific tasks, especially those involving basic administrative or manual skills, the learning will be more effective if job instruction techniques are used. HR professionals may possibly be involved in providing direct instruction but their most typical role is that of promoting effective instruction techniques for use by line managers and others involved in workplace learning or running formal training programmes. They should therefore be aware of the sequence of instruction, as described below.

Preparation

Preparation for each instruction period means that the trainer must have a plan for presenting the subject matter and using appropriate teaching methods, visual aids and demonstration aids. It also means preparing trainees for the instruction that is to follow. They should want to learn. They must perceive that the learning will be relevant and useful to them personally. They should be encouraged to take pride in their job and to appreciate the satisfaction that comes from skilled performance.

Presentation

Presentation should consist of a combination of telling and showing – explanation and demonstration.

Explanation should be as simple and direct as possible: the trainer explains briefly the ground to be covered and what to look for. He or she makes the maximum use of charts, diagrams and other visual aids. The aim should be to teach first things first and then proceed from the known to the unknown, the simple to the complex, the concrete to the abstract, the general to the particular, the observation to reasoning, and the whole to the parts and back to the whole again.

Demonstration

Demonstration is an essential stage in instruction, especially when the skill to be learnt is mainly a 'doing' skill. Demonstration can take place in three stages:

1 The complete operation is shown at normal speed to show the trainee how the task should be carried out eventually.

2 The operation is demonstrated slowly and in correct sequence, element by element, to indicate clearly what is done and the order in which each task is carried out.

3 The operation is demonstrated again slowly, at least two or three times, to stress the how, when and why of successive movements.

The learner then practises by imitating the instructor and constantly repeating the operation under guidance. The aim is to reach the target level of performance for each element of the total task, but the instructor must constantly strive to develop coordinated and integrated performance – that is, the smooth combination of the separate elements of the task into a whole job pattern.

Follow up

Follow up continues during the training period for all the time required by the learner to reach a level of performance equal to that of the normal experienced worker in terms of quality, speed and attention to safety. During the follow-up stage, the learner will continue to need help with particularly difficult tasks or to overcome temporary set-backs that result in a deterioration of performance. The instructor may have to repeat the presentation for the elements and supervise practice more closely until the trainee regains confidence or masters the task.

Key learning points: Learning and development skills

The requirement

HR professionals need skills in coaching and mentoring to fulfil their important responsibilities for enhancing the knowledge and skills of employees and for providing guidance to line managers on conducting their learning and development activities.

Coaching

Coaching is a personal (usually one-to-one) approach that enables people to develop their skills and knowledge and improve their performance.

The approach to coaching

- To succeed in coaching you need to understand that your role is to help people to learn and to see that they are motivated to learn.

- Coaching is sometimes informal but it has to be planned. It is not simply checking from time to time on what people are doing and then advising them on how to do it better, or occasionally telling people where they have gone wrong and throwing in a lecture.

- Coaching should provide motivation, structure and effective feedback. As a coach, you should believe that people can succeed and that they can contribute to their own success.

Mentoring

Mentors offer guidance, pragmatic advice and continuing support to help those allocated to them to learn and develop. It is a method of helping people to learn as distinct from coaching, which can be a relatively directive means of increasing people's competence. Mentors provide people with:

- advice in drawing up self-development programmes or learning contracts;

- general help with learning programmes;

- guidance on how to acquire the necessary knowledge and skills to do a new job;

- advice on dealing with any administrative, technical or people problems individuals meet, especially in the early stages of their careers;

- information on 'the way things are done around here' – the corporate culture in terms of expected behaviour;

- coaching in specific skills;

- help in tackling projects – not by doing it for them but by pointing them in the right direction, helping people to help themselves;

- a parental figure with whom individuals can discuss their aspirations and concerns and who will lend a sympathetic ear to their problems.

Job instruction

When people learn specific tasks, especially those involving basic administrative or manual skills, the learning will be more effective if job instruction techniques are used. The sequence of instruction is.

- Preparation for each instruction period means that the trainer must have a plan for presenting the subject matter and using appropriate teaching methods, visual aids and demonstration aids. It also means preparing trainees for the instruction that is to follow.

- Presentation should consist of a combination of telling and showing – explanation and demonstration.

- Demonstration is an essential stage in instruction, especially when the skill to be learnt is mainly a 'doing' skill.

- Follow up continues during the training period for all the time required by the learner to reach a level of performance equal to that of the normal experienced worker in terms of quality, speed and attention to safety.

Questions

1 What is coaching?

2 What approach should be adopted to coaching?

3 What is mentoring?

4 What do mentors do?

5 What is the job instruction sequence?

References

Clutterbuck, D (2004) *Everyone Needs a Mentor: Fostering talent in your organization*, 4th edn, London, CIPD

Clutterbuck, D and Megginson, D (2005) *Making Coaching Work: Creating a coaching culture*, London, CIPD

Gray, D A (2010) Building quality into executive coaching, in (eds) J Gold, R Thorpe and A Mumford, *Gower Handbook of Leadership and Management Development*, Farnham, Gower, pp 367–85

Whitmore, J (2002) *Coaching for Performance*, 3rd edn, London, Nicholas Brealey

50
Negotiating skills

KEY CONCEPTS AND TERMS

Bargaining

Negotiating

Corridor negotiations

Zero-sum game

LEARNING OUTCOMES

On completing this chapter you should be able to define these key concepts. You should also know about:

- The process of negotiation
- The stages of a negotiation
- Negotiating and bargaining skills

Introduction

HR practitioners who are involved in industrial relations may conduct or take part in negotiations with trade union representatives or officials. Negotiating is a process that requires considerable skill to do well.

Negotiation involves bargaining, which is reaching the most advantageous position in discussion with another party through a process of offer and counter-offer. It is a process in which two parties – management and the trade union – get together with the aim of getting the best deal possible for their business or their members.

Negotiations involve a conflict of interest. In pay negotiations unions want the highest settlement they can get; management wants the lowest. In negotiations about other terms and conditions, unions will want the best result for their members while management will want to avoid agreeing to anything other than what they think is reasonable from their viewpoint. It can be a zero-sum game – what one side gains the other loses. No one likes to lose, so there is scope for conflict, which has to be managed if an amicable agreement is to be achieved. And negotiators do, or should, try to end up on friendly terms, whatever differences of opinion have occurred on the way. After all, they may well meet again.

TABLE 50.1   Commercial and industrial relations negotiations compared

Industrial relations negotiations	Commercial negotiations
• Assume an ongoing relationship – negotiators cannot walk away. • The agreement is not legally binding. • Conducted on a face-to-face basis. • Carried out by representatives responsible to constituents. • Make frequent use of adjournments. • May be conducted in an atmosphere of distrust, even hostility.	• Negotiators can walk away. • The contract is legally binding. • May be conducted at a distance. • Carried out directly with the parties being responsible to a line manager. • Usually conducted on a continuing basis. • Usually conducted on a 'willing buyer/willing seller' basis.

The process of negotiation

Negotiating takes place when two parties meet to reach an agreement concerning a proposition, such as a pay claim, one party has put to the other. Negotiation can be convergent when both parties are equally keen to reach a win-win agreement (in commercial terms, a willing buyer/willing seller arrangement). It can be divergent when one or both of the parties aim to win as much as they can from the other while giving away as little as possible. Negotiations in an industrial relations setting differ from commercial negotiations in the respects shown in Table 50.1.

In negotiations on pay or other terms and conditions of service, management represents the employer's interests and employee representatives represent the interests of employees. Both sides are of equal status. Negotiations take place in an atmosphere of uncertainty. Neither side knows how strong the other side's bargaining position is or what it really wants and will be prepared to accept.

Stages of negotiation

Negotiations are conducted in four stages: initial steps, opening, bargaining and closing.

Initial steps

In a pay negotiation, unions making the claim will define for themselves three things: a) the target they

would like to achieve, b) the minimum they will accept, and c) the opening claim they believe will be most likely to achieve the target. Employers define three related things: 1) the target settlement they would like to achieve, 2) the maximum they would be prepared to concede, and 3) the opening offer that will provide them with sufficient room to manoeuvre in reaching their target. The difference between a union's claim and an employer's offer is the negotiating range. If the maximum the employer will offer exceeds the minimum the union will accept the difference will be the settlement range, in which case a settlement will be easily reached. If, however, the maximum the employer will offer is less than the minimum the union will accept, negotiations will be more difficult and a settlement will only be reached if the expectations of either side are adjusted during the bargaining stage. The extent to which this will happen depends on the relative power of the two parties. The strength of the arguments put forward by either party will also be a factor, but the major consideration is usually power.

Preparation for negotiation by either party involves:

- deciding on the strategy and tactics to be used;
- listing the arguments to be used in supporting their case;
- listing the arguments or counter-arguments the other party is likely to use;
- obtaining supporting data;

- selecting the negotiating team, briefing them on the strategy and tactics and rehearsing them in their roles.

Opening

Tactics in the opening phase of a negotiation can be as follows:

- open realistically and move moderately;
- challenge the other side's position as it stands; do not destroy their ability to move;
- observe behaviour, ask questions and listen attentively in order to assess the other side's strengths and weaknesses, their tactics and the extent to which they may be bluffing;
- make no concessions at this stage;
- be non-committal about proposals and explanations – do not talk too much.

Bargaining

After the opening moves, the main bargaining phase takes place in which the gap is narrowed between the initial positions and the attempt to persuade each other that their case is strong enough to force the other side to close at a less advantageous point than they had planned. Bargaining is often as much about concealing as revealing – keeping arguments in reserve to deploy when they will make the greatest impact. The following tactics can be used:

- Always make conditional proposals: 'If you will do this, then I will consider doing that' – the words to remember are: 'if ... then ...'.
- Never make one-sided concessions: always trade off against a concession from the other party: 'If I concede x, then I expect you to concede y'.
- Negotiate on the whole package: negotiations should not allow the other side to pick off item by item (salami negotiation).
- Keep the issues open to extract the maximum benefit from potential trade-offs.

There are certain bargaining conventions that experienced negotiators follow because they appreciate that by so doing they create an atmosphere of trust and understanding that is essential to the sort of

stable bargaining relationship that benefits both sides. Some of the more generally accepted conventions are as follows:

- Whatever happens during the bargaining, both parties are hoping to reach a settlement.
- Negotiators should show that they respect the views of the other side and take them seriously even if they disagree with them.
- While it is preferable to conduct negotiations in a civilized and friendly manner, attacks, hard words, threats and controlled losses of temper may be used by negotiators to underline determination to get their way and to shake their opponent's confidence and self-possession. But these should be treated by both sides as legitimate tactics and should not be allowed to shake the basic belief in each other's integrity or desire to settle without taking drastic action.
- Off-the-record discussions ('corridor negotiations') can be mutually beneficial as a means of probing attitudes and intentions and smoothing the way to a settlement, but they should not be referred to specifically in formal bargaining sessions unless both sides agree in advance.
- Each side should be prepared to move from its original position.
- It is normal, although not inevitable, for the negotiation to proceed by alternate offers and counter-offers from each side, leading steadily towards a settlement.
- Third parties should not be brought in until both sides agree that no further progress can be made without them.
- Concessions, once made, cannot be withdrawn.
- If negotiators want to avoid committing themselves to 'a final offer' with the risk of devaluing the term if they are forced to make concessions, they should state as positively as they can that this is as far as they can go. But bargaining conventions allow further moves from this position on a *quid pro quo* basis.
- Firm offers must not be withdrawn.
- The final agreement should mean exactly what it says. There should be no trickery and the agreed terms should be implemented without amendment.

- So far as possible the final settlement should be framed and communicated in such a way as to reduce the extent to which the other party loses face or credibility.

When bargaining, the parties have to identify the basis for a possible agreement; that is, the common ground. One way of doing this is to use the aspiration grid technique. The grid sets out the parameters for the anticipated outcome of the negotiations. It shows the expected issues one of the parties is prepared to trade as well as the anticipated attitude to the bargaining agenda of the other party. The grid also gives the parameters within which the forthcoming bargaining sessions might be expected to develop. It helps to identify the information required from the other party and the information required to be conveyed by one party to the other party. If the receipt of this information shows expectations as to the behaviour of the other party to be wrong, then the aspiration grid has to be reassessed and modified.

Closing

There are various closing techniques:

- Make a concession from the package, preferably a minor way, which is traded off against an agreement to settle. The concession can be offered more positively than in the bargaining stage: 'If you will agree to settle at x then I will concede y.'

- Do a deal, split the difference or bring in something new, such as extending the settlement timescale, agreeing to back-payments, phasing increases, or making a joint declaration of intent to do something in the future.

- Summarize what has happened so far, emphasize the concessions that have been made and the extent of movement from the original position, and indicate that the limit has been reached.

- Apply pressure through a threat of the dire consequences that will follow if a 'final' claim is not agreed or a 'final offer' is not accepted.

Employers should not make a final offer unless they mean it. If it is not really their final offer and the union calls their bluff, they may have to make further concessions and their credibility will be undermined. Each party will attempt to force the other side into revealing the extent to which they have reached their final position. But negotiators should not allow themselves to be pressurized. They have to use their judgement on when to say 'this is a far as we can go'. That judgement will be based on their understanding that the stage when a settlement is possible has been reached.

Negotiating and bargaining skills

The skills required to be effective in negotiations and bargaining are:

- *Analytical ability* – the capacity to assess the factors that affect the negotiating stance and tactics of both parties.

- *Empathy* – the ability to put oneself in the other party's shoes.

- *Interactive skills* – the ability to relate well with other people.

- *Communicating skills* – the ability to convey information and arguments clearly, positively and logically.

- *Keeping cards close to the chest* – not giving away what you really want or are prepared to concede until you are ready to do so (in the market place it is always easier for sellers to drive a hard bargain with buyers who have revealed somehow that they covet the article).

- *Flexible realism* – the capacity to make realistic moves during the bargaining process to reduce the claim or increase the offer, which will demonstrate that the bargainer is seeking a reasonable settlement and is prepared to respond appropriately to movements from the other side.

> ## Key learning points: Negotiating skills
>
> ### The process of negotiation
>
> Negotiation is the process of coming to terms and, in so doing, getting the best deal possible. Negotiation involves bargaining, which is reaching the most advantageous position in discussion with another party through a process of offer and counter-offer.
>
> Negotiating takes place when two parties meet to reach an agreement on a proposition, such as a pay claim, one party has put to the other. Negotiation can be convergent when both parties are equally keen to reach a win-win agreement (in commercial terms, a willing buyer/willing seller arrangement). It can be divergent when one or both of the parties aim to win as much as they can from the other while giving away as little as possible.
>
> ### Stages of negotiation
>
> Negotiations are conducted in four stages: initial steps, opening, bargaining and closing.
>
> ### Negotiating and bargaining skills
>
> - *Analytical ability* – the capacity to assess the factors that affect the negotiating stance and tactics of both parties.
> - *Empathy* – the ability to put oneself in the other party's shoes.
> - *Interactive skills* – the ability to relate well with other people.
> - *Communicating skills* – the ability to convey information and arguments clearly, positively and logically.
> - *Keeping cards close to the chest* – not giving away what you really want or are prepared to concede until you are ready to do so.
> - *Flexible realism* – the capacity to make realistic moves during the bargaining process to reduce the claim or increase the offer, which will demonstrate that the bargainer is seeking a reasonable settlement and is prepared to respond appropriately to movements from the other side.

Questions

1 What is the process of negotiation?

2 What are the main stages of a negotiation?

3 What are the required negotiating and bargaining skills?

Questions

1 What is the role of HR in leading and facilitating change?

2 What does leading change involve?

3 What does facilitating change involve?

4 What is the change process?

5 What are the main problems in implementing change?

6 What is Lewin's change model?

7 What is field force analysis?

8 Why do people resist change?

9 How can resistance to change be overcome?

10 What is the role of a change agent?

11 What are the key guidelines for change management?

References

Alfes, K, Truss, C and Gill, J (2010) The HR manager as change agent: evidence from the public sector, *Journal of Change Management*, **10** (1), pp 109–27

Balugon, J and Hope-Hailey, V (2004) *Exploring Strategic Change*, 2nd edn, London, Prentice Hall

Beckhard, R (1969) *Organization Development: Strategy and models*, Reading, MA, Addison-Wesley

Beer, M, Eisenstat, R and Spector, B (1990) Why change programs don't produce change, *Harvard Business Review*, November–December, pp 158–66

Brown, S L and Eisenhardt, K M (1997) The art of continuous change: linking complexity theory and time-paced evolution in relentlessly shifting organizations, *Administrative Science Quarterly*, **42** (1), pp 1–24

Caldwell, R (2001) Champions, adapters, consultants and synergists: the new change agents in HRM, *Human Resource Management Journal*, **11** (3), pp 39–52

Caldwell, R (2003) Models of change agency: a fourfold classification, *British Journal of Management*, **14** (2), pp 131–42

Carnall, C (1991) *Managing Change*, London, Routledge

Hamlin, B and Davies, G (2001) Managers, trainers and developers as change agents, in (eds) B Hamlin, J Keep and K Ash, *Organizational Change and Development: A reflective guide for managers, trainers and developers*, Harlow, Pearson Education, pp 39–60

Keep, J (2001) The change practitioner: perspectives on role, effectiveness, dilemmas and challenges, in (eds) B Hamlin, J Keep and K Ash, *Organizational Change and Development: A reflective guide for managers, trainers and developers*, Harlow, Pearson Education, pp 13–38

Kotter, J J (1996) *Leading Change*, Boston, MA, Harvard University Press

Lawler, E E and Mohrman, S A (2003) HR as a strategic partner: What does it take to make it happen?, *Human Resource Planning*, **26** (3), pp 15–29

Lewin, K (1951) *Field Theory in Social Science*, New York, Harper & Row

Nadler, D A and Tushman, M L (1980) A congruence model for diagnosing organizational behaviour, in (ed) R H Miles, *Resource Book in Macro-organizational Behaviour*, Santa Monica, CA, Goodyear Publishing

Pettigrew, A and Whipp, R (1991) *Managing Change for Competitive Success*, Oxford, Blackwell

Quinn, J B (1980) Managing strategic change, *Sloane Management Review*, **11** (4/5), pp 3–30

Thornhill, A, Lewis, P, Saunders, M and Millmore, M (2000) *Managing Change: A human resource strategy approach*, Harlow, FT Prentice Hall

Thurley, K (1979) *Supervision: A reappraisal*, London, Heinemann

Ulrich, D (1997) *Human Resource Champions*, Boston, MA, Harvard Business School Press

Ulrich, D (1998) A new mandate for human resources, *Harvard Business Review*, January–February, pp 124–34

Vere, D and Butler, L (2007) *Fit for Business: Transforming HR in the public service*, London, CIPD

Woodward, J (1968) Resistance to change, *Management International Review*, **8**, pp 78–93

52
Leadership skills

KEY CONCEPTS AND TERMS

Authentic leaders

Charismatic leaders

Contingent leadership

Distributed leadership

Emotional intelligence

Leadership

Leadership development

Situational leadership

Trait

Transactional leaders

Transformational leaders

Visionary leaders

LEARNING OUTCOMES

On completing this chapter you should be able to define these key concepts. You should also know about:

- The meaning of leadership
- The main leadership theories
- What leaders do
- The main leadership styles
- The qualities of a good leader
- The process of leadership development
- What makes an effective leader

Introduction

HR professionals need to know about leadership for four reasons: they have to exercise leadership in persuading others to do things; they are, or should be, concerned with the development of leaders in the organization; at a senior level they have to lead their own function; and they are involved in leading change. The purpose of this chapter is to meet this need by analysing the process of leadership and the skills involved.

The meaning of leadership

To lead people is to inspire, influence and guide. Leadership can be described as the ability to persuade others willingly to behave differently. It is the process of getting people to do their best to achieve a desired result. It involves developing and communicating a vision for the future, motivating people and securing their engagement. As Stogdill (1950: 3) explained, leadership is an 'influencing process aimed at goal achievement'.

Leadership theories

Leadership is a complicated notion and a number of theories have been produced to explain it. These theories, as summarized below, have developed over the years and explore a number of different facets of leadership and leadership behaviour. In many ways they complement one another and together they help to gain a comprehensive understanding of what the process of leadership is about.

Trait theory, which explains leadership by reference to the qualities leaders have, is the basic and to many people the most familiar theory. But it has its limitations, and pragmatic research was carried out to identify what types of behaviour characterized leadership rather than focusing on the personalities of leaders. The key leadership behaviour studies conducted by the Universities of Michigan and Ohio State led to the identification of two dimensions of leadership behaviour, respectively: employee as distinct from job-centred behaviour, and the processes of consideration and initiating structure.

The next step in the development of leadership theory was the recognition by researchers that what leaders did and how they did it was dependent or contingent on the situation they were in (Fiedler, 1967). Different traits became important; different behaviours or styles of leadership had to be used to achieve effectiveness in different situations. These studies resulted in the theories of contingent and situational leadership.

Next, traits theory was in effect revived by Goleman (2001) in the notion of emotional intelligence as a necessary attribute of leaders. Most recently Ulrich put his oar in alongside his colleague Smallwood (2007) with the notion of the leadership brand as a comprehensive approach to leadership by organizations.

The problem with leadership theories

Despite of all the research and theorizing, the concept of leadership is still problematic. As Meindl

et al (1985: 78) commented: 'It has become apparent that, after years of trying, we have been unable to generate an understanding of leadership that is both intellectually compelling and emotionally satisfying. The concept of leadership remains elusive and enigmatic.'

These problems may arise because, as a notion, leadership is difficult to pin down. There are many different types of situations in which leaders operate, many different types of leaders and many different leadership styles. Producing one theory that covers all these variables is difficult if not impossible. All that can be done is to draw on the various theories that exist to explain different facets of leadership without necessarily relying on any one of them for a comprehensive explanation of what is involved.

Perhaps leadership is best defined by considering what leaders do and how they do it (the different styles they adopt), examining what sort of leaders carry out these activities and practise these styles, and looking at any empirical evidence available on what makes them good leaders. These are all covered in the next four sections of this chapter.

What leaders do

The most convincing analysis of what leaders do was produced by Adair (1973). He explained that the three essential roles of leaders are to:

1 *Define the task* – they make it quite clear what the group is expected to do.

2 *Achieve the task* – that is why the group exists. Leaders ensure that the group's purpose is fulfilled. If it is not, the result is frustration, disharmony, criticism and, eventually perhaps, disintegration of the group.

3 *Maintain effective relationships* – between themselves and the members of the group, and between the people within the group. These relationships are effective if they contribute to achieving the task. They can be divided into those concerned with the team and its morale and sense of common purpose, and those concerned with individuals and how they are motivated.

He suggested that demands on leaders are best expressed as three areas of need which they must satisfy. These are: 1) task needs: to get the job done; 2) individual needs: to harmonize the needs of the individual with the needs of the task and the group; and 3) group maintenance needs: to build and maintain team spirit. As can be seen in Figure 52.1, he modelled these demands as three interlocking circles.

FIGURE 52.1
John Adair's model of leadership

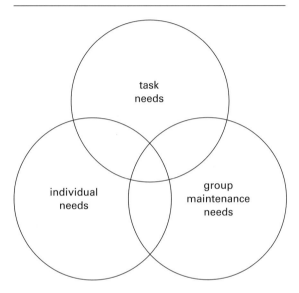

This model indicates that the task, individual and group needs are interdependent. Satisfying task needs will also satisfy group and individual needs. Task needs, however, cannot be met unless attention is paid to individual and group needs, and looking after individual needs will also contribute to satisfying group needs, and vice versa. There is a risk of becoming so task-oriented that leaders ignore individual and group or team needs. It is just as dangerous to be too people-oriented, focusing on meeting individual or group needs at the expense of the task. The best leaders are those who keep these three needs satisfied and in balance, according to the demands of the situation.

Leadership styles

Leadership style is the approach managers use in exercising leadership when they are relating to their team members. It is sometimes called 'management style'. There are many styles of leadership and no one style is necessarily better than the other in any situation. To greater or lesser degrees, leaders can be autocratic or democratic, controlling or enabling, task-oriented or people-centred. The Hay/McBer research reported by Goleman (2000) identified the following six styles and indicated when they might be used:

1 *Coercive* – demands compliance (use in a crisis or with problem people).

2 *Authoritative* – mobilizes people (use when new vision and direction is needed).

3 *Affiliative* – creates harmony (use to heal wounds and to motivate people under stress).

4 *Democratic* – forges consensus (use to build agreement and get contributions).

5 *Pacesetting* – sets high standards (use to get fast results from a motivated team).

6 *Coaching* – develops people (to improve performance and develop strengths).

In line with contingency and situational theories it should not be assumed that any one style is right in any circumstances. There is no such thing as an ideal leadership style. It all depends. The factors affecting the degree to which a style is appropriate will be the type of organization, the nature of the task, the characteristics of the individuals in the leader's team (the followers) and of the group as a whole and, importantly, the personality of the leader.

Effective leaders are capable of flexing their style to meet the demands of the situation. Normally democratic leaders may have to shift into more of a directive mode when faced with a crisis, but they make clear what they are doing and why. Poor leaders change their style arbitrarily so that their team members are confused and do not know what to expect next.

Good leaders may also flex their style when dealing with individual team members according to their characteristics. Some people need more positive directions than others. Others respond best if they are involved in decision making with their boss. But there is a limit to the degree of flexibility that should be used. It is unwise to differentiate too much between the ways in which individuals are treated or to be inconsistent in one's approach.

Types of leaders

To understand the process of leadership (and, incidentally, provide a basis for leadership development programmes) it is useful not only to analyse the styles that leaders can adopt but also to classify the different types of leaders that apply those styles. As described below, leaders can be charismatic, visionary, transformational, transactional or 'authentic'. However, typical leaders may exhibit any or even all of these characteristics either consistently or in response to the situation in which they find themselves.

Leadership may be exercised by a few selected authoritative individuals and many studies focus on top managers as 'charismatic' or 'visionary' leaders. But it may and indeed should take the form of distributed leadership, which is spread through the organization amongst people working together by processes of influence and interdependencies. As Huczynski and Buchanan (2007: 720) commented: 'leadership is a widely distributed phenomenon. Leadership functions are best carried out by those who have the interest, knowledge, skills and motivation to perform them effectively'. The possibility that people who become managers may not have these qualities to a desirable extent creates a need for systematic leadership development programmes.

Charismatic leaders

Charismatic leaders rely on their personality, their inspirational qualities and their 'aura' to get people to follow them. Burns (1978), who coined the term, suggested that charismatic leaders were set apart from ordinary people and treated as being endowed with exceptional powers or qualities that inspire followers.

Conger and Kanungo (1998) described charismatic leadership as a process of formulating an inspiring vision of the future and then demonstrating the importance of the articulated vision. This may involve unconventional behaviour that conveys important goals that are part of the vision and demonstrates means to achieve these goals. Charismatic leaders also take risks and motivate followers by setting a personal example. In this sense, charismatic leaders operate as visionary and transformational leaders, as described below.

But Carey (1992: 232) charged that, 'when the gifts of charisma, inspiration, consideration and intellectual strength are abused for the self-interest of the leader, the effect on followers ceases to be liberating and moral and becomes instead oppressive and ideological'. And Bennis (2010: 4) commented that: 'the ability to inspire trust, not charisma, is what enables leaders to recruit others to a cause'.

Visionary leaders

Visionary leaders are inspired by a clear vision of an exciting future and inspire their followers by successfully conveying that vision to them. Bennis and Nanus (1985: 89) defined a vision as 'a target that beckons'. Their notion of visionary leadership was explained as follows:

> To choose a direction, a leader must first have developed a mental image of a possible and desirable future state of the organization. This image, which we call a vision, may be as vague as a dream or as precise as a goal or mission statement. The critical point is that a vision articulates a view of a realistic, credible and attractive future for the organization, a condition that is different in some important ways from one that now exists. (ibid: 89)

Kouzes and Posner (2003: 112) claimed that: 'One of *the* most important practices of leadership is giving life and work a sense of meaning and purpose by offering an exciting vision.'

Transformational leaders

Transformational leaders are able, by their force of personality, to make significant changes in the behaviour of their followers in order to achieve the leader's vision or goals. As described by Burns (1978), what he called 'transforming leadership' involves motivating people to strive for higher goals. He believed that good leadership implies a moral responsibility to respond to the values and needs of people in a way that is conducive to the highest form of human relations. As he put it: 'The ultimate test of moral leadership is its capacity to transcend the claims of the multiplicity of everyday needs, wants and expectations' (ibid: 46).

Another researcher, Bass (1985), extended the work of Burns by explaining the psychological mechanisms that underlie transforming leadership. He pointed out that the extent to which leaders are transformational is measured by their influence on their followers in terms of the degree to which they feel trust, admiration, loyalty and respect for the leader and are willing to work harder than originally expected. According to Bass, this occurs because the leader transforms and motivates through an inspiring mission and vision and gives them an identity. Tichy and Devanna (1986) concluded that the transformational leader has three main roles: recognizing the need for revitalization, creating a new vision and institutionalizing change.

Yukl (1999) advised transformational leaders to:

- develop a challenging and attractive vision together with employees;

- tie the vision to a strategy for its achievement;

- develop the vision, specify and translate it to actions;

- express confidence, decisiveness and optimism about the vision and its implementation;

- realize the vision through small planned steps and small successes on the path to its full implementation.

Transactional leaders

Transactional leaders trade money, jobs and security for compliance. As Burns (1978: 19) noted: 'Such leadership occurs when a person takes the initiative in making contact with others for the purpose of an exchange of valued things.' Tavanti (2008: 169) stated that: 'Transactional leaders exhibit specific leadership skills usually associated with the ability to obtain results, to control through structures and processes, to solve problems, to plan and organize, and work within the structures and boundaries of the organization.' Put like this, a transactional leader conforms to the stereotype of the manager rather than the leader. Bass (1985) argued that leaders can display both transformational and transactional characteristics. Tavanti (2008) also observed that transactional leadership behaviour is used to one degree or another by most leaders, but that: 'Particular instances of transactional leadership are motivated simply by people's wants and preferences. This form of leadership uncritically responds to our preferences, that is, even when they are grounded in base motivations or an undeveloped moral sense' (ibid: 171).

Authentic leaders

The concept of the authentic leader was originally defined by George (2003: 12) as follows:

> Authentic leaders genuinely desire to serve others through their leadership. They are more interested in empowering the people they lead to make a difference than they are in power, money or prestige for themselves. They lead with purpose, meaning and values. They build enduring relationships with them. Others follow them because they know where they stand. They are consistent and self-disciplined.

Authenticity was defined by Harter (2002: 382) as 'owning one's personal experiences, be they thoughts, emotions, needs, preferences, or beliefs, processes captured by the injunction to know oneself and behaving in accordance with the true self'. Authentic leadership is based on a positive moral perspective characterized by high ethical standards that guide decision making and behaviour (May et al, 2003). As Avolio et al (2004) explained, authentic leaders act in accordance with deep personal values and convictions to build credibility and win the respect and trust of followers. By encouraging diverse viewpoints and building networks of collaborative relationships with followers, they lead in a manner that followers perceive and describe as authentic.

George et al (2007: 129) set out the basis of authentic leadership as follows:

> We all have the capacity to inspire and empower others. But we must first be willing to devote ourselves to our personal growth and development as leaders … No one can be authentic by trying to imitate someone else. You can learn from others' experiences, but there is no way you can be successful when you are trying to be like them. People trust you when you are genuine and authentic, not a replica of someone else.

Authentic leadership is, in essence, ethical leadership. Walumbwa et al (2008) claimed that it can lead to enhanced trust, job satisfaction and performance.

The reality of leadership

The reality of leadership is that many first-line managers and supervisors are appointed or promoted to their posts with some idea, possibly, of what their managerial or supervisory duties are, but with no appreciation of the leadership skills they need. They see their role as being to tell people what to do and then see that they do it. They may tend to adopt a transactional approach, focusing on getting the job done and neglecting everything else. They are unlikely to be charismatic, visionary or transformational leaders because even if they have the latent qualities required, their situation does not seem to require or encourage any of these approaches.

However, the better ones will rely on their know-how (authority goes to the person who knows), their quiet confidence and their cool, analytical approach to dealing with problems. Any newly appointed leader or individual who is progressing to a higher level of leadership will benefit from a leadership development programme, which will help them to understand and apply the skills they need.

The qualities of a good leader

As mentioned earlier, the trait theory of leadership has its limitations but there is still some value in studying the qualities required by good leaders. It is generally accepted that one of the key skills a leader or manager needs is an ability to analyse and read situations and to establish order and clarity in situations of ambiguity. Gold *et al* (2010: 6) stated that: 'Leadership demands a sense of purpose, and an ability to influence others, interpret situations, negotiate and express their views, often in the face of opposition'.

Research conducted by the Work Foundation (Tamkin *et al*, 2010), involving 260 in-depth interviews conducted with 77 business leaders from six high-profile organizations, found that outstanding leaders:

- viewed things as a whole rather than compartmentalizing them;
- connect the parts through a guiding sense of purpose;
- are highly motivated to achieve excellence and are focused on organizational outcomes, vision and purpose;

- understand they cannot create performance themselves but are conduits for performance through their influence on others;
- watch themselves carefully and act consistently to achieve excellence through their interactions and their embodiment of the leadership role.

Effective leadership

Effective leaders are confident and know where they want to go and what they want to do. They have the ability to take charge, convey their vision to their team, get their team members into action and ensure that they achieve their agreed goals. They are trustworthy, effective at influencing people and earn the respect of their team. They are aware of their own strengths and weaknesses and are skilled at understanding what will motivate their team members. They appreciate the advantages of consulting and involving people in decision making. They can switch flexibly from one leadership style to another to meet the demands of different situations and people. They have to answer the following questions about the individuals in the group and the team.

Individuals in the group

- What are their strengths and weaknesses?
- What are their needs, attitudes, perspectives and preferences?
- What are likely to be the best ways of motivating them?
- What tasks are they best at doing?
- Is there scope to increase flexibility by developing new skills?
- How well do they perform in achieving targets and performance standards?
- To what extent can they manage their own performance and development?
- Are there any areas where there is a need to develop skill or competence?
- How can I provide them with the sort of support and guidance that will improve their performance?
- What can be done to improve the performance of any individuals in the group by coaching or mentoring?

The team

- How well is the team organized?
- Is the team clear about what is expected of it?
- Do the members of the team work well together?
- If there is any conflict between team members, how can I resolve it?
- How can the commitment and motivation of the team be achieved?
- Are team members flexible – capable of carrying out different tasks?

- To what extent can the team manage its own performance?
- Is there scope to empower the team so that it can take on greater responsibility for setting standards, monitoring performance and taking corrective action?
- Can the team be encouraged to work together to produce ideas for improving performance?
- What is the team good and not so good at doing?
- What can I do to improve the performance of the team through coaching and mentoring?

Key learning points: Leadership skills

Leadership defined

Leadership is the process of influencing the behaviour of others to achieve results.

Leadership theories

The main leadership theories are trait theory, leadership behaviour theory, contingent and situational theories, emotional intelligence theory and the leadership brand.

What leaders do

Adair (1973) explained that the three essential roles of leaders are to define the task, achieve the task, and maintain effective relationships. Leaders have to satisfy interdependent task, individual and group needs.

Types of leaders

Leaders can be charismatic, visionary, transformational, transactional or 'authentic'.

The qualities of a good leader

Leaders need the ability to analyse and read situations and to establish order and clarity in situations of ambiguity. Leadership demands a sense of purpose and an ability to influence others, interpret situations, negotiate and express their views, often in the face of opposition (Gold *et al*, 2010: 6).

The reality of leadership is that many first-line managers and supervisors are appointed or promoted to their posts with some idea, possibly, of what their managerial or supervisory duties are, but with no appreciation of the leadership skills they need to get the results they want with the help of their team.

Leadership development

Leadership development programmes prepare people for leadership roles and situations beyond their current experience. 'Leadership development in the widest sense involves the acquisition, development and utilization of leadership capability or the potential for it' Burgoyne (2010: 43).

Questions

1 What is leadership?

2 What is the trait theory of leadership?

3 What are the two dimensions of leadership behaviour?

4 What is the contingent theory of leadership?

5 What is a transactional leader?

6 What is a transformational leader?

7 What is a charismatic leader?

8 What is an authentic leader?

9 What do leaders do – their essential roles?

10 What are the three needs that leaders must satisfy, as defined by Adair?

11 What are the main types of leadership styles?

12 What are the leadership styles identified by Hay/McBer?

13 What choice of style do leaders have?

14 What qualities do good leaders have?

References

Adair, J (1973) *The Action-centred Leader*, London, McGraw-Hill

Avolio, B J, Gardner, W L, Walumbwa, F O, Luthans, F and May, D R (2004) Unlocking the mask: A look at the process by which authentic leaders impact follower attitudes and behaviours, *Leadership Quarterly*, **15**, pp 801–23

Bass, B M (1985) *Leadership and Performance*, New York, Free Press

Bennis, W (2010) We need leaders, *Leadership Excellence*, **27** (12), p 4

Bennis, W and Nanus, B (1985) *Leadership: The strategies for taking charge*, New York, Harper & Row

Burgoyne J (2010) Crafting a leadership and management development strategy, in (eds) J Gold, R Thorpe and A Mumford, *Gower Handbook of Leadership and Management Development*, Farnham, Gower, pp 42–55

Burns, J M (1978) *Leadership*, New York, Harper & Row

Carey, M R (1992) Transformational leadership and the fundamental option for self-transcendence, *Leadership Quarterly*, **3**, pp 217–36

Conger, J A and Kanungo, R N (1998) *Charismatic Leadership in Organizations*, Thousand Oaks, CA, Sage

Fiedler, F E (1967) *A Theory of Leadership Effectiveness*, New York, McGraw-Hill

George, B (2003) *Authentic Leadership*, San Francisco, CA, Jossey-Bass

George, B, Sims, P, McLean, A N and Mayer, D (2007) Discovering your authentic leadership, *Harvard Business Review*, February, pp 129–38

Gold, J, Thorpe, R and Mumford, A (2010) *Gower Handbook of Leadership and Management Development*, Farnham, Gower

Goleman, D (2000) Leadership that gets results, *Harvard Business Review*, March–April, pp 78–90

Goleman, D (2001) *What Makes a Leader*, Boston, MA, Harvard Business School Press

Harter, S (2002) Authenticity, in (eds) C R Snyder and S J Lopez, *Handbook of Positive Psychology*, Oxford, Oxford University Press, pp 382–94

Huczynski, A A and Buchanan, D A (2007) *Organizational Behaviour*, 6th edn, Harlow, FT Prentice Hall

Kouzes, J and Posner, B (2003) *The Leadership Challenge*, San Francisco, CA, Jossey-Bass

May, D R, Chan, A, Hodges, T and Avolio, B J (2003) Developing the moral component of authentic leadership, *Organizational Dynamics*, **32** (3), pp 247–60

Meindl, J R, Ehrlich, S B and Dukerich, J M (1985) The romance of leadership, *Administrative Science Quarterly*, **30** (1), pp 78–102

Stogdill, R M (1950) Leaders, membership and organization, *Psychological Bulletin*, **25**, pp 1–14

Tamkin, P, Pearson, G, Hirsh, W and Constable, S (2010) *Exceeding Expectation: The principles of outstanding leadership*, London, The Work Foundation

Tavanti, M (2008) Transactional leadership, in (eds) A Marturano and J Gosling, *Leadership: The key concepts*, London, Routledge, pp 166–70

Tichy, N M and Devanna, M A (1986) *The Transformational Leader*, New York, Wiley

Ulrich, D and Smallwood, N (2007) *Leadership Brand: Developing customer-focused leaders to drive performance and build lasting value*, Boston, MA, Harvard Business School Press

Walumbwa, F O, Avolio, B J, Gardner, W L, Wernsing, T S and Peterson, S J (2008) Authentic leadership: development and validation of a theory-based measure, *Journal of Management*, **34** (1), pp 89–126

Yukl, G (1999) An evaluation of conceptual weaknesses in transformational and charismatic leadership theories, *Leadership Quarterly*, **10**, pp 285–305

53
Influencing skills

LEARNING OUTCOMES

On completing this chapter you should be able to define these key concepts. You should also understand:

- How to persuade
- How to make a business case
- Coordinating discussion
- How to present a case
- Facilitating meetings

Introduction

HR professionals are in the business of influencing people. They have to persuade senior management, line managers and employees generally to accept their advice or proposals. Influencing involves case presentation and submitting business cases. HR professionals can often be concerned with more subtle forms of influencing people by acting as facilitators and leading discussions.

Persuading people

HR specialists spend a lot of time persuading other people to accept their ideas and suggestions. Persuasion is akin to selling. You may feel that good ideas should sell themselves, but life is not like that. People resist change and anything new is usually treated with suspicion. Here are 10 rules for effective persuasion:

1 *Define your objective and get the facts.*
If you are persuading someone to agree to
a proposal, first decide what you want to
achieve and why. Assemble all the facts
you need to support your case. Eliminate
emotional arguments so that you and others
can judge the proposition on the facts alone.

2 *Define the problem.* If there is a problem to
resolve and you are trying to persuade
someone to accept your views on what
should be done about it, first decide whether
the problem is a misunderstanding (a failure
to understand each other accurately) or
a true disagreement (a failure to agree even
when both parties understand one another).
It is not necessarily possible to resolve a true
disagreement by understanding each other
better. People generally believe that an
argument is a battle to understand who is
correct. More often, it is a battle to decide
who is more stubborn.

3 *Find out what the other party wants.*
The key to all persuasion is to see your
proposition from the other person's point
of view. Find out how they look at things.
Establish what they need and want.

4 *Accentuate the benefits.* Present your case in
a way that highlights the benefits to the other
party or at least reduces any objections or fears.

5 *Predict the other person's response.*
Everything we say should be focused on that
likely response. Anticipate objections by
asking yourself how the other party might
react negatively to your proposition and
thinking up ways of responding to them.

6 *Create the other person's next move.* It is not
a question of deciding what we want to do
but what we want the other person to do.

7 *Convince people by reference to their own
perceptions.* People decide on what to do on
the basis of their own perceptions, not yours.

8 *Prepare a simple and attractive proposition.*
Make it as straightforward as possible.
Present the case 'sunny side up', emphasizing
its benefits. Break the problem into
manageable pieces and deal with them one
step at a time.

9 *Make the other person a party to your ideas.*
Get them to contribute. Find some common

ground so that you can start with agreement.
Don't try to defeat them in an argument –
you will only antagonize them.

10 *Clinch and take action.* Choose the right
moment to clinch the proposal – don't
prolong the discussion and risk losing it.
But follow up promptly.

Case presentation

Persuasion frequently means making a case for what
you think should be done. You have to convince
people to believe in your views and accept your
recommendations. To do this, you must have a clear
idea of what you want, and you have to show that
you believe in it yourself. Above all, the effectiveness of your presentation will depend upon the care
with which you have prepared it.

Thorough preparation is vital. You must think
through not only what should be done and why,
but also how people will react. Only then can you
decide how to make your case: stressing the benefits
without underestimating the costs, and anticipating
objections. The four steps you should take are:

1 Show that your proposal is based on
a thorough analysis of the facts and that the
alternatives were properly evaluated before
the conclusion was reached. If you have
made assumptions, you must demonstrate
that these are reasonable on the basis of
relevant experience and justifiable
projections, which allow for the unexpected.
Bear in mind that a proposal is only as
strong as its weakest assumption.

2 Spell out the benefits – to the company and
the individuals to whom the case is being
made. Wherever possible, express benefits in
financial terms. Abstract benefits, such as
customer satisfaction or workers' morale,
are difficult to sell. But don't produce 'funny
numbers' – financial justification that will
not stand up to examination.

3 Reveal costs. Don't try to disguise them in
any way. And be realistic. Your proposition
will be destroyed if anyone can show that
you have underestimated the costs.

4 Remember, senior management decision
makers want to know in precise terms what

they will get for their money. Most are likely to be cautious, being unwilling and often unable to take much risk. For this reason, it can be difficult to make a case for experiments or pilot schemes unless the decision maker can see what the benefits and the ultimate bill will be.

Making a business case

You may be asked specifically to produce a business case. This will set out the reasons why a proposed course of action will benefit the business, how it will provide that benefit and how much it will cost. A business case is a particular form of persuasion and all the points made above apply to its preparation and presentation. But there are some special features about business cases, as described below.

A business case is typically made either in added-value terms (ie the income generated by the proposal will significantly exceed the cost of implementing it), or on the basis of the return on investment or ROI (ie the cost of the investment, say in training, is justified by the financial returns in such areas as increased productivity). Clearly, a business case is more convincing when it is accompanied by realistic projections of added value or return on investment. When people make out a case for capital expenditure they analyse the cash flows associated with the investment and calculate the benefits – in financial terms as far as possible – that are likely to arise from them. The objective is to demonstrate that in return for paying out a given amount of cash today, a larger amount will be received over a period of time.

It can be more difficult to make out a business case for an HRM innovation in financial terms. The costs can and should be calculated but the benefits may have to be expressed in qualitative terms. A business case will be enhanced if:

- Data is available on the impact the proposal is likely to make on key areas of the organization's operations, eg customer service levels, quality, shareholder value, productivity, income generation, innovation, skills development, talent management.
- It can be shown that the proposal will increase the business' competitive edge, for example enlarging the skill base or multi-skilling to ensure that it can achieve competitive advantage through innovation and/or reducing time-to-market.

- There is proof that the innovation has already worked well within the organization (perhaps as a pilot scheme) or represents 'good practice' that is likely to be transferable to the organization.

- It can be implemented without too much trouble, for example not taking up a lot of managers' time, or not meeting with strong opposition from line managers, employees or trade unions (it is as well to check the likely reaction before launching a proposal).

- It will add to the reputation of the company by showing that it is a 'world class' organization, ie what it does is as good as, if not better than, the world leaders in the sector in which the business operates (a promise that publicity will be achieved through articles in professional journals, press releases and conference presentations, will help).

- It will enhance the 'employer brand' of the company by making it a 'best place to work'.

- The proposal is brief, to the point and well argued – it should take no more than five minutes to present orally and should be summarized in writing on the proverbial one side of one sheet of paper (supplementary details can be included in appendices).

Making the business case is obviously easier where management is preconditioned to agree to the proposition. For example, it is not hard to convince top managers that performance-related pay is a good thing – they may well be receiving bonus payments themselves and believe, rightly or wrongly, that because it motivates them it will motivate everyone else. Talent management is another process where top management needs little persuasion that things need to be done to enhance and preserve the talent flow, although they will have to be convinced that, in practice, innovations will achieve that aim. Performance management may be slightly more difficult because it is hard to demonstrate that it can produce measurable improvements in performance, but senior managers are predisposed towards an approach that at least promises to improve the level of performance.

The toughest area for justification in added-value terms can be expenditure on learning and development (L&D) programmes. This is where an ROI approach is desirable. The business case for learning and development should demonstrate how learning, training and development programmes will meet business needs. The following points could be made to support an L&D initiative:

- Improve individual, team and corporate performance in terms of output, quality, speed and overall productivity.
- Attract high-quality employees by offering them learning and development opportunities, increasing their levels of competence and enhancing their skills, thus enabling them to obtain more job satisfaction, to gain higher rewards and to progress within the organization.
- Provide additional non-financial rewards (growth and career opportunities) as part of a total reward policy in order to enhance engagement.
- Improve operational flexibility by extending the range of skills possessed by employees (multi-skilling).
- Increase the commitment of employees by encouraging them to identify with the mission and objectives of the organization.
- Help to manage change by increasing understanding of the reasons for change and providing people with the knowledge and skills they need to adjust to new situations.
- Provide line managers with the skills required to manage and develop their people.
- Help to develop a positive culture in the organization, one, for example, that is oriented towards performance improvement.
- Provide higher levels of service to customers.
- Minimize learning costs (reduce the length of learning curves).

Facilitating

Facilitating in this context is the process of helping a group reach conclusions in the shape of ideas and solutions. Facilitators do not exist to 'chair' the meeting in the sense of controlling the discussion and pressurizing the group to agree to a course of action. The group is there to make up its own mind and the facilitator helps it to do so. The facilitator is exerting influence, but indirectly.

Help in reaching conclusions is provided by asking questions that encourage the group members to think for themselves. These can be challenging and probing questions but the facilitator does not provide the answers – that is the role of the group. Neither do facilitators allow their own opinions to intrude – they are there to help the group marshal its opinions, not to enforce their own ideas. However, by using questioning techniques carefully, facilitators can ensure that the group thoroughly discusses and analyses the issues and reaches conclusions by consensus rather than allowing anyone to dominate the process.

Facilitators ensure that everyone has their say and that they are listened to. They step in quickly to defuse unproductive arguments. They see that the group defines and understands its objectives and any methodology they might use. They summarize from time to time the progress made in achieving the objectives, without bringing their own views to bear. Facilitators are there to ensure that the group makes progress and does not get stuck in fruitless or disruptive argument – but they encourage the group rather than drive it forward.

The aim of the facilitator is to guide the group's thinking. He or she may, therefore, be more concerned with shaping attitudes than convincing people about what to do or imparting new knowledge. The facilitator has unobtrusively to stimulate people to talk, guide the discussion along predetermined lines (there must be a plan and an ultimate objective), and provide interim summaries and a final summary.

Coordinating discussions

Coordinating discussions is a matter of getting active participation and then ensuring that the discussion informs people of the issues related to the subject and leads to a conclusion that satisfies the participants. HR practitioners lead discussions when they are taking part in L&D activities. Importantly, discussion is also a means of persuading people to do or accept something by getting them to participate in analysing the issues and reaching a joint and acceptable conclusion.

The following techniques can be used to get active participation and to coordinate the process:

- Ask for contributions by direct questions.
- Use open-ended questions that will stimulate thought.
- Check understanding; make sure that everyone is following the argument.
- Encourage participation by providing support rather than criticism.
- Prevent domination by individual members of the group by bringing in other people and asking cross-reference questions.

- Avoid dominating the group yourself. The leader's job is to guide the discussion, maintain control and summarize from time to time. If necessary, 'reflect' opinions expressed by individuals back to the group to make sure they find the answer for themselves. The leader is there to help the group reach a conclusion, not to do it for them.

- Maintain control – ensure that the discussion is progressing along the right lines towards a firm conclusion.

Key learning points: Influencing skills

Influencing people

HR professionals are often involved in influencing other's thinking and decision making. They must know about persuading people and case presentation.

Persuading people

HR specialists spend a lot of time persuading other people to accept their ideas and suggestions. Persuasion is akin to selling. You may feel that good ideas should sell themselves, but life is not like that. People resist change and anything new is usually treated with suspicion.

Case presentation

Persuasion frequently means making a case for what you think should be done. You have to convince people to believe in your views and accept your recommendations. To do this, you must have a clear idea of what you want, and you have to show that you believe in it yourself.

Making a business case

A business case sets out the reasons why a proposed course of action will benefit the business, how it will provide that benefit and how much it will cost.

Facilitating

Facilitating is the process of helping a group reach conclusions in the shape of ideas and solutions.

Coordinating discussions

Coordinating discussions is a matter of getting active participation and then ensuring that the discussion informs people of the issues related to the subject and leads to a conclusion that satisfies the participants.

Questions

1 What are the most important rules for effective persuasion?

2 What are the key steps required for effective case presentation?

3 How should a business case be made?

4 What is facilitating?

5 How should facilitation be carried out?

6 How should discussions be conducted?

54
Handling people problems

KEY CONCEPTS AND TERMS

Capability procedure   Disciplinary procedure

Improvement period   Return to work interview

LEARNING OUTCOMES

On completing this chapter you should be able to define these key concepts. You should also know about handling:

- Disciplinary issues
- Poor timekeeping
- Under-performance
- Absenteeism
- Negative behaviour

Introduction

An important part of the transactional role of HR professionals is handling people problems directly or by providing advice and guidance to line managers. Problem-solving skills, described in Chapter 43, are required but it is also necessary to advise overall on how to handle disciplinary problems and more specifically on how to deal with absenteeism, poor timekeeping, negative behaviour and under-performance.

Disciplinary issues

Employees can be dismissed because they are not capable of doing the work, or for misconduct. It is normal to go through a formal disciplinary procedure containing staged warnings, but instant dismissal can be justified for gross misconduct (eg serious theft), which should be defined in the company's disciplinary procedure or employee handbook. Anyone with a year's service or more can claim unfair dismissal if their employer cannot show that one of these reasons applied, if the dismissal was not reasonable in the circumstances, if a constructive dismissal has taken place, or if there has been a breach of a customary or agreed redundancy procedure and there are no valid reasons for departing from that procedure.

Even if the employer can show to an employment tribunal that there was good reason to dismiss the employee, the tribunal will still have to decide whether or not the employer acted in a reasonable way at the time of dismissal. The principles defining 'reasonable' behaviour are in line with the principles of natural justice and are as follows:

- the employee should be informed of the nature of the complaint;
- the employee should be given the chance to explain;
- the employee should be given the opportunity to improve, except in cases of particularly gross incapability or misconduct;
- the employee should be warned of the consequences in the shape of dismissal if specified improvements do not take place;
- the employer's decision to dismiss should be based on sufficient evidence;
- the employer should take any mitigating circumstances into account;
- dismissal should only take place if the offence or misbehaviour deserves it rather than some lesser penalty.

The organization should have a statutory disciplinary procedure (see also Chapter 39). Managers need to know what that procedure is and the part they are expected to play in implementing it. Whether or not there is a formal procedure, if it is believed that disciplinary action is necessary the following steps should be taken by the manager, as guided by HR, in planning and conducting a disciplinary interview.

If all the stages in the disciplinary procedure have been completed and the employee has to be dismissed, or where immediate dismissal can be justified on the grounds of gross misconduct, a manager may have to carry out the unpleasant duty of dismissing the employee. This should be as guided by HR and it is advisable that an HR specialist is involved in the dismissal meeting. This is best conducted as follows:

Planning and conducting a disciplinary meeting

1. Get all the facts in advance, including statements from the people involved.

2. Invite the employee to the meeting in writing, explaining why it is being held and that he or she has the right to have someone present at the meeting on his or her behalf.

3. Ensure that the employee has reasonable notice (ideally at least two days).

4. Plan how to conduct the meeting.

5. Line up another member of management to attend the meeting to take notes (they can be important if there is an appeal), generally provide support and witness the proceedings.

6. Start the interview by stating the complaint to the employee and referring to the evidence.

7. Give the employee plenty of time to respond and state his or her case.

8. Take a break as required to consider the points raised and to relieve any pressure in the meeting.

9. Consider what action is appropriate, if any. Actions should be staged, starting with a recorded warning followed, if the problem continues, by a first written warning, then a final written warning and lastly, if the earlier stages have been exhausted, disciplinary action, which would be dismissal in serious cases.

10. Deliver the decision, explaining why it has been taken and confirm it in writing.

- If possible, meet when everything is quiet, preferably on a Friday.
- Keep the meeting formal and organized.
- Write down what is going to be said in advance, giving the reason and getting your facts, dates and figures right.
- Be polite but firm – read out what has been written down and make it clear that it is not open for discussion.

- Ensure that the employee clears his or her desk and has no opportunity to take away confidential material or use his or her computer.

- See the employee off the premises – some companies use security guards as escorts; this might be rather heavy-handed, although it could be useful to have someone on call in case of difficulties.

Absenteeism

A frequent people problem managers and HR professionals have to face is absenteeism. It may be necessary to deal with recurrent short-term (one or two days) absence or longer-term sickness absence.

Recurrent short-term absence

Dealing with people who are repeatedly absent for short periods can be difficult. This is because it may be hard to determine when occasional absence becomes a problem or whether it is justifiable, perhaps on medical grounds.

So what can be done about it? Many organizations provide guidelines to managers on the 'trigger points' for action (the amount of absence that needs to be investigated), perhaps based on analyses of the incidence of short-term absence and the level at which it is regarded as acceptable (there may be software to generate analyses and data that can be made available direct to managers through a self-service system). If guidelines do not exist, HR specialists should be available to provide advice.

It is necessary to decide when something needs to be done and then what to do about it. A day off every other month may not be too serious, although if it happens regularly on a Monday (after weekends in Prague, Barcelona, etc?) or a Friday (before such weekends?) you may feel like having a word with the individual, not as a warning but just to let him or her know that you are aware of what is going on. There may be a medical or other acceptable explanation. Return-to-work interviews can provide valuable information and an opportunity to discuss any problems. The individual is seen and given the chance to explain the absence.

In persistent cases of absenteeism an absence review meeting can be held. Although this would be more comprehensive than a return-to-work interview it should not at this stage be presented as part of a disciplinary process. The meeting should be positive and constructive. If absence results from a health problem it can be established what is being done about it, and if necessary suggest that his or her doctor should be consulted. Or absences may be caused by problems facing a parent or a carer. In such cases it is right to be sympathetic but it would be reasonable to discuss with the individual what steps can be taken to reduce the problem or whether flexible working could be arranged. The aim is to get the employee to discuss as openly as possible any factors affecting his or her attendance and to agree any constructive steps.

If after holding an attendance review meeting and, it is to be hoped, agreeing the steps necessary to reduce absenteeism, short-term absence persists without a satisfactory explanation, then another meeting can be held that emphasizes the employee's responsibility for attending work. Depending on the circumstances (each case should be dealt with on its merits), at this meeting it can be indicated that absence levels should improve over a defined timescale (an improvement period). If this does not happen, the individual can expect more formal disciplinary action.

Dealing with long-term absence

Dealing with long-term absence can also be difficult. The aim should be to facilitate the employee's return to work at the earliest reasonable point while recognizing that in extreme cases the person may not be able to come back. In that case he or she can fairly be dismissed for lack of capability as long as:

- the employee has been consulted at all stages;

- contact has been maintained with the employee – this is something you can usefully do as long as you do not appear to be pressing him or her to return to work before he or she is ready;

- appropriate medical advice has been sought from the employee's own doctor, but the employee's consent is needed and employees have the right to see the report – it may be desirable to obtain a second opinion;

- all reasonable options for alternative employment have been reviewed as well any other means of facilitating a return to work.

The decision to dismiss should only be taken if these conditions are satisfied. It is a tricky one and it may be advisable to seek advice from an employment law expert.

Handling poor timekeeping

Faced with persistent lateness and when informal warnings to the individual concerned seem to have little effect, it may be necessary to invoke the disciplinary procedure. If timekeeping does not improve, this could go through the successive stages of a recorded oral warning, a written warning and a final written warning. If the final warning does not work, disciplinary action would have to be taken; in serious cases this would mean dismissal.

Note that this raises the difficult question of time limits – when a final warning is given that timekeeping must improve by a certain date (the improvement period). If it does improve by that date, and the slate is wiped clean, it might be assumed that the disciplinary procedure starts again from scratch if timekeeping deteriorates again. But it is in the nature of things that some people cannot sustain efforts to get to work on time for long, and deterioration often occurs. In these circumstances, is it necessary to keep on going through the warning cycles time after time? The answer ought to be no, and the best approach seems to be to avoid stating a finite end date to a final warning period that implies a 'wipe the slate clean' approach. Instead, the warning should simply say that timekeeping performance will be reviewed on a stated date. If it has not improved, disciplinary action can be taken. If it has, no action will be taken, but the employee is warned that further deterioration will make him or her liable to disciplinary action, which may well speed up the normal procedure, perhaps by only using the final warning stage and by reducing the elapsed time between the warning and the review date. There will come a time, if poor timekeeping persists, when you can say 'enough is enough' and initiate disciplinary action.

Handling negative behaviour

Negative behaviour may take the form of lack of interest in the work, unwillingness to cooperate with team leaders or other members of the team, making unjustified complaints about the work or working conditions, grumbling at being asked to carry out a perfectly reasonable task, objecting strongly to being asked to do something extra (or even refusing to do it) – 'It's not in my job description', or, in extreme cases, insolence. People exhibiting negative behaviour may be quietly resentful rather than openly disruptive. They mutter away in the background at meetings and lack enthusiasm.

Managers have to tolerate a certain amount of negative behaviour as long as the individual works reasonably well and does not upset other team members. They have simply to say to themselves, 'It takes all sorts…' and put up with it, although they might calmly say during a review meeting, 'You're doing a good job but…'. If, however, they take this line they have to be specific. They must cite actual instances. It is no good making generalized accusations that will either be openly refuted or internalized by the receiver, making him or her even more resentful.

If the negative behaviour means that the individual's contribution is not acceptable and is disruptive, action has to be taken. Negative people can be quiet but they are usually angry about something; their negative behaviour is an easy way of expressing their anger. To deal with the problem it is necessary to find out what has made them angry.

Causes of negative behaviour

There are many possible causes of negative behaviour, which could include one or more of the following:

- a real or imagined slight from their manager or a colleague;
- a feeling of being put upon;
- a belief that the contribution they make is neither appreciated nor rewarded properly in terms of pay or promotion;
- resentment at what was perceived to be unfair criticism;
- anger directed at the company or their manager because what was considered to be a reasonable request (such as for leave or a transfer) was turned down, or because of an unfair accusation.

Dealing with the problem

It is because there can be such a variety of real or imagined causes of negative behaviour that dealing with it becomes one of the most difficult tasks line managers and HR people have to undertake. If the action taken is crude or insensitive the negative behaviour will only be intensified. This might mean having to invoke the disciplinary procedure, which should be a last resort.

In one sense, it is easier to deal with an actual example of negative behaviour. This can be handled on the spot. If the problem is one of general attitude rather than specific actions it is more difficult to cope with. Hard evidence may not be available. When individuals are accused of being, for example, generally unenthusiastic or uncooperative, they can simply go into denial and accuse you of being prejudiced. Their negative behaviour may be reinforced.

It is best to deal with this sort of problem informally, either when it arises or at any point during the year when it is felt that something has to be done about it. An annual formal performance review or appraisal meeting is not the right time, especially if it produces ratings that are linked to a pay increase. Raising the issue then will only put individuals on the defensive and a productive discussion will be impossible.

The discussion may be informal but it should have three clear objectives:

1 To review the situation with individuals, the aim being if possible to get them to recognize for themselves that they are behaving negatively. If this cannot be achieved, then the objective is to bring to the attention of individuals your belief that their behaviour is unacceptable in certain ways.

2 To establish the reasons for the individuals' negative behaviour so far as this is feasible.

3 To agree any actions individuals could take to behave more positively, or what you or the organization could do to remove the causes of the behaviour.

Discussing the problem

The starting point should be general questions about how individuals feel about their work. Do they have any problems in carrying it out? Are they happy with the support they get from you or their colleagues? Are they satisfied that they are pulling their weight to the best of their ability?

This generalized start provides the basis for the next two stages – identifying the causes and remedies. It is best if individuals are encouraged to identify for themselves that there is a problem, but in many, if not the majority of cases, this is unlikely to happen. Individuals may not recognize that they are behaving negatively or will not be prepared to admit it.

It is then necessary to discuss the problem. They should be given time to say their piece. The response should spell out how justifiable grievances will be dealt with or why no action is necessary. In the latter case, an explanation should be given as to why the individual's behaviour gives the impression of being negative. This should be specific, bringing up actual instances. For example, a discussion could be based on the following questions: 'Do you recall yesterday's team meeting?', 'How did you think it went?', 'How helpful do you think you were in dealing with the problem?', 'Do you remember saying… ?', 'How helpful do you think that remark was?', 'Would it surprise you to learn that I felt you had not been particularly helpful in the following ways… ?'

Of course, even if this careful approach is adopted, individuals may still refuse to admit that there is anything wrong with their behaviour. If this impasse is reached, then there is no alternative but to spell out where it is believed they have gone wrong. But this should be done in a positive way: 'Then I think that it is only fair for me to point out to you that your contribution (to the meeting) would have been more helpful if you had…'.

Establishing causes

If the negative behaviour is because of a real or imagined grievance about what the manager, colleagues or the organization have done, then the individual has to be persuaded to spell this out as precisely as possible. At this point, the job of the manager or HR practitioner is to listen, not to judge. People can be just as angry about imaginary as real slights. You have to find out how they perceive the problem before you can deal with it.

It may emerge during the discussion that the problem has nothing to do with the manager or the company. It may be family troubles or worries about health or finance. If this is the case a sympathetic approach is appropriate, which may involve suggesting remedies in the form of counselling or practical advice from within or outside the organization. If the perceived problem is the manager, colleagues or the organization, try to get chapter and verse on what it is so that remedial action can be taken.

Taking remedial action

If the problem rests with the individual, the objective is, of course, to get them to recognize for themselves that corrective action is necessary and what they need to do about it – with help as necessary. In some situations you might suggest counselling or a source of advice might be recommended. But care needs to be taken: there should be no implication that there is something wrong with them. It is best to go no further than suggesting that individuals may find this helpful – they don't *need* it but they could *benefit* from it. Managers or HR specialists should not offer counselling themselves. This is better done by professional counsellors.

If there is anything specific that the parties involved in the situation can do, then the line to take is that the problem can be tackled together: 'This is what I will do', 'This is what the company will do', 'What do you think you should do?' If there is no response to the last question, this is the point where it is necessary to spell out the necessary action. This should be as specific as possible and expressed as suggestions, not commands. A joint problem-solving approach is always best.

Dealing with under-performance

Poor performance can be the fault of the individual but it could arise because of poor leadership or problems in the system of work. In the case of an individual, the reason may be that he or she:

- could not do it – ability;
- did not know how to do it – skill;
- would not do it – attitude; or
- did not fully understand what was expected of him or her.

Ten approaches to managing negative behaviour

1 Define the type of negative behaviour being exhibited. Make notes of examples.

2 Discuss the behaviour with the individual as soon as possible, aiming to get agreement about what it is and the impact it makes.

3 If agreement is not obtained, give actual examples of behaviour and explain why you believe them to be negative.

4 Discuss and so far as possible agree reasons for the negative behaviour, including those attributed to the individual, yourself and the organization.

5 Discuss and agree possible remedies – actions on the part of the individual, yourself or the organization.

6 Monitor the actions taken and the results obtained.

7 If improvement is not achieved and the negative behaviour is significantly affecting the performance of the individual and the team, invoke the disciplinary procedure.

8 Start with a verbal warning, indicating the ways in which behaviour must improve, and give a timescale and offers of further support and help as required.

9 If there is no improvement, issue a formal warning, setting out as specifically as possible what must be achieved over a defined period of time, indicating the disciplinary action that could be taken.

10 If the negative behaviour persists and continues seriously to affect performance, take the disciplinary action.

Inadequate leadership from managers can be the cause of poor performance from individuals. It is the manager's responsibility to specify the results expected and the levels of skill and competence required. As likely as not, when people do not understand what they have to do it is their manager who is to blame.

Performance can also be affected by the system of work. If this is badly planned and organized or does not function well, individuals cannot be blamed for the poor performance that results. This is the fault of management and things must put it right.

If inadequate individual performance cannot be attributed to poor leadership or the system of work, there are seven steps that can be taken to deal with it.

A seven-step approach to managing under-performance

1 Identify the areas of under-performance – be specific.

2 Establish the causes of poor performance.

3 Agree on the action required.

4 Ensure that the necessary support (coaching, training, extra resources, etc) is provided to ensure the action is successful.

5 Monitor progress and provide feedback.

6 Provide additional guidance as required.

7 As a last resort, invoke the capability or disciplinary procedure, starting with an informal warning.

Key learning points: Handling people problems

The HR role in handling people problems

An important part of the transactional role of HR professionals is handling people problems by providing advice and guidance to line managers or directly.

Disciplinary issues

Employees can be dismissed because they are not capable of doing the work or for misconduct. It is normal to go through a formal disciplinary procedure containing staged warnings, but instant dismissal can be justified for gross misconduct (eg serious theft), which should be defined in the company's disciplinary procedure or employee handbook.

The organization should have a statutory disciplinary procedure. Managers need to know what that procedure is and the part they are expected to play in implementing it.

Absenteeism

A frequent people problem managers and HR professionals have to face is that of dealing with absenteeism. It may be necessary to deal with recurrent short-term (one or two days) absence or longer-term sickness absence.

Many organizations provide guidelines to managers on the 'trigger points' for action (the amount of absence which needs to be investigated), perhaps based on analyses of the incidence of short-term absence and the level at which it is regarded as acceptable. If guidelines do not exist, HR specialists should be available to provide advice.

Handling poor timekeeping

Faced with persistent lateness and when informal warnings to the individual concerned seem to have little effect, it may be necessary to invoke the disciplinary procedure. If timekeeping does not improve this could go through the successive stages of a recorded oral warning, a written warning and a final written warning. If the final warning does not work, disciplinary action would have to be taken; in serious cases this would mean dismissal.

Handling negative behaviour

Negative behaviour may take the form of lack of interest in the work, unwillingness to cooperate with team leaders or other members of the team, making unjustified complaints about the work or working conditions, grumbling at being asked to carry out a perfectly reasonable task, objecting strongly to being asked to do something extra (or even refusing to do it), or, in extreme cases, insolence.

It is because there can be such a variety of real or imagined causes of negative behaviour that dealing with it becomes one of the most difficult tasks line managers and HR people have to undertake. If the action taken is crude or insensitive the negative behaviour will only be intensified. This might mean having to invoke the disciplinary procedure, which should be a last resort.

In one sense, it is easier to deal with an actual example of negative behaviour. This can be handled on the spot. If the problem is one of general attitude rather than specific actions it is more difficult to cope with. It is best to deal with this sort of problem informally, either when it arises or at any point during the year when it is felt that something has to be done about it.

Dealing with under-performance

Poor performance can be the fault of the individual, but it could arise because of poor leadership or problems in the system of work. To deal with it:

1   Identify the areas of under-performance – be specific.

2   Establish the causes of poor performance.

3   Agree on the action required.

4   Ensure that the necessary support (coaching, training, extra resources, etc) is provided to ensure the action is successful.

5   Monitor progress and provide feedback.

6   Provide additional guidance as required.

7   As a last resort, invoke the capability or disciplinary procedure (see Chapter 39), starting with an informal warning.

Questions

1   What are the principles of natural justice?

2   How should a disciplinary meeting be conducted?

3   How should short-term absence be dealt with?

4   How should long-term absence be dealt with?

5   How should poor timekeeping be dealt with?

6   How should negative behaviour be handled?

7   How should under-performance be dealt with?

55
Managing conflict

KEY CONCEPTS AND TERMS

Conflict resolution   Constructive confrontation

Creative conflict

LEARNING OUTCOMES

On completing this chapter you should be able to define these key concepts. You should also know about:

● Handling inter-group conflict

● Handling interpersonal conflict

● Handling conflict between team members

Introduction

Conflict is inevitable in organizations because they function by means of adjustments and compromises among competitive elements in their structure and membership. Conflict also arises when there is change, because it may be seen as a threat to be challenged or resisted, or when there is frustration – this may produce an aggressive reaction: fight rather than flight.

Conflict is not to be deplored. It results from progress and change and it can and should be used constructively. Bland agreement on everything would be unnatural and enervating. There should be clashes of ideas about tasks and projects, and disagreements should not be suppressed. They should come out into the open because that is the only way to ensure that the issues are explored and conflicts are resolved.

There is such a thing as creative conflict – new or modified ideas, insights, approaches and solutions can be generated by a joint re-examination of different points of view, as long as this is based on an objective and rational exchange of information and opinions. But conflict becomes counterproductive when it is based on personality clashes, or when it is treated as an unseemly mess to be hurriedly cleared away, rather than as a problem to be worked through. Conflict resolution deals with ways of settling differences between groups, individuals and team members.

Handling inter-group conflict

There are three principal ways of resolving inter-group conflict: peaceful coexistence, compromise and problem solving.

Peaceful coexistence

The aim here is to smooth out differences and emphasize the common ground. People are encouraged to learn to live together, there is a good deal of information, contact and exchange of views, and individuals move freely between groups (for example, between headquarters and the field, or between sales and marketing).

This is a pleasant ideal, but it may not be practicable in many situations. There is much evidence that conflict is not necessarily resolved by bringing people together. Improved communications and techniques such as briefing groups may appear to be good ideas but are useless if management has nothing to say that people want to hear. There is also the danger that the real issues, submerged for the moment in an atmosphere of superficial bonhomie, will surface again later.

Compromise

The issue is resolved by negotiation or bargaining and neither party wins or loses. This concept of splitting the difference is essentially pessimistic. The hallmark of this approach is that there is no 'right' or 'best' answer. Agreements only accommodate differences. Real issues are not likely to be solved.

Problem solving

An attempt is made to find a genuine solution to the problem rather than just accommodating different points of view. This is where the apparent paradox of 'creative conflict' comes in. Conflict situations can be used to advantage to create better solutions.

If solutions are to be developed by problem solving, they have to be generated by those who share the responsibility for seeing that the solutions work. The sequence of actions is: first, those concerned work to define the problem and agree on the objectives to be attained in reaching a solution; second, the group develops alternative solutions and debates their merits; and third, agreement is reached on the preferred course of action and how it should be implemented.

Handling interpersonal conflict

Handling conflict between individuals can be even more difficult than resolving conflicts between groups. Whether the conflict is openly hostile or subtly covert, strong personal feelings may be involved. However, interpersonal conflict, like inter-group conflict, is an organizational reality that is not necessarily good or bad. It can be destructive, but it can also play a productive role. The approaches to dealing with it are withdrawal, smoothing over differences, reaching a compromise, counselling and constructive confrontation.

Withdrawal

The reaction to interpersonal conflict may be the withdrawal of either party, leaving the other one to hold the field. This is the classic win/lose situation. The problem has been resolved by force, but this may not be the best solution if it represents one person's point of view that has ignored counter-arguments, and has, in fact, steamrollered over them. The winner may be triumphant but the loser will be aggrieved and either demotivated or resolved to fight again another day. There will have been a lull in, but not an end to, the conflict.

Smoothing over differences

Another approach is to smooth over differences and pretend that the conflict does not exist, although no attempt has been made to tackle the root causes. Again, this is an unsatisfactory solution. The issue is likely to re-emerge and the battle will recommence.

Reaching a compromise

Yet another approach is bargaining to reach a compromise. This means that both sides are prepared to lose as well as win some points and the aim is to reach a solution acceptable to both sides. Bargaining, however, involves all sorts of tactical and often counterproductive games, and the parties are often more anxious to seek acceptable compromises than to achieve sound solutions.

Counselling

Personal counselling is an approach that does not address the conflict itself but focuses on how the two people are reacting. It gives people a chance to release pent-up tensions and may encourage them to think about new ways of resolving the conflict. But it does not address the essential nature of the conflict, which is the relationship between two people. That is why constructive confrontation offers the best hope of a long-term solution.

Constructive confrontation

Constructive confrontation is a method of bringing the individuals in conflict together with a third party whose function is to help build an exploratory and cooperative climate. Constructive confrontation aims to get the parties involved to understand and explore the other's perceptions and feelings. It is a process of developing mutual understanding to produce a win/win situation. The issues will be confronted but on the basis of a joint analysis, with the help of the third party, of facts relating to the situation and the actual behaviour of those involved. Feelings will be expressed but they will be analysed by reference to specific events and behaviours rather than inferences or speculations about motives. Third parties have a key role in this process, and it is not an easy one. They have to get agreement to the ground rules for discussions aimed at bringing out the facts and minimizing hostile behaviour. They must monitor the ways in which negative feelings are expressed and encourage the parties to produce new definitions of the problem and its cause or causes and new motives to reach a common solution. Third parties must avoid the temptation to support or appear to support either of those in contention. They should adopt a counselling approach, as follows:

- listen actively;
- observe as well as listen;
- help people to understand and define the problem by asking pertinent, open-ended questions;
- recognize feelings and allow them to be expressed;
- help people to define problems for themselves;

- encourage people to explore alternative solutions;
- get people to develop their own implementation plans but provide advice and help if asked.

To conclude, conflict, as has been said, is in itself not to be deplored: it is an inevitable concomitant of progress and change. What is regrettable is the failure to use conflict constructively. Effective problem solving and constructive confrontation both resolve conflicts and open up channels of discussion and cooperative action.

Many years ago, one of the pioneering and most influential writers on management, Follett (1924), wrote something on managing conflict that is as valid today as it was then. She said that differences can be made to contribute to the common cause if they are resolved by integration rather than domination or compromise.

Resolving conflict between team members

To resolve conflict between team members the following actions can be taken:

1 Obtain an overview of the situation from your own observations.

2 Find out who is involved.

3 Talk to each of the parties to the conflict to obtain their side of the story.

4 Talk to other members of the group to get their views, being careful to be dispassionate and strictly neutral.

5 Evaluate what you hear from both parties and other people against your knowledge of what has been happening, any history of conflict and the dispositions and previous behaviour of the people involved.

6 Reach preliminary conclusions on the facts, the reasons for the dispute and the extent to which either of the parties or both of them are to blame (but keep these to yourself at this stage).

7 Bring the parties together to discuss the situation. The initial aim of this meeting would be to bring the problem out into the open, get the facts and defuse any emotions that may prejudice a solution to the problem.

Both parties should be allowed to have their say but, as the facilitator of this meeting, you should do your best to ensure that they stick to the facts and explain their point of view dispassionately. You should not even remotely give the impression that you are taking sides.

8 Try to defuse the situation so that a solution can be reached that on the whole will be acceptable to all concerned. Ideally, this should be an integrated solution reached by agreement on the basis of collaboration along the lines of. 'Let's get together to find the best solution on the basis of the facts.' It may be necessary to reach a compromise or accommodation – something everyone can live with.

9 Only if all else fails or the parties are so recalcitrant in holding an untenable position that no integrated, compromise or accommodating solution can be reached, should you resort to direct action – instructing one or both of the parties to bury their differences and get on with their work. If the worst comes to the worst this may involve disciplinary action, beginning with a formal warning.

Key learning points: Managing conflict

The manifestation of conflict

Conflict is inevitable in organizations because they function by means of adjustments and compromises among competitive elements in their structure and membership. Conflict also arises when there is change, because it may be seen as a threat to be challenged or resisted, or when there is frustration – this may produce an aggressive reaction: fight rather than flight.

Handling inter-group conflict

There are three principal ways of resolving inter-group conflict: peaceful coexistence, compromise and problem solving.

Handling interpersonal conflict

The approaches to dealing with interpersonal conflict are withdrawal, smoothing over differences, reaching a compromise, counselling, and constructive confrontation.

Resolving conflict between team members

- Obtain an overview of the situation.
- Find out who is involved.
- Talk to each of the parties to the conflict to obtain their side of the story.
- Talk to other members of the group.
- Evaluate what you hear.
- Reach preliminary conclusions on the facts and the reasons for the dispute.
- Bring the parties together to discuss the situation.
- Only resort to direct action if all else fails.

Questions

1 What are the three main ways of handling inter-group conflict?

2 What approaches can be used to deal with interpersonal conflict?

3 How should counselling be handled when dealing with interpersonal conflict?

4 How can conflict between team members be resolved?

Reference

Follett, M P (1924) *Creative Experience*, New York, Longmans Green

56
Political skills

KEY CONCEPTS AND TERMS

Dominant coalition   Networking

Politics

LEARNING OUTCOMES

On completing this chapter you should be able to define these key concepts. You should also know about:

● Typical political approaches
● Using political means to get things done
● Political sensitivity
● Dangers of politics
● Dealing with organizational politics

Introduction

To be politic, according to the *Oxford English Dictionary*, you can be sagacious, prudent, judicious, expedient, scheming or crafty. So political behaviour in an organization could be desirable or undesirable.

Organizations consist of individuals who, while they are ostensibly there to achieve a common purpose, will, at the same time, be driven by their own needs to achieve their own goals. Effective management is the process of harmonizing individual endeavour and ambition to the common good. Some individuals will genuinely believe that using political means to achieve their aims will benefit the organization as well as themselves. Others will rationalize this belief. Yet others will unashamedly pursue their own ends. They may use all their powers of persuasion to legitimize these ends to their colleagues, but self-interest remains the primary drive. These are the corporate politicians the *Oxford English Dictionary* describes as 'shrewd schemers, crafty plotters or intriguers'. Politicians within organizations can be like this. They manoeuvre behind people's backs, blocking proposals they do not like. They advance their own reputation and career at the expense of other people's. They can be envious and jealous and act accordingly. They are bad news.

But it can also be argued that a political approach to management is inevitable and even desirable in any organization where the clarity of goals is not absolute, where the decision-making process is not clear-cut and where the authority to make decisions is not evenly or appropriately distributed. And there can be few organizations where one or more of these conditions do not apply.

It was suggested by Kakabadse (1983) that politics in an organization is a process of influencing individuals and groups of people to your point of view, where you cannot rely on authority. In this sense, a political approach can be legitimate as long as the ends are justifiable from the viewpoint of the organization. Whether or not that is the case, political skills and political sensitivity, as described in this chapter, are required to thrive and sometimes even survive in organizations. This applies particularly to HR specialists who may lack the power-base others possess and may feel they have to pursue the achievement of their ends and exert influence through political as well as more open means. But it is also essential for them to gain insight into the political situation in their organization in order to understand what is happening, why it is happening and what they need to do about it.

Typical political approaches

Kakabadse (1983) identified seven approaches that organizational politicians adopt, some of which are more legitimate than others:

1 Identify the stakeholders, those who have commitment to act in a particular way.

2 Keep the stakeholders comfortable, concentrating on behaviour, values, attitudes, fears and drives that the individuals will accept, tolerate and manage (comfort zones).

3 Fit the image – work on the comfort zones and align their image to that of the people with power.

4 Use the network – identify the interest groups and people of influence.

5 Enter the network – identify the gatekeepers, adhere to the norms.

6 Make deals – agree to support other people where this is of mutual benefit.

7 Withhold and withdraw – withhold information as appropriate and withdraw judiciously when the going gets rough.

Using political means to get things done

People acting politically get things done by lobbying decision makers and doing deals. This may not always be desirable, but it does happen, and some people rationalize it on the basis that the end justifies the means (always a dubious stance). Other ploys include withholding information, which is not legitimate, but people do indulge in it in recognition of the fact that knowledge is power. Organizational politicians can go behind people's backs, hatch up plots in dark corners, 'sew things up' before meetings (lobbying) and exert undue influence on weaker brethren. You may not deign to practise these political black arts but it is useful to be aware of the possibility that others will so that you are prepared for that eventuality.

The reality of politics in organizational life means that HR specialists who are proposing new initiatives to managers need to identify the key decision makers before coming to a final conclusion and launching a fully fledged proposal at a committee or in a memorandum. It makes good sense to test opinion and find out how other people may react, especially when it is possible that there will be some opposition or indifference. This testing process enables the anticipation of counter-arguments and the modification of proposals, either to meet legitimate objections or, when there is no alternative, to accommodate other people's requirements.

Political sensitivity

Organizational politicians exert hidden influence to get their way, and 'politicking' in some form takes place in most organizations. A degree of political sensitivity is desirable – knowing what is going on so that influence can be exerted properly. This means that it is necessary to:

- know how 'things are done around here';
- know how key decisions are made and who makes them;
- understand the factors that are likely to affect decisions;
- know where the power base is in the organization (sometimes called the 'dominant coalition') – who makes the running, who are the people who count when decisions are taken;
- be aware of what is going on behind the scenes;
- know who is a rising star and whose reputation is fading;
- identify any 'hidden agendas' – try to understand what people are really getting at beneath the surface by getting answers to the question: 'Where are they coming from?';
- find out what other people are thinking and seeking;
- network – identify the interest groups and keep in contact with them.

Dangers of politics

Much of this behaviour is legitimate, but there are dangers. Politicking can be carried out to excess, and it can then seriously harm the effectiveness of an organization. The signs of excessive indulgence in political behaviour include:

- back-biting;
- buck-passing;
- secret meetings and hidden decisions;
- feuds between people and departments;
- e-mail or paper wars between armed camps – arguing by e-mail or memoranda rather than meeting people face-to-face is a sign of distrust;
- a multiplicity of snide comments and criticisms;
- excessive and counterproductive lobbying;
- the formation of cabals – cliques that spend their time intriguing.

Dealing with organizational politics

One way to deal with this sort of behaviour is to find out who is going in for it and openly confront them with the damage they are doing. They will, of course, deny that they are behaving politically (they wouldn't be politicians if they didn't), but the fact that they have been identified might lead them to modify their approach. It could, of course, only serve to drive them further underground, in which case their behaviour would have to be observed even more closely and action taken to restrain it.

A more positive approach to keeping politics operating at an acceptable level is for the organization to manage its operations as transparently as possible. The aim should be to ensure that issues are debated fully, that differences of opinion are dealt with frankly and that disagreements are de-personalized, so far as this is possible. Political processes can then be seen as a way of helping to maintain the momentum of the organization as a complex decision-making and problem-solving entity. In their organization development role, HR professionals can exert influence in achieving these aims.

Key learning points: Political skills

Organizational politics

Politics in an organization is a process of influencing individuals and groups of people to your point of view, where you cannot rely on authority (Kakabadse, 1983). In this sense, a political approach can be legitimate as long as the ends are justifiable from the viewpoint of the organization.

Approaches adopted by organizational politicians

1 Identify the stakeholders.

2 Keep the stakeholders comfortable, concentrating on their comfort zones.

3 Work on the comfort zones and align their image to that of the people with power.

4 Use the network – identify the interest groups and people of influence.

5 Enter the network – identify the gatekeepers, adhere to the norms.

6 Make deals – agree to support other people where this is of mutual benefit.

7 Withhold information as appropriate and withdraw judiciously when the going gets rough.

Using political means to get things done

People acting politically get things done by lobbying decision makers and doing deals. Other ploys include withholding information, which is not legitimate, in recognition of the fact that knowledge is power. Organizational politicians can go behind people's backs, hatch up plots in dark corners, 'sew things up' before meetings and exert undue influence on weaker brethren.

Political sensitivity

To be politically sensitive it is necessary to:

● know how 'things are done around here';

● know how key decisions are made and who makes them;

● understand the factors that are likely to affect decisions;

● know where the power base is in the organization;

● be aware of what is going on behind the scenes;

● know who is a rising star and whose reputation is fading;

● identify any 'hidden agendas' – try to understand what people are really getting at beneath the surface;

● find out what other people are thinking and seeking;

● network – identify the interest groups and keep in contact with them.

Dealing with organizational politicians

To keep politics operating at an acceptable level the organization should manage its operations as transparently as possible. The aim should be to ensure that issues are debated fully, that differences of opinion are dealt with frankly and that disagreements are de-personalized.

Questions

1 What are organizational politics?

2 What are typical political approaches?

3 How can political sensitivity be achieved?

4 How should organizational politics be dealt with?

Reference

Kakabadse, A (1983) *The Politics of Management*, Aldershot, Gower

PART X

HRM toolkits

PART X CONTENTS

Introduction

The purpose of the HRM toolkits in this part is to provide practical guidance on the steps required to develop and implement HRM innovations and to manage key HR practices. The toolkits consist of questionnaires and checklists that can be used to conduct surveys, to analyse HR practices and the context in which they take place, to assist in the diagnosis of problems and issues, and to plan development and implementation programmes.

The toolkits set out a step-by-step process of analysis and diagnosis. Questionnaires and checklists are provided to elicit views, summarize arrangements and issues, and provide a framework for decision making. However, the processes are in practice not always as sequential as the layouts of the toolkits suggest. The toolkits should not, indeed cannot, be used rigidly. It is often a case of using the toolkit flexibly in accordance with the circumstances.

It is useful in the first place to read through the whole toolkit to understand its structure and gain familiarity with the instruments it contains. How it is used can then be planned in accordance with the requirements presented by the situation facing the organization. They need to take account of priorities imposed by internal and external pressures. A speedy solution may be required to a pressing problem and this will mean selecting the relevant parts of the toolkits and focusing on these. Only a limited number of the instruments may therefore be used.

The toolkits have been designed to provide a choice of instruments from which a selection can be made. These instruments contain statements or questions that are likely to be generally relevant, but these are only intended to provide guidelines and can be amended to suit the requirements of the situation. Thus questions could be added or deleted, or the instrument could be shortened to ease administration.

Used on this selective basis, the toolkits can provide the basis for programme planning, whether it is a survey, a risk assessment exercise, a fundamental strategic review, a study of particular aspects of reward management or the evaluation of reward effectiveness. Instruments from within the toolkits can be selected for use in surveys and in involvement activities. They can elicit the information upon which communication plans can be based.

57
Strategic HRM

Purpose of the toolkit

Strategic HRM is concerned with how the organization's goals will be achieved through its human resources by means of integrated HR strategies, policies and practices. It involves a systematic analysis of the business context and needs, and the effectiveness of existing HRM policies and practices in operating within the context and satisfying the needs. The purpose of this toolkit is to describe the methods of analysis that can be used within a strategic HRM framework.

The strategic HRM framework

Strategic HRM involves a sequence of activities as set out in Figure 57.1.

Analyse:
- what's happening?
- what's good and not so good about it?
- what are the issues?
- what are the problems?
- what's the business need?

Diagnose:
- why do these issues exist?
- what are the causes of the problems?
- what factors are influencing the situation (competition, environmental, political, etc)?

Conclusions and recommendations:
- what are our conclusions from the analysis/diagnosis?
- what alternative strategies are available?
- which alternative is recommended and why?

Action planning:
- what actions do we need to take to implement the proposals?
- what problems may we meet and how will we overcome them?
- who takes the action and when?

Resource planning:
- what resources will we need (money, people, time)?
- how will we obtain these resources?
- how do we convince management that these resources are required?

Benefits:
- what are the benefits to the organization of implementing these proposals?
- how do they benefit individual employees?
- how do they satisfy business needs?

FIGURE 57.1
The sequence of strategic HRM

Strategic HRM activities

The strategic HRM activities conducted within this framework as set out in the rest of the toolkit are to:

- analyse the internal environment (Exhibit 57.1);
- analyse the external environment (Exhibit 57.2);
- analyse the HR implications of business strategy and business drivers (Exhibit 57.3);
- conduct a human resource management attitude survey (Exhibit 57.4);
- analyse the effectiveness of existing HR strategies (Exhibit 57.5);
- conduct a strategic HRM gap analysis (Exhibit 57.6);
- develop a diagnostic framework (Exhibit 57.7).

EXHIBIT 57.1   Analysis of internal environment

Question	Response	Implications for HR strategy
What are the key objectives of our business strategy?		
What are the main drivers of success in our business?		
What are the core values of the organization?		
What evidence is there that these values are used in the everyday life of the organization?		
What are the implications of the type of business we are in on our reward strategy?		
To what extent do we manage centrally or devolve responsibility?		
What is it like to work for this organization?		
What characteristics do we look for in our people?		
What do the people we want, want?		
What is our employee value proposition and does it help to attract and retain high quality people?		
What do we do to ensure the engagement of our people, and is it enough?		

EXHIBIT 57.2   Analysis of external environment

External factor	Impact on HR policy and practice
Competitive pressures	
Business/economic downturn	
Globalization	
Employment and demographic trends	
Legislation/regulations	
Availability of key skills	
Market rates of pay and trends	

EXHIBIT 57.3   HR implications of business strategy and business drivers

	Content	Possible HR supporting activities	To what extent do we have the effective HR activities required?			What should we do about it?
			Wholly	Partly	Not at all	
Business strategy	• Growth – revenue/profit • Maximize shareholder value • Growth through acquisitions/ mergers • Product development • Market development • Cost leadership	• Workforce planning				
		• Talent management				
		• Skills development				
		• Targeted recruitment				
		• Retention policies				
		• Leadership development				
Business drivers	• Innovation • Maximize added value • Productivity • Customer service • Quality • Satisfy stakeholders – investors, shareholders, employees, elected representatives	• Total reward management				
		• Performance management				
		• High performance working				
		• Enhance engagement				

EXHIBIT 57.4   Human resource management attitude survey

Please state the extent to which you agree or disagree with the following statements about human resource management in this organization by placing a circle around the number which most closely matches your opinion.

		Strongly agree	Agree	Disagree	Strongly disagree
1.	I think this organization is a great place in which to work	1	2	3	4
2.	I am happy about the values of this organization and the ways in which it conducts its business.	1	2	3	4
3.	I get plenty of opportunities to learn in this job.	1	2	3	4
4.	I get good advice on how I can develop my career.	1	2	3	4
5.	I am given plenty of opportunities to achieve in my job.	1	2	3	4
6.	I get ample opportunity to use my skills in my job.	1	2	3	4
7.	I have been properly trained to do my job.	1	2	3	4
8.	My contribution is adequately rewarded.	1	2	3	4
9.	My performance is recognized properly.	1	2	3	4
10.	The performance pay scheme encourages better performance.	1	2	3	4
11.	I understand how the job evaluation scheme works.	1	2	3	4
12.	Pay increases are handled fairly.	1	2	3	4
13.	I get good feedback on my performance throughout the year.	1	2	3	4
14.	I am kept well informed about changes that affect me in the organization.	1	2	3	4
15.	I feel that management is prepared to listen to employees.	1	2	3	4
16.	The organization treats me fairly.	1	2	3	4
17.	The organization makes every effort to achieve job security.	1	2	3	4
18.	The organization makes every effort to ensure the wellbeing of its employees.	1	2	3	4
19.	The organization is committed to ensuring the health and safety of its employees.	1	2	3	4
20.	The working conditions in my department encourage good work.	1	2	3	4

EXHIBIT 57.5   Analysis of the effectiveness of existing HR strategies

	Wholly	Partly	Not at all	If partly or not at all, what needs to be done about it?
To what extent does the HR strategy support the achievement of business goals?				
To what extent does the HR strategy promote the wellbeing of all employees?				
To what extent are the HR strategies in different areas integrated with one another?				
To what extent does HR strategy enable the organization to recruit and retain the skilled people it needs?				
To what extent does HR strategy enable the organization to develop the talented people it needs?				
To what extent does HR strategy ensure that people are rewarded according to their contribution?				
To what extent does HR strategy contribute to the creation of a positive employee relations climate?				

EXHIBIT 57.6   A strategic HRM gap analysis

| Effective high performance work system in place | | No systematic attempt is made to encourage high performance |

| Integrated talent management programmes are operating effectively | | Talent management, if it happens at all, is haphazard or ineffective |

| Sophisticated techniques are used to recruit employees | | A traditional approach is adopted to recruitment |

| Focus on using blended learning and development processes | | Reliance on the delivery of traditional training courses |

| A total reward approach is used successfully | | Reward programmes limited to financial incentives |

| Employees given a voice on all matters that concern them | | Only lip service is paid to employee participation and involvement |

| Employee wellbeing given the close attention of management | | Little or no concern by management for employee wellbeing |

Mark on the scale X for current,   0 for desired–eg

| High quality HR practices | | Poor quality HR practices |

EXHIBIT 57.7   Diagnostic framework

Issues identified by analysis in exhibits 57.3 to 57.6	Reasons for issues	Action proposed to deal with issues

Strategic HRM gap analysis

A strategic HRM gap analysis compares the current and desired HRM characteristics in the organization, using the framework set out in Exhibit 57.6.

Comparing the largest gaps with the current situation helps to indicate the priority issues to be addressed. It can be used in workshops and focus groups as a means of obtaining the views of line managers and employees on where things need to be done.

59
Organization design

Purpose of the toolkit

This toolkit provides a set of analytical and diagnostic organization design tools for use in a design and organization development programme, as set out in Figure 59.1.

FIGURE 59.1   Organization design programme

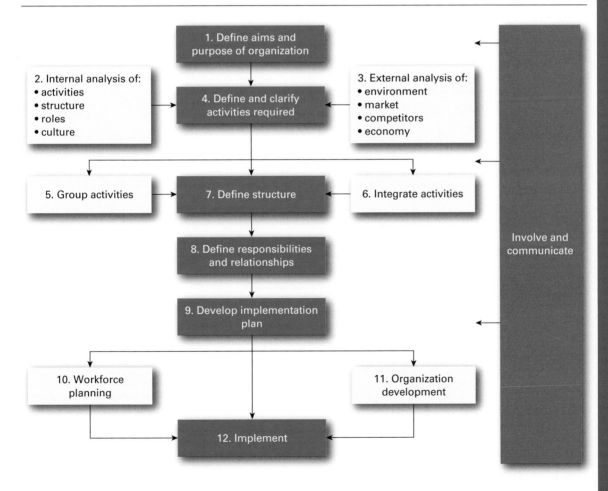

Aims and purpose of organization

Use Exhibit 59.1 to analyse the aims and purpose of the organization.

EXHIBIT 59.1   Analysis of overall aims and purpose

Question	Answer
1. What business are we in?	
2. What is our business model?	
3. How do we make money?	
4. What is our mission?	
5. What are our main business goals?	
6. What are our core values?	
7. What are our main activities?	
8. Who are our customers/clients?	
9. Who are our other main stakeholders?	
10. How appropriate, well-defined and understood are our mission and business goals?	

Activities and structure analysis

Use Exhibit 59.2 to analyse activities and structure.

EXHIBIT 59.2   Activities and structure analysis

	Question	Answer
Activities	Are all the activities required to achieve objectives properly catered for?	
	Are any unnecessary activities being carried out?	
	Is there any unnecessary duplication of activities?	
Structure	On what basis are activities grouped together – by product, by function or process, by region or area, by customer or client or by a combination of any of these?	
	Is the basis upon which activities are grouped appropriate in relation to the markets and customers of the organization and its technology, environment and geographical coverage?	
	If grouping is on a product, customer or regional basis, has this resulted in too much duplication of activities, unnecessary numbers of staff or duplication of group or central service functions?	
	If grouping is on a functional or process basis has this resulted in too much task specialization, insufficient identification with the end product and the consultant, or managers not having adequate responsibility for the range of resources they need?	
	Does the basis upon which activities are grouped create boundary difficulties between them?	
	Is the organization a process-based one, in the sense defined by Ghoshal and Bartlett (1995)? 'Managers are beginning to deal with their organizations in different ways. Rather than seeing them as a hierarchy of static roles, they think of them as a portfolio of dynamic processes. They see core organizational processes that overlay and often dominate the vertical, authority-based processes of the hierarchical structure.' Or should it be?	
	Is the flow of work across organizational boundaries smooth and uninterrupted?	
	Is there sufficient degree of flexibility in grouping activities and defining group boundaries to facilitate rapid adjustments to changing requirements?	
	Is there any scope for grouping activities more closely together or removing boundaries between them to facilitate integration and smooth, economical workflows?	
	Does the nature of the work indicate that a looser form of boundaryless organization or a matrix organization would be more appropriate?	
	Should the emphasis be more on creating a climate in which networking can take place and hierarchical decision making becomes less important?	
	Are there too many levels in the organization and if so, what is the scope for reducing them?	
	Are there any 'one-over-one' situations in which managers have an assistant manager between them and the next level, creating confusion and duplication?	
	Do any managers have more people reporting to them than they can conveniently and effectively control?	
	Does the structure inhibit in any way clear and rapid communications on matters affecting the business and how it is managed?	

Role analysis

Use Exhibit 59.3 to conduct role analysis.

EXHIBIT 59.3   Role analysis

Question	Answer
Are any role holders unclear about what they are expected to do?	
Are any role holders unclear about who they report to for what?	
Are any role holders unclear about their reporting relationship to their line manager and to any other person with whom they have a functional relationship?	
Are any role holders expected to do too much or too little?	
Are any role holders carrying out a range of miscellaneous tasks that do not seem to be logically grouped together?	
Do any role holders lack the authority, resources or information that would enable them to carry out their job effectively?	
Are there any role holders who are clearly unable to carry out their work properly?	
Is there a sufficient degree of flexibility in the ways in which roles are defined to enable role holders to adjust readily to new or changed demands?	
To what extent are roles designed to provide an appropriate degree of challenge, responsibility, autonomy and scope for growth?	
Are managers aware of the principles of job design and do they take them into account in designing jobs in their departments?	
Are there any cases where roles have been inappropriately structured round the capacities or personalities of role holders?	

Reference

Ghoshal, S and Bartlett, C A (1995) Changing the role of top management: beyond structure to process, *Harvard Business Review*, January–February, pp 86–96

60
Organization development

Purpose of the toolkit

The purpose of this toolkit is to provide the basis for organizational development programmes through a number of diagnostics and checklists covering major aspects of organizational culture and behaviour.

The toolkit contains the following exhibits:

Exhibit 60.1   Culture analysis

Exhibit 60.2   Values analysis

Exhibit 60.3   Norms analysis

Exhibit 60.4   Artefacts analysis

Exhibit 60.5   Management style analysis

Exhibit 60.6   Teamwork analysis

Exhibit 60.7   Organizational development action plan

EXHIBIT 60.1   Culture analysis

Types of culture (Handy, 1981)	To what extent does the culture of the organization correspond to any of these types?
The power culture is one with a central power source that exercises control. There are few rules or procedures and the atmosphere is competitive, power-oriented and political.	
The role culture in which work is controlled by procedures and rules and the role, or job description, is more important than the person who fills it. Power is associated with positions not people.	
The task culture in which the aim is to bring together the right people and let them get on with it. Influence is based more on expert power than in position or personal power. The culture is adaptable and teamwork is important.	
The person culture in which the individual is the central point. The organization exists only to serve and assist the individuals in it.	

EXHIBIT 60.2   Values analysis

Question	Answer
Is it possible to say that the organization has a set of core values? If so:	
What are they? eg: • Care and consideration for people • Competence • Competitiveness • Customer service • Innovation • Performance • Quality • Teamwork	
Have they been articulated?	
Have employees been involved in describing them?	
To what extent are they 'values in use' rather than just 'espoused values'?	
Have any efforts been made by the organization to operationalize the values?	
Does anything more need to be done to operationalize the values?	

EXHIBIT 60.3   Norms analysis

Possible norms	To what extent do they apply?
How managers treat the members of their teams (management style) and how the latter relate to their managers.	
The prevailing work ethic, eg 'work hard, play hard', 'come in early, stay late', 'if you cannot finish your work during business hours you are obviously inefficient', 'look busy at all times', 'look relaxed at all times'.	
Status – how much importance is attached to it; the existence or lack of obvious status symbols.	
Ambition – naked ambition is expected and approved of, or a more subtle approach is the norm.	
Performance – exacting performance standards are general; the highest praise that can be given in the organization is to be referred to as very professional.	
Power – recognized as a way of life; executed by political means, dependent on expertise and ability rather than position; concentrated at the top; shared at different levels in different parts of the organization.	
Politics – rife throughout the organization and treated as normal behaviour; not accepted as overt behaviour.	
Loyalty – expected, a cradle to grave approach to careers; discounted, the emphasis is on results and contribution in the short term.	
Anger – openly expressed; hidden, but expressed through other, possibly political, means.	
Approachability – managers are expected to be approachable and visible; everything happens behind closed doors.	
Formality – a cool, formal approach is the norm; the atmosphere is relaxed and highly informal.	

EXHIBIT 60.4   Artefacts analysis

Examples of artefacts	How are they evidenced?
The working environment	
The tone and language used in e-mails, letters or memoranda	
The manner in which people address each other at meetings, in e-mails or over the telephone	
The welcome (or lack of welcome) given to visitors	
The way in which receptionists deal with outside calls	

EXHIBIT 60.5   Management style analysis

Indicate the prevailing management style in each of the listed categories on a scale of 1 to 10

1   2   3   4   5   6   7   8   9   10

Charismatic managers rely on their personality, their inspirational qualities and their 'aura'. They are visionary leaders who are achievement-oriented, calculated risk takers and good communicators.

Non-charismatic managers rely mainly on their know-how (authority goes to the person who knows), their quiet confidence and their cool, analytical approach to dealing with problems.

Autocratic managers impose their decisions, using their position to force people to do as they are told.

Democratic managers encourage people to participate and involve themselves in decision making.

Enablers inspire people with their vision of the future and empower them to accomplish team goals.

Controllers manipulate people to obtain their compliance.

Transactional leaders trade money, jobs and security for compliance.

Transformational leaders motivate people to strive for higher level goals.

EXHIBIT 60.6   Teamwork analysis

High suspicion	1	*Degree of mutual trust*	10	High trust

Guarded, cautious	1	*Communications*	10	Open, authentic

Everyone for themselves	1	*Degree of mutual support*	10	Genuine concern for each other

Not understood	1	*Team objectives*	10	Clearly understood

Through denial, avoidance	1	*Handling conflict within team*	10	Acceptance and 'working though' conflicts

Competencies used by team	1	*Use of member resources*	10	Competencies not used

Control is imposed	1	*Control methods*	10	Control from within

Restrictive, pressure for conformity	1	*Organizational environment*	10	Free, supportive, respect for differences

Adapted from McGregor, 1960

EXHIBIT 60.7 Organizational development action plan

Area of analysis	Implications for organizational development
Culture analysis	
Values analysis	
Norms analysis	
Artefacts analysis	
Management style analysis	
Teamwork analysis	

References

Handy, C (1981) *Understanding Organizations*, 3rd edn, Harmondsworth, Penguin Books

McGregor, D (1960) *The Human Side of Enterprise*, New York, McGraw-Hill

References

Alfes, K, Truss, C, Soane, E C, Rees, C and Gatenby, M (2010) *Creating an Engaged Workforce*, London, CIPD

Balain, S and Sparrow, P (2009) *Engaged to Perform: A new perspective on employee engagement*, Lancaster, Lancaster University Management School

Conference Board (2006) *Employee Engagement: A review of current research and its implications*, New York, Conference Board

Macey, W H, Schneider, B, Barbera, K M and Young, S A (2009) *Employee Engagement*, Malden, MA, Wiley-Blackwell

MacLeod, D and Clarke, N (2009) *Engaging for Success: Enhancing performance through employee engagement*, London, Department for Business Innovation and Skills

Maslach, C, Schaufeli, W B and Leiter, M P (2001) Job burnout, *Annual Review of Psychology*, **52**, pp 397–422

Murlis, H and Watson, S (2001) Creating employee engagement – transforming the employment deal, *Benefits and Compensation International*, **30** (8), pp 6–17

Robinson, D, Perryman, S and Hayday, S (2004) *The Drivers of Employee Engagement*, Brighton, Institute for Employment Studies

Towers Perrin (2007) *Global Workforce Study*, at http://www.towersperrin.com, accessed 1.8.2011

Truss, C, Soane, E, Edwards, C, Wisdom, K, Croll, A and Burnett, J (2006) *Working Life: Employee attitudes and engagement*, London, CIPD

62
Workforce planning

Purpose of the toolkit

The purpose of the toolkit is to provide a guide to workforce planning, defined as a process in which an organization attempts to estimate the demand for employees and evaluate the size, nature and sources of supply that will be required to meet the demand. Workforce planning often focuses on key categories of staff, for example doctors, nurses and radiographers in the National Health Service, or skilled operatives in a manufacturing company. A workforce planning flowchart is shown in Figure 62.1.

FIGURE 62.1 Workforce planning flowchart

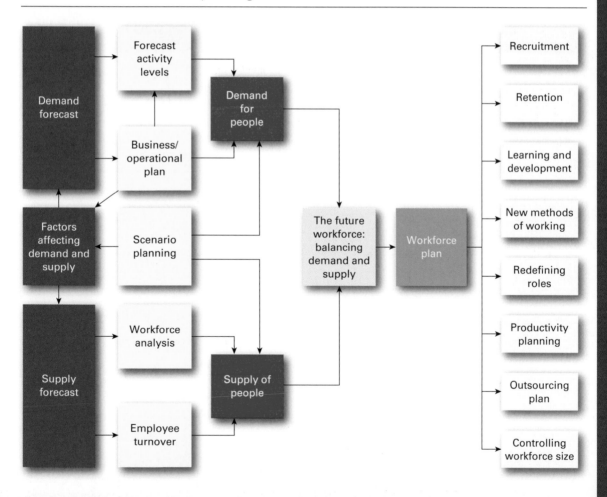

The following tools are provided:

Factors affecting demand and supply

The starting point of the workforce planning process is an analysis of the factors affecting the demand and supply of people. Exhibit 62.1 shows the internal factors that need to be considered by reference to business and organizational plans. The external factors are identified by means of scenario planning (Exhibit 62.2).

EXHIBIT 62.1   Internal factors affecting demand and supply of people

Factor	Occurrence in organization	Impact on demand and supply of people
Changes in working arrangements – hours, flexibility		
Changes in organization – different structures, new functions		
Changes in roles – new jobs, greater role flexibility, amalgamation of existing roles, enlargement of roles		
New activities or services		
New skills – demand for new or different skills		
More part-time working		
More outsourcing of work		

Scenario planning

Scenario planning assesses the environmental changes that are likely to affect the organization so that the implications of these changes on the organization's labour markets and the supply of people can be taken into account in the workforce plan. The PESTLE scanning approach, as shown in Exhibit 62.2, can be used.

Forecasting activity levels

The raw data for preparing demand forecasts is provided by forecast activity levels. Obviously, the activities will vary according to the type of business or organization. The following are examples of different types of activities for which forecasts could be made:

- call outs;
- claims dealt with;
- customers/clients/patients;
- deliveries;
- despatches;
- enquiries dealt with;
- examinations/inspections made;
- orders processed;
- policies underwritten;
- routes/journeys undertaken;
- telephone calls received/made;
- tests conducted;
- transactions;
- units manufactured or processed;
- volume of items/material manufactured or processed.

An analysis should be made of the current level of activity. The number of people involved and the ratio of people to activity levels are included to provide data for demand forecasts (see Exhibit 62.3).

EXHIBIT 62.2   Scenario planning

Factors	Assessment of developments that are likely to affect the organization	Workforce plan implications
Political		
Economic		
Social		
Technological		
Legal		
Environmental		

EXHIBIT 62.3   Forecasting activity levels

Activity	Applicable role(s)	Current level of activity	Current number in role(s)	Ratio: roles to activity*	Forecast level of activity on:		
					Date:	Date:	Date:

* For use in ratio-trend analysis (see Exhibit 62.5)

EXHIBIT 62.4   Workforce implications of the business plan

Question	Answer
What are the key features of the business/ operational plan?	
What are the implications of the business/ operational plan for the need for new or different skills?	
What are the implications of the business/ operational plan for the numbers of different categories of people required?	

Workforce implications of business plan

Business or operational plans indicate projected levels of activity, which feed into the activity level forecast and through that to the demand forecast. They also provide information on the likely demands for new or different skills to meet plans for business model innovation or the introduction of new technology. A checklist is set out in Exhibit 62.4.

Demand forecast methods

Demand forecasts are based on data relating to forecast activity levels and the implications of business and operational plans, together with information from scenario planning. There are three basic forecasting methods, as set out in Exhibit 62.5. Of these, managerial judgement is the most typical, followed by ratio trend analysis.

EXHIBIT 62.5   Demand forecasting methods

Method	Description	Advantages	Disadvantages
Managerial judgement	Managers think about their future workloads and other factors affecting the demand and estimate how many people they need on the basis of judgement and experience. Potential changes in productivity can be factored in.	Simple and quick and makes use of the experience of line managers. An assessment, albeit a qualitative one, can be made of the impact of other factors affecting demand as set out in Exhibit 62.1.	Highly judgemental – the forecasts can be generalized and misleading and may not provide an accurate basis for recruitment planning.
Ratio-trend analysis	Existing ratios between an activity level and the number of employees working on that activity are analysed. The ratio is applied to forecast activity levels to determine an adjusted number of people required. The analysis may be extended to cover employees connected to but not directly involved in the activity, for example indirect workers who support direct workers. The existing ratio of directs to indirects would be applied to the forecast number of directs needed to deal with the new activity levels to determine the number of directs. Potential changes in productivity can be factored in.	Based on factual data about ratios, which can then be linked to quantified estimates of future activity levels. At least gives the appearance of being reasonably scientific.	Relies on forecasts of activity levels that could be little more than inspired guess work. The existing ratios may be related to poor levels of productivity, which the forecast would perpetuate unless real efforts were made to factor in specific productivity improvement plans. Ignores other factors affecting demand because account is only taken of activity levels.
Work study	Work study techniques are used in association with activity level forecasts to calculate how long operations should take and the number of people required.	In the right circumstances, this can produce accurate forecasts.	Limited to situations (eg manufacturing) when work study techniques can be applied.
Choice	Managerial judgement is the easiest although limited option. At least some attempt can be made to allow for the less quantifiable factors that will affect demand. Ratio-trend analysis provides quantified information that could be combined with more qualitative managerial judgements covering the other factors.		

EXHIBIT 62.6   Demand forecast schedule

Occupation	Present number	Forecast numbers required on:			Basis for forecast
		Date:	Date:	Date:	

Demand forecast schedule

A demand forecast schedule, as shown in Exhibit 62.6, shows the forecast number of people requirements for specified occupations based on one of the forecasting methods listed in Exhibit 62.5. An explanation should be made of the basis for the forecast, covering the ratios if ratio-trend analysis is used and the other factors taken into account.

Workforce analysis

Workforce analysis is the first step in assessing the supply of people. It sets out the numbers available in each major occupational group, as in the examples illustrated in Exhibit 62.7.

Employee turnover

The number of existing people as determined by workforce analysis will be eroded by employee turnover (labour attrition or wastage). It is therefore necessary to decide how to measure turnover and then collect and analyse the data before adjusting forecast supply figures to take account of wastage. Different methods of measuring wastage are itemized in Exhibit 62.8.

EXHIBIT 62.7   Workforce analysis

Occupational group	Number
Senior managers	
Middle managers	
Junior managers	
Supervisors/team leaders	
Senior professional staff	
Professional staff	
Senior technical staff	
Technical staff	
Senior sales and service staff	
Sales and service staff	
Senior administrative staff	
Administrative staff	
Skilled operatives	
Semi-skilled operatives	
Unskilled operatives	
Senior support and service staff	
Support and service staff	
Drivers	
Others	

EXHIBIT 62.8   Measuring employee turnover

Type of measure	Description	Advantages	Disadvantages
Employee turn over index	$$\frac{\text{Number of leavers in a specified period (usually 1 year)}}{\text{Average number of employees during the same period}} \times 100$$	Easily understood and applied – most commonly used index.	The percentage may be inflated by the high turnover of a relatively small proportion of the workforce, especially in times of heavy recruitment.
Stability index	$$\frac{\text{Number with 1 year's service or more}}{\text{Number employed 1 year ago}} \times 100$$	Provides an indication of the tendency for longer-service employees to remain with the company, and therefore shows the degree to which there is continuity of employment.	The index will not reveal the different situations that exist in an organization with a high proportion of long-serving employees in comparison with one where the majority of employees are short service.
Survival rate	The proportion of employees who are engaged within a certain period who remain with the organization after so many months or years of service.	Useful as a means of tracking a cohort of recruits, eg graduates, to assess the effectiveness of recruitment and retention policies.	Cannot be used as a means of measuring the turnover rates of whole populations in order to allow for future wastage as a basis for supply forecasts.
Half-life index	The time taken for a group or cohort of starters to reduce to half its original size through the wastage process.	A simpler form of survival rate. Comparisons can then be made for successive entry years or between different groups of employees to show where action may have to be taken to counter undesirable wastage trends.	As for survival rate.
Leavers' length of service analysis	An analysis is made of the average length of service of leavers. A more refined analysis compares, for designated length of service categories, the numbers leaving with the numbers employed.	An alternative survival rate measure that can be used to assess the effectiveness of recruitment and retention policies.	As for survival rate.

EXHIBIT 62.9   Forecasting the supply of people

Occupation	Present number available	Forecast numbers available on:			Basis for forecast
		Date:	Date:	Date:	

Forecasting internal supply of people

Supply forecasting measures the number of people likely to be available from within the organization, having allowed for the output of training programmes, internal movements and promotions, and the impact of employee turnover and changes in hours and other conditions of work. It involves taking the existing numbers in major employment categories (if this is a comprehensive plan), or in the specific categories to be covered by the plan, and adjusting the numbers to take account of losses through employee turnover. Because turnover rates may vary according to the type of occupation, ideally figures for different types would be available. This initial analysis may need to be adjusted to take into account other factors affecting the supply, as listed in Exhibit 62.1. The basis upon which this is done should be explained. A supply forecast schedule is shown in Exhibit 62.9.

Balancing demand and supply

Balancing demand and supply involves taking the demand and supply forecasts and identifying the gaps in the form of deficits or surpluses. This provides the basis for preparing a workforce plan to deal with gaps. A schedule for recording the balance and indicating in headline form the proposed planning actions is shown in Exhibit 62.10. The planning actions are defined in Exhibit 62.11 but would, of course, need to be expanded in more detail in the full plan with explanations of the actions required, timescale, responsibilities for the action and the costs and benefits of the proposed action.

EXHIBIT 62.10   Balancing demand and supply

Occupation	Forecast for (date):			Forecast for (date):			Proposed action heading(s)*
	Demand	Supply	Deficit (–) or surplus (+)	Demand	Supply	Deficit (–) or surplus (+)	

*Headings:
- Recruitment/procurement plan
- Retention plan
- Learning and development plan
- New methods of working
- Redefining roles
- Productivity plan
- Controlling workforce size

EXHIBIT 62.11   Action planning

Action plan headline	Summary of possible actions
Recruitment/ procurement plan	<ul><li>Numbers and types of people needed to make up any deficits and when needed</li><li>Likely sources of external recruits</li><li>Proposals for attracting good candidates</li><li>Proposals for dealing with any recruitment problems</li><li>The recruitment programme</li><li>Other sources of people from training programmes or by retraining/reallocation</li><li>Develop talent management programmes</li></ul>
Retention plan	<ul><li>Analysis of the factors affecting retention</li><li>Plans for overcoming weaknesses in policies and practices leading to wastage</li></ul>
Learning and development plan	<ul><li>New skills required and how they will be developed</li><li>Number of trainees/apprentices required and proposals for recruiting and training them</li><li>Number of existing staff who need training or retraining and the programmes required</li><li>New courses to be developed or changes to be made to existing ones</li></ul>
New methods of working	<ul><li>Increase operational flexibility by introducing flexible patterns of work</li><li>Provide more scope for flexible hours</li><li>Review traditional employment patterns</li><li>More outsourcing</li><li>More sub-contracting</li><li>Use more temporary and part-time staff and job-sharing</li></ul>
Redefining roles	<ul><li>Enhance role flexibility</li><li>Encourage multitasking and multi-skilling</li></ul>
Productivity plan	<ul><li>Improve or streamline methods, procedures and systems</li><li>Deploy more technology including computers</li><li>Reduce duplication and waste</li><li>Enhance engagement</li></ul>
Controlling workforce size	If a reduction in numbers is unavoidable (ie if methods mentioned above are insufficient) consider the following options (in order of preference): <ul><li>Freeze recruitment</li><li>Reduce working hours</li><li>Encourage voluntary redundancy</li><li>As a last resort, use compulsory redundancy</li></ul>

63
Talent management

Purpose of the toolkit

Talent management is the process of ensuring that the organization has the talented people it needs to attain its business goals. It involves the management of the flow of talent through an organization by creating and maintaining a talent pipeline, as shown in Figure 63.1.

FIGURE 63.1 The talent management pipeline

Talent management strategy

A talent management strategy consists of a declaration of intent on how the talent management process of planning, auditing, resourcing, succession planning and development should mesh together to achieve an overall objective – to acquire and nurture talent wherever it is and wherever it is needed by using a number of interdependent policies and practices. The rating framework shown in Exhibit 63.1 can be used to obtain overall views and generate discussion on the strategy.

EXHIBIT 63.1   Rating framework for talent management strategy goals

Objectives	Importance*	Effectiveness*
• Reinforce the achievement of organizational goals		
• Identify talented people through performance management and potential assessment processes		
• Recruit and retain talented people		
• Ensure that the talent required is available within the organization		
• Provide for management succession		
• Design jobs and develop roles which give people opportunities to apply and grow their skills and provide them with autonomy, interest and challenge		
• Guide career management		
• Provide talented staff with opportunities for career development and growth		
• Develop leadership and management skills through systematic leadership and management development programmes		
• Recognize those with talent by rewarding excellence, enterprise and achievement		
• Communicate talent management policies to employees		
• Manage programmes effectively		
• Involve experienced line managers in talent management activities		

* Scale: 10 = high; 1 = low

Talent management policy

Talent management policy can be reviewed by answering the questions set out in Exhibit 63.2.

EXHIBIT 63.2   Talent management policy checklist

Policy question	Answer
What do we mean by talent in this organization?	
What do we mean by talent management in this organization?	
Who should be included in a talent management programme?	
Who should be responsible for talent management?	
To what extent is the policy to make or buy, ie develop internally or recruit from outside?	

Talent planning

Talent planning is the process of establishing how many and what sort of talented people are needed now and in the future. The questions set out in Exhibit 63.3 deal with what should be covered.

EXHIBIT 63.3   Talent planning checklist

Question	Answer	
How is talent classified in the organization?		
How many people have we now in each talent category?		
How many people in each category will we need:	In one year's time?	
	In two years' time?	
	In three years' time?	
	In five years' time?	
What problems could we have in obtaining the talent required?		
How should we deal with these problems?		

Talent audit

A talent audit identifies those with talent and potential, often through performance management. It provides the basis for career planning and development – ensuring that talented people have the sequence of experience supplemented by coaching and learning programmes that will equip them to carry out more demanding roles in the future. A talent audit checklist is set out in Exhibit 63.4.

EXHIBIT 63.4   Talent audit checklist

Question	Answer
Does a system for assessing talent and potential exist?	
To what extent is the system used properly by line managers?	
How are talented people classified by the system?	
How many people have been assessed in each category?	
Is the number in the higher categories adequate?	
What needs to be done about any problems raised in the answers to the above questions?	

Resourcing talent

Resourcing policies and programmes ensure that the organization gets and keeps the talent it needs. Attraction policies influence programmes for external resourcing. Retention policies are designed to ensure that people continue as engaged and committed members of the organization. Line managers can be asked to carry out separate 'risk analyses' for any key staff to assess the likelihood of their leaving so that steps can be taken to encourage them to stay. The outcome of these policies is a talent flow, which creates and maintains the talent pool. An analysis of the effectiveness of resourcing practices can be made by using the checklist in Exhibit 63.5.

EXHIBIT 63.5   Analysis of effectiveness of resourcing practices

Resourcing aims	Extent to which achieved			Actions required
	Fully	Partly	Not at all	
Identify the talents/skills required				
Plan and implement recruitment activities and programmes that deliver the talented people required in accordance with make-or-buy policy				
Develop talented people within the organization in accordance with make-or-buy policy				
Formulate a retention strategy designed to minimize the loss of talented people				
Conduct risk analyses of the likelihood of talented people leaving				
Take action to retain talented people, especially those who are at risk				

Succession planning

Succession planning is the process of identifying successors for key posts and then planning career moves and/or development activities for these potential successors. The questions set out in Exhibit 63.6 can be used to assess the effectiveness of succession planning.

EXHIBIT 63.6   Succession planning checklist

Question	Answer	Action required
Is there a formal process for identifying those with potential to succeed more senior managers?		
Is the process based on a comprehensive analysis of the qualities/competencies required to progress to higher positions generally or to be appointed to a specified post?		
Are those under consideration in the succession planning process identified as being ready to do the next job now or as being ready for a certain higher-grade position within a specified period?		
Are steps taken to develop those with potential through leadership and management development programmes and/or by means of career planning programmes involving planned experience?		
To what extent do succession planning arrangements work in the sense that they provide a flow of talented people to succeed those in higher positions?		

Talent development

Learning and development policies and programmes are essential components in the process of talent management – ensuring that people acquire and enhance the skills and competencies they need. Policies should be formulated by reference to 'employee success profiles', which are described in terms of competencies and define the qualities that need to be developed. Employee success profiles can be incorporated in role profiles. A talent development checklist is provided in Exhibit 63.7.

EXHIBIT 63.7   Talent development checklist

Question	Answer	Action required
Are there well-established leadership and management development programmes?		
Has the effectiveness of any programmes been evaluated and, if so, what was the result?		
Do development programmes include executive coaching or mentoring? If so, how effective are they?		
Do career planning/management procedures exist that provide those with promise a sequence of experience and learning activities that will equip them for whatever level of responsibility they have the ability to reach?		
Are those with potential given the opportunity to broaden their experience and develop their skills through lateral moves (job rotation) or special assignments?		

Overall analysis

An overall analysis can be carried out using the questionnaire in Exhibit 63.8 to assess how effectively talent management is being carried out.

EXHIBIT 63.8   Overall analysis and assessment of talent management practice

What should be happening	What is happening	What needs to be done?
1. The strategic management of the flow of talent through an organization is achieved by creating and maintaining a talent pipeline.		
2. The organization is clear on what is meant by talent in its environment and who the talented people are who will be covered by talent management policies.		
3. Talent management starts with the business strategy and what it signifies in terms of the talented people required by the organization.		
4. A well-defined talent pipeline exists, consisting of the processes of resourcing, retention planning, succession and career planning and learning and development (especially leadership and management development) that maintain the flow of talent needed by the organization.		
5. Talent planning processes are in place that lead to the development of policies for attracting and retaining talent and the determination of future requirements as monitored by talent audits. They also influence the development of the roles talented people carry out.		
6. A talent audit process successfully identifies those with potential and provides the basis for career planning and development.		
7. Talent relationship management activities build effective relationships with people in their roles. They recognize the value of individual employees, provide opportunities for growth, treat them fairly and achieve 'talent engagement', ensuring that people are committed to their work and the organization.		
8. Performance management processes, including 360-degree feedback, provide a means of building relationships with people, identifying talent and potential, planning learning and development activities and making the most of the talent possessed by the organization.		
9. 'Employee success profiles' are prepared that set out the competencies and qualities required to be classified as having high potential.		
10. Talented people are provided with the sequence of experience supplemented by coaching, mentoring and learning programmes that will equip them to carry out more demanding roles in the future.		

64
Planning and delivering learning events

Purpose of the toolkit

Learning events or formal training courses need to be planned and delivered with care. The purpose of this toolkit is to provide a basis for putting the sequence of activities into effect.

Planning learning events

The sequence of activities required is:

1 Establish learning needs.
2 Define objectives.
3 Decide on content and delivery.
4 Decide on arrangements.
5 Distribute information on the event.
6 Deliver the learning.
7 Evaluate.

Establish learning needs

Learning events should be planned to meet well-established and clearly defined learning needs. There are a number of ways of doing this, as listed in Exhibit 64.1, together with an assessment of their advantages and disadvantages. In practice, the methods may be used in combination to provide an overall picture.

EXHIBIT 64.1   Establishing learning needs

Method	Description	Advantages	Disadvantages
Assumption of need	Needs established on the basis of general assumptions about what people in certain occupations should know and be able to do, for example, managers need to learn about leadership.	The needs can be readily defined, especially if they are related to common requirements such as leadership, teamworking, communicating and business awareness.	No evidence of what the real needs are for particular occupations. The result could be a generalized programme that satisfies nobody.
Gap analysis	The gap between what people know and can do and what they should know and be able to do is identified so that the learning needs to fill the gap can be described. Information on the nature of the gap may be obtained by one or more of the methods described below.	Specifies what needs to be learnt so that deficiencies can be remedied by tailored training programmes.	This 'deficiency model' of training – only putting things right that have gone wrong – is limited. Learning is much more positive than that. It should be concerned with identifying and satisfying development needs – equipping people to take on extra responsibilities or acquire new skills.

EXHIBIT 64.1   *Continued*

Method	Description	Advantages	Disadvantages
Analysis of business and HR plans	Business and HR plans are analysed to indicate in general terms the types of skills and competencies that may be required in the future and the numbers of people with those skills and competencies who will be needed.	Ensures that learning plans and events are rooted firmly in business needs thus ensuring that they are business-driven. For example, a business model innovation programme may indicate what new skills will be required.	May be too generalized. Learning events need to be planned to meet specific learning needs. It is not enough for them just to aim to further the business. It is *how* they will do this that matters.
Surveys	Surveys can obtain the views of managers and other employees about what needs to be learnt.	Provide factual information on learning needs as perceived by people in the front line.	The material gathered from a survey may be unspecific and when interviewed people often find it difficult to articulate learning needs.
Performance and development reviews	Assessments are made of development needs and the extent to which the individual meets role requirements. This identifies what sort of development programme is required and what needs to be done to remedy any deficiencies. An overall analysis of performance and development review reports can reveal any common learning needs, which can be satisfied by tailored learning events.		
Role analysis	Role analysis is the basis for preparing role profiles, which provide a framework for analysing and identifying learning needs. Role profiles define the competencies required to perform the role. This can be used to assess and agree the level of competency displayed and, where necessary, what needs to be done to improve it.	A good method of assessing individual learning needs, which can generate information on common learning needs. This can be related to the organization's competency framework and used to inform the design of competency-based learning events.	The analysis can be time-consuming. It may not always be easy to obtain reliable information.
Skills analysis	Determines the skills required to achieve an acceptable standard of performance. It is mainly used for technical, craft, manual and office jobs to provide the basis for devising learning and training programmes.	If carried out properly it can provide a comprehensive and accurate basis for planned and systematic training.	Needs considerable expertise to be done properly.

Define objectives

It is essential to be clear about what the programme or event is required to achieve – its learning objectives and outcomes. These are defined to satisfy established learning needs and to provide the basis for planning content and evaluating results.

Objectives can be defined as criterion behaviour (the performance standards or changes in behaviour on-the-job to be achieved if a learning process is to be regarded as successful) and terminal behaviour (what actually happened following the learning event). Any gap between criterion and terminal behaviour will indicate deficiencies in the programme. A behavioural objective could be set out as follows.

> At the end of the programme managers will be able to take greater responsibility for the development of their staff. Indicative activities will include:
>
> - the conduct of satisfactory performance and development reviews;
> - the agreement of personal development plans;
> - enabling team members to carry out self-directed learning activities;
> - the ability to use coaching skills to improve performance.

Decide on content and delivery

A checklist of the points to be considered when deciding on the overall content of the event, the content of individual sessions and methods of delivery is set out in Exhibit 64.2.

EXHIBIT 64.2 Planning learning events checklist

Question	Answer
1. What are the overall learning objectives of the event?	
2. How long should the event be, how many sessions a day and what are the specific learning objectives and contents of each session? It is usual for a lecture session to last a maximum of 60 minutes allowing 30–40 minutes for the presentation (never any more) and time for discussion, A normal day could have three such sessions in the morning and two to three in the afternoon. There is a limit to how much people can absorb in a day and it is often best to have exercises or discussions sessions in the afternoon, especially after lunch (the graveyard shift).	
3. What are the key learning points in each session?	
4. How could these be converted into action points?	
5. What is it expected that participants will do that they could not do at all or do very well before they attended the programme?	
6. What will be done to ensure that the learning is cumulative by building sessions on each other to emphasize that they are related and that each one contributes to achieving the overall learning objectives of the programme?	

EXHIBIT 64.2   *Continued*

Question	Answer
7. What is the policy on the delivery of learning, eg the amount devoted to discussions and exercises rather than lectures? (The more of the former the better.)	
8. What steps will be taken to ensure that learning is transferred to the workplace?	
9. How will learning be linked to the context of those attending the event?	
10. How will the specific learning needs of individuals attending the programme be identified and met?	
11. What learning activities and exercises will be incorporated in the programme to extend and reinforce learning and ensure that active learning takes place?	
12. Is it certain that participants will be able to absorb and use the volume of material included in the programme?	
13. How will participants be encouraged to put what they have learnt into practice?	
14. How will the interest of participants be maintained throughout the programme?	
15. How will learning be checked and the pace adjusted to ensure progressive learning?	
16. How will visual aids be used to support learning?	
17. What will be done to brief speakers on content, length (no more than 30–40 minutes) and use of visual aids (no more than 15 PowerPoint slides each with no more than six bullet points of six words, and simple diagrams).	
18. What material should participants take away with them after the event?	
19. How will the immediate reactions of participants be obtained?	
20. How will the impact of the programme after the event be evaluated?	

Decide on arrangements

A checklist on points to consider when arranging the event is set out in Exhibit 64.3.

EXHIBIT 64.3   Event arrangements checklist

Question	Answer
1. Who is running the event – in-house or outsourced?	
2. How many people will be attending?	
3. Where will the event be held – in-house or at an external location?	
4. What rooms will be required, eg a main conference or lecture rooms and smaller (syndicate) rooms for 'breaking out sessions' (groups of participants breaking out from the main session to conduct an exercise or hold a discussion)?	
5. What facilities will be required such as projectors, flipcharts or any other equipment to be used for training purposes?	
6. Will there be a technician available to facilitate the use of projectors for PowerPoint presentations?	
7. What arrangements need to be made for eating (lunch) and refreshments (tea and coffee)?	
8. What is the budget for the event?	
9. What is the estimated expenditure?	
10. Who is to direct or chair the event?	
11. Who are the speakers/trainers?	
12. Who will invite them?	
13. Have the chair and the speakers/trainers been briefed?	
14. What advance information on the event (notice, programme or brochure) needs to be prepared?	
15. What material to be used in the event (handouts, discussion or exercise briefs or case studies) needs to be prepared in advance?	

EXHIBIT 64.4   Evaluation form

EVALUATION FORM

Name of event..

Date...

Evaluation of sessions

For each session assess on a scale of 1 to 5 (1 = poor, 5 = excellent):

- the content of the session: how interesting, how useful
- how well the session was presented
- the quality of the visual aids

Session	Rating			Comments
	Content	Presentation	Visual aids	
1				
2				
3				
4				
5				
6				

Evaluation of arrangements

	Rating: 1 to 5	Comments
Joining instructions		
Food and refreshments		
Accommodation		

Overall evaluation of the event

How would you rate the overall value of the event on a scale of 1 to 5?	Comments (please give reasons for your evaluation)

Distribute information on the event

Information in the form of notices, programmes and brochures are distributed to those who are likely to nominate participants for the event. The information should make it clear who should attend and why they should attend, ie the benefits to them and the organization.

Deliver the learning

This should not present too many problems if the planning and preparation for the event have been carried out systematically. However, a flexible approach is desirable because all learning events differ according to the characteristics of the learners, whose learning needs and reactions will vary. Fine tuning will be necessary throughout the programme.

Evaluate

Evaluation can take the form of an immediate assessment of the reactions of participants by getting them to complete an evaluation form (a 'happy sheet'), as illustrated in Exhibit 64.4. A more searching evaluation can be carried out by adding the other three Kirkpatrick levels (see Chapter 24) to the first 'reactions' level and also summing up the extent to which the event met expectations (Exhibit 64.5). A final overall evaluation can be made using the checklist set out in Exhibit 64.6.

EXHIBIT 64.5   Evaluation levels and return on expectations assessment

Level or type of evaluation	Evaluation
1. *Reactions*: how those who participated in the training have reacted to it. In a sense, it is a measure of immediate customer satisfaction.	
2. *Learning*: this level obtains information on the extent to which learning objectives have been attained. It will aim to find how much knowledge was acquired, what skills were developed or improved, and the extent to which attitudes have changed in the desired direction.	
3. *Behaviour*: this level evaluates the extent to which behaviour has changed as required when people attending the programme have returned to their jobs.	
4. *Results*: this is the ultimate level of evaluation and provides the basis for assessing the benefits of the training against its costs. The objective is to determine the added value of learning and development programmes – how they contribute to raising organizational performance significantly above its previous level.	
5. *Return on expectation*: this is the extent to which the anticipated benefits of any learning investment have been realized. This starts with a definition of expectations – a statement of what the learning event is aiming to achieve at the individual, departmental and, importantly, the organizational level. This would also involve deciding how achievement will be measured – the success criteria. These criteria would be used as the basis for evaluation.	

EXHIBIT 64.6   Overall evaluation of a learning event

Questions *To what extent have*:	Answers
1. Learning needs been evaluated as a basis for the event?	
2. Clear objectives been set for the outcomes of the event or programme?	
3. Success criteria and methods of measuring success been established?	
4. A blend of learning methods been used that are appropriate for the established needs of those taking part?	
5. The responsibilities for planning and delivering the event been clarified?	
6. Those responsible for the learning activity been well-qualified in whatever role they are expected to play?	
7. Adequate resources have been allocated to the event?	
8. Arrangements ensured that the event was implemented effectively as planned, within its budget and in accordance with defined standards?	
9. Arrangements been made to monitor the planning and delivery of the event to ensure that it meets the defined objectives and standards?	
10. The achievements of the event been evaluated against the success criteria and swift corrective action taken to deal with any problems?	

65
Performance management

Purpose of the toolkit

The purpose of this toolkit is to provide practical guidance to those who want to review existing performance management systems and processes or to develop and implement new ones. The toolkit can be used by line managers as a guide to their performance management practices. It can also be the basis for developing understanding and skills through coaching, mentoring, formal training and e-learning.

Structure of the toolkit

The toolkit is divided into the five sections described below and illustrated in Figure 65.1.

1 The analytical and diagnostic toolkit covers the analysis of present arrangements and the diagnosis of the causes of any problems. It provides the basis for the design or modification of a performance management system.

2 The design toolkit covers the development of the constituents of a performance management system – performance planning and agreements, goal setting, feedback, performance analysis and assessment, rating, coaching, and the link to reward and personal development.

3 The implementation toolkit covers the processes of communicating, briefing, training and pilot testing, which must be carried out to ensure the successful operation of performance management.

4 The operations toolkit covers the main performance management activities of completing performance agreements, goal setting, performance review, managing managerial performance and dealing with under-performers.

5 The evaluation toolkit covers methods of evaluating the effectiveness of performance management through checklists and surveys.

Analysis and diagnosis

It is necessary to analyse and understand the strengths and weaknesses of the present arrangements. As far as possible the analysis and diagnosis should involve line managers and employees through surveys, workshops and focus groups, using the checklists in Exhibits 65.1 to 65.3.

Performance management goals

Possible goals for performance management are set out in Exhibit 65.1.

FIGURE 65.1   The performance management design, development, implementation and maintenance pathway

EXHIBIT 65.1   Performance management goals

Possible goals	Importance	Effectiveness
Align individual and organizational objectives		
Improve organizational performance		
Develop a high performance culture		
Improve individual performance		
Provide basis for personal development		
Increase motivation and engagement		
Inform contribution/performance pay decisions		
Measure performance against quantified objectives		
Encourage appropriate behaviours – 'living the values'		
Clarify performance expectations in the role		
Identify potential		
Identify poor performers		

Scale: 10 = high, 1 = low

Performance management gap analysis

The gap analysis shown in Exhibit 65.2 assesses the extent to which desirable characteristics of performance management exist in the organization. It provides the basis for the design and development of performance management systems and processes.

Start gap analysis with senior management, line managers and staff by getting them to complete the grid individually or in groups by marking with an X the position in which they think the organization is at present and an O where it is believed the organization should be placed. A gap between X and O – between what is and what should be – reveals areas for development. The next step is to get those involved to discuss and agree priorities.

EXHIBIT 65.2   Gap analysis of performance management practices

Desirable characteristics	X = current O = desired	Undesirable characteristics
Performance management is perceived by top management as a key process for managing the business.		Top management pays lip service to performance management.
Line managers are committed to performance management.		Line managers see performance management as a chore.
Line managers have the skills to manage performance effectively.		There are serious deficiencies in the skill levels displayed by line managers.
Performance management is owned and driven by line managers.		Performance management is seen as owned by and the preserve of HR.
Employees believe that performance management operates fairly.		Employees do not trust line managers to review their performance fairly.
There is hard evidence that performance management improves business performance in our organization.		There is no evidence that performance management improves business performance in our organization.
Performance management is based on agreed definitions of roles in terms of key result areas and competency requirements.		Performance management is not related to the reality of what people are expected to do and how they are expected to behave.
Clear objectives and performance standards are agreed at the performance planning stage.		Objectives and standards, if agreed at all, are vague or undemanding.
Methods of measuring performance (key performance indicators) and assessing levels of competence are agreed at the performance planning stage.		No attempt is made to agree performance or competency indicators.
Performance development plans are agreed at the planning stage.		Performance development planning is generally neglected.
Performance management in the form of review and feedback is practised throughout the year.		Performance appraisal takes place, if at all, as a dishonest annual ritual.
Line managers provide helpful feedback and support during formal reviews.		The quality of feedback and support is generally inadequate.
Line managers recognize their responsibility for coaching people and act accordingly.		Coaching by line management is sparse and often inadequate.

Analysis of performance review practices

The checklist in Exhibit 65.3 can be used to analyse performance review practices.

EXHIBIT 65.3　Analysis of performance review practices

Review practice	Fully in place	Partly in place	Not in place	Action
1. The content of the performance review is based on a role profile.				
2. Performance expectations are agreed with employees.				
3. Performance objectives are aligned with business goals.				
4. The review is based on evidence in the form of observable job behaviours.				
5. The review process is clearly defined for everyone involved.				
6. Employees participate fully in the review process.				
7. Reviewers are capable of making fair and consistent assessments.				
8. The review focuses on development and improvement needs.				
9. A higher authority checks and comments on reviews.				
10. Reviewers are trained in feedback and assessment techniques.				

Diagnosis

Following the analysis of any problems, their causes and possible remedies should be identified. Exhibit 65.4 shows how they can be summarized.

EXHIBIT 65.4   Diagnostic summary

List any significant problems identified by the analysis and indicate the likely causes of the problems and their possible remedies.		
Problem	**Likely cause**	**Possible remedy**

Design toolkit

The design should be based on the initial analysis and diagnosis and should involve stakeholders, ie senior management, line managers, employees and their representatives. It is advisable to build on existing practices in order to promote acceptance and assimilation. The steps in the design programme are illustrated in Figure 65.2.

FIGURE 65.2   Steps in the design programme

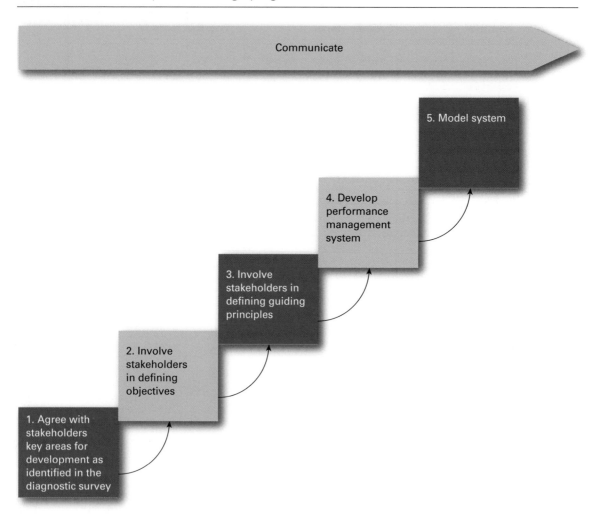

Areas for development

The areas for development will have been identified if a diagnostic survey has been undertaken. They can be summarized under the headings shown in Exhibit 65.5.

EXHIBIT 65.5   Areas for development

Area for development	What needs to be done	How it can be done
Performance planning and agreement		
Goal setting		
Providing feedback		
Conducting performance reviews		
Assessment and rating		
Coaching		
Documentation		
Use of computers		
Increasing the commitment of line managers to performance management		
Developing performance management skills of line managers		
Educating employees generally on the purpose of performance management, how it works, how it affects them and what part they play		

Analysis of possible objectives and success criteria

It is essential that everyone involved is clear about the objectives of performance management and the criteria that will be used to evaluate the extent to which the objectives have been successfully achieved. Managers and employees should be involved in setting objectives and success criteria. They should consider not only what performance management will do for the organization but also what they hope it will do for them. It is advisable, however, not to try to attempt too much, especially when this is a new development. Some prioritization of objectives may therefore be required. A framework for analysis is given in Exhibit 65.6.

EXHIBIT 65.6 Analysis of possible objectives

Possible objectives	For the organization	For line managers	For employees	Possible success criteria
	Rate the possible objective on a scale of 1–5 where: 1 = crucial, 2 = important, 3 = not sure, 4 = not very important, 5 = irrelevant			
Improve performance	1 2 3 4 5	1 2 3 4 5	1 2 3 4 5	
Develop a performance culture	1 2 3 4 5	1 2 3 4 5	1 2 3 4 5	
Identify people with high potential	1 2 3 4 5	1 2 3 4 5	1 2 3 4 5	
Identify under-performers	1 2 3 4 5	1 2 3 4 5	1 2 3 4 5	
Align individual and organizational objectives	1 2 3 4 5	1 2 3 4 5	1 2 3 4 5	
Provide the basis for personal development	1 2 3 4 5	1 2 3 4 5	1 2 3 4 5	
Enable people to know where they stand	1 2 3 4 5	1 2 3 4 5	1 2 3 4 5	
Provide the basis for performance pay decisions	1 2 3 4 5	1 2 3 4 5	1 2 3 4 5	
Other	1 2 3 4 5	1 2 3 4 5	1 2 3 4 5	

Development of performance management system

The development of a performance management system involves selecting and describing the components of the system; see Exhibit 65.7.

EXHIBIT 65.7 The components of the performance management system

Component	Contents	Considerations
Performance planning and agreement	• Agreeing role profiles • Agreeing objectives (see also goal setting) • Agreeing performance measures • Agreeing development needs (see also personal development planning) • Agreeing areas for performance improvement • Recording decisions in an agreement	• Format of role profiles • Methods of preparing and updating role profiles • Choice of measures • Format of agreement
Goal setting	• Identifying key result areas • Identifying key performance indicators • Agreeing targets and standards of performance	• Methods of goal setting • Ensuring 'SMART' goals are agreed • Selecting appropriate measures
Personal development planning	• Deciding areas for development • Planning methods of development	• Format of development plan • Approaches to development • Emphasis on self-directed development
Feedback	• Provision during year • Provision during formal review	• Developing feedback skills • Use of informal and formal feedback
Performance reviews	• Purpose • Content • Timing	• Use of informal reviews throughout year • Preparation for formal reviews • Conduct of formal reviews
Performance analysis	• Methodology • Use of metrics	• Performance analysis skills • Data collection and analysis
Performance assessment and rating	• Use of overall assessment • Use of rating • Use of forced distribution rating	• Provision of guidelines for overall assessments • Arguments for and against rating • Decisions on type of rating to be used, if at all • Developing assessment/rating skills • Providing rating guidelines, if appropriate • Arguments for and against forced distribution
Link to performance pay	• How assessment/ratings will inform performance pay decisions • The timing of pay reviews and performance reviews	• Arguments for and against performance pay
Coaching	• Methods • Responsibility of line managers	• Developing coaching skills
Administration	• Documentation • Use of computers	• Design of documentation • Design of computer system • Decision on extent to which a standard approach to performance management should be used

Implementation toolkit

The implementation programme, as illustrated in Figure 65.3, should start with a pilot test of the performance management process and approaches to communication and training that can inform full communication and training programmes and, subject to any modifications required, the launch of the system.

FIGURE 65.3   Implementation programme

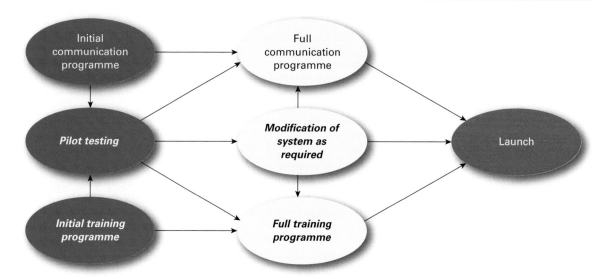

Pilot testing

Before embarking on full implementation it is essential to pilot test the process. This should be done in two or three departments where the managers are sympathetic to performance management and will therefore give it their backing. The test should be preceded by a briefing and training for participants in the processes and skills they should use. Ideally, it should extend over the whole of the performance management cycle, ie 12 months, but a period of between six and 12 months will provide an adequate test. The purpose of the test, which should be explained to those taking part, is to ensure that an appropriate and acceptable form of performance management is introduced. Another way of testing is to do it top-down – get senior managers to try it out first so that they know all the wrinkles before cascading it throughout the organization.

The rating questionnaires shown in Exhibits 65.8 and 65.9 can be used to evaluate the test.

EXHIBIT 65.8   Pilot test questionnaire for managers

Rate the following statements on a scale of 1–5 where:
11 = fully agree, 2 = agree, 3 = not sure, 4 = disagree, 5 = strongly disagree

1. The objectives and processes of performance management were described clearly to me.	1 2 3 4 5
2. I received good training in performance management skills.	1 2 3 4 5
3. I had no difficulty in agreeing role profiles.	1 2 3 4 5
4. I had no difficulty in agreeing objectives.	1 2 3 4 5
5. I had no difficulty in agreeing performance and development plans.	1 2 3 4 5
6. I was able to monitor performance well, providing feedback and coaching as required.	1 2 3 4 5
7. The performance review meeting went very well.	1 2 3 4 5
8. I was able to assess performance accurately and fairly.	1 2 3 4 5
9. I believe that performance management will enable me to do my job as a manager better.	1 2 3 4 5
10. I believe that performance management is a waste of time.	1 2 3 4 5

EXHIBIT 65.9   Pilot test questionnaire for employees

Rate the following statements on a scale of 1–5 where:
1 = fully agree, 2 = agree, 3 = not sure, 4 = disagree, 5 = strongly disagree

1. The objectives and processes of performance management were described clearly to me.	1 2 3 4 5
2. I received good training in performance management skills.	1 2 3 4 5
3. I had no difficulty in agreeing my role profile.	1 2 3 4 5
4. I had no difficulty in agreeing my objectives.	1 2 3 4 5
5. I had no difficulty in agreeing my performance and development plans.	1 2 3 4 5
6. I was able to monitor my own performance well and was provided with feedback and with coaching as required.	1 2 3 4 5
7. The performance review meeting went very well.	1 2 3 4 5
8. I was able to assess performance accurately and fairly.	1 2 3 4 5
9. I believe that performance management will enable me to do my job better.	1 2 3 4 5
10 I believe that performance management is a waste of time.	1 2 3 4 5

Performance management operations toolkit

The operations toolkit is concerned with the major performance management process of agreeing performance and development plans, goal setting, providing feedback, preparing for and conducting performance reviews, coaching and dealing with under-performers. A summary of performance management activities over the year is given in Exhibit 65.10.

EXHIBIT 65.10   Summary of performance management activities over the year

Start of year	Performance and development agreement	• Define role profiles, updating as necessary. • Ensure that role profiles set out updated key result areas and competency requirements. • Define goals and standards of performance. • Identify and define key performance indicators. • Draw up performance development plans. • Draw up personal development plans.
Continuing dialogue	Managing performance throughout the year	• Monitor progress and review evidence of achievement. • Provide informal feedback as required. • Provide coaching as required. • Update role profiles and objectives as necessary.
End of year	Performance review	• Prepare for performance review by analysing achievements (work and learning) against objectives. • Identify specific strengths and weaknesses on the basis of evidence. • Assess overall performance. • Provide feedback. • Use conclusions of performance review as the basis for next year's performance and development agreement.

The evaluation toolkit

It is essential to evaluate the effectiveness of performance management in meeting its objectives.

Evaluation against success criteria

The performance management activities need to be evaluated against success criteria, as shown in Exhibit 65.11. Unless such evaluation takes place regularly and leads to any remedial action required, the system is likely to decline.

EXHIBIT 65.11   Evaluation of performance management against success criteria

Evaluate effectiveness as follows: 1 = high level of achievement, 2 = acceptable level of achievement, 3 = poor level of achievement			
Measures of improved performance by reference to key performance indicators in such terms as output, productivity, sales, quality, customer satisfaction, return on investment.	1	2	3
Achievement of defined and agreed objectives for performance management.	1	2	3
Measures of employee engagement before and after the introduction of performance management and then at regular intervals.	1	2	3
Assessments of reactions of managers and employees to performance management.	1	2	3
Assessment of the extent to which managers and employees have reached agreement on goals and performance development plans.	1	2	3
Performance development plans agreed and implemented.	1	2	3
Personal development plans agreed and implemented.	1	2	3

Evaluation by survey of reactions

The questionnaires shown in Exhibits 65.8 and 65.9 for managers and employees respectively can be used to evaluate how well performance management is functioning on a continuing basis.

66
Strategic reward

Purpose of the toolkit

Strategic reward means using a systematic approach to ensuring that reward policy and practice support the achievement of business goals and provide fair and equitable pay for employees. This is achieved by analysing the context and needs, assessing the alternatives available, and developing and implementing reward strategies. This toolkit aims to provide the framework and means for making such an approach.

The reward strategy development framework

A framework for developing reward strategy is shown in Figure 66.1.

FIGURE 66.1   The reward strategy development framework

Analysis of reward strategy and practice

The analysis of current reward strategy and practice is the starting point. It can be conducted using the following tools:

Exhibit 66.1   Analysis of reward strategy
Exhibit 66.2   Analysis of current reward practices
Exhibit 66.3   Reward attitude survey

EXHIBIT 66.1   Analysis of reward strategy

The reward strategy:	In full	Mostly	Partly	Not at all
Is aligned to business strategy.				
Has clearly defined goals based on business objectives.				
Well-articulated guiding principles exist.				
Provides a framework for reward decisions.				
Is long term.				
Is flexible enough to change when circumstances require.				

EXHIBIT 66.2   Analysis of current reward practices

Statement	Fully agree	Partly agree	Partly disagree	Fully disagree	Comments
1. We have well-defined and understood reward guiding principles.					
2. Our reward system effectively enhances the engagement of people.					
3. We implement our policy on levels of pay compared with market rates.					
4. We pay insufficient attention to non-financial rewards.					
5. We are satisfied with our methods of deciding on internal relativities.					

EXHIBIT 66.2   *Continued*

Statement	Fully agree	Partly agree	Partly disagree	Fully disagree	Comments
6. There is an unacceptable incidence of grade drift (unjustified upgradings).					
7. We are vulnerable to an equal pay claim.					
8. Our rates of pay are uncompetitive.					
9. We do not have adequate data on market rates.					
10. We have too many grades in our pay structure.					
11. Our grade structure is too complex.					
12. People are fairly rewarded according to their contribution.					
13. Our reward system does not succeed in motivating people.					
14. Our reward system helps to attract and retain high quality people.					
15. We get value for money from our reward system.					
16. Our performance management processes work well.					
17. We have an excellent and competitive range of employee benefits.					
18. There is room for more choice by employees on benefits.					
19. We spend too much on employee benefits.					
20. Our pension scheme is too expensive.					

EXHIBIT 66.3   Reward attitude survey

Please state the extent to which you agree or disagree with the following statements by placing a circle around the number that most closely matches your opinion.

	Strongly agree	Agree	Disagree	Strongly disagree
1. My contribution is adequately rewarded	1	2	3	4
2. Pay increases are handled fairly	1	2	3	4
3. I feel that my pay does not reflect my performance	1	2	3	4
4. My pay compares favourably with what I could get elsewhere	1	2	3	4
5. I am not paid fairly in comparison with other people doing similar work in the organization	1	2	3	4
6. I think the organization's pay policy is overdue for a review	1	2	3	4
7. Grading decisions are made fairly	1	2	3	4
8. I am not clear how decisions about my pay are made	1	2	3	4
9. I understand how my job has been graded	1	2	3	4
10. I get good feedback on my performance	1	2	3	4
11. I am clear about what I am expected to achieve	1	2	3	4
12. I like my job	1	2	3	4
13. The performance pay scheme encourages better performance	1	2	3	4
14. I am proud to work for the organization	1	2	3	4
15. I understand how my pay can progress	1	2	3	4
16. The job evaluation scheme works fairly	1	2	3	4
17. The benefits package compares well with those in other organizations	1	2	3	4
18. I would like more choice about the benefits I receive	1	2	3	4
19. I feel motivated after my performance review meeting	1	2	3	4
20. I do not understand the pay policies of the organization	1	2	3	4

Developing and implementing reward strategy

The formulation of reward strategy can be described as a process for developing a sense of direction and making the best use of resources. The steps required to develop it are:

1   Ensure that the reward strategy supports the achievement of the business and HR strategies by considering the implications of the business strategy and how integration can be achieved (Exhibits 66.4 and 66.5).

2   Define reward goals (Exhibit 66.6).

3   Review reward options in relation to reward goals and practicality (Exhibit 66.7).

4   Formulate strategy with reference to guidelines (Exhibit 66.8).

5   Implement (Exhibit 66.9).

EXHIBIT 66.4   Implications for reward of business strategy

	Possible elements	Actual elements	Implications for reward strategy
Business strategy	• Growth – revenue/profit • Maximize shareholder value • Growth through acquisitions/ mergers • Growth in production/servicing facilities • Product development • Market development • Price/cost leadership		
Business drivers	• Innovation • Maximize added value • Productivity • Customer service • Quality • Satisfy stakeholders – investors, employees, elected representatives • Price/cost leadership		

EXHIBIT 66.5 Integration of HR and reward strategies

HR strategy area	Possible reward strategy contribution	Proposed action
Resourcing	• Total reward approaches that help to make the organization a great place in which to work. • Competitive pay structures that help to attract and retain high quality people.	
Performance management	• Contingent pay schemes that contribute to the motivation and engagement of people. • Performance management processes that promote continuous improvement and encourage people to uphold core values.	
Talent management	• Non-financial rewards such as recognition and opportunities for growth and development. • Policies that recognize talented people for their contribution. • Career-linked grade and pay structure, for example a career family structure.	
Learning and development	• Performance management processes that identify learning needs and how they can be satisfied. • Career family structures that define career ladders in terms of knowledge and skill requirements.	
Work environment	• Total reward approaches that emphasize the importance of enhancing the work environment. • Work–life balance policies.	

EXHIBIT 66.6   Rating framework for reward strategy goals

Goals	Importance*	Effectiveness*
Reinforce the achievement of organizational goals.		
Recruit and retain staff of the required calibre.		
Facilitate staff mobility.		
Strong relationship between pay and performance.		
Reinforce organizational values.		
Motivating for employees.		
Cost-effective.		
Well communicated and understood by employees.		
Managed effectively in practice by line managers.		
Efficient to operate/maintain.		
Flexible, to react to change.		
Others (list).		

* Scale: 10 = high; 1 = low

EXHIBIT 66.7   Review reward options in relation to reward goals and practicality

Strategy area		Examples of possible solutions	Yes √	No √	Modify
Financial	Total reward	Introduce total reward approach			
	Job evaluation	Develop new analytical scheme			
		Develop new non-analytical scheme			
		Modify existing scheme			
		Rely on analytical matching			
	Grade and pay structure	Reduce number of grades considerably (broad-grading)			
		Introduce broad-banding			
		Develop job or career family structure			
		Replace pay spine			
	Contingent pay	Introduce performance-related pay (not pay spine)			
		Introduce contribution-related pay (not pay spine)			
		Introduce variable pay (bonus) scheme			
	Employee benefits	Revise benefits provision			
		Introduce flexible benefits			
	Pensions	Change to defined contribution scheme			
Non-financial	Recognition	Introduce formal recognition scheme			
	Scope for development and growth	Improve learning and development programmes			
	Autonomy	Encourage, guide and train line managers to increase autonomy			
	Working environment	Develop 'great place to work' policies			
	Work–life balance	Introduce more comprehensive work–life balance policies			

EXHIBIT 66.8   Formulating strategy with reference to guidelines

To what extent does the reward strategy:	Answer
Support the business strategy?	
Support the HR strategy?	
Have clearly defined goals, success criteria and deliverables?	
Provide a clear basis for future action?	
Demonstrate that it can readily be implemented?	

EXHIBIT 66.9   Implementation checklist

Have you:

- Specified the objectives of the project, its success criteria and its deliverables?
- Defined who is to be responsible for directing and managing the project and the degree of authority they have?
- Set out what should be done (activities), who does what, and when it will be done?
- Involved senior managers/heads of department as sponsors, to provide comment, guidance, support and encouragement?
- Involved line managers and staff in the strategy development, planning and implementation programme?
- Communicated to all concerned the objectives of the programme, how it will take place and how they will be affected?
- Broken down the project into stages with defined starting and completion dates to produce the programme?
- Clarified inter-dependencies?
- Defined resource requirements – people, outside advisers, finance?
- Defined methods of control and risk management, eg progress reports, meetings?
- Ensured that everyone knows what is expected of them and has the briefing, guidance and resources required?
- Seen that progress is monitored continuously against the plan as well as at formal meetings?
- Ensured that corrective action is taken as required; for example, amending timings, re-allocating resources?
- Evaluated progress and the end result against objectives, success criteria and deliverables?

68
Job evaluation

Purpose and contents of the toolkit

The toolkit deals with the steps required to develop the most popular form of job evaluation, ie point-factor rating. However, it also refers to the design of analytical matching schemes, which can function independently but are often associated with a point-factor scheme. A typical method is to design and test a point-factor scheme and then use the factors included in that scheme as the basis for analytical matching. Point-factor and analytical matching schemes are described in Chapter 29.

The job evaluation review and development sequence

The following sequence of actions is required to develop a point-factor scheme with an associated analytical matching process:

1 Analyse present job evaluation arrangements.

2 Decide approach to job evaluation in principle.

3 Decide on features of new scheme.

4 Prepare project programme.

5 Develop basic factor plan.

6 Test basic factor plan.

7 Amend basic factor plan as necessary.

8 Decide on weighting.

9 Produce full factor plan.

10 Consider use of computer-aided evaluation.

11 Apply scheme to benchmark jobs.

12 Develop analytical matching approach.

These steps are described below.

Analyse present job evaluation arrangements

A preliminary assessment, using the questionnaire shown in Exhibit 68.1, can be made of whether or not the present arrangements for job evaluation should be replaced or whether to introduce formal job evaluation.

Decide approach to job evaluation in principle

The choices available and the factors to be taken into account in making them are set out in Exhibit 68.2.

EXHIBIT 68.1   Analysis of current job evaluation scheme

Statement	Fully agree	Partly agree	Partly disagree	Fully disagree
1. The present arrangements for valuing and grading jobs are quite satisfactory.				
2. Our scheme ensures that there are no grading problems.				
3. The factors in our scheme are no longer appropriate.				
4. Our scheme has decayed.				
5. Our scheme prevents grade drift.				
6. Our scheme would provide a good defence in an equal pay case.				
7. The weightings of factors in the scheme are inappropriate.				
8. There is no gender bias in the scheme's factors and weightings.				
9. The scheme is bureaucratic, paper-intensive and time wasting.				
10. People generally understand how the scheme works.				

EXHIBIT 68.2   Choice of approach to job evaluation

Choice	Factors to be taken into account	Decision
Make no change	• Extent to which present arrangements are satisfactory • Need to avoid disruption • Cost considerations	
Introduce new point-factor scheme or substantially amend existing one	• Advantages – analytical, provide equal pay claim defence • Disadvantages – time-consuming, bureaucratic • The fact that this is by far the most popular approach	
Introduce analytical matching	• Advantages – analytical, much less time-consuming than point-factor rating • Disadvantages – may not resolve equity problems, not a guaranteed defence in an equal pay case, need to be underpinned by point-factor evaluation	
Introduce combined scheme, ie an underpinning point-factor scheme used to develop grade structure and as back-up and an analytical matching scheme for ongoing evaluations	• Provides support to analytical matching • Reduces time for ongoing evaluations • Provides defence in equal pay case • Can be complex and difficult to understand	
Purchase 'ready-made' scheme from consultant	• Scheme well-established • Consultants experienced in implementation • Linked to market rate database • May not fit culture and circumstances of organization • Could be expensive	
Develop own 'tailor-made' scheme	• Scheme should fit • Those involved in development should 'own' scheme • But, untried and could be time-consuming and expensive to develop in terms of the human resources required	
Consider using a computer-aided approach	• The development of a computer-aided approach usually takes place after the factor plan has been finalized and a paper scheme (ie one that has not been computerized) has been produced. • A final decision is not required at this stage although it may be agreed that one of the proprietary brands should be tested when the paper scheme is ready.	

Decide on features of new scheme

The options are listed in Exhibit 68.3. The decisions made at this stage are interim and could be amended later.

EXHIBIT 68.3   Choice of features

Design area	Options	Interim decision
Job evaluation factors	There will be a choice on the number and types of factors. The number of factors can range from 3 to 14 and the average is 6.	
Factor levels	There will be choice on the number of levels and whether or not there should be the same number of levels in each factor. Typically, there are five or six levels.	
Scoring progression	Scoring intervals between levels can be either arithmetic or geometrical	
Weighting	Schemes can be unweighted, or if they are weighted, this can be explicit or implicit.	

Prepare project programme

A project programme should be prepared in as much detail as possible. This will provide the basis for managing the project. A programme set out as a bar chart is illustrated in Exhibit 68.4.

EXHIBIT 68.4   Project plan bar chart

Activities	Months
	1 2 3 4 5 6 7 8 9 10 11 12 13 14 15 16 17 18 19 20 21 22 23 24
1. Agree deliverables	
2. Design and test scheme	
3. Evaluate benchmark jobs	
4. Design grade structure	
5. Evaluate remaining jobs	
6. Conduct market survey	
7. Design the pay structure	
8. Implement	

Amend basic factor plan as necessary

The initial test will almost certainly reveal the need to amend factor-level definitions and it may indicate that more radical changes to the factor plan are required, for example in the choice of factors or the number of levels. Following any amendments it is desirable to retest the basic plan. This is time-consuming, which is why a job evaluation exercise can be a lengthy process. But this is the time to get it right.

Decide on weighting

Weighting recognizes that there are differences in the importance of factors by allocating more or less points to them. The choice is between weighting and not weighting factors. If weighting is considered desirable, possibly on the basis of the initial test of the basic factor plan, there is a choice between explicit and implicit weighting. *Explicit weighting* means increasing the maximum points available for what were regarded as more important factors. *Implicit weighting* means allocating more levels, and therefore points, to some factors than others.

The most common but highly judgemental approach is for the project team to discuss and agree subjective views on which factors are more important and allocate additional points or extra levels accordingly. Another method of deciding on explicit weighting, ie extra points, is to get each member of the team to distribute 100 points amongst the factors, which are then revealed to the whole team, who reach an agreement on the most acceptable distribution. This discussion may be expected to take account of guiding principles such as that no factor will have a weighting of less than 5 per cent or more than 30 per cent.

The weighted plan should be retested on the test jobs to ensure that it produces valid results.

Produce full factor plan

The basic factor plan (the range of factors and level definitions) produced after the initial test will be finalized, taking into account decisions on weighting.

Consider use of computer-aided evaluation

Consideration at this stage can be given to the possibility of introducing computer-aided evaluation. The advantages and disadvantages of computer-aided evaluation are set out in Exhibit 68.8.

EXHIBIT 68.8 Advantages and disadvantages of computer-aided job evaluation

Advantages	Disadvantages
• Greater consistency may be achieved – the same input information gives the same output result. • The speed of evaluations can be increased. • Facilities are provided for sorting, analysing, reporting on the input information and system outputs and for record-keeping on a database. • The resources required are reduced.	• May be expensive. • May be elaborate or have the feel of a 'black box'. • May lack transparency. • Means abandoning the involvement of employees and their representatives in the traditional panel approach.

A computer-aided system is usually based on the paper-based system's factor plan. So it needs to be tested on the same jobs used for testing the paper-based system to ensure that it replicates the paper scheme's results.

Apply scheme to benchmark jobs

The final paper or computer-aided scheme is used to evaluate benchmark jobs (except in a small organization, where all jobs may be evaluated). These are typical jobs that represent the different occupations and levels of work in an organization and are used as points of reference with which other jobs can be compared and evaluated. The evaluated benchmark jobs provide the basis for designing a grade structure and are used in analytical matching, as described below. They will include the test jobs but it may be necessary to select additional ones to provide a sufficient number for designing a grade structure.

Develop analytical matching approach

Analytical matching involves matching jobs to be evaluated on a factor-by-factor basis, either with analytical grade definitions (grade profiles) or analytical job descriptions for benchmark posts (role profiles). The development sequence is illustrated in Figure 68.1.

FIGURE 68.1 Development sequence for analytical matching job evaluation scheme

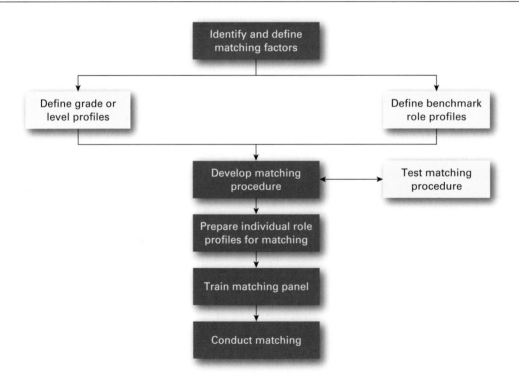

Where analytical matching is developed to support a point-factor scheme, the first two steps will involve looking at the pattern of evaluation results for each grade and developing grade/level profiles that reflect the typical pattern of results, factor by factor.

Matching procedure

The matching procedure may be defined as a formal protocol that specifies:

- What constitutes a perfect match, ie where all the elements in the role profile match all the elements in the grade or benchmark role profile.

- The number of matches of individual elements required to indicate that a profile match is justified, for example six out of 10, but it is usual to restrict the mismatches allowed to fairly small variations – if there are any large ones, the match would be invalidated.

- Any elements that must match for there to be a profile match, for example it may be decided that there must be a match for an element covering knowledge and skills.

- The procedure for grading if there has been a mismatch; this may specify a full evaluation of the role if the matching process is underpinned by a point-factor or proprietary analytical scheme.

69
Grade and pay structure design

Purpose of the toolkit

Graded pay structures are a fundamental aspect of base pay management. This toolkit focuses on the design of the most common form of grade and pay structures, namely broad-graded, career family and job family.

The grade and pay structure design sequence

The process of grade and pay structure design is shown in Figure 69.1.

FIGURE 69.1   The grade and pay structure design sequence

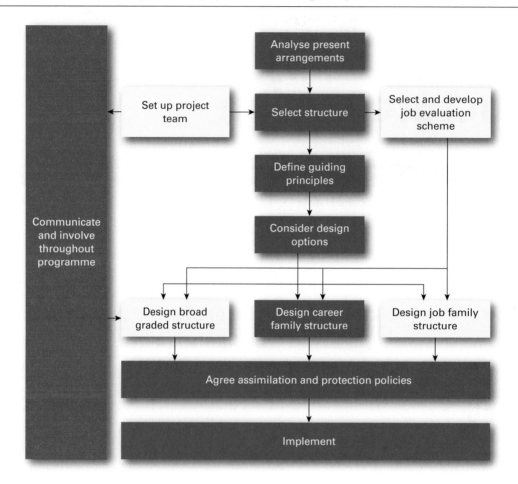

Analysis of present arrangements

Line managers, staff and staff representatives should be involved in an analysis of the present arrangement to indicate where changes may have to be made. The analysis could be based on the questionnaire set out in Exhibit 69.1. Use could be made of surveys, special workshops or focus groups, or it could be discussed in a consultative committee.

EXHIBIT 69.1   Analysis of present grade and pay structure arrangements

Statement	Fully agree	Partly agree	Partly disagree	Fully disagree
1. The present grade and pay structure is quite satisfactory.				
2. We have no problems in grading jobs within the structure.				
3. There are too many anomalies (under- or over-graded jobs).				
4. The structure no longer fits the way work is organized.				
5. Pay levels are competitive.				
6. The structure is easy to manage and control.				
7. The structure provides adequate scope for pay progression.				
8. The structure does not contribute to the creation of a gender gap.				
9. The structure is inflexible.				
10. People generally understand and accept how their jobs are graded.				

Choice of structure

Assuming that the analysis indicates that radical action is required, a choice needs to be made on which type of structure is appropriate. The choice can be based on an analysis of the features and advantages and disadvantages of different structures, as summarized in Exhibit 69.2, and an assessment of the criteria for when they are appropriate (Exhibit 69.3).

EXHIBIT 69.2 Summary description of most common grade and pay structures

Type of structure	Features	Advantages	Disadvantages
Broad-graded	• A sequence of between 6 and 9 grades • Fairly broad pay ranges eg 40–50% • Progression linked to contribution and may be controlled by thresholds or zones	As for narrow-graded structures but in addition: • the broader grades can be defined more clearly • better control can be exercised over grade drift	• Too much scope for pay progression • Control mechanisms can be provided but they can be difficult to manage • May be costly
Career family	• Career families identified and defined • Career paths defined for each family in terms of key activities and competence requirements • Same grade and pay structure for each family	• Clarify career paths within and between families • Facilitate the achievement of equity between families and therefore equal pay • Facilitate level definitions	• Could be difficult to manage • May *appear* to be divisive if 'silos' emerge
Job family	• Separate grade and pay structures for job families containing similar jobs • Progression linked to competence and/or contribution	• May inhibit lateral career development • May be difficult to maintain internal equity between job families unless underpinned by job evaluation	• Facilitate pay differentiation between market groups • Define career paths against clear criteria • Can appear to be divisive

EXHIBIT 69.3   Criteria for assessing the extent to which a structure is appropriate

Type of structure	The structure is more likely to be appropriate when:
Broad-graded	• It is believed that if there is a relatively limited number of grades it will be possible to define and therefore differentiate them more accurately as an aid to better precision when grading jobs. • An existing narrow-graded structure is the main cause of grade drift because the structure cannot accommodate market factors. • A broad-banded structure has led to pay drift due to lack of management control. • It is considered that pay progression through grades can be related to contribution and that it is possible to introduce effective control mechanisms.
Career family	• There are distinct families and different career paths within and between families can be identified and defined. • There is a strong emphasis on career development in the organization. • Robust methods of defining professional, specialist and technical competencies exist. • It is believed to be inappropriate to vary pay structures between families.
Job family	As for career family plus: • There are distinct market groups that need to be rewarded differently. • The range of responsibility and the basis upon which levels exist vary between families.

Definition of guiding principles

Guiding principles for the design of the grade and pay structure need to be defined at this stage. An example of a set of guiding principles is given in Exhibit 69.4.

EXHIBIT 69.4   Example of grade and pay structure guiding principles

Grade and pay structures should:

- be appropriate to the culture, characteristics and needs of the organization and its employees;
- facilitate the management of relativities and the achievement of equity, fairness, consistency and transparency in managing gradings and pay;
- be capable of adapting to pressures arising from market rate changes and skill shortages;
- facilitate operational flexibility and continuous development;
- provide scope as required for rewarding performance, contribution and increases in skill and competence;
- clarify reward, lateral development and career opportunities;
- be constructed logically and clearly so that the basis upon which they operate can readily be communicated to employees;
- enable the organization to exercise control over the implementation of pay policies and budgets.

Design options

Whichever structure is selected, there will be a number of design options, as summarized in Exhibit 69.5.

EXHIBIT 69.5   Grade and pay structure design options

Design feature	Design considerations
Number of grades, levels or bands	• The range and types of roles to be covered by the structure. • The range of pay and job evaluation points scores to be accommodated. • The number of levels in the organizational hierarchy (this will be an important factor in a broad-banded structure). • Decisions on where grade boundaries should be placed following a job evaluation exercise that has produced a ranked order of jobs – this might identify the existence of clearly defined clusters of jobs at the various levels in the hierarchy between which there are significant differences in job size. • The potential for 'grade drift' (unjustified upgradings in response to pressure, lack of promotion opportunities or because job evaluation has been applied laxly), which can be increased if there are too many narrow grades.
Pay range spans	• Views on the scope that should be allowed for performance, contribution or career progression within grade. • Equal pay considerations – wide spans, especially extended incremental scales, are a major cause of pay gaps between men and women because women, who are more likely to have career breaks than men, may not have the same opportunity as men to progress to the upper regions of the range. • In a broad-banded structure, the range of market rates and job evaluation scores covering the jobs allocated to the band.
Differentials between pay ranges	• Differentials between pay ranges should provide scope to recognize increases in job size between successive grades. • If differentials are too close – less than 10% – many jobs become borderline cases, which can result in a proliferation of appeals and arguments about grading. • Large differentials below senior management level of more than 25% can create problems for marginal or borderline cases because of the amount at stake. • In most organizations with conventional grade structures a differential of between 15 and 20% is appropriate except, perhaps, at the highest levels.
Pay range overlap	• There is a choice on whether or not pay ranges should overlap and, if so, by how much. • Large overlaps can create equal pay problems if men are clustered at the top of their grades and women are at the lower end.
Pay progression	• There is a choice of methods of pay progression between the various forms of contingent pay, namely performance, competence or contribution-related and the fixed service-related increments common in the public sector.

Graded pay structure design

A graded pay structure involves first designing the grade structure and then deciding on the pay ranges that should be attached to it.

The two approaches to designing the grade structure are, 1) the derived method in which decisions on the grade structure are led by point-factor job evaluation, and 2) the pre-emptive method in which the number of grades is determined first and each grade is then defined as a basis for analytical matching or market pricing.

The derived method (use of point-factor job evaluation)

The derived method consists of the following steps:

1 Use point-factor job evaluation to produce a rank order of jobs according to their job evaluation scores.

2 Either, a) take a preliminary view on the preferred number of grades, or b) analyse the rank order to establish by inspection where jobs might be grouped into grades and how many grades emerge from this procedure.

3 Decide where the boundaries that will define grades should be placed in the rank order by analysing the rank order to identify any significant gaps in the points scores between adjacent jobs. These natural breaks in points scores will then constitute the boundaries between clusters of jobs, which can be allocated to adjacent grades. This is the preferred approach, but in many cases there will be no significant gaps. If so, the following method can be used:

   - Jobs with common features as indicated by the job evaluation factors are grouped together so that a distinction can be made between the characteristics of the jobs in different grades: it should be possible to demonstrate that the jobs grouped into one grade resemble each other more than they resemble jobs placed in adjacent grades. All the jobs placed in a grade should be clearly smaller than the jobs in the next higher grade and larger than the jobs placed in the next lower grade.

   - The grade hierarchy should take account of the organizational hierarchy, ie jobs in which the job holder reports to a higher level job holder should be placed in a lower grade, although this principle should not be followed slavishly when an organization is over-hierarchical with, perhaps, a series of one-over-one reporting relationships.

   - There would need to be good justification for placing any boundaries between jobs mainly carried out by men and jobs mainly carried out by women.

   - Caution should be exercised in placing any boundaries immediately above jobs in which large numbers of people are employed because this may result in a large number of appeals against the grading.

4 The grade width in terms of job evaluation points should represent a significant step in demands on job holders as indicated by the job evaluation scheme.

The grades in a structure established in this manner can be defined in the form of grade profiles using the job evaluation factors as the headings for each profile. These can form the basis for analytical matching, as described in Chapter 29.

Pre-emptive method

The pre-emptive method takes place in the following steps:

1 *Assume number of grades.* The assumption on how many grades are required is based on an analysis of the existing hierarchy of roles and a judgement on how many levels are needed to produce a logical grouping of those roles, level by level. A logical grouping is one in which each grade contains roles whose levels are broadly comparable in terms of responsibility and decision making, and there is a step difference in the degree of responsibility between each level.

2 *Define grades.* There is choice between a simple non-analytical or semi-analytical job classification approach, and a full analytical approach. A non-analytical job classification

approach involves preparing an overall definition of the grade to enable 'job slotting' to take place. This means slotting 'whole jobs' (ie ones that have not been analysed under job evaluation factor headings) into grades by comparing the whole job description with the grade. A full analytical approach involves the preparation of grade profiles. These use job evaluation factors as the headings for the profile of each grade, which can be compared with role profiles set out under the same headings so that analytical matching can take place.

3 *Revise initial assumption as necessary.* The process of definition may reveal that the number of grades assumed to be required initially was either too many (the distinctions between them could not be made with sufficient clarity), or too few (it becomes apparent that the range of roles to be fitted into the structure was too great to be accommodated in the number of grades available). If this is the case, the number of grades would have to be adjusted iteratively until a satisfactory result is obtained.

4 *Match benchmark roles.* The benchmark roles are matched to grades in accordance with a pre-determined analytical matching protocol, as described in the job evaluation toolkit (Chapter 68). When matched, the information on the benchmark roles may suggest changes to the grade profiles.

5 *Match remaining roles.* The remaining roles can be matched to the grade profiles using the protocol. A confirmation of the match can be obtained by comparing them with the graded benchmark roles.

Pay range design

The steps required to determine pay ranges are:

1 Obtain information on the market rates for benchmark jobs, where available. If possible this should indicate the median rate and the upper and lower quartiles. Remember that there may be some key jobs for which market rate data is not available.

2 List the jobs placed within each grade on the basis of job evaluation (these might be limited to benchmark jobs that have been evaluated, but there must be an adequate number of them if a proper basis for the design is to be provided).

3 Establish the actual rates of pay of the job holders.

4 For each grade, set out the range of pay for job holders and calculate their average or median rate of pay (the pay practice point). It is helpful to plot this pay practice data, as illustrated in Figure 69.2, which shows pay in each grade against job evaluation scores and includes a pay practice trend line.

5 Agree policy on how the organization's pay levels should relate to market rates – its 'market stance'. This could be at the median, or above the median if it is believed that pay levels should be more competitive.

6 Calculate the average market rates for the benchmark jobs in each grade according to pay stance policy, eg the median rates. This produces the range market reference point.

7 Compare the practice and market reference points in each range and decide on the range reference point. This usually becomes the mid-point of the pay range for the grade and is regarded as the competitive rate for a fully competent job holder in that grade. This is a judgemental process that takes into account the difference between the practice and policy points, the perceived need to be more competitive if policy rates are higher, and the likely costs of increasing rates.

8 Examine the pay differentials between reference points in adjacent grades. These should provide scope to recognize increases in job size and, so far as possible, variations between differentials should be kept to a minimum. If differentials are too close – less than 10 per cent – many jobs become borderline cases, which can result in a proliferation of appeals and arguments about grading. Large differentials below senior management level of more than 25 per cent can create problems for marginal or borderline cases because of the amount at stake. Experience has shown that in most

FIGURE 69.2   Scattergram of evaluations and pay

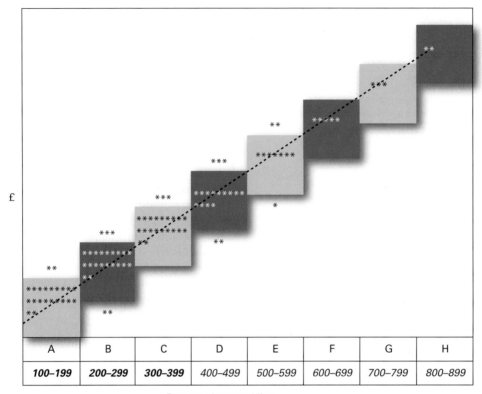

A	B	C	D	E	F	G	H
100–199	*200–299*	*300–399*	*400–499*	*500–599*	*600–699*	*700–799*	*800–899*

Pay practice trend line- - - - - - - - -

organizations with conventional grade structures a differential of between 15 and 20 per cent is appropriate except, perhaps, at the highest levels.

9 Decide on the range of pay around the reference point, eg 20 per cent on either side of the reference point. Thus, if that point is 100 per cent, the range is from 80 to 120 per cent. The range will, however, vary in accordance with policy on the scope for progression and, if a given range of pay has to be covered by the structure, the fewer the grades the wider the ranges.

10 Decide on the extent, if any, to which pay ranges should overlap. Overlap recognizes that an experienced job holder at the top of a range may be making a greater contribution than an inexperienced job holder at the lower end of the range above. Large overlaps can create equity issues

between jobs that have the same salary but are in different grades. This is particularly pronounced if it means that individuals with the same pay could fit within more than two grades.

11 Review the impact of the above pay range decisions on the pay of existing staff to calculate implementation costs. Establish the number of staff whose present rate of pay is above or below the pay range for the grade into which their jobs have been placed, and the extent of the difference between the rate of pay of those below the minimum and the lowest point of that pay range. Calculate the costs of bringing them up to the minimum. Pay-modelling software or Excel spreadsheets can be used for this purpose.

12 When the above steps have been completed it may be necessary to review the decisions made on the grade structure and pay

reference points and ranges, especially when the costs calculated in stage 11 are too high. Iteration is almost always necessary to obtain a satisfactory result that conforms to the criteria for grade and pay structures mentioned earlier, and minimizes the cost of implementation. Alternatives can be modelled using the software mentioned above.

Career family structure design

The steps required to design a career family structure are:

1   Select and define career families. Decide on what career families are required. Typically, not more than four or five families are identified. The choice of families is between functions, eg marketing, finance; or activities, eg administration, support staff; or a combination of functions and activities.

2   Decide on number of levels in the career family structure and define them with level profiles. Level profiles are required that apply to all the families in the structure, bearing in mind that the defining characteristic of a career family is that the levels and the pay ranges attached to them are common to all the families in the structure (as distinct from job family structures in which levels and ranges differ between some or all of the families).

3   Identify, define and match benchmark roles. A representative sample of benchmark roles are identified, defined as role profiles, and matched with the level profiles, as described above for a graded structure.

4   Conduct analytical matching. Analytical matching procedures are used to allocate the remaining roles to levels. It is advisable to test the process first in one family – this will not only test the procedure but will also enable model career family structures to be used when dealing with the other career families.

5   Attach pay ranges to levels. Pay ranges are established for each level, as described above for graded structures.

6   Validate relativities between career families. The allocation of jobs to levels through matching across the career families is validated by reference to job evaluation scores to ensure that the relativities between them look reasonable. Some adjustment may need to be made as a result of this cross-check if it exposes inequities between families.

Job family structure design

The process of designing job family structures is essentially the same as that used for career family structures. The difference is that, because some individual families will have their own pay and level structure, the analysis of market rates and the organization of work in families will have a stronger influence on the design.

Assimilation policy

It is necessary to have a policy on where staff will be assimilated into the new structure. This is usually at their existing salary or, in the case of a revised pay spine, on the nearest point in a new incremental scale above their existing salary.

Protection policy

Protection policy limits any loss in pay arising from the introduction of a new graded pay structure. 'Indefinite protection', that is maintaining the difference between current pay and range maximum for as long as the employee remains in the job, is highly undesirable, first because it will create permanent anomalies and, second, if there are a lot of men in this situation it will perpetuate unacceptable gender gaps.

Because of these considerations, the most common approach is now to protect pay for a period of between two to four years. During this time the employees will 'mark time' (ie receive no pay increases until their rate of pay falls within the new scale for their job. They will then be entitled to the same increases as any other staff in their grade, up to the grade maximum. Alternatively, during the protection period affected employees may receive a general increase/cost of living rise, but where this is the case it is less likely that an individual's pay will fall back within the new pay range during the protection period.

Where there is an incremental pay structure, staff may continue to earn increments to which they are entitled under existing arrangements, up to the maximum of their present scale, until the pay protection period ends, or their entitlement is bought out.

Protection policy limits any loss in pay arising from the introduction of a new graded pay structure. Individuals who are provided with protection are said to be 'red-circled'. If a red-circled individual leaves the job, the scale of pay for the job reverts to the standard range as set up following job evaluation.

Implementing new grade and pay structures

Implementation can be challenging and must be planned. The steps required are:

1 Decide at the planning stage the overall change/transition strategy and timing.

2 Model the transition to the new structure and develop policies to manage it.

3 Develop detailed operating responsibilities and guidelines for the new structure, including the procedures for grading or re-grading jobs and managing pay progression. The authority to make pay and grading decisions and methods of budgetary control should also be covered.

4 Negotiate the introduction of the new arrangements with staff representatives and trade unions, if appropriate. They should have been involved throughout the process, but the detailed 'nitty-gritty' of actual pay levels and assimilation policies and procedures needs to be thrashed out now.

5 Produce and distribute communications about the new structure – how it works, who will be involved in managing it and how people will be affected.

6 Design and run training workshops for managers, and possibly all staff.

7 Run a pilot or simulation exercise if feasible, operating the new approach in parts of the organization, to test its workability and robustness.

8 Full implementation and rollout. This will include giving every person information on how the new structure affects them and on their right to ask for a review of their grading if they are dissatisfied.

70
Attitude surveys

Introduction

Attitude surveys are being increasingly used by organizations to measure engagement and obtain the views of employees about particular HR policies and practices. This toolkit provides a practical guide to the development and use of such surveys.

Developing and conducting an attitude survey

The steps required to develop and conduct an attitude survey are as follows.

Set up survey team

One individual should be given the overall responsibility for planning and conducting the survey, but it is useful to appoint two or three other people to form a survey team that can discuss how the survey can be developed and share in its management.

Define objectives and scope

It is essential to be clear about what the survey is expected to achieve. In general terms it could be any of the reasons mentioned above. In particular, the objectives can be specified in terms of the area they are intended to cover, for example:

- To assess levels of engagement in order to identify any areas in which improvements could be made to people management processes with a view to increasing those levels.

- To measure trends in engagement levels and benchmark the levels against those achieved in comparable organizations.

- To evaluate the impact of the new performance management system.

- To obtain the views of employees about the reward system.

- To evaluate the effectiveness of e-learning.

- To obtain the views of employees about their benefits package as a basis for introducing a flexible benefits system.

The scope of the survey could be a census of all employees or cover a representative sample. A census has the advantage of giving everyone an opportunity to participate and, subject to response rates, information from a larger proportion of employees. A sample survey may be easier to manage in large organizations, but selecting a representative sample may be difficult and some important information may be missed. The scope of a survey may be limited to a category of staff such as senior managers or sales representatives and again, can be conducted on either a census or a sample basis.

When defining the scope, an estimate should be made of the number of people who will be contacted so that the scale of the survey can be calculated.

In-house, with external support or outsourced

There is a choice at the extremes between planning and administering the survey entirely in-house or entirely outsourced to consultants. In between there is a choice of activities that can be carried out in-house, possibly with outside advice. If a decision is made to outsource, wholly or partly, care has to be taken in selecting an external provider.

Choice between in-house and outsourcing

The factors to be considered when making a choice between in-house and outsourcing to external consultants are set out in Exhibit 70.1, which suggests that, apart from cost considerations, the advantages of using external help for all or part of the survey outweigh the disadvantages.

EXHIBIT 70.1   Advantages and disadvantages of planning and conducting surveys in-house or outsourcing

In-house		Outsourced	
Advantages	*Disadvantages*	*Advantages*	*Disadvantages*
Save costs	Time and trouble taken in planning and administering survey	Resources available to plan and administer survey; relieve organization of time and trouble	Cost
Complete control of survey	Lack of internal expertise	Expertise	Less control
Management visibly involved	Employees may suspect confidentiality	Confidentiality	
		Database available for benchmarking	

Choice of responsibility for activities

The choice for each of the main activities involved in planning and conducting a survey is between carrying it out entirely in-house, carrying it out in-house with advice and possibly some support from an external provider, and outsourcing the whole activity to an external provider. The choices can be mapped out with the help of Exhibit 70.2.

EXHIBIT 70.2   Choice of responsibility for activities

Activity	Wholly in-house	In-house with external advice/support	Wholly external
Decide on objectives and scope			
Decide on content			
Draft survey items			
Draw up survey			
Plan and administer online survey, and/or distribute survey questionnaire			
Follow up to increase level of response			
Analyse responses			
Prepare report			
Issue and discuss report with employees			
Plan and implement action			

Criteria for external adviser

A checklist of the points to consider when choosing an external adviser is set out in Exhibit 70.3.

A list of survey providers is given in the appendix at the end of this chapter.

EXHIBIT 70.3   Criteria for selecting an external adviser

Criteria	Comments
Relevant experience in the planning, advisory and administration activities the adviser is to carry out.	
Adequate resources available to carry out the work.	
Qualified, skilled and experienced staff who will conduct the work under proper supervision.	
References from satisfied clients.	
Estimated time to complete work.	
Ability to deliver on time.	
Fee structure and total cost of fees and expenses.	
Acceptability to management and employees and ability to fit in with the organization's culture.	

Identify survey content

It is necessary to decide what subject matter should be covered by the survey in order to achieve its objectives. The areas covered by a specialist survey are usually fairly obvious. But more care is necessary in deciding on what should be included in a more general engagement or attitude survey. The views of senior management and employees should be sought.

The outcome can be a checklist, as illustrated in Exhibit 70.4, which is used as the basis for interviews and focus group discussions, leading to the production of an outline list of survey topics.

EXHIBIT 70.4   Issues checklist

Possible survey issue	Very important – should be covered	Not so important – might be covered	Unimportant
Commitment to the organization			
Leadership			
Line manager effectiveness			
Communications			
Job content and clarity			
Autonomy			
The work environment			
Resources and equipment			
Use of skills and capabilities			
Opportunities for advancement and development			
Job security			
Pay and benefits			
Recognition			
Quality of feedback and guidance available			
Opportunities for involvement and participation			
Teamwork			
Cooperation and relationships with co-workers			
Fair treatment			
Discrimination, harassment and bullying			
Other			

Survey topics

An outline list of survey topics can be prepared by reference to the outcomes of the interviews and focus group findings. This list provides the basis for drawing up questions and constructing the survey.

Draft survey items

Format

The most commonly used format for survey items is a request to respondents to indicate the extent to which they agree or disagree with a statement, for example: 'My work is very satisfying.' The response can be on a five-point scale: 'Strongly agree', 'Inclined to agree', 'Neither agree nor disagree', 'Inclined to disagree' and 'Strongly disagree'. This is the most common approach but there is some support for using a four-point scale, leaving out the middle 'Neither agree nor disagree' on the grounds that respondents may be too inclined to select the central choice, which is not really an expression of opinion.

Scoring

Whichever scale is adopted, the responses can be scored – 5 or 4 for the most positive one; 1 for the most negative one. Adding these item scores can produce an overall score for, say, engagement, which can be used to assess trends as measured by successive surveys.

Positive or negative statements

A decision has to be made on the use of positive or negative statements. For example, a positive statement could be: 'My work is very satisfying', while a negative one would be: 'I get very little satisfaction from my work' (the latter are reverse-scored, ie a 'fully disagree' gets the maximum points and a 'fully agree' gets the minimum).

The argument for including negative as well as positive statements (sometimes called a 'balanced-scale approach') is that it makes people think about their responses, forces them to read the items more carefully and use both ends of the response scale, and prevents them from agreeing or disagreeing with items indiscriminately The counter-argument is that mixing positive and negative statements can confuse people, and there is no evidence that it does

make them think harder about their response. A negative response to a negatively worded item may not be equivalent to a positive response to a positive item. It is best to stick to positive statements.

Guidelines for wording items

The following are the guidelines for wording items:

- *Ask what you want to know* – be certain that the item will convey information relevant to the purpose of the survey and the issues raised in the content analysis.

- *Keep items simple and short* – the aim is to encourage responses and this will not happen if the items are complex or lengthy. Avoid compound sentences and subsidiary clauses. As a rule of thumb, an item should not be longer than 20 words.

- *Cover only one topic per item* – double-barrelled statements confuse respondents who do not know which one of them they are agreeing or disagreeing with.

- *Avoid ambiguous statements* – the aim is to ensure that as far as possible all respondents interpret the item in the same way. Define terms where necessary.

- *Be specific* – the test of a good item is to answer the question: 'If we get a poor rating on this item, will we be clear what needs to be done about it?' A general item such as, 'Our performance management scheme is very effective' may possibly be useful as a broad indicator of satisfaction or dissatisfaction, but it needs to be followed up by more specific items on such aspects of performance management as the quality of feedback, the fairness of performance ratings, or how well managers conduct performance review meetings.

- *Use appropriate, everyday language* – avoid words that may be unfamiliar to respondents. Item compilers should subject each item to a readability analysis.

Open-ended items

Open-ended or unstructured items are invitations to respondents to provide comments or opinions in their own words, for example: 'Please provide any ideas you have on how the performance management system could be improved.' They can be used to produce in-depth information that would not be available from the prescribed survey items and enable people to vent their feelings on emotion-laden topics such as the operation of a performance-related pay scheme. Respondents can be asked to list the three best or worst things associated with an issue such as the quality of communications.

Quotes from open-ended responses can liven up a report by providing an insight into real feelings. The disadvantage is that they are more difficult to process and analyse. They can serve a useful purpose in a survey but their use should be limited. It is, however, a good idea to at least include an item at the end of the survey asking for general comments such as: 'Please provide any other comments you would like to make on the issues covered by this survey.'

Construct the survey

The main areas for consideration when constructing a survey are the length of the survey, the order of items, the demographic information required and the introduction and explanatory notes to the survey.

Length of the survey

Clearly, the length of a survey will vary according to the breadth of issues it deals with. But it is advisable to limit the number of items in order to encourage good response by not putting off or confusing participants and by reducing the amount of time they take to complete it. An excessive number of items will increase the problems of analysing the outcome of the survey.

It is probably best not to have more than 50 items and to ensure that the survey can be completed within 30 minutes; a trial run can be used to check this. (An example of an engagement survey is given in Chapter 14, Table 14.2.)

The order of items

There is a choice in ordering the items in a survey between positioning them at random and clustering (grouping related items together). The argument for random ordering is that biases are better controlled if the topic areas covered are not too obvious.

The arguments for clustering are stronger. If the survey items are placed randomly, this may seem illogical to respondents who could find it difficult to follow and become annoyed or frustrated or even fail to complete the survey. Respondents find it easier to follow a survey where items are clustered. A typical approach when clustering items such as views about the job is to start with questions dealing with particular characteristics, followed by items concerned with general characteristics of the job, followed by an overall assessment of the job.

Demographics

Some information on the demographics of survey respondents is required to enable more detailed analysis. But the information should not be so specific as to threaten the survey's anonymity. The starting point is to consider what forms of analysis are required. Demographic data should only be sought if it is believed that it will produce useful analyses. Results are typically analysed by occupation (usually expressed in broad categories, eg manager, team leader, administrator), function or department, gender and length of service.

Introduction

The introduction to the survey should cover the following points:

- the purpose of the survey;
- how the survey will be conducted;
- how the results of the survey will be communicated (full disclosure of the analysis should be promised);
- the benefits of the survey to the organization and its employees;
- how anonymity will be preserved (this will be more convincing if the survey is conducted by a third party who carries out the analysis away from the organization);
- contact details for queries about the survey or help in completing it;
- confirmation that the survey can be completed during working hours;
- the date by which the survey should be completed.

Instructions for completing the survey

Clear instructions should be given on how to complete the survey. If care has been taken to adopt a simple and consistent approach (eg a five-point scale to indicate the extent to which a respondent agrees or disagrees with a statement) these instructions need not be too complex. But they should be pilot tested to ensure that they are understood.

Plan survey

The steps required to prepare for a survey are:

1 Plan an initial communications programme for employees.
2 Decide on how results will be analysed and the format of the report.
3 Decide on the use of online technology.

Communicate to employees

It is essential to convey to employees that a survey is to be carried out, its purpose, and how the organization and they will benefit. Details of how the survey will be conducted need to be explained; this should cover the role of the external provider if one is engaged. Employees should be informed that the survey can be completed in working hours and that help will be available in completing the survey if required. Employees need to be assured that their completed surveys will be anonymous and that the survey will therefore be completely confidential. If an outside provider is to be used, assurances can be given that confidentiality will be maintained. The impact of the survey can be enhanced by giving it an identity, such as 'Have your say'.

Analysis

The demographic categories for analysis should have been considered when designing the survey. At this stage, further consideration can be given to the detailed analysis and how the results will be presented in the report – tabulations, graphics, trend analysis, etc. Decisions can also be made on the need for any cross-analyses, for example how responses to an item dealing with career prospects varied between men and women, or between managers and support staff or, more elaborately, how responses varied between male and female managers and male and female support staff.

Use of online technology

Most surveys are conducted online, especially in larger organizations. Web-based software is used. Online surveys are typically operated by external providers. Respondents access the online questionnaire by following an e-mail link, which takes them directly to the provider's site. Some suppliers can set up the survey on the organization's intranet site rather than hosting it remotely. Instructions are given on how to respond to survey items.

Respondents are usually given one practice item. The software may present only one item at a time together with the alternative responses. When an item is completed the next item is displayed.

The software is used to collect completed surveys, analyse responses and prepare reports. External providers can produce elegant reports, complete with graphics.

Online surveys save time and trouble and enable more sophisticated analyses and reports to be produced. When they are conducted by an external provider they can convince employees that their responses will be confidential. They are also easier to complete than paper-based surveys (even the minority of people unfamiliar with computers seldom have any difficulty, and help can be provided if necessary). The only problem is where employees do not have immediate access to a computer. Some companies have overcome this by installing special computer stations with staff available to give advice. Alternatively, a paper-based survey can be carried out.

Pilot testing

It is essential to pilot test the survey to evaluate its content and to assess the administration time. The purposes of the pilot test would be to:

- obtain initial reactions from employees on the proposed survey and its content;
- find out generally if members of the test group have any problems with completing the survey;
- identify specific weaknesses in the draft survey, eg ambiguous or badly worded survey items, inadequate instructions on how

to complete the survey, illogical sequence of items, complexity, too many items;

- identify any unnecessary items or any additions that need to be made;
- check on the time taken to complete the survey and identify any need to shorten it.

The pilot test can usefully be conducted with a group of eight to12 people consisting of a balanced sample of employees (or more groups in large or complex organizations). The individuals in the group complete the draft survey under broadly the same conditions as they would experience in an actual survey. Their opinions under the headings listed above would be obtained by the survey team, who would make any necessary changes to the survey.

Conduct survey

Conducting a survey is simply a matter of implementing the plan. The steps required are:

1 Use the outcomes of the pilot test to make final amendments to the survey document and prepare the software or the paper survey.

2 Inform employees that the survey is to be carried out and remind them of its purpose, how it will be conducted and the arrangements to ensure confidentiality. This will confirm advance communications about the survey.

3 Make arrangements to deal with queries and, if necessary, provide computers and support.

4 Issue the survey online or on paper.

5 Maximize the response rate (the percentage of people who complete and submit a survey). Aim for a minimum of 70 per cent by contacting non-respondents two or three times to remind them to submit the survey.

Analyse responses

The initial analysis should describe the population of respondents. The basic analysis then describes the number and percentage of people who chose each response for each item. To simplify the findings, some analysts combine 'strongly agree' and 'inclined to agree' into one category called 'agree', and 'inclined to disagree' and 'disagree' into one category called 'disagree'.

If the choices are scored from, say, 1 to 5 in increasing order of agreement, an average score for each item and the survey as a whole can be calculated. This provides an index that can be used to assess trends in successive surveys, as long as the score relates to the same items. Cross-analyses can be carried out in addition to the basic analysis to describe results in more detail by identifying variations in the responses between different groups, for example managers and support workers.

More sophisticated analysis can be used to test statistical significance, analyse variance, test the relationship between sub-groups (chi-square test) and assess reliability (internal consistency reliability).

Assessing results

It is an interesting fact that when people are asked directly if they are satisfied with their job, most of them will probably say that they are. This is regardless of the work being done and often in spite of strongly held grievances. A possible reason for this phenomenon is that while most people are willing to admit to having grievances – in fact, if invited to complain, they will complain – they may be reluctant to admit, even to themselves, to being dissatisfied with a job they have no immediate intention of leaving. Many employees have become reconciled to their work, even if they do not like some aspects of it, and have no real desire to do anything else. So they are, in a sense, satisfied enough to continue, even if they have complaints. Finally, many people are satisfied with their job overall, although they grumble about some aspects of it.

Overall measures of satisfaction do not, therefore, always reveal anything interesting. It is more important to look at particular aspects of satisfaction or dissatisfaction to decide whether or not anything needs to be done. In these circumstances, a survey will only indicate a line to be followed up. It will not provide the answers. Hence the advantage of individual meetings or focus group discussions to explore in depth any issue raised.

Post-survey activities

The three essential post-survey activities are to:

1 Feed back summaries of the results, including negative views, to all employees.

2 Hold discussions with employees in focus groups and workshops to obtain views on what needs to be done about any of the negative outcomes of the survey.

3 Plan and implement action to deal with problem areas, involving employees as far as possible and keeping everyone informed of what has been accomplished as a result of the survey.

Appendix: survey providers

AF Associates, **sales@ASassociates.co.uk**

Alexandra Surveys, **Alexandrasurveys.com**

BDI Surveys, **research@bdisurveys.com**

Direct Data Analysis, **direct-data-analysis.co.uk**

Electoral Reform Services, **electoralreform.co.uk**

Fargus Consulting Partnership, **fargus.co.uk**

The Gallop Organization, **gallop.com**

Ipsos MORI, **ipsos-mori.com**

ORC International, **orc.co.uk**

People in Business, **pib.co.uk**

TNS, **tnsglobal.com**

SUBJECT INDEX

AUTHOR INDEX